P9-BJP-764

Gendered Worlds

THIRD EDITION

JUDY ROOT AULETTE

UNIVERSITY OF NORTH CAROLINA-CHARLOTTE

JUDITH WITTNER

LOYOLA UNIVERSITY CHICAGO

New York   Oxford

OXFORD UNIVERSITY PRESS

Oxford University Press is a department of the University of Oxford.
It furthers the University's objective of excellence in research,
scholarship, and education by publishing worldwide.

Oxford   New York
Auckland   Cape Town   Dar es Salaam   Hong Kong   Karachi
Kuala Lumpur   Madrid   Melbourne   Mexico City   Nairobi
New Delhi   Shanghai   Taipei   Toronto

With offices in
Argentina   Austria   Brazil   Chile   Czech Republic   France   Greece
Guatemala   Hungary   Italy   Japan   Poland   Portugal   Singapore
South Korea   Switzerland   Thailand   Turkey   Ukraine   Vietnam

Copyright © 2015, 2012, 2009 by Oxford University Press.

For titles covered by Section 112 of the US Higher Education
Opportunity Act, please visit www.oup.com/us/he for the
latest information about pricing and alternate formats.

Published in the United States of America by
Oxford University Press
198 Madison Avenue, New York, NY 10016
http://www.oup.com

Oxford is a registered trade mark of Oxford University Press.

All rights reserved. No part of this publication may be reproduced,
stored in a retrieval system, or transmitted, in any form or by any means,
electronic, mechanical, photocopying, recording, or otherwise,
without the prior permission of Oxford University Press.

Library of Congress Cataloging-in-Publication Data
Aulette, Judy Root.
   Gendered worlds / Judy Root Aulette, University of North Carolina-Charlotte, Judith Wittner,
Loyola University Chicago. -- Third edition.
      pages cm
   ISBN 978-0-19-933561-9
 1. Sex role. 2. Women--Social conditions. 3. Feminist theory. I. Wittner, Judith G. II. Title.
   HQ1075.A95 2015
   305.3--dc23
                                                                           2014008903

Printing number: 9 8 7 6 5 4 3 2 1

Printed in the United States of America
on acid-free paper

CONTENTS

CHAPTER 14 GLOBALIZING, ORGANIZING, AND MAKING THE WORLD A BETTER PLACE

GENDER IN EVERYDAY LIFE

PREFACE

The first edition of this book was a work of faith—faith that we could grasp the massive theoretical and empirical work of feminist scholars in one brief volume. This third edition is our continued effort to tap into the global discussions on gender and to introduce our readers to an even broader array of empirical research and theory-building that increasingly makes feminist scholarship so vital today.

Much of the popular discourse on gender consists of sound bites about feminism and women, platitudes about gendered work and violence, and ideologies about sex and gender. Widely circulated in the popular media and among students are such notions as "feminism is sexist," "feminism is no longer necessary," and "the differences between men and women are an inevitable feature of our biology," alongside assertions that "I'm not a feminist, but . . ." and "this generation has pretty much eliminated gender inequality." We hope that introducing students to feminist scholarship will produce a better understanding of these issues.

This book is our attempt to bring together the multiple strands of gender and associated research from local and everyday manifestations of masculinities and femininities to the gendered global forces that lie beneath today's political and social crises. To do so, each chapter builds on five principles.

First, we weave together theory and empirical data rather than segregate them into separate chapters. The book gathers together much of the scholarship—mainly sociological, but also interdisciplinary—that has accumulated in many substantive areas. For example, readers will learn about research on violence, families, media, sports, politics, sexuality, religion, education, health, and bodies. Theories that have grown up alongside this research and help to interpret its meanings are woven into each chapter, so that students are able to see how theory emerges from and helps to explain empirical studies.

Second, we connect personal experience with sociological conceptualizations. We offer both social constructionist and social structural approaches that explain the production of inequality in face-to-face interaction within constraining organizational and institutional structures. We ask how the gendered features of our everyday lives are given life, shape, and meaning by the larger organizations and institutions that contain them and how we, in turn, act back on these structures, shaping new forms of gendered relationships, challenging gendered worlds, and perhaps even eliminating gendered differences.

Third, this is a book about gender and gendered relationships, and not only about women. Men's lives are shaped by gender relations as much as the lives of women. In addition, we call our readers' attention to the ways that the categories of "men" and "women" are constructs that conceal other sexualities and genders. Our task is to uncover and attempt to understand how the binary of man and woman are constructed and how it might be eliminated in the ways we think, interact with and treat one another, and the ways we construct and maintain our social institutions.

Fourth, this book takes seriously the understanding that there are important differences among women and among men. The "intersectionality" that differentially locates individuals and groups in what black feminist theorist Patricia Hill Collins (2000) called a "matrix of domination" is a core feature of each chapter. There is no way to understand gender inequality as a phenomenon that can be separated from the multiple cross-cutting inequalities of class, race, sexuality, and nation. Gendered identities are accomplishments, not fixed states of being, and they include dynamic relationships of privilege and subordination. Some men may be privileged as men, but many are subordinated along racial ethnic, national, sexual, and class lines. At the same time, women have varied relationships with one another and with men along these same lines. In each chapter, we explore these advantages and disadvantages, as well as actors' complicity with and resistance to them.

Fifth, this book takes the world as its starting point. Our goal is to help readers gain a sense of the similarities and differences in gender across the globe. We hope to encourage students to see the many ways gender is experienced as well as the many ways in which gender injustice is being challenged around the world.

CHANGES TO THE THIRD EDITION

- Updated all of the data, especially statistics, and streamlined the presentation of information to make it more readable.
- Separated the Media and Sports chapter into two chapters.
- Incorporated clarification and further explanation of topics suggested by the hundreds of students who have used this book in courses taught by the authors.
- Added critical thinking questions and key terms at the end of each chapter and a glossary defining the key terms at the end of the book.
- Added content on: the cult of the virgin, the intersection of gender and sexuality in media, the Bechdel Test for films, gender in reality TV, mothers and youth sports, theoretical models of assimilation and reform to sports, benefits of sports for women, women in combat, fair sentencing, sexual assault in the military, gender politics in rural China, child brides, lesbian parents, and images of motherhood in recent political campaigns.

PLAN OF THE BOOK

Chapter 1 provides a brief overview of the assumptions we make and the tools we use to proceed with our exploration of gender. Chapter 2 begins with the question of biology. Agree or disagree: no matter how much gender relations have changed and are changing, biological sex—the underlying differences between human males and females—are important natural facts. If you agree with this statement, chapter 2 will try to convince you that you are mistaken. Even at the most basic level of genes and hormones, not everyone fits into one of the two standard and supposedly exclusive sex categories of male and female. Historically, the conventional idea of "opposite" sexes turns out to be a relatively recent invention, and cross-culturally, different societies employ different and sometimes more numerous sex categories. The chapter concludes with a section on a gender-bending movements of intersexual and transgendered people, movements which underscore the political nature of so-called biological categories. The chapter makes the case that biological sex is a continuum, not a dichotomy between male and female, and suggests that by relinquishing our faith that male and female bodies are naturally and forever different in consequential ways, we make space for the "playful exploration" of the many possibilities of embodiment (Fausto-Sterling 2000).

If biology is not the basis of gender difference, racial variation, or alternative sexualities, then what is? Chapter 3 reviews three answers to that question. Regarding gender, one answer is that we learn appropriate ways of being gendered from our parents, teachers, and friends. We see examples of gendered behavior on television and in books. From our first days, we are schooled in gender roles, and most of us are good students. A second answer to the question of how gender differences arise draws on the idea that by interacting with one another we actively produce the worlds in which we live. Instead of "being" a gender, we "do" gender in social encounters. A third answer points to the ways organizations and institutions build gender and other inequalities into the ways they function. As you read this chapter, test these theories against your own experiences and observations of the ways you have become gendered, raced, sexualized, and turned into a member of your class. Have you ever resisted some of these identities? How, and in what contexts?

Chapter 4 explores sexuality through intersecting dimensions of gender, race ethnicity, class, and nation. Normatively, men and women are expected to be heterosexual, to be sexually attracted to and engage in sexual activity only with each other. In fact, actual sex practices offer much more complicated and interesting examples of the ways racial ethnic and gender identities enter into and produce sexuality and sexual identity. Feminist and antiracist studies of sexuality have exposed the very political character of constructions of sexuality. The chapter moves from discussing the construction of conventional sexualities by means of sexual scripts and gendered double standards to describing the global sexual politics of sex tourism and sex trafficking, and exploring the queer movement's resistances and challenges to normative sexualities mounted by queers and others demanding sexual human rights.

What does water have to do with education? In chapter 5, you'll read about how lack of access to water and sanitation in poor countries directly affects girls' ability to enter and remain in school. In the global North, girls' education has become similar to that of boys in terms of attendance, graduation, and choice of studies, and in some ways girls have surpassed boys. Globally, however, the story is quite different. In the poorest countries of Haiti, Colombia, Malawi, Madagascar, Surinam, Tanzania, and Lesotho, boys are less likely than girls to go to school, but in these countries school is a luxury many children cannot afford, and many boys as well as girls do not go to school. Worldwide, two-thirds of children not attending schools are girls, and 60 percent of illiterate young people are girls. Illiteracy, low education, and poverty mean higher mortality rates, decreased income, hunger, and even death. The intersections of gender, race ethnicity, and nation can be deadly.

You've been students now for at least fourteen or fifteen years, and perhaps longer. Can you recall the ways that you and your teachers relied on gender in your classrooms? Most studies show that for many years, teachers often consciously and unconsciously built on the dichotomy between boys and girls for purposes of teaching and to exercise control over their students. Did you make separate girls' and boys' lines at lunchtime? Did girls and boys play separate games in the schoolyard during recess? Did boys and girls compete at spelling and geography in class? Did the teacher listen more attentively to boys' answers or give more time in class to unruly boys than to well-behaved girls? These were common practices in American classrooms of the past and perhaps in some classrooms today. Chapter 5 shows that assuming differences between boys and girls in the classroom becomes a self-fulfilling prophecy, another piece of the puzzle that helps to explain how gender differences are created. Racial/ethnic differences also matter in classrooms, and the crosscutting dimensions of race ethnicity and gender construct hierarchies of educational success. This chapter makes clear that gendering in education is not a simple story. Gendering creates problems for boys, too, exemplified by the greater proportion of boys who are diagnosed and treated for hyperactivity. Racism and poverty contribute to the diminished educations that many children receive. Overall, chapter 5 shows how gender, class position, and race ethnicity intertwine to play central roles from kindergarten through higher education, and that we all pay a price for these inequalities.

Chapter 6 turns the lenses of gender, race ethnicity, class, and nation on local and global economies and on the gendered and raced character of work. For example, the relationship between paid and unpaid work is also a relationship between men and women in the gendered division of labor. Much of domestic labor—cleaning, cooking, shopping, and caring for children and other dependents—was for a long time, and to a certain extent still is, invisible. The only work that was visible and therefore appeared to be "real" was that done by men, for pay, outside families. Was domestic work invisible because it was the work of women? Was it invisible because it was done inside the home? Was it invisible because it was not paid? Or, were all three factors interrelated?

The gender perspective has contributed many useful concepts to the study of working lives, concepts that you will learn about in chapter 6. The glass ceiling is a term for the invisible obstacles facing women who try to make it up the ladders that professional men have been climbing for generations. The glass escalator signifies the seemingly effortless ways men rise to top positions in women's professions such as elementary-school teaching or nursing. Emotional labor refers to some of the invisible tasks required of workers—being nice and absorbing abuse from customers in the service economy; being tough and instilling fear in bill collecting and policing. The former is work more likely to be required in jobs assigned to women; the latter, in jobs assigned to men. The pay gap and the feminization of poverty describe the consequences of gender, class, and racial inequalities in the labor force; to remedy such disparities, activists promoted the policy of comparable worth. In recent decades, the global economy has come into view as a reality directly connecting the fates of workers around the world. Despite the better situation of some women in the global North, women around the world have less status, power, and wealth than men. The implementation of free-trade agreements has meant the loss of jobs in the United States to countries in which labor is vastly cheaper. It has also meant that workers in those nations with cheap labor are toiling for wages that aren't sufficient to support themselves or their families. Moreover, it has meant the impoverishment of millions of third-world farmers, who cannot compete with subsidized American goods from corporate farms that undersell their products and drive local growers out of business.

The family has been a loaded political issue in the United States for the past forty years, as conservatives hold its so-called decline responsible for the ills of contemporary life. In chapter 7, you will have a chance to draw your own conclusions about family life today. Does marriage prevent poverty, as those who promote marriage among the poor believe? Will allowing same-sex marriage undermine marriage as an institution, or give it new life? Promoting marriage for the poor and prohibiting it for gay men and lesbians dispensed with love as the basis of marriage. The gay/lesbian community fought back, and the right to marry whomever you love has been their increasingly successful rallying cry. Not so for poor families. A similar contradiction separates middle class and poor mothers. Middle-class women have been and still are exhorted to be good mothers by staying home with their children, even as mothers on welfare are required to enter the labor force.

Chapter 7 demonstrates that the massive entry of women into the labor force is producing significant conflicts between the needs of families and the requirements of jobs. Among other things, these conflicts have produced a child-care crisis in the United States. Mothering and caregiving are examples of invisible and unpaid labor, absolutely vital to the well-being of families and absolutely necessary to sustain the labor force. Comparative data from other industrial countries shows that the United States provides the least family and parental support for child care and gender equity.

Chapter 8 shows that gender is a central feature of the continuum of violence that stretches from our most intimate lives to the ongoing global tragedies of militarism and war. Street harassment, rape, domestic violence, gendered violence in prisons, militarist masculinity, wartime rape, the enslavement of women by militias, sex trafficking, and growing civilian casualties in wartime of women, children, and elderly—what do you think can explain such relentless and pervasive gendered violence? And a related question: are these different kinds of violence related in any way? Some observers have attempted to naturalize violence as evolutionarily or psychologically necessary. Some feminists have evoked biology as an explanation for violence by characterizing it as men's violence against women. Feminist antiracist research has broadened and complicated this simplistic naturalized picture of gendered violence. Some women—poor, working class, of color—are at greater risk of sexual and gendered violence than others. Likewise, inequalities of race ethnicity, class, gender, and sexuality shape men's relationship to violence, both as victims and as perpetrators. These new understandings of the ways gendered violence enters into the lives of individuals, communities, and nation states suggest innovative remedies and courses of action, which we explore in the chapter.

Chapter 9 recounts the many ways that illness and health are gendered around the globe. Everything you have learned up to this chapter helps to structure the distribution of health and illness: the sexual division of paid and unpaid labor, race ethnicity, the political economies and ruling orders of the nations in which people live, membership in particular sexual communities, and so forth. After reading this material, you will understand why health is a collective good requiring collective action to secure it for all people. This chapter also describes feminist and antiracist social movements around reproductive rights that have grown from local actions into transnational movements linking reproductive and general health to a wide range of rights: housing, education, employment, freedom from violence, and health services, with the goal of prioritizing human interests over those of market forces.

Is changing the gender of officeholders sufficient to make positive political change? According to the studies reported in chapter 10, the evidence is mixed. The question of women's impact on politics remains open, because men dominate all channels of contemporary politics around the world: electoral politics, the news media, and the metaphors of political discourse, war, and sports. Despite the prevalent belief of Americans that they are leaders in and teachers of democracy and equal participation, the participation of U.S. women in legislative and executive positions is close to that of women in Chad or Morocco. It is Rwanda, Andorra, Cuba, Sweden, Seychelles, and Senegal that have the largest proportion of women in government leadership. Politics is not just about elections and offices. There is a gender politics of women in prisons, girls in gangs, and women in combat. Some suggest that politics is even broader, including all activities in which people engage to link public and private concerns and to develop power that brings about change in their everyday lives. Given the broader definition, think about the ways your activities and those of your friends and family could be seen as political.

You are the media generation. Your daily lives are saturated with media. Try this test: keep a diary of all the media-connected contacts you have from the time you wake up in the morning until the time you go to bed. Note when and how long you listen to the radio or watch television. Don't forget to list the advertisements you encounter, including those that come to you in the mail, on bulletin boards at school and work, on billboards along the roads you travel, and on the Internet. Remember to include the papers and books you look at today. The thousands of images and messages we receive in these ways exhort us overtly or subtly to view, experience, and act on the world in certain ways.

Chapter 11 explores the gendering of these messages. Women are still missing as subjects of media stories and behind the scenes as reporters and writers. Stereotypes of women and men abound. The ads show some differences in different countries. Women outnumber men in Japanese and Turkish ads, although men are, unsurprisingly, the primary characters in automobile, financial services, and food and drink advertisements. One consistent image is that women are nearly always young. Middle-aged and older women have been "annihilated" globally in such ads. In the United States, the images are of powerful white men, white women as sex objects, aggressive black men, and inconsequential black women. Men and women who are Latino, Asian American, and First Nations people are nearly nonexistent in the ads. Similar stereotypes and absences can be found in movies, magazines, video games, song lyrics, and televised sports.

Chapter 12 covers the topic of sports. For women, athletics have been a place of exclusion, expressing the idea that femininity does not include athletic ability and experience. Learning to be athletes and learning to be masculine are closely related. Critics of organized sports cite violence, disrespect for human bodies, and excessive competitiveness that damages athletes. Athleticism for women is different. One student of women in sports claims that women's athletics create new images and new ways of being women that challenge men's dominance (Messner 1992). Ironically, sports are a way men prove they are masculine, but participation in sports often forces women to prove they are feminine. Studying gender and sports forces comparisons between the highly organized and competitive fan-supported sports that have become big business today and participation sports, comprised of more loosely defined and organized activities, the former the sport of spectacle, the latter its democratic and participatory alternative.

In chapter 13, we focus on gender and religion, one of the most loaded topics of debate today, as the rise of religious fundamentalism has put the roles of women in the spotlight. Although fundamentalist religions restrict women, it might surprise you to learn that more women than men are fundamentalists. Women's support of these religions makes sense when we realize that religious communities, regardless of doctrine, can be places where women find collective support and the social space for expression—arenas of freedom in otherwise restrictive societies. Not all forms of spirituality and religious organization constrain women. Women often resist the constraints imposed on them religiously. For example, some Catholic women are calling for an end to the ban on women priests. Also, religion has played important positive roles in movements for social justice. The black church in the American South, with its high level of women members, played a pivotal role in the civil rights movement, for example. The peace and antiwar movements of the past century attracted many religious activists who were women. Finally, ancient and indigenous societies created forms of worship that were egalitarian and that revered women's bodies for their life-giving abilities. In this chapter, we ask if these partnership forms of worship could provide the models of more humane and socially constructive forms of religion.

Chapter14 returns to some of the questions we have posed throughout the book, by developing our thoughts on the future of gender and gender studies. What can we conclude about the gender gap, and what intellectual and political tools will we need to not only understand but change our gendered world?

Our world is filled with injustice, inequality, and pain. It is also filled with the hope and promise that grows from the many who contribute to resisting injustices, promoting equality, and creating a world of that promotes our potentials and our pleasures. We dedicate this book to furthering those ends.

REFERENCES

Collins, Patricia Hill. 2000. *Black Feminist Thought: Knowledge, Consciousness, and the Politics of Empowerment.* 2nd edition. New York: Routledge.

Fausto-Sterling, Anne. 2000. *Sexing the Body: Gender Politics and the Construction of Sexuality.* New York: Basic Books.

Messner, Michael.1992. *Power at Play: Sports and the Problem of Masculinity.* Boston: Beacon Press.

ACKNOWLEDGMENTS

Writing a book such as this one requires the authors to learn new areas of research about which they may initially have known little. Judy Aulette thanks Anna Aulette-Root, Elizabeth Aulette-Root, and Albert Aulette for their careful reading and essential feedback on many drafts of chapters, especially regarding issues related to gender and religion and gender and the media. In addition, she thanks them for living with this project for so many years. She also thanks Claude Teweles and Phong Ho for inviting her to consider the original project for Roxbury Press and for patiently waiting for the project to be completed. Most important, she thanks her coauthor, Judy Wittner, for her knowledge, creativity, tenacity, and especially her friendship.

Judith Wittner thanks the members of her writing group, Susan Stall and Martha Thompson, for their encouragement and support. Her thanks also go to Judy Aulette for hand holding and great patience and to Kristin Blakely for the intelligence and energy she brought to our project. Special thanks to Jenny Wittner, Jorge, Nathaniel, and Alex Pinheiro, Liz Wittner, and John, Mollie, Mario, and Lily Pepper.

We both thank Sherith Pankratz from Oxford University Press for choosing to continue the project and inviting us to write a second and now a third edition. And we thank Katy Albis for her careful attention to all of the details in the final stages. Special thanks to the terrific copy editor, Debbie Ruel. We also are grateful to the reviewers who provided vital and supportive suggestions that helped make this text something of which we are very proud:

- Dana Berkowitz, Louisiana State University
- Tara Lampert, University of Alaska, Anchorage
- Megan Titus, Rider University
- Thea Alvarado, College of the Canyons
- Nancy Porter, Chestnut Hill College
- Dianne Dentice, Stephen F. Austin State University
- JoAnn Rogers, Clarkson University
- Sharon Preves, Hamline University
- Jennifer Woodruff, Heartland Community College

GENDERED WORLDS

INTRODUCTION

Many people believe that gender inequality no longer exists. Natural disasters like
the Tsunami that devastated Indonesia, however, reveal that gender continues
to have a powerful influence on the ways we live and die.

Source: Associated Press.

A FEW MORE INCONVENIENT TRUTHS

Climate change and the environmental disasters that accompany it would seem to be one issue
that touches all human beings in the same way. But in 2004, when a tsunami in Indonesia
killed more than a quarter of a million people, 75 percent of them were women (Oxfam 2005).
This scenario is not unusual. Women typically far outnumber men in mortalities resulting
from environmental disasters. This effect is strongest in countries with very few social and economic rights for women (Neumayer and Pluemper 2007; Juran 2012).

Physical differences between men and women are unlikely to explain the higher mortality rate for women. For example, women are sometimes even at an advantage in famines because they can cope better with food shortages due to their lower nutritional requirements
and higher levels of body fat (Neumayer and Pluemper 2007). In the case of the tsunami,
some men may have survived because of greater physical strength that allowed them to hang
on to trees or to stay afloat. However, social factors were far more significant, especially the
social factor of gender (Oxfam 2005; Doocy, Rofi, Burnham, and Robinson 2007). Reports on
the tsunami identify a number of social factors that contributed to the fact that women were
so much more likely to have died:

- Swimming and tree climbing are taught mainly to boys. These skills, of course,
  were essential to survival when the waves of the tsunami hit.

- Women were indoors, whereas men were more likely to be outside working, shopping, and socializing; therefore, information warning residents to leave the area reached the women later than it did men who were out in public.
- Responsibilities for others, especially children, prevented women from moving fast enough to escape the floods. In Aceh, for example, many women were found dead with babies still clutched in their arms. Some personal accounts from survivors tell of mothers pushing their children to safety on buildings or trees that withstood the tsunami, but being swept away themselves.
- The clothing women wore, long dresses, inhibited their ability to run or swim to save themselves from the floods. In addition, some who were in their homes but casually dressed when the first wave struck ran to put on "acceptable" outdoor clothes before seeking safety, and as a result were drowned or barely escaped.
- A division of labor placed men in fishing boats at sea (a tsunami wave is not as dangerous at sea as when it crashes to shore), farming in agricultural areas away from the beach, or serving as soldiers in conflict areas away from those affected by the tsunami, making them less likely to be affected (Juran 2012).

Are you surprised that gender played such an important role in determining whether people lived or died in this environmental disaster? Do the differences in gender seem relatively insignificant if they are taken out of context? For example, would you have thought that gender differences in clothing or play activities like swimming and tree climbing could be so important?

This scenario emphasizes gender differences, but you are probably familiar with images of Hurricane Katrina floods and the importance of race ethnicity and social class in that disaster. How does gender add to or interact with the variation in our experience by race ethnicity and social class?

The researchers who studied the tsunami argue that biology had little to do with differences in survival. What do you think of this argument in general? Is gender mostly a function of biology? Or are social factors most important?

What exactly is gender? Is gender only a problem for women? Or does gender cause problems for men, too? Some researchers have noted that in some environmental disasters, such as Hurricane Mitch in Central America, men were more likely to die because of the expectation that they take more risks trying to save others from the mudslides and floods. In that case, gender was still important but it disadvantaged men.

The tsunami scenario describes a situation in Asia. How does gender vary around the globe? How are gender expectations being challenged locally and globally? How is gender changing?

These are the kinds of questions we will be asking in this text. Our goal is to explore the ways that gender appears in every corner of our lives and of our globe. Before the tsunami, very few scholars had ever considered the connections among gender, environmental disasters, and mortality (Enarson and Morrow 1998). Every day, researchers are "discovering" new situations in which gender plays a role. We will be trying to keep up with them as we travel around the world looking for gender and seeking ways to understand how it works, what its effects are, and the ways we might address the problems it causes.

SOME GROUND RULES FOR STUDYING GENDER

Trying to determine a place to begin answering questions about gender is difficult. How to consider the subject, what to focus on, and what to ignore are all challenging issues. In this book, we approach the subjects with a few important assumptions: social life is socially based and politically structured, gender is part of a network of social inequalities, and scholarship is political.

Social Life Is Socially Based and Politically Structured

Like many features of social life, gender is a factor that has been seen and felt by all of us, and in some ways that experience makes us all "experts" about it. Our familiarity with the topic, however, may make us prone to look only at the surface or to accept the conventional wisdom of the time and, therefore, to have distorted or superficial views of issues. One especially important aspect of conventional wisdom about gender is the belief that these views are bedrock biological certainties: all humans can be placed into one of two categories and these categories are inborn, natural, unchanging givens. This book challenges this idea by emphasizing the social character of gender.

In addition, we propose that gender does not stand alone and that in order to understand its social construction we also must look at the social construction of other relations of power, especially race ethnicity and sexuality. You will notice in this book that we use the term "race ethnicity" rather than separating these two factors. We do this because the distinction between the two terms implies that race is a biological factor while ethnicity is a social one. Since we regard both race and ethnicity as social factors that are intertwined we have combined the terms to remind us that neither has anything to do with biology but both are socially constructed and enormously socially consequential. We add, there is no gender or sexuality— just bodies—before they are socially constructed. This book is dedicated to showing how and with what consequences gender, race ethnicity, and sexuality are social constructions, not biological truths. In addition, we explain how these constructions work together to create the "ruling relations" of society helping to maintain the status quo in the power systems that make up our social lives.

Gender Is Part of a Network of Social Inequalities

This book explores inequalities of gender, their consequences, and the movements challenging them. However, gender analysis alone will not help us to understand the ways that this particular inequality shapes our lives and the lives of people around the globe. We live in a world built atop gendered differences entertwined with hierarchies of race ethnicity and sexuality, but also put together by class-based systems of power at the global level: patriarchal oppression, **heterosexual privilege**, the racist repercussions of colonization and slavery, and the dynamic of global capitalism that continues to feed the growing gap between the rich and powerful few and the excluded many.

Sometimes scholars use the word *lenses* to talk about the complexity of social life. If you were to put on a pair of glasses that allowed you to see only objects that were green, and

TABLE 1-1 The Global Gender Gap Index 2010 Rankings (highs and lows)

Country	Highest Ranks	Score
Iceland	1	.85
Finland	2	.85
Norway	3	.84
Sweden	4	.82
Ireland	5	.78
New Zealand	6	.78
Denmark	7	.78
Philippines	8	.77
Nicaragua	9	.77
Switzerland	10	.77
Netherlands	11	.77
Belgium	12	.77
Germany	13	.76
Lesotho	14	.76
Latvia	15	.75
South Africa	16	.75
Luxembourg	17	.74
Cuba	18	.74
United Kingdom	19	.74
Cuba	20	.74
Austria	21	.74
United States	22	.74

another pair blocked everything but blue or red, and so on, then each time you took off one pair of glasses and put on another, you would see only a piece of the total view and never be able to see the whole picture. Similarly, if we investigate this world using only one lens, whether it be the lens of gender or of race ethnicity or that of class, nation, or sexuality, we have a distorted view of history as well as of the present. In this book, we put on our "rainbow glasses" and try to see the whole picture with all of its variations and intersections.

In this book, we also try to see the whole picture by taking into consideration not only diversity within the United States but the variation and contrasts among nations. Table 1-1 provides us with some data with which to start to get a global view of gender. Box 1-1 explains what information is being provided in the table and what some of the key comparisons are. Throughout the book you will read about gender as it is socially constructed in many different ways around the world.

Scholarship Is Political

Sociologists have long debated whether the study of human beings can be based on a model that demands distanced objectivity from the scholar-observer and promotes the idea that only

TABLE 1-1 The Global Gender Gap Index 2010 Rankings (highs and lows)

Country	Lowest Ranks	Score
Guatemala	113	.63
Bahrain	114	.62
Ethiopia	115	.62
India	116	.62
Burkina Faso	117	.62
Cameroon	118	.61
Mauritania	119	.61
Algeria	120	.61
Jordan	121	.61
Lebanon	122	.60
Nepal	123	.60
Turkey	124	.60
Oman	125	.60
Egypt	126	.60
Iran	127	.59
Mali	128	.58
Morocco	129	.58
Côte d'Ivoire	130	.58
Saudi Arabia	131	.57
Syria	132	.56
Chad	133	.56
Pakistan	134	.55
Yemen	135	.51

Source: Hausmann, Tyson, and Zahidi (2012).

GENDER IN EVERYDAY LIFE   BOX 1-1
GENDER GAP AROUND THE GLOBE

One of the most important goals we have in this book is to broaden our view of gender to a global one. The gender gap is one that affects everyone's life all over the world, but the way in which gender is constituted and experienced varies across many social and political borders. Table 1-1 summarizes some of the latest information on the gender gap in 135 of the approximately 194 nations in the world (Hausmann, Tyson, and Zahidi 2012).

The nations are ranked on the basis of how unequal men and women are within them. These rankings were obtained by assigning scores for four factors: economic participation and opportunity; educational attainment; political empowerment; and health and survival. The highest possible score a nation could receive was 1.0000, which would mean that all four factors were 100 percent equal in regard to gender.

This table reports only some of the data: the top twenty-two nations and the bottom twenty. If you would like to see all of the nations' rankings as well as much more information on the individual countries, check out the website that contains the full report, http://www3.weforum.org/docs/WEF_GenderGap_Report_2012.pdf.

In the nations represented in the full table—which include 95 percent of the world's countries—equality ranges from .51 in Yemen to .85 in Iceland. Some of the highest-ranked nations are what most people would expect. They are located in Europe and Scandinavia, which are known to value gender equality and to have implemented strong policies to encourage it. Other high-ranking nations may be more surprising, since we don't hear about them as often. In the past six years, since these numbers have been compiled annually, 88% of the nations have shown improvement in gender equity, while 12 percent have seen the gap grow. These numbers give us a snapshot for making comparisons around the globe, but we also don't want to forget the gaps that exist within nations and the complexities that are summarized in the individual numbers.

the experts can tell us all we need to know about social life. More than three decades of feminist activism and research have developed the idea that researchers cannot and should not claim to be neutral outside observers and that knowledge is best produced collaboratively among scholars and others, including the people being observed. In particular, our knowledge should be grounded in the experience of people at the bottom of the power systems of gender, race ethnicity, sexuality, and class. Beginning to build knowledge from the perceptions and lives of the marginalized and least powerful members of society produces knowledge *for*—in contrast with knowledge *about*—people (Smith 1999). It is this knowledge for, rather than about, people that brings us closest to seeing the broadest and most valid view of social life.

This book is written in the tradition of those scholars who take this political view of scholarship. We seek to replace the "view from above" with the "view from below" by exploring the lives of people who have often been invisible, ignored, censored, or oppressed (Mies 1986). The topics we examine and the perspective we take attempt to see the world from the point of view of those who are marginalized by gender, as well as by race ethnicity, sexuality, social class, and nation. In addition, our exploration seeks not only to describe and explain the social world, but also to discover ways to transform it by making those groups and individuals who have been marginalized by race ethnicity, gender, sexuality, and citizenship central to producing knowledge of the social world.

THE OVERARCHING THEORY OF INTERSECTIONALITY

In our explorations in this text, we look at a wide range of gendered practices and institutions, assembling knowledge that shows the distribution of inequality, its consequences, and the ways people organize to challenge it. Throughout the book, we present the most current research, bringing in data from qualitative and quantitative studies. In addition to describing the issues and providing empirical data, we also offer an analysis to explain the issues from a range of theoretical perspectives. In each chapter, we look at the crosscutting inequalities that complicate gendered differences, a method that is called **intersectional analysis** (Collins 2000).

Intersectional analyses focus on the attributes assigned to members of oppressed communities of gender, race ethnicity, class, sexuality, and nation. The gender order is hierarchical: overall, men dominate women in terms of wealth, power, and social position, but not all men dominate all women. The racial ethnic order is a hierarchy in which whites have power over people of color. It crosscuts gender so that, for example, some white women are richer, more powerful, and more privileged than many men who are not white. The sexual order makes heterosexuality supreme and puts gay men, lesbians, transgender people, and members of other sexual communities at a decided disadvantage. Through its wealth and power, the **global North** (nations and regions of the world that are mostly at the "top" of the globe, such as the United States and Europe) still dominates the **global South** (poorer, less powerful nations and regions such as Africa, Latin America, and India, which are in the Southern Hemisphere).

The lesson of intersectional analysis is this: gender arrangements create relationships of inequality between women and men, but these arrangements also cause disadvantages for both women and men. Most important, not all women suffer oppression in the same way, nor do all men always benefit from patriarchal privilege simply because they are men. Being a white, wellborn man opens doors, offers privileges, and produces rewards. Being poor and black increases the difficulties and barriers a woman faces in her life. However, no person is completely oppressed or completely privileged, because oppressions and privileges shift with the social context. A working-class man may be privileged in the context of his family, where he dominates his wife and children by virtue of his paycheck and patriarchal privilege. In the workplace, however, he in turn may be dominated by his boss and may be relatively powerless to change the terms of his employment. Intersectionality, then, focuses attention on the ways that multiple and sometimes conflicting sources of oppression and power are intertwined.

Hegemonic Masculinities and Emphasized Femininities

The insights of intersectional analyses help us to see that there cannot be only one, universally valid way to be a man or a woman, but there are certainly images of the "right" way to be a man or a woman that dominate our thinking and our experience. Australian sociologist Robert (Raewyn) Connell (1987) first introduced the idea of hegemonic masculinity—idealized, culturally ascendant masculinity—into feminist men's-studies scholarship. The word *hegemony* means "dominance," and Connell uses the term *hegemonic masculinity* to refer to the culturally exalted form of masculinity that is linked to institutional power, such as that displayed at the top levels of the military, business, and government. This form of masculinity regularly appears in the media and as a component of our image of political leaders. Think of the film personas of John Wayne, "Indian" fighter and tough soldier in America's wars, or "Rambo," Sylvester Stallone, who won the on-screen Vietnam War for the United States, or Tony Stark (Robert Downey Jr.), the billionaire arms contractor and playboy turned Iron Man to fight terrorists in Afghanistan. Is the patriotic, violent, tough, uncompromising hero still hegemonic, or are there other ideals of manhood competing with it? If there are competing ideals, what is their message (Connell and Messerschmidt 2005)?

In the real world, dominant men are usually white, heterosexual citizens of the global North from elite schools with professional, managerial, or political careers. Hegemonic men are the powerful members of national and increasingly global orders. Some men are hegemonic within local or specific orders. The coach and the drill sergeant, for example, are usually working-class men with authority only over their soldiers or their team and fans. Connell also identifies "**subordinated**" **masculinities**, among which he includes sexually marginalized gay men, "sissies," "mother's boys," and "wimps." The intersections of class and race ethnicity produce other forms of subordinated or marginalized masculinity, men rendered socially invisible or outside the gender order.

There are different sorts of femininity as well. What Connell named *emphasized femininity* is the media version of womanhood that is "organized, financed, and supervised by men" (Connell 1987, 188). Women in TV-land are white, young, thin, conventionally beautiful, heterosexual, and often nurturant. Other forms of femininity resist and remake femininity, hidden in the experiences of women in the margins: "spinsters, lesbians, unionists, prostitutes, madwomen, rebels and maiden aunts, manual workers, midwives and witches" (Connell 1987, 188). The recovery of these marginalized forms of masculinity and femininity has been the work of feminism. Throughout the text, we look at the hegemonic forms of masculinity and emphasized femininity as well as the way masculinities and femininities vary and are challenged.

MAKING HISTORY

At the core of sociology is the idea that although individuals make choices about their destinies, they make them within the limits of the society in which they live. We are all constrained by the ideas and social institutions that surround us. The laws that protect equality (or not), the media messages we are sent about what are acceptable ways for women and men to behave, the technology available for health care or warfare, and the pay scales and the jobs available in our economic system, for example, all shape, limit, and sometimes even determine the "choices" we make as we interact with one another.

It is unlikely that we can successfully challenge these constraints as long as the systems are in place. We cannot live "outside" society and therefore we have to live at least to some extent within the rules. We can, however, change the systems. C. Wright Mills was one sociologist who explained that our laws, ideas, technology, social institutions, and ways of doing things did not drop from the sky or emerge as a fact of nature, but were invented and implemented by human beings and are constantly being reinvented and re-created. Mills wrote, "By the fact of his living he [each individual within a society] contributes, however minutely, to the shaping of this society and to the course of its history, even as he is made by society and by its historical push and shove" (Mills 1959, 11).

This quote has two important implications. First, it means that our experience of gender and our gendered relationships with one another are subjects of constant debate and struggle among all the people who are seeking to maintain or to change the status quo. Second, it means that we have the opportunity to shape the course of history—our own and our society's—by entering into these disputes and the social movements that have surrounded them. Sociologists use the term *agency* to describe the ways that people seek to change their social circumstances, to dismantle existing ways of thinking and acting, and to create new ideas and new social institutions. Throughout the text, we call attention to the ways organizations, small and large, local and global, are challenging systems of gender inequality as they intersect with other systems of inequality. In confronting systems of gender inequality, feminists have been at the forefront of both revisioning and reinvention.

Feminist Scholars Seeking Answers

Why are we writing about gender, and why are you reading about it? Women's and gender studies is a field that emerged in the United States in the late 1960s. The social movement that shaped the invention of the discipline and continues to influence it has a long history that is often argued to be rooted in the abolitionist and women's suffrage movements of the late nineteenth and early twentieth centuries. The development of these social movements, along with others and along with social activism and scholarship in places outside the United States, not only invented the discipline of gender studies but have continued to shape the scholarship and pedagogy of the field.

Both U.S. feminist history and the movement for racial justice developed from similar starting points—abolition and suffrage—but these two movements began to move along different tracks in the post–Civil War era. A common starting point was the women, black and white, who tried to act publicly as abolitionists in interracial coalitions to end slavery at a time when middle-class women's place was firmly restricted to their homes. When women attempted to conduct abolitionist meetings or even attend them, they were not allowed to speak in public and frequently had to hide behind curtains while the men spoke.

After the Civil War abolished slavery, Congress had to decide who would be able to vote among the newly emancipated black men and women. Some white woman suffragists chose to support "expedient" racism, by making arguments that white women should not be given less power than black men (Eisenstein 2010, 10). And some black activists insisted that although the women's vote was a worthy goal, fighting for it should not jeopardize the voting rights of black men. The history of these tensions and the perceived and actual slights and betrayals of black women by white feminists is long. Even if many white feminists were not actively racist, their failure to strongly condemn suffragist racism was an early betrayal with enormous ramifications for both the rights of women and the rights of black Americans, as well as for the persistent difficulties in organizing coalitions of all people who had been marginalized.

Although the intellectual and activist tradition of African American women remained hidden to most, throughout the nineteenth century and well into the twentieth, black women were active in the defense of their communities and families. Ida B. Wells, for example, was a leader in the anti-lynching movement at the turn of the century. In contemporary terms, lynching was a form of terrorism employed by white southern men to retain control over black people and white women. Anna Julia Cooper, a contemporary of Wells, was instrumental in organizing women to resist race and gender control as well as an advocate of the anti-lynching campaign. Early practitioners of what later would come to be called "intersectional analysis," Wells, Cooper, and others like them urged women to challenge racism.

Black domestic workers organized to improve their pay and working conditions. Others resisted the powerful eugenics movement in the early twentieth century and the "sterilization abuse" of the 1970s that routinely sterilized women of color and poor women in the name of "improving" the race. Many promoted black women's access to education. Well before white middle-class women began to demand entry into the labor force, black women were employed and contributing to the economic support of their families (Guy-Sheftall 1995, 78).

In the middle of the twentieth century, calls for gender equality by white women began to emerge, and white feminists of the nineteenth and early twentieth centuries were rediscovered by activists in the early days of the Women's Liberation Movement, which is sometimes called the "**second wave**" of feminism. This "second wave"—the feminism of predominantly white women—was in fact two conjoined movements. One, spearheaded by the **National Organization for Women (NOW)**, focused on reform of the political and economic system. It was founded by a group of lawyers, academics, writers, business executives, and government employees in 1966 to work for the elimination of legal barriers to women in government, the work force, educational institutions, and labor unions. NOW and its allies helped to establish affirmative action programs that opened universities, professions, and many "men's" occupations to women. They pressed for the passage of **Title IX** of the Education Amendments of 1972, which mandated equal funding for girls' and women's sports, a law that has been responsible for women's gains in educational institutions and in high school and collegiate athletics. They exhorted women to run for political office and supported their efforts to do so.

The second arm of second-wave feminism was made up of young women, many of whom identified themselves as socialist feminists and/or lesbian feminists. They were former civil rights activists, Vietnam War protesters, community advocates, and student militants. Many had gone south in the 1960s to join the **Student Nonviolent Coordinating Committee (SNCC)**, the younger wing of the civil rights movement noted for its leadership of sit-ins, freedom rides, and the dangerous work of registering black voters in the rural South. Women's historian Sarah Evans notes how the leadership of women's liberation in the North drew inspiration from local southern black women who were "the core of the local civil rights insurgency" (Evans 1979, 51):

> The most important models for the young volunteers were the older black women in local communities. Living in their homes, eating from their tables, civil rights workers often became temporary members of the family, even to the point of being introduced to friends as "my adopted daughter." . . . In addition to their warmth and courage in taking in civil rights workers, these black women also furnished the backbone of leadership in local movements. Volunteers wrote home of "Mama" doggedly attempting to register again and again or of a rural woman attending a precinct meeting, and no one showed up. With a neighbor as a witness, she called the meeting to order, elected herself delegate and wrote up the minutes. Like the white southern women who had preceded them, female volunteers in the field found these "mamas" vital examples of courage and leadership. (Evans 1979, 75–76)

History repeated itself! The civil rights movement, like the abolitionist movement before it, was a seedbed of white feminism. And despite the fact that black women "struck the first blow for female equality" in that movement (Eisenstein 2010), by the 1970s that community of young civil rights activists had split into separate movements, often based on their singular sexual or racial identities. Winifred Breines succinctly characterizes the period in American feminist history:

> From the civil rights movement into the **Black Power movement**, the New Left, and the student movement, young women went forward to create the socialist feminist movements, white and black. The central trajectory of those years saw them first working together politically in solidarity in the civil rights movement and then dramatically shifting toward separation based on new definitions of distinct identities, eventually moving into a provisional reconciliation very different from their earlier bonds. White feminists believed there could be universal sisterhood, that black women would join their movement. But that didn't happen. The 1970s were filled with efforts at reconciliation and failures, work at understanding how race operates in the United States and recriminations—far from the earlier, easier times of idealism and high expectations. White and black feminism developed on parallel tracks, distant from earlier notions of solidarity and integration. But socialist feminists persevered, in part because of their deep desire for an inclusive women's movement. (Breines 2006, 4)

Black and white socialist feminism grew from the civil rights, antiwar, and **New Left** movements. Socialist feminists cast a critical eye on capitalism, class relations, and imperialism as the foundation of gender inequalities, and often on race, gender, and sexuality as divisions that weakened feminist and other struggles for justice and equality. Unlike the women's rights/NOW feminist project, which concentrated on creating more opportunities for women within existing social structures, socialist feminists wanted to build a new society in which everyone shared power and resources equally; where people, not corporations, governed our lives; and where neither sexism nor racism divided women and men, people of color and whites.

Another strand of the women's movement that emerged in that period was radical and lesbian feminism. Radical feminists saw women's oppression as the first and most fundamental oppression. The New York radical feminist group Redstockings argued that "[T]he conflicts between individual men and women are political conflicts that can only be solved collectively. . . . *All men* receive economic, sexual, and psychological benefits from male supremacy" (Baxandall and Gordon 2000, 90). The idea that many men (though not all, and not in the very radical sense conveyed by Redstockings) benefit socially, politically, and economically as men has entered contemporary feminist theory as the concept of "patriarchal privilege." Other groups focused on the oppressiveness to women of the institutions of love, marriage, and sex. One radical feminist group, who called themselves the Feminists, limited the number of married women who were allowed to join the group, believing that marriage weakened women's feminist commitments. A famous member of this group, Ti-Grace Atkinson, wrote that love was a pathological state, the pivotal point in the persecution of women, a psychological phenomenon that supported the "pairing" of oppressor and oppressed (Baxandall and Gordon 2000, 91–93).

Lesbian feminism was an extension of radical feminism. In the 1970 statement "The **Woman-Identified Woman**," the group Radicalesbians treated lesbianism as a political choice, a necessary step "at the heart of women's liberation." We can detect the roots of lesbian separatism, yet another extension of radical feminism, in this statement:

> As long as the label "dyke" can be used to frighten women into a less militant stand, keep her separate from her sisters, keep her from giving primacy to anything other than men and family—then to that extent she is controlled by the male culture. Until women see in each other the possibility of a primal commitment which includes sexual love, they will be denying themselves the love and value they readily accord to men, thus affirming their second-class status. As long as male acceptability is primary—both to individual women and to the movement as a whole—the term lesbian will be used effectively against women. Insofar as women want only more privileges within the system, they do not want to antagonize male power. They instead seek acceptability for women's liberation, and the most crucial aspect of the acceptability is to deny lesbianism—i.e., deny any fundamental challenge to the basis of the female. (Radicalesbians 1970, cited in Baxandall and Gordon 2000, 107–109)

In the mid-twentieth century, Chicanos, Native Americans, and Puerto Ricans, also inspired by the civil rights movement, formed radical and activist groups dedicated to their rights and liberation. Women were central participants in these movements. Their demands, such as ending sterilization abuse, lowering infant mortality rates, and reducing school dropout rates, reflected their particular experiences as women of color. Eisenstein reminds us that

> . . . black women and other women of color often argued that their main issues were the struggle against racism, against high infant mortality rates, and for decent education, housing, and health care. If many white women were eager to get out of their kitchens into the paid workforce, many black women wanted nothing more than the opportunity to leave the workforce and raise their own children, rather than the children of white mothers. (Eisenstein 2010, 76; see also hooks 1999)

FEMINISM IN THE UNIVERSITIES. Not surprisingly, all of the social upheaval of the period affected the university. Feminists entered the universities as students and young faculty, opening up new areas for study and theorizing in the 1970s. Women's Studies programs emerged and feminism affected every field, especially in the social sciences and humanities.

Feminist scholars began to theorize on the issues around them. At first, they divided feminist thought into liberal, socialist, and radical/lesbian approaches, but ideas have continued to develop. Since the 1970s, many different feminist theories have been added to the original three, including postcolonial feminism, black feminism, ecofeminism, lesbian feminism, psychoanalytic feminism, standpoint feminism, multiracial/multiethnic feminism, feminist studies of men, social construction feminism, postmodern feminism or queer theory, and third-wave feminism (Lorber 2009). New concepts have been introduced to theorize gender relations and structures.

At the same time social activism has continued to shape our scholarship. In 1992, Rebecca Walker, the daughter of African American novelist Alice Walker, first used the term ***third wave*** in an article in *Ms.* magazine. She argued that the third-wave movement embraced women from all backgrounds and identities, young women who had entered a variety of occupations and activities, who took for granted the privileges won by their mothers' generation, embraced racial ethnic and global differences among women, and lived feminism in their everyday lives. She and the people about whom she wrote reminded us once again that gender does not exist in isolation and brought our attention to the diversity of gender especially within the United States and the persistence in particular of racial ethnic inequality and its ties to gender inequality. In addition, women's studies became gender studies as we became more aware of gendered character of men's lives as well as women's. Box 1-2 shows another version of waves based on the experience of many activists in Africa.

Gender activists and scholars from outside the United States have also continued to influence gender studies theorizing and practicing transnational feminism. The critique of white Western feminism stimulated the growth of **transnational feminism**, based on networks of women in the global South who are critical of the hegemony of the North and of its capitalist economies and militarist policies. A less militant globalism has developed under the aegis of the United Nations. The **Commission on the Status of Women (CSW)**, established in 1946 by the UN Economic and Social Council to promote the rights of women in political, economic, civil, social, and educational fields, successfully lobbied the UN General Assembly to designate **1975 International Women's Year**, and in that year the UN sponsored the first of a series of international women's conferences in Mexico City. The conference participants recommended that the UN declare 1976–1985 the Decade for Women, during which the UN would address the needs of women in the first (The United States and its allies), second (the Soviet Union and its allies), and third worlds (the non-aligned nations). The second conference in 1980 took place in Copenhagen. In 1985 the Nairobi conference reviewed the achievements of the Decade for Women and created a ten-year action plan for their advancement. In 1995 the Fourth World Conference on Women was held in Beijing, China, and in 2000, a five-year review ("Beijing + 5") took place in New York. Despite having begun with divergent goals, the UN Decade for Women attempted to find common ground between activists in the North and the South and to legitimize activities to promote women's rights within the UN system and beyond. The Platform for Action, approved at the Fourth World Conference on Women in Beijing, called for action in twelve critical areas of concern, including women and poverty, education and training, women's health, and violence against women. Another feature of the international system is the increasing numbers of **nongovernmental organizations (NGOs)** dedicated to assisting women in the global South and in stressed areas such as Eastern Europe. And yet, as subsequent chapters will show, women throughout the world remain marginalized, poor, and under threat of violence to an alarming degree.

WOMEN'S MOVEMENTS: A BROAD LOOK. After reading this brief history, what do you think will be the future of feminism, and what will be the future of feminist gender studies? Feminist political theorist Nancy Fraser (2009) argues that the feminist movement arose in the context of **welfare-state capitalism**, toward which it directed compelling critiques of androcentric labor and welfare policies and was often either ignored or ridiculed. Fraser points out that feminism now has become an acceptable piece of the dominant political economy of neoliberal capitalism. Is feminism no longer a significant challenger to the global power structures? Has feminism toned down its critiques and accommodated to **neoliberalism**? If so, does feminism need to find its edge again?

GENDER IN EVERYDAY LIFE   BOX 1-2
WAVES OF AFRICAN FEMINISM

The American women's movement has been divided into waves by some scholars. The first wave was focused on suffrage and emerged out of the abolitionist movement of the nineteenth century. The second wave was the women's liberation movement of the 1960s that had roots in the civil rights and anti-war movements. The third wave is more nebulous but emerged from within the women's movement itself and was identified in the 1990s as feminists pointed to the diversity of women as well as the gendered character of men's lives as critical issues that we should highlight.

African women's activism has also been divided into waves, but the turning points and the focal issues are quite different from the three waves identified with the American women's movement. Using the model of the waves, scholars of African history have proposed a postcolonial timeline of African women's activism running from 1950 to 1970. During this period, the focus was on development issues such as "integrating women into development, promoting women's cooperatives, developing small-scale industries, training rural women to take on leadership positions, and establishing national mechanisms for integrating women in development projects" (Adams 2006, 189).

A second wave of regional activism in Africa began in 1980 and continues today. This period is marked by global debt, structural adjustment, and economic crisis. The globalized economy introduced problems to the people of Africa, but it also facilitated international communication and organization that helped increase gender equity in Africa, such as the growth of nongovernmental organizations (NGOs) committed to solving women's problems and providing alternatives to the official views and activities of governments. Peace and the elimination of poverty have dominated the agendas of these NGOs.

At the beginning of the twenty-first century, another turning point emerged suggesting that perhaps a third wave is developing. In 2002 the launching of the African Union (AU) gave impetus to the struggle for gender justice. The AU is modeled after the European Union and "seeks to promote unity among African countries and peoples, political and economic integration, peace and respect for democracy and human rights" (Adams 2006, 196). A centerpiece of the AU is its commitment to gender equity. Women

Neoliberals support free (unregulated) markets and the privatization of state welfare provisions. They believe that corporations should have total freedom to pursue profits around the globe, that trade unions should be curbed, and that the social safety net should be greatly reduced or eliminated. As neoliberalism has become policy, first in the global South and more recently in the industrial economies of the North, social programs providing protections such as welfare grants, unemployment insurance, and free education have been slashed, and others, such as Social Security, are under attack.

make up fully half of the executive body of the organization. In 2003 it passed the Protocol on the Rights of Women in Africa, which explicitly endorsed quotas to increase women's representation in decision-making bodies, prohibition of female genital cutting, setting of the minimum age of marriage at 18, and guarantee of a woman's right to terminate a pregnancy in the case of rape, incest, or to save the mother's life (Adams 2006).

Africa's waves of feminist activism show different turning points and different activities and organizations than those of women in the United States. They also show a different trajectory, for the gains made by African women seem to be occurring at the same time as American women are losing ground, for example, on the issue of reproductive rights and access to abortion.

A number of explanations have been given for why the United States in particular has fallen from its leadership role (Tripp 2006):

- A growing complacency among Americans about defending gender equality
- The demise of the labor movement, which has been the seedbed of much of American reform
- A general increase in the position of conservative political forces
- Few feminists in public office
- Poor media coverage, resulting in a lack of awareness of international initiatives and of how far the United States has fallen behind

Throughout this text, we explore the organized activism of people seeking to change the gendered context of their lives. This look at African waves tells us that we need to be careful to remember that one size does not fit all and that the experience of gender in other regions and nations, or even within a nation by race ethnicity or social class, might be quite different. This comparison of waves also reminds us of another important issue in this text: the tendency of people from the global North to think about themselves as providing a model to which the rest of the world needs only to "catch up." Activism by women in Africa and other places today tells us that we will find models of equality all over the world and that the United States may sometimes be a leader but may also often be a nation that could benefit by looking at solutions that have developed in other areas of the world.

Even though the new labor force of neoliberal, **transnational capitalism** is a largely female labor force (see chapter 6), most feminists have not developed extensive critiques of this system from the standpoint of gender, nor have they envisioned a broad struggle of women and men for economic and political justice. Instead, "dreams of emancipation," observes Fraser, "[are] harnessed to wage labor." In other words, there is no movement against capitalism, only struggles to find accommodation within it. Fraser maintains that feminism must reconnect with its former critique of capitalism and with its roots as a movement for gender justice.

"I am suggesting," she concludes, "we have an opening now in which to reclaim [our best ideas]. In seizing this moment, we might just bend the arc of the impending transformation in the direction of justice—and not only with respect to gender" (Fraser 2009). In other words, Fraser believes that it is time to look beyond capitalism to a new social order.

As you read through this book, think about Fraser's viewpoint. For example, she may be correct about feminisms of the North, but what about the critical work of transnational feminists working through the United Nations, the African Union, and international and local NGOs (nongovernmental organizations)? Perhaps the momentum of feminist movements is now located in the global South. By the time you reach the last chapter of this book, you will have knowledge that helps you evaluate the theories and evidence that you are about to encounter here.

Our world is filled with injustice, inequality, and pain. It is also filled with the hope and promise that grows from the many who contribute to resisting injustices, promoting equality, and creating a world that promotes our potentials and our pleasures. We dedicate this book to furthering those ends.

KEY TERMS

agency
Black Power movement
Commission on the Status of Women (CSW)
emphasized femininities
1975 International Women's Year
  and Decade for Women
Global North and South
hegemonic masculinity
heterosexual privilege
intersectional analysis
National Organization for Women (NOW)
neoliberalism

New Left
nongovernmental organizations (NGOs)
Student Nonviolent Coordinating
  Committee (SNCC)
subordinated masculinities
Title IX
transnational capitalism
transnational feminism
waves of feminism
welfare-state capitalism
Woman-Identified Woman

CRITICAL THINKING QUESTIONS

1. The text states: "At the core of sociology is the idea that although individuals make choices about their destinies, they make them within the limits of the society in which they live." What does this mean in regard to gender?
2. Look at the numbers in the table on the global gender gap. Which of the rankings surprise you? Why did you think certain nations might rank higher or lower than they do? What do you think now that you see the rankings?
3. With which category of gender, race ethnicity, social class, and nation do you identify? How does the theory of intersectionality help you make sense of the social categories with which you identify?
4. How does the example of the Tsunami in 2004 in Indonesia illustrate the social character of gender? How does it illustrate the political character of gender?

REFERENCES

Adams, Melinda. 2006. "Regional Women's Activism: African Women's Networks and the African Union." In *Global Feminism: Transnational Women's Activism, Organizing, and Human Rights*, edited by Myra Marx Ferree and Aili Mari Tripp, 187–218. New York: New York University Press.

Baxandall, Rosalyn, and Linda Gordon, eds. 2000. *Dear Sisters: Dispatches from the Women's Liberation Movement*. New York: Basic Books.

Breines, Winifred. 2006. *The Trouble Between Us: An Uneasy History of White and Black Women in the Feminist Movement*. New York: Oxford University Press.

Collins, Patricia Hill. 2000. *Black Feminist Thought: Knowledge, Consciousness, and the Politics of Empowerment*. 2nd edition. New York: Routledge.

Connell, Robert W. 1987. *Gender and Power*. Stanford, CA: Stanford University Press.

Connell, Robert W., and James Messerschmidt. 2005. "Hegemonic Masculinity: Rethinking the Concept." *Gender and Society* 19 (6): 829–59.

Doocy, Shannon, Abdur Rofi, Gilbert Burnham, and Courtland Robinson. 2007. "Tsunami Mortality in Aceh Province, Indonesia." *Bulletin of the World Health Organization* 85 (4): 245–324.

Eisenstein, Hester. 2010. *Feminism Seduced: How Global Elites Use Women's Labor and Ideas to Exploit the World*. Boulder, CO: Paradigm.

Enarson, Elaine, and Betty Hearn Morrow, eds. 1998. *The Gendered Terrain of Disaster: Through Women's Eyes*. Westport, CT: Greenwood.

Evans, Sarah. 1979. *Personal Politics: The roots of Women's Liberation in the Civil Rights Movement and the New Left*. New York: Alfred A. Knopf.

Fraser, Nancy. 2009. "Feminism, Capitalism, and the Cunning of History." *New Left Review* 56 (March-April): 97–117.

Guy-Sheftall, Beverly. 1995. *Words of Fire: An Anthology of African-American Feminist Thought*. New York: New Press.

Hausmann, Ricardo, Laura Tyson, and Saadia Zahidi, eds. 2012. *The Global Gender Gap Report, 2012*. Geneva: World Economic Forum. http://www3.weforum.org/docs/WEF_GenderGap_Report_2012.pdf

hooks, bell. 1999. *Ain't I a Woman: Black Women and Feminism*. Cambridge, MA: South End Press.

Juran, Luke. 2012. The gendered nature of disasters: Women survivors in post-tsunami Tamil Nadu. *Indian Journal of Gender Studies* 19 (1): 1–29.

Lorber, Judith. 2009. *Gender Inequality: Feminist Theories and Politics*. 4th edition. New York: Oxford University Press.

Mies, Maria. 1986. *Patriarchy and Accumulation on a World Scale: Women in the International Division of Labour*. London: Zed Books.

Mills, C. Wright. 1959. *The Sociological Imagination*. New York: Oxford University Press.

Neumayer, Eric, and Thomas Pluemper. 2007. "The Gendered Nature of Natural Disasters: The Impact of Catastrophic Events on the Gender Gap in Life Expectancy, 1981–2002." *Annals of the American Association of Geographers* 97 (3): 551–66. http://ssrn.com/abstract=874965. Accessed March 18, 2011.

Oxfam. 2005. *Gender and the Tsunami*. Oxfam briefing note, March 30. London: Oxfam.

Smith, Dorothy E. 1999. *Writing the Social: Critique, Theory, and Investigations*. Toronto: University of Toronto Press.

Tripp, Aili Mari. 2006. "The Evolution of Transnational Feminisms: Consensus, Conflict, and New Dynamics." In *Global Feminism: Transnational Women's Activism, Organizing, and Human Rights*, edited by Myra Marx Ferree and Aili Mari Tripp, 51–78. New York: New York University Press.

2

BODIES AND GENDERS

Caster Semenya from South Africa celebrates becoming the women's 800m world champion.
Source: Associated Press.

Becoming a person who is comfortable standing up in public, literally, on television and saying, "No matter what you think of how I look or how I speak, no matter what I've done to fit into this world, I am not male and I am not female. And probably neither are you."

Sharon Preves, *Intersex and Identity: The Contested Self*

Sex by definition will be shown to have been gender all along.

Judith Butler, *Gender Trouble*

In 1985 Maria Patino got the surprise of her life when she traveled to Kobe, Japan, to compete in the World University Games. Since 1966, women who compete in international games have been required to take a sex test to prove they are not really men disguised as women. In the first years, the women were required to parade naked before a gynecologist to prove they were female. Eventually, a new procedure called the buccal smear was developed to test the women athletes. A lab technician scrapes a few skin cells from the inside of a woman's cheek, stains the tissue sample, and examines it under a high-powered microscope. If the cells have two X chromosomes—the mark of a genetic female—then the technician will see a dark spot, called a Barr body, inside the cells' nuclei. If only one X is present, as is the case with genetic males, no dark spot appears.

Patino was not concerned with the test, because she had spent her life living and training as a woman. Her body appeared to herself and to everyone else as female, but the genetics test showed that she had only one X chromosome, while the other was a Y, which meant that genetically she was male. Patino found out that she was androgen insensitive, which means that before she was born, her body was not able to use the hormone androgen to transform her XY genetics into a male body with a penis and scrotum. Instead, she was born appearing to be a female; and as her body matured, it acquired female attributes such as breasts and a vagina. Her body, however, did not have a uterus, and hidden inside she had two testes (Peel 1994). Patino was disqualified from the games in 1985, although she was later reinstated. International athletic organizations, however, are still debating the question of how to define a female. Their arguments are shaped by what we might call "**the standard story.**"

What is the standard story? And what is its effect on how we think about ourselves and others? How is the standard story being challenged by activists and by scholars in history, genetics, and cross-cultural studies?

This chapter describes the standard story and the ways it is being challenged. We begin by critically examining the claim, convincingly disputed by feminist and queer theorists, that our chromosomes, hormones, and genitalia work together to create "purely" female or "purely" male bodies. In some quarters even now, nonconforming bodies—those that do not easily fit the categories of male or female—are seen as "mistakes of nature" that require correction. However, increasingly, activists, scholars, physicians, and others argue that multiple sex statuses and sexed bodies are arrayed along a continuum, with fully male and fully female at the extreme ends of a range containing three, four, five, or more mixed "sexes" (Fausto-Sterling 2000b). An even more radical perspective is that "male" and "female" are not two extreme poles of a continuum, but instead are "orthogonal" to each other, "independent variables in 'perpendicular dimensions,' so that a person could be high or low in both scales at once" (Kimmel, Connell, and Hearn 2004, 46; Sedgwick 1991).

The chapter explores the emergent multiplicities of sex and gender that have only recently become more widely visible. It reviews the historical and anthropological evidence that shows how, in other times and other places, people perceived sexed bodies differently and treated them differently from the way they are seen and treated today. In fact, gender historians have shown how our once seemingly immutable ways of seeing and understanding the sexes developed as recently as the nineteenth century, alongside new divisions of labor, new forms of production, and new patterns of social relations (D'Emilio 1983). In contrast, many ancient and medieval naturalists and physicians compared male and female anatomy to prove there was only one sex, not two. Likewise, many anthropologists described cultures in which life was built around the existence of three or more sexes. To the people of these other worlds, the shape and functions of sexed bodies seemed just as obvious to them as our two-sex system has appeared to us. In fact, some historians have made the case that the West has had its own three-sex system (something on the order of male, female, and queer) (Trumbach 1996, Chauncy, 1995).

Next, the chapter examines dualist and biological explanations of sexuality and bodies and compares these to current research claiming that sexuality and desire have histories, and that they are constructed socially out of bodily potentials. Finally, the chapter examines the public emergence of intersexuals and transsexuals and their increasingly influential impact on thinking about gender and sex.

What these developments in ideas about embodiment, sexuality, and gender suggest is that our ways of seeing and ways of being sexed and gendered are evolving. Instead of considering ambiguously sexed bodies as mistakes of nature or disorders of personality that modern medical science and psychiatry should try to correct, intersexuals and transsexuals have begun to challenge beliefs that "sex categories are binary, that there are only males and females, and that anything not clearly one or the other is abnormal" (Dreger 1998, 8). As these gender and sexual stories reach wider audiences, and as the previously shared assumptions about sex and gender differences are questioned, we may see a **paradigm shift** (Kuhn 1996) in the way we understand sexed and gendered bodies and selves.

THE STANDARD STORY

In the not-too-distant past, many of us believed that there were clear connections among sex, sexuality, and gender. An infant with a female body would grow up to be a woman who is sexually attracted to men. An infant with a male body would become a man who is sexually attracted to women. There was no in-between or "other" status, such as that claimed by the speaker in the first epigraph. This was once the story most of us learned about sex, what philosopher Judith Butler (1990) has named the **heterosexual matrix**, or what we might call the standard story line. The epigraphs that begin this chapter suggest that new story lines about sex are emerging to challenge the standard.

The old story line contains several tacit assumptions (Oyama, Griffiths, and Gray 2001):

- *Biology is destiny.* Underlying social behavior (gender) and sexual choice (normatively, heterosexuality) is the substratum of nature. One's biological sex determines one's sexual and social identity, one's needs and desires, and one's sexual potentials.
- *There are only two sexes, male and female.* Male infants will become boys and men; female infants will become girls and women. This is the "normal" and "natural" course of development dictated by our genes, hormones, and gonads (testes or ovaries). A person with a penis and testes is a man; a person with a vagina and ovaries is a woman.
- *The two-sex order is universal, a fact of nature.* Deviations from this natural order are mistakes of nature or of culture. They require intervention to restore this order, lest we "subvert nature's plan."

THE INTERPLAY OF SEX, GENDER, AND SEXUALITY

At one time, scholars agreed that binary sex differences were the sum and substance of embodied sex, asking only if nature or culture was responsible for turning sex (the biological substratum) into gender (the social arrangements built on sex differences). Now growing numbers of scholars are trying to disentangle the complex interplay of sex, gender, and sexuality. For example, Edward Stein suggests using the term *sex-gender* to reflect the fact that some things we attribute to biological sex might turn out to be the outcome of social gender. For him, the boundary between what is sex (nature) and what is gender (society and culture) is dissolving. His category sex-gender "includes all the characteristics (biological, psychological, cultural, and social) that are supposed to distinguish males/men from females/women" (Stein 1999, 33).

Social psychologists Suzanne Kessler and Wendy McKenna (1978) go even further than Stein. They treat sex as an aspect of gender, where even genes, chromosomes, and hormones are socially constructed. They begin from the **ethnomethodological premise** that in our everyday lives we proceed on the basis of a **natural attitude**, a belief in the objectivity and rationality of the world as we apprehend it. In other words, reality is what we see and experience directly. In the natural attitude, gender (and, similarly, race) is a biological, universal, and unchanging reality in which, unerringly, men are men and women are women.

Kessler and McKenna assert that most scientific approaches to sex have failed to question the premise that there are two, and only two, sexes. Instead, scientists use the "everyday attribution process" that nonscientists use in daily interaction. They mean that scientists, like the rest of us, assign individuals to one or the other sex category based on their observations of a person's demeanor, clothing, mannerisms, name, and so forth. Scientists, like the rest of us, adopt the natural attitude that there are, objectively, only two sexes.

Kessler and McKenna, however, argue that the natural attitude assumes what scientists should question. They offer an example of how that assumption produces circular reasoning about the reality of sex difference. To know if women and men differ in brain structures, they write, we would need to get a group of (deceased) women and a group of (deceased) men, label their brains according to the donor's gender, and then examine the brains for differences. But if this group of dead men and women is assembled by asking the morgue to supply brains from male and female corpses, the research will be tainted. As in Maria Patino's case, a person who looks female might have undescended testicles and an XY genetic makeup; similarly, a person who looks male could have ovaries and an enlarged clitoris. If scientists base their tests of brain structure simply on corpses that look female or male, they are likely to contaminate the categories of analysis and thus render their conclusions meaningless (Kessler and McKenna 1978, 75).

Judith Lorber (1994) suggests that women and men are fairly alike biologically and that social and cultural selection processes produce individuals we see as men or women. Gendered people, she writes, "do not emerge from physiology or hormones but from the exigencies of the social order." Quoting philosopher Judith Butler, she continues:

> There is no core or bedrock human nature below these endlessly looping processes of the social production of sex and gender, self and other, identity and psyche, each of which is a "complex cultural construction" (Butler 1990, 36). The paradox of "human nature" is that it is always a manifestation of cultural meanings, social relationships, arid power politics—[quoting Butler again] "not biology, but culture, becomes destiny." (Lorber 1994, 568)

Sex, gender, sexuality—these are terms that can confuse us now because what they refer to in the real world is becoming blurred. Following Lorber (2005b, 9), we use the terms in the following ways:

- **Sex** is "a complex interplay of genes, hormones, environment, and behavior with loopback effects between bodies and society." We use the adjectives *male*, *female*, and *intersex* when referring to apparent biological—chromosomal, gonadal, or genital (phenotype of one's genitalia)—features of sex.

- **Sexuality** involves "lustful desire, emotional involvement, and fantasy." We use the terms *homosexuality, lesbianism, heterosexuality, bisexuality, omnisexuality,* and *asexuality* when referring to sexuality. Studies of sexual orientation suggest that there are no hard-and-fast divides among individuals in the objects of their sexual desires. An individual's feelings of homosexuality, lesbianism heterosexuality, and bisexuality need not be "fixed for life" nor mutually exclusive. These ideas are explored further in chapter 4.
- **Gender** is "a social status, a legal designation, and a personal identity." Gender divisions and their accompanying norms and expectations are part of major social institutions. We use the terms *women* and *men* and *boys* and *girls* when referring to gender.

CHROMOSOMES, HORMONES, AND GENES

What sex are you? How do you know? One way we could categorize you is in terms of your chromosomes, as international athletics organizations such as the World University Games did to Maria Patino and the International Olympic Committee (IOC) began to do in 1968. They policed female competitors to make sure no "men" competed in women's events; the rules they established required that women's events be restricted to people with two X chromosomes. The IOC based its action on the idea that a person is either a man or a woman, an XX or an XY. However, the biology of sex is more complicated than this single either–or test suggests. The decision to rule that Patino was not a woman was based on cultural beliefs about gender, not scientific facts. As Fausto-Sterling describes her, Patino had breasts, a narrow waist, and broad hips. She had the strength of a woman, was raised as a woman, and felt herself to be a woman. Despite her Y chromosome, she had grown up female.

When you read the story of Maria Patino in the opening scenario, did you agree with the committee's decision about her eligibility to compete as a woman? By the time you finish reading this chapter, your answer may change. The fact is that the IOC has changed its approach to athletes whose chromosomes or appearance seem ambiguous, abandoning as unreliable the chromosome testing that led to Patino's disqualification. The problem of defining what is a female (and what is a male) persists, however, for international athletic organizations. In 2009 Caster Semenya, the South African world champion in the 800-meters race, was tested and retested, removed from competition and reinstated, without definitive answers (see Box 2-1). In 2012 the Olympic Committee revised its sex verification standards to end genetic tests, but also to prohibit from competition women whose levels of testosterone reach a man's normal levels. Critics called this revision a "farce" that is still a "sex test" (Macur 2012). In fact, definitive answers about sex are now more, not less, difficult to unearth. Alice Dreger, professor of clinical medical humanities and bioethics at Northwestern University School of Medicine, stated that it is not possible to designate what constitutes the essential difference between a man and a woman. "This is not a solvable problem. People always press me: 'Isn't there one marker we can use?' No. We couldn't then and we can't now, and science is making it more difficult, not less, because it ends up showing us how much blending there is and how many nuances, and it becomes impossible to point to one thing, or even a set of things, and say that's what it means to be male" (Levy 2009).

GENDER IN EVERYDAY LIFE   BOX 2-1

CASTER SEMENYA AIN'T 8 FEET TALL

If you aspire to be a star woman athlete but have no aspirations to appear in *Playboy*'s Women of the Olympics issue, you are far better off being from South Africa than the United States. The Western media's handling of the story of Caster Semenya, the gold-medal-winning eighteen-year-old South African runner, has been at best simplistic and at worst repellent. In a salacious, drooling tone, "Is she really a he?" is the extent of their curiosity. On various radio shows, I've been asked, "Why does she talk like a man?" No one defines what "a man" is supposed to talk like. Or, "Do you think she's really a dude? Is this a *Crying Game* thing?" I've heard it all this week, and most of the questions say far more about the insecurities of the questioners than about Semenya's situation.

It's not just in the confederate confines of sports radio. I appeared on Campbell Brown's CNN show, where my co-panelist, Dr. Jennifer Berman, said that suspicion of Semenya's gender was justified because she is "8 feet tall" (she's 5-foot-7). How an eighteen-year-old runner became Yao Ming in Dr. Berman's mind was never addressed. This is hysteria, pure and simple, and it is born out of people's own discomfort with women athletes who don't conform to gender stereotypes. In South Africa, however, the response could not be more different. Semenya was greeted by thousands of people in a celebration that included signs and songs from the antiapartheid struggle.

She was even embraced by former South African first lady Winnie Mandela. "We are here to tell the whole world how proud we are of our little girl," Mandela told cheering fans. "They can write what they like—we are proud of her."

As Patrick Bond, a leading South African global justice activist, said to me, "To order Semenya tested for gender seems about as reasonable as ordering IAAF officials like Philip Weiss tested for brain cells—which actually isn't a bad idea given his recent off-field performance. And if Weiss doesn't have a sufficient number of brain cells to know how to treat women athletes, it would only be fair to relieve him of his functions for the good of world athletics."

It's not just national political figures with global profiles who are embracing Semenya. The people have rallied around her fiercely, particularly in the very rural, impoverished, subsistence-farming community where Semenya was raised. Her home village, Masehlong, has an unemployment rate near 80 percent. They only recently acquired electricity.

As *The Guardian* recently wrote:

> The loyalty of Semenya's friends and neighbours is striking. South Africa's rural communities are typically regarded as bastions of social conservatism divided into traditional gender roles and expectations of femininity. But there is no evidence that Semenya, an androgynous tomboy who played football and wore trousers, was

ostracised by her peers. Instead, they are shocked at what they perceive as the intolerance and prurience of western commentators. "They are jealous," said Dorcus Semenya, the athlete's mother, who led villagers in jubilant singing and dancing on Friday. "I say to them, go to hell, you don't know what you're saying. They're jealous because they don't want black people improving their status." It perhaps shouldn't be so surprising that they recognize the West's "intolerance and prurience." Unlike the United States, South Africa has same-sex marriage.

The African National Congress Home Affairs Minister Nosiviwe Mapisa-Nqakula, while arguing in favor of legalizing same-sex marriage, said, "In breaking with our past . . . we need to fight and resist all forms of discrimination and prejudice, including homophobia." Unlike the United States', South Africa's Constitution formally prohibits discrimination based on sexuality. The Constitution reads:

> The state may not unfairly discriminate directly or indirectly against anyone on one or more grounds, including race, gender, sex, pregnancy, marital status, ethnic or social origin, colour, sexual orientation, age, disability, religion, conscience, belief, culture, language and birth. This does not to mean South Africa is some sort of Shangri-La for LGBT people. But it does suggest the United States can stand to learn a thing or two about discrimination and human sexuality.

There is currently no definitive information regarding Semenya's sexual orientation or gender choice. We know she identifies herself as an 18-year-old woman and she can run like the wind while not looking like a conventional pinup.

Unfortunately for women athletes, you can't be too masculine for fear you'll be called a lesbian. You can't be too aggressive for fear that you will be called mannish. You must be an outdated stereotype of a woman before you are an athlete. You must market yourself as nonthreatening and blazingly heterosexual.

The most famous female athlete of the first half of the twentieth century was Mildred Ella "Babe" Didrikson. She won three medals in track and field in the 1932 Olympics and also became the standard for all women golfers. Yet despite her towering athletic accomplishments, Didrikson was denounced as "mannish," "not-quite female" and a "Muscle Moll" who could not "compete with other girls in the very ancient and time honored sport of mantrapping."

Hearing that in addition to track and field she also played basketball, football and numerous other sports, an astonished journalist asked Didrikson, "Is there anything you don't play?" Without missing a beat, she reportedly answered, "Yeah, dolls."

From Babe Didrikson to Caster Semenya, to paraphrase the ad for Virginia Slims: you've come a long way . . . maybe.

SOURCE: Reprinted with permission from Zirin (2009).

Biological sex is complicated, and chromosomal makeup is only one part of it. Usually, human beings have twenty-three pairs of chromosomes, one pair of which are called sex chromosomes. In most instances, the egg contributes only X chromosomes to the embryo, and the sperm contributes either an X or a Y chromosome. The resulting individual, then, is chromosomally either an XX (a female) or an XY (a male). However, that is not the end of the story. In a number of instances, a person will inherit only one chromosome, an X; in others, she or he will have an extra X or Y chromosome (notice that language forces us to accept the male–female dichotomy). The result is that there is a range of solely X-chromosome people (XO, XX, XXX), as well as XYs and XYYs and XXYs. Chromosomally, then, we could say that there are five sexes, not two, which is the point Fausto-Sterling made, tongue in cheek, in her famous article, "The Five Sexes" (Fausto-Sterling 1993).

Not all reasons for variations in biological sex are chromosomal. Congenital adrenal hyperplasia (CAH), a condition related to steroid hormone production, masculinizes XX individuals. Androgen insensitivity syndrome (AIS), the condition that made Patino and Semanya feminine despite their Y chromosomes, causes XY children to develop female genitalia. Embryonically, we all develop our sex from an unsexed body. In the first six weeks of gestation, an embryo has undifferentiated external genitalia that will usually develop either into a penis, testicles, and scrotum or into a clitoris, labia, and vagina. Some individuals are born with the genitalia of both sexes, or their genital makeup does not match their chromosomal category, as with Patino. There are people who are born with both ovarian and testicular tissue, and others who have the external genitalia of one sex and the internal gonads (ovaries or testes) of the other. Until recently in the United States, many of these individuals did not survive intact to adulthood. Instead, they were surgically and hormonally altered at birth to appear more "normal" or fully and unambiguously male or female. Fausto-Sterling has attempted to estimate the frequencies of such births (see Table 2-1), but with some difficulty due to the shame and secrecy that has surrounded them. Nonetheless, it is clear that such births are more

TABLE 2-1 Frequencies of Various Causes of Ambiguous, Nonnormal, or Unclear Sexual Development

Cause	Estimated Frequency/100 Live Births
Non-XX or non-XY (except Turner's or Klinefelter's)	0.06390
Turner syndrome	0.03690
Klinefelter syndrome	0.09220
Androgen insensitivity syndrome	0.00760
Partial androgen insensitivity syndrome	0.00076
Classic congenital adrenal hyperplasia (omitting very high frequency population)	0.00779
Late-onset congenital adrenal hyperplasia	1.50000
Vaginal agenesis	0.01690
True hermaphrodites	0.00120
Ideopathic	0.00090
Total	1.72800

Source: Fausto-Sterling (2000a, 53).

common than most people believe. In the last analysis, the epigraph to this chapter becomes more intelligible: In more than a few instances, biological makeup is far from clear, far from either simply male or female. The binaries of sex and gender may seem eternal to you. But science shows that behind what we "see" and "know" is a different reality.

Moreover, historians have found that our "eternal" categories of sex and gender originated relatively recently, as the next section of this chapter demonstrates.

SEXED BODIES IN OTHER TIMES AND OTHER PLACES

How do we get beyond the natural attitude, the conviction that everyone is either a male or a female? One way to make visible our unexamined commonsense beliefs is to compare social worlds in other times and places. Are the sexes "opposite?" Not in medieval Europe, where naturalists and physicians demonstrated that women were like men, although biologically inferior. How many sexes are there? In some societies there can be more than two sex statuses that are socially relevant, if not biologically "real," categories. Such examples show that what we "see" and "know" is rooted in our specific histories, contexts, and practices. Different times and places have their own common sense and their own ways of seeing. Freud reputedly claimed that "biology is destiny." Thanks to the examples presented in this section, readers might counter with Judith Butler's (1990) claim that it is not biology, but culture and history that are destiny.

Regardless of whether biology is fixed and immutable, the way we understand the biology of sex is not. Historian Thomas Laqueur shows that how we view, understand, and use bodies is enmeshed in social and cultural ways of seeing and acting, and not simply in some nonsocial biological core. Today the conventional understanding is that there are two sexes and that biological sex is the underpinning of gender. Laqueur reverses this conventional understanding. In his view, our gender relations and ideologies shape observed sex and sexuality. Our ways of seeing, our tacit understandings of reality, our suppositions about men and women—indeed the very idea that men and women exist—affect how bodies appear to laypersons and scientists alike. To demonstrate this truth, his book shows that many doctors, naturalists, and anatomists from ancient times until the dawn of the modern scientific era in the late eighteenth century believed in a one-sex world, not the seemingly self-evident two-sex world with which we are so familiar. This difference in perspective is linked to a society's more general understandings of social reality.

Laqueur shows that the way people saw (and continue to see) biology and sexuality mirrored the social order. Medieval scientists and doctors saw bodies as miniature societies that corresponded to the society's gendered hierarchies of power. Bodily structures reflected and legitimized men's social dominance:

> In a public world that was overwhelmingly male, the one-sex model displayed what was already massively evident in culture more generally: man is the measure of all things, and woman does not exist as a . . . distinct category. Not all males are masculine, potent, honorable, or hold power, and some women exceed some men in each of these categories. But the standard of the human body and its representations is the male body. (Laqueur 1990, 62)

Within the bodily and social hierarchy, there was only one sex: the male sex. Women were like men, but lesser and less perfect. Naturalists and physicians of the time offered "proof" of this assumption in female reproductive anatomy and wrote many treatises proving the likenesses between men and women. For example, Aristotle believed that the vagina and cervix looked like an internal penis. Five centuries after Aristotle, Galen, the second-century Roman physician and philosopher whose studies of anatomy remained influential into the nineteenth century, wrote that women's reproductive organs were like men's "turned outside in."

Similarly, bodily fluids—semen, menstrual blood, and milk—were seen as male and female versions of the same substance, but hierarchically ordered according to their power. Again, the female versions of these fluids were not essentially different, but instead were lesser, weaker, and corrupted versions of male secretions. Orgasm, also, was common to both men and women, although male orgasm was believed to be more intense and more violent than female orgasm. Renaissance anatomical illustrators—Vesalius, Berengario da Carpi, and even the great artist, Leonardo—represented the vagina as an internal penis (see Figure 2-1).

FIGURE 2-1

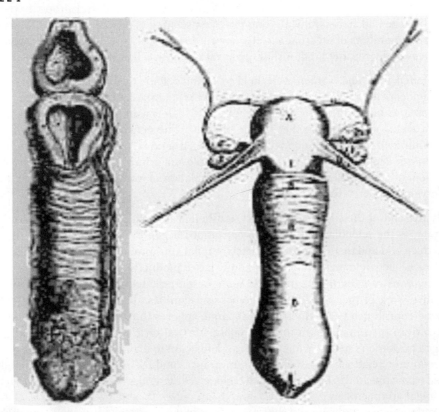

(left) Vagina as penis, from Vesalius, *Fabrica*, sixteenth century. (right) Vagina and uterus from Vidus Vidius, *De anatome corporis humani* (1611).

Source: Laqueur (1990, 82).

Such beliefs about the hierarchy of the sexes helped to determine how people saw actual bodily organs. Ideologies about sex guided how people interpreted the evidence presented by actual male and female bodies.

To summarize, Laqueur's study of premodern views of sexed bodies showed how ideas and beliefs about men and women shaped the ways people understood sexual anatomy and its functions, how **believing is seeing** (Lorber 1994). A belief in male perfection and dominance contributed to a vision of sexed bodies that reflected and supported those beliefs. Men were the standard against which women's bodies were compared; women's bodies, the metaphorical "rib" springing from men.

Metaphors About Bodies in the New World

The male–female polarity came into being in a very different social world from the world of the premodern naturalists. As industrial capitalism grew, it brought with it a new division of labor between women and men. Prior to this great transformation, in the precapitalist agricultural economies of the American colonies, women partnered with men in producing the family's subsistence, as had been true of peasants in premodern Europe. In the New World, like the Old, a hierarchical, "one-sex" view seemed to prevail. Historian Mary Ryan claims that members of colonial society viewed differences between men and women as differences of degree, not kind, just as medieval naturalists had viewed them:

> Colonial men and women were held to a single standard of good behavior and equipped with a will free to perfect the temporal manifestations of their character. Therefore, unlike their progeny, early Americans rarely wrote or spoke of the "nature of woman" as opposed to the "nature of man." The concepts of masculinity and femininity remained ill-defined in agrarian America. . . . The agrarian frontier economy kept the sexual division of labor simple and primitive, while the household system of social organization precluded the isolation of women in a private and undervalued sphere. (Ryan 1975, 63–64)

By the end of the eighteenth century, a different understanding of sexual natures was emerging, as the scientific and capitalist revolutions began to change how Westerners perceived the world and themselves. Commercial capitalism—production for the market, not for subsistence—began to undermine rural, family-based production. The new system instituted novel divisions of labor that segregated the domestic productive work of women from the productive work of men outside their homes and families. The development of scientific medicine contributed to **the doctrine of separate spheres** the idea that women's bodily differences from men made them unfit for public life and civic responsibilities. Healing had belonged to women's sphere before physicians laid claim to it and usurped women's position. New economic relations separated men from women, and the new sciences of the body uncovered what appeared to be fundamental biological differences between the sexes that made these social arrangements mandatory.

Contemporary medicine still shows the traces of these early modern views of sex. Emily Martin explored how women's biological differences from men were presented in modern medical science as pathologies. For example, medical models of menstruation, pregnancy, and menopause implied "failed production, waste, decay, and breakdown." A 1984 medical text described menstruation as follows:

> Much of the endometrial tissue dies and sloughs into the uterine cavity. Then, small amounts of blood ooze from the denuded endometrial wall, causing a blood loss of about 50 ml during the next few days. The sloughed endometrial tissue plus the blood and much serous exudates from the denuded uterine surface, all together called the menstrum, is gradually expelled by intermittent contractions of the uterine muscle for about 3 to 5 days. (Martin 1992, 47)

Perhaps you think that this description of the biology of menstruation sounds accurate and objective. Not according to Martin, who contrasts it with accounts of the shedding of the lining of the stomach, a more neutral bodily location shared by women and men. When it comes to stomachs, medical texts represent the process of shedding as a process of renewal, not of degeneration. Couldn't menstruation be represented just as legitimately in this way, too? The case is even stronger when Martin compares descriptions of menstruation with passages describing male sexual processes. Such passages are celebratory, gushing (pardon the pun) over the wonder of ejaculation. But there is no reason, except for the ideology of male bodily supremacy, that female bleeding should appear as degenerative whereas male ejaculate seems glorious. The truth is that a large proportion of male ejaculate is shredded cellular material (Martin 1992, 51). Martin quotes a medical explanation of spermatogenesis, which makes the point quite well:

> The mechanisms which guide the *remarkable* cellular transformation from spermatid to mature sperm remain uncertain. . . . Perhaps the most *amazing* characteristic of spermatogenesis is its *sheer magnitude*: the normal human male may manufacture several hundred million sperm per day. (Martin 1992, 48; emphasis in original)

In another article, Martin appraises the imagery of eggs and sperm. She writes that where once the gendered metaphors were of passive eggs invaded by active sperm, by the 1980s, scientific and medical texts were offering a more interactive view, but one that nevertheless preserved the idea of the sperm as the active party, the one that penetrates and fertilizes. In the more contemporary version, however, the egg is not passive matter waiting to be chosen by the active sperm, but a "female aggressor who 'captures and tethers' the sperm . . . rather like a spider lying in wait in her web" (Martin 1997, 1992). This image resonates with the backlash against feminist politics that emerged in the 1980s.

Martin concludes that we must pay attention to such hidden metaphors and biased attitudes in matters that claim to be objective and scientific. If we fail to become aware of the cultural imagery that shapes the scientific discourses about bodies, such discourses retain the power to make our social conventions about gender seem natural. If we become aware of these metaphors and their implications, we rob them of their power (Martin 1992, 1997).

How Many Genders Are There? The Evidence from Other Cultures

Recall Lorber's distinction between sex and gender (2005b). Sex is "a complex interplay of genes, hormones, environment, and behavior with loopback effects between bodies and society," whereas gender is "a social status, a legal designation, and a personal identity." We have seen how in everyday life, sex is not as straightforward and as clearly distinct from gender as it has been made out to be. Ancient and medieval naturalists and physicians looked at male and female bodies and saw them as a hierarchy of more and less perfect expressions of the same (male) anatomy. Modern observers looked at the same male and female bodies and saw that there were fundamental differences between them. This is not to deny the materiality of bodies. Sexed bodies are not simply what we think they are. Certainly, medieval bodies were not actually different from modern bodies. But to explain, we invoke a somewhat different proposition from sociology.

In the 1920s, University of Chicago sociologist W. I. Thomas wrote what came to be known as the "Thomas theorem": "If men [and women] believe things to be real, they are real in their consequences" (Thomas 1928, 571–72). Using the Thomas theorem to explain the science of sex, we might say, "If we believe men and women are biologically different, then we build social institutions and practices that embed and honor this belief." The consequences are that such institutions and practices create a world organized around gendered differences. In this way, embodied sex grows from our beliefs about masculinity and femininity. History shows that maleness and femaleness, the bodily expressions of gender, are socially malleable. Part of what we see grows from our expectations about what exists, and part of what we see is the consequence of acting on those expectations, acting as if gender differences were real. As socially competent members of our own society, we see bodies through the cultural lenses of sex and gender, and we shape actual bodies to our expectations (Connell 1999).

Just as the historical record demonstrates the socially malleable character of sex and gender, so too does the cross-cultural evidence. Many cultures recognize multiple gender categories that seem different from those of modern Western culture. Consider, for example, the **"two-spirit" people** or "women-men" that eighteenth- and nineteenth-century Europeans reported to have found in some First Nations societies.

The term "two-spirit" originated in Winnipeg, Canada, in 1990, during the third annual intertribal Native American/First Nations gay and lesbian conference, and refers to people whose bodies house both a feminine and a masculine spirit. The term was designed to replace the terms *berdache* and *gay*, which were standard ways to refer to such individuals. *Berdache* is a French word meaning "male prostitute," and it was used disparagingly by Europeans as they tried to make sense of the tribal societies they encountered in the New World. *Gay* is a term coming out of the struggles of homosexual and lesbian communities in twentieth-century Europe and North America, and it distorts the experiences and self-understandings of two-spirit people in seventeenth-, eighteenth-, and nineteenth-century tribal societies.

Two-spirit people were well integrated into their communities and were held in high regard as "beings of potentially great power and blessing" (Miller 1998). In many First Nations societies, two-spirit women-men took up occupations designated as women's, dressed as women, and had sexual relations with men. A possible fourth category was that of "men-women," biological females who lived as men, hunted, took up men's work, fought in wars with the men of the tribe, and married women (Lang 1998; Roughgarden 2004). As young girls such women showed an interest in learning boys' roles and avoided girls' tasks. In our society we might label these children "tomboys" and perhaps guide them to take up more feminine pursuits. In some First Nations societies, adults accepted their children's choices and taught such girls the skills boys learned. In some cases, a family with no sons might select one of their daughters and encourage her to be "like a man." As adults, cross-gender females hunted, trapped, cultivated crops, and fought in wars.

In these societies, native gender categories did not equate gender with biological sex or sexual identity. A woman who married a cross-gender woman was not considered lesbian or cross-gender herself. If the relationship ended in divorce, the ex-wife could enter into any number of possible arrangements, including heterosexual marriage (Blackwood 1984, 30).

Blackwood connects the possibilities for third-sex and fourth-sex status to the political and economic context within which these genders appeared. For example, prior to contact with Europeans, several First Nations societies in western North America were egalitarian subsistence societies. In these communities, there was no accumulation of wealth or private wealth holding. The sexual division of labor was not highly developed, and all members of the group contributed to production. Both men's and women's tasks were valued by the wider community, and men and women often worked at the same or similar tasks. Note, by the way, how this minimal gender division of labor is similar to that of peasant-based European societies and rural colonial American societies before the advent of industrial capitalism.

Contact with the westward-moving whites in North America brought catastrophic changes to many First Nations societies. By introducing guns, horses, and the fur trade to the First Nations people, the white settlers disrupted First Nations society. By the early nineteenth century, some First Nations men were able to accumulate wealth through trade in hides. Such trade required that they acquire additional wives who could handle the tanning and preparation of the hides for trade. As women lost control over production and men gained authority over women's labor, women's status declined, and their autonomy was limited. In addition, First Nations men were killed in significant numbers due to the constant state of war with whites. Under these circumstances, the First Nations communities were less tolerant of losing women's reproductive capacities to cross-gendering. Finally, Western sexual ideologies of female inferiority and heterosexuality replaced First Nations beliefs. Cross-gender women were harassed, accused of not being real men, and not equipped to satisfy a wife. In these later developments, gender roles and sexuality were associated with an ideology and a practice of male dominance (Blackwood 1984).

Many other cultures have institutionalized multiple genders. One well-known example is that of the hijras of India, studied by Serena Nanda. The common view in India is that **hijras** are neither men nor women, and neither are they seen as homosexuals. The key defining characteristic of this group is the absence of male external genitalia (often a result of elective surgery) or "imperfect genitals" (ambiguous genitalia at birth). Culturally, hijras are "not-men" and view themselves as "man minus maleness" (Nanda 1990). Hijras also claim an identity as "man plus woman." They dress as women when they perform on ritual occasions such as weddings, or when they beg, engage in prostitution, or visit the temple of their goddess, Bahuchara Mata. They wear their hair long, pluck out their facial hair, and adopt what they claim is "female" behavior.

Some hijras work as electricians or in construction—men's jobs—but they are more likely to take jobs that are held by both men and women, such as household servants and cooks. They take feminine names and sometimes insist they be counted as women in the census (Nanda 1990, 16–17). Despite their naming practices and their occasional demand to be counted as women, hijras see themselves and are seen by others as "not-women," as well as "not-men." Their performances as women are over-the-top parodies of femininity, outrageous practices that no ordinary woman would dare to enact. Hijras swear and threaten others, expose their genitals, smoke, and dance in public. No "decent" Hindu woman would behave in these ways.

In contrast to the West, where intersex children have been subjected to "normalizing" surgeries, intersex children in India may be categorized as "born hijras." However, many if not most hijras are chromosomal and gonadal males who have elected as adults to be surgically emasculated. These surgically altered individuals are known as "made hijras."

As discussed in the final sections of this chapter, many Westerners are uncomfortable with such in-between sexual and gender categories, and try to resolve such ambiguities. However, Indian culture has a long tradition of accommodating alternative sexes and genders. For example, the Hindu deity Shiva combines both male and female characteristics, and Vishnu and Krishna are deities who are sexually ambiguous. Telling the story of her childhood, Salima, a "real" hijra, treats her status matter-of-factly and as a real third sex (Nanda 1990, 99):

> My parents felt sad about my birth, but they realized it was their fate to have me born to them. They were looking forward to my birth—I was the eldest child—and they were sad that I was born "neither here nor there." From my birth, my organ was very small. My mother felt, as I grew up, naturally it will grow also. But it didn't, so she tried taking me to doctors and all that. But the doctors said, "No, it won't grow, your child is not a man and not a woman, this is God's gift." I am a real hijra, not like those converts—those men who have the operation.

Other examples of alternative sexes and genders can be found around the world. In Islamic Oman on the Saudi Arabian peninsula, there is a group of cross-gender-behaving "not-men," known as Xanith. Xanith retain the rights of men—for example, they have the right to worship in the mosque with men and to move about freely outside during the day (but not at night)—but they do women's work and are judged according to feminine standards of beauty. Xanith eat and socialize with women. Only they, but not other men, may view brides on their wedding nights.

In Omani society, manliness rests on men's active, penetrating role in sexual intercourse. Xanith, like women in that society, are passive receivers. However, there are ways in which Xanith are neither women nor men. Their clothing is a mixture of men's and women's styles. Unlike most Muslim women in Oman, they are often prostitutes. Xanith are not men, but they are not women either. They have some of the privileges of men, some of the restrictions of women, and their own particular place in society (Nanda 1990, 130–31).

Clearly, some men and women have taken up "third gender" roles throughout southern Asia and among some groups in the Americas and Africa. However, third genders are not only the "exotic" creation of indigenous and non-Western societies. Some students of gay history suggest that we in the West also support third genders, although we do not know them by that term. They contend that until about three hundred years ago, most men in the West had legitimate sexual relations with adolescent boys, as well as with women, a practice at least as old as that of the ancient Greeks. In such systems of sexual relations, age differences maintained older men's dominance over younger lovers. The practice of licit sex between men persisted well into the twentieth century and has been documented among working-class

Italian, Irish, and Australian men, who were able to engage in homosexual relations without acquiring a homosexual identity (Chauncy, 1995, Connell 2001). But around 1700, the dominant Western system of gender and sexuality began to change to one in which a minority of men were cast into lifelong homosexual roles. In the late nineteenth century, such individuals were called "fairies," and "queers," in contrast to the majority, who were named "heterosexuals," or, simply, "men." Historian Randolph Trumbach (1996) suggests that this was "the language in which Western societies have increasingly over the past century described the operation of our system of three genders." Homosexual men were not seen simply as masculine-gendered men who had sex with other men, as is the case with contemporary gay men. Rather, "fairies" were understood to be more broadly different from other men, woman-like and feminine in the cultural as well as the sexual roles they assumed. At the same time, men whom they successfully solicited were not considered homosexual as long as they adhered to masculine gender conventions. Since the mid-twentieth century, and owing to gay liberation movements, the early twentieth-century division between "queers" and "men," who differed in their gender identity, has changed to "homosexuals" and "heterosexuals," who differ principally in their choice of sex objects.

Historical and cross-cultural research shows that sex and gender are not static. Western beliefs that sex categories are fixed and universalistic are challenged by this evidence of the fluidity of sexuality and gender. Today the cultural and ideological conviction that sex is an unchanging bedrock of bodily constitution linked to gender in determinate ways is being shaken by new claims and new evidence.

SEXUALITY AND SEXUAL ORIENTATION: GENDERING DESIRE

The contrast in the belief that gender is rooted in biological sex (essentialism) and the belief that gender is a product of social relationships (social constructionism) also shapes debates about the foundations of sexuality. Among those on the side of biology are sociobiologists and evolutionary psychologists who directly connect the Darwinian process of natural selection—a process favoring those organisms that adapt to assure species survival—with specific sexual and gendered practices. For example, some evolutionary psychologists and sociobiologists have argued that rape may be a male adaptation assuring that human beings will reproduce successfully (see chapter 4). They contend that particular gendered arrangements between the sexes (male dominance, female passivity) and particular gendered sexualities (heterosexual desire, male competitiveness for women) are naturally selected, genetically programmed adaptive survival mechanisms benefiting the human race. Feminists, as well as most biologists, disagree with this conflation of gender power relations with Darwin's theory of natural selection, but some feminists have also used biologically based logic to make their own case, as when they claim that men are naturally aggressive and women naturally peaceful. On the other side are those who claim new and newly valued identities that are beginning to cross the once seemingly impermeable biological divide between male and female sex and sexuality.

At first inspired by the civil rights movement of the 1960s, gays, lesbians, transsexuals, intersexuals, and queers have "come out" publicly to question long-standing beliefs in the determinate male–female sexual story and in the forms of "properly sexual" bodies. Their questions are challenges to the power relations underpinning these beliefs (Lancaster 2003). Chapter 4 explores the many issues surrounding gender and sexuality. Here we focus on some of the ways that scholars have advanced the claim that sexuality is structured socially, not by nature.

Of course the genetic, hormonal, and physiological makeup of bodies is a material reality that cannot be willed away. What then does it mean to claim that sexuality—the array of bodily responses that seem to originate in the deepest, nonconscious part of ourselves and are experienced as "coming from within" (Simon 1996, 138)—is, in some measure, a social construction? How do social scientists reconcile the physicality of sexuality with its social forms? One line of thinking tries to marry biology and society. A second uses the metaphor of scripting to explain gendered sexuality. A third tries to show how sexed bodies are socially produced. And a fourth explores the changing histories of sexuality.

The Basis of Sexuality Is Not "Either–Or" but "Both–And"

Binary thinking demands that you are either male *or* female and that traits are either biologically given *or* culturally constructed. But some social scientists encourage "both–and" ways of thought. To anthropologist Clifford Geertz, humans are "incomplete or unfinished animals who complete or finish ourselves through culture" (quoted in Lancaster 2003, 204). Geertz means that sexuality is part of the animal world; and we are certainly members of that world. But we take the raw material of animal sexuality and craft it into something uniquely human through our various cultures. Sociologists Pepper Schwartz and Virginia Rutter (1998, 22) make a similar point. They write:

> Although people tend to think of sex as primarily a biological function—tab B goes into slot A—biology is only one part of the context of desire. Such sociological factors as family relationships and social structure also influence sex. A complex mix of anatomy, hormones, and the brain provides the basic outline for the range of acts and desires possible, but biology is neither where sexuality begins nor where it ends.

Schwartz and Rutter (1998) describe several experimental studies that show how social and biological processes together produce sexual desire. In one experiment men were connected to a phony heartbeat monitor and told that the heartbeat "surges" they heard when viewing photos of women models would indicate their preference for one photograph over the others. In fact, the fake heartbeats they heard were randomly produced by the experimenters. Nonetheless, the men chose the women based on hearing what they believed was their own speeding heartbeat. In a second experiment, a group of men were asked to cross an unstable bridge. When the men reached the other side, an attractive researcher spoke with them and gave them her phone number. In this experiment the men confounded their anxiety on crossing an unstable bridge with the sexual arousal caused by meeting a desirable person, measured by the numbers of men who phoned the woman later. In this experiment, anxiety—the physiological response—was interpreted as sexual desire.

A third study found that testosterone levels among a group of homosexual men and a group of military men were similarly low. What common situation influenced testosterone levels among men traditionally reputed to be lower and higher, respectively, on indexes of "masculinity"? The researchers suggested that the common denominator that depressed both groups' hormone levels was stress and anxiety—the impact on a gay man of life in a straight world, and on a military man of constant direction from superiors. They theorized that a stressful social situation produced a biological response. Geertz, Schwartz, and Rutter and the researchers who conceived of the experimental research believe biology is implicated in the bodily sensations that we call "desire." However, they also believe that the social context in which we feel desire organizes and gives meaning to these sensations (Schwartz and Rutter 1998, 25).

Sexuality Is Socially Scripted

In 1973, sociologists John Gagnon and William Simon proposed that sexuality was governed by sexual "scripts" derived from socially learned gender roles. This idea was at odds with the popular notion that sexuality was innate, inborn, and nonsocial. It also contradicted the Freudian concept of the id, the source of libido or sexual energy. According to Freud, the id—the primitive, irrational, and ungovernable part of the mind—functioned on the basis of the "pleasure principle" and in opposition to the "reality principle," which he believed was the basis of society and civilization. Becoming a member of society in Freud's view entailed reigning in and repressing sexuality. Gagnon and Simon did not treat sexuality as a drive that needed containment and repression. Quite the contrary, they envisioned sexuality as the outcome of learning a sexual "**vocabulary of motives**" in adolescence, when young people are socially defined as potential sexual actors. Hormonal changes may be taking place at the time, but newly sexualized actors must learn the meaning of their feelings and internal states, the specifically sexual acts they must deploy, the situations in which sexuality is expected and appropriate, the limits and boundaries of sexual responses, and the like:

> Without the proper elements of a script that defines the situation, names the actors, and plots the behavior, nothing sexual is likely to happen. . . . Combining such elements as desire, privacy and physically attractive person of the appropriate sex, the probability of something happening will, under normal circumstances, remain exceedingly small until either one or both actors organize these behaviours into an appropriate script. (Gagnon and Simon 1973, quoted in Jackson and Scott 1996, 71)

Gagnon and Simon believed that we must be educated to recognize sexual feelings and desires and learn how to translate them into socially validated actions. To whom are we supposed to be attracted? What sexual cues must we learn and interpret? Where and when are we supposed to have sex? When they developed their theory of sexual scripts several decades ago, boys and girls were perhaps learning to be sexual differently from what and how they learn to be sexual today. Then, girls' scripts centered on romantic love; boys' scripts, on sexual interest and getting sex from girls. The sexual scripts Simon and Gagnon encountered have probably changed since that time. Do girls still learn to be romantic about sex? Do boys still learn that men are expected to be sexually predatory? Are hook-ups today's ruling sexual scripts?

Bodies Are Produced Within Society

A third way of thinking about the social production of sexuality holds that specific bodies are produced through what sociologist Raewyn Connell calls "body-reflexive practices." In Connell's view, the physical body is enmeshed in a social world of practices and activities that have physical outcomes regarding reproduction, sexuality, and masculinity or femininity. She views bodies as the sites or arenas of social practice, in which "bodies are brought into social processes" (Connell 2002, 10), rather than, as the "both–and" theorists see it, the biological starting points or underpinning of that practice. In Connell's view, bodies are materially transformed through social practices.

Think about the ways that class transforms bodies. Working-class men have higher accident rates and fatal injuries; working-class women have higher rates of repetitive strain injuries. Race ethnicity transforms bodies. African American men and women have increased incidence of high blood pressure, a condition linked by medical research to the effects on black people of living in a racist society (see chapter 9). Gender also transforms bodies. Sexually, steroids and diet pills shape bodies. Genital surgeries and cosmetic surgeries shape bodies. Some of us sit "like men," taking up the space around us; others sit "like women," with arms folded and legs crossed. We informally learn gestures and nonverbal forms of communication—the hip-swaying walk, the swagger—that become our sometimes unconscious repertoires of gendered and sexualized bodily practice. Formal learning also marks our bodies, as we learn to build or to knit, to play some sports and not others, to do math or to type, even to engage in sex. In regard to the last item, scan the magazine racks while you are waiting in line in the grocery store, and note the many articles on how to "please your man" or enjoy "the best sex ever." Sexuality is learned. Sexual arousal and sexual "turnoffs" are bodily responses mediated by social relationships. Our sexed bodies are produced in society and often announce to society our gendered identities and our sexual selves (Connell 2001, 27).

Connell's biography of the iron-man athlete Steve illustrates the interplay between bodies and social processes. In childhood and adolescence, Steve was physically big and did well in sports. By the age of 13, he began to specialize in swimming. In adulthood, Steve's day centered on maintaining his body in ways that enabled him to be a successful competitive swimmer. The irony of Steve's life, writes Connell, is that because "the business of winning has consumed his life," he cannot live the kind of ideally masculine life of a young, handsome bachelor. His training regimen requires that he go to bed early, exercise daily, avoid drink, and even avoid sex. Because of his athletic career, he has become socially isolated, uninvolved in the wider world, unable to maintain relationships with women, and without inner direction. Connell writes that "hegemonic masculinity [the dominant and idealized form of masculinity in contemporary Western culture] appropriates Steve's body and gives it a social definition" (Connell 2001, 69–85). In other words, Steve's bodily practices, propelled by parents, coaches, fans, and his own ambitions, have created a person who looks the part of the handsome, virile, charismatic athlete, but whose life has been stolen by these very practices.

Erotic Relations Are Historical Relations

The fact that sexuality has changed and evolved historically—that it is not universal and fixed—removes bodies from the biological realm and places them firmly in the social realm. You have read that heterosexuality and homosexuality and the identities "heterosexual" and "homosexual" were historical inventions. Before these labels took hold, people engaged in heterosexual and homosexual acts, but their acts did not adhere to them as identities. Sometime in the late nineteenth century, however, a new group of people was identified, people interested in sex only for pleasure. These people were first called heterosexuals to distinguish them from that generation's "normals," who were people who reputedly only used sex for procreation. Only later did heterosexuality become the "natural" norm.

John D'Emilio (1983) situates this sexual history within the wider political economy of industrializing America. According to D'Emilio, capitalist industrialization created the conditions that allowed some men and women to leave their families and to organize their personal lives around erotic or emotional attractions, whether in relation to the other sex or to their own sex. As the rural economy declined and wage labor spread in nineteenth-century America, production brought people together in factories and offices, where family oversight and family ties were less controlling. Ideologically, heterosexual and homosexual expression came to be understood as a way to pursue intimacy, promote happiness, and experience pleasure, contributing to the release of sexuality from the imperative to procreate. In these ways, the growth of cities as the locations of industry made possible transformations of sexuality, its emergence as a central feature of individual identity, the formation of urban communities of lesbians and gay men, and a politics based on sexual identity (D'Emilio 1983, 104). In other words, the socioeconomic organization of society—not genes, not brains—created the conditions for living heterosexual and gay or lesbian lives.

SEXUALITY IS RACIALIZED, RACE IS SEXUALIZED. Think about this: racial ethnic boundaries are sexual boundaries; race ethnicity and sex are integrally bound together. As more fully discussed in chapter 4, sexual stereotypes, sexual fears, and sexual identities are central components of race relations. Racial ethnic differences serve to heighten or dampen sexual desire, to place some groups off limits sexually, or to fuel secret longings and underground connections for others (Nagel 2003). Colonialism and slavery were the contexts within which the bodies of subjugated peoples were controlled, exploited, and dominated. The racial past of colonialism and slavery has contributed to sexual images of black women as promiscuous and black men as dangerous (A. Davis 1983). In fact, most sexual danger comes from white men's violence against black women or the long history of lynching and violence against black men for presumed interest in white women.

Constructing social worlds on the idea of essential differences between groups is dangerous business. We remain unaware of the intersecting inequalities and divisions that together construct our commonsense understandings and everyday practices at our peril.

INTERSEX AND TRANSGENDER BODIES

Intersexuals are (1) individuals born with ambiguous genitalia such as penises that look small enough to be clitorises or clitorises that look large enough to be penises and (2) people whose bodies develop sexually along unexpected paths, such as infants with "5-alpha reductase deficiency," who may be categorized as girls at birth, but who at puberty develop beards, lower voices, and larger penises. At the very least, such persons, neither fully male nor fully female, make evident that sex is not sharply dichotomous.

Transsexuals and transgender people also challenge the dichotomous categories of sex and gender. In his book about female-to-male (FTM) transsexuals, Henry Rubin (2003) identified transsexuals as people who reject their assigned sex category and believe that their bodies betray their core identity as transwomen or transmen. But these are not the only people gathered under the umbrella of transsexual and transgender. Whittle (2006) includes among the "trans" population

> a butch or a camp, a transgender or a transsexual, an MTF [male to female], an FTM [female to male], or a cross-dresser; they might, in some parts of the world, consider themselves a lady boy, *katoey*, or even the reclaimed Maori identities *whakawahine* or *whakatane*. Some communities and their terms are ancient, such as the Hijra from Northern India, but many are more modern. The word "trans," referring to a "trans woman" or a "trans man" (of whatever subtype of trans identity) is a very recent take on the umbrella term "transgender.". . . Cultural spaces and historiographies are constantly reframing the community, the identities, the cultures, and the language. (Whittle 2006, xi)

When and how did these boundary-violating embodiments and ideas emerge into public awareness? What is their history? Are they, as some claim, "disorders" that need correction by scientific and medical experts? Or are they harbingers of a new order of things (Foucault 2001)—a new system of knowledge and practice—that is challenging long-standing assumptions about gender and sexuality?

Intersexuality and Ambiguity

Each year about seventeen ambiguously sexed infants are born for every one thousand births (see Table 2-1). What is the social place of intersex individuals in a two-sex world? What has been the lived experience of intersexuality in the century since the condition was named? In the past two decades, many intersex adults and their supporters have joined with other activists to challenge the two-sex model of sexuality. What accounts for the new politics of intersex, and what does that politics suggest about the future? In recent years a growing number of intersex adults have "come out" to speak about their experiences.

Embodiment and Intersexuality

The National Institutes of Health divides intersex into four categories (U.S. National Library of Health and National Institutes of Health 2009):

- *XX intersex* (formerly female pseudohermaphroditism). A person with the chromosomes and ovaries of a woman, but with external genitals that appear male.
- *XY intersex* (formerly male pseudohermaphroditism). A person with XY chromosomes, but with ambiguous, or clearly female, external genitals.
- *True gonadal intersex*. A person has both ovarian and testicular tissue in one or both gonads. In most people with true gonadal intersex, the underlying cause is unknown, although in some animal studies it has been linked to exposure to common agricultural pesticides.
- *Complex or undetermined intersex*. Many chromosome configurations other than simple XX or XY can result in ambiguous sex development. These include XO (only one X chromosome), and XXY and XXX (both cases have an extra sex chromosome, either an X or a Y).

What is the social relevance of these physical states? Recall Geertz's statement that we are "incomplete or unfinished animals who complete or finish ourselves through culture." The physical condition of most infants born intersex is not life threatening or even unhealthy. But the intersex infant will be completed—that is, turned into a woman, man, or "intersexual"—in society. In this sense, the categories just described are not in any meaningful sense descriptions of intersex conditions. They are the raw material from which society constructs the meanings and practices surrounding people identified as intersex.

In contemporary Western societies, our bodies have become cultural projects and extensions of our selves. We act on our bodies to remake ourselves through makeup, hair dyes, shaving, tanning salons, cosmetic surgery, dieting, nutrition, transplants, workouts, and a host of other practices. In many respects the project to transform ambiguously sexed infants and children into members of one or the other "natural" sex, described later, is no different from these other body projects. The project to remake intersex children into "real" girls and boys is a product of historically specific, socially constructed, and institutionalized networks and practices around binary sex difference. There is, however, one important difference between most other projects of the self and the project to remake ambiguously sexed infants' and children's bodies into acceptably sexed bodies. The project to eliminate intersex was almost always chosen *for* intersex individuals, not *by* them. That vital difference raises issues that bring these bodies clearly into the realms of politics and ethics.

We begin with a look at how obstetricians have been counseled by their professional association to cope with an intersex birth. As late as 2000, the American Academy of Pediatrics called the birth of a child with ambiguous genitals a "social emergency" and recommended that doctors immediately and carefully explain to parents that the condition is correctible and that their children can become boys or girls, "as appropriate":

> Because words spoken in the delivery room may have a lasting impact on parents and their relationship with their infant, it is important that no attempt be made to suggest a diagnosis or offer a gender assignment.
>
> The infant should be referred to as "your baby" or "your child"—not "it," "he," or "she." It is helpful to examine the child in the presence of the parents to demonstrate the precise abnormalities of genital development, emphasizing that the genitalia of both sexes develop from the same primordial fetal structures, that both incomplete development or overdevelopment of the external genitalia can occur, and that *the abnormal appearance can be corrected and the child raised as a boy or a girl as appropriate.* (American Academy of Pediatrics 2000, 138; emphasis added)

No doubt, there are still many physicians and parents who are moved to act out of the fear that intersex children are so psychologically at risk and so physically grotesque that anything that helps to normalize them is worth the cost. This attitude has justified what Dreger (1998) has called "monster ethics," which accepts treatment of intersex in ways that would be considered unethical under any other circumstances: lying to patients, performing risky procedures without follow-up, and failing to obtain informed consent (see Box 2-2).

Today it is no longer routine for intersex infants to undergo surgical and hormonal sex assignment, although sex assignment surgery is still practiced (Davis, 2011, Nakhal et al., 2013). Only six years after the previously quoted statement appeared, the Academy significantly changed its recommendations to physicians confronted with an intersex infant.

GENDER IN EVERYDAY LIFE   BOX 2-2
NO CHOICE AT ALL

When the child identified in court papers only as "M.C." was 16 months old and a ward of the state, doctors and health officials in South Carolina decided that he would become a girl. Born intersex (a term encompassing individuals with some variation of sexual and/or reproductive anatomy that falls outside of society's male-or-female "standard"), M.C. had "ambiguous genitals" and "both male and female reproductive organs," according to Reuters.

Doctors removed M.C.'s male reproductive organs and eliminated any potential he had "to procreate as a male," said court filings.

But that surgery did not so neatly turn M.C. into a girl. Now age 8, he identifies as a boy.

A lawsuit filed earlier this month by M.C.'s adoptive parents contends that medical professionals sworn to protect the child failed him catastrophically.

Represented by the Southern Poverty Law Center and Advocates for Informed Choice, they argue that doctors convinced the child's state-appointed guardians to go through with surgery without fully disclosing the procedure's enormous risks, which include sterilization and diminished sexual sensation.

The lawsuit also alleges that the state of South Carolina in turn violated M.C.'s constitutional rights by failing to hold a court hearing to determine whether surgery was in the child's best interest. The plaintiffs go on to argue that beyond questions of procedural due process, the government does not have any legitimate, defensible claim to the kind of life-altering power that South Carolina exercised over M.C.

That last bit is most crucial when evaluating the case's implications, because to see this simply as an instance of medical malfeasance and negligence is to miss the larger cultural point. Doctors didn't just treat a condition or a disease incorrectly or too hastily. They didn't treat a medical disease at all. The procedure was done without any medical justification whatsoever, as is historically the case with most intersex infants who undergo such operations.

Instead, they treated a social illness, for which the remedy is making bodies deemed "abnormal" conform to society's strict sex and gender guidelines, and in the process they mutilated a child in their care.

M.C. will spend the rest of his life paying for his caretakers' actions. Should he choose reparative surgery, he'll face multiple expensive operations that might be categorized as elective procedures by an insurance carrier determined not to cover them. He also faces psychological peril. As sociologist Sharon Preves writes in an essay titled "Intersex Narratives: Gender, Medicine, and Identity," "intersexuals who [unknowingly] underwent medical sex assignment in childhood experienced consistently negative and confusing messages about their bodies and their identities."

However, putting aside for a moment the flawed instinct to mourn the fact that M.C. is a boy without a penis, we should recognize that M.C. was violated and victimized long before his identity as a boy emerged. The tragedy is not only physical and psychic; his disfigurement symbolizes his denied right to control his own body and identity. Even if M.C. had grown up to identify as a girl, identify with her surgically altered genitalia and live out her days as a female-bodied woman, the surgery would have been just as problematic and alarming.

To think otherwise is to consent to systemic forces that force us into boxes of pink and blue. These are the same forces that justify reparative therapy or gay "cures," limit women's reproductive rights and so dehumanize intersex bodies that, like M.C., they essentially become science experiments.

After all, it's easier to alter or defile a vulnerable body like M.C.'s to enforce an entrenched social norm than it is to change that norm. For decades, doctors rationalized these surgeries by saying that they saved children from a lifetime of torment. Granted, medical consensus is now a bit vaguer. In 2006, around the time of M.C.'s surgery, the journal *Pediatrics* published a paper signed by 50 international experts that stated that no proof exists that infant cosmetic genital surgery improves the recipient's quality of life.

Obviously, we have a long way to go from that. And M.C.'s case only challenges the state's ability to take such medical action. It does not address the wide legal dominion that parents have over medical decisions for their children. Either way, the lawsuit will send a strong message. It's fair to assume that parents want what's best for their children, but too often, "best" is interpreted as forcing children (of any stripe) to fit social expectations.

Instead, we need to fight against the norms that rationalize violence against those who, like M.C., fail to fit within arbitrary boundaries of what's "normal," or who present a threat to those boundaries, more precisely. Make no mistake: M.C., with his heretical little body, was a threat. And as an infant unable to give consent and articulate what he wanted, he was, and is, a victim of institutionalized violence, not just bureaucratic error and negligence.

There's nothing Earth-shatteringly new about the current way society polices sex and gender, or about the fact that many find it unnerving when they can't read a human being's gender or, in the case of infants, aren't privy to his or her sex. (Perhaps the internalized debate goes something like, "Do I pick up this mushy body mass gently or *really gently*?")

For proof, one need only look at the hostile response over the last few years to parents who refused to reveal the sex of their children. They were ridiculed, ostracized, even accused of child abuse, simply because they didn't want to limit their kids to such arbitrary and strict gender distinctions.

Why such an outcry? Infants and, until a certain age, toddlers all look and act pretty much the same. The only things that notably differ are our *own* reactions to their blue or pink bows, their short or long hair, or their skirts or pants.

That doctors should advise families to postpone surgery for intersex infants and toddlers is so obvious that it's almost not worth mentioning. But let's be sure that they're not waiting because there's an inevitable choice to be made between those pink or blue boxes. There should be no expectation of choice, because not only are there too many options to name but there is also this choice: none at all. (M.C. might have been perfectly content enjoying sex from a less limited perspective and labeling himself as he saw fit.) There is nothing wrong with a body that defies social expectations, but there is something abhorrent and ghastly about a compulsion for and obsession with clear gender and sex distinctions that shortchange us all and result in victimizing and mutilating people like M.C.

SOURCE: Erica K. Landau, "Carolina Infant's Mistaken Sex Assignment Surgery More Than a Case of Malpractice." *The Huffington Post*, May 31, 2013. Reprinted by permission from Erica K. Landau.

Participants in the International Consensus Conference on Intersex published a lengthy "Consensus Statement on Management of Intersex Disorders" (Lee, Houk, Ahmed, and Hughes, 2006), which began:

> Optimal clinical management of individuals with DSD should comprise the following: (1) gender assignment must be avoided before expert evaluation in newborns; (2) evaluation and long-term management must be performed at a center with an experienced multidisciplinary team; (3) all individuals should receive a gender assignment; (4) open communication with patients and families is essential, and participation in decision-making is encouraged; and (5) patient and family concerns should be respected and addressed in strict confidence.

What accounts for this transformation in the medical treatment of intersex infants? The study's authors have learned new attitudes and practices from an international activist community of adults who are intersex or who have children with intersex conditions.

A Brief History of Intersex

Until recently, the medicalized management of intersexuality rested on cultural beliefs that living within the normative sex and gender categories was the best life strategy. Many, if not most, surgeries and hormonal treatments of intersex infants were performed for cosmetic reasons rather than to correct life- or health-threatening medical conditions. How genitals and secondary sex characteristics might look to others took primacy over assuring the potential of genitalia for pleasure or even for reproduction (Kessler 1990).

For many years, if a baby was born with a "micropenis" (less than 1.5 centimeters long and 0.7 centimeters wide), the baby was a candidate for sex assignment surgery. Doctors reasoned that such a penis was too small to allow the child to urinate standing up (a condition they believed could lead to psychologically damaging ridicule once the child was in school) and too short to penetrate a vagina during sexual intercourse. Similarly, babies born with large clitorises have also been surgically altered to make their sex organs "look right," a treatment that people in the global North, the rich nations, have criticized when it is named female genital mutilation (FGM) and occurs in the global South or the so-called underdeveloped world. Wherever it is done, excision of the clitoris severely limits a woman's ability to experience orgasm. Remaking a boy's penis into a vagina does away with that child's ability to have children. Critics call these surgeries "social surgeries," akin to face lifts and nose jobs. Will the girl look right to others? Will the boy perform adequately during sexual intercourse?

The physical facts of intersex bodies do not translate directly into the identity of intersexual. The concept of ambiguously sexed bodies can only exist if there is a companion concept of normally sexed bodies. When, where, and how did the *social* category intersexual emerge? Around the turn of the twentieth century, bodies came under the scrutiny of men of science and medicine, who helped to create sex as a new object of study and to identify sexuality (homo or hetero) as a fundamental personal identity. Experts' strong belief in a two-sex system brought intersexuality into view as a problem that called for medical intervention. Before this time, most intersexuals lived lives generally free from public attention, medical intervention, or state oversight. By the late nineteenth century, however, the new specialty of gynecological medicine and state-mandated medical supervision of soldiers and prostitutes in wartime revealed that there were many nonstandard sexual anatomies. How was it possible to categorize people who did not fit comfortably into the categories of male or female? Doctors named the variations they discovered hermaphroditism (after the Greek god Hermaphroditus) and pseudohermaphroditism and designated them as pathological abnormalities. The discovery of intersexual bodies did not prompt experts to rethink the two-sex system. Instead they sought to uphold it by remaking individuals with healthy but nonconforming bodies into bodies that appeared to be 100 percent male and female.

By the 1920s, experts were beginning to use surgery to bring bodies into line with their belief in a two-sex system. Their project was delayed during two decades of depression and war but was resurrected in the 1950s at Johns Hopkins University, where an interdisciplinary team of surgeons, endocrinologists, and psychologists developed an "**optimum gender of rearing" model** to eliminate intersexuality. Their goal was to work with a child's body, mind, and upbringing to create a standard, heterosexual gender identity.

Why heterosexual? In the 1950s, many feared the consequences of living outside normative sexual boundaries. Vice squads regularly raided gay and lesbian bars and hangouts. Senator Joseph McCarthy paired his crusade against Communists in the government and in Hollywood with the persecution of gay men and lesbians. He charged that there was a "homosexual underground" that was "abetting the Communist conspiracy," and the national media regularly supported his charges with stories on the "pervert peril." As a consequence, businessmen and heads of government agencies, afraid of being accused of protecting "subversives," began to dismiss homosexuals and lesbians from their jobs (Reeves 1997). However, more than political fear drove the project to eliminate intersex. Doctors working with intersex infants believed that such babies were doomed to a life of misery if they did not have surgery. In this postwar world in which nuclear families were the white norm and ideal, it is no wonder that an intersex baby would precipitate a crisis.

Harvard-trained psychologist John Money provided theoretical support for the project. Money believed that when it came to sex and sexuality, society trumped biology. He was certain of the infinite malleability of infants' sexed bodies and minds. The case that supported his ideas, but that ultimately produced serious challenges to his project, was the famous case of John/Joan. In 1965, at the age of eight months, John (who came forward in the 1990s as David Reimer) was the victim of a botched circumcision that destroyed his penis. Money advised David's parents to make him a girl through surgery and hormonal treatments, a course of action Money had been advising for children born intersex. Money continued to see David each year and claimed that the boy, now called Brenda, had developed a successful feminine gender identity. Word of Money's success was broadcast widely among sex researchers. The case of John/Joan became the "hallmark case" around the globe for legitimizing sex assignment for newborns with ambiguous genitalia (Colapinto 1997). However, David Reimer later revealed that his childhood had been miserable and that the primary architect of his misery was John Money. As a teen, Reimer underwent surgery to restore his penis, later married, and adopted children. In his thirties he committed suicide.

Intersex as Lived Reality

The ways that intersexuality was a social invention should now be clear. Rather than a physiological problem demanding active intervention, as for example an infant born with a serious heart defect would require, intersex was *constructed* as a medical and social problem by a particular group of medical experts at a particular historical moment and in a particular sociohistorical context. What impact has the medicalization of intersex had on the generation of children born in the second half of the twentieth century and raised in the shadow of Money's "optimum gender of rearing" model? Based on her interviews with thirty-seven intersex adults between 1997 and 1998, Sharon Preves (2005, 9) summarized what they told her of their childhood struggles:

> [In] interview after interview, participants shared stories of feeling scrutinized and sexualized by medical professionals, of being treated as oddities and freaks, of lacking control over their own bodies, and of the resulting shame and secrecy of such experiences. They also spoke of arduous battles to gain accurate information about their bodies and attempts to find other intersexuals—aiming to piece together a puzzle whose solution was sure to hold the key to identity.

The stories Preves heard also show that a confluence of events and opportunities helped intersex adults reinterpret their biographies, make contact with others like themselves, and build networks, support groups, and political associations that have become the basis of the intersex rights movement. In the process, participants in the movement have joined feminists, queers, and transsexuals in posing compelling challenges to the two-sex system.

Preves's study chronicles the "careers" as intersexuals of the study's participants. Their collective story is the story of their advance from being "objects" of other people's design and practice to becoming self-directed individuals and collective actors determined to challenge and change the social conditions that once entrapped them.

Study participants begin their stories with accounts that describe their "prehistory," the time in their lives when they were more acted upon than actors, a period when others determined their fates. During this time, doctors regularly lied to patients about their condition, their surgeries, and their ongoing treatment and withheld vital information from their parents and guardians. Doctors' intentions were good—to save patients from the shame and pain that they believed would be their fate if they were not "fixed." However, normalizing surgeries and body-changing hormone treatments created, rather than alleviated, the children's feelings of difference and of their own freakishness. Despite the treatments—many say because of them—participants felt isolated, shamed, stigmatized, and abused, but also powerless to bring the treatments to an end. They looked back on childhoods filled with visits to doctors, group medical exams, hospitalizations, and surgeries as invasions of their bodies, over which they had no control. Here is how Gaby remembers her regular checkups:

> I was the local dog and pony show. "Come here. You wanna see something interesting?" Yeah, definitely medical traumatization. I probably went about once every three months up 'til a certain age. Then I went twice a year. The worst thing [about] being in a clinic is the dog and pony show. The worst thing is being put in a prone position, half-naked, [and] told to spread your legs while five or six other people look in your crotch and probe. (Preves 2005, 67)

Making these treatments even more traumatizing, no one—not parents, not doctors—told the children what was happening to them and why. At the age of nineteen, Carol went to the hospital for what she thought was a checkup and overheard members of the staff discussing her surgery:

> [I said to the doctor] as he was leaving, "Excuse me, the nurse said I'm having surgery." And he said, "Yes, it'll be first thing in the morning." And I said, "For what?" And he said, "Don't worry, everything will be fine." And I said, "Why? Fine from what? Why am I having surgery?" And he said, "Well your condition has gonads that could have abnormal cell growth and we must remove them before it gets out of hand." And I said, "I have cancer, don't I?" And he said, "Oh, don't worry about it. Don't worry about it, you're just fine. No, no, no don't be silly. No, you don't have cancer. Don't worry." I said, "Well, then why do I have . . .?" "Don't worry about it, you're just fine." And I thought, "He's lying; I have cancer." Cause that was the best diagnosis I'd come up with yet. (Preves 2005, 68)

Lies and evasions by doctors about the reasons for this intense medical scrutiny were, ironically, carried out in the interest of "normalizing" intersex patients. Quite the contrary, this treatment sent the unmistakable message to the children that they were so horrifically different and so freakish, that no one, not even they, could know the cause. Childhood mysteries did not end when the children grew up. Flora was twenty-four years old, but even then, she told Preves, her genetic counselor refused to tell her about her condition:

> [The geneticist] said, "I'm obliged to tell you that certain details of your condition have not been divulged to you, but I cannot tell you what they are because they would upset you too much." So she's telling us we don't know everything, but she can't tell us what it is because it's too horrible. (Preves 2005, 75)

GENDER IN EVERYDAY LIFE   BOX 2-3
ORGANISATION INTERSEX INTERNATIONAL (OII) OFFICIAL POSITIONS

ON HEALTH CARE

Our societies have accepted a binary construct between male and female which does not reflect Nature and the enormous variety of possible sexes which overlap one another in various gradations on a spectrum with male at one end and female at the other. The arbitrary division of biological sex into only two categories makes all sex assignments of an individual problematic. Neither the genitalia, nor the chromosomes helps one determine the "true" sex of an infant. The gonads, hormones and the internal reproductive organs of the infant are also not reliable indicators for determining conclusively the sex of a child. Each child is born with a unique combination of all these factors and the different possible combinations are very numerous, making all sex assignments of infants a mere conjecture.

We campaign against all non-consensual normalisation treatments of infants that are not medically necessary and favour the right of all intersexed children to determine their own sex identity once they are capable of communicating it to us. Furthermore we advise parents to respect the sex identity of their children and to do all that is necessary so that their children can live according to their choice.

Once the child has communicated clearly their own sex identity, it is crucial that the child's identity be respected both by the parents, physicians and therapists who are caring for the child. All steps should be taken to respect the child's own sense of self by

Imagine how you might respond to hearing such news.

The stories of intersexuals reveal a tragic history of people being subjected to all manner of medical and social abuse because their bodies did not fit normative ideas of what humans are supposed to be like. Real human bodies are variable. Conventional ideas about human bodies, however, have recently demanded that we all belong to one of two sexes. It would seem that the sensible solution to finding that many people do not fit into one of the two "proper" slots would be to question the slots themselves. Instead, as we have seen in these accounts about intersexuals, real people's bodies and lives were forcibly altered so that they would fit into someone's idea about what it means to be human. Should we continue to surgically reconstruct real people? Or should we change our ideas about sex? Intersex activists have answered this last question with a resounding yes by challenging dominant ideas about sex and demanding that doctors stop surgically altering intersexuals without their consent (as is the case with infants and children; see Box 2-3).

being given access to all health care necessary to facilitate life in the sex the child considers most appropriate.

Therefore, we are campaigning in favour of changing the current medical paradigm concerning nonconsensual normalisation treatments and against the diagnosis of gender dysphoria or GID in intersex individuals who feel they were assigned the wrong sex. OII affirms that the true sex of the child is determined by their own inner psychological perceptions and that the right of individual intersex persons to affirm their own sex without medical or governmental interference should be a basic human right.

ON A THIRD SEX

The creation of a new category to be designated intersex poses several problems. First of all, how do we define intersexuality? OII believes that there will be never [sic] a clear definition and at the same time, that it is not necessary to have a legal definition for intersex. We have no clear definitions for what a woman is or a man is. We only assume this to be the case.

The purpose of OII is to work in favour of human rights for the intersexed by helping people to understand that there are not just two pre-existing sexes. There is an infinite combination of possibilities on the spectrum of sex and gender.

The creation of a specific category for the intersexed risks even more marginalisation of a group which is poorly understood. We base our legal arguments on the right of every person to determine her/his own identity in the binary system in the hope that eventually there would be no attempt to impose legal sex categories on anyone.

SOURCE: Reprinted with permission from Organisation Intersex International.

Intersex Activism

The convergence of several factors set off the growing resistance to medical interventions for the purpose of maintaining gender polarity. The outcome has been to interpret gender polarity—not intersexuality itself—as pathological. In the 1990s, increasing publicity about sex assignment surgeries that turned out to be failures accounted for growing public concern. The pivotal case was that of David Reimer. Despite Money's claim that the sex assignment of Reimer had been successful, that was far from the truth. Reimer's childhood was harsh, troubled, and lonely because of his sex assignment, and when he learned at the age of fourteen what had been done to him, he reclaimed his identity as a boy. In the 1990s, Reimer gave up his anonymity to tell his story in a widely circulated account in *Rolling Stone* (Colapinto 1997; 2000). The story produced widespread coverage in the media, ending forty years of silence on intersexuality. In that year alone, periodicals such as *Newsweek, Time,* and

Mademoiselle featured stories about sex assignment, and television news featured Reimer, leaders of intersex groups, and biologist Anne Fausto-Sterling as guests.

In 1993, Anne Fausto-Sterling had published "The Five Sexes," in which she argued that the two-sex system was too narrow to encompass the many varieties of human sexuality. Several years later, Fausto-Sterling recalled the reaction to her article (Fausto-Sterling 2000b, 19):

> I had intended to be provocative, but I had also written with tongue firmly in cheek. So I was surprised by the extent of the controversy the article unleashed. Right-wing Christians were outraged. . . . At the same time, the article delighted others who felt constrained by the current sex and gender system. Clearly, I had struck a nerve. *The fact that so many people could get riled up by my proposal to revamp our sex and gender system suggested that change—as well as resistance to it—might be in the offing.* (emphasis added)

Moved by Fausto-Sterling's article, Cheryl Chase, who had suffered under the medical regime for intersexuals as a child, announced the formation of the Intersex Society of North America (ISNA). Born with an enlarged clitoris, Chase had been raised as a boy until the age of eighteen months, when doctors performed a cliterodectomy on her. After the operation, her parents changed her name and began to raise her as a girl. It was not until she was twenty-three that she learned she had been diagnosed as a "true hermaphrodite" and surgically altered to be female (Fausto-Sterling 2000a, 80–81). In a few short years, Chase and the organization she founded went from picketing outside medical conventions in which physicians discussed intersexuality to being invited to address these conventions and participate in task forces trying to establish ethical treatments and courses of action (Dreger 1998). Fairly rapidly, ISNA became an important advocate for the human rights of intersexuals. ISNA ceased operation in 2008, and Chase went on to help found Accord Alliance, to promote "care that enhances the health and well-being of people and families affected by sex development" (www.accordalliance.org). The Organisation Intersex International (OII) claims to be the largest intersex organization in the world, with members representing almost all known intersex variations and with members in North and South America, Europe, Asia, Africa, and Australia. OII is critical of ISNA founders and supporters such as Cheryl Chase and Alice Dreger for their championing of medical involvement and the term "Disorders of Sex Development" (DSD) as the new designation of intersexuality.

Based on her interviews with medical professionals, Georgiann Davis (2011) found that almost all believe that a person's gender ought to be in line with that person's sex and sexuality. In other words, they are "**gender essentialists**." For these specialists, who are "in a position of authority to define and treat these social constructions [as] they see fit," the label "disorders of sex development" reasserts medical jurisdiction over intersexuality in the face of activists' challenges to doctors' authority. In effect, through this label, intersexuality is removed from activists' ability to define it and has, once more, become medicalized (Davis, 170).

But the battle is still joined. For example, instead of medical treatment for intersexuals, OII champions intersexual cultural pride. On its website, OII announces that it "resists all efforts to make intersex invisible, including genital mutilation, medicalization and normalization without consent and offers another face to intersex lives and experience by highlighting the richness and diversity of intersex identities and culture." (For OII's position statement, see Box 2-3.) Other advocacy groups are Intersex Initiative (IPDX), founded in 1999, and Bodies Like Ours (BLO).

Beginning in the late 1980s, and continuing today with the help of the World Wide Web, intersexuals and their families have formed networks of support, bringing together similarly affected people from around the globe, challenging medical secrecy, eroding the isolation that made intersexuals vulnerable to accepting conventional medical assessments, and establishing conditions that allow intersexuals and their families to challenge conventional wisdom about treatment.

Dreger (1998, 170–73) identified a host of other factors, which she called "postmodernism," that helped to give voice to the growing community of intersexuals and their families. These factors included the rising regard for the testimonies of ordinary people, who are encouraged to speak out about their experiences; the recognition that there are many stories about intersex, in addition to the once-dominant medical story featuring nature's mistakes and bodily pathologies; challenges to the imbalance of power between doctors and patients; patients' demands for active roles in their own health care; and an awareness among intersex patients of the ways their problems with medical experts recapitulate the problems experienced by gay men and lesbians and by women who were once also labeled as "fundamentally unacceptable or flawed."

The Umbrella of Transgender

Few of us are born intersexual, but we are all affected by gender norms that naturalize the two-gender system. As we have tried to demonstrate in this chapter, it's a system that creates the very conditions—in embodiment, in behavior, in identities—that appear to us as its cause. In other words, we act in the belief that there are only two sexes and two genders, and in doing so we materialize a world that confirms our beliefs. Throughout our lives, most of us embrace the sex we are assigned at birth, and we are held accountable to the expectations of others who police our performances of gender (see chapter 3). For many if not most of us, our bodies, our interactions, and our self-feelings have validated the existence of a two-gendered world and our place within it.

Nevertheless, there are growing numbers of people who transgress these gender boundaries. Some boys and men feel feminine within their male bodies. **MTFs** or **transwomen** are those male-born individuals who, feeling this way, elect to live their lives as women. Some girls and women feel essentially male at the core of their female bodies. **FTMs** or **transmen** are those female-born individuals who elect to live their lives as men. Some FTMs and MTFs use hormones and surgery to mold their bodies to be the "opposite" of their birth sex, and some do not. Do transmen and transwomen transition to become just "men" and just "women?" Not according to some transmen and transwomen themselves. They argue that their biographies, bodies, sexualities, and identities are different from the biographies, bodies, sexualities, and identities of nontransgender men and women. A transman interviewed by Jason Cromwell (2006) explained, "I didn't have the experiences of boys growing into manhood; I don't identify as a man, I identify as a transman."

Scholars and service providers often place MTFs and FTMs under the umbrella term **"transgender,"** which covers all those who reject normative gender and sexual identities and who challenge the sexual and gender logics embedded in social institutions (Halperin 1997; Warner 1993). The transgender community is an "imagined community" (Valentine 2007) of transsexuals, drag queens, butches, hermaphrodites, cross-dressers, masculine women, effeminate men, sissies, and tomboys. David Valentine (2007), who studied various groups of transgender women when he was a researcher and a safer-sex outreach worker for the Lesbian and Gay Community Services Center in Manhattan, notes the recent and rapid rise of the term "to incorporate all and any variance from imagined gender norms" (14) and worries that when outreach workers institutionalize this term to identify their client base, they may ignore important differences among those so labeled. He fears that privileging one unifying identity—transgender—can erase "racial, ethnic, sexual, gendered, and other kinds of differences" (Valentine 2007, 132). Intersecting inequalities then disappear under the label.

In Valentine's New York, those most erased or marginalized—not surprisingly—are the young black and Latino male-bodied girls who stroll the night streets of the meat market, the gentrifying New York neighborhood on the outskirts of Greenwich Village. They are targets for police action and are harassed and endangered by those who buy their services. The girls' lives are structured by racism and poverty, and their consciousness of who they are is very different from the consciousness of those among the cross-dressers, gays, and drag queens who value "whiteness, middle classness, and respectability" (2007, 245). And yet, writes Valentine, the idea that there is a transgender community has helped to provide those on its margins with sensitive and available medical services, schools, workplaces, and laws respecting their human rights.

Of course, there have always been people who refused to live in their birth-gender and people who refused the strictures of both genders. But the modern history of the trans phenomenon begins with the "coming out" of surgically altered transsexuals such as Christine Jorgenson, whose sex reassignment surgery (SRS) in the 1950s was a media sensation, and Renee Richards, an American ophthalmologist who, after SRS in the 1970s, sued the United States Tennis Association and won the right to play in the US Open despite a rule restricting competition to "women-born women" (WBW). Like the "prehistory" of intersexuals that began with surgical and hormonal interventions, biomedical science and clinical practice reinforced a two-gender system and the conventional norms of sex and gender on transmen and transwomen. But in the 1990s, after a long period in which medical/psychiatric diagnoses defined their identities and treatments, gender and sexual rebels began to speak for themselves. Since then, scholarship and activism has moved "from the clinic to the streets" (and to the universities) (Stryker 2006).

The rapid rise of the term "transgender" and of the transgender activism that began in the 1990s was facilitated in part by the expansion of the World Wide Web, which you should recall also contributed to the political organization of intersexuals. One flashpoint came at the Michigan Womyn's Music Festival in 1991, when a transsexual woman was denied entry because she was "actually" a man. The festival organizers maintained that it was a site for "women-born women" only. The policy reflected longstanding reservations among lesbian feminists regarding male-to-female transsexuals. In her widely circulated 1979 book, *The Transsexual Empire: The Making of the She-Male*, Janice Raymond wrote that "all transsexuals rape women's bodies by reducing the real female form to an artifact, appropriating this body for themselves" (Raymond 1979, 104). Raymond believed that male-to-female transsexuals were involved in a plot by men to infiltrate the women's movement. In 1999, after yearly demonstrations by transwomen outside the gates, a small group of transgender activists were admitted to the festival, and a compromise was negotiated under which only postoperative transwomen would be admitted. This policy, like the WBW policy that preceded it, was criticized by Emi Koyama as oppressive, exclusionary, and racist. For instance, she wrote, it excluded poor women who could not afford expensive genital surgeries or who were not covered by health insurance. Moreover, the policy reproduced the logic of exclusion of women of color:

> Speaking from the perspective and the tradition of lesbians of color, most if not all rationales for excluding transsexual women are not only transphobic, but also racist. To argue that transsexual women should not enter the Land [the site of the music festival] because their experiences are different would have to assume that all other women's experiences are the same, and this is a racist assumption. The argument that transsexual women have experienced some degree of male privilege should not bar them from our communities once we realize that not all women are equally privileged or oppressed. To suggest that the safety of the Land would be compromised overlooks, perhaps intentionally, ways in which women can act out violence and oppression against each other. Even the argument that "the presence of a penis would trigger the women" is flawed because it neglects the fact that white skin is just as much a reminder of violence as a penis. The racist history of lesbian-feminism has taught us that any white woman making these excuses for one oppression have made and will make the same excuse for other oppressions such as racism, classism, and ableism. (Koyama 2000, 702–703)

Despite these differences and disputes, transgender scholars and activists have adopted a feminist agenda of rethinking gender and sexuality. In turn, transgender activism and reflection about gender and sexuality has affected feminist thought. Influential philosopher Judith Butler acknowledges the influence of transgender and transsexual movements on her work. In the introduction to *Undoing Gender*, she writes, "My own thinking has been influenced by the 'New Gender Politics' that has emerged in recent years, a combination of movements concerned with transgender, transsexuality, intersex, and their complex relations to feminist and queer theory" (2004, 4).

Lesbian feminist of color Gloria Anzaldua (1987) provided the concept of the "mestiza," which may help to explore the meanings and potentials of transgender. The **mestiza** is a person who lives with multiple competing, conflicting, and interconnected identities and uses the insights of her position and experience to challenge the boundaries between different cultures, race ethnicities, and genders. Anzaldua wrote:

> As a *Mestiza* I have no country, my homeland cast me out; yet all countries are mine because I am every woman's sister or potential lover. (As a lesbian I have no race, my own people disclaim me; but I am all races because there is the queer of me in all races.) I am cultureless because, as a feminist, I challenge the collective culture because I am participating in the creation of yet another culture, a new story to explain the world and our participation in it, a new value system with images and symbols that connect us to each other and to the planet. *Soy un amasamiento*, I am an act of kneading, of uniting, and joining that not only has produced both a creature of darkness and a creature of light, but also a creature that questions the definitions of light and dark and gives them new meanings." (Anzaldua 2003)

The many gender- and sex-variant people collected under the umbrella of transgender are among the "new mestizas." Their lives demonstrate that the categories of sex and gender are no longer as stable as they once were. They present us with new possibilities and new hope that we might be able to "degender" society (Lorber 2005a), and thereby end one of our most basic and enduring inequalities. We should celebrate this growing area of human diversity.

GENDER MATTERS

Intersex and transgender are human rights issues. The intersex and transgender rights movements of the twenty-first century have joined the gay, lesbian, bisexual movements that emerged in the late twentieth century to compel many of us to rethink our basic cultural assumptions about sex and gender, maleness and femaleness, and femininity and masculinity. Instead of hiding in shame and isolation, which was once their fate, many intersexuals and transgender people are publicly challenging the domination of a two-sex-only view. Their challenge suggests that we may be moving from a system based on sexual dimorphism—male–female difference—to one that includes many sexualities and multiple genders. Social scientists have described gender and sexual diversity in the non-Western world and are giving these sex and gender variations in our own society more attention and respect today, undoubtedly because gay, lesbian, bisexual, and transgender movements have given voice to their members and power to such analyses.

The idea that men are men and women are women, a modern (as opposed to postmodern) conception of sex, gender, and sexuality, is no longer as safely part of our definition of reality as it once was. Here we have tried to capture recent sociological thinking about the role of the social in the creation of our embodied selves. Under the guidance of sex- and gender-bending movements, we are more than ever able to relinquish the biological straightjackets of the past. As gender variations become normalized, they become arenas "for playful exploration" of our possibilities (Fausto-Sterling 2000b), and we are made freer.

People come in a wide array of sexual identities, and they practice social selection by inventing an exploding array of gendered and sexual possibilities. This practice may ultimately put an end to sex and gender as relevant categories of existence. Nevertheless, the attempt to free ourselves from older normative sexual and gender identities can be dangerous, as the murder of Matthew Shepard shows (see Box 4–3). This danger is the reason why, according to Fausto-Sterling, legal protection is necessary in the transition to a more gender-diverse world. The excerpts from the International Bill of Gender Rights shown in Box 2-4 speak to these needs.

GENDER IN EVERYDAY LIFE   BOX 2-4
FROM THE INTERNATIONAL BILL OF GENDER RIGHTS, ADOPTED
JUNE 17, 1995, HOUSTON, TEXAS, USA

The International Bill of Gender Rights (IBGR) strives to express human and civil rights from a gender perspective. However, the ten rights enunciated below are not to be viewed as special rights applicable to a particular interest group. Nor are these rights limited in application to persons for whom gender identity and gender role issues are of paramount concern. All ten sections of the IBGR are universal rights which can be claimed and exercised by every human being.

- All human beings have the right to define their own gender identity regardless of chromosomal sex, genitalia, assigned birth sex, or initial gender role; and further, no individual shall be denied Human or Civil Rights by virtue of a self-defined gender identity which is not in accord with chromosomal sex, genitalia, assigned birth sex, or initial gender role.
- All human beings have the right to free expression of their self-defined gender identity; and further, no individual shall be denied Human or Civil Rights by virtue of the expression of a self-defined gender identity.
- Individuals shall not be denied the right to train for and to pursue an occupation or profession, nor be denied the right to secure and retain employment, nor be denied just compensation for their labor, by virtue of their chromosomal sex, genitalia, assigned birth sex, or initial gender role, or on the basis of a self-defined gender identity or the expression thereof.
- No individual shall be denied access to a space or denied participation in an activity by virtue of a self-defined gender identity which is not in accord with chromosomal sex, genitalia, assigned birth sex, or initial gender role.
- Individuals shall not be denied the right to change their bodies as a means of expressing a self-defined gender identity; and further, individuals shall not be denied Human or Civil Rights on the basis that they have changed their bodies cosmetically, chemically, or surgically, or desire to do so as a means of expressing a self-defined gender identity.
- Individuals shall not be denied the right to competent medical or other professional care when changing their bodies cosmetically, chemically, or surgically, on the basis of chromosomal sex, genitalia, assigned birth sex, or initial gender role.
- Individuals shall not be subject to psychiatric diagnosis or treatment as mentally disordered or diseased solely on the basis of a self-defined gender identity or the expression thereof.
- No individual shall be denied Human or Civil Rights for expression of a self-defined gender identity through sexual acts between consenting adults.
- Individuals shall not be denied the right to form committed, loving relationships with one another or to enter into marital contracts by virtue of their own or their partner's chromosomal sex, genitalia, assigned birth sex, or initial gender role, or on the basis of their expression of a self-defined gender identity.
- Individuals shall not be denied the right to conceive, bear, or adopt children, nor to nurture and have custody of children, nor to exercise parental capacity with respect to children, natural or adopted, on the basis of their own, their partner's, or their children's chromosomal sex, genitalia, assigned birth sex, initial gender role, or by virtue of a self-defined gender identity or the expression thereof.

SOURCE: As drafted by Sharon Stuart during the International Conference on Transgender Law and Employment Policy.

KEY TERMS

believing is seeing
the doctrine of separate spheres
gender essentialists
heterosexual matrix
hijra
mestiza
MTFs and FTMs, or transwomen
and transmen

natural attitude
the "optimum gender of
rearing" model
paradigm shift
the standard story
transgender
two-spirit people
vocabularies of motives

CRITICAL THINKING QUESTIONS

1. What is the "standard story" regarding sex, gender, and sexuality? What is significant about it? On what assumptions is the "standard story" based?
2. What do some First Nations cultures believe and practice regarding gender? How do their perceptions and actions regarding gender challenge the dominant beliefs in most Western cultures?
3. Who are hijras, and how does their treatment differ from the treatment of intersex children in the West?
4. How did the intersex movement emerge in the late twentieth century?
5. Imagine that you have been asked to advise some researchers about the importance of distinguishing between sex and gender in their work. How would you advise them?

REFERENCES

American Academy of Pediatrics. 2000. "Evaluation of the Newborn with Developmental Anomalies of the External Genitalia." *Pediatrics* 106 (1, Pt 1): 138–42.

Anzaldúa, Gloria E., 2003. "La Conciencia de la Mestiza: Towards a New Consciousness." In *Feminist Theory Reader: Local and Global Perspectives*, edited by Carole R. McCann and Seung-Kyung Kim, 179–87. New York: Routledge.

Blackwood, Evelyn. 1984. "Sexuality and Gender in Certain Native American Tribes: The Case of Cross-Gender Females." *Signs: Journal of Women in Contemporary Society* 10 (1): 27–42.

Butler, Judith. 1990. *Gender Trouble*. New York: Routledge.

Chauncy George. 1995. *Gay New York: Gender, Urban Culture, and the Making of the Gay Male World, 1890–1940*. New York: Basic Books.

Colapinto, John. 1997. "The True Story of John/Joan." *Rolling Stone*, December 11, 54–97.

———. 2000. *As Nature Made Him: The Boy Who Was Raised as a Girl*. New York: HarperCollins.

Connell, R. W. 1999. "Making Gendered People: Bodies, Identities, Sexualities." In *Revisioning Gender*, edited by Myra Marx Ferree, Judith Lorber, and Beth Hess, 449–71. Thousand Oaks, CA: Sage.

———. 2001. *The Men and the Boys*. Berkeley: University of California Press.

———. 2002. *Gender*. Cambridge, UK: Polity Press.

Cromwell, Jason. 2006. "Queering the Binaries: Transsituated Identities, Bodies, and Sexualities." In *The Transgender Studies Reader*, edited by Susan Stryker and Stephen Whittle, 509–21. New York: Routledge.

Davis, Angela. 1983. *Women, Race, and Class*. New York: Random House.

Davis, Georgiann. 2011. "DSD is a Perfectly Fine Term": Reasserting Medical Authority Through a Shift in Intersex Terminalogy. *Sociology of Diagnosis*, edited by P. J. McGann and David J. Hutson, 155–82.

D'Emilio, John. 1983. "Capitalism and Gay Identity." In *Powers of Desire: The Politics of Sexuality*, edited by Ann Snitow, Christine Stansell, and Sharon Thompson, 100–16. New York: Monthly Review Press.

Dreger, Alice Domurat. 1998. *Hermaphrodites and the Medical Invention of Sex*. Cambridge, MA: Harvard University Press.

Faustino-Sterling, Anne. 1993. "The Five Sexes: Why Male and Female Are Not Enough." *The Sciences* 33 (2): 20–24.

———. 2000a. *Sexing the Body: Gender Politics and the Construction of Sexuality*. New York: Basic Books.

———. 2000b. "The Five Sexes, Revisited." *The Sciences* 40 (4): 19–23.

Foucault, Michel. 2001. *Order of Things: An Archaeology of the Human Sciences*. 2nd edition. New York: Routledge.

Frye, Phyllis Randolph. 2000. "The International Bill of Gender Rights vs. the Cider House Rules: Transgenders Struggle with the Courts over What Clothing They Are Allowed to Wear on the Job, Which Restroom They Are Allowed to Use on the Job, Their Right to Marry, and the Very Definition of Their Sex," William & Mary Journal of Women and the Law 7 (1): 133, Appendix B.

Gagnon, John, and William Simon. 1973. *Sexual Conduct: The Social Sources of Human Sexuality*. Chicago: Aldine.

Halperin, David. 1997. *Saint Foucault: Towards a Gay Hagiography*. New York: Oxford University Press.

Jackson, Stevi, and Sue Scott, eds. 1996. *Feminism and Sexuality: A Reader*. New York: Columbia University Press.

Kessler, Suzanne. 1990. "The Medical Construction of Gender: Case Management of Intersexed Infants." *Signs* 16 (1): 3–26.

Kessler, Suzanne, and Wendy McKenna. 1978. *Gender: An Ethnomethodological Approach*. New York: Wiley.

Kimmel, Michael, Robert S. Connell, and Jeff Hearn. 2004. *Handbook of Studies on Men and Masculinities*. Thousand Oaks, CA: Sage.

Koyama, Emi. 2006. "Whose Feminism Is It Anyway? The Unspoken Racism of the Trans Inclusion Debate." Susan Stryker and Stephen Whittle, eds. *The Transgender Studies Reader*. NY: Routledge. 698–705.

Kuhn, Thomas S. 1996. *The Structure of Scientific Revolutions*. 3rd edition. Chicago: University of Chicago Press.

Lancaster, Roger. 2003. *The Trouble with Nature: Sex in Science and Popular Culture*. Berkeley: University of California Press.

Lang, Sabine. 1998. *Men as Women, Women as Men: Changing Gender in Native American Cultures*. Austin: University of Texas Press.

Laqueur, Thomas. 1990. *Making Sex: Body and Gender from the Greeks to Freud*. Cambridge, MA: Harvard University Press.

Lee, Peter A., Christopher P. Houk, S. Faisal Ahmed, and Iquan Hughes. 2006. "Consensus Statement on Management of Intersex Disorders." *Pediatrics* 118. 488–50.

Levy, Ariel. 2009. "Either/Or: Sports, Sex, and the Case of Caster Semenya." *The New Yorker*, November 30. http://www.newyorker.com/reporting/2009/11/30/091130fa_fact_levy. Accessed March 19, 2011.

Lorber, Judith. 2005a. *Breaking the Bowls: Degendering and Feminist Change*. NY: W.W. Norton and Company.

Lorber, Judith. 1994. *Paradoxes of Gender*. New Haven: Yale University Press.

——. 2005b. *Gender Inequality: Feminist Theories and Politics*. 3rd edition. Los Angeles: Roxbury.

Macur, Juliet. 2012. "Sex Verification Policy Is Criticized as a Failure." *New York Times*, June 25.

Martin, Emily. 1992. *The Woman in the Body: A Cultural Analysis of Reproduction*. Boston: Beacon Press.

——. 1997. "The Egg and the Sperm: How Science Has Constructed a Romance Based on Stereo-typical Male-Female Roles." In *Situated Lives: Gender and Culture in Everyday Life*, edited by Louise Lamphere, Helena Rogone, and Patricia Zavella, 85–98. New York: Routledge.

Miller, Eleanor. 1998. "Celebrating, Deconstructing, Historicizing, and Theorizing Transgenderism and the Transgendered." *Feminist Collections* 19 (2).

Nagel, Joane. 2003. *Race, Ethnicity, and Sexuality: Intimate Intersections, Forbidden Frontiers*. New York: Oxford University Press.

Nakhal, Rola S., Margaret Hall-Craggs, Alex Freeman, Alex Kirkham, Gerard S. Conway, Rupali Arora, Chistopher R. J. Woodhouse, Dan N. Wood, and Sarah M. Creighton. 2013. Evaluation of Retained Testes in Adolescent Girls and Women with Complete Androgen Insensitivity Syndrome. *Radiology* 268 (1) July: 153–60.

Nanda, Serena. 1990. *Neither Man nor Woman: The Hijras of India*. Belmont, CA: Wadsworth.

Organisation Intersex International (OII). "Official Positions." http://www.intersexualite.org/English-Offical-Position.html. Accessed March 20, 2011.

Oyama, Susan, Paul E. Griffiths, and Russell D. Gray, eds. 2001. *Cycles of Contingency: Developmental Systems and Evolution*. Cambridge, MA: MIT Press.

Peel, Robert. 1994. *Eve's Rib—Searching for the Biological Roots of Sex Differences* New York: Crown.

Preves, Sharon. 2005. *Intersex and Identity: The Contested Self*. New Brunswick, NJ: Rutgers University Press.

Raymond, Janice. 1994. *The Transsexual Empire*. Boston: Beacon Press.

Reeves, Thomas. 1997. *The Life and Times of Joe McCarthy: A Biography*. New York: Madison Books.

Roughgarden, Joan. 2004. *Evolution's Rainbow: Diversity, Gender, and Sexuality*. Berkeley: University of California Press.

Rubin, Henry. 2003. *Self-Made Men: Identity and Embodiment Among Transsexual Men*. Nashville: Vanderbilt University Press.

Ryan, Mary P. 1975. *Womanhood in America: From Colonial Times to the Present*. New York: New Viewpoints.

Schwartz, Pepper, and Virginia Rutter. 1998. *The Gender of Sexuality*. Thousand Oaks, CA: Pine Forge.

Sedgwick, Eve Kosofsky. 1991. *Epistemology of the Closet*. 2nd edition. Berkeley: University of California Press.

Simon, William. 1996. *Postmodern Sexualities*. New York: Routledge.

Stein, Edward. 1999. *The Mismeasure of Desire: The Science, Theory, and Ethics of Sexual Orientation*. New York: Oxford University Press.

Stryker, Susan. 2006. "(De)Subjugated Knowledges: An Introduction to Transgender Studies." In *The Transgender Studies Reader*, edited by Susan Stryker and Stephen Whittle, 1–17. New York: Routledge.

Thomas, W. I. 1928. *The Child in America: Behavior Problems and Programs*. New York: Knopf.

Trumbach, Randolph. 1996. "The Third Gender in Twentieth-Century America." *Journal of Social History* 30 (2): 497–501.

U.S. National Library of Medicine and National Institutes of Health. 2009. "Intersex." http://www
.nlm.nih.gov/medlineplus/ency/article/001669.htm. Accessed March 18, 2011.

Valentine, David. 2007. *Imagining Transgender: An Ethnography of a Category.* Durham, NC: Duke
University Press.

Warner, Michael. 1993. *Fear of a Queer Planet: Queer Politics and Social Theory.* Minneapolis: University of Minnesota Press.

Whittle, S. 2006. "Foreword." In *The Transgender Studies Reader,* edited by Susan Stryker and Stephen
Whittle, xi–xvi New York: Routledge.

Zirin, Dave. 2009. "Caster Semenya Aint 8 Feet Tall," *ZNet,* August 26. http://www.zcommunications
.org/caster-semenya-aint-8-feet-tall-by-dave-zirin. Accessed 2-20-2014.

3

SOCIALIZATION AND THE SOCIAL CONSTRUCTION OF GENDER

Barbie in 1959 (left) and 2009 (right), the portrait of pop femininity. Since her first appearance in 1959, Barbie has been an astronaut, TV news reporter, veterinarian, UNICEF ambassador, aerobics instructor, NASCAR driver, gulf war soldier, basketball player in the WNBA, presidential candidate, pop star, and producer, all the while maintaining her impossible physique.

Source: Associated Press.

Not long ago a university professor in Indiana asked more than 1,200 college students to participate in a study about toys and socialization (Blakemore and Centers 2005). The students were shown pictures of a large number of common American toys and told to label each toy according to how feminine or masculine they believed them to be. They sorted the toys into these categories:

- Strongly masculine: G.I. Joe, footballs, Matchbox cars, miniature weapons, and toolboxes
- Moderately masculine: Big Wheel, basketball hoop, Lincoln Logs, and microscope
- Neutral: wagon, Play Doh, doctor kit, trampoline

- Moderately feminine: toy kitchen, Ken doll, costume, horses
- Strongly feminine: Easy-Bake Oven, Barbie doll, ballerina costume, vanity set

In a second part of the study, another group of more than seven hundred students was asked to describe the characteristics of the toys. The students came up with descriptors such as violent, competitive, exciting, and somewhat dangerous for the masculine toys. They described the feminine toys as associated with physical attractiveness, nurturance, and domestic skill. The toys rated as most likely to be educational and to develop children's physical, cognitive, artistic, and other skills were typically rated as neutral or moderately masculine.

This study illustrates an important area of study for scholars who have been interested in uncovering the social sources of gender. In the last chapter we argued that biology does not seem to provide a valid explanation for the origins of gender. We asserted that gender is socially structured, but what does that mean?

How does the way we socialize our children help to create and perpetuate gender? How do toys, for example, teach children about what is expected of them as "properly" gendered people? Is social learning the only social source of gender? Is gender also something we create and perpetuate as we interact with others? Adults do not usually play with children's toys, but we do express gender, perpetuating it as we interact with one another.

What about social structure? What role does it play? If children were all given the same toys and socialized in the same way, would they still face gendered social institutions and social structures that would demand that they "choose" a gender and play the role?

How do all of these social factors—social learning, social interaction, and social structure— fit together to create our gendered experience?

This chapter seeks to answer these questions by describing how social psychologists and sociologists have attempted to explain the emergence and persistence of gender differences. We begin by exploring the tacit assumptions, or lenses, that perpetuate views of gender differences. Then we look at three levels at which gender differences have been constructed: (1) at the *individual* level of social learning and psychological sex differences; (2) at the *interactional* level of social relations in everyday life; and (3) at the level of *structural, organizational, and institutional forces* that constrain and shape action. We conclude by comparing these approaches and suggesting how an integration of the three perspectives can help us explain how gender differences and similarities are produced, how they persist, and how they may be transformed.

THE GENDER LENSES OF ANDROCENTRISM, GENDER POLARIZATION, AND ESSENTIALISM

The women's movement that arose in the 1960s challenged a number of tacit assumptions about sex and gender, assumptions that shaped both individual perceptions and social institutions. In her book *The Lenses of Gender*, Sandra Bem (1993) likened these assumptions to gender lenses that filter what we see and color how we see it. In particular, Bem identified three such lenses.

The lens of **androcentrism**, or male-centeredness, makes everything male appear to be the neutral norm, the universally human. Viewed against this standard, women appear deviant, less than human, and "other" or alien. One of many possible examples of androcentrism we could cite is the use of the generic "he" to refer to men *and* women, or "mankind" to refer to all human beings.

A second lens, the lens of *gender polarization*, refers to the ways that diverse aspects of human experience are culturally linked to sex differences. Cultural items, emotions, social positions, and needs are *either* male or female. For example, it has been a North American cultural mandate that only women should wear pink. A gender-polarized view holds that men are authoritative, rational, and unemotional, whereas women are submissive, irrational, and highly emotional. Men and women supposedly have different inborn capacities that fit them for different kinds of work. Engineering is properly men's work, just as child care is appropriately women's work. Women need romance; men need to "score." As discussed in chapter 2, gender scholars argue that these polarities or binaries in men's and women's emotions, needs, abilities, and desires are socially constructed, not biologically determined.

A third lens, *essentialism*, is the view that gender is a fixed biological or psychological trait that does not vary among individuals or over time. Essentialist thinking has also been used to argue that racial ethnic capacities and traits are inborn and immutable. In fact, it may be easier for many people to understand how essentialism in matters of race supports racist thinking than to understand the sexism implicit in gender essentialism. In both cases, a human-made or socially constructed but powerful fiction about race or gender is treated as if it were an indisputable biological reality. It is always helpful to remember the Thomas theorem, a theory formulated by Chicago sociologist W. I. Thomas (1863–1947) in 1928: "If men [*sic*] define situations as real, they are real in their consequences." Based in reality or not, beliefs about gender and race have tremendous consequences for people's lives and for the maintenance of inequalities of race and gender. Box 3-1, "Trayvon Martin and the Thomas Theorem," shows the lethal effects of defining boys of color as dangerous.

GENDER IN EVERYDAY LIFE   BOX 3-1
TRAYVON MARTIN AND THE THOMAS THEOREM

Situations defined as real are real in their consequences. If you believed the hotel you were staying at was experiencing a gas leak and the only way to save your life was to break the sprinkler system with a porcelain toilet lid, would you do it? [There follows a video showing hotel guests tricked by prank calls into believing they were endangered by a gas leak in the hotel in which they were staying.]

For these unsuspecting hotel guests, they truly believed there was a gas leak and that if they didn't break the sprinkler heads people were going to die. They believed the gas leak was real and they believed the person on the phone was really the authorities. Clearly they were manipulated by pranksters, but we see the same type of reality construction every day.

These prank calls illustrate two important sociological concepts, the social construction of reality and the Thomas Theorem. Sociologists argue that reality is whatever we all agree it is. The Thomas Theorem contends that situations defined as real are real in their consequences. If we believe our hotel needs us to break a window, we are likely to do it.

A far more horrific example of this theorem can be seen in the killing of 17 year old Trayvon Martin. On the night of February 26th [2012] Martin was walking to his father's house after purchasing a bag of skittles and an iced tea from a convenience store when George Zimmerman, a captain with the neighborhood watch program in the area, spotted him. Zimmerman called 911 from his truck and reported that a "real suspicious guy" was walking in his neighborhood. "This guy looks like he's up to no good or on drugs or something," Zimmerman continued. At this point Zimmerman had not yet verbally interacted with Martin or even got out of his truck, but already he had decided Martin was dangerous. Around this time Trayvon Martin pulled up his dark gray hoodie and covered his head.

"He's got his hand in his waistband," Zimmerman told the operator as Martin walked toward his truck, "something's wrong with him." After another moment, Zimmerman said, "these [expletive] they always get away." Zimmerman then got out of his car and started following Martin. Despite the 911 operator telling him not to chase Martin, Zimmerman continued.

What happened then is still being debated. All we know for certain is Zimmerman pulled out his gun, shot and killed Trayvon Martin that rainy night. As of this writing he has not been charged with a crime and is still in possession of the gun used in the killing. Zimmerman claimed it was self-defense and was released that night.

Martin's killing and Zimmerman's freedom have sparked a national outrage and while we wait to see what will ultimately happen to Zimmerman little is certain, except that Zimmerman acted based on the reality he had constructed for himself. [Note: On July 13, 2013, Zimmerman was acquitted of second-degree murder and of manslaughter charges.]

Despite never meeting Martin before, Zimmerman was certain that he was, "up to no good." With one look Zimmerman felt compelled to call 911 because he knew Trayvon was one of the "[expletives]" that "always get away." Zimmerman defined his situation as real (Martin was a dangerous criminal) and this distorted perception was real in it's [sic] consequences.

Except, by all accounts Trayvon Martin wasn't a criminal. He was a good kid who wanted some Skittles and an iced tea while he watched the NBA All Star Game. Zimmerman saw something suspicious, but there was no evidence to suggest his perception was accurate.

Reality is what we believe it to be. If we are mislead or if our bias, prejudice, or ignorance cloud our perception of reality the consequences can be profound. To be clear, the Thomas Theorem doesn't excuse any behavior, but rather it only helps us understand how tragic events like this can occur.

Source: Palmer, Nathan. "Trayvon Martin & the Thomas Theorum." Pearson Education Sociology in Focus [blog] April 2, 2012. www.sociologyinfocus.com/2012/04/02/trayvon-martin-the-thomas-theorem/#more-1802.

As a claim based on innate biological or psychological attributes, essentialism poses logical problems. First, as we saw in the previous chapter, not all individuals can be categorized as either male or female. What would be the *essential* sex or gender characteristics of people who are born with ambiguously sexed bodies or those with the bodies of one sex who envision themselves as members of the other ("opposite") sex?

Second, essentialist thinking is akin to stereotyping, which categorizes and judges groups of individuals according to a few shared characteristics such as sex, skin tone, or age. An early form of what is now discredited essentialism is the claim that all women are emotional and all men are rational due to their biological or psychological makeup. Feminist research has by now undermined this broad generalization. The work of Arlie Hochschild (1983) on the sociology of emotions explored masculine emotionality as feelings of anger and fear. Feminist studies of militarism and war making suggest that the narrow rationality of military tactics and strategies exists within an irrational context of gendered violence and threat (Cohn 1987). In the wake of such studies, it is more difficult to explain gender as an inborn and universal quality dividing male from female, masculinity from femininity, and men from women.

If gender difference isn't inborn, where does it come from? We know from chapter 2 that ideas about gender have evolved historically. The feminist movements of the nineteenth and twentieth centuries have made important contributions to understanding the evolution of thinking about gender. Earlier feminist movements in the United States—women's demands for the vote, for the right to hold property, and access to education and the professions— challenged prevailing beliefs that women were men's natural inferiors. Such challenges raised questions about the origins of the sexual division of labor and laid the groundwork for a social science of gender (Connell 1987, 25).

Later in the century, feminist activists (the second and third waves) again contested academic and popular representations of women's place and initiated studies of hidden assumptions, shifting categories, and processes of gender production, in the hope that revealing how gender is organized would be the first step toward "de-gendering" society (see Lorber 1994).

INDIVIDUAL-LEVEL THEORIES: SOCIAL ROLES AND SOCIAL LEARNING

Role theory flourished in the mid-twentieth century, when the functionalist paradigm was predominant in sociology. **Functionalists** described society as a system of interdependent parts—the family, the economy, the political system, the educational system—that worked together to meet the system's "functional needs" and keep it stable. Individuals who were socialized into roles that fulfilled societal needs were the key to maintaining the social system. Their socialization involved internalizing social norms as expectations about how to feel, think, and behave in the social roles they inhabited as parents and children, husbands and wives, employers and workers, teachers and students.

In white middle-class American families fifty years ago, it was normative, valued, and expected that a single male breadwinner would support his family; and it was equally normative, valued, and expected that a wife and mother would exclusively care for her children and make a home for her husband. Scholars and ordinary middle class people alike believed that failing to live up to the requirements of these roles would not only create a deviant family but would undermine the social system itself. For example, if women were to abandon their roles as full-time wives and mothers, men would not be free to fulfill their functions in the public sphere as breadwinners. In many ways, functionalist theory supported the status quo as the best and perhaps the only way to organize an ongoing, stable society.

Until the second wave of the women's movement, there had been few challenges to the idea that complementary sex roles in families and in society were socially required. In keeping with the perception that women's lives in the private sphere were less important than men's public roles, the small amount of research done on women's lives focused primarily on women's family responsibilities. If there were people who did not live according to the functionalist view of a socially harmonious and socially necessary division of labor, they usually were labeled deviant.

One exception to this consensus was the research of sociologist Mirra Komarovsky, who found that educated women were greatly dissatisfied with their allotted roles. In a 1946 study, she showed that college women were torn between the injunction to commit their lives exclusively to marriage and motherhood and their interests in successful academic and professional careers. In another study, published a full ten years before Betty Friedan's *Feminine Mystique*, Komarovsky (1953) noted that full-time mothers were wondering "what is wrong with me that home and family are not enough?" (127).

Komarovsky was almost alone in the sociological study of the conflicts and dilemmas of conventional sex roles until the 1970s, when the women's movement stimulated an explosion of research questioning the desirability and social utility of complementary sex roles. Although not yet departing from the focus on individual learning of sex roles, feminist scholars argued that sex roles were unequal and oppressive. Many of their studies showed how girls were socialized to concentrate on marriage and motherhood by parents, schools, and the media and attributed women's lesser status to such learning. As women moved into the labor force, it became increasingly apparent that there were serious conflicts between women's family and work roles, between being adequate wives and mothers on the one hand, and pursuing satisfying public careers on the other. Something would have to change.

In its feminist version, sex-role research remained focused on the individual level. Like the functionalists before them, feminist scholars argued that sex roles were rooted in individuals' social positions or statuses and the expectations that accompanied those positions (West and Fenstermaker 1995, 17). They explained that children were socialized into roles by families, textbooks, teachers, and the media. Sex-role learning, they argued, produced girls and women who were nurturant, child centered, dependent on husbands, and family oriented and boys and men who were work oriented, competitive, aggressive, and ambitious. Their focus was on the differences between boys and girls, men and women.

This new research tended to concentrate narrowly on white and middle-class women who were pioneering in men's professions (see, for example, Epstein 1970; Lorber 1975). Almost no one studied the lives and work of African American women, whose generations-long involvement in paid labor seriously challenged the conventional wisdom that most women were exclusively housewives, that employment for women was something new, and that the breadwinner–housewife family was the norm (Landry 2002; Cole 1971; Hochschild 1973). Some social scientists called nonnormative single-parent families or those without lone male breadwinners pathological, disorganized, and out of step with mainstream society (Hill 2005, 63). In particular, some social scientists blamed strong black mothers, whom they called "matriarchs," for emasculating black husbands and failing to provide black sons with the authority figures that would allow them to learn appropriate masculine roles (Coontz 1992).

In the 1970s, revisionist family scholars (those who rewrote the stories of African American families) rejected this view of black families, noting their strengths, their rich, extended family life, and the adaptive strategies they devised to relieve the impact on black people of racist social policies that supported housing, education, and job discrimination (see, for example, Stack 1997). But the "social problems focus" of scholarship on black families returned in the late 1980s with studies of teen pregnancy, welfare dependency, and family violence (Hill 2005, 148). An explosion of feminist and antiracist research that emerged in the latter years of the twentieth century addressed the intersecting issues of race and gender. For example, feminists of color argued that it was misguided to build theory solely around the opposition between women and men. Instead, they argued, we must attend to the crosscutting dimensions of race and class inequalities that complicate that story. As we discussed in chapter 1, many sociologists are now engaged in studies of the ways interactions among many factors, especially race/ethnicity, class, citizenship, and sexuality affect sexism and gendered behavior.

Patricia Hill Collins (2000, 66), an important theorist of intersectionality, suggests that it is important to understand how intersecting oppressions of class and gender differentially position black women nationally and globally:

> Large numbers of U.S. Black women in the working poor are employed as cooks, laundry workers, nursing home aides, and child-care workers. These women serve not only U.S. Whites, but more affluent U.S. Blacks, other people of color, and recent immigrants. Dependent on public services of all sorts—public schools for their children, health-care clinics for their checkups, buses and other public transportation to get them to work, and social welfare bureaucracies to fill in the gap between paychecks and monthly bills—these women can encounter Black middle-class teachers, nurses, bus drivers, and social workers who are as troublesome to them as White ones.

These experiences challenge simplistic hierarchies of domination and resistance and the binary thinking that makes opposition between women and men the central problem of power and inequality. All of us are in some ways privileged and in other ways oppressed, writes Collins. Privilege and oppression are context dependent. In some settings, white women may be oppressed by their gender but privileged by their race. In developing countries and international settings, U.S. black women may be privileged by their citizenship but racially oppressed. In some situations, men may be oppressed by their racial/ethnic and class position and yet still privileged by their gender (Collins 2000, 245–46).

Issues of power are front and center in more recent research on sex roles. Glick and Fiske (1999) suggest that sex categorization, a form of stereotyping of occupants of social roles, is resilient because it functions as a "cognitive labor-saving device" and is "the most automatic, pervasive, and earliest learned way we classify others on first encounter" (368–71; see also Ridgeway and Correll 2004). Knowing a person's role—mother, secretary, wife—tells us what to expect from that person. However, according to the authors, this knowledge is not "inno-cent," because power is embedded in these sex-role relationships, based as they are on a sexual division of labor in which men monopolize high-status positions that sustain their dominance in interpersonal interactions. Bringing power into the research on role relation-ships is important, because it offers a more accurate portrait of how such relationships work. At the same time, recent research also considers how women's subordinate statuses may posi-tion them to resist men's control even in the most conservative patriarchal societies.

Individual-level research on gender and race ethnicity helps us explore the ways we and others shape and are shaped by our identities in everyday life. However, this research cannot answer many questions. Where do sex roles come from? How do they persist and change? Interactionist analyses provide some of the answers.

INTERACTIONIST THEORIES: DOING GENDER

The interactionist approach to gender as an "ongoing product of everyday social practice" (Glenn 1999), arose as an alternative to biological and individualist explanations. Interaction-ist explanations of gender emphasize how people together "do gender" in the context of cul-turally based, interactional expectations of others. From this point of view, people produce (or "do") gender in specific situations and contexts. That is, the situations and context in which we interact with others elicit from us particular ways of acting and particular identities. When you are with your family, you act as a daughter or a son. When you are in class, you act as a student. When you are with your friends, you act as a friend, or if not, you may sacrifice the friendships you have by not doing what is expected of you in that status. Of course, we often improvise within the broad channels marking what is expected of us, and sometimes we move beyond these channels and reshape them. History, past practice, and the communi-ties within which we act, interact, and shape our worlds create boundaries outside of which our actions may shock, confuse, or anger the audiences for whom we perform. Interaction is, therefore, infused with cultural meanings, because it requires that we understand the mean-ings of the actions of others in order to respond to them appropriately. Herbert Blumer, who coined the term "symbolic interactionism," wrote:

> Human beings interpret or "define" each other's actions instead of merely reacting to each other's actions. Their "response" is not made directly to the actions of one another but instead is based on the meaning which they attach to such actions.
>
> Thus, human interaction is mediated by the use of symbols, by interpretation, or by ascertaining the meaning of one another's actions. This mediation is equiva-lent to inserting a process of interpretation between stimulus and response in the case of human behavior. (Blumer 1969, 180)

Symbolic interaction de-emphasizes socialization (past learnings) to focus on the active construction of meaning in the present. Of course, appropriate construction of meaning re-quires that interactants have learned the cultural understandings of other participants and that they know how to interpret the meanings conveyed by these others. How people define the situation that confronts them is the key. To some extent, the individualist theory of social-ization emphasizes a more passive process of learning social rules, learning to conform to these rules, and learning to take one's place in prescribed relations. Interactionist theory focuses on how people in interaction interpret and respond to the expectations and meanings of other participants in the interaction. A key aspect of the social order, according to interactionists, is that it is a **negotiated order**, which social actors construct together. From this perspective, gender differences are created in social interaction throughout our lives. It is that repetitive and continual social production of gender relations that produces the appearance that these relations are natural.

In *Gender Blending,* a book about women who are often mistaken in public for men, author Holly Devor shows how these women negotiate with strangers in public spaces to create these gendered views of themselves. Here is one woman's account:

> The first time that I realized that I could pass was when I was living . . . in a rooming house near the university. And it was pretty much the first I'd been off for any length of time where no one would know if I ever disappeared. So I was a bit concerned about walking around on the streets at night. . . .
>
> I had a jacket that could've looked like a leather jacket, and I had short hair. And I put the jacket on and I sort of greased my hair back and put my hands in my pockets and I really startled myself because I looked like such a young punk. . . . I really looked like a guy. . . . It worked. Nobody hassled me. . . . I thought it was a great joke. I was really chuckling away to myself. And also I thought I felt a lot of freedom. This was great. I could pass. I didn't have to worry about it.
>
> I used it to my benefit. . . . I would take longer steps and hunch my shoulders up. . . . Once I decided that it would work I put on this "I'm not afraid" business and took big steps. You know there's a posture that you use to show that you're casual in the situation, and that's what I did. (Devor 1989, 111)

This woman and others Devor interviewed for her book could not take their gender identity for granted. On the contrary, they were often forced to consider consciously a matter that normally goes without saying. They had to think strategically about their appearance and negotiate with their audiences about who they "really" were. In public restrooms, for example, other women often challenged these women's right to be there. Sometimes they called the police to remove them.

Because most people assume that there are only two sexes, they conclude that if a person is not clearly female, that person must be male (and vice versa). If actors display and perform gender with skill, using dress and demeanor to present themselves to others as men or women, audiences generally take their displays and performances as evidence of an underlying, appropriate biology. Devor's informants took advantage of the widespread belief that gender is biological, permanent, and transparent. The woman quoted earlier remade her gender identity through clothing, body language, and hairstyle. She designed this strategy to make herself safer on the streets. In the language of interactionist sociology, this young woman was consciously ***doing gender***.

Some women might choose to "do" gender by adopting the manner and dress that signals male identity. The performance, of course, can also go in the other direction. Harold Garfinkel (1967) provides a famous example of doing gender in his description of Agnes, who was born and raised as a boy "with normal-appearing male genitals." Although Agnes believed that her femininity was ascribed by nature, and that her genitals and other bodily signs of masculinity were mistakes to be surgically corrected, she was forced by her situation to *achieve* the status of "natural normal female" (157). Agnes's claims to female status required her to manage the impressions of others about her. To do so meant that she had to present herself as a woman in everyday interaction, to display and perform femininity in a conscious and purposeful manner.

To learn what her past life as a male had failed to teach her, Agnes actively set out to study how to act feminine by imitating and apprenticing to others who had the appropriate social skills. From her boyfriend's mother, she learned how to cook, what clothes to wear, and how to manage a household. From her boyfriend, she learned not to "display" herself in front of other men; not to insist on her own way; to be sweet, innocent, and uncomplaining; and to serve rather than to demand service. Not only did Agnes have to *act* like a woman—the external manifestation of her sexual status—she had to manage her internal emotional states to *feel* like a woman as well, a kind of method acting. For example, from her roommates and girlfriends, she learned both to accept instructions passively and to value "passive acceptance as a desirable feminine character trait" (Garfinkel 1967, 147).

Agnes had to accomplish consciously what most adult women and men know how to do without thinking about it. Because we are tutored in femininity and masculinity from in-fancy, and because gendered actions are supported or required in many social contexts, our performances feel instinctive and natural. Agnes did not possess the background knowledge that generally resides below conscious awareness and shapes feminine (and masculine) be-havior and interaction. To appear feminine, Agnes had to pay close attention to the ways "natural" women acted. On the basis of what she observed, Agnes monitored her appearance and calculated her actions. She was attentive to subtle cues and clues about what others ex-pected from her and what they understood to be "normal" female behavior. Garfinkel (1967) called Agnes a *practical methodologist*. By that he meant that Agnes turned a sociological eye on the "trivial but necessary social tasks" that women enacted to appear "normally" female (180). Agnes made conscious what most of us do as a matter of course: she made gender "happen." Garfinkel explains:

> The scrutiny she paid to appearances; her concerns for adequate motivation, rele-vance, evidence, and demonstration; her sensitivity to devices of talk; her skill in detecting and managing "tests" were attained as part of her mastery of *trivial but necessary social tasks*, to secure ordinary rights to live. Agnes was self-consciously equipped to teach normals *how normals make [gender] happen in commonplace settings* as an obvious, familiar, recognizable, natural, and serious matter of fact. Her specialty consisted of treating the "natural facts of life" of socially recognized, so-cially managed sexuality as a managed production . . . in short, so as unavoidably in con-cert with others to be making these facts of life visible and reportable—*accountable*—for all practical purposes. (Garfinkel 1967, 180, emphasis added)

The studies by Devor and Garfinkel report on how people on the margins of society negotiate with their audiences over their appearance as masculine or feminine and their ac-ceptance as men or women. However, as is often the case, extraordinary lives can tell us about ourselves and about the processes that hold our own worlds together. Garfinkel called attention to two essential aspects of Agnes's performance. First, representing herself as female required Agnes to master the trivia of everyday life. That Agnes adopted a willingness to serve exposed to what extent this trait was a subtle but important dimension of femininity in public. Devor's informant mastered the walk and hunched shoulders that signaled the "young punk" form of masculinity. Probably most of us could understand the meaning of the walk, part of our own everyday knowledge about the types of people we see on the streets. Devor and Garfinkel show how gendered identities rest on a foundation of mundane and trivial acts, noticeable only, perhaps, in their absence.

Second, Garfinkel showed that Agnes was *accountable* to her audience (which was also true for Devor's women, and is the case for other female and male "impersonators," and for the rest of us). If she was to be accepted as the woman she claimed to be, Agnes had to perform femininity in expected, adequate, and recognized ways. By successfully achieving femininity on the basis of acting and feeling appropriately, as defined by her audiences, Agnes reinforced the femininity she sought to embody. For Agnes and for the women Devor studied, gender was an *achieved* status, an accomplishment, rather than something affixed to them at birth by virtue of their chromosomes or genitals or learned by them once and for all at home or in school. In a sense, Agnes and the women who passed for men were making false, albeit successful, claims. What do these accounts suggest about our own gendered selves? Do we also display and perform our gender? The concept of doing gender suggests that we do—that all of us, in a sense, are in drag.

The Social Implications of Doing Gender

The mannerisms, speech, dress, and demeanor of the women who passed for men and of Agnes, the biological male who passed for a woman, were performances that broadcast to their audiences the essential gendered natures of these individuals. These actors achieved or earned their gendered status by learning how to be and to act feminine or masculine. They did not receive their gendered status as women or men as a birthright, nor did they adopt it as a role and status laid out for them to fill as they matured. Their dress and demeanor signaled that the unseen body parts determining male or female status were actually there, although they in fact were not.

The studies reviewed in this chapter and the previous one show that (1) *sex*: our biological sex, (2) *sex category*: our status as males or females, and (3) *gender*: the ways we live our lives as sexed beings, with all the appropriate demeanors, emotions, understandings, and practices such living entails, need not coincide. Candace West and Don Zimmerman (1987) published a highly influential article in which they distinguished among these three analytically distinct but overlapping categories. These categories are slightly different from the ones presented in chapter 2. As in that chapter, the category *sex* refers to a person's biology—whether a person has a penis and testicles or a vagina and clitoris. *Sex* may be a biological category, but in practice it depends on social cues. As argued in chapter 2, the fact that we "know" that there are two and only two sexes is based on our belief that this is the case. Our "moral certainty" leads us to deduce sex from what we see before us. We do not ask people to disrobe in front of us to ascertain their biological sex. In everyday life, we take their appearance at face value. A person wearing a suit and tie probably has a penis; a person in a dress or lipstick probably has a vagina. Of course, these categories are becoming less distinct where clothing, hairstyles, and body language have become more "unisex" and possibly because there are growing challenges from scientists, and even from the popular media, to the belief that every individual is *either* a man or a woman.

Sex category refers to the status of male or female that most persons inhabit unambiguously. However, some people with a penis are able to claim the status of woman. Their clothing, their demeanor, and their claims to womanhood help their audiences to locate them in the category of female. If people around these individuals had known that they possessed penises, that knowledge would have discredited their claims, no matter how skilled their performance. *Gender* refers to the performance itself, the ways people accomplish being a man or a woman, a boy or a girl. Agnes's gender problem, according to West and Zimmerman, was to learn to behave and think like a "normal" woman, as defined by her audiences. Agnes had to act in the presence of "normals" and interact with them in ways that validated her claim to female status. If men and women do not act in gender-appropriate ways, they risk being found socially incompetent or, worse, fraudulent. In this way, people are accountable for their performances. The sanctions imposed on people who act "inappropriately" in the opinion of their audience have ranged from ridicule and ostracism to imprisonment and even death, as the story in Box 3-2 of Brandon Teena's murder illustrates.

Viewing gender in this manner directs attention toward the interactional contexts of social life and away from the biological and psychological states of individuals. From this

GENDER IN EVERYDAY LIFE   BOX 3-2
TRANSGENDERED COMMUNITY REMEMBERS DEATH
THAT SPARKED A MOVEMENT

Ten years ago, a handsome, brown-haired 21-year-old named Brandon Teena was raped and later murdered by two men after they discovered he wasn't born a man. The New Year's Eve tragedy in rural southeastern Nebraska inspired the award-winning 1999 film, *Boys Don't Cry*. It also touched off a movement in the transgendered community.

In the days after Teena was killed, a new generation of activists banded together to demand greater civil rights protections. Ten years later, 65 municipalities and states have hate crime laws that specifically include transgendered people, according to the Transgender Law Policy Institute. California became the fourth state to adopt such a law earlier this year. Big corporations, such as Hewlett-Packard and Nike, have adopted similar rules. And 145 members of Congress have banned such discrimination from their offices, said Riki Wilchins, executive director of the Washington-based Gender Public Advocacy Coalition. "How many times do you get to see a giant sea change like this in people's perceptions? But you look at Congress, corporate America, and cities and states . . . and you see this enormous change in how people are looking at gender as a civil rights issue," Wilchins said.

Nebraska passed a hate-crime law in 1997, but it did not refer specifically to transgendered people. It was found unconstitutional after a 2000 U.S. Supreme Court ruling in another case involving sentencing provisions. One problem for the transgendered community—which encompasses a range of identities including cross-dressers and transsexuals—is that allies have been hard to come by. Although they were at the forefront of New York City's 1969 Stonewall Riots, which led to the gay rights movement, the relationship between the transgendered and gay communities hasn't always been easy. "For a long time, the gay movement was like, 'Well, that's an interesting problem, but it's not our problem. You folks are too weird. We don't want to talk to you.' " said Paisley Currah, executive director of the Center for Lesbian and Gay Studies at Brooklyn College in New York.

The national attention given to Teena's murder also helped introduce the idea of being transgendered to mainstream America, said Shannon Minter, a board member of the Transgender Law and Policy Institute in New York. "People are just much less freaked out about the concept, and see us more as human beings with partners, families, children," said Minter, who is transgendered. Many activists say Teena's murder attracted so much attention because of its brutality and the failure of law enforcement to protect Teena. John Lotter and Marvin Nissen were convicted of murdering Teena, who had dated a female friend of the two men. They also killed Lisa Lambert, 24, and Philip DeVine, 22, who had witnessed Teena's death in a farmhouse. A week before the killing, Teena had told the local sheriff the men had raped him, but the sheriff took no action.

In a scathing court opinion in 2001, Nebraska Supreme Court Chief Justice John Hendry said former Richardson County Sheriff Charles Laux showed indifference by referring to Teena as "it" and not immediately arresting the suspects. Laux, reached by telephone at his home, decline to comment. A judge initially awarded Teena's mother, Joann Brandon, $17,360 in damages, saying that Teena's own lifestyle was partly responsible for his death. The state Supreme Court ordered him to reconsider, and he later awarded Brandon $98,223. Brandon's lawyer, Herb Friedman, said she no longer wanted to talk about case. Lotter is now on Nebraska's death row. Nissen was sentenced to life in prison.

Though much has improved for the transgendered community in the last 10 years, there is still a long way to go, Minter said. In the past year alone, Remembering Our Dead, an online memorial that tracks bias killing of transgendered people around the world, recorded 17 deaths in the United States. The few people in Falls City willing to talk about the case voiced a desire to move on and frustration at its cost to the county. "Every town's got some weird people," said resident Mary Symonds.

About 25 miles from Falls City in the tiny town of Humboldt, the small farmhouse where Teena, Lambert and DeVine were killed attracts a regular stream of sightseers. "They just drive and stare and I guess get a thrill out of that," said Dagmar Jansen, who moved into the house about two years ago with her family. "It's horrible. It probably comes from prejudice and people not being open-minded," Jansen said. "I think by the year 2003 people should be able to live for who they are and not for what people think they should be."

SOURCE: Reprinted with permission from Associated Press (2003).

perspective, gender is a property of and emerges in social situations. Doing gender involves acting appropriately in specific contexts and for specific audiences. For example, recall that Agnes was counseled not to insist on having her way. A woman who insists on her way is considered "unfeminine" in some circles. Agnes did gender during a time when feminist ideas were less accepted than they are today. Certainly today there are contexts in which it would *not* be unfeminine to insist on one's way. Nonetheless, doing gender involves managing one's emotions, goals, and desires, as well as one's actions. Agnes's teachers also coached her to value passive acceptance, to embrace emotionally their understanding that this was an appropriately feminine way of living.

How have you been held accountable for your gendered behavior? Think about a time when you refrained from acting in a particular way because you worried that observers or those who know you might think you were being unfeminine or not manly enough. In these cases, you were being held accountable or were holding yourself accountable for your actions. You can be held accountable for doing gender almost anywhere. Try to imagine situations where your performance as a man or a woman would never be relevant. It's not easy! In fact, Garfinkel's work with Agnes led him to claim that **gender is "omnirelevant"** (relevant in every situation) and that doing gender is unavoidable.

The concept of doing gender was a major advance in sociological thinking about gender. It showed how we create gender differences between men and women, boys and girls in social interaction. It demonstrated the ways in which gender is a social category. Genitalia, hormones, and genes cannot tell us what is sociologically interesting about gender differences.

The real news about gender can be found in the ways local contexts and social institutions shape gender identities and relations in systematic ways.

Props and Resources for Doing Gender

People enact gender by drawing on the "resources" that are features of local settings and that guide actions that produce and reproduce gender difference. For example, public bathrooms differentiate men from women, although as Erving Goffman explains, there is no biological reason for them. In fact, he suggests that these arrangements produce the difference they are meant to respect:

> The *functioning* of sex-differentiated organs is involved, but there is nothing in this functioning that biologically recommends segregation; *that* arrangement is a totally cultural matter . . . toilet segregation is presented as a natural consequence of the difference between the sex-classes when in fact it is a means of honoring, if not producing, this difference. (Goffman 1977, 316; quoted in West and Zimmerman 1987, 137; emphasis in original)

Other **resources for doing gender** cited by Goffman (1977) are organized sports and "assortative mating practices." This phrase refers to the practices that produce, in couples, older, taller, and stronger boys and men and younger, smaller, and weaker girls and women. Take notice of the heterosexual couples you encounter in your daily life who do or do not conform to this expectation. Perhaps a few of you are part of such a couple, or you are one of a same-sex couple. Have you had any thoughts, feelings, or discussions with your partner about being in such a nonnormative relationship? If you have, we might say that you were involved in doing gender or trying to escape it.

Almost any situation can be an occasion for doing gender. A flat tire can become such an occasion. How many women have you passed on the highway fixing their flat tires? How many women do you see mowing their lawns? When men and women are together in an automobile, who drives? When parents are walking with their babies, who is pushing the stroller or holding a child's hand? A decade or two ago it would be rare to observe a woman changing a tire or a man pushing a stroller. Men were likely to be in charge of the car and outdoor work. Women were in charge of the children. Lately, these boundaries seem to be disintegrating. Could this change be driven by changing attitudes toward women? Possibly, but certainly one factor driving this change is the fact that women are now about half the labor force, while jobs that historically have employed men are declining. Such major structural changes have an impact on family arrangements. Perhaps as more women become economically independent of their husbands' wages or become the major financial supporters of their families, husbands may be more likely to take up domestic and child-care duties.

What maintains gender differences? For interactionists, interaction is the process through which we create and maintain ourselves and our society. **Accountability** is one explanation for why gender is a central and persistent feature of everyday life. Think about a time when you worried about how others might respond to something you did or planned to do. In these cases, you were being held accountable for your actions by others in your social world. Accountability is one of the mechanisms that holds gender differences and gender relationships in place. Moreover, interactionists believe, with Garfinkel, that in everyday life, sex category is almost always relevant (Ridgeway and Correll 2004). Often what we do is designed with an eye toward how it will look to others—a concern that Agnes took to necessary extremes—or it is done for reasons that Devor's informant gave, so as not to attract attention by passing as a man. There is virtually no activity for which you could not be held accountable for performance as a woman or a man. That means that doing gender is unavoidable. At stake is the management of our most valued identities.

Doing gender reinforces the illusion that there are essential differences between women and men when, in fact, the *doing* is what creates these very differences. Gender is a fundamental category for the allocation of resources and power in many contexts, from interpersonal interaction and the household division of labor to global political and economic relations. So even as we do gender at the local, interactional level of social life, that activity supports, reinforces, and re-creates broader structural and institutional processes. It is those processes, with their seeming natural ways of organizing work, family, love, war, and all the other dimensions of our collective lives that support, reinforce, and re-create our production of gender in the interactional sphere. In other words, we interactionally create the social worlds we are part of, but we are, in turn, constrained and pressed into certain courses of action as our creations take on a life of their own. Let's take Agnes's experience as an example. Some women and men believed it was unfeminine for a woman to insist on having her own way. This belief and practice arose in a definite historical period and among certain people—the middle classes of North America in the late nineteenth century—but it has persisted into our own time. By the time Agnes appeared on the scene, it was institutionalized as part of feminine behavior. Agnes could choose to flout that practice—but only at her peril.

Since the publication of *Doing Gender* (West and Zimmerman) in 1987, the concept has been widely adopted. Francine Deutsch (2007) examined all the articles published in

2005 that drew on the idea of doing gender and found that almost all were about how gender inequalities were maintained and reproduced in the course of interaction. Maybe it's time, she wrote, that we begin to study how we might "undo" gender. To that end, she proposed that we change our questions about gender so that we begin looking for the moments when gender inequalities decline and for the conditions under which gender becomes irrelevant. Erving Goffman believed that we are always doing gender. Deutsch suggests that gender may not be omnirelevant under some conditions and that we should turn our attention to discovering those conditions so that we might discover how gender might be "undone."

Isn't rape men's problem? The organization Men Can Stop Rape believes it is.

Source: www.mencanstoprape.org. © Copyright 2011 Men Can Stop Rape, Inc.

STRUCTURALIST THEORIES: ROSABETH MOSS KANTER

There is much evidence—including evidence from our own daily lives—to support interactionist theories that locate the production of gender in everyday social conduct. But what accounts for the strength and persistence of gendered inequality in interaction, its occurrence across social situations and contexts, and its reproduction over time? Some sociologists focus on the way that gender inequalities are produced and maintained at the level of institutions, organizations, and social structures. Where interactionists concern themselves with the everyday world and the social meanings of actors in it, structuralists maintain that the rules and resources that frame local action should take a central place in social theories about gender.

The concept of "social structures" is notoriously slippery. A common mistake is to be too literal in conceptualizing social structure and to imagine it as a sort of permanent edifice that determines our thoughts and acts. Social theorist Anthony Giddens (1984), who focuses on the social processes that create and change structures, avoids this mistake by bringing to our attention the dynamic character of social structure. Structures, to Giddens, are both the outcome and the medium of acting subjects. We interact with one another to produce gender, for example, and the gendered social relations we produce over and over again (or, to put it another way, reproduce) push us to continue acting in these gendered ways. In other words, we are the product of structures that we ourselves create. In *The Eighteenth Brumaire of Louis Bonaparte*, Karl Marx explained it this way:

> Men [*sic*] make their own history, but they do not make it just as they please; they do not make it under circumstances chosen by themselves, but under circumstances directly encountered, given and transmitted from the past. The tradition of all the dead generations weighs like a nightmare on the brain of the living (1972, 10).

Marx meant that we make the worlds we share; but we cannot just create anything that comes to mind (in fact, what will come to mind is limited by what we know and how we think about that). What Marx called the "the tradition of all the dead generations" limits us and shapes what is possible. Understanding that we are the producers of the very structures that limit our social action is vitally important. For example, we have invented war as a way to resolve conflict. If war is a human creation and not a fact of nature, and if we can imagine an end to war, then we may be capable of actually putting an end to it. Likewise, once we understand how gendered action creates structures of femininity and masculinity, then we may be capable of changing or eliminating those structures as well (see Connell 1987).

Sociologists often use the concept of structure to refer to the constraints built into social organizations and relationships. Think about how you have acceded to the rules and demands of the education system in your lifetime as a student. As a child, you had to follow rules that may have seemed arbitrary, but about which you could do little. You had to wake up at a certain time to get to school on time, and you had to forgo playing in the park on school days. As a college student, you must accumulate credit hours by writing papers, taking exams, and reading what your instructors tell you to read (if you want your education to count for future employment or graduate school). Historically, structured racial/ethnic, class, and gender inequalities in education have meant that schooling has not provided a level playing field to girls and boys, young men and women, students of color and white students, or people of different classes. Gender, racial ethnic, and class inequalities have also been a part of your education. These inequalities often take the form of "**microinequities**" (Sandler 1986), the small and not so small ways we are treated differently because of our race ethnicity, gender, age, class, or sexuality. Sandler identified more than fifty ways that women and men are treated differently in the classroom. For example, teachers call on men more often, ask men more questions, nod and gesture when men speak, and look elsewhere when women speak.

Not surprisingly, race ethnicity enters into these microinequities. White men get the most questions, then minority men, then white women, with black women receiving the least attention in classrooms. Such classroom structures limit and restrict your education, whether you are a man or a woman. Another way structure restricts us is that it shapes our choices and interests. Maybe you are a man interested in nursing, but you consider it too feminine, too low-status, or too low-paying to be a reasonable career choice. The gender-segregated structure of occupations in the United States means that women's pay is, on the average, lower than men's by about 30 percent. Working conditions differ for women and men as well. Women's jobs and professions such as nursing have lower mobility structures. On the other hand, although men are also disadvantaged in terms of pay, prestige, and working conditions when they enter women's occupations, they also retain certain advantages because they are men, often riding the "glass escalator" to the top echelons of management in these occupations (Williams 1995).

The gendered division of labor is a structural concept. It refers to the ways in which women and men are sorted into jobs and occupations in the labor force, as well as to who is responsible for unpaid work. In the early days of the second wave of the women's movement, feminists focused on the gendered division of labor and the exclusion of women from better-paid and more interesting men's jobs. Rosabeth Moss Kanter studied a corporation to learn how "organizational structure forms people's sense of themselves and of their possibilities" (Kanter 1977, 3). Her project was to show that gender differences in organizational behavior were the result of structures rather than the result of personality differences between men and women. She identified three structural features of the corporation that explained the differences she observed between women and men in their workplace performance, relations on the job, and attitudes toward work. The three structural features were (1) the structure of opportunity offered by the organization, (2) the structure or distribution of power, and (3) the **relative numbers** of men and women employed, especially as managers, professionals, and executives.

Opportunity Structures

The principle measure of success in the corporation was upward mobility through promotion. Kanter asked, Why aren't more women in top-level managerial positions? Most women, it appeared, did not have the aspirations, commitment, and dependability that would have earned them promotions. They cared more about relationships with others on the job and less about occupational success. Most observers attributed these differences to deficiencies women brought with them to the job. Note that this is an individual-level explanation of women's failure to rise in the corporate hierarchy.

Kanter suggested a different reason for women's immobility at work. She argued that opportunity is not a result of behavior on the job. Quite the opposite, **opportunity structures** produce gendered behavior:

> When women seem to be less motivated or committed, it is probably because their jobs carry less opportunity. There is evidence that in general the jobs held by most women workers tend to have shorter chains of opportunity associated with them and contain fewer advancement prospects. (Kanter 1977, 159)

Kanter cited studies that contradicted the picture of women as less committed to work than men (in the 1970s, when Kanter's study was done, stereotypes and beliefs about women as workers were somewhat different from what they are today). She showed that when men's opportunity structures were also limited, their behavior resembled women's:

> Women can also be more committed than men at upper levels when they have had to work harder to overcome barriers; effort helps build commitment. At the same time, *men with low opportunity look more like the stereotype of women in their orientations toward work*, as research on blue-collar men has shown; they limit their aspirations, seek satisfaction in activities outside of work, dream of escape, interrupt their careers, emphasize leisure and consumption and create sociable peer groups in which interpersonal relationships take precedence over other aspects of work. (Kanter 1977, 160–61, emphasis in original)

Kanter's point is that people with little opportunity behave in one way, and people with a great deal of opportunity behave in another way. Not only do low-opportunity people not aspire to more exalted positions at work, but they have low self-esteem and feel resigned to staying where they are. In contrast, people with substantial opportunity have high aspirations as well as high self-esteem, are more interested in work, and are more competitive with their co-workers. It is the structure of opportunity, not the gender of workers, that makes the difference.

Power Structures

Power—"the ability to get things done, to mobilize resources, to get whatever it is that a person needs for the goals he or she is attempting to meet"—is also the result of structural position rather than gender (Kanter 1977, 167). People with fewer resources available to them, a function of their position in networks, have little power. If women or men in supervisory positions are excluded by others from the knowledge and means to do their jobs, their responses are likely to include closely supervising workers under them and jealously guarding their domain—features of the stereotypic woman boss. People who can mobilize resources to get the job done are less rigid and authoritarian, better liked, seen as helpful, more cooperative, and exercise fewer strong controls. Again, what look like gender differences at work are actually produced by differential access to resources to get the job done, a structural problem.

Relative Numbers

Relative numbers of men and women in networks also contribute to outcomes that look like—but do not originate in—gendered social relations at the individual level. When Kanter was studying the Industrial Supply Corporation, pioneering women were fighting for the right to be police officers, firefighters, mechanics, doctors, attorneys, and corporate leaders. These forerunners faced a phenomenon that Kanter labeled *tokenism*, the social relations that grow from belonging to a tiny minority amid a large majority. At the upper levels of corporate management, token women were highly visible, and their work—especially their perceived missteps and mistakes—were subject to public scrutiny. They were treated as representatives of all women. They were under pressure to perform well and also under the conflicting pressure not to make the dominant group look bad by performing too well. Their presence stimulated the men of the company to magnify their own group solidarity against such intruders. Here is what Kanter observed:

> Around token women . . . men sometimes exaggerated displays of aggression and potency: instances of sexual innuendos, aggressive sexual teasing, and prowess-oriented "war stories." When a woman or two were present, the men's behavior involved "showing off," telling stories in which "masculine prowess" accounted for personal, sexual, or business success. They highlighted what they could do, as men, in contrast to the women. (Kanter 1977, 223)

Men interrupted women, reminded them that they made the workplace different ("Can we still swear?"), kept them out of informal meetings, and subjected them to other forms of "boundary heightening" behavior. Women were stereotyped—treated as mothers, temptresses, pets, or iron maidens. Kanter's observations about token women also seem to apply to racial/ethnic, religious, and other minorities within larger, homogeneous groups. For example, in some majority white colleges where students of color are "tokens," they may be called on in class to represent all members of their group or held accountable for stereotypes of the group's supposed cultural behaviors.

Kanter saw the corporation as a gender-neutral setting. Anyone in the same low-status position would be likely to behave and be treated similarly, regardless of their sex. However, studies of men who are tokens in majority female occupations suggest otherwise. Whereas the work of men in low-status positions in hierarchical organizations may be "feminized," white men who are token workers in women's occupations (nursing and elementary education, for example) are likely to be evaluated positively and to move rapidly into positions of authority. Such findings suggest that gendering is not an accident of structure, but integral to its existence. In the excerpt from *Men and Women of the Corporation*, "The Secretary's Desk" (Box 3-3), we see how secretaries accumulate resources for doing gender as the structures of work at INDSCO push them into wifelike relationships with their bosses.

GENDER IN EVERYDAY LIFE   BOX 3-3
THE SECRETARY'S DESK

Secretaries added a personal touch to Industrial Supply Corporation workplaces. Professional and managerial offices tended to be austere: generally uniform in size and coloring, and unadorned except for a few family snapshots or discrete artworks. ("Welcome to my beige box," a rising young executive was fond of saying to visitors.) But secretaries' desks were surrounded by splashes of color, displays of special events, signs of the individuality and taste of the residents: postcards from friends' or bosses' travels pasted on walls, newspaper cartoons, large posters with funny captions, huge computer print-outs that formed the names of the secretaries in gothic letters. It was secretaries who remembered birthdays and whose birthdays were celebrated, lending a legitimate air of occasional festivity to otherwise task-oriented days. Secretaries could engage in conversations about the latest movies, and managers often stopped by their desks to join momentarily in a discussion that was a break from the more serious business at hand. It was secretaries who were expected to look out for the personal things, to see to the comfort and welfare of guests, to show them around and make sure that they had what they needed. And it was around secretaries that people at higher levels in the corporation could stop to remember the personal things about themselves and each other (appearance, dress, daily mood), could trade the small compliments and acknowledgments that differentiated them from the mass of others and from their formal role. In many ways—visually, socially, and organizationally—the presence of secretaries represented a reserve of the human inside the bureaucratic.

Nowhere were the contradictions and unresolved dilemmas of modern bureaucratic life more apparent than in the secretarial function. The job, made necessary by the growth of modern organizations, lay at the very core of bureaucratic administration, yet it often was the least bureaucratized segment of corporate life. The product of the rationalization of work and the vast amount of paperwork that entailed, it still remained resistant to its own rationalization. At INDSCO, secretarial positions were unique in a number of ways: for one thing, they were the only jobs in the company ranked merely by the status of the manager, and attempts to change this arrangement were resisted. The secretarial job involved the most routine of tasks in the white-collar world, yet the most personal of relationships. The greatest time was spent on the routine, but the greatest reward was garnered for the personal.

Understanding the nature of this bureaucratic anomaly sheds light on several features of life in the corporation: the functions served by pockets of the personal inside the bureaucratic, but the tradeoffs for people who become trapped as an underclass in those pockets; the sources of both the intensity and the awkwardness that can emerge in relationships between bosses and secretaries; and the origin, in job conditions, of those work orientations that tend to be adopted by secretaries. Secretaries' characteristic ways of managing their organizational situation—their strategies for attaining recognition and control—as well as the behaviors and attitudes they develop, can all be seen as a response to the role relations surrounding the secretarial function. Here also are found the sources of resistance to change in the secretarial function: by the organization at large, by managers, and by secretaries themselves. From awareness of the resistances can come better designs for change.

Source: Reprinted with permission from Kanter (1977).

GENDERED ORGANIZATIONS: JOAN ACKER

To Kanter, organizational structures were gender neutral. If there were differences in women's and men's jobs, opportunities, or experiences, Kanter believed those differences were just as likely to be produced between any two differently situated and unequal groups in the organization: blue-collar versus managerial employees, majority versus token workers. She recognized that the masculine culture at the corporation she studied was incited to resist the entry of a few women into managerial positions. She acknowledged that men in general were overwhelmingly dominant in corporate positions of power and prestige, that men's work was valued (and paid) more highly than was women's work, and that token women faced many forms of gender harassment on the job, from sexist joking and stereotyping to overt hostility. Nonetheless, she reasoned that gender inequality grew out of more generic hierarchical rules and practices. Gender was not intrinsic to organizational structure.

For many scholars, however, gendered inequalities were too pervasive to be explained away as the random effects of neutral structures and impartial organizational practices. Everywhere one looked, one saw differences between women and men that made a difference: the gendered segregation of work and the boundary between paid and unpaid labor; the income and status inequality between men and women; and the male dominance and masculine culture of many large, hierarchical organizations. After reviewing the research of Kanter, Joan Acker (1990) wrote, "Gender is not an addition to ongoing processes, conceived as gender neutral. Rather, it is an integral part of those processes, which cannot be properly understood without an analysis of gender" (146).

What does it mean to say that organizational structures are gendered? Acker identified several ways that gender difference creates and sustains inequalities in organizations:

- Organizational processes create gendered divisions—of labor, of space, of behavior, of power. One spatial difference that has come into view recently is the ladies [*sic*] room as the corporate space for nursing infants.
- Organizational processes construct symbols and images that support gender differences in organizations—the masterful business leader, the difficult female boss.
- Organizations promote gendered components of individual identity—appropriate (gendered) clothing, workplace demeanor, language.
- There is a gendered logic discernable in the work rules, labor contracts, and other documents that are part of organizational discourses.

An example of the gendered logic implicit in organizations is the category of the job, the basic unit of work. On its face, a job is a neutral thing, a set of tasks and responsibilities that has no particularly gendered aspect to it (except for a few jobs such as wet nurse—the woman who takes on the task of nursing another woman's baby—or surrogate mother). However, Acker asks us to consider the fact that we all think about jobs as separate from family life. The job itself presupposes the existence of a split between unpaid domestic labor and child care (the so-called private sphere) and social labor, which takes place in a separate location, away from families and communities. That split, of course, is built on a gendered division of labor that assigns women to the domestic sphere even when they are also employed. In other words, the category "job," although apparently neutral, implicitly rests on the gendered division of labor in society. Acker argues that although the category "worker" also appears neutral, in fact "ideal" workers are gendered. Who are the ideal workers? Individuals who are committed to work, who have no outside responsibilities that distract them from the tasks at hand, and who need not concern themselves with caring for sick members of their households, delivering children to and from day care, or shopping for and cooking the family's daily meals. Ideal workers have no obligations outside the job. Ideal workers "exist only for [their] work" (Acker 1990, 149). Who, then, are the ideal workers? Men with stay-at-home wives.

Another indicator that jobs depend on the sexual division of labor and assume that workers are male is the fact that women's bodily needs and rhythms are excluded from the ideal workplace. Emotions, reproduction, and women's bodies disrupt the efficient ordering of the workday, whereas men's bodies fit organizational demands and symbols.

> It is the man's body, its sexuality, minimal responsibility in procreation, and conventional control of emotions that pervades work and organizational processes. Women's bodies—female sexuality, their ability to procreate and their pregnancy, breast-feeding, and child care, menstruation, and mythic "emotionality"—are suspect, stigmatized, and used as grounds for control and exclusion. . . . While women's bodies are ruled out of order, or sexualized and objectified, in work organizations, men's bodies are not. Indeed, male sexual imagery pervades organizational metaphors and language, helping to give form to work activities. For example, the military and male worlds of sports are considered valuable training for organizational success and provide images for teamwork, campaigns, and tough competition. The symbolic expression of male sexuality may be used as a means of control over male workers, too, allowed or even encouraged within the bounds of the work situation to create cohesion or alleviate stress. Management approval of pornographic pictures in the locker room or support for all-male work and play groups where casual talk is about sexual exploits or sports are examples. (Acker 1990, 153)

Acker makes a strong case for the inherent gendering of organizational structures and for understanding the ideal worker as male. As more women enter the workforce, these gendered underpinnings of jobs and workers create crises of care and a time crunch for women workers and their families. The abstract, deceptively gender-neutral classifications and systems of work conceal a gendered substructure that controls both women and men workers and their work. Through Acker's theory we can see how gender is a product of large-scale organizations and organizational processes.

INSTITUTIONAL THEORIES

The term "social institution" refers to a persistent constellation of practices, power relations, norms, interactional dynamics, and ideologies surrounding social phenomena. Some sociologists identify particular substantive areas as institutions. They study the institutions of family, education, work, religion, or media. Others conceptualize institutions as processes. Interacting human beings create social institutions, and these in turn create us. Using this view of institutions, some scholars argue that gender is an institution. As processes, institutions entail recurring and predictable social practices, ways to distribute scarce resources, ways to care for those who cannot care for themselves, ways of identifying and legitimating leaders, and so forth. Gender is the process by which we accomplish these tasks.

Institutions are not "out there" but are inside of and around us. Through the recurring practices and ever-present pressures of institutional processes, we live out the constraints and possibilities that they make thinkable and possible. We feel these constraints and potentials as parts of our selves, as emotions, desires, and goals. Acting on these feelings, we reproduce the very institutions that have made us. As the early twentieth-century American sociologist Charles Horton Cooley (1962, 5) wrote, "self and society are twin-born." We give birth to our world, and our world gives birth to us. These births are ongoing, not one-time events. Neither selves nor societies are static. C. Wright Mills (1967, 6) called the individual and social forms of existence "biography" and "history." Biography, the history of an individual life, is always in a state of transformation or "becoming." History is the story of groups, peoples, and national entities that are constantly evolving and changing. As we produce and reproduce the institutions that shape us and our worlds, we change them and ourselves, sometimes consciously, more often subtly and without conscious intent. Through our collective actions, then, we maintain, but also resist and change, institutions.

The vignette "Tom, Betsy, and the Telephone" (Box 3-4) shows the unconscious operation of gender in a workplace and demonstrates (1) how gender is a part of our psychological makeup, (2) how we act to reproduce the institution that shapes us, and (3) how resistance emerges and leads to changes in the institution of gender.

GENDER IN EVERYDAY LIFE   BOX 3-4
TOM, BETSY, AND THE TELEPHONE: AN ORGANIZATIONAL STORY

In this excerpt from "'Said and Done' versus 'Saying and Doing': Gendering Practices, Practicing Gender at Work," Patricia Yancey Martin shows how attention to the ways people "do gender" in the workplace "produces insights into how inequalities are created in workplaces." Martin was interested in the ways that gender is socially constructed in large organizations, and she shows how subtle forms of gendering practice reproduce inequalities between Tom and Betsy in the telecommunications company in which they are both vice presidents (2003, 345). Martin argues that the "sayings and doings" of gender must be incorporated into organizational theory and research:

Tom and Betsy, both vice-presidents in a Fortune 100 company, stood talking in a hallway after a meeting. Along the hallway were offices but none was theirs. A phone started to ring in one office and after three or so rings, Tom said to Betsy, "Why don't you get that?" Betsy was surprised by Tom's request but answered the phone anyway and Tom returned to his office. Afterwards, Betsy found Tom to ask if he realized what he had done. She told him: "I'm a vice-president too, Tom, and you treated me like a secretary. What were you thinking?" Betsy's reaction surprised Tom. He did not mean anything by his action, he said, commenting: "I did not even think about it." Tom apologized to Betsy. She told Tom his behavior was "typical of how men in High Tech Corporation [a pseudonym] treat women. You're patronizing and [you] don't treat us as equals." Tom was again surprised and decided to ask other women if they agreed with Betsy. (Field notes, *Fortune* 100 telecommunications company 1994, quoted in Martin 2003)

Tom discussed this event with eighteen women from the organization, who told him "about the hurtfulness of their experiences" at High Tech. Tom was inspired to start a group of eighteen men and eighteen women to discuss gender issues in the corporation. Martin comments,

According to everyone who knew this story . . . Betsy became angry with Tom for asking and with herself for answering the telephone. Tom and Betsy were both familiar with and skilled in gender practices; thus they simply "hopped into the [gender] river and swam." . . . They did not reflect. They did not analyze the situation; they were "practiced" in gender; they practiced gender. The gender institution holds women accountable to pleasing men; it tells men/boys they have a (gender) right to be assisted by women/girls; Tom and Betsy knew this. Tom's request and Betsy's behavior are thus unsurprising. Without stopping to reflect, Tom practiced a kind of masculinity that the gender institution makes available to him, which is to request practical help from women; Betsy responded in kind by complying with his request. (Martin 2003)

Martin explains that such requests (and others, such as "cook my food," "raise my kids," and "wash my clothes") are usually not articulated, but rather are built into the language of institutionalized positions such as secretary "that are gendered over time and across situations." Notice that Betsy did not object to the assumptions about secretaries ("like a subordinate" and "like a woman"). "In Judith Butler's terms," Martin explains, "Tom's and Betsy's actions were citational of the gender order. They showed awareness and skill in reinstituting the gender institution within which they live—as man, as woman." Nevertheless, Betsy's subsequent complaints shifted the gender order in that workplace.

SOURCE: Reprinted with permission from Martin (2003).

Studying institutions involves understanding their history and the power relations that constitute them. Gender relations have changed radically over time—gender has a history. Institutions involve power, and the institution of gender is suffused with power relations. For example, the claim that gender is natural is a political claim that suppresses gender's history and dismisses the possibility of gender equality. Gender history is about changes in gender relations produced by our collective and individual actions in the world. We do not simply react to the world, we actively make it. That is what sociologists mean by *agency*. Institutions are social creations that constrain their creators, but their creators also have agency and can change institutions.

"Gender is done from birth, constantly and by everyone" and "one of the major ways people organize their lives; where there is gender difference there is inequality and stratification" (Lorber 1994, 14–15). This is true, to a greater or lesser extent, in every known society. The more power, prestige, and wealth is at stake, the more gender difference is the case. Within contemporary class societies, gender inequality is more pronounced among the wealthy than among the poor. In the gender stratification system of the United States, wealthy businessmen and corporate executives control more resources, and are more likely to be in political and economic leadership positions, than are wealthy women. Gender stratification is evident even at the highest levels of business. Lorber (1994, 34) summarizes a variety of studies of inequality and stratification as follows:

> The more economic resources, such as education and job opportunities, are available to a group, the more they tend to be monopolized by men. In poorer groups that have few resources (such as working-class African Americans in the United States), women and men are more nearly equal, and the women may even outstrip the men in education and occupational status.

In a gender-structured and gender-stratified society, what elite men do is more highly valued than what women and lower class, lower status men do. Women are systematically worse off than men of their race and class, except at the very poorest levels of society. However, it is important to remember that women of the professional and managerial middle classes and from the upper class are better off in terms of security, wealth, and opportunity than, for example, are working-class and poor men of color.

If money is the measure of value in our capitalist society, then women are of lesser value as workers than men are. Are men's jobs more vital, more central to the economy? Try this thought experiment. Think for a minute about one of the least valued and most dishonored forms of work: domestic labor. Think now about a world in which no one did that work. Make a list of what would not get done if there were not a group of people, unpaid or underpaid, who do housework. Think now about child care and the care of old people. Imagine that there was not a group—whether unpaid or severely underpaid—who did the work of caring. What would happen to the wealthy and powerful members of society if there were no such group?

INTEGRATING SOCIALIZATION, INTERACTION, AND INSTITUTIONS

This chapter has explored the many ways sociologists have tried to understand the creation and maintenance of inequalities of gender, race, and class. So far, we have looked at three frameworks for thinking about the production and reproduction of gender: socialization, social interaction, and social structures, organizations, and institutions. How do individuals develop their understandings and preferences regarding gender? How do they internalize gendered and racialized norms and expectations? Questions about individual orientations and practices are best answered by looking at the processes of socialization. How do differently situated groups collaborate, negotiate, and conflict in ways that produce everyday practices and expectations? To answer these questions we must look at interactional processes. When we are concerned with the history and current distributions of material and cultural resources and the gendered, racial, and class consequences of this distribution, we are raising questions at the institutional level of analysis.

Ann Arnett Ferguson (2000 has conducted research that shows us how someone might think about children in schools from each of these perspectives. In 2007 she published a study, based on three years of interviews and observation in classrooms, about the ways fourth-, fifth-, and sixth-grade African American schoolboys are identified by their teachers as troublemakers, delinquents, and children destined for prison. How do the perspectives offered by theories of socialization, interaction, and institutions help Ferguson to tell her story?

Across the nation, public schools are sites in which African American boys are labeled as behavior problems. Many school personnel believe these boys are less intelligent and less able to learn than are girls and white children. Black schoolboys are more likely than other students to be punished or expelled from schools, less likely than other students to be supported by educators, and unlikely to actively engage with their schools as learning environments from which they can benefit (Noguera 2010). This stigmatization certainly takes place at the Rosa Parks Elementary School, a California middle school described by Ferguson in her ethnography *Bad Boys: Public Schools in the Making of Black Masculinity*.

Explaining Bad Boys in the Language of Socialization

Socialization theories are attempts to explain how individual gender and race differences originate and are internalized by individuals, usually children, creating gendered and raced selves that become long-lasting, even lifelong, identities. Many teachers and administrators at Rosa Parks attached the identity of "insubordinate" and "threatening troublemaker" to a sizable proportion of the black youth at Rosa Parks and believed that the boys brought these behaviors to school from their apathetic and dysfunctional families and neighborhoods. A long tradition in American social science and popular thought explains the causes of poverty in this way. In the 1960s, social scientists promulgated a **"culture of poverty" thesis** to explain the persistent poverty experienced by African Americans in the deteriorating urban ghettos of the North. Scholars defined the culture of poverty as a set of values, attitudes, and behaviors that differed from those of the middle class. Where middle-class people delayed gratification and saved for the future, the poor were said to be overly "present oriented" and impulsive. Where the middle class aspired to better positions in life or to better jobs, the poor, scholars argued, had few such ambitions. Where middle-class families had breadwinner-fathers and stay-at-home mothers who stabilized families and raised law-abiding and successful sons, poor black households were seen as disorganized entities loosely held together by single mothers dependent on welfare to survive. Boys in such families, these observers argued, had no stable male "role models" to guide them into manhood. Socialized to adopt these poverty-sustaining cultural attitudes and practices, boys perpetuated their parents' lifestyle into the next and future generations (see Moynihan 1965). According to the culture of poverty thesis, therefore, such boys were raised to become unproductive, antisocial, and criminal adults.

Most sociologists have by now rejected as racist the culture of poverty thesis, but Ferguson's study shows that teachers and administrators at the Rosa Parks School found it a useful explanation of the sources of black boys' school troubles. As a result, even though most pupils sent out of the classroom to the "punishing room" or expelled for bad behavior were black and male, teachers did not recognize the racist and sexist understandings at the foundation of the school's policy. Rather, the gender and race of the troublemakers seemed to be an accident of each child's individual choice to be "good" or "bad." It was the cultural and natural differences kids brought with them to school, not the school itself, that explained their failures and troubles. It was an individual problem of the boys, not an interactional problem between the boys and school staff or an institutional problem of race in the American system of education that appeared to cause this problem.

We can reject the notion that the boys were "socialized" by their families to behave badly at school. However, Ferguson tells us how local "knowledge" the boys learned in their families and neighborhoods helped to shape their understanding of the school environment. Based on that knowledge, their response to school practices seems reasonable. Indeed, we can see how we too might respond as they did. Here is Ferguson's more sympathetic, indeed heartbreaking, view of the knowledge that boys brought with them to school, information that they believed they needed in order to protect themselves from a world that is, by and large, hostile to them (and which, by the way, the fate of Trayvon Martin affirms as rational):

> The boys are alerted by family to the dangers of "the real world" for black males through admonitions, object lessons from direct personal experience, and electrifying moments such as watching the videotape of Rodney King[1] being beaten senseless by the police. The constant reiteration of this danger and the need to be on guard or to handle dreadful encounters by themselves saturates their daily journeys through school and neighborhood. . . . The very boys who were being constituted in school and in the media as demonic, terrifying, and unsalvageable were themselves fearful. . . . This social terror permeates the daily life of which the school day is a part. It constitutes the feeling component of the popular, illegitimate knowledge that the boys bring into school, which informs their practices, their relationships, what they accept as truth, what they shut out, suspect, question, or challenge. (116)

The Interactional Construction of Bad Boys and Disciplinarian Teachers

Interactionists focus on how identities are created within the social relations of everyday life. They don't believe that girls and boys or women and men are simply socialized to behave in particular ways and then apply these fixed beliefs and practices to new situations. Instead, they see social actors as agents who collaborate, bargain, and strategize within specific contexts, "exerting power and producing effects in their lives" (Courtenay 2000). Ferguson shows that this happens at the Rosa Parks Elementary School as boys and their teachers negotiate ways to interpret and apply the school rules.

Of course, teachers have the upper hand in their contest with ten-, eleven-, and twelve-year-old boys. They can and do send troublesome boys out of the classroom to the "punishing room" or expel them from the school altogether for days at a time. But the boys do not submit without a challenge to the teachers' and the school's authority. Based on their experiential knowledge, which is more real and more seemingly relevant to them than anything taught in the classroom, "they expect to be engaged in confrontations with authority, to be able to stand up for themselves, to talk back, to defend themselves physically" (133). Through daily resistance (what teachers call "making trouble"), the boys challenge the system that devalues them. In so doing, they engage in contests that further demonize them in the eyes of the teachers while confirming the teachers' lack of respect for their language, their homes, and their interactional styles. The outcome is that teachers see the boys as confirmed troublemakers who may be on their way to criminal careers. In these ways, teachers and pupils create the effects that the rules and authority structures exist to diminish.

Explaining How Institutions Create Bad Boys

Institutional racism and sexism form the backdrop to the daily drama of confrontation and resistance at Rosa Parks Elementary School. Racialized and gendered practices and ideologies sort and rank the children into categories that have consequences for them on a daily basis and for their futures. Singling out some children as troublemakers who need discipline conveys messages about racial and gender identities. At Rosa Parks, it is African American boys who are overrepresented in the punishing room and who are most likely to be expelled for their confrontational behavior. This fact reinforces the cultural message, regardless of their teachers' intention, that these boys aren't as smart, as well brought up, or as civilized as their white counterparts. Noguera (2010) writes that

> such messages are conveyed even when responsible adults attempt to be as fair as possible in their handling of sorting and disciplinary activities. Because the outcomes of such practices often closely resemble larger patterns of success and failure that correspond with racial differences in American society, they invariably have the effect of reinforcing existing attitudes and beliefs about the nature and significance of race. (xx)

What is the purpose of the social construction of gender, and how can we challenge it? We have come a long way from the idea of gender as a function of individual psychology. Far from a necessity external to the social order, rooted perhaps in our biological or psychological makeup, feminist sociologists see gender as a construction within and of society. The implication of this perspective is radical. It forces us to ask, What is the point of constructing a social order that distinguishes men from women? Lorber suggests that the point is to create a class of subordinates:

> Gender inequality—the devaluation of "women" and the social domination of "men"—has social functions and a social history. It is not the result of sex, procreation, physiology, anatomy, hormones, or genetic predispositions. It is produced

and maintained by identifiable social processes and built into the general social structure and individual identities deliberately and purposefully. The social order as we know it in Western societies is organized around racial, ethnic, class, and gender inequality. I contend, therefore, that the continuing purpose of gender as a modern social institution is to construct women as a group to be the subordinates of men as a group. (Lorber 1994, 35)

At this juncture, we must consider whether gender is a relationship with a future. Holly Devor imagines a future in which gender is "obsolete and meaningless." If sex and gender were to become as meaningless as eye color, she writes,

> the social entities we now call women and men would become archaic and the basis for gender as a meaningful concept would become irreparably eroded. Were people to become no longer distinguishable on the basis of sex, were all gender choices open to all people, were there to cease to be a cognitive system which measured the world in gendered units, the material basis for sexism would cease to exist. (Devor 1989, 154)

GENDER MATTERS

This chapter has presented three stories about gender difference. Stories based on social roles and social learning tell us about the ways individuals learn gender norms and behave in gendered ways. Interactionist stories move beyond the individual level of explanation to focus on the relationships among individuals and within groups in daily life. Stories at the structural and institutional levels inform us about the gendered distribution of material and social resources and the gendered ideologies and discourses that support these gender inequalities. Do we need to decide which one is the "best" story? Perhaps not. Each story tells us something we need to know, and each story is linked to the others in important ways. One way to think about these linkages is to imagine that there are three chapters in the story of gender differences and inequalities: (1) gender roles are internalized and adopted by individuals through gender socialization; (2) they are sustained by social expectations, gender categorization, and accountability (doing gender) at the interactional level; and (3) they are shaped by constraints and possibilities at the structural and institutional levels. Each chapter of this story adds a dimension to our understanding of the whole, but since no chapter tells us all of what we need to know, we can't restrict ourselves to a single point of view. Nor can we limit the story to just the study of gender. As intersectional theories demonstrate, gender inequalities are interwoven at the very least with inequalities of class and race structures. Tying these pieces together is the process Anthony Giddens called "**structuration**."

Giddens (1984) developed this term to refer to the relationship between human agency and social structure, between the individual level of action, in which we exercise choice, and the structural or institutional level of tradition, moral codes, organizations, and established ways of doing things, which constrains our choices. In Giddens's theory, human agency and social structure are two sides of the same coin, or, to use Cooley's metaphor, "twin-born." Structures shape individuals, and individuals shape structures. Human action reproduces structure but also creates new conditions of action. Sociologist Barbara Risman puts it this way:

> Gender is deeply embedded as a basis for stratification not just in our personalities, our cultural rules, or institutions but in all these, and in complicated ways. The gender structure differentiates opportunities and constraints based on sex category and thus has consequences on three dimensions: (1) At the individual level, for the development of gendered selves; (2) during interaction as men and women face different cultural expectations even when they fill the identical structural positions; and (3) in institutional domains where explicit regulations regarding resource distribution and material goods are gender specific. (Risman 2004, 433)

When sociologists argue that gender is a social construction, they are referring to this complex, multilevel process. At the individual level, we grow up with gender expectations, gender rules, and gendered practices that we may or may not come to question. Where do such expectations come from? Studies of social learning have shown how adults socialize children into existing gender arrangements. Our own recollections remind us of the strong influence families have on most of us when we are very young. Sometimes parents and others select toys or clothing for children that mark gender differences (or, as likely, are persuaded to do so by their own children): baby dolls and pretend make-up for small girls; militarized and muscled "action figures" for boys. Perhaps the kids on the block or in the schoolyard create gendered forms of play and interaction or make fun of and bully nonconforming children. However, that answer only pushes the question back a notch, for we must then ask where our parents and our friends got their ideas. When they were very young, they learned a lot from their own parents and other caretakers, as you learned from yours. But social contexts and gendered expectations are historical phenomena, and they are constantly changing, as are the problems we confront and the solutions to them that we devise collectively.

In *Gender Play*, her ethnographic study of the ways schoolchildren construct and overcome gendered boundaries, Barrie Thorne (1997) shows how an individual-level framework that explains gender as a system learned through socialization pushes us to see gender differentiation but makes invisible the nongendered social activity in children's play. Good researchers know that the questions one asks determine the answers one gets. If researchers believe that there are differences between boys and girls and devise tests to capture those differences, they probably will not notice all the moments when boys and girls are similar. Just as public restrooms create the differences they exist to honor, as Goffman pointed out, studies based on the assumption of difference will probably find the difference they assume exists. In her study of children's play, Thorne asks and answers a different question, one that does not assume difference:

> In shifting the focus from individual to social relations, I move away from the question, Are girls and boys different? which centers most of the research on children and gender. Instead I ask: How do children actively come together to help create, and sometimes challenge, gender structures and meanings? (Thorne 1997, 4)

Such questions can help us to see the dimension of socially constructed differences in the wider context of our similarities and common interests. Imagine a world without gender. Barrie Thorne does in Box 3-5.

GENDER IN EVERYDAY LIFE   BOX 3-5

IMAGINING A DIFFERENT FUTURE

Twenty years ago, when the second wave of feminism was just beginning, we were preoccupied with countering biological arguments that had long been used to justify gender divisions and inequalities. Now many of us are concerned less about biology than about the hold of existing arrangements on our imaginations and desires. How do we become invested in particular forms of femininity and masculinity, in oppositional gender, in arrangements based on domination? What are sources of resistance, of opposition, of alternative arrangements based on equality and mutuality? How can we imagine, and realize, other possibilities?

When I grasp for a concrete image to hold an abstraction like gender equality and mutuality, I sometimes think about Hansel and Gretel, extracted, if they can be, from the adults of the story—the wicked stepmother, the witch, the irresponsible father. Gretel and Hansel (I exchange the order of their names to animate the image of equality) provide mutual support as they go through the dangers of the forest. They each take the lead, Hansel in gathering and scattering the pebbles and, later, the bread crumbs to mark their path, and Gretel in tricking the witch. They confront the vicissitudes of life as brother and sister, as caring friends.

In fact, in our culture the model of sisters and brothers offers one of the few powerful images of relatively equal relationships between girls and boys, and between adult men and women. It is not by chance that relationships between brothers and sisters begin in childhood, a period in which gender relations are relatively egalitarian. Boys of elementary school age lack major sources of adult male privilege, such as access to greater income and material resources, control of political and other forms of public power, and the legal and labor entitlements of husbands compared with wives. The "protected" status of children (which, from another vantage point, constitutes a pattern of legal, economic, and political subordination) cuts across gender and mutes male privilege. The dominance of boys over girls may, as a result, be more anxious, but it also has a weaker material and legal base than the dominance of men over women.

The painfully sparse language that kids have for relationships between girls and boys—"like" charged with romantic connotations, "hate" as a quick nullification—underscores the need for more images of, and more experience with, cross-gender relationships based on friendship and collegiality. The culture of heterosexual romance needs fundamental reconstruction so that it no longer overshadows other possibilities for intimacy and sexuality. Friendship and equality are a much better basis for intimate relationships than mistrust and a sense of being strangers.

As adults we can help kids, as well as ourselves, imagine and realize different futures, alter institutions, craft new life stories. A more complex understanding of the dynamics of gender, of tensions and contradictions, and of the hopeful moments that lie within present arrangements, can help broaden our sense of the possible.

SOURCE: Reprinted with permission from Thorne (1997).

KEY TERMS

androcentrism

accountability

culture of poverty thesis

doing gender

functionalists

gender is omnirelevant

microinequities

negotiated order

opportunity structures and relative numbers

resources for doing gender

structuration

tokenism

CRITICAL THINKING QUESTIONS

1. In your own words, briefly describe the lenses of androcentrism, gender polarization, and gender essentialism and provide examples of each from something you have noticed at work, on campus, from a magazine, popular song, or TV program.

2. Imagine that you are visiting a hospital and you notice that the jobs are divided by gender. Men are often orderlies and physicians, while most of the nurses are women. How would theorists from the three perspectives—social learning, social interaction and social structure—explain the variation?

3. Spend the day observing how gender is a part of your life. Walk around with a notebook and notice all the ways gender is expressed in your everyday life. Try to imagine what the people and events around you would be like if everyone "reversed gender." Spend the next day observing how you express gender. What do you do to perform gender? How do people know you are a man or a woman? If you are a man, for example, how would you look different if you decided to present yourself to the world as a woman? What might you do differently? How would others treat you? What would they say if they determined that you were not really a woman but a man "in drag"? How are you held accountable?

4. Go to www.youtube.com and find some advertisements for children's toys. How is gender expressed in the ads? What colors or words are used? What toys are being sold to boys or girls? What are the children doing in the ads? How do the activities and toys relate to adult activities? You can also do this by taking a field trip to a large toy store such as Toys R Us. How are the toys organized in the store? How do you know some toys are for boys and some are for girls? What toys seem to be for both boys and girls?

5. Read Catherine Connell's article, "Doing, Undoing, or Redoing Gender: Learning from the Workplace Experiences of Transpeople" in Gender & Society 24, Februrary 2010: 31–55. How does the article elaborate on Deutsch's idea of "undoing gender"? What would a world without gender look like?

NOTE

1. Rodney King was brutally beaten by Los Angeles police on March 3, 1991, an incident that was videotaped by a bystander and aired by news agencies around the world. When the police officers were later tried and acquitted for the beating, announcement of the acquittals sparked the 1992 Los Angeles riots. Two of the officers were later convicted in a federal trial for civil rights violations and sent to prison.

REFERENCES

Acker, Joan. 1990. "Hierarchies, Jobs, Bodies: A Theory of Gendered Organizations." *Gender and Society* 4 (2): 139–58.

Associated Press. 2003. "Transgendered Community Remembers Murder," December 28. http://www.usatoday.com/news/nation/2003–12-27-teena_x.htm.

Bem, Sandra. 1993. *The Lenses of Gender: Transforming the Debate on Sexual Inequality.* New Haven, CT: Yale University Press.

Blakemore, Judith, and Renee Centers. 2005. "Characteristics of Boys' and Girls' Toys." *Sex Roles* 53 (9/10): 619–33.

Blumer, Herbert. 1969. *Symbolic Interactionism: Perspective and Method.* New York: Prentice Hall.

Cohn, Carol. 1987. "Sex and Death in the Rational World of Defense Intellectuals." *Signs: Journal of Women in Contemporary Society* 12 (4): 687–718.

Cole, Johnneta. 1971. "Black Women in America: An Annotated Bibliography." *Black Scholar* 3 (December): 42–53.

Collins, Patricia Hill. 2000. *Black Feminist Thought: Knowledge, Consciousness, and the Politics of Empowerment.* 2nd edition. New York: Routledge.

Connell, R. W. 1987. *Gender and Power.* Stanford, CA: Stanford University Press.

Cooley, Charles Horton. 1962. *Social Organization.* New York: Schocken.

Coontz, Stephanie. 1992. *The Way We Never Were: American Families and the Nostalgia Trap.* New York: Basic Books.

Courtenay, Will H. 2000. "Engendering Health: A Social Constructionist Examination of Men's Health Beliefs and Behaviors." *Psychology of Men and Masculinity* 1 (1): 4–15.

Deutsch, Francine. 2007. "Undoing Gender." *Gender and Society* 21(1): 106–127.

Devor, Holly. 1989. *Gender Blending: Confronting the Limits of Duality.* Bloomington: University of Indiana Press.

Epstein, Cynthia. 1970. *Women's Place: Options and Limits in Professional Careers.* Berkeley: University of California Press.

Ferguson, Ann Arnett. 2000. *Bad Boys: Public Schools in the Making of Black Masculinity.* Ann Arbor, MI: University of Michigan Press.

Garfinkel, Harold. 1967. *Studies in Ethnomethodology.* New York: Prentice-Hall.

Giddens, Anthony. 1984. *The Constitution of Society: Outline of the Theory of Structuration.* Berkeley: University of California Press.

Glenn, Evelyn Nakano. 1999. "The Social Construction and Institutionalization of Gender and Race: An Integrated Framework." *Revisioning Gender.* Myra Marx Ferree, Judith Lorber, and Beth B. Hess, eds. Thousand Oaks, CA: Sage.

Glick, Peter, and Susan T. Fiske. 1999. "Gender, Power Dynamics, and Social Interaction." In *Revisioning Gender,* edited by Myra Marx Ferree, Judith Lorber, and Beth Hess, 365–98. Thousand Oaks, CA: Sage.

Goffman, Erving. 1977. "The Arrangement Between the Sexes." *Theory and Society* 4 (3): 301–31.

Hill, Shirley. 2005. *Black Intimacies: A Gender Perspective on Families and Relationships.* Walnut Creek, CA: Altamira.

Hochschild, Arlie. 1973. "A Review of Sex Role Research." *American Journal of Sociology* 78 (4): 1011–29.

———. 1983. *The Managed Heart: Commercialization of Human Feeling.* Berkeley: University of California Press.

Kanter, Rosabeth Moss. 1977. *Men and Women of the Corporation.* New York: Basic Books.

Komarovsky, Mirra. 1953. *Women in the Modern World: Their Education and Their Dilemmas.* Boston: Little Brown.

Landry, Bart. 2002. *Black Working Wives: Pioneers of the American Family Revolution.* Berkeley: University of California Press.

Lorber, Judith. 1975. "Women and Medical Sociology: Invisible Professionals and Ubiquitous Patients." In *Another Voice: Feminist Perspectives on Social Life and Social Science,* edited by Marcia Millman and Rosabeth Moss Kanter, 75–105. New York: Anchor.

———. 1994. *Paradoxes of Gender.* New Haven, CT: Yale University Press.

Martin, Patricia Yancey. 2003. " 'Said and Done' vs. 'Saying and Doing': Gendering Practices, Practicing Gender at Work." *Gender and Society* 17 (3): 342–66.

Marx, Karl. 1972. *The Eighteenth Brumaire of Louis Bonaparte.* Moscow: Progress.

Mills, C. Wright. 1967. *The Sociological Imagination.* New York: Oxford University Press.

Moynihan, Daniel. 1965. *The Negro Family: The Case for National Action,* Washington, D.C., Office of Policy Planning and Research, U.S. Department of Labor.

Noguera, Pedro. 2010. "Closing the Achievement Gap: Racial Inequality and the Unfinished Legacy of Civil Rights in America." *In Motion Magazine,* March 23.

Ridgeway, Cecilia, and Shelley Correll. 2004. "Unpacking the Gender System: A Theoretical Perspective on Gender Beliefs and Social Relations." *Gender and Society* 18 (4): 510–31.

Risman, Barbara. 2004. "Gender as Social Structure." *Gender and Society* 18 (4): 429–50.

Sandler, Bernice. 1986. "The Campus Climate Revisited: Chilly for Women Faculty, Administrators, and Graduate Students" Washington, DC: Association of American Colleges, Project on the Status and Education of Women.

Stack, Carol. 1997. *All Our Kin: Strategies for Survival in a Black Community.* New York: Basic Books.

Thorne, Barrie. 1997. *Gender Play: Girls and Boys in School.* New Brunswick, NJ: Rutgers University Press.

West, Candace, and Don H. Zimmerman. 1987. "Doing Gender." *Gender and Society* 1 (2): 125–51.

West, Candace, and Sarah Fenstermaker. 1995. "Doing Difference." *Gender and Society* 9 (1): 8–37.

Williams, Christine. 1995. *Still a Man's World: Men Who Do Women's Work.* Berkeley: University of California Press.

4

SEXUALITIES

Hooking up on college campuses is a familiar activity. Does it represent greater gender equality and freedom from the double standard for college women? Or, is it a new version of sexual oppression?

Source: ImageSource.com.

I bet you're worried. *I* was worried. That's why I began this piece. I was worried about vaginas. I was worried about what we think about vaginas, and even more worried that we don't think about them. I was worried about my own vagina. It needed a context of other vaginas—a community, a culture of vaginas. There's so much darkness and secrecy surrounding them—like the Bermuda Triangle. Nobody ever reports back from there. . . .

Let's just start with the word "vagina." It sounds like an infection at best, maybe a medical instrument: "Hurry, Nurse, bring me the vagina." "Vagina." "Vagina." Doesn't matter how many times you say it, it never sounds like a word you want to say. It's a totally ridiculous, completely unsexy word. If you use it during sex, trying to be politically correct—"Darling, could you stroke my vagina?"—you kill the act right there.

The Vagina Monologues

This excerpt is from *The Vagina Monologues*, a one-woman play based on interviews about sex conducted by Eve Ensler (2001) with more than two hundred women from diverse backgrounds. The play is a series of first-person vignettes or monologues that address such topics as pubic hair, thong underwear, pap smears, and tampons, as well as the more serious subjects of rape and incest. The play challenges the dominant discourse on sexuality for women and offers alternative ideas that celebrate the diversity of women's bodies, identities, sexualities, and sexual experience at the same time as it acknowledges the difficulties women face when it comes to sex, such as exploitation, the **double standard**, stigma, and violence. *The Vagina Monologues* first debuted off Broadway in New York City in 1996. There are now more than a thousand productions of the play performed each year, with half of them at universities and colleges (Marklein 2004).

The Vagina Monologues is often a source of campus controversy. The play has been cancelled at more than fifteen Catholic universities in the United States and banned altogether in Uganda. A prayer vigil was held outside the production at Loyola Marymount University in Los Angeles by a small group of students, parents, and alumni whose objections to *The Vagina Monologues* were based on their moral and religious convictions (Marklein 2004). Protests, boycotts, heated debates, and strongly worded editorials about the play in student, local, and national newspapers have become a part of *The Vagina Monologues* phenomenon. Why? For starters, there is the title, which makes many people uncomfortable. The word *vagina* is not often spoken in public outside of a medical setting. Women are not given many words to talk about their genitals, and they are not supposed to talk about their vaginas, unless it is to their gynecologist *The Vagina Monologues* is often performed as a V-Day benefit event in February around Valentine's day as a way to raise awareness about violence against women and to raise funds for antiviolence work. The importance of the play is illustrated when, in television promotions of the opening of upcoming productions, speakers have been instructed by news directors not to use the word "vagina" on the air, especially during daytime programming. One news director explained, "In the morning, we recognize that a lot of parents are watching the show with their kids. As a parent, I'm not sure I'd be comfortable hearing that word in front of my kids. I think a lot of people would find it objectionable. Children might ask what it means" (Ryan 2002). The discomfort around *The Vagina Monologues*, or even speaking of women's vaginas, reveals a discomfort around women's sexuality. Gender expectations and gender norms for women tell us that women's sexuality should be kept under wraps.

In 2012, *The Vagina Monologues* was used by women political leaders to draw attention to the problem of legislating about women's bodies without ever acknowledging women's sexuality or even female anatomy. Representative Lisa Brown was censored for using the word "vagina" on the floor of the Michigan state legislature during a debate about an abortion bill. Representative Brown said, "Finally Mr. Speaker, I'm flattered that you're all so interested in my vagina, but 'no' means 'no.'" The speaker responded by barring her from speaking on the floor the next day on any bills, arguing that her comments and actions the previous day failed to maintain the decorum of the Michigan House of Representatives. One of her colleagues, Representative Mike Callton, told the press that what she had said was so vile, so disgusting, that he could never bear to mention it in front of women or "mixed company." Representative Brown and some of her colleagues responded to the her censure by reading *The Vagina Monologues* on the front steps of the Michigan Legislature (*Telegraph* 2012).

For whom does *The Vagina Monologues* speak? Although *The Vagina Monologues* has been an important vehicle for bringing women's sexuality into the open as a legitimate and important subject, feminists in nations outside the United States have asserted that the play's point of view is too narrowly from the global North and have soughtto localize the play by changing it in ways that make it more appropriate to their particular community (Cheng 2004). To protect Ensler's intellectual property rights, however, strict rules are in place for anyone who uses the script. No changes are allowed in the dialogue, and if someone wishes to present it in a language other than English, they must use the "official translation" provided by the publishers. This has ironically meant that the play, which was written to represent a broad spectrum of women's experiences, is in fact imposing on the rest of the world a universal model of a set of very American experiences and a very American point of view.

One artist in Hong Kong, Sealing Cheng (2004), has conducted her own smaller series of interviews of Chinese women to try to create a Hong Kong version that she has entitled *Little Sister* because Hong Kong women frequently refer to their vaginas as "little sister." Her research has resulted in a version of *The Vagina Monologues* that includes scenes such as "Labia Dance" because of her finding that Hong Kong women had never seen a vagina, including their own. In the dance, she positions her body, head, and arms to depict a vagina. In addition, Cheng eliminated stories about motherhood because she felt that this aspect of vaginas was overemphasized in Hong Kong culture. Cheng was also critical of the inclusion of **female genital mutilation** (**FGM**) in the original *Monologues* because she felt that Americans discussing FGM created a perception that cruel **misogyny** was something only other/othered cultures did. Instead, Cheng included stories of cruelty and control of Hong Kong women's sexuality and bodies that came from within their own culture.

- What is the message about sexual liberation for women in *The Vagina Monologues*? What would this play look like if it were about male bodies and men's experience of sexuality? The play was originally written almost twenty years ago. Is the double standard it presents still valid for men and women today? Or is the double standard a thing of the past?
- What does Cheng's critique of Ensler's play tell us about the diversity of sexuality? Does Ensler's play represent the new woman in the United States? In the world? Who is left out of the picture? How does the experience of sexuality intersect with race ethnicity, social class, and nation? Do the problems described in the play represent the issues women around the world face regarding sex? What might their stories be like?
- Much, but not all, of *The Vagina Monologues* is about heterosexuality. How would the play be different if it emphasized Lesbian, Gay, Bisexual, Transgender, and Questioning (**LGBTQ**) experience?

The Vagina Monologues and *Little Sister* are examples of how popular culture can be used to combat oppressive images of sexuality. Popular culture, especially advertising, however, often uses sexuality as a way to sell products at the same time as it sells exploitative images. What is the connection between sex and sales? This chapter tries to answer this question. As we will see, many of our attitudes and beliefs about gender are reflected in our opinions, ideas, and expression of sexuality. In other words, sexuality is gendered in our thinking and in practice. Different standards, expectations, and experiences exist about sex for women and men, and these are further complicated by other factors such as race ethnicity, social class, sexual identity, and global political economics. We begin this chapter by looking at some statistics from empirical studies of ideas and behaviors related to sex around the world. We then move to the United States, where we explore sexual politics, the cult of virginity, "hooking up," and sexual rights. The chapter continues with an exploration of diversity by race ethnicity and social class, followed by a consideration of where sexuality fits in. We then confront the problems of heteronormativity, homophobia, and heterosexism as they intersect with gender. Our attention then moves to the theoretical approaches of biology, sexual scripts, and queer theory as frameworks that have been developed to understand the organization of sexuality in human societies. And finally, we look at the intersection of sex and global capitalism.

COMPARING SEXUAL ATTITUDES AND BEHAVIORS AROUND THE GLOBE

Ideas about sex vary across many social lines, such as age and nation. One study of ideas about sexual issues among more than 33,000 people in twenty-four nations found that the respondents from the various nations clustered into categories on the basis of people's attitudes about sexual behavior (Widmer, Treas, and Newcomb 1998). The questions asked whether they believed that teen sex (under age sixteen), premarital sex, extramarital sex, and homosexual sex were always wrong, almost always wrong, only sometimes wrong, or not wrong at all. The researchers determined the average for all of the participants and then looked at how the clusters differed from the average.

The first cluster included Australia, Great Britain, Hungary, Italy, Bulgaria, Russia, New Zealand, and Israel. Respondents from these nations believed that extramarital sex and teen sex were always or almost always wrong. Sex before marriage was only sometimes or not at all wrong, and respondents were somewhat evenly divided on whether homosexual sex was wrong or not. A second cluster included people from Germany, Austria, Sweden, and Slovenia. People in these nations had the most liberal attitudes about premarital sex, extramarital sex, and teens under sixteen having sex, but their opinion of homosexual sex was more divided. A third category included the United States, Ireland, and Poland. This was the most conservative group, with high proportions believing that sex outside of marriage, teen sex, and homosexual sex were always or almost always wrong. A fourth group included people from the Netherlands, Norway, the Czech Republic, Canada, and Spain. They believed that extramarital sex was wrong and were about evenly divided about teen sex. They were the most likely to say that premarital sex and homosexual sex were not wrong at all (Widmer et al. 1998).

This study looked at ideas about sex, but sexual behavior can sometimes seem to contradict opinions. For example, the United States is one of those countries that is especially critical of premarital sex. By age thirty, however, 93 percent of both women and men in the United States have had premarital sex. Despite the more conservative opinions of sex, young Americans have sex at the same age or earlier than Europeans and have more sexual partners. Americans also have higher rates of teen pregnancy, abortion, and sexually transmitted diseases (STDs), including **HIV** (Finer 2007). In other words, American teens may be at least as sexually active as European teens, but they pay a higher price for it. And, the price they pay may be related to the ideas about sex that do not match behavior. The dangers of sexuality in the United States have been linked to the absence of adequate government policies, little openness about teen sexuality, little or no access to information about sex, and restricted availability of services. Ironically, in European nations where young people have access to information and services and where tolerance for teen nonmarital sex is high, rates of adolescent sexual activity are lower than in the United States (Feijoo 2001).

The U.S. government has spent more than a billion dollars on **abstinence-only sex education** programs in spite of the fact that there is no evidence that the programs work (Schwartz 2010). The programs may in fact be dangerous to the health of the young people who participate in them. Eighty percent of abstinence-only curricula funded by the federal government has been found to include false, misleading, or distorted information. One study, furthermore, found that young people who had taken vows of abstinence were less knowledgeable about sex, less likely to use condoms, and had the same rates of **sexually transmitted diseases (STDs)** as those who had participated in sex education programs that were not abstinence-only and had not taken vows of abstinence (Bruckner and Bearman 2005).

Young people are not the only ones who have sex. Edward Laumann and his colleagues (2006) studied the sexual activities of more than 27,000 adults over age forty in twenty-nine nations to see what their experience was and how it varied by nation and gender. The researchers asked people, "In the past twelve months, how physically pleasurable did you find your relationship with your partner to be?" They found that the average responses for each nation could be organized into categories centered around regions in the world: West (Austria, Belgium, France, Germany, Spain, Sweden, United Kingdom, Mexico, Australia, Canada, New Zealand, South Africa, and the United States), Middle East (Algeria, Egypt, Israel, Italy, Morocco, Korea, Turkey, Malaysia, and the Philippines), and East Asia (China, India, Japan, Taiwan, and Thailand).

Table 4-1 shows how the responses differed for women and men in these three categories for three issues: satisfaction with sexual relations, satisfaction with their own sexual ability, and how important sex was for them. The table shows that relationships among

TABLE 4-1 Sexual Satisfaction by Region for Men and Women Over 40

Region	Satisfying sexual relations	Satisfied with sexual ability	Sex is very or extremely important
Western			
Men	67%	80%	50%
Women	67%	80%	33%
Middle Eastern			
Men	50%	70%	60%
Women	38%	70%	37%
East Asian			
Men	25%	67%	28%
Women	25%	50%	12%

N = 27,500.

Source: Laumann et al. (2006).

region, gender, and sexual issues are complex, with differences between women and men for most questions in most of the regions, and differences from one region to the next on all three questions.

Laumann and his colleagues (2006) argue that the differences from one nation to another are related to ideas about gender equality. In nations in the West, where women have relatively more equality with men, sexual satisfaction is relatively high for both women and men. In nations where women have less equality with men, in the Middle East and East Asia, men and especially women have less sexual satisfaction. In East Asia, sexual satisfaction is particularly low, as is the proportion who say that sex is important to them. But what does Laumann mean by "gender equality," and how do specific aspects of gender equality relate to the factors identified in the table? We should also wonder how the respondents in the study were defining sexual relations and sexual satisfaction. The numbers are intriguing, but it will take much theoretical analysis to sort out how gender is both a cause and an effect of sexual satisfaction, sexual ability, and how important we regard sex and how and why these relationships vary from one culture, nation, or region to another.

CHANGING ATTITUDES TOWARD SEXUALITY IN THE UNITED STATES

Although Americans are more conservative than people from many other nations regarding ideas about sex, national survey data reveal that they are much more liberal than they were forty or fifty years ago (Reiss 2006). In 1937 and 1959, 22 percent of adult Americans approved of men and women having had sexual experience before marriage. By 1973, 43 percent of Americans surveyed felt that premarital sex was not wrong, and by 1985, this proportion had reached 52 percent (Smith 1994). Today 59 percent of people in the United States say they believe that premarital sex is morally acceptable (Saad 2010).

Americans' attitudes toward premarital sex have become increasingly liberal since the "sexual revolution" of the 1960s and 1970s. The slogan "Make love, not war" captured the essence of this time of great political and moral change. Young people were protesting not only against the war in Vietnam, but also against dominant values in post–World War II America. The cracks in the moral terrain that developed into the free-love era of the 1960s and 1970s had appeared in the 1950s during the *"Playboy* revolution" (Ehrenreich 1984).

Playboy, an iconic men's magazine that began publication in 1953, depicted a lifestyle of carefree sex and fun devoid of consequences. For many middle-class men in the 1950s, becoming an adult meant marrying and settling down. *Playboy* presented the alternative option of the bachelor playboy surrounded by beautiful women who were willing sex partners. *Playboy* assured us that men could be "real" men—adults, successful in their careers, heterosexual—without being married. For women, the introduction of the oral contraceptive pill in the early 1960s also played a role in this massive social change, reflecting and contributing to transformed sexual practices and ideas about sex without marriage and sex for pleasure (Rosen 2000; May 2010). Equally significant was the women's liberation movement of the 1960s and 1970s which challenged ideas about sex and campaigned for women's rights of sexual expression and control of their own bodies.

In rap groups (women meeting to talk about themselves and issues they found troubling), women's liberation teach-ins, pamphlets, and protests, women discovered that their private troubles were shared. They learned that the "experts" on sex did not know much about sexuality. Women's actual experiences were very different from the experts' discourse. In rap groups, women learned to explore their worlds from their own experiences by coming together in small groups to tell their stories about sexuality and domestic life. For the first time, they spoke with others about the disappointments of their sex lives with husbands and boyfriends, about faked orgasms and their fears of being "frigid," about the need to please one's man or any man, and about sex on men's terms.

In the early days of the women's liberation movement, the discussion about sex was centered on **heterosexuality** and women's relationships with men. A central focus was on penetrative sex and on the vaginal orgasm. Freud, whose ideas were a powerful force in the middle of the twentieth century, held that mature female sexuality entailed relinquishing clitoral for vaginal orgasms. Based on listening to one another and learning from their own experience, feminists challenged the claim that "mature" orgasms were exclusively located in the vagina, asserting that this idea came out of a focus on men's sexual needs and on vaginal sexual intercourse with men as the only "right" way for women to have sex.

Anne Koedt's (1996) 1970 paper "The Myth of the Vaginal Orgasm" challenged this point of view and was widely circulated among rap groups around the country. Koedt wrote, "Women have thus been defined sexually in terms of what pleases men; our own biology has not been properly analyzed. Instead, we are fed the myth of the liberated woman and her vaginal orgasm—an orgasm that in fact does not exist" (Koedt 1996, 115). Koedt argued that the Freudian distinction between clitoral ("immature") and vaginal ("mature") orgasms privileged men's pleasure, and she questioned the supposed "naturalness" or inevitably of heterosexuality. "It would thus open up the whole question of *human* sexual relationships beyond the confines of the present male-female role system" (Koedt 1996, 116).

At the same time that feminists were criticizing male-centered heterosexuality, critical discussion of the institution of heterosexuality itself was part of the growing lesbian movement of the day. For lesbian feminists, lesbianism was a political statement, a rejection of the patriarchal institutions of heterosexuality and marriage, and an expression of women's sexual liberation. Adrienne Rich (1996) contributed the concept of "**compulsory heterosexuality**" to the discussion, arguing that social institutions and popular culture assume heterosexuality and that heterosexuality maintains women's subordination. Rich was one of the first scholars to question the existence of the **sexual binaries** of heterosexuality and homosexuality. She placed women on a "lesbian continuum." One pole of this continuum included women's friendships and loving connections to other women, and active lesbian sexuality was at the other pole. Rich maintained that the alliances of women throughout the continuum were a key factor in overturning patriarchy.

The politics of sexuality was a central aspect of women's struggles for gender equality in the emerging feminism of the 1970s. Mid-twentieth-century feminists asserted that to be truly free and equal, women needed to be sexually liberated. Sexual liberation included (1) access to birth control and safe, legal abortions; (2) free sexuality, including the right to pleasure; (3) the right to say no to sex; and (4) the sexual option of lesbianism.

Calling, Dating, and Hooking Up

A number of scholars have observed that a new form of heterosexual interaction began to develop in the 1970s in the United States that has remained the dominant form today (Bogle 2008; Kimmel 2008). In the early twentieth century, young women and men in the upper and middle classes met each other through "calling," an arrangement where the woman and her mother would choose a suitable man and ask him to call on her. This process didn't work very well with the majority of the population that did not have large enough spaces, or parlors, where men could visit the women. Meeting in public places, "dating," was more popular among the working class, and eventually dating became the norm for most Americans. Both calling and dating were expected to lead to increased sexual intimacy after the couple got to know each other and also were perceived as a stepping stone to finding a husband or wife (Bailey 1988).

Dating began to change in the 1960s and 1970s. Young people increasingly met with each other as groups in informal settings rather than as couples in prearranged activities, or dates. At the same time, attitudes about sex became more liberal, the birth control pill was developed, and sexual repertoires may have broadened as activities such as oral sex became more common among unmarried couples. In addition, the organization of college campuses changed so that women and men now found it easier to spend time with each other. For example, before the 1960s, most colleges had curfews, gender-segregated dorms, and restrictions against women being in men's quarters or men in women's. In addition, the ratio of men to women has changed on college campuses, as women have flooded into higher education (a phenomenon we explore in chapter 5).

Today, especially on college campuses, dating is not a customary social practice, and instead, college students talk about "hooking up" as the most common way of meeting with others and of experiencing sexual intimacy, whatever that may include (Kimmel 2008). Hooking up is "when a girl and guy get together for a physical encounter and don't expect anything further" (Bogle 2008, 2). The term ***hooking up*** has a wide range of meanings. The tricky part of the definition is what exactly the physical encounter is. Interviews with students reveal that hooking up can mean anything from a kiss to sexual intercourse to sexual assault. One study showed that 78 percent of students had hooked up at least once since they started college and that 28 percent had hooked up ten times or more. Only 38 percent of those who had hooked up, however, said that sexual intercourse was a part of their hookup (Bogle 2008).

Today hooking up is sometimes perceived as a continuation of the movement toward the liberation of women's as well as men's sexuality that emerged in the middle of the twentieth century. The earlier inequality persists, however, and in many ways hooking up "retains certain features of the old dating patterns: male domination, female compliance, and double standards" (Kimmel 2008, 197). For example, men initiate sexual behavior most (two-thirds) of the time, hookups are twice as likely to take place in the man's room, and hooking up enhances the man's reputation while it can damage the woman's. Armstrong, England, and Fogarty (2010) argue furthermore that if we use orgasm as a measure of the value of various kinds of sexual arrangements for women, hooking up falls short. They asked college women and men about their experience with hookups and found a gender gap in the proportion of times they had an orgasm. The percentage of orgasms for women compared to men was 32 percent for first hookups, 39 percent if they had hooked up with the same person once or twice before, 49 percent if they had repeat hookups with the same person, and 79 percent if they were in a relationship with the person. This means that women had an orgasm only about a third as often as men for first hookups, but that the gap narrowed to nearly 80 percent as often as men when the women were in a relationship. The researchers argue that the reason sex in a relationship tends to be better is that there is greater incentive to treat one's partner well since a repeat is likely, and good sex takes practice.

Two specific factors were associated with the sexual encounters that did result in orgasm for women. The first was cunnilingus (women receiving oral sex). Women received oral sex in 46 percent of the first hookups, 55–59 percent of the repeat hookups, and 68 percent of the relationships. Oral sex was more likely to be received by men than given by men. Men received oral sex about 80 percent of the time in all contexts (Armstrong et al. 2010).

Self-stimulation was the second important factor associated with sex where women had orgasms. Those women who self-stimulated (masturbated) while having sex with their partners were more likely to orgasm. In one kind of encounter, women's and men's orgasm rates nearly converged and were nearly universal (92 percent of women and 96 percent of men): when they were in a relationship and the women received oral sex and engaged in self-stimulation (Armstrong et al. 2010). Self-stimulation, like receiving oral sex, however, is less likely among women than among men.

Norms about masturbation provide an example of the persistence of the double standard. Masturbation for men continues to be less stigmatized, reflecting the rule that holds that men's sexual expression is expected and encouraged. Men must masturbate to be masculine. Masturbation for men is unavoidable, a rite of passage during puberty, and socially tolerated as part of a traditional view of sexuality that places entitlement and pleasure at the center of men's sexuality. For women, however, masturbation is more likely to be discouraged as shameful and unfeminine. In a recent study of sexual behavior in the United States, masturbation rates for men ranged from a low of 46 percent (among men over 70) to a high of 84 percent (among men 25–29). For women, the range was from 33 percent (among women over 70) to 72 percent (among women 25–29).

How can we respond to these findings on orgasm from the perspective of improving the experience of sex for women? One way is to argue that since much of the hooking-up sex in which college women engage does not lead to orgasm, bringing sex back to relationships rather than encouraging sex with no strings attached would be a move toward gender equality as well as a way to provide better sex for women. But relationships are not without difficulties for women who are trying to succeed academically and have professional goals that don't include a permanent partner, at least not yet. An alternative solution is to keep the hookup but also address the factors that degrade the experience for women, such as a double standard that inhibits women from self-stimulation during sex and the lack of reciprocity in oral sex. Women deserve sexual pleasure and sexual respect in hookups as well as in relationships. Men will need to be challenged to treat their hookup partners generously and with respect, and women will need to grow into adulthood with a sense of entitlement about sex and an understanding of their own sexual response through masturbation (Armstrong et al. 2010).

What does hooking up do to or for men? Early feminists in the mid-twentieth century would have argued that hooking up is just one more way for men to exploit women, and this may be true in many cases. But a closer look reveals that asserting that hooking up is somehow a natural aspect of men's sexuality assumes that heterosexual men's sexuality and sexual preferences are not socially structured themselves and do not limit men's sexual experience. What are some of the problems hooking up poses for men? One feature of the social construction of sexuality for men is the belief that men are always looking for sex, which means they are always available and must perform on demand as often as possible in order to be properly gendered men. Almost all the men in one study of hooking up said that they believed the stereotype that college men cannot avoid being preoccupied by sex because it is part of the "natural" makeup of men. One man described his fraternity house: "You are in a big house, a lot of beer, you have lot of friends and have parties and if that results in [sex, so be it]. . . . I think all guys want to have a lot of sex [not just fraternity men]. It's just testosterone" (Bogle 2008, 75). Perhaps one of the reasons the term "hookup" is so vague is that it hides the lack of sexual intercourse in many encounters. While the stereotype of men is that they are insatiable, real men can claim to have hooked up, implying that they had intercourse, when in fact they had kissed or fondled partners without intercourse (Bogle 2008).

A second problem with hooking up for men is that it does not seem to create the best sex in terms of quantity or quality. In the statistics on orgasm, we noted that women were less likely than were men to orgasm in all forms of encounters from first hookup to relationships, but that women were much more likely to orgasm when they were in a relationship than in a hookup. The same was true for men. About 30 percent of men experienced an orgasm in first hookups, but more than 85 percent had an orgasm when they were in a relationship (Armstrong et al. 2010). Quantity for men is also undoubtedly enhanced in relationships compared to hookups, because a partner is a surer bet than a chance encounter with finding "someone" at a fraternity party (Kimmel 2008).

The Cult of the Virgin

Despite changes in ideologies and behaviors that appear to have liberalized sexuality in the United States, the identification of morality with virginity for women persists. "While boys are taught that the things that make them men—good men—are universally accepted ethical ideals, women are led to believe that our moral compass lies somewhere between our legs. Literally. Whether it's the determining factor in our "cleanliness" and "purity" or the marker of our character, virginity has an increasingly dangerous hold over young women. It affects not only our ability to see ourselves as ethical actors outside of our own bodies, but also how the world interacts with us through social mores, laws, and even violence" (Valenti 2010, 13).

American culture is marked by a prevalent and growing obsession with virginity. In 2006, for example, 1,400 **purity balls** were held. At these promlike events, which have often been funded by federal grants, girls are escorted by their fathers to whom they pledge their virginity. A focus on virginity on Facebook, at school assemblies, and in the popular culture are an expanding feature of American life. Girls are encouraged to take chastity vows and to wear **promise (abstinence) rings** and should they falter and have intercourse, cosmetic surgeons across the country offer hymen reconstruction (despite warnings from the medical community that the surgeries can be dangerous) (Committee on Gynecological Practice 2007; Valenti 2010).

The United States is not alone in its obsession with virginity. Women protesters in Egypt during the Arab Spring in 2011 were forced by soldiers to submit to "virginity tests" so that the soldiers could argue that the women were morally corrupt and therefore not credible political activists. The Indian government has been criticized for requiring some rape victims to submit to a medical virginity test as part of their legal case. Virginity testing has been banned is South Africa, but it persists in some population groups, particularly in Zulu communities.

The focus on virginity brings with it many problems. Among the most important is the way in which it dismisses anything else girls and women do with their lives. Women are not judged by their intelligence, their talents, their altruism, or their success. Rather, an intact hymen becomes the sole criteria for seeing women or for women seeing themselves as good, worthy, moral humans. In addition, it defines women as bad, unworthy, and immoral if they are not virgins, regardless of anything else they are accomplishing in their lives.

Another problem with the focus on virginity is that no one seems to have a clear idea of what "virgin" means. In reports comparing sexual activity between those teens who have taken vows of abstinence and those who haven't, one critical difference is that those who claim to be leading virginal lives have in fact participated in more anal and oral sex than those who haven't. "Virgin" for these people is defined as not having had vaginal intercourse, while other sex acts are not considered unchaste. Beyond being a problem in semantics, defining sex so narrowly results in riskier behavior. The virginity movement has become the new authority on sexuality dominating the discourse of sex education and the policies being put in place (Valenti 2010). Abstinence-only sex education both denies information about condoms to young people and promotes virginity in the hopes that teens will abstain from sex. Instead, sex has been redefined as vaginal intercourse while oral and anal sex, which are more likely to result in **sexually transmitted infections** (**STIs**), are more prevalent (Bruckner and Bearman 2005).

While both women and men are purportedly admonished to remain virgins until marriage, women are given the greater responsibility to maintain both theirs and their boyfriends' chastity. Promise rings and purity balls are not held for young men, and nearly all of the books, speeches, sex education courses, and websites promoting virginity focus on women based on the incorrect assumption that females are naturally less interested in sex and therefore the inevitable gatekeepers.

One of the most horrific results of valuing virginity more than women are so-called **honor crimes**. About 5,000 honor crimes are reported (most scholars believe the numbers committed are much higher) every year in which women and girls are "shot, stoned, buried alive, strangled, smothered and knifed to death" (Kienan 2011, 184). The murder victms have been accused of immoral behavior that has brought shame on the family. Immoral behavior is most often associated with having sex outside of marriage. While honor crimes kill or mutilate women for many reasons, at the heart of the rationale is that women and girls who are not chaste virgins must be punished.

Sexual Rights

A new concern in international human rights forums that addresses these issues of sexual liberation and the right to quality in our sexual lives "marks a historic achievement that feminist, and gay and lesbian, movements should proudly claim" (Petchesky 2000, 100). This concept is sexual rights. Discussions of sexual and reproductive rights have a short history on the international political stage. In fact, there is no mention of sexuality in any human rights document prior to 1993. Rosalind Petchesky (2000) sees this as related to the dualistic nature of the *negative* right not to be sexually abused and the *affirmative* right to enjoy sex. She asks,

> Why is it so much easier to assert sexual freedom in a negative than in an affirmative, emancipatory sense; to gain consensus for the right not to be abused, exploited, raped, trafficked, or mutilated in one's body, but not the right to fully enjoy one's body? (82)

At the 14th World Conference of Sexology in 1999, Petchesky's question was answered when a declaration of sexual rights, shown in Box 4-1, was adopted.

GENDER IN EVERYDAY LIFE   BOX 4-1
DECLARATION ON SEXUAL RIGHTS

1. *The right to sexual freedom.* Sexual freedom encompasses the possibility for individuals to express their full sexual potential. However, this excludes all forms of sexual coercion, exploitation, and abuse at any time and situations in life.

2. *The right to sexual autonomy, sexual integrity, and safety of the sexual body.* This right involves the ability to make autonomous decisions about one's sexual life within a context of one's own personal and social ethics. It also encompasses control and enjoyment of our own bodies free from torture, mutilation, and violence of any sort.

3. *The right to sexual privacy.* This involves the right for individual decisions and behaviors about intimacy as long as they do not intrude on the sexual rights of others.

4. *The right to sexual equity.* This refers to freedom from all forms of discrimination regardless of sex, gender, sexual orientation, age, race, social class, religion, or physical and emotional disability.

5. *The right to sexual pleasure.* Sexual pleasure, including autoeroticism, is a source of physical, psychological, intellectual, and spiritual well-being.

6. *The right to emotional sexual expression.* Sexual expression is more than erotic pleasure or sexual acts. Individuals have a right to express their sexuality through communication, touch, emotional expression, and love.

7. *The right to sexually associate freely.* This means the possibility to marry or not, to divorce, and to establish other types of responsible sexual associations.

8. *The right to make free and responsible reproductive choices.* This encompasses the right to decide whether or not to have children, the number and spacing of children, and the right to full access to the means of fertility regulation.

9. *The right to sexual information based upon scientific inquiry.* This right implies that sexual information should be generated through the process of unencumbered and yet scientifically ethical inquiry, and disseminated in appropriate ways at all societal levels.

10. *The right to comprehensive sexuality education.* This is a lifelong process from birth throughout the life cycle and should involve all social institutions.

11. *The right to sexual health care.* Sexual health care should be available for prevention and treatment of all sexual concerns, problems, and disorders.

SOURCE: World Association for Sexual Health (1999).

THE RACIAL SUBTEXT OF THE SEXUAL DOUBLE STANDARD

The sexual double standard is racialized as well as gendered in the United States. The two factors of gender and race are intertwined creating variations in stereotypes and experience for men and women of different racial ethnic groups. For African Americans, the sexual double standard means that both black men and women are **hypersexualized**; that is, the stereotypes of black people portray them as overly engaged in sex. Racist ideologies include the notions that black people are animal-like in their sexual appetites and expression. Black sexuality is portrayed by the media and even by scholars as "generally excessive, deviant, diseased, and predatory" (Ford, Whetten, Hall, Kaufman, and Thrasher 2007, 209).

In addition, black men are subject to sexual surveillance and restriction and are severely punished if they do not follow the rules or if they are falsely accused of breaking the norms (Staples 2006). Moreover, they are subjected to sexual exploitation and violence by white men (Nagel 2003). Prior to the Civil War, during slavery, both black men and women were stereotyped as sexually promiscuous. After the Civil War, black men were further stereotyped as sexual predators (Nagel 2000).

Until the 1960s, **anti-miscegenation laws** in the southern United States were enacted to prevent interracial marriages and sexual encounters. White men, however, were not obligated to follow the laws, and white men raped black women at will, often impregnating them. The description in Box 4-2 of the sexual relationship between Thomas Jefferson and one of his adolescent slaves illustrates the impunity of white men. From 1865 well into the twentieth century, no Southern white man was convicted of raping a black woman (White 1985).

GENDER IN EVERYDAY LIFE   BOX 4-2
SALLY HEMINGS AND THOMAS JEFFERSON

For a long time, historians have been debating whether President Thomas Jefferson had sexual relations with his slaves that produced slave children. During Jefferson's presidency, a journalist named James Callender was the first to publicly make such charges. Many others have debated the issue since then. Recently, biologists have provided empirical evidence of these relationships through DNA tests. The tests conclude that at least one of Sally Hemings' seven children was fathered by Jefferson (Lander and Ellis 1998).

Sally Hemings was a slave who was owned by Jefferson. She was the half-sister of his wife, because Mrs. Jefferson's father had sexual relations with Hemings's mother, who was also a slave. When Jefferson first engaged in sex with Hemings, she was only about fourteen years old, thirty years younger than he was. Their sexual relationship lasted for a long time, and at least one of the children she bore was his. Jefferson never freed Hemings or his children who were born to her (Burstein, Isenberg, and Gordon-Reed 1999).

> Some scholars have portrayed the relationship between Hemings and Jefferson as a love affair. Others have questioned whether a teenage slave who had no right to refuse her master's sexual advances could enter into a relationship of love or even consent to sex. What do you think of this debate? Were slave women who were subjected to sex with their owners sometimes their lovers? Or were these encounters always a form of rape because the women could not voice their own feelings and, regardless of their feelings, they did not have the right to refuse the slave owner (Aulette 2007)?

Powerful myths about black sexuality served as justifications for racial oppression and to this day act as controlling images "designed to make racism, sexism, poverty, and other forms of social injustice appear to be natural, normal, and inevitable parts of everyday life" (Collins 2000, 69). The controlling images either depict black men and women as sexually powerful and threatening (images of **Bigger Thomas** and **Jezebel**) or as harmless, desexed subordinates of white society (**Uncle Tom** and **Aunt Jemima**) (West 1993; Collins 2000).

Sexualized Images of Black Men

The Bigger Thomas image of black men's sexuality is particularly important because of its connection to sexual violence and to the myth of the black rapist (Davis 1990). In fact, accusations of rape were common and used to justify lynchings in the United States well into the twentieth century. It is estimated that between 1882 and 1968, 539 African Americans were lynched in Mississippi alone (Payne 1994, 7).

The death of Emmett Till in 1955 was a brutal demonstration of a modern-day lynching. While visiting family in Mississippi during his summer vacation, fourteen-year-old Emmett Till went into a grocery store to buy some candy. As he left, Emmett reportedly whistled at Carolyn Bryant, the white clerk and the wife of the store's owner. A few days later, Carolyn's husband, Roy Bryant, along with his half-brother, John W. Milam, kidnapped and murdered Emmett Till. His mutilated body was recovered from the Tallahatchie River. A 75-pound electric fan was tethered to his neck with barbed wire, his nose was crushed, his right eye was hanging down to the middle of his face, and there was a bullet hole through his head (Hudson-Weems 1994). Bryant and Milam were charged with the murder of Emmett Till and were acquitted by a jury of twelve white men. They confessed to the murder in a magazine article published in 1956 but were never brought up on any additional charges. Milam died in 1980 and Bryant in 1990. They lived out the rest of their natural lives in Mississippi. Emmett Till is an important figure in the **civil rights** movement because his death ignited black communities across the South that were outraged not only by the savagery of this modern-day lynching but by the failure of the legal system to provide justice. Some historians even regard Till's murder as the catalyst for the civil rights movement (Hudson-Weems 1994).

Today the myth of the black rapist continues. Davis (1990) argues that white women in the United States are socialized to fear black men, even though they are statistically more likely to be raped by men of their own race. Approximately 90 percent of all rapes in the

United States are intraracial, which means that the perpetrator and the victim are of the same racial ethnic group (Greenfield 1997). The frequent portrayal of black men in movies and on television as brutish and aggressive, whether as rapists, pimps, gangsters, drug dealers, or wife abusers, however, perpetuates the fear that white women will be assaulted by black men (Entman and Rojecki 2001).

The myth of the black rapist, however, is not just an image on the screen. Differential treatment of black and white men in the criminal justice system also reflects and perpetuates a racialized sexual double standard. Davis (1990) points out that in the United States, rape laws were framed to protect the daughters and wives of upper-class men. Few of these men have been prosecuted for the considerable sexual violence they have inflicted on working-class women, particularly black women. In contrast, nearly all of those men convicted of rape have been African American. Furthermore, many of the African American men convicted have subsequently been proveninnocent. Of the 455 men executed between 1930 and 1967 on the basis of rape convictions, 405 were black. The history of lynching shows that what Davis calls the "frame-up rape charge," or the "myth of the black rapist," has incited and justi-fied racist aggression against black men while erasing the sexual violence that white men have inflicted on black women (Davis 1983).

Accusing black men of rape is the most extreme version of the sexualization of black men. Black men, however, are sexualized in less violent racist stereotypes as well. Kevin McGruder (2009), for example, reviewed all the research on sexuality in scientific journals between 1998 and 2008 that included black subjects. Researchers presented images of black sexuality as nonnormative and linked to disease and pathology. The general image offered in the published studies was that black sexuality itself is a problem rather than the behaviors practiced by people across gender and race ethnicity lines that are linked to the spread of HIV and other STDs.

The popular media also promotes stereotypes of black men as hypersexed and sexual predators. Accounts of Tiger Woods, Kobe Bryant, or Magic Johnson, for example, make it appear that their behavior speaks for all black men. Rather than presenting the problems as those of individuals, they come to stand for all black men, therefore implying that black men's sexuality is over the top (Staples 2006). In contrast, Bill Clinton's or Woody Allen's sexual behavior is never offered as representing the behavior of all white men or of all Christian or Jewish men.

Racialized Images of Women's Sexuality

The sexual stereotypes of women of color reflect two extremes of sexual expression. Black women are either Aunt Jemimas or Jezebels. Latinas are Madonnas or whores (Espín 1986; Almquist 1994; Cofer 1993). First Nations women are often labeled as Pocahontas, the Indian princess who assists white men, or squaw (a derogatory word), an untamed sexual being.

The legend of Pocahontas, as told in the 1995 Disney movie, is based on the relationship between a young Native American princess and a Virginia colonist, Captain John Smith. Pocahontas is said to have convinced her father, Chief Powhatan, to spare Smith's life and also to have warned whites of First Nations attacks. At the other end of the spectrum from the "helper" image, Native American women are also stereotyped as the "savage squaw." The term "squaw" is an Algonquin word that literally means "woman." It is used derogatorily, often on its own, to mean female genitalia or as a negative term for First Nations women in general. The "savage squaw" is the untamed, highly sexual whore who lacks Pocahontas's beauty and civility.

Stereotypes of black women in the United States have developed from early images of Aunt Jemimas and Jezebels to now include additional images of the diva, who uses sex to enhance her social status; the gold digger, who uses sex in exchange for money and material goods; the freak, who is wild and "kinky" for her own gratification; the dyke, a self-sufficient woman who rejects men; the gangster bitch, who has sex to signal her solidarity with her man who is also of the streets; the sister savior, who rejects all but marital procreative sex; the earth mother, whose sexuality is linked to her support of the race or the nation; and the baby mama, who has sex to maintain a connection to her child's father. All of these images are presented in hip-hop youth culture (Stephens and Few 2010).

What is, of course, most remarkable is the number of sexual images of black women. Black women in the popular media are hypersexualized in an inordinate number of ways. In addition, the images are also mostly degrading, making black women appear to be manipulative and inhuman. Black women's sexuality is portrayed as selfish or that of foolish victims. The images are also remarkable because of their distance from real women's lives. Not surprising, their ubiquitous media presence in the everyday lives of young black women and men has a profound effect on self-identity, behaviors, and experiences—especially of young people who are the target audience of those images (Stephens and Few 2010). Stephens and Few (2010) argue that the images facilitate the formation of a double standard in the minds of young black people, who believe that the diva and the sister savior are the most appropriate models for young black women. Not only do youth seem to buy into this limiting set of stereotypes, but when choosing which images to emulate or to look for in the young women they know, they tend to select those that restrict women the most.

Asian women in the United States are also stereotyped as sexually threatening dragon ladies, cunning femmes fatales who seduce white men, or geishas, who exist to please white men sexually and domestically (Tajima 1989; Espiritu 1997). These images of Asian women as sexual and submissive have helped fuel the demand for Asian **mail-order brides**, which we discuss in chapter 7. In addition, governments in Thailand, Vietnam, and the Philippines have built sex tourism on this image of exotic Asian female sexuality to bring foreign exchange into their countries.

The **sex tourism** industry is based on sexual and racial/ethnic stereotypes. Sex tourism typically involves men from the global North traveling to countries and regions in the global South such as Thailand, the Philippines, Central and South America, and the Caribbean for the purpose of engaging in sexual acts with local sex workers, many of whom are illegally trafficked or are children.

Very little research has been done on sex tourism for women seeking men. A growing population of single-women tourists, however, appears to be increasing the numbers of white women from the global North trading money for sex, intimacy, and romance with black men in the Caribbean, for example in Costa Rica. These exchanges are more ambiguous than sex tourism for heterosexual men. Negotiations between white women tourists and local black men place more emphasis, at least for the women tourists, on intimacy compared to encounters between men tourists and local women. Exchanges between women tourists and local men are also more ambiguous in regard to the money to be paid in the interactions (Frohlick 2007).

Social Class and Sexuality

So far we have reviewed the intersection of gender and sexuality and race ethnicity and sexuality. Social class also intersects with sexuality to create images and stereotypes of various strata of communities. You should recall from chapter 3 that gender is embedded in social institutions. The work of scholars such as Joan Acker has shown us, for example, how the office workplace is gendered. The organization of physical structures and social relationships that make up social institutions create notions and expressions of gender that include elements of power and inequality between women and men. Trautner (2005) has examined another example of a workplace that illustrates the intersection of gender, social class, and sexuality in the organization of a social institution: the exotic dance club.

Exotic dance clubs are obviously gendered. The clubs are premised on the assumption that women's sexuality can and should be commodified for the consumption of men customers. Social class, however, also plays an important role in distinguishing among the clubs. The women present themselves as feminine, (hetero)sexual, and as representatives of working-class or middle-class tastes. The music, the costumes, the dances, the drinks, and the décor all work together to create specific versions of sexuality, gender, and social class. In the middle-class clubs, feminine sexy women are required to be thin, young, and tanned, with breast implants and natural-appearing makeup. Their costumes are themed (such as schoolgirl, cowgirl, or dominatrix), and the music is contemporary pop music. Their interaction with customers is mostly looking and little touching (Trautner 2005).

In the working-class clubs, feminine sexiness is given a broader scope. The women are much more diverse in terms of age, weight, ethnicity, breast size, and hairstyle. Their makeup is heavier and accentuates their mouths rather than their eyes as is popular in the middle-class clubs. Performers wear lingerie rather than costumes, and the music covers a range of tastes from country and rap to metal and classic rock. Tipping the dancers includes more touching than in the middle-class clubs. The contrast in the two types of clubs illustrates the construction of gendered and classed sexuality. Sex is a performance in both places, but that performance varies by class and race ethnicity, as well as gender (Trautner 2005).

Trautner's work illustrates the construction of classed, raced, and gendered sexuality with a focus on women. Other scholars have looked at the consequences of this structuring of sexuality in beliefs about masculinity and sexuality and the ways in which social class shapes ideas and behaviors. Interviews with men and women about their perceptions of sexuality show that respondents expect men to enact their masculinity by demonstrating a strong sexual appetite (Higgins and Browne 2008). But respondents differ by social class in their interpretations of where these appetites come from. Working-class participants believe that men's sex drives are rooted in biology and pretty much beyond the control of individual men. One woman explained, "Men, you know, need to spread their seed" (Higgins and Browne 2008, 234). Another working-class woman related the problems that could develop if men didn't have an outlet for their physical needs: "Nothing happens to a women if she doesn't have sex. But men get so messed up with sex that they'll wreck somebody. This can lead to rape sometimes. We can't avoid rape. It isn't right. But sometimes men get all pent up and they can't help it" (Higgins and Browne 2008, 236).

Middle-class participants believe that men's sexual appetites are influenced by the social position of men and therefore are more controllable. Middle-class respondents argued that men's social privilege allows them to expect sex. In addition, expectations that men should not express themselves emotionally may cause them to seem more interested in sex. One man explained, "There's a stereotype about sexual interest or libido, that men in general may be hornier than women. But men may want to express things sexually instead of emotionally. Demonstrating their feelings sexually is more appealing to men. Women have other outlets for emotion than men" (Higgins and Browne 2008, 235). Both social classes construct masculinity as closely connected to active sexuality. Because middle-class people believe that men's sexuality is less inevitable and more controllable by men, however, they also are more likely to incorporate ideas about making decisions about sex.

Higgins and Browne (2008) argue that these distinctions create important differences in the consequences of sex. The element of control allows for more effective decision making in sexual experience. As a result, middle-class men have a greater tendency to avoid risky behavior and are therefore more likely to practice birth control or to use condoms to protect themselves from STDs. For poorer men, however, the gender-class association of uncontrolled sex with masculinity encourages them to make bad decisions regarding both contraception and sexual health.

WHAT IS YOUR SEXUALITY?

This discussion of sexuality so far has focused on diversity among heterosexuals by gender, race, and class. Where does sexuality fit into the picture? The "ideal" heterosexual fantasizes, feels attracted to, and engages in sexual behavior only with members of the other sex. The "ideal" homosexual fantasizes, feels attracted to, and engages in sexual behavior only with members of the same sex (Jay 1996). But who is to say that there is such a thing as a "pure" heterosexual or homosexual? Fausto-Sterling (1993) argues that there are no universal categories of sex, gender, or sexuality that hold up over time and across cultures. You should recall from our discussion of sex and gender in chapter 2 that it is impossible to slot everyone into the two-sex model of man or woman. Similarly, not everyone is either gay or straight. Sex and gender do not fit together into an inevitable package, and sexuality and sex or sexuality and gender do not always fit together the same way. The range of real people and their actual sexual experiences challenges the conventional categories. Intersex, transgender third gender, bisexual, omnisexual, asexual, and transsexual are all part of the landscape of sexuality.

The terms **"sexual identity"** and **"sexual orientation"** refer to how people identify or classify themselves sexually. In the United States, we tend to assume that sexual behaviors and desires are consistent with identity or orientation. Most people in North America identify as heterosexual, gay, lesbian, or bisexual. Although these labels or categories have cultural currency—that is, we all understand their meanings—peoples' behaviors are not always consistent with their sexual identity. Table 4-2 shows the data from a recent study of sexuality in the United States. The study found that the numbers of people who identify as gay, lesbian, or bisexual are lower than the proportion that have had sex with someone of the same sex or who are attracted to those of the same sex (Mosher, Chandra, and Jones 2005). These contrasts have caused researchers to rethink categories and develop concepts that capture such behavior and identity differences, such as "men who have sex with men" and "lesbian or bisexual chic" (King 2004).

TABLE 4-2 Sexuality in the United States, 2002

	Women	Men
Identify as gay or lesbian*	1.3%	2.3%
Identify as bisexual*	2.8%	1.8%
Identify as heterosexual*	90.0%	90.0%
Identify as transgender**	0.3% (includes women and men)	
Had homosexual or lesbian experience*	11.2%	6.0%
Had sex with same-sex partner in last year	4.0%	3.0%
Had sex with same-sex partner and opposite sex in last year	3.0%	1.0%
Sexually attracted to opposite sex only*	86.0%	92.0%
Find the fantasy of homosexual or lesbian experience appealing	5.5%	6.0%

Source: Laumann et al. (1994); *Mosher, Chandra, and Jones (2005); **Gates (2011).

Lesbian or Bisexual Chic

The phenomenon in the United States and Canada referred to as "lesbian or bisexual chic" illustrates a mismatch between sexual behavior and sexual identity. Paula Rust (2002, 5) defines the phenomenon as "same-sex behavior engaged in by essentially heterosexual individuals under certain extenuating circumstances, in keeping with the cultural belief that there are only two true forms of sexuality" (Rust 2002, 2). She argues that the behavior is most likely found "in a cultural milieu favoring sexual experimentation." This includes bars, nightclubs, and teenage and college parties. Such "girl-on-girl" action was popularized by the *Girls Gone Wild* franchise, Hollywood star publicity such as the Madonna–Britney Spears kiss at the 2003 MTV Video Music Awards, and radio shock jocks such as Howard Stern.

In a popular advice book, Jen Sincero (2005) argues that getting physical with a woman does not imply what it used to—lesbianism. Sincero reports more than a hundred interviews with women who still think of themselves as heterosexual even though they have kissed or engaged in other sexual behaviors with women.

Some critics have suggested that the increasing cultural acceptance of "girl-on-girl" sexual relations is not necessarily progressive. They maintain that the images are marketed for audiences of heterosexual men and are focused on using women to please men (Luscombe 2004). Others are concerned that its popularization might perpetuate the myth that bisexuality is a phase and not a real sexual identity. On the other hand, it can be seen as subversive in its challenge to heterosexist social norms and patriarchal restrictions of "compulsory heterosexuality."

Bisexuality also creates challenges within gay and lesbian communities. According to a survey of 835 men and women, 35 percent of those who currently self-identified as bisexual had considered themselves gay or lesbian earlier in their lives (Fox 1995). Theories of lesbian and gay development have typically regarded bisexuality as a transitional phase on the way to establishing a lesbian or gay identity. Fox argues that bisexuality can be an endpoint stage itself, however. It is society's polarization of the categories of homosexual versus heterosexual that reinforce the idea that bisexuals are confused and that there cannot be any "in-between" categories of sexual identity.

Ochs and Deihl (1992) refer to the fear of the space between categories as *biphobia*. They argue that bisexuals are relegated to a "netherworld by heterosexuals and homosexuals alike," ostracized by the heterosexual community as well as by the lesbian and gay communities. Rust (1995) suggests that bisexuality poses a personal and political threat to lesbians because it undermines the political identity of the lesbian community as an oppressed **sexual minority** struggling for their civil rights. Rust's study of lesbian and bisexual women found that the majority of lesbian participants were reluctant to engage politically and socially with bisexual women. This unwillingness stems from a distrust of heterosexuals and heterosexist politics. As Rust explains, "To people who feel threatened, trust is a very important issue; in a heterosexual world, lesbians are threatened, and they do not trust bisexual women because bisexual women appear to be connected to that world" (101).

Ostracism of bisexuals within the gay and lesbian community is ironic because "the gay and lesbian liberation movement in the United States is united around the right to love whomever we please, and to have our relationships validated and recognized, even when they do not conform to society's norms. Bisexuals are often pushed into a closet within a closet" (Deihl and Ochs 2004, 183–84).

Men Who Have Sex with Men

One of the important examples of the disconnect between sexual identity and sexual behavior is men who do not identify as homosexual or bisexual but who engage in sex with other men. The popular term for this is the "down low (DL)" or "trade," and although it exists across many different racial ethnic communities in the United States, it has been identified in the both popular media and social science literature most closely with African American men (Lapinski, Braz, and Maloney 2010). People who exist on the down low are believed to do so, in part, because of their concerns over the social stigma attached to homosexuality. "**Stigma**" is a negative label that sets a person apart from others, links the labeled person to supposedly undesirable characteristics, and then discriminates against them (Goffman 1963). The stigmatizing of men who have sex with men is compounded by the stigmatizing of African American men whose sexuality has also been stereotyped as hypersexed and predatory by racist ideologies. In addition, Christian churches have been particularly critical of gay men, and the church is a powerful force in the black community. The confluence of these factors can create difficult restrictions for men. One DL man explained to interviewers:

> It makes me feel angry only in the sense that um . . . when our society makes them (DL men) feel that way. Because they're in denial about themselves. Our society says that men should be quote-un-quote masculine. They have to make the money, they can't have emotions, they can't . . . they can't be themselves. They must be this perfect being and they're not. They have feelings, they are real people, and there are different facets of men. And so . . . because they're on the DL they can't be themselves. So, that's why they're on the DL. (quoted in Lapinski et al. 2010, 620)

Most of the participants in the study by Lapinski et al. (2010), like the man quoted, believed that behavior was more important than identity. They contended that DL men were either in denial, ashamed of their homosexuality, or afraid that others would look down on them. It is possible, of course, that at least some DL men are not homosexual. Rather, they are bisexual. Or perhaps they are heterosexual men who have sex with men. Their experience suggests that we need to think more about the distinction between identity and behavior as two separable factors in our sexuality.

The quote reflects an important consequence of the stigma against homosexuality coupled with racist ideologies about African American men's sexuality—the emotional impact of marginalization. Another critical result is the inhibition of DL men to protect themselves from STDs, especially HIV. The term **"men who have sex with men"** (**MSM**) first appeared in the 1990s among health researchers who needed to find a way to tap into real sexual behavior in order to understand and promote healthy sex. If health care providers or researchers only ask people whether they are gay or heterosexual, they will have insufficient information to provide health care and health education that is appropriate to their patients' sexual activities.

Homophobia

Most people know that Jewish people in Germany were forced to wear arm bands with the symbol of a yellow star during the Nazi regime; fewer know about the arm bands with pink triangles. These were assigned to homosexual men and those suspected of being homosexual. It is estimated that one hundred thousand gay men were arrested, fifty thousand were imprisoned, and as many as fifteen thousand were sent to concentration camps, where many were killed. Heinrich Himmler, head of the Nazi police and security forces, was strongly homophobic. He created a special division of the Gestapo (secret state police) called the Reich Central Office for the Combating of Homosexuality and Abortion. Himmler's homophobia was connected to his sexism (Plant 1986). Himmler believed that homosexuals were "like women," who were weak and inferior to men. To Himmler, homosexuals were a disgrace to the state, and their presence, like that of Jewish and Roma peoples, would contaminate and demoralize the pure Aryan race. These were Himmler's justifications for annihilating homosexuals during the Nazi regime.

George Weinberg (1972) coined the term *homophobia* to describe the hatred Himmler expressed toward gay men and lesbians. Weinberg used this term because he thought it captured the "fear of contagion" he observed in clinical psychological situations where patients expressed fear of being tainted with the stigma of homosexuality and fear of being "gay by association" due to contact with homosexuals (Koch 2007).

Homophobia is intimately connected to sexism and the devaluation of anything feminine (Schwartz 2010). Gay men are stereotyped as effeminate in our culture, and lesbians are stereotyped as masculine "butches." When a girl who likes sports is called a "tomboy" and accused of being a "dyke," or a boy who does not like sports is called a "sissy" and accused of being a "faggot," it demonstrates the interplay between homophobia and sexism.

Suzanne Pharr (1988) expands on these links among heterosexuality, patriarchal power, and homophobia, arguing that homophobia is a weapon of sexism. To Pharr, hatred of gay men is based on fears that men who fail to uphold hegemonic masculinity will "bring down

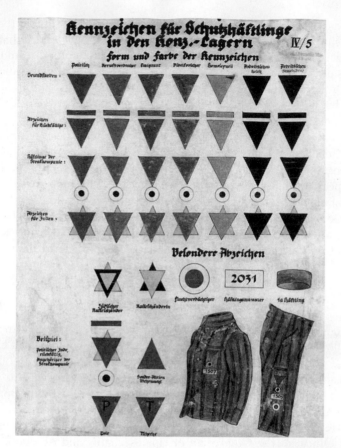

In concentration camps run by the Nazis during World War II, prisoners were designated as belonging to certain categories including Jews, Jehova's Witnesses, union organizers, communists, immigrants, and homosexuals. Each group was made to wear insignia identifying their category. The pink triangle was the symbol assigned to gay people.

Source: Deutsches Bundesarchiv.

the entire system of male dominance and compulsory heterosexuality" (18). Lesbian baiting is a way to control women who are independent, who struggle for women's human rights, and who "resist male dominance and control."

Heterosexism

As scholars and activists have developed their understanding of homophobia, they have come to feel that the concept is no longer sufficient. First, the term "homophobia" literally means "fear of homosexuals." Although fear may be a feature of what we see as homophobic behavior, hatred, anger, and aggression are even stronger components (Logan 1996; Herek 2004). See Box 4-3, for example, for a tragic story of a young man who was beaten and left to die.

GENDER IN EVERYDAY LIFE   BOX 4-3
VIOLENCE AGAINST GAY MEN: THE CASE OF MATTHEW SHEPARD

Last Saturday morning, while Matthew Shepard lay comatose from a beating, a college homecoming parade passed a few blocks from his hospital bed in Fort Collins, Colo. Propped on a fraternity float was a straw-haired scarecrow labeled in black spray paint, "I'm Gay."

Few people missed the message. Three days earlier, Mr. Shepard, a gay University of Wyoming freshman, was savagely beaten and tied to a ranch fence in such a position that a passer-by first mistook him for a scarecrow.

Today, officials at Colorado State University in Fort Collins reacted with outrage, opening an investigation and disciplinary procedures against the fraternity, Pi Kappa Alpha. The fraternity chapter immediately suspended seven members and said they had acted independently.

But in a week when candlelight vigils for Mr. Shepard were being held on campuses across the nation, the scarecrow incident highlighted how hostility toward homosexuals often flourishes in high schools and universities, gay leaders said today.

"People would like to think that what happened to Matthew was an exception to the rule, but it was an extreme version of what happens in our schools on a daily basis," said Kevin Jennings, executive director of the Gay, Lesbian and Straight Education Network, a New York group dedicated to ending anti-gay bias in the schools.

Mr. Shepard, a slightly built 21-year-old was beaten so severely that he died on Monday. He never regained consciousness after being discovered on Oct. 7, 18 hours after he was lashed to the fence. Two men, Russell A. Henderson, 21, and Aaron J. McKinney, 22, were arraigned on first degree murder charges late Monday night. Their girlfriends, Chasity V. Pasley, 20, and Kristen L. Price, 18, have been arraigned as accessories after the fact.

In response to the killing, about 50 candlelight vigils were scheduled this week, from Texas to Vermont, from Wayne, Neb., to New York City.

At the Poudre Valley Hospital in Fort Collins where Mr. Shepard was in intensive care for five days, his parents, Dennis and Judy Shepard, received about 6,000 electronic messages of condolences. Today, when funeral arrangements were announced for Friday in Casper, Wyo., the hospital Web site received 30,000 hits an hour.

University friends in Laramie, Wyo., have set up the Matthew Shepard Memorial Fund to raise money to pressure the state Legislature to pass legislation against hate crimes.

"I see his name going down in gay history as a catalyst for renewed activism," said Matt Foreman, a former Wyomingite who directs Empire State Pride Agenda, a gay political organization in New York.

From around the nation today, gay leaders emphasized that campus homophobia was not restricted to college towns in the Rocky Mountain West.

Last year, in a survey of almost 4,000 Massachusetts high school students, 22 percent of gay respondents said they had skipped school in the past month because they felt unsafe there, and 31 percent said they had been threatened or injured at school in the past year. These percentages were about five times greater than the percentages of heterosexual respondents. The survey was conducted at 58 high schools by the Massachusetts Department of Education.

In a separate study of nearly 500 community college students in the San Francisco area, 32 percent of male respondents said they had verbally threatened homosexuals and 18 percent said they had physically threatened or assaulted them. The study was conducted this year by Karen Franklin, a forensic psychologist who is a researcher at the University of Washington.

Surveys of gay college students conducted in the late 1980's at Yale University, Oberlin College, Rutgers University and Pennsylvania State University found that 16 percent to 26 percent had been threatened with violence, and that 40 percent to 76 percent had been verbally harassed, said the National Gay and Lesbian Task Force, a lobbying group based in Washington.

Last year, a Des Moines student group, Concerned Students, recorded hallway and classroom conversations at five high schools on 10 "homophobia recording days." They estimated that the average Des Moines high school student heard about 25 anti-gay remarks every day.

"Nine out of 10 'teaching tolerance' courses weed out gays," Mr. Foreman said. "There are a lot of people preaching anti-racism and anti-Semitism. But it is still very much O.K. to make anti-gay jokes, to express anti-gay sentiments."

A survey of the nation's 42 largest school districts found that 76 percent did not train teachers on issues facing gay students and 42 percent lacked policies to protect students from discrimination based on sexual orientation, said the Gay, Lesbian and Straight Education Network, which did the study last month.

In Fort Collins, while the hospital officials struggled with an electronic avalanche of condolences, city police detectives were investigating a different kind of E-mail.

On Monday, hours after Mr. Shepard's death, two gay organizations, the Rainbow Chorus and the Lambda Community Center, received identical messages applauding the killing of Mr. Shepard. The messages closed with the words, "I hope it happens more often."

SOURCE: James Brooke, "Homophobia Often Found in Schools, Data Show," *New York Times*, Oct. 14, 1998, http://www.nytimes.com/1998/10/14/us/homophobia-often-found-in-schools-data-show .html?src=pm. Copyright 2002 The New York Times Company. Used with permission.

Some scholars have argued that the continued use of the term "homophobia" may not only be a mislabel, it may even help to excuse hostile behavior as the (understandable) result of inescapable fear (Logan 1996).

Another reason why the term is inadequate is that *homophobia* refers only to individual beliefs and behaviors, not to institutionalized discrimination. A concept that directs us to consider the antihomosexual beliefs and practices embedded in social institutions is ***heterosexism***. A list of examples of heterosexism is given in Box 4-4.

A good way to understand heterosexism is by looking at another form of prejudice and privilege, racism and white privilege, that has been explained by scholars. Peggy McIntosh (1988) uses the metaphor of an "invisible knapsack" to illustrate how white privilege functions:

> I have come to see white privilege as an invisible package of unearned assets that I can count on cashing in each day, but about which I was "meant" to remain oblivious. White privilege is like an invisible weightless knapsack of special provisions, assurances, tools, maps, guides, codebooks, passports, visas, clothes, compass, emergency gear, and blank checks. (95)

McIntosh argues that white people are not taught to see how racism puts them in a position of privilege but rather come to view it only as something that puts racial/ethnic minorities at a disadvantage. Take the issue of routine police stops that have been labeled "driving while black." According to the U.S. Department of Justice, African Americans are more

---

GENDER IN EVERYDAY LIFE   BOX 4-4
EXAMPLES OF HETEROSEXISM

- Assuming that everyone that you meet is heterosexual
- Assuming that everyone has or is interested in having an opposite-sex partner
- Assuming that all mothers and fathers are heterosexual
- Assuming all sexually active women use birth control
- Assuming that all unmarried people are "single" while in reality they may have a same-sex partner
- Assuming all children live in families with a man–woman couple as parental roles
- Using language that presumes heterosexuality in others, such as husband or wife, instead of gender-neutral language, such as partner
- Using official forms that allow only for designation as married or single
- Denying equal employment benefits to people with same-sex partners, such as spousal insurance
- Omitting any discussion of LGBTQ persons as part of educational curricula

SOURCE: Out Wilmington On-Line Community and Resource Center (2011).

GENDER IN EVERYDAY LIFE   BOX 4-5

EXAMPLES OF HETEROSEXUAL PRIVILEGE

- Ability to talk openly, comfortably, and without fear of judgment about one's friends, social activities, and personal relationships
- Never having one's normalcy questioned
- Ability to show affection in public with one's partner without fear of negative reactions or hostility
- Ability to have children without any questions of one's fitness to do so
- Right to legally marry
- Right to purchase insurance benefits for a partner, such as health care
- Right to job security and freedom from sanctioned discrimination
- Right to take family or medical leave for a partner
- Ability to purchase family memberships in health clubs or other recreational activities
- Validation of one's human dignity by one's chosen religion

SOURCE: Out Wilmington On-Line Community and Resource Center (2011).

likely to be pulled over by the police than are whites. During a traffic stop, police are almost three times more likely to carry out some type of search on an African American (9.5 percent) or a Latino motorist (8.8 percent) than they are on a white motorist (3.6 percent) (U.S. Department of Justice 2007). Searches of whites in traffic stops are four times more likely to find criminal evidence (14.5 percent) than their African American counterparts (3.3 percent) and slightly more than their Latino counterparts (13 percent) (U.S. Department of Justice 2005).

The racial discrepancy is often explained as an illustration of racism in policing. An overlooked aspect of this form of racial discrimination is the advantage to white people who are pulled over and searched less frequently. This is white privilege.

Similarly, if we were to look in the heterosexual invisible knapsack we would see hospital policies that allow heterosexuals to visit their spouses in the hospital without the worry that they might be kicked out because of their sexual orientation or forced to pose as their loved one's relative; this is heterosexual privilege. Box 4-5 lists several examples of other invisible heterosexual privileges we might find in the knapsack.

COMPETING PERSPECTIVES ON GENDERED SEXUALITY

A central theme in research on sexualities has been understanding gender differences in sexual behaviors and attitudes. Scholars have created several positions on this question, including a biological framework, a sexual script framework, and a queer theory framework.

Biology

The biological framework focuses on the physiological aspects of sex. The underlying assumption of this framework is that sex is primarily a biological experience, and therefore if we wish to understand it, we need to examine the body's response to sexual stimulation. This perspective is represented by William Masters, a gynecologist, and Virginia Johnson, a psychologist, who were pioneers in sexuality research and founded the field we know today as sex therapy. They focused exclusively on physical sexuality to understand bodily differences in sexual arousal of males and females. Their research involved extensive laboratory observations of more than 10,000 sexual encounters from a sample of 382 women and 312 men (Masters and Johnson 1966). Photographs and measurement instruments recorded muscular and vascular changes in vaginas and penises, revealing that the key difference in patterns of arousal is in the timing of the excitement. The male cycle of arousal from excitement to plateau to orgasm is much quicker than the female cycle. However, the male refractory period (or the time needed before sexual excitement and erection can be resumed) is much slower, in comparison. This led Masters and Johnson to highlight women's capacity for multiple orgasms and to take note of their sexual stamina. These differences in arousal cycles formed the basis of their theory of the mismatch of mating styles. They advocated sexual counseling that would enable men and women to become more synchronized with each other sexually. In other words, they advocated teaching men to slow down.

Masters and Johnson were not concerned with the social environment and external factors that affect sexuality. Instead, their exploration of male and female sexual response focused on biological factors. They did not question what males and females might have experienced prior to their visit to their labs or how they thought and felt about sex. In our review of hooking up, for example, we noted that women were more likely to orgasm if they engaged in self-stimulation during sex. Masturbation, however, is more taboo for women in American society, and therefore women may appear in a lab experiment to be slower to arouse because they have less knowledge about their bodies and feel less comfortable being sexual. These issues, however, are not part of the work of researchers whose concern is biology alone. The research of Masters and Johnson is important, but it cannot be taken out of the specific historical, social, and political context in which their subjects lived and be generalized to all human beings.

Masters' and Johnson's work is recognized as scientifically sound, and although it is narrow in its view of sexuality, it is not explicitly political. Another example of a biological perspective can be found in the work of scientists who have attempted to explain homosexuality as biologically determined. This work is methodologically flawed and controversial in its political implications. The work of Simon LeVay (1991), a neurobiologist, is one example. LeVay examined the brain tissues of forty-one deceased people in his research on homosexuality. He found that the anterior hypothalamus was twice the size in the men believed to be heterosexual than in the men who identified as homosexual and bisexual. The anterior hypothalamuses of the homosexual and bisexual men were the same size as those of the six deceased women in the sample. From these findings, LeVay deduced that there is a biological basis to sexual orientation.

LeVay's work has been strongly criticized, because nearly half of his sample had died of AIDS, including all of the gay men in the study. HIV is known to reduce testosterone and affect the brain. This means that LeVay might only have been measuring the dual effect of

HIV infection and high-strength formaldehyde solution (in which the brains of gay men were preserved out of fear of HIV transmission) and not differences in brain structure of heterosexuals and homosexuals (Kimmel 2004).

Claims that there is a "gay gene" or that homosexuals show androgen deficiencies have been put forward to show that sexual orientation has its basis in biology. None of these studies search for the "straight gene" or for hormonal imbalances among heterosexuals. Because heterosexuality is posited as the norm, the hormones, brain structures, and genetic composition of heterosexual people become the standard from which all other sexualities are measured and judged. This **"othering"** of sexual minorities is part of "heterosexism," which privileges the position of heterosexuals.

Nevertheless, the view that our sexuality is innate is increasingly common in popular discourse and has been an important part of much gay rights activism (Wolf 2009). D'Emilio (2009), a gay rights activist and scholar, explains:

> The idea that people are born gay—or lesbian, or bisexual—is appealing for lots of reasons. Many of us experience the direction of our sexual desires as something that we have no control over. We just are that way, it seems, so therefore we must be born gay. The people who are most overt in their hatred of queer folks, the religious conservatives, insist that being gay is something we choose, and we know we can't agree with them. Hence, again, born gay. Liberal heterosexual allies love the idea. If gays are born that way, then of course they shouldn't be punished for it. "Born gay" is also a relief to any of us who have some doubts about our ourselves or feel ourselves sinking under the weight of the oppression. If we're born gay, then it's not our fault, and we're certainly not choosing to be oppressed: we just can't help it so leave us alone. It also answers those who worry about the effect of too many out-of-the-closet gay men and lesbians: if people are born this way, then young people won't be influenced by us. (D'Emilio 2009)

The argument that sexuality is a matter of biology—the argument that we are born gay or heterosexual—has been an important piece of the political rhetoric of gay rights activists. But the research on which it is based is not valid, and the argument is problematic because it ignores the plasticity of human sexuality and the broad range of ways people identify and experience their sexuality across time and place.

Sexual Scripts

A second framework has been developed by scholars who take a **social constructionist** view of the issues. They argue that the categories that we often take for granted and accept as real are in fact, socially constructed; that is, people and groups interact within particular sociohistorical contexts. John Gagnon and his collaborator William Simon were the first to apply social constructionism to sexual behavior, and their theory of social scripts became the dominant view in the last half of the twentieth century in the United States (Kimmel 2007).

Gagnon and Simon's (1973) theory of **sexual scripts** holds that sexual relations are scripted interactions based on prevailing gender ideologies. It is based on the dramaturgic sociology of Erving Goffman (1959), who argued that in their everyday lives people are like actors performing on a stage, playing roles for an audience. In the dramaturgical tradition,

Gagnon and Simon (1973) apply the notion of the "script" to show how sexual interactions follow a sequence of dialogue and actions like those in a play. Gagnon (1977) argued that although sex sometimes appears to be something special, biologically determined, and apart from the rest of our social selves, sex really isn't very different from anything else we do:

> In any given society, at any given moment, people become sexual in the same way as they become everything else. Without much reflection, they pick up directions from their social environment. They acquire and assemble meanings, skills, and values from the people around them. Their critical choices are often made by going along and drifting. People learn when they are quite young a few of the things that they are expected to be, and continue slowly to accumulate a belief in who they are and ought to be through the rest of childhood, adolescence and adulthood. Sexual conduct is learned in the same way through the same processes: it is acquired and assembled in human interaction, judged and performed in specific cultural and historical worlds. (Gagnon 1977, 2)

Gagnon and Simon distinguished among three different levels of sexual scripts: cultural scenarios, interpersonal scripts, and intrapsychic scripts. Cultural scenarios refer to the large social-context issues that tell us what sex is and how it should make us feel or behave. The messages we receive from schools, religious institutions, and the media would be examples of cultural sources of the frameworks and roles through which we experience sex. Intrapsychic scripts are the ones that play out in our heads as we go about collecting, assembling, and reflecting on our experiences. Interpersonal scripts are the more microlevel interactions and relationships we have with family and friends, from which we pick up cues or lessons about sexuality.

Nicholas Solebello and Sinikka Elliott (2011) explored the particular role that fathers play in these interpersonal scripts by interviewing twenty-five fathers about their beliefs and experiences in regard to sex education of their teenage children. They found that the fathers care a great deal about their sons being heterosexual and work hard to shape their sons' behavior to fit conventional models of **heteronormativity**. The fathers look for evidence that their sons are heterosexual and blame themselves if the sons do not seem to be sexually interested enough in girls. The fathers are more accepting of the idea that their daughters might be lesbians, but they also take their daughters' sexuality less seriously. For example, when one father was asked about how he would feel if he found out his daughter or son was gay, he said, "I don't think it would make any difference if it was my daughter but with a son . . . I think I would feel like I had failed in coaching in some way . . . that I didn't coach, advise, [or] lead in a way to help clarify some of those thoughts." (302)

Another father explained that although he would be accepting of his son if he were gay he would be relieved if the son showed a sexual interest in girls as it would be a clear sign that he was heterosexual. He explained,

> There were moments when I wondered if he was going to be gay . . . and if I had my choice I wish that he wouldn't be, but if he was I knew that my wife and I would both be fine with it. . . . And then just watching for clues you know? Is he more interested in men than women? And then he started to move very clearly into the female direction so there was a sense of OK! [Paul does a fist pump in the air.] Chip off the old block. (303)

In contrast, the fathers of daughters were more concerned with what they perceived to be their daughters' sexual vulnerability. The fathers of daughters did not express a sense of accountability for their daughters' sexual orientation as they did for the sons, but they strongly expressed feeling responsible for protecting their daughters from boys and sexual harm. One of the fathers explained that he tells his daughter, "'Okay, honey, right now you have something that's valuable. Right? You have your sex. And the guys, they want it'" (307). And, on the other hand, some of the fathers spoke of joking with their daughters about their close friendships with their girlfriends. The fathers' concern that their daughters show the right signs of heterosexuality is less pronounced. Solebello and Elliot (2011) however, argue that the professed acceptance of lesbianism by the fathers may stem from their belief that it is just the way some girls try to gain attention from boys or a phase some girls go through before permanently establishing their true heterosexual identities.

HOW TO BE A HETEROSEXUAL

The conventional script for contemporary heterosexual performance in the United States contains eight overarching requirements. Pepper Schwartz (2007) outlined the rules for properly playing the role of a heterosexual:

1. In order to be truly heterosexual we must be a masculine man or a feminine woman dressed properly and behaving in a manner that will sexually attract people of the other gender.
2. When we play this properly gendered heterosexual role correctly, we can expect applause and we are protected from the stigma of being identified as gay or lesbian.
3. We must have certain kinds of bodies to play the role properly. It is not just a matter of costuming. Our bodies must conform to ideals of femininity or masculinity. Our sexual identity as heterosexual means that that our breasts are a certain size, our shoulders have a specific amount of bulk, and our bodies are covered with hair in only the proper places, for example.
4. In order to be heterosexual, we must always be aroused and only be aroused by the opposite sex.
5. Heterosexual arousal must be strong and unambiguous. We cannot slip from our sexual performance. If we are unable to meet this requirement, but wish to maintain our heterosexuality, we might be required to seek medical help or take drugs, such a Viagra (Tiefer 2007).
6. The opposite sex must be attracted to us. If they are not, we might be counted as either desexed or homosexual.
7. Once we have established our heterosexuality (or not), it is stable and unconflicted. One cannot be heterosexual at one point in one's life and then gay, lesbian, or bisexual at another. We only have one true sexuality.
8. Heterosexuals must have intercourse. Other forms of sexual interaction are foreplay, afterplay, or tangential, they are not real sex for heterosexuals.

In addition to playing these roles as individuals, we live out scripts in our heterosexual interactions with others. These follow predictable, prescribed sequences of events that have been popularized in our culture, where men are supposed to be the dominant sexual initiators, and women are supposed to be sexually shy and submissive but also the sexual gatekeepers (deciding if and how far the sexual encounter will go).

As discussed in chapter 3, sexual scripts are shared cultural instructions for "normal" sexual behaviors. These behaviors are different for men and women. Men must adopt a dominant role in the sexual encounter both as the verbal initiator and even in their sexual position (Steedman 1987). They must appear more "into" the sex, or at least vocalize their desire more than women do. According to sexual script theorists, in Western culture sex means love and intimacy for women and orgasm and physical pleasure for men. The actors' roles in a traditionally scripted sexual encounter are thus extensions of a society's expectations of gender. Women initiating sex and embracing sexual pleasure, men who wait for women to initiate, and gay men and lesbians are all deviants from their "proper roles."

These descriptions of all of the social rules associated with being a heterosexual show us how unnatural sexuality is. Sex is not something that appears to be driven by biological inevitability. Rather, it appears to be something that requires a lot of social learning. Being a heterosexual and engaging in heterosexual encounters necessitates careful study and much practice. Since we go about this study and practice in our daily lives, and because we do so usually with little reflection, it appears to be natural. Schwartz's outline, however, shows us just how much effort goes into the production of heterosexuality. Schwartz's outline also emerges from her observations of sexuality in contemporary American society. How might the rules and roles, costuming, and dialogue be different in other times and places?

Besides limiting our experience and expression of sexuality, scripts can also have direct negative consequences. For example, feminists have used the concept of sexual scripts to explain gendered patterns of violence. The emphasis on men's initiation and pleasure in traditional sexual scripts is thought to be linked to men's sexual aggression. Men are supposed to be demanding sex and women are supposed to be the sexual gatekeeper as well as the passive recipient "on the bottom," making men more likely to think they must aggressively seek sexual encounters and making it more difficult for women to refuse unwanted sex (Tolman and Higgins 1996, 209).

These sexual scripts create barriers to egalitarian heterosexual relationships, and there is some evidence that they play a part in rape and sexual violence. For example, in rape trials before the feminist reforms of the 1980s, women's actions, dress, and words could become implicated in the rape. Often the rape victim herself was on trial, as rapists' excuses and justifications—"she asked for it" or "no *really* means yes"—blamed the victim for the crime (Smart 1989). Although the laws have changed regarding rape trials, today, these same ideas have emerged in the debates around abortion. Todd Akin, a member of the House of Representatives for 12 years, for example, argued in a campaign speech that in a "legitimate rape" female bodies "shut down" and block conception. Women who were adhering to a supposedly legitimate sexual script, therefore, cannot become pregnant if they are raped. This assertion, of course, is not valid, but it shows the persistence of beliefs about what is legitimate feminine sexuality.

Traditional sexual scripts are also associated with decreased condom usage and thus increased risk of HIV and other STDs. Research shows that most women want men to use condoms, but because men control the sexual activity, they also control condom use. And, because men are supposed to be risk takers and desperate for sex, they do not want anything to create a barrier to their pleasure. In this way, stereotyped versions of masculinity and femininity work together to inhibit the use of condoms.

Queer Theory

"As far as I'm concerned, being any gender is a drag" (musician Patti Smith, quoted in Levine 1998). The third framework for exploring the connections between genders and sexualities is called **queer theory**. The term "queer" was once used as an insult against gay men and lesbians, but it has been appropriated as a source of pride and reclaimed to unify all sexual minorities, not just gay men and lesbians. This includes other marginalized sexual identities such as bisexuality, transsexualism, and transgenderism, as well as discredited sexual communities such as sadomasochism (S&M) and other fetish communities. Queerness is subversive because it challenges sexual norms—what might be called the "regime of normalization"—from the position of outsiders (Epstein 1994). The "regime of normalization" refers to the domination of the "shoulds" and "musts" and sanctions that hold society and its members in place. In this way, queer theory serves an important political function, as well as an important theoretical function, helping us understand ties among genders and sexualities.

Queer theorists, like social constructionists, assert that sexualities are created through social interaction. Queer theorists go further, however, rejecting traditional categories of sexual orientation like homosexuality, heterosexuality, or any fixed identity. Kinsey and his colleagues were among the first to try to capture queer theorists' insights about the dynamic and diverse character of sexuality. More than fifty years ago, before queer theory had become a theoretical perspective, Kinsey (Kinsey, Pomeroy, and Martin 1948; Kinsey, Pomeroy, Martin, and Gebhard, 1953) proposed a continuum that recognized the fluidity of sexuality and more accurately described peoples' sexual experiences.

Building on the work of Kinsey and Michel Foucault (1978), one of the original theorists to explore the social construction of sexuality and gender, contemporary queer theorist Judith Butler (1990) challenges the naturalness of sexuality. Like other theorists who use the idea of sexual script, Butler sees gender and sexuality as an act or a performance, a form of "drag" where people play the role of a man or a woman, and sometimes a "sexy" man or woman. If we see a male wearing a wig and makeup and a tight, low-cut, pink satin gown, we understand it as a performance of gender and sexuality; and many people would laugh because it seems inconsistent with the man's true gender. But how is he any different from a female wearing the same costume? Isn't she performing sexual femininity also?

Butler goes further with this concept, noting how the roles are scripted in ways that create and maintain structures of power and inequality. In addition to privileging men over women, the performance privileges heterosexuality by making it appear natural. The male in the pink gown appears to be gay (because he is appearing to be trying to attract a man) and feminine and therefore laughable. The female in the pink gown appears to be feminine and heterosexual and therefore attractive. Butler's ideas recall Rich's concept of "compulsory heterosexuality." Butler challenges the gay and lesbian claim that homosexuality is as natural as heterosexuality. She claims that all of it—heterosexuality and homosexuality—is unnatural. All "identities" are performances, not essences.

In her book *Gender Trouble*, Butler (1990) writes, "There is no gender identity behind the expressions of gender; . . . identity is performatively constituted by the very 'expressions' that are said to be its results" (25). In other words, we produce the illusion of gendered essences in performing them. The essences are no more "real" than the performance. Gender is nothing but the performance of gender. Queer theory totally severs biological sex, social gender, and desire. Therefore, according to Butler, we cannot be slotted into a few categories. Rather, our sexuality—identity, feelings, opinions, fantasies, and behavior—creates complex variations of many types. Furthermore, these feelings, identities, fantasies, and behaviors are socially constructed, acted, and reenacted as we relate with one another.

SEX FOR SALE

Sex sells. Advertising products such as cars or beer in a commercial with a thin, attractive, big-breasted model has become a cliché in American culture—sex, itself, really does sell. The business of sex or how sex is bought and sold like a commodity in the marketplace is an important dimension of gendered sexuality. In the global marketplace, **sex work** is one of the largest and fastest-growing industries. Although men and women are involved in both the provision and consumption of sex through prostitution, pornography, stripping and exotic dancing, and for-profit telephone sex and cybersex, men make up the majority of consumers and women are the majority of workers. Take pornography as an example.

Pornography

In the United States alone, the pornography industry totals $13.3 billion in sales each year, which is more than the profits of the NBA, the NFL, and Major League Baseball combined. The porn industry is bigger than ABC, NBC, and CBS combined, and adult bookstores in the United States outnumber McDonald's restaurants by a margin of three to one (Kimmel 2008). Worldwide, the pornography industry is worth close to $60 billion (Ropelato 2007). The sheer volume of videos, websites, and magazines produced each year is staggering. In the Los Angeles area—the center of U.S. porn production—11,000 hard-core pornographic movies are produced annually. Hollywood, in comparison, produces an average of 400 major movies each year (Jensen 2010). Pornography on the Internet increased from 14 million websites in 1998 to 260 million in 2003, and by 2005, there were 1.5 billion porn downloads a month (Kimmel 2008).Video pornography is the most popular and profitable sector of the industry, with an average of 700 million pornographic videos rented each year (F. Rich 2001). Recently, revenue from pornographic videos has declined. But the numbers suggest that while less money may be generated because of the availability of free or pirated videos on the Internet, popularity hasn't waned (Dines and Bialer 2012). Table 4-3 shows the breakdown in terms of revenue of the industry as a whole.

Because the sources are industry insiders like *Adult Video News*, an industry trade magazine, some skepticism about these statistics may be warranted. According to David Klatell, associate Dean of the Columbia Graduate School of Journalism, "[pornography] is an

TABLE 4-3 Pornography Industry Revenue in the United States for 2006 (in Billions)

Video sales and rental	$3.62
Internet	$2.84
Cable/pay-per-view/in-room/mobile/phone sex	$2.00
Exotic dance clubs	$2.19
Novelties	$1.73
Magazines	$0.95
Total	$13.33

Source: Ropelato (2007).

industry where they exaggerate the size of everything" (Ackman 2001). Nevertheless, pornography is a pervasive industry all over the world.

GENDERED PORN. The number of adult films, magazines, websites, and clubs targeted for heterosexual women has risen in recent years, as has the entire gay and lesbian porn industry. The latter is one of the fastest-growing sectors of the entire industry. In addition, pornography not explicitly geared toward women and gay men and lesbians does not mean, however, that it is not consumed by them. For instance, *Playboy*—the grandfather of heterosexual men's magazines—estimates that 17 percent of the magazine's readers are women (Frontline 2002). Nevertheless, most pornography is targeted to heterosexual men. Naked or partially naked women are presented in sexual poses or engaging in sex acts catering to men's sexual fantasies. Seventy-two percent of visitors to pornographic websites are men (Ropelato 2007), and men, on average, consume more (both in terms of volume and duration) pornographic materials than women.

Heterosexual video pornography is the largest genre of pornography and comprises two types of films: (1) features that mimic a Hollywood film in terms of a script, set, and characters and often in their titles, such as *Pulp Friction*, *Saving Ryan's Privates*, and *There's Something In and Out of Mary*, and (2) gonzos, which are amateur films of recorded sex with no story lines. Three main themes dominate in heterosexually focused pornographic film (Dines and Jensen 2004):

1. All women want sex from men.
2. Women like all the sexual acts that men perform or demand.
3. Any woman who does not at first realize her desire for sex can be easily persuaded with a little force. Such force is rarely necessary, however, for most of the women in pornography are "nymphomaniacs," always on the lookout for sexual encounters and hyperorgasmic sex.

Heterosexual video pornography perpetuates stereotyped sexual scripts, with men as the subjects in control of the sexual situation and women as objects whose role is to fulfill men's desires (Dines and Jensen 2004). The focus in this genre is on vaginal, oral, and anal penetration, women performing fellatio on men and cunnilingus on other women, and ejaculations onto women—the cum, or money shot—as indicators of men's heterosexual fantasies in the films. Common sexual positions in this genre such as the "reverse cowgirl," with the woman on top and facing away from the man, and "double penetration," in which two men simultaneously enter the woman (vaginally and anally), maximize the visibility of women's bodies and facilitate getting close-ups of women's genitals. Men's bodies, on the other hand, are not scrutinized in the same way. Their penises are only focused on at the point of ejaculation, and men often remain clothed in the films up until the sex requires them to undress.

For young men, pornography may serve as the primary form of sex education, and the images may be the first they see of sex or even women's bodies. They learn that " 'the world of pornography is easy.' It makes few relationship demands; it asks little of men morally, intellectually, politically, and offers so much in return: the illusion of power and control. Pornography allows 'gratification without vulnerability, without risk to the self' " (Beneke 1983, 84, cited in Kimmel 2008, 178). Kimmel argues that men in America are told that the fundamental way they must prove they are men is to have sex with women, many women, many conventionally beautiful women. The young men he interviewed found that real women were not the compliant and willing partners to which they had been led to believe they were entitled.

> Pornography is a moment of reassuring voyeurism for these almost-men. Most of them have certainly had less experience than they'd like, and they are still trying to figure out how they measure up. Women in pornography are portrayed as the fantasized ideal—always ready and willing, always orgasmic, completely satisfied with you and always wanting more. (Kimmel 2008, 173)

Pornography provides a vehicle for getting back at or getting around the real women in men's lives who do not respond to the entitlement demands of men trying to prove their manhood.

THE FEMINIST CENSORSHIP DEBATE. "The objectification of women in pornography is a foundation of the genre, and the gender hierarchy that pervades the wider culture is, if anything, more intense in the pornographic world" (Dines and Jensen 2004, 370). This view is shared by a number of antipornography scholars, including many feminists. However, not all feminists agree. Pornography is a divisive issue among feminists (Segal 1993). At the heart of the debate is whether or not pornography is oppressive and contributes to violence against women. Also at issue is the extent to which pornography should be controlled by the government or censored.

There are three positions held by feminists in the debate over pornography. Antiporn feminists hold that pornography is an expression of men's sexual dominance that commodifies, objectifies, and exploits women. They assert that sexuality is the source of women's subordination in society and claim that pornography is an instrument of power that reinforces women's oppression. Catharine MacKinnon (1987), a major spokesperson for this point of view, writes that pornography is "sexual terrorism" that eroticizes rape and sexual abuse and promotes violence against women. She and radical feminist Andrea Dworkin (1981) believe that the laws should emphasize women's rights and the courts should protect those rights. They argue that pornography should be treated as a violation of women's civil rights and the courts should allow women harmed by pornography to seek damages through civil suits (Barnett 2013). Ironically, antiporn feminists have aligned with the religious right on the subject of pornography.

A second point of view is held by liberal feminists who argue that on the basis of free speech and civil liberties, pornography should not be regulated, despite the fact that some (including many liberal feminists themselves) find it personally offensive or morally reprehensible. They argue that feminists have a lot to lose by supporting censorship. These feminists are anticensorship but not pro-pornography.

The least understood and, perhaps, least heard position in the pornography debate is that of the third position, pro-sex feminists. **Pro-sex feminists**, like liberal feminists, are against censorship because they view it as an attack on free speech and civil rights. Pro-sex feminists argue further that pornography can have benefits for women (McElroy 1995; Strossen 1995). Judith Kegan Gardiner (1993) sees several positive aspects for women. She writes:

> For some women, pornography may actually de-objectify women because they can use it to validate their own desires and pleasures. They can also reinterpret or take control of the fantasy. For example, they may point out that a particular pictured position is not fun, but awkward and uncomfortable. Furthermore, women too can make comparisons between their lovers and the performers, for instance to the male stars' larger organs or more sustained erections, and they can use the pornography to encourage or instruct their partners how to please them. (331)

McElroy (1995) suggests that pornography benefits women politically in ways similar to feminism:

> Pornography is one of the windows through which women glimpse the sexual possibilities that are open to them. It is nothing more or less than freedom of speech applied to the sexual realm. Feminism is freedom of speech applied to women's sexual rights.
>
> Both pornography and feminism rock the conventional view of sex. They snap the traditional ties between sex and marriage, sex and motherhood. They both threaten family values and flout the status quo. (128)

Instead of viewing women as degraded and exploited in pornography as anti-porn feminists and liberal feminists do, pro-sex feminists claim that women are sexual agents, subjects and not objects, who make choices and decisions about their bodies and sexualities. The questions over whether women are victims or agents in controversial sexual practices is also part of the debate over another important feminist issue—prostitution.

Sex Workers

Many people think of "hookers" or "streetwalkers" when they think of sex work: young, scantily clad women walking a downtown street in search of a "trick" or a "date." But most sex work is off the street, in saunas and spas, brothels, massage parlors, and through escort services and exotic dancing venues. Most people also think of women when they think of sex workers, but not all sex workers are women. In the United States, 67.2 percent of all people arrested for prostitution are women (Federal Bureau of Investigation 2010).

Clients of sex workers are almost exclusively men, and that holds true for both men and women sex workers. It is estimated that 16 percent of adult men in the United States have paid for sex (Laumann, Gagnon, Michael, and Michaels 1994). Nevada, where prostitution is legal in ten counties, is home to thirty-five licensed brothels. The clientele consists of men construction workers, military personnel, truckers, and tourists. Aside from the occasional heterosexual couple who come to one of the brothels, the industry is geared toward serving men. The Chicken Ranch, a brothel in Pahrump, Nevada, also known as "The Best Little Whorehouse in the West," offers special promotions for "birthday boys." The Bunny Ranch offered free sex to the first fifty soldiers to arrive at the ranch who had served in Iraq. This unique patriotic gesture amounted to $50,000 in sexual services (BBC News 2003).

LEGAL PROSTITUTION. There are around three hundred legally registered sex workers in Nevada. All are women. Plans for opening a Stud Farm—a brothel with men as sex workers—in Nye County, Nevada, to be owned and operated by legendary Hollywood madam Heidi Fleiss, fell through and she has now decided to open a string of laundromats instead (Brean 2009). Sex workers in Nevada are legal, they are tested weekly for STDs and monthly for HIV, and they must use condoms. Brothels typically take half the sex workers' earnings and enforce health and safety laws. Since the mid- to late 1980s, when the mandatory health testing and condom laws took effect, not a single licensed brothel sex worker in Nevada has ever tested positive for HIV (Albert 2001). In the remaining counties of Nevada and all other states in the United States, prostitution is against the law and classified as a misdemeanor.

In many countries, however, such as Australia, Canada, Israel, Mexico, Singapore, Brazil, Venezuela, New Zealand, and most of Europe, prostitution is legal. It is often heavily regulated, with restrictions on advertising and soliciting. In Denmark, prostitution is not illegal as long as it is not a woman's sole means of income. The Netherlands restricts prostitution to brothels. In the famous Red Light District of Amsterdam, several hundred one-room shops are rented out by sex workers who typically sit in the windows to attract passersby. Sex workers are treated as self-employed tradespersons in the Netherlands. They are unionized, pay taxes, and have full access to health and social services.

In Canada, recent changes in the laws have made important alterations to sex work. Buying and selling sex in Canada is not illegal, but until recently, soliciting and running a brothel was. The recent court decision invalidates the prohibition on "bawdy houses," which advocates believe will improve the safety of sex workers by allowing them to legally work together indoors without fear of eviction or arrest. A second law that prohibited living on the income of another person's sex work was also invalidated. This law was intended to protect sex workers from pimps. In practice, however, it made the sex workers' family members (e.g., live-in partners or even the sex workers' elderly parents) and employees (e.g., drivers and receptionists) susceptible to being charged, convicted, and serving up to ten years in prison. The third law that was invalidated had prohibited "communication for the purposes of prostitution," including the use of cell phones, the Internet, hotel lobbies, bars, and even rooms with an open door or window. Sex workers argued that the law endangered them because it limited their ability to communicate with clients to determine whether they were safe or not. Activists in Canada are pleased with the new decisions but continue to seek complete delegalization of sex work (Sex Professionals of Canada SPOC 2010).

THE FEMINIST PROSTITUTION DEBATE. Are sex workers victims or agents? Some feminists argue that sex workers are victims of sexual and economic exploitation, whereas others claim that sex workers have agency and are in control of their lives. They are neither better nor worse off than most women workers. One organization, COYOTE (Call Off Your Old Tired Ethics), is a sex workers' rights group that claims that sex workers have the "right to engage in sex work." They advocate **decriminalizing** prostitution in the United States because that would give sex workers more control over their bodies. However, COYOTE opposes legalization because it implies regulation—licensing or registration, zoning of street prostitution, legal brothels, mandatory medical exams, and special business taxes. COYOTE activists argue that such regulations would allow the state to control what a woman does with her body (Weitzer 2000).

WHISPER (Women Hurt in Systems of Prostitution Engaged in Revolt) is a leading organization in the antiprostitution campaign in the United States. Unlike the pro–sex work stance taken by COYOTE, WHISPER holds that prostitution is never freely chosen by women. They believe that prostitution is inherently traumatizing to the sex worker and is not a valid career that should be organized or regulated by the state (Weitzer 2000). Some critics even label prostitution an act of violence against women and a form of female sexual slavery (Barry 1979; MacKinnon 1993).

Instead of seeing sex workers as either victims or agents, Carpenter (2000) recommends embracing the contradictions by recognizing the ways that sex workers are both victims and agents. There can be violence, exploitation, and substance abuse in sex workers' lives as well as autonomy, free will, and job satisfaction, depending on who the sex worker is, where she works, and how much control she has over her work.

Although WHISPER and COYOTE disagree on many points, they do agree that the current conditions under which sex workers work must be improved. A study of 475 sex workers (which included men, women, and transgender persons) in five countries (South Africa, Thailand, Turkey, the United States, and Zambia) found that violence marked the lives of the majority of sex workers (Farley, Baral, Kiremire, and Sezgin 1998), including those who are trafficked and forced into prostitution and those under the control of pimps and brothel owners. Here are some of the highlights from the study:

- 73 percent of sex workers reported being physically assaulted in prostitution, and 68 percent reported being threatened with a weapon.
- 62 percent reported being raped since entering prostitution, and of those who were raped, 46 percent were raped more than five times.
- 54 percent of sex workers reported being physically abused as children, and 58 percent reported being sexually abused as children by an average of four perpetrators.
- 72 percent reported current or past homelessness.
- 61 percent reported current physical health problems.
- 52 percent reported a problem with alcohol addiction, and 45 percent with drug addiction.
- 92 percent stated that they wished to leave prostitution.
- 24 percent supported the legalization of prostitution.

GLOBALIZATION AND SEX TRAFFICKING. Most of the discussion so far in this chapter has looked at the connections between major social systems of inequality by race ethnicity, social class, sexual identity, and nation, as they intersect with the focus of the book, gender inequality.

These systems and their intersections take place in the context of a global political economy, and that context has a profound effect on our ideas and experiences of sex.

Globalization has created a global labor force in every industry, including sex work. It has also created systems of communication and transportation that move workers, including sex workers, around the world. In a global economy, human **trafficking** moves people around the world for a range of industries including not only prostitution, but sweatshop labor, street begging, domestic work, marriage, adoption, agricultural work, construction, armed conflicts (child soldiers), and other forms of exploitative labor or services (Jones, Engstrom, Hilliard, and Diaz 2007). Some people who are trafficked as sex workers choose to be sex workers and choose to migrate, but their choices are seriously constrained by the poverty and desperation they find if their homecountries have few economic opportunities. Furthermore, many of them are trafficked in order to be exploited against their will. They have neither chosen to be sex workers nor chosen to move to other nations.

Women and girls make up a large proportion (about 80 percent), although not all, of those who are trafficked as sex workers (UNODC 2006). About four million women and girls are trafficked every year around the world. One-fourth of them are forced to work in the sex industry. With profits of $7 billion to $12 billion a year, sex trafficking has become the third most profitable illegal industry behind drugs ($150–$400 billion in profits) and arms smuggling ($56 billion in profits) (Farr 2005).

Most of the sex-trafficked women and girls come from Thailand, Bangladesh, the former Soviet Union, and Brazil (Farr 2005). Many are kidnapped or sold to brokers who move them to another country. The highest prices are paid for girls from ten to twelve years old. A typical situation is where a young woman learns from a newspaper or a friend about a job in a wealthy nation working in a restaurant, or as a nanny or a dancer. When she arrives, she finds that she is part of a debt-bondage system that requires her to pay back the expenses of her transportation, passport, and room and board. The job turns out to be sex work, and she is held captive until she pays off her debt. She is never told how much she owes, how much she makes, or what her expenses are, so she never gets out of bondage. Her work is to service twelve to thirty men a night. She is fined and beaten if she breaks house rules such as turning down a customer, trying to escape, gaining weight, or failing to get customers to buy drinks (Farr 2005).

Finding accurate information on sex trafficking, sorting through the issues, and creating policies to address the problems are surrounded by much controversy. One of the first problems is the identification of sex trafficking as something that affects women and girls only. Although boys and men comprise a portion of those exploited by sex traffickers, they are nearly invisible in the discussions of the issue (Dennis 2008). One review of the social science research on sex trafficking found that 84 percent of the published articles identified women as the only people trafficked, 6 percent mentioned both women and men, and only 10 percent discussed men only. The characterization of men and women who were trafficked also differed. Men sex workers were assigned considerably more agency than women sex workers. The men were described more often as having chosen to be trafficked, and the women were described as having been forced into their work. The assumptions about the dangers of the work also differed by gender, with men perceived as being most threatened by HIV and women seen to be most threatened by violence. These accounts of sex trafficking are not necessarily reflective of the real experience. Although men and boys are nearly invisible in the research, they undoubtedly make up a significant proportion of those who are trafficked. Twenty percent of people arrested for sex work in the United States and 30 percent of those arrested in France are men. In addition, the literature may not accurately reflect the real dangers faced by sex workers (Dennis 2008).

Controversies around trafficking also parallel those regarding sex work in general (Jones et al. 2008). Is sex work, including that done by immigrant sex workers, a form of gender violence, or is it a legitimate career choice? On the one hand, some paint a grim picture of sex workers as victims of inhuman treatment by traffickers, clients, and immigration officers. On the other hand, some argue that this image ignores the possibility that some sex workers cross national borders by their own choice as a way to improve their working conditions. And, like the Canadian sex workers' organizations described previously, some call for decriminalization of sex work and protection from international agencies and governments, rather than treating sex workers as criminals and creating more dangerous conditions through repressive laws.

Recent changes in policy in Europe that are designed to address trafficking reflect these disagreements (Hubbard, Matthews, and Scoular 2008). Non-EU nationals now constitute the majority of sex workers in the European Union: 75 percent in Germany, 50 percent in Britain, 90 percent in Italy, 60 percent in France, and 66 percent in the Netherlands.

Sex work in the Netherlands has been legal for some time, although it has been restricted to certain areas that are highly policed, and brothels were illegal until recently. In response to the recognition of the growing problem of trafficking, the Dutch made brothels legal and made the government responsible for issuing working permits for those who work in them. This has resulted in a growing problem for the most vulnerable sex workers, immigrants, who often work in unlicensed and uncontrolled settings. "The mayor of Amsterdam . . . concluded bluntly, 'the aims of the law have not been reached as we've received more and more signals that abuse still continues'" (Hubbard et al. 2008, 147). Sweden passed laws in the late 1990s as part of their Violence Against Women Act, making it illegal to purchase sexual services. As a result, "the situation on the street is described as more difficult for sex workers due to greater policing, a drop in customers leading to lower prices, less choice of clients, a need for quicker transactions and greater risk-taking in client selection" (Hubbard et al. 2008, 147). In Britain, both selling and buying sex is illegal, although it is tolerated by the police in restricted areas. Sex workers face similar problems to those in Sweden. Sex trafficking is troubling policy makers who claim to be concerned about protecting women and immigrants at the same time as they wish to protect sexual rights of sex workers and their clients. In all three nations, however, policy does not seem to be protecting sex workers, especially immigrants, nor does it seem to be inhibiting the prevalence of the industry.

The underlying problem of a global economy that forces some people to choose to become sex workers and to move to wealthier nations coupled with more restrictive immigration laws that prevent immigrants from legally obtaining other kinds of work is not being addressed. Because of the organization of sex and gender, and because of the higher levels of poverty among women and the lower wages in other kinds of work, women are most likely to be trafficked as sex workers. The global capitalist system appears to be the underlying, but thus far invisible, issue that must be addressed.

GENDER MATTERS

Sexuality and gender are closely tied to one another in our thinking. To be a woman or a man still normally includes the requirement to be heterosexually identified and active. This connection between sexuality and gender is shaped by systems of inequality by race ethnicity, social class, nation, and sexual identity as well as by the global political economy that commodifies everything, including sexual relationships. Various social activists have challenged the organization of sexuality and the ways in which it connects to these various social forces, but controversy persists about how the community should or can intervene to evaluate and regulate our sexual lives.

Some of the most difficult issues are regulation of pornography, sex work, and sex trafficking. Advocates on many sides of these questions debate whether they should be illegal, legal but controlled by the government, or decriminalized. Although their arguments are strongly oppositional, they often are equally valid in their concern for justice and equality.

Rules about sexuality not only affect sex workers. They also affect nearly all of us as we attempt to develop our own sexual identity, engage in sexual activities, and create sexual relationships. Recent changes in heterosexual arrangements among young people in the form of hooking up, for example, challenge some of the rules established in the last century. The changes, however, also leave in place persistent questions about gender justice. Schwartz's work reminds us that no matter how the rules change or remain the same, sexuality is not natural but is absolutely shaped by ideologies and social rules.

The experience of LGBT people also challenges dominant ideas about what is legitimate sexuality and how sexuality should be experienced by properly feminine women and masculine men. The experience of men who have sex with men further challenges the rules by separating identity from behavior as well as sexuality and gender. Like many of the issues related to gender, sexuality appears to be in the midst of important changes, and organizations from across the political spectrum are seeking to control the outcome of these transitions.

KEY TERMS

abstinence-only sex education
binaries, sexual
Bigger Thomas, Jezebel, Uncle Tom, Aunt Jemima
biphobia
civil rights
compulsory heterosexuality
decriminalize
double standard
female genital mutilation (FGM)
globalization
heteronormativity

heterosexism
heterosexuality
HIV
homophobia
honor crimes
hooking up
hypersexualized
LGBTQ
mail-order/cyber brides
miscegenation/anti-miscegenation laws
misogyny
MSM (men who have sex with men)

prosex feminists

purity balls and promise (abstinence) rings

queer theory

sex tourism

sex work

sexual identity/orientation

sexual minority

sexual scripts

social constructionist

stigma/othering

STD/STI

trafficking

CRITICAL THINKING QUESTIONS

1. Look at Table 4–1, "Sexual Satisfaction by Region for Men and Women Over 40," and imagine that you had to describe the information in the table to someone over the phone. They wouldn't be able to see the numbers, so you would need to mention some of the key numbers but you couldn't just recite the lines of data. How would you summarize the key information?

   After thinking about the numbers, what questions do you feel are left unanswered? What kinds of research might be generated by trying to understand what the numbers in the table mean?

2. How does racism intersect with images and myths of sexuality? What are the images? What do they convey about racial inequality? How do they help maintain systems of inequality?

3. What are the main differences in the three major approaches to sexuality: biological explanations such as the gay gene; sexual scripts; and queer theory. Which of these comes closest to your own thinking? Why do you think it is the most powerful explanation?

4. What is the debate among feminists over pornography? What social policies might feminists from the different perspectives support?

5. What is the debate among feminists over sex work/prostitution? What social policies might feminists from the different perspectives support?

REFERENCES

Ackman, Dan. 2001. "How Big Is Porn?" *Forbes*, May 25. http://www.forbes.com/2001/05/25/0524porn .html. Accessed March 19, 2011.

Albert, Alexa. 2001. *Brothel: Mustang Ranch and Its Women*. New York: Random House.

Almquist, E. 1994. "The Experience of Minority Women in the United States." In *Women: A Feminist Perspective*, 5th edition, edited by Jo Freeman, 573–606. Mountain View, CA: Mayfield.

American Congress of Obstetricians and Gynecologists, Committee on Gynecological Practice. 2007. "ACOG Committee Opinion No. 378: Vaginal 'rejuvenation' and cosmetic vaginal procedures." *Obstetrics & Gynecology* 110 (3): 737–38. http://www.ncbi.nlm.nih.gov/pubmed/17766626.

Armstrong, Elizabeth, Paula England, and Alison Fogarty. 2010. "Orgasm in College Hookups and Relationships." In *Families as They Really Are*, edited by Barbara J. Risman, 362–77. New York: Norton.

Aulette, Judy. 2007. *Changing American Families*. 2nd edition. Boston: Allyn and Bacon.

Bailey, Beth. 1988. *From Front Porch to Back Seat: Courtship in Twentieth Century America*. Baltimore: Johns Hopkins University Press.

Barnett, Hillaire. 2013. *Introduction to Feminist Jurisprudence*. New York: Routledge.

Barry, Kathleen. 1979. *Female Sexual Slavery*. New York: Avon Books.

BBC News. 2003. "Free Sex Offer for US Troops." BBC News, June 4. http://news.bbc.co.uk/2/hi/americas/2961288.stm. Accessed March 19, 2011.

Beneke, Tim. 1983. *Men on Rape: What They Have to Say about Sexual Violence*. New York. St. Martin's.

Bogle, Kathleen. 2008. *Hooking Up: Sex, Dating and Relationships on Campus*. New York: New York University Press.

Brean, Henry. 2009. "Heidi Fleiss Gives Up on Plan for Brothel for Women." *Las Vegas Review Journal*, February 10. http://www.reviewjournal.com/news/heidi-fleiss-gives-plan-brothel-women.

Brooke, James. 1998. "Homophobia Often Found in Schools, Data Show." *New York Times*, October 14. http://www.nytimes.com/1998/10/14/us/homophobia-often-found-in-schools-data-show.html?src=pm. Accessed March 19, 2011.

Bruckner, Hannah, and Peter Bearman. 2005. "After the Promise: The STD Consequences of Adolescent Virginity Pledges." *Journal of Adolescent Health* 36 (4): 271–78.

Burstein, Andrew, Nancy Isenberg, and Annette Gordon-Reed. 1999. "Three Perspectives on America's Jefferson Fixation." *Nation*, January 16.

Butler, Judith. 1990. *Gender Trouble: Feminism and the Subversion of Identity*. New York: Routledge.

Carpenter, Belinda J. 2000. *Re-thinking Prostitution: Feminism, Sex, and the Self*. New York: Peter Lang.

Cheng, Sealing. 2004. "Vagina Dialogues?: Critical Reflections from Hong Kong on *The Vagina Monologues* as a Worldwide Movement." *International Feminist Journal of Politics* 6 (2): 326–34.

Cofer, Judith Ortiz. 1993. "The Myth of the Latin Woman: I Just Met a Girl Named María." In *The Latin Deli: Prose and Poetry*, edited by Judith Ortiz Cofer, 148–54. Athens, GA: University of Georgia Press.

Collins, Patricia Hill. 2000. *Black Feminist Thought: Knowledge, Consciousness, and the Politics of Empowerment*. New York: Routledge.

Davis, Angela. 1983. *Women, Race and Class*. New York: Random House.

———. 1990. *Women, Culture and Politics*. New York: Vintage Books.

Deihl, Marcia, and Robyn Ochs. 2004. "Biphobia." In *Readings for Diversity and Social Justice: An Anthology on Racism, Antisemitism, Sexism, Heterosexism, Ableism, and Classism*, edited by Maurianne Adams, Warren J. Blumenfeld, Rosie Castañeda, Heather W. Hackman, Madeline L. Peters, and Ximena Zúñiga, 267–75. New York: Routledge.

D'Emilio, John. 2009. "LGBT Liberation: Build a Broad Movement." Interview with Sherry Wolf. *International Socialist Review* 65 (May-June): 21–22. http://www.isreview.org/issues/65/feat-demilio.shtml. Accessed March 19, 2011.

Dennis, Jeffery. 2008. "Women Are Victims, Men Make Choices: The Invisibility of Men and Boys in the Global Sex Trade." *Gender Issues* 25 (1): 11–25.

Federal Bureau of Investigation, Department of Justice. 2010. "Table 33: Ten-Year Arrest Trends by Sex." *Crime in the United States, 2009*. http://www2.fbi.gov/ucr/cius2009/data/table_33.html. Accessed March 19, 2011.

Dines, Gail, and Dana Bialer. 2012. "Porn Is in Rude Health." *The Guardian*, June 7. http://www.guardian.co.uk/commentisfree/2012/jun/07/porn-rude-health-louis-theroux.

Dines, Gail, and Robert Jensen. 2004. "Pornography and Media: Toward a More Critical Analysis." In *Sexualities: Identities, Behaviors, and Society*, edited by Michael Kimmel and Rebecca F. Plante, 369–79. New York: Oxford University Press.

Dworkin, Andrea. 1981. *Pornography: Men Possessing Women*. New York: Perigee.

Ehrenreich, Barbara. 1984. *The Hearts of Men: American Dreams and the Flight from Commitment*. New York: Doubleday.

Ensler, Eve. 2001. *The Vagina Monologues: The V-Day Edition.* New York: Villard.

Entman, Robert, and Andrew Rojecki. 2001. *The Black Image in the White Mind: Media and Race in America.* Chicago: University of Chicago Press.

Epstein, Steven. 1994. "A Queer Encounter: Sociology and the Study of Sexuality." *Sociological Theory* 12 (2): 188–202.

Espín, O. M. 1986. "Cultural and Historical Influences on Sexuality in Hispanic/Latina Women." In *All American Women,* edited by Johnnetta B. Cole, 272–84. New York: Free Press.

Espiritu, Yen E. 1997. *Asian American Women and Men.* Thousand Oaks, CA: Sage.

Farley, Melissa, Isin Baral, Merab Kiremire, and Ufuk Sezgin. 1998. "Prostitution in Five Countries: Violence and Post-Traumatic Stress Disorder." *Feminism and Psychology* 8 (4): 405–26.

Farr, Kathryn. 2005. *Sex Trafficking: The Global Market in Women and Children.* New York: Worth.

Fausto-Sterling, Anne. 1993. "The Five Sexes: Why Male and Female Are Not Enough." *The Sciences* 33 (2): 20–24.

Federal Bureau of Investigation, Department of Justice. 2010. "Table 33: Ten-Year Arrest Trends by Sex, 2000–2009." *Crime in the United States.* http://www2.fbi.gov/ucr/cius2009/data/table_33 .html. Accessed March 19, 2011.

Feijoo, Ammie N. 2001. *Adolescent Sexual Health in Europe and the U.S.—Why the Difference?* 3rd ed. Advocates for Youth. www.advocatesforyouth.org/storage/advfy/documents/fsest.pdf.

Finer, Lawrence. 2007. "Trends in Premarital Sex in the United States, 1954–2003." *Public Health Reports* 122 (1): 73–78.

Ford, Chandra L., Kathryn D. Whetten, Sue A. Hall, Jay S. Kaufman, and Angela D. Thrasher. 2007. "Black Sexuality, Social Construction, and Research Targeting 'the Down Low.'" *Annals of Epidemiology* 17 (3): 209–216.

Foucault, Michel. 1978. *The History of Sexuality.* Vol. 1: An Introduction, translated by Robert Hurley. New York: Pantheon.

Fox, Ron C. 1995. "Bisexual Identities." In *Lesbian, Gay, and Bisexual Identities Across the Lifespan,* edited by Anthony R. D'Augelli and Charlotte J. Patterson, 48–86. New York: Oxford University Press.

Frohlick, Susan. 2007. "Fluid Exchanges." *City and Society* 19 (1): 139–68.

Frontline. 2002. "Playboy Magazine Demographics." http://www.pbs.org/wgbh/pages/frontline/shows/ porn/business/havedemos.html. Accessed March 19, 2011.

Gagnon, John. 1977. *Human Sexualities.* Glenview, IL: Scott Foresman.

Gagnon, John, and William Simon. 1973. *Sexual Conduct: The Social Sources of Human Sexuality.* Chicago: Aldine.

Gardiner, Judith Kegan. 1993. "What I Didn't Get to Say on TV about Pornography, Masculinity, and Representation." *New York Law School Law Review* 38:319–33.

Gates, Gary. 2011. "How many People are Lesbian, Gay, Bisexual and Transgendered?" The Williams Institute. http://williamsinstitute.law.ucla.edu/wp-content/uploads/Gates-How-Many-People-LGBT- Apr-2011.pdf. Accessed March 3, 2014.

Goffman, Erving. 1959. *The Presentation of Self in Everyday Life.* Garden City, NY: Doubleday.

———. 1963. *Stigma: Notes on the Management of Spoiled Identity.* Englewood Cliffs, NJ: Prentice-Hall.

Greenfield, Lawrence A. 1997. *Sex Offenses and Offenders: An Analysis of Data on Rape and Sexual Assault.* Washington, DC: U.S. Department of Justice, Bureau of Justice Statistics.

Herek, Gregory. 2004. "Beyond 'Homophobia': Thinking about Sexual Prejudice and Stigma in the Twenty-First Century." *Sexuality Research and Social Policy* 1 (2): 6–24.

Higgins, J. A., and Browne, I. 2008. "Sexual Needs, Control, and Refusal: How 'Doing' Class and Gender Influences Sexual Risk Taking." *Journal of Sex Research* 45 (3): 233–45.

Hubbard, Phil, Roger Matthews, and Jane Scoular. 2008. "Regulating Sex Work in the EU: Prostitute Women and the New Spaces of Exclusion." *Gender, Place and Culture* 15 (2): 137–52.

Hudson-Weems, Clenora. 1994. *Emmett Till: The Sacrificial Lamb of the Civil Rights Movement*. Troy, MI: Bedford.

Jaco, Charles. 2012. "Jaco Report: Full Interview with Todd Akin." Fox 2 Now, August 19.

Jay, Paul. 1996. "Bisexuality." In *The Lives of Lesbians, Gays, and Bisexuals*, edited by Ritch C. Savin-Williams and Kenneth M. Cohen, 436–61. New York: Harcourt Brace.

Jensen, Robert. 2010. "Just a John? Pornography and Men's Choices." In *Doing Gender Diversity: Readings in Theory and Real-World Experience*, edited by Rebecca F. Plante and Lis M. Maurer, 280–84. Boulder, CO: Westview.

Jones, Loring, David Engstrom, Tricia Hilliard, and Mariel Diaz. 2007. "Globalization and Human Trafficking." *Journal of Sociology and Social Welfare* 34 (2): 107–24.

Kienan, Robert. 2011. Honor killings. *Global Researcher* 5:183–208. Globalresearcher.com

Kimmel, Michael. 2004. *The Gendered Society*. 2nd edition. New York: Oxford University Press.

———. 2007. "Introduction: John Gagnon and the Sexual Self." In *The Sexual Self: The Construction of Sexual Scripts*, edited by Michael Kimmel, vii–xvi. Nashville, TN: Vanderbilt University Press.

———. 2008. *Guyland: The Perilous World Where Boys Become Men*. New York: Harper Collins.

King, J. L. 2004. *On the Down Low: A Journey into the Lives of "Straight" Black Men Who Sleep with Men*. New York: Broadway Books.

Kinsey, Alfred C., Wardell B. Pomeroy, and Clyde E. Martin. 1948. *Sexual Behavior in the Human Male*. Philadelphia: Saunders.

Kinsey, Alfred C., Wardell B. Pomeroy, Clyde E. Martin, and Paul H. Gebhard. 1953. *Sexual Behavior in the Human Female*. Philadelphia: Saunders.

Koch, Stephanie. 2007. *Is She Heterosexual, Bisexual, or Lesbian?* MA thesis, University of North Carolina, Charlotte.

Koedt, Anne. (1970) 1996. "The Myth of the Vaginal Orgasm." In *Feminist Sexualities: A Reader*, edited by Stevi Jackson and Sue Scott, 111–16. New York: Columbia University Press.

Lander, Eric, and Joseph Ellis. 1998. "Founding Father." *Nature* 396:13–14. doi:10.1038/23802.

Lapinski, Maria Knight, Mary E. Braz, and Erin K. Maloney. 2010. "The Down Low, Social Stigma, and Risky Sexual Behaviors: Insights from African-American Men Who Have Sex with Men." *Journal of Homosexuality* 57 (5): 610–33.

Laumann, Edward, Anthony Paik, Dale Glasser, Jeong-Han Kang, Tianfu Wang, Bernard Levinson, Edson Moreira, Alfredo Nicolosi, and Clive Gingell. 2006. "Cross National Study of Subjective Sexual Well-Being among Older Women and Men." *Archives of Sexual Behavior* 35 (2): 143–59.

Laumann, Edward O., John H. Gagnon, Robert T. Michael, and Stuart Michaels. 1994. *The Social Organization of Sexuality: Sexual Practices in the United States*. Chicago: University of Chicago Press.

LeVay, Simon. 1991. "A Difference in Hypothalamic Structure Between Heterosexual and Homosexual Men." *Science* 253:1034–37.

Levine, Martin. 1998. *Gay Macho*. New York: New York University Press.

Logan, Colleen. 1996. "Homophobia? No, Homoprejudice." *Journal of Homosexuality* 31 (3): 31–53.

Luscombe, Richard. 2004. "U.S. Girls Embrace Gay Passion Fashion." *Observer*, January 4. http://www.guardian.co.uk/gayrights/story/0,12592,1115656,00.html. Accessed March 19, 2011.

MacKinnon, Catharine. 1987. *Feminism Unmodified: Discourses on Life and Law*. Cambridge, MA: Harvard University Press.

———. 1993. "Prostitution and Civil Rights." *Michigan Journal of Gender and Law* 1:13–31.

Marklein, Mary Beth. 2004. " 'Vagina Monologues' Becoming College Phenomenon." *USA Today*, March 1. http://www.usatoday.com/life/theater/2004-03-01-monologues-usat_x.htm. Accessed March 19, 2011.

Masters, William, and Virginia Johnson. 1966. *Human Sexual Response*. London: Churchill.

May, Elaine. 2010. *America and the Pill: A History of Promise, Peril, and Liberation*. New York: Basic Books.

McElroy, Wendy. 1995. *A Woman's Right to Pornography*. New York: St. Martin's Press.

McGruder, Kevin. 2009. "Black Sexuality in the U.S.: Presentations as Non-normative." *Journal of African American Studies* 13 (3): 251–62.

McIntosh, Peggy. 1988. "White Privilege and Male Privilege: A Personal Account of Coming to See Correspondences through Work in Women's Studies." In *Race, Class, and Gender: An Anthology*, 4th edition, edited by Margaret L. Andersen and Patricia Hill Collins, 70–81. Belmont, CA: Wadsworth.

Mosher, William, Anjani Chandra, and Jo Jones. 2005. "Sexual Behavior and Selected Health Measures: Men and Women 15–44 Years of Age, United States, 2002." Advance Data from Vital and Health Statistics, No. 362, September 15. Atlanta, GA: Centers for Disease Control. http://www.cdc.gov/nchs/products/pubs/pubd/ad/361–370/ad362.htm. Accessed March 19, 2011.

Nagel, Joane. 2000. "Ethnicity and Sexuality." *Annual Review of Sociology* 26:107–33.

———. 2003. *Race, Ethnicity, and Sexuality: Intimate Intersections, Forbidden Frontiers*. New York: Oxford University Press.

Ochs, R., and M. Deihl. 1992. "Moving Beyond Binary Thinking." In *Homophobia: How We All Pay the Price*, edited by Warren Blumenfeld, 67–78. Boston: Beacon.

Out Wilmington On-Line Community and Resource Center. 2011. "Heterosexism 101." http://www.outwilmington.com/8001/8043.html. Accessed March 19, 2011.

Payne, Charles. 1994. *I've Got the Light of Freedom: The Organizing Tradition and the Mississippi Freedom Struggle*. Berkeley: University of California Press.

Petchesky, Rosalind P. 2000. "Sexual Rights: Inventing a Concept, Mapping an International Practice." In *Framing the Sexual Subject: The Politics of Gender, Sexuality, and Power*, edited by Richard Parker, Regina Maria Barbosa, and Peter Aggleton, 81–103. Berkeley: University of California Press.

Pharr, Suzanne. 1988. *Homophobia: A Weapon of Sexism*. Inverness, CA: Chardon.

Plant, Richard. 1986. *The Pink Triangle: The Nazi War Against Homosexuals*. New York: Henry Holt.

Reiss, Ira. 2006. *An Insider's View of Sexual Science Since Kinsey*. New York: Rowman and Littlefield.

Rich, Adrienne. 1996. "Compulsory Heterosexuality and Lesbian Existence." In *Feminism and Sexuality—A Reader*, edited by Stevi Jackson and Sue Scott, 130–43. New York: Columbia University Press.

Rich, Frank. 2001. "Naked Capitalists: There's No Business Like Porn Business." *New York Times Magazine*, May 20. http://www.nytimes.com/2001/05/20/magazine/20PORN.html?ex=1168232400&en=6d1d58426e373abd&ei=5070. Accessed March 19, 2011.

Ropelato, Jerry. 2007. "Internet Pornography Statistics." *TopTenReviews*. http://internet-filter-review.toptenreviews.com/internet-pornography-statistics.html. Accessed March 19, 2011.

Rosen, Ruth. 2000. *The World Split Open: How the Modern Women's Movement Changed America*. New York: Penguin.

Rust, Paula C. 1995. *Bisexuality and the Challenge to Lesbian Politics: Sex, Loyalty, and Revolution*. New York: New York University Press.

———. 2002. "Bisexuality: The State of the Union." *Annual Review of Sex Research* 6:1–57.

Ryan, Joan. 2002. "A 6-Letter, 4-Letter Word." *San Francisco Chronicle*, February 19. http://www.sfgate.com/opinion/article/A-6-letter-4-letter-word-2872685.php . Accessed February 19, 2014.

Saad, Lydia. 2010. "Four Moral Issues Sharply Divide Americans." *Gallup*, May 26. http://www.gallup
.com/poll/137357/Four-Moral-Issues-Sharply-Divide-Americans.aspx. Accessed March 19, 2011.

Schwartz, Pepper. 2007. "The Social Construction of Heterosexuality." In *The Sexual Self: The Construction of Sexual Scripts*, edited by Michael Kimmel, 80–92. Nashville, TN: Vanderbilt University Press.

———. 2010. "Why Is Everyone So Afraid of Sex?" In *Families as They Really Are*, edited by Barbara J.
Risman, 120–30. New York: Norton.

Segal, Lynne. 1993. "Introduction." In *Sex Exposed: Sexuality and the Pornography Debate*, edited by
Lynn Segal and Mary McIntosh, 1–14. London: Virago.

Sex Professionals of Canada (SPOC). 2010. "Status on Our Constitutional Challenge for Decriminalization." November 28. http://www.spoc.ca/. Accessed March 19, 2011.

Sincero, Jen. 2005. *The Straight Girl's Guide to Sleeping with Chicks*. New York: Fireside.

Smart, Carol. 1989. *Feminism and the Power of the Law*. New York: Routledge.

Smith, Tom W. 1994. "Attitudes Toward Sexual Permissiveness: Trends, Correlates, and Behavioral
Connections." In *Sexuality Across the Life Course*, edited by Alice S. Rossi, 63–98. Chicago: University of Chicago Press.

Solebello, Nicholas Paul, and Sinikka Elliott. 2011. "'We want them to be as heterosexual as possible':
Fathers talk about their teen children's sexuality." *Gender and Society* 25:293–315.

Staples, Robert. 2006. *Exploring Black Sexuality*. New York: Rowman and Littlefield.

Steedman, Mercedes. 1987. "Who's on Top? Heterosexual Practices and Male Dominance During the
Sex Act." In *Who's on Top? The Politics of Heterosexuality*, edited by Varda Burstyn, Howard
Buchbinder, Dinah Forbes, and Mercedes Steedman, 83–111. Toronto: Garamond.

Stephens, Dionne, and April Few. 2010. "The Effects of Images of African American Women in Hip
Hop on Early Adolescents' Attitudes toward Physical Attractiveness and Interpersonal Relation-
ships." In *Doing Gender Diversity: Readings in Theory and Real-World Experience*, edited by
Rebecca F. Plante and Lis M. Maurer. Philadelphia: Westview.

Strossen, Nadine. 1995. *Defending Pornography: Free Speech, Sex, and the Fight for Women's Rights*.
New York: Scribner.

Tajima, Renee E. 1989. "Lotus Blossoms Don't Bleed: Images of Asian Women." In *Making Waves: An
Anthology of Writings by and about Asian American Women*, edited by Asian Women United of
California, 308–17. Boston: Beacon.

The Telegraph. 2012. "Politician barred for saying 'vagina' performs 'The Vagina Monologues' outside
Congress." *The Telegraph*, June 19. http://www.telegraph.co.uk/news/worldnews/northamerica/
usa/9342194/Politician-barred-for-saying-Vagina-performs-The-Vagina-Monologues-outside-
state-congress.html.

Tiefer, Leonore. 2007. "Sexuopharmacology: A Fateful New Element in Sexual Scripts." In *The Sexual
Self: The Construction of Sexual Scripts*, edited by Michael Kimmel, 239–48. Nashville, TN:
Vanderbilt University Press.

Tolman, Deborah L., and Tracy E. Higgins. 1996. "How Being a Good Girl Can Be Bad." In *Bad
Girls/Good Girls: Women, Sex, and Power in the Nineties*, edited by Nan Bauer Maglin and Donna
Perry. New Brunswick, NJ: Rutgers University Press.

Trautner, Mary Nell. 2005. "Doing Gender, Doing Class: The Performance of Sexuality in Exotic
Dance Clubs." *Gender and Society* 19 (6):771–88.

U.S. Department of Justice, Bureau of Justice Statistics. 2005. "Contacts between the Police and the
Public: Findings from the 2002 National Survey." http://bjs.ojp.usdoj.gov/index.cfm?ty=
pbdetail&iid=656. Accessed March 19, 2011.

———. 2007. "Contacts between Police and the Public, 2005." http://bjs.ojp.usdoj.gov/index
.cfm?ty=pbdetail&iid=653. Accessed March 19, 2011.

United Nations Office on Drugs and Crime (UNODC). 2006. *Trafficking in Persons: Global Patterns.* November. http://www.unodc.org/pdf/traffickinginpersons_report_2006ver2.pdf. Accessed March 19, 2011.

Valenti, Jessica. 2010. *The purity Myth: How America's Obsession with Virginity Is Hurting Young Women.* Berkeley, CA: Seal.

Weinberg, George. 1972. *Society and the Healthy Homosexual.* New York: St. Martin's.

Weitzer, Ronald. 2000. "The Politics of Prostitution in America." In *Sex for Sale: Prostitution, Pornography, and the Sex Industry,* edited by Ronald Weitzer, 159–80. New York: Routledge.

West, Cornel. 1993. "Black Sexuality: The Taboo Subject." In *Gender Basics: Feminist Perspectives on Women and Men,* edited by Anne Minas, 299–303. Belmont, CA: Wadsworth.

White, Deborah Gray. 1985. *Ar'n't I a Woman? Female Slaves in the Plantation South.* New York: Norton.

Widmer, Eric D., Judith Treas, and Robert Newcomb. 1998. "Attitudes Toward Nonmarital Sex in 24 Countries." *Journal of Sex Research* 25 (4): 349–58.

Wolf, Sherry. 2009. *Sexuality and Socialism: History, Politics, and Theory of LGBT Liberation.* Chicago: Haymarket Books.

World Association for Sexual Health. 1999. *Declaration on Sexual Rights.* Adopted in Hong Kong at the 14th World Congress of Sexology, August 26. http://www.sexology.it/declaration_sexual_rights.html Accessed February 19, 2014.

5

EDUCATION

Drought and inadequate infrastructure for access to water can mean that girls are not educated because carrying water is a gendered task in many places in the world and it is mostly girls and women who do this work. If girls must spend hours waiting for their turn at the wells and carrying the water home, they do not have time to attend school.

Source: UNDESA 2013.

SNAPSHOT 1: Keisha and Jessica sit with hands raised, while Andrew blurts out the answer to a question.

SNAPSHOT 2: The teacher reprimands Ernesto, telling him to stay in his seat.

SNAPSHOT 3: Brittany answers a question. The teacher responds with a nod and moves on.

SNAPSHOT 4: The teacher praises Marcus for skill in reading.

SNAPSHOT 5: The teacher helps Sam with a spelling mistake, telling him to sound out the word.

SNAPSHOT 6: The teacher compliments Annalisa on her new shoes.

SNAPSHOT 7: Students line up to go to lunch. Boys are one side of the room, girls on the other (M. Sadker and Sadker 1994).

SNAPSHOT 8: Mr. Chang goes to visit his daughter's "graduation" from kindergarten. He notices that the boys are given awards for "Very Best Thinker" and "Most Eager Learner," while the girls are awarded "Sweetest Personality" and "Best Helper"(Deveny 1994).

School takes up much time in children's lives, and most of us attend school for many years. Not surprising, our experience in education is an important force in shaping our personalities, skills, and interactions in the rest of our lives. These snapshots show that gender is an important part of the lessons we learn in school, although these "lessons" may be unintentional and largely "hidden agendas" in the school curriculum (M. Sadker and Sadker 1994).

This chapter reviews the ways in which gender shows up in schools, from our first day in kindergarten to the moment we receive our PhD, and even after if we choose to become teachers ourselves. Although gender inequity remains in schools, education is an area where great strides in equality have been made in the United States. Especially in higher education, women have caught up to and surpassed men in many ways.

This chapter explores gender in the classroom through the different levels from primary to secondary to higher education, examining the ways students are treated, the courses they take, the materials used to educate them, and the ways teachers are evaluated. It introduces readers to ethnographic studies that paint a picture from the standpoint of their daily lives from primary schools to high schools. Finally, the chapter looks at policies designed to address inequities in education the United States, such as Title IX, and at the surprising factors, including access to water, that contribute to illiteracy around the globe. The last section of the chapter focuses on the theoretical idea of the correspondence principle as a way of understanding why our schools are so hierarchical and gendered.

GENDER IN THE K–12 CLASSROOM

About the same number of girls and boys attend school at all levels from preschool through high school in the United States. In terms of attendance, girls and boys seem to be equal in their participation in education. Does that mean that gender equity has been achieved? In the past two decades, researchers have entered public school classrooms to find out what is happening with gender equity there (Orenstein 1994; American Association of University Women [AAUW] 1999). As the opening scenario reveals, their studies have found that teachers treat boys and girls differently.

Differential treatment begins with a segregation of children by gender that is done automatically and with little thought. You will see in this chapter that thinking about children, and treating students, as two distinct and very different categories by gender is so pervasive in schools that it is difficult to write about education and gender without repeating this kind of dichotomous thinking. The world of education appears to be divided into two apparently natural, exhaustive, and fairly separate categories, girls and boys. As you read, think about how schools create the dichotomy of boys and girls rather than how they reflect some "natural" distinction among children.

Children are perceived as two groups, and the two categories are treated differently. Teachers, for example, respond to boys more frequently than to girls; and when they do call on girls, they wait less time to allow girls to reply before interrupting them with an answer or moving on to another topic or student. Girls, however, are often less assertive than boys and like to think about their answers. The boys, therefore, often beat them to the punch, and the teacher ends up interacting with the boys while the girls sit in silence (M. Sadker and Sadker 1994). The end result is that teachers pay more attention to boys, allowing them to speak out of turn, praising and helping them more often, and calling on them more. Sometimes teachers respond positively to boys and sometimes negatively, but boys successfully demand their time more often, whereas girls more often sit quietly, wait patiently, and become fringe elements in the classroom action.

The amount of attention paid to students also varies by race ethnicity. White boys receive the most attention, followed by minority boys, then white girls. Minority girls are least likely to gain the teachers' attention.

The type of interaction teachers have with children also differs by the gender of the student. Teachers engage in fewer complex interactions with girls. When boys speak out in class, teachers comment on their observations. They encourage boys to correct a wrong answer or expand a correct one. With girls, teachers more often respond with a nod or a brief "OK" and then move on to the next topic (M. Sadker and Sadker 1994).

Another difference in interactions with students occurs when students ask for help. When a girl asks for help, teachers show her how to do things by doing it themselves. A teacher might take the pencil and write on the girl's paper to show her how to solve a math problem, for example. In contrast, when a boy asks for help, teachers give elaborate instructions to the student as he does the work (M. Sadker and Sadker 1994).

Teachers are also more apt to comment on the appearance and clothing of girls. This kind of attention is probably intended to be complimentary and supportive. Focus on appearances, however, may be an important source of the feelings of self-consciousness girls experience, which interfere with their self-confidence and academic performance.

These kinds of gender biases vary from one course to another, with math and science classes showing the most bias against girls. Chemistry classes, in particular, have boys dominating the discussion and teachers favoring boys and humiliating girls (Lee, Marks, and Byrd 1994). However, most of these discrepancies occur without the teachers or the students being aware of them. Teachers are not consciously creating discrimination and are usually stunned to see the differences when they view themselves on videotape (M. Sadker and Sadker 1994; Ridgway and Healy 1997).

In addition to this kind of discrimination against girls by teachers, girls are also often subjected to **sexual harassment** by some boy classmates, who tease them about their bodies and do things when the teacher leaves the room such as surround girls and simulate sexual intercourse with them. Although most schools have written policies against such kind of harassment, social pressures keep girls from reporting the incidents (United Nations 2006c).

But the situation for boys may be changing. More recent data show that teachers devalue boys in their classrooms. Since the early 2000s, boys have been doing less well in school than girls. A 2013 study on data collected by the federal government on ten thousand students as they moved from kindergarten to eighth grade found that teachers' grades favored girls. Boys who scored well on tests did not get grades from teachers that represented their abilities (measured by these tests) in reading, math, and science. Analysis of these data showed that teachers downgraded boys when they didn't show "an aptitude for learning." There are other indicators that boys, more than girls, are in trouble. They are expelled from preschool at five times the rate of girls, they are more likely to be held back, and they are more often identified as having ADHD. They get more Cs and Ds than girls, and they are more likely to drop out of school. Boys do not do as well as girls in reading and writing, but girls have caught up to boys in math and science (Aud et al. 2013). And, as we have seen in chapter 3, teachers are likely to rank poor boys of color the furthest behind in schools (Ferguson 2001). Are boys trading places with girls in educational ranking? Or, as Ferguson's study suggests, is the downgrading of boys an indicator of the ways that the power of race and class position shape teachers' impressions of their students?

Another ethnographic study calls into question the tendency to ignore the part children themselves play in the production of gender differences in elementary schools. Barrie Thorne (1993) studied the group life of elementary school children and its place in the production of gender differences. Much of the scholarly work on gender is firmly located in psychology and begins with individuals, asking how boys and girls are different. Thorne, a sociologist, begins instead with group life. She asks, "How do children actively come together to help create, and sometimes challenge, gender structures and meanings?" (4). Thorne found her answers by spending time observing children in two elementary schools, one in Michigan and the other in California. She observed children's everyday social practices, such as organizing a "boys-against-the-girls" game on the playground, exchanging insults ("boys are stupid"), and inventing heterosexual couples (Cindy likes Bill), practices that heighten differences between the sexes. Thorne argues that children's play creates and enacts consequential relations of gendered power. Both divisions—the division between adult and child and the division between "male" and "female"—are "socially created, historically changing, filled with ambiguity and contradiction, and continually renegotiated" (6).

Using the concept of "**borderwork**," Thorne explores moments when children activate gender boundaries and times when they have little sense of gender differences. Contests, chasing, pollution rituals ("cooties"), and invasions serve to strengthen borders and reveal the dynamics of power in schoolchildren's worlds. **Neutralization**, the opposite of borderwork, indicates moments when the sense of division and opposition does not come into play. As a good ethnographer, Thorne's focus is always on *how* children produce or erase the divisions between them.

Thorne's study shows gender and its absence as an active and ongoing accomplishment of social relations among children and between children and teachers in two elementary schools. Of course, the school exists in the wider context of male dominance and of feminist resistance, as well as struggles over class and race inequalities, of which we must also be mindful. But an important lesson of Thorne's work is that through collective practices, we produce gender differences in schools and elsewhere, and that sociological understanding depends on attending to the processes and products of group life.

What Difference Does Differential Treatment in Schools Make?

These differences are strongly felt by girls in schools. The decline in self-confidence among girls during their school years, especially during adolescence, is remarkable (AAUW 2001). Researchers maintain that a drop in positive feelings about themselves and their achievements is a critical aspect of nearly all children's school careers. When self-esteem is measured in students in elementary, middle, and high school, the scores decline for both boys and girls, but the slide is greater for girls. In addition, girls are much lower at all three levels. On a self-esteem index where higher scores indicate stronger self-esteem, the numbers go from 4 to about 2.8 for girls as they move from elementary school to high school. The scores for boys go from 5 to about 4.8.

This change in self-esteem varies by race ethnicity as well as by gender. Black girls see a decline, but it is not as sharp as that for white girls. Black girls, for example, are twice as likely as other girls to say they are "happy with the way I am" and "pretty good at a lot of things." They may also be more likely to assert their opinions and stand up for themselves as ways to overcome constraints to success in school (O'Connor, Lewis, and Mueller (2011) Latina girls' self-esteem falls further than that of either white or black girls (Orenstein 2002).

How is self-esteem measured in these kinds of surveys? Boys are more likely than girls to say they are pretty good at a lot of things and twice as likely to name their talents as the thing they like best about themselves. Girls name aspects of their appearance as what they like about themselves. Teenage girls are much more likely than boys to also say that they are "not smart enough" or "not good enough" to achieve their dreams (Orenstein 2002).

Although school can be a place that constructs and reinforces gender stereotypes and inequities, it can also be a place where children learn to challenge gender. In addition, access to equal education can have important positive effects not only for individual students but for promoting change in the broader society. Jennifer Rothchild (2006) argues that schools can help create what she calls **"gender troublemakers."** She maintains that the best schools could and should provide an atmosphere for intellectual development facilitating awareness of structures of domination and subordination. Classrooms can provide a space in which to identify and develop skills and connections to create social change (Staudt 1998). Rothchild's interviews with girls in Nepal, for example, revealed the barriers they faced getting to go to school and the measures they took to demand an education, which necessitated that they challenge ideas about what girls are capable of and how they should spend their time. The interviews also showed how education further pushed the girls along to continue to make changes in themselves and their communities. Sanu Kamari, a ninth-grade girl, told Rothchild, "If I pass [ninth grade], I will study further and so on. Then after that I will go to look for some work. I will earn my own living, and then try to support my family since I am the eldest." Sanu went on to explain that if she became an elected official in her community, she would "talk about the village problems like water, electricity, and even girls' education" (Rothchild 2006, 127, 129).

Taming Warriors in the Kindergarten Classroom

Schools seem to be a place where girls and boys alike are harmed by gender inequality. Little boys enter preschool or kindergarten already well versed in masculine activities involving guns, fighting, and fast cars. The boys bring with them behaviors that reflect an ideology in which violence is legitimate and even honorable as long as it occurs in a struggle between good and evil and they are on the proper side. Schools, however, are places where children are supposed to learn the ideals of rationality, responsibility, and decorum. What happens when the boys enter kindergarten and find that their favorite activities violate the schools' rules of decorum?

Researchers in Australia tried to answer this question by sitting in on kindergarten classes to observe boys and the transition they made as they progressed through the program (Jordan and Cowan 2004). They found that boys actively participated in what the researcher called **"warrior narratives."** The stories in their play acting centered around fighting, destroying, and identifying "good guys" and "bad guys" even in the most unlikely of places, turning teddy bears into the enemy, plastic cutlery from tea sets into swords, and cupboards in the play kitchen into jails. The toys and activities offered by the teacher were designed to encourage them to develop skills in cooperation and positive productivity by playing house, farm, and shop, or using tools and toys to construct roads and cities. The boys, however, transformed the available objects into symbolic ones that they could use for their warrior activities. This process of transforming objects and putting something together from whatever happens to be available is called *bricolage*. In this example, bricolage occurs when a boy creates a car/weapon from a doll carriage:

> Mac threw a doll into the largest pram in the Doll Corner. He walked the pram [baby carriage] out past a group of his friends who were playing "crashes" on the Car Mat. Three of the five boys turned and watched him wheeling the pram toward the classroom door. Mac performed a sharp three-point turn; raced his pram past the Car Mat group, striking one boy on the head with the pram wheel. (Field notes quoted in Jordan and Cowan 2004, 107)

The teacher responded by gently but persistently attempting to control the boys' behavior and showing them the "proper" use of the objects. She argued that the rules of "no shouting," "no running," and "no using classroom materials inappropriately" were rational ways of preventing the toys from being damaged and the children from being hurt. Because their behavior directly contradicted these ideas, the boys' warrior narratives became part of a "'deviant' masculine subculture" (Jordan and Cowan 2004, 110).

At the same time, the girls' feminine games "of nurturing and self-display—mothers, nurse, brides, princesses—were accommodated easily within the classroom" (Jordan and Cowan 2004, 110). The girls' favorite activities and their ways of expressing themselves were in line with the rules of rationality, responsibility, and decorum the school wanted to establish.

The perception of boys in Australia is similar to the ways in which white boys are seen in the United States—boys are naturally naughty. Their behavior may be exasperating, but it is also endearing. "Boys will be boys: they are mischievous, they get into trouble, they can stand up for themselves" (Ferguson 2011, 439). African American boys, in contrast, are not given this dispensation. Their behavior is more quickly perceived as dangerous, vicious, and a threat to order as well as a sign that they are "at risk" for total failure. You should recall the discussion of black boys in school from chapter 2 describing the boys as a problem. In her fieldwork in a school with African American children, Ann Ferguson heard teachers speak of boys as "on the fast track to San Quentin prison," and make observations such as "That one has a jail-cell with his name on it" (Ferguson 2011, 440).

We learned in chapter 2 that sometimes schools engage in a continuous battle with the boys by punishing them for their behavior. Other times schools are able to drive the boys' warrior narratives underground or transfer them to the sports fields. And sometimes the boys' behavior is diagnosed as **attention deficit hyperactivity disorder** (**ADHD**), and they are medicated.

Medicalizing and Medicating Boys in Schools

Ritalin, a medication used to treat ADHD, is one of the top-selling drugs today. Diagnosis for ADHD increased by 700 percent in the 1990s, and Ritalin is now the drug most often dispensed in school to students in the United States (Rafalovich 2005). Of all the Ritalin prescriptions in the world, 90 percent are written for Americans (Leo 2002). It is mostly boys who are diagnosed with the disorder and prescribed the drugs; boys are three to ten times more likely to be identified with ADHD than are girls (Biederman et al. 2002).

ADHD is a cluster of problems that include hyperactivity and difficulty concentrating. Children who are diagnosed have symptoms such as inability to sit and focus on their school-work or to get along in a classroom setting that demands that they wait their turn, raise their hand, and stay in their seat.

A brochure for teachers about identifying ADHD describes a typical case:

> John, a third grade student, is often noncompliant and does not begin tasks when asked. During a two week observation period, he exhibited the following behaviors on a routine basis: John sharpened his pencil three times before beginning work. John fell out of his chair when given an assignment with 50 problems. He pretended to be the class clown. The class laughed. After leaving his reading group on the way back to his seat for independent work, John tripped Sally. He was sent to the corner of the room. (Leo 2002)

Some psychologists argue that ADHD is a serious problem and that Ritalin has saved children like John from failure and helped them be happier and more successful in every area of their lives, especially school. They argue that, if anything, we should be concerned with the underdiagnosis of girls. They assert that a particular type of the disorder, the "inattentive type," is more prevalent in girls and may be overlooked by teachers because it is marked less by disruptive, impulsive behavior and more by disorganized, unfocused performance (Hinshaw 2002). The disorder may be equally destructive to the girl's life, but it is not as disruptive to the classroom and, therefore, is ignored and goes untreated.

Others, however, worry that ADHD is an excuse for medicating children, especially boys, for behavior that is in the normal range or is caused by social factors rather than neurological ones (Goldman et al. 1998; Timimi 2002). The critics point out that Ritalin and other ADHD drugs are given to children at two to three times the rate one might normally expect. Although ADHD is estimated to affect 3 percent to 5 percent of school-age children, some 8 percent to 10 percent of children have been diagnosed with ADHD and are taking drugs for it (Shaw 2002). Others have noted the geographic disparity of prescription rates, suggesting that children, at least in some states (the highest rates are in North Carolina and Louisiana; the lowest, in California, Nevada, and Colorado) are being overprescribed (Cox, Motheral, Henderson, and Mager 2003).

Troubling recent findings of studies from New York to California have linked rising rates of ADHD in children to common pesticides on food. If this is the case, treating the victims of chemical exposure with other chemicals (medication), rather than eliminating the sources of the problem, is particularly reprehensible (Pesticide Action Network 2010).

Geographic variation and the gap between the numbers of those who randomly might be expected to exhibit the disorder and the numbers that are being treated for it suggest that factors in the social context may be responsible for the incorrect labeling of children as disabled (Diller 1996). Critics argue that the social structure of schools constrains children for long periods of time and leaves little room for individual variation. They also assert that our culture gives a double message to boys, in particular, who are supposed to be active, assertive, and outspoken—boisterous—but who are made to set aside these boyish traits when they go to school (Hart, Grant, and Riley 2006).

Teaching Materials

Reading materials in schools are another critical feature of the gendered terrain. Books and other resources that are used for instruction, compared to other sources of information, are especially powerful because they are presented to students as authoritative and students are asked to see them uncritically (Stewart, Cooper, Stewart, and Friedley 2003). According to Philip Smith (1985):

> Students are less free to disregard or be critical of educational materials than they are of the media. In fact, they are frequently required to absorb and assimilate the material in minute detail. Second, people attach a great deal of credibility and authority to educational and reference material and are, therefore, probably much more attentive to the messages they convey and susceptible to the sway of their influence. (37)

In the 1970s, a number of studies were done in the United States on the books children read, and remarkable gender differences were found (Weitzman and Rizzo 1975). Three times as many men and boys were characters in reading books, six times as many men and boys were subjects of autobiographies, and pictures showed fifteen times more boys and men than girls and women (Milner 1977). In collections of essays and stories for English class, six times as many men authors were included (Arlow and Froschel 1976).

These studies were replicated in the 1990s, and the ratio of women and girls to men and boys had improved, but men and boy characters were still more visible and more likely to be active and involved in important areas of social life. Boys and men were portrayed as participating in a wider range of occupations and as being more adventurous and were often depicted rescuing girls and women. Pictures in high school chemistry books in the 1990s still showed three times as many boys and men as women and girls (Bazler and Simonis 1991). Literature anthologies also continued to show a preponderance of men authors (Stewart et al. 2003).

What are the messages that such enduring differences transmit to schoolchildren? In 2011 McCabe, Fairchild, Grauerholz, Pescosolido, and Tope (2011), who reviewed the presentation of gender in 5,618 books published in the United States throughout the twentieth century, concluded that children's literature "**symbolically annihilated**" girls and women thereby helping to reproduce a patriarchal gender system. The character of this body of children's literature is one more element assuring the continuance of gender inequality by means of its subtle influence on our understanding of the parts girls and boys, women and men play in our world.

In China, similar findings have been made in research on gender in textbooks. One study of reading texts used for grades 2 through 6 in 2008 showed that 75 percent of the characters in the books were boys or men. In addition, when girls and women were shown, they were more likely to be in minor or supporting roles to a masculine main character. The roles that the adult characters took were also gendered. Both boys and girls were most likely to be shown as students, but men were most likely to be government officials, soldiers, and professionals, while women were most likely to appear as housewives and teachers. Gender was also expressed in the place of the characters' activity. More than half the women and girls

(56 percent) were shown in their homes, and girls and women were much less likely to be shown outdoors (24%), at school (17%), or inside someplace other than their homes (3%). In contrast, men and boys were most likely to be shown outdoors (49%) rather than in their homes (27%), indoors (19%), or at school (5%) (Liew 2008).

These problems persist into higher education. A review of the photographs in introductory sociology texts for college students showed a similar invisibility of women (Ferree and Hall 1990). Forty-four percent of the photos included only men, while just 19 percent included only women. And while pictures of women were likely to occur in chapters on family, sexuality, education, and gender inequality, they were underrepresented in chapters on politics (Spade 2001).

One result of the invisibility of women in students' reading material is ignorance about the contribution women have made to our ideas, social institutions, and history. For example, one (Fournier and Wineburg 1997) study explored the effect of the invisible woman in textbooks by asking fifth to eighth graders to illustrate passages from a history book. The boys drew all men—mostly warriors. The girls drew families with women in them, but they also always included at least one man. The children's view of history reflected the words and illustrations they had seen in the text, and while that view sometimes showed women as participants in history, it always showed men.

Bullying

C. J. Pascoe (2007) shows that the terrain of bullying in the California high school she studied was shaped and sustained by homophobia, sexism, and inequality. Gendered insults— "fag!!'—were central disciplinary mechanisms shoring up masculinity among the white boys in the school. Pascoe argues that this harassment was fundamental to the formation of a gendered identity among these boys. Fearing that the fag identity could become permanent, they "policed" each other's behaviors to avoid it. In the high school usage, "fag" was another word for non-masculine. Not homosexuality, but **effeminacy**, was the problem.

Bullying is a problem that creates enormous problems for children in schools the world over (United Nations 2006c). Bullying stigmatizes various categories of boys and girls by race ethnicity, social class, and many other attributes and can create long-term psychological pain. At its worst it can lead to suicide, physical abuse, and murder. Because of its pervasiveness and the problems it causes, bullying has been identified as one of the important aspects of violence against children that needs to be addressed at every level of the global community. But what exactly does bullying do? Pascoe's study shows that bullies bully to shore up their own gendered identity. A second important consequence of bullying is that it maintains segregation among people in different social categories such as gender; and, thereby, it helps to maintain gender inequality by presenting rules and punishing children who step outside the lines.

Much of the creation of gender expectations in schools is in the hands of people other than students, such as teachers and textbook writers. Bullying, however, is an arena in which children police each other. Many scholars have discovered the ways children perceive rules about gender and the ways they go about demanding that everyone follow those rules: for instance, by using ostracism, ridiculing, and hitting. Kowalski and Kanitkar (2003), for example, studied kindergarteners by asking teachers to take handheld recorders into their classrooms and record the conversations their students had about gender over a three-month period. They found that 97 percent of the gender comments included gender stereotypes.

For example, a boy playing with a butterfly puppet was told by another boy in his peer group, "You need to have a boy puppet, and give that girl puppet to a girl!" (Lamb, Bigler, Liben, and Green 2009, 362). Bullying, of course, can include much more devastating comments and even physical abuse, but Kowalski and Kantikar's (2003) research shows how pervasive and incessant the problems are.

Lindsay Lamb and her colleagues (2009) created a technique to try to help children confront gender bullying by offering strategies to respond to six forms of sexist comments they encounter: (1) gender-based exclusion from peer interaction (e.g., "Only boys can play this game."), (2) role-based biases (e.g., "You can't be the doctor, you have to be the nurse."), (3) comments about a child's counterstereotypic characteristics (e.g., "Why do you have a boy's haircut?"), (4) comparative judgments (e.g., "Boys are better at math than girls."), (5) trait stereotyping (e.g., "Girls are gentle."), and (6) highlighting gender in a neutral context (e.g., "Boys sit over here and girls sit over there.").

First, the children were given a brief presentation about what bullying is, how it might affect them, and how it is related to stereotyping and prejudice. Next, six lessons (one for each type of sexist remark) were presented. The lessons consisted of the following phrases that the children practiced with the researcher: (1) "You can't say that boys [girls] can't play!" (gender-based exclusion from peer interaction), (2) "Not true, gender doesn't limit you!" (role-based biases), (3) "There's no such thing as a girls' [boys'] —!" (comments about a child's counterstereotypic characteristics), (4) "Give it a rest, no group is best!" (comparative judgments), (5) "I disagree! Sexism is silly to me!" (trait stereotyping), and (6) "That's weird, being boys and girls doesn't matter here!" (highlighting gender in a neutral context) (Lamb et al. 2009, 367).

To test the effectiveness of the lessons, the children were asked to return a misplaced item to the school office. Each girl was asked to carry a tool-belt to the school office, and each boy was asked to carry a purse. On their way to the office, a same-gender confederate child stopped the participant and made a sexist remark: "Purses [tool belts] are for girls [boys]!" Responses were recorded by an observer who was out of sight and coded as: (a) implicitly agreeing with the sexist remark by minimizing involvement in the behavior (e.g., "I'm just taking this to the office."), (b) explicitly agreeing with the sexist remark (e.g., "I know!"), (c) ignoring the sexist remark (e.g., staring at or walking past the confederate), (d) objecting to the unfair/antisocial nature of the sexist remark (e.g., "That's mean!"), or (e) specifically challenging the sexist nature of the remark (e.g., "There is no such thing as something being just for boys.") (Lamb et al. 2009, 369).

Lamb and her colleagues (2009) found that before the lessons, children rarely challenged their peers' sexist remarks; but after the intervention, their challenges were significantly more common and a six-month posttest revealed that not only was the lesson retained, but it had in fact become more widespread. Furthermore, among the girls at least, these changes in behavior were accompanied by decreases in gender typing.

HIGH SCHOOL

You have just read how the "**fag discourse**" regulated high school boys' performance of masculinity in the school studied by C. J. Pascoe. In general, ethnographic accounts of high school life and teenage cultures focus on boys (Willis 1981; MacLeod 2009), and this is to some extent true of Pascoe's work as well. An exception is the work of Julie Bettie, who explores the ways girls "perform" class in a small town California high school (Bettie 2000, 2003). Bettie notes that women had not been well-represented in analyses of class or of race (Bettie's study was published about ten years ago). Rather, most observers looked at girls and women only as gendered subjects, a correction that owed much to thirty prior years of feminist research. Bettie was one of a number of researchers who wanted research on women to include inquiries about multiple inequalities besides gender. In her own work, Bettie examined how girls in a small town high school deployed gender, color, and ethnicity to shape their "lived culture" and their "subjective identity" (Bettie 2000, 7).

This attention to how girls manage multiple inequalities and identities draws on the feminist concept of "intersectionality," which holds that oppressive institutionalized inequalities (racism, sexism, homophobia, for example) are interconnected and need to be analyzed together. In the high school Bettie studied, students arrived with and built upon many identities and experiences. For example, about 60 percent of the students in this school were white, and 40 percent were Mexican or Mexican American. Most were from working class families, but some were the children of middle class professionals. Some working class girls were from "settled-living" (relatively secure) families, and others were from "hard-living" families (whose home lives were "chaotic and unpredictable") (Bettie 2000, 8; Howell 1972). Over the year that Bettie "hung out" in the school, she came to understand the informal groupings and hierarchy that girls constructed from and within their differences. Among whites they included "preps" (middle class), "skaters/alternatives" (settled-living), "hicks" (settled- and hard-living), and "smokers/rockers/trash" (hard-living); among Mexican-American students there were "Mexican preps" (middle class and settled- and hard-living), "*las chicas*" (settled-living), and "*cholas/os*" or "hard-cores" (hard-living).

The girls' group memberships set them on particular life trajectories: to four-year colleges, to vocational programs at junior colleges, to low-wage jobs right out of high school. Performing the particular race and class cultures of each group enabled the girls to sort themselves out along class and racial lines.

Bettie imagines the class futures of the girls who will graduate from high school into "the deindustrializing U.S. economy" in which only low-income service jobs will be available to them. She wonders how they will understand and act in this new world order as classed, raced, and gendered subjects faced with declining opportunities.

Counting Gender Differences in High School

Most people in the United States finish high school. The numbers of students who did not complete high school declined from about 27.2 percent in 1960 to 9 percent in 2005, but these numbers vary by gender and race ethnicity. Boys in the United States drop out of school more often (8.5%) than do girls (7.5%), but race ethnicity makes an even bigger difference than gender (National Center for Education Statistics 2009). Table 5-1 shows the dropout rate for boys and girls of different racial/ethnic groups. Hispanic people, in particular, are likely to drop out of high school. Latinas are a little more likely to graduate than Latinos, but both are much less likely to graduate than white or black students—and the racial/ethnic gap is growing (National Center for Education Statistics 2009).

TABLE 5-1 High School Dropout Rates in the U.S. by Gender and Race Ethnicity, 2008

	Boys	Girls
White	5.4%	4.20%
Black	8.70%	11.10%
Hispanic	19.90%	16.7%

Source: National Center for Education Statistics (2009).

TABLE 5-2 Participation in High School Extracurricular Activities by Gender, 2001

	Girls	Boys
Newspaper/yearbook	13%	6%
Music and performing arts	31%	9%
Athletic teams	32%	45%
Academic clubs	19%	12%
Student government	13%	8%
Other activities	44%	26%

Source: Freeman (2004).

The reasons for these gaps are the subject of much debate. Perhaps the most significant determinant of the gap between racial ethnic groups is the unequal amounts of money spent across school systems from one neighborhood to the next. Wealthy neighborhoods are more likely to be white; and because of a larger tax base, they are able to spend more on education, including programs to retain students. The gap between boys and girls is also difficult to explain. In the discussion that follows on why women are more likely to complete college degrees, several explanations are suggested that might also help us understand the gender gap among high school students. Not only are girls more likely to complete high school, but they also seem to be more involved in school activities. Table 5-2 shows that, compared to boys, high school girls are more often involved in all extracurricular activities except sports; and we will see in chapter 11 that girls are making gains in athletics as well.

Math and Science and Gender

Math and science are areas of particular concern because so many jobs are attached to success in these disciplines. Girls now outnumber boys in college preparatory courses. About 2 percent of girls and boys were in these courses in the early 1980s, but today 33 percent of girls are, and 29 percent of boys are. Table 5-3 shows that high school girls have caught up and now surpass boys in the proportion enrolled in geometry, algebra II, biology, and chemistry courses. They are only slightly behind boys in calculus and physics.

Girls are catching up with boys in all disciplines. Forty years ago in the United States, for example, boys were much more likely than girls to take courses in math and science. Today, however, girls are just as likely or even more likely to take courses in math and science than are boys.

Source: Associated Press NEA Policy Brief 2008.

TABLE 5-3 Percentage of Students Enrolled in High School Math and Science Classes by Gender, 2000

	Geometry	Algebra II	Calculus	Biology	Chemistry	Physics
Girls	81%	71%	11%	93%	66%	29%
Boys	75%	65%	12%	83%	58%	34%

Source: Freeman (2004).

College women are also catching up with men in their participation in math and science in almost every field. Women are nearly half the graduates in math (48 percent), agriculture and natural resources (45 percent), physical sciences (41 percent), and business (39 percent), and they are the majority in biology (60 percent). Only in engineering are women (20 percent) still significantly less likely to earn a degree, and even there, the numbers increased 2,000 percent between 1969 and 2001 (see Box 5-1 for a discussion of the significance of the Mars rover *Opportunity* for women in science).

GENDER IN EVERYDAY LIFE   BOX 5-1
MARS MISSION

When the second robotic rover, *Opportunity,* landed on Mars, it represented an important landmark for women scientists. Only a century ago, women were not allowed to look into a telescope, and a half century ago, women were not hired at observatories, with the excuse that there were no women's bathrooms. But 10 percent of the engineers and 20 percent of the 154-member team of scientists who put *Opportunity* on Mars are women. The numbers are still small, but they are growing; and women are now in every category at the National Aeronautics and Space Administration (NASA). Even more important, in the younger ranks, women are equal to or even surpassing men in their numbers. Fifty-seven percent of astronomers under age twenty-three and the majority of graduate assistants and research fellows in the field are women (Ginty 2004).

Although women are equaling men and in some cases surpassing them in obtaining degrees in math and science, ideas about gender still identify these fields as masculine. One of the important results of the identification of math and science as masculine is that women may be less likely to recognize their abilities in these fields.

Shelley Correll (2001) examined this question by looking at the math exam scores and course grades of eighth-grade students in the United States. She then looked at how the students assessed their skill by asking true–false questions such as, "Mathematics is one of my best subjects," "I have always done well in math," and "I get good marks in math." In addition, she looked at students' exam scores and course grades in English and their answers to the same questions about their success in English courses.

She found that when she compared boys and girls with similar scores and grades in math courses, the boys were more likely to perceive themselves as good at math. The boys did not, however, assess themselves better than girls did who had similar scores and grades in English. In other words, the boys did not think they were better at everything; they just thought they were better at math.

Correll (2001) argues that our feelings about our competence may have a powerful effect on our future choices. She writes, "Boys do not pursue mathematical activities at a higher rate than girls do because they are better at mathematics. They do so, at least partially, because they think they are better" (2001, 1728). The association of math and math-related skills with masculinity may allow boys to assess themselves as more competent and may therefore lead them to pursue further education and career paths in these fields. The association of math with masculinity may, at the same time, be holding back equally competent or more competent girls.

Vocational Education

Girls have made impressive strides in education, but vocational education programs continue to reflect patterns that existed twenty years ago. Surveys show that young women are still clustered in a few programs and that those vocations have median hourly wages of about $9 an hour. Young men, in contrast, are likely to be training in skilled trades with median hourly wages of about $30 an hour (*Washington Post* 2002, A8). Table 5-4 shows the proportion of men and women in the different areas of study in vocational education programs in twelve regions.

The table shows that women account for nearly all the students in cosmetology (96 percent) and a large proportion of those in courses in child care (87%) and health aide (86 percent), all of which are highly stereotyped occupations. Young men make up the over-whelming majority of students in courses in plumbing (94 percent), electrician (94 percent), welding (93 percent), carpentry (93 percent), and automotive (92 percent). The picture we get from the numbers is similar to the images in the movie *Grease*, which was supposed to depict the quaint gender divisions in high school of the 1950s. In voc-ed not much has changed.

Title IX, No Child Left Behind, and Single-Sex Schools

Civil rights laws passed in the 1960s began to protect women from discrimination at work, but the protection did not extend to education. Title IX, which we examine more fully in chapter 11, was passed in 1972 to try to fill this gap by addressing gender inequity in schools from kindergarten through graduate school. Title IX made it illegal for schools that received any federal assistance, including universities that received federally funded scholarships or research grants, to discriminate against girls and women. Title IX was a turning point in gender in education in the United States. Before 1972, public universities restricted the entrance of women through quotas and higher standards. For example, women who applied to study at some colleges needed to present scores thirty to forty points higher on achievement tests than did men who applied. Even in fields dominated by women, women students were restricted. For example, nursing schools before Title IX often did not permit married women to be students (General Accounting Office 2001).

Title IX outlaws treating boys and girls differently in school in the United States. It currently permits select single-sex classes—in physical education, for example—but it does not

TABLE 5-4 Gender Segregation in Vocational and Technical Courses, 2002

	Men Enrolled	Women Enrolled
Cosmetology	4%	96%
Child care	13%	87%
Health aide	14%	86%
Drafting	77%	23%
Automotive	92%	8%
Carpentry	93%	7%
Welding	93%	7%
Electrician	94%	6%
Plumbing	94%	6%

Source: *Washington Post* (2002, A8).

allow schools to segregate students arbitrarily. This is because when groups have been segregated in the past, the least valued group has ended up with fewer resources and fewer opportunities. In looking at the problems in K–12 classrooms, some educators are now suggesting that we should establish more same-sex schools. Single-sex schools are unusual in the United States, but they have been established to try to create gender equity in Australia, England, Ireland, and Jamaica (Streitmatter 1999).

The **No Child Left Behind Act** is an education policy established by the George W. Bush administration in 2002 to improve academic achievement of disadvantaged students. It appears to conflict with Title IX and may increase same-sex schools in the United States because it encourages schools to try same-sex classrooms. Which policy will supersede the other will be decided in the courts. In the meantime, about 250 schools in the United States accept only one sex or have some same-sex classrooms. This number has increased from just three classrooms in 1996. In 2006 the federal government began to actively promote same-sex classrooms. The government predicts that about 10 percent of the nation's 90,000 public schools will eventually become same-sex schools (Toppo 2006).Those who support boys-only classrooms assert that boys are less distracted and that the curriculum can be better designed in ways that fit their interests and talents. Although this approach is popular, the research doesn't support it. Boys do not do better in single sex-schools and classrooms, and in fact some studies have shown that boys gain more language skills in coed classrooms (Van de Gaer, Pustjens, Van Damme, and De Munter 2004). Differences in boys' academic performance in coed and boys-only classrooms seem to wash out when intake criteria are considered. This means that while some studies have found higher performance among boys in same-sex schools, those differences are more likely a result of the higher standards in admissions to exclusive boys' schools than they are of the experience of attending classes without girls present (Tsolidis and Dobson 2006).

Those who support girls-only classrooms assert that girls feel like outsiders in coeducational classrooms, their voices are silenced, and their confidence is diminished (Streitmatter 1999). They maintain that coeducation only appears to be equal. Girls may sit side by side with boys, but they are not fully integrated and they do not have the same educational experience that boys do.

Some research on all-girls schools provides support for this point of view. The research shows that students in all-girls schools speak out in class and participate more. In all-girls physics classes, the girls understand the material better, work together more often, and are not afraid to ask questions. When physics classes are coeducational, the boys tend to dominate the discussion and create a climate of competition (Blair and Northway 2001).

Another study of all-girls physics classes reported similar positive results (Illinois Mathematics and Science Academy [IMSA] 1995). This study found that, compared to girls in coeducational classes, students in all-girls classes scored higher on physics tests, improved their problem-solving and analytical skills, and decided to take more physics and math classes in subsequent semesters. The girls who attended these schools also spoke more freely in class, and they more often attended college and graduate school and majored in math and science.

An especially interesting result of the study was that the all-girls classes created a "girl culture" in which the classroom dynamics were altered. Students in the all-girls classes had more influence over classroom dynamics, and a special rapport developed in which the students took greater responsibility for their own learning as well as that of their classmates.

Studies have also shown a shift in class participation by women and men in higher education courses as the proportion of men in a class increases. The more men there are in a class, the less the women enter into sustained discussion, and the more active the men become (Canada and Pringle 1995). In addition, single-sex classrooms report less gender stereotyping and fewer explicit sexual harassment incidents such as drawing unflattering pictures of the girls (Lee et al. 1994).

Not all researchers agree, however. Some studies have found little difference in achievement between single-sex schools and coeducational schools (Carpenter and Hayden 1987; Bell 1989). Furthermore, one large study concluded that all-girls schools are detrimental to girls. It found that, in contrast to all-boys schools and coeducational schools, teachers in all-girls schools talked down to the students, encouraged students in hard work rather than correct work, and created dependency (Lee et al. 1994).

What accounts for the disagreements in the research on girls-only education? One answer might be that the high levels of performance reported in some girls-only classrooms are due to factors other than just the absence of boys. The differences may not be related to the gender of classmates. Rather, they may be a result of spending more money on education. For example, single-sex classrooms that report higher levels of learning are also of higher quality in other ways. They have smaller class sizes, more engaged parents, better-trained teachers, and stronger academic emphasis (D. Sadker and Zittleman 2004).

In addition, even if all-girls classes are sometimes more effective in teaching girls, this solution may still be a dangerous one. Civil rights advocates are concerned that recent changes in federal policy that allow schools to set up same-sex schools and classrooms might mean that school districts will begin segregating girls and boys based on "outdated and dangerous stereotypes" (Toppo 2006, 1). Barrie Thorne (1993) also warns that the underlying assumption of much of this research—if girls are left alone they will create a different kind of classroom atmosphere that reflects "girl culture," with more turn taking and supportive learning groups—may not be valid. Her research shows that the picture is more complex. Many or maybe even most boys are not really part of "boy culture" because they, too, are dominated by more aggressive boys. And, all girls do not participate in the cooperative classrooms that make up the picture of girl culture.

Michael Kimmel (2000), a critic of single-sex education, asserts that the promotion of single-sex schools is a sign that we have abandoned the goal of transforming our social institutions into safe, equal places for both women and men. He maintains that if we believe that the only way for girls and women to be safe and enjoy access to social benefits like education is to establish single-sex "safe havens," we have given up critical efforts to create a more human-friendly society. He cites John Dewey (1911), who scoffed at single-sex schools, asking whether we have " 'female botany,' 'female algebra' and for all I know a 'female multiplication table.' " Dewey argued that coeducated girls attained "greater self-reliance and a desire to win approval by deserving it instead of 'working' [manipulating] others." In addition, Dewey maintained that boys in coeducational settings learned gentleness, unselfishness, courtesy, and more-helpful channels for expression than "lawless boisterousness" (Kimmel 2000, 59).

Kimmel (2000) agrees with Dewey, arguing that single-sex schools may challenge men's domination of our educational institutions but that they also perpetuate and reproduce that masculine dominance. Single-sex schools imply that women must have special schools because they cannot do well without special treatment, and they imply that men cannot change. Single-sex schools insult both women and men.

SAT Scores

As all American college students know, SATs are an important gateway to higher education. SAT I assesses students' potential for learning about a subject. SAT II is an achievement test that measures what students have already learned in a particular subject area. SAT I is the test we normally think of when we say "SAT," and it is the test that large numbers of students take as a requirement for entrance into college.

These standardized tests are usually a key feature in each student's college application, and decisions about who will be admitted are frequently determined by their scores. Besides surpassing men in the proportion who enter college, women are now the majority of those students who take SATs (55 percent). Men, however, score higher on average on the test.

Table 5-5 shows recent scores of boys and girls on SAT I tests in reading, writing, and mathematics. The scores show that they are nearly identical on reading, that girls outscore boys a little in writing, and that boys outscore girls quite a bit in math. These numbers have not varied much in the past few decades. Overall, boys earned an average of 1,512 points and girls 1,486 on all three tests. Why do men receive higher numbers on SATs?

One explanation is that women do not do as well because more women take the test, which means that a more select group of men take SATs. However, men have scored higher than women for a long time, even before women were the majority of test takers.

Some people believe that the test is gender biased, although the College Board, which designs the questions, claims to make every effort to eliminate gender and racial ethnic bias. Gender bias in the questions may, however, be an issue at least in the past results. In 1998, after persistent complaints about gender bias in the test, the College Board changed the exam, and the gender gap narrowed. Gender bias appears in the questions, for example, when activities with which boys might be more familiar, such as sports or auto racing, are used in word problems in the math section. Girls do better on questions that relate to relationships, aesthetics, and the humanities (Rosser 1989).

The history of the SAT is interesting in this regard. When the test was first developed and given to high school students, boys did better than girls on the math section, whereas girls out-performed boys on the verbal section. The test makers went back to readjust the questions to close the gap on the verbal sections. The company that designed the test, ETS (Educational Testing Service), believed that the verbal score gap showed a bias against boys, so they added more questions pertaining to politics, business, and sports, topics in which boys tended to do

TABLE 5-5 National SAT Scores by Gender, 2013

	Reading	Writing	Mathematics
Girls	494	493	499
Boys	499	482	531

Source: College Board (2013).

better. They did not adjust the math test, perhaps believing that when girls are superior, balancing is required but that when boys are superior, no adjustment is necessary (Dwyer 1996).

Another explanation for the gap is the format of the test, which coincides with a masculine style of test taking. Boys tend to do better on multiple-choice exams, whereas girls are better at short-answer, essay, and constructed-response questions. The math and reading sections of the SAT I are multiple-choice.

The SAT also deducts a fraction of a point for wrong answers but not for leaving an answer blank. Boys are more likely to take the risk and guess rather than leave a question blank. The ACT does not have a guessing penalty, and the gender gap on that test is much smaller (FairTest 2002).

Furthermore, SATs are timed tests, rewarding speed. Research shows that boys and girls approach problem solving differently. Girls are more likely to work a problem out completely, to consider more than one possible correct answer, and to check their answers. These are probably good study skills, but they are not useful for achieving high SAT scores. Studies show that when the time constraint is removed, girls do much better, whereas boys' scores remain about the same (FairTest 2002).

The most important explanation for why boys have higher scores in math on the SAT I is that boys are better prepared in high school for taking SATs because of the kinds of courses they take. As students move through middle school and high school, girls used to be less likely to take math classes and often took only the minimum requirement. When boys and girls with identical backgrounds in math take standardized tests, their scores on math tests are more similar (Entwisle, Alexander, and Olson 1994). As girls catch up with boys in the courses they take in math and science, they are also catching up on the standardized tests in these areas.

Not only is the gap diminishing, but the distribution of SAT I math scores for boys and girls is becoming more similar. Scores for boys are more variable, with more boys at the extremes with very high scorers and very low scorers, whereas girls tend to have scores in the middle. This difference, however, is also changing. In the 1980s, thirteen times more boys than girls scored 700 or more out of a possible 800 in math on the SAT. Today boys are about three times more likely than girls to score in this high range. Although girls have not completely caught up with boys, the number of girl "junior math wizards" has soared in the last two decades. This improvement has corresponded with a change in educational opportunities for girls, in which special programs and mentoring have increasingly encouraged girls to take higher level math and science courses (Halpern et al. 2007). Girls are now nearly identical to boys in the level and number of high school math and science courses they take, and their math scores on SATs are similar, although still not identical.

These tests, however, remain important gatekeepers, and because women still do not score quite as well, women may be prevented from entering the most prestigious institutions or receiving scholarships. However, are standardized-test scores valid criteria for making these kinds of decisions about prospective students? The purpose of SATs is to try to predict which students will be successful in college. Because girls score lower than boys on the tests, we might expect that girls would not do as well in college and would receive lower grades or fail to complete their degrees. Women, in fact, get better grades in college courses on average and are more likely to finish their degrees. Boys' SAT scores are on average thirty-three points higher than the scores of girls who receive the same grades in the same college courses

(Wainer and Steinberg 1992). The SATs, therefore, appear to be measuring something other than skills required for success in college, or at least they are measuring them differently for women and men. The best predictor of success in the college classroom is high school grade point average (GPA), followed by SAT II. SAT I is not a good predictor.

INTERNATIONAL COMPARISONS ON STANDARDIZED TESTS

Since 1995, forty-one countries representing 14 percent of the world's population have reported education data by gender for eighth-graders (Nicholson 2010). The data from these reports show that in eleven countries there are no gender gaps in math or science: the United States, Singapore, Russia, Thailand, Australia, Ireland, Romania, Flemish Belgium, Cyprus, Colombia, and South Africa.

You might be thinking that these data seem to contradict the SAT I score report for the United States cited in the previous section. The reason that the SAT I shows a **gender gap in math** while the international reports do not show a gender gap in math (or science) in the United States is that the SAT I assesses the *potential* for someone to do well in a course. The international scores are of tests of *achievement* assessing how much a student knows after having taken a course in math. Given the same background in course work, therefore, it appears that boys and girls in many nations score about the same when given exams in those subjects.

Although the gender gap in math has disappeared in many nations, there are still important differences by gender in language skills. For example, in literacy scores of girls and boys in fourth grade, girls scored above boys in all sixty-eight nations reporting. The largest gaps were in Kuwait, Iran, New Zealand, and Belize. Remember, of course, that these tests were only given to children attending school.

The international educational reports, however, point to many other inequities besides gender. The biggest gaps are not between boys and girls within a country but the gap from one country to the next. For example, the very highest scores from students in the United States in math are about equal to the average score of students in the top-scoring nations such as Singapore, Korea, Japan, the Czech Republic, and Hungary.

HIGHER EDUCATION AND GENDER

Higher education is one place where women in many places in the world have made remarkable gains in the past few decades. In Algeria, for example, 70 percent of lawyers and 60 percent of judges are women, and women dominate in medicine as well. These changes have been spurred by increasing numbers of women in higher education. Sixty percent of all college students in Algeria are women (Slackman 2007).

Women and Higher Education in the United States

The United States now has the highest proportion of women attending college of any nation in the world. At the turn of the twentieth century, however, education experts in the United States claimed that women should not become too educated because it diverted energy from

TABLE 5-6 BA, MA, and PhD Degrees Earned by Gender, 1985–2010

	Bachelor's Degrees		Master's Degrees		Doctoral Degrees	
	Women	Men	Women	Men	Women	Men
1965–1966	220,228	299,287	47,521	93,081	2,116	16,121
1974–1975	418,092	504,841	130,880	161,570	7,266	26,817
1999–2000	659,000	502,000	227,000	187,000	19,000	27,400
2009–2010	919,824	682,656	382,920	228,773	74,889	65,616

Source: Blair and Northway (2001, 62); U.S. Department of Education (2012).

their uteruses to their brains and made them too feeble to bear healthy children. The first university to integrate by gender in the United States was Oberlin College in 1833. Oberlin officials originally decided to allow women in because they believed that coeducation would enhance the education of men. University officials argued that as part of a solid education, men students needed a "more wholesome and realistic view of women," which could be accomplished by permitting them to be educated along with women (Stock 1978, 190).

In 1870 the first survey of college graduates in the United States showed that about 85 percent of the 9,400 bachelor of arts degrees (BAs) were awarded to men. During the twentieth century, women began to catch up with men and are now pulling ahead in admissions to college and completion of college degrees. The gap between women and men is expected to continue to grow with women in the lead as they pass men in their pursuit of higher education. Table 5-6 shows the way these numbers changed.

In addition to women's catching up and surpassing men in the total number of degrees obtained, the gender balance in many fields of university study has also become more equal as women enter fields once thought to be for men only. For example, in 1971 only about 1 percent of dentistry degrees went to women, but in 1997, 37 percent of the graduates of dental schools were women. In business degrees, women have almost caught up with men. In 1971 10 percent of business degrees went to women, and in 1997 49 percent went to women. Women students have surpassed the numbers of men in law school. Women have made some headway in engineering, computer sciences, and physical sciences, although the numbers of women receiving degrees in these fields remains low. At the same time, between 1971 and 1996, men became more likely to earn degrees in fields dominated by women, such as nursing (from 3 percent to 11 percent), elementary education (from 9 percent to 12 percent), and home economics (from 4 percent to 12 percent). Table 5-7 shows the proportion of women receiving degrees in several disciplines in 2008.

Important differences within fields, however, remain. For example, the number of degrees awarded in social sciences is about the same for women and men, but women are more likely to receive a degree in sociology or anthropology, whereas men receive them in economics and geography. Business management is also nearly equal, but women are concentrated in the specialty of human resource management and men in finance. Law is gender stratified with women in family law and men in taxes; physicians divide themselves into women in family practice and men in anesthesiology specialties (Sapiro 2003).

TABLE 5-7 Undergraduates by Age, Race Ethnicity, and Gender, 2004

	Under 24			Over 25		
	Total%	*Men*	*Women*	*Total%*	*Men*	*Women*
All	61%	28%	33%	39%	15%	24%
White	63%	29%	34%	37%	15%	22%
African American	50%	20%	30%	50%	16%	34%
Hispanic	61%	26%	35%	39%	15%	24%
Asian American	65%	32%	33%	35%	14%	21%
American Indian	49%	21%	28%	51%	16%	35%

Source: U.S. Department of Education (2004).

The gender gap in enrollment and graduation in higher education is most pronounced in the **historically black colleges**, where women compose 70 percent of the student body despite efforts to recruit men. However, the trend for women to increasingly outnumber men exists in universities across the board, and some institutions are concerned. In 1990 the University of Georgia became so disturbed that women were the majority of graduates (55 percent) they began giving an edge to men applicants, who were admitted with lower high school grades and scores on SATs. The practice was discontinued when they were threatened with a federal lawsuit (Fletcher 2002). Other colleges and universities, especially private ones, are still using different criteria for choosing men and women for admission into their institutions.

Race ethnicity is not the only variable that intersects with gender, however. Age is also important. Table 5-8 shows the proportion of undergraduate degrees by gender, race ethnicity, and age. Read the rows across to see that nontraditional students (over twenty-five years old), who make up a growing proportion of college students, are much more likely to be women. African American and Native American women undergraduates particularly fall into this over-twenty-five category.

Social class also intersects with gender to create different rates of college attendance. In Table 5-9, the data are divided by race ethnicity and by income level. A quartile refers to one-fourth of the population. The lowest quartile indicates the poorest 25 percent of the population, and the highest quartile the richest. The middle quartiles are the rest of the population. Table 5-9 allows us to look at the different racial ethnic groups in the four groups. The number in each cell is the proportion of college students who are men in a specific quartile and racial ethnic group. For example, the number in the right column on the first line tells us that if we look at the category of white students in the highest income bracket, 51 percent of them are men. Women are not the majority in this socioeconomic group. The left column shows the proportion of men in the lowest income group. In all racial ethnic categories, men are in the minority (less than 50%). Table 5-9 tells us that women have made the greatest strides in catching up and surpassing men in college attendance in the poorest households.

In the United States, both men and women are increasingly likely to enter and complete college. In 1940 about one-quarter of Americans finished high school and 5 percent received

TABLE 5-8 Percentage of Dependent Undergraduates Who Are Men by Race Ethnicity and Income, 2003–2004

	Lowest Quartile	Middle Quartiles	Highest Quartile
White	44%	47%	51%
African American	42%	44%	54%
Hispanic	43%	46%	51%
Asian American	48%	52%	54%

Source: U.S. Department of Education (2004).

TABLE 5-9 Percentage of Women Teachers and Administrators at Various Positions in Education

Position	% Women
Teachers' aides, elementary school teachers	91%
Pre-K and kindergarten teachers	98%
Elementary school teachers	83%
Secondary school teachers	58%
Principals	34%
College and university instructors	51%
Assistant professors	45%
Associate professors	30%
Professors	17%
College and university administrators	20%

Sources: National Center for Education Statistics (2001); Spade (2001).

a bachelor's degree. In 1999 83 percent completed high school and 25 percent received a bachelor's degree. Both women and men have increased their participation in postsecondary education, but women have increased their participation much more rapidly than men have, and no one knows why.

Several possible reasons have been suggested for why women have made so much progress in college attendance and graduation while men's participation has remained more stagnant:

- Women's learning styles may fit better into the typical college classroom.
- Men may be more enticed by the popular culture to avoid further education and to enter the labor market.
- Men may have more pressure on them, especially in low-income families, to choose a paid job rather than college (Fletcher 2002). Girls are more likely to enter college right after high school (almost 70 percent of high school grads in 2003) compared to boys (a little over 60 percent). Entering college immediately after high school is strongly associated with staying in college and graduating (King 2006).

- Girls are more serious about their education. The annual survey of U.S. college freshmen, for example, finds that boys often spend large amounts of time watching television, partying, and exercising during their senior year of high school. High school girls spend more time studying and doing homework, talking with teachers outside of school, and participating in volunteer work. And, as we saw in Table 5-2, girls participate in more extracurricular activities. In addition, girls more often take honors courses and college prep courses and have higher academic aspirations (Fletcher 2002).

This section has presented a lot of data on the changes in the experience and participation of women and men in higher education. As you read through the material, be sure to take time to look at the tables to see what they are reporting. Tables are a way to present a large amount of information in a condensed form, which means that the reader needs to look carefully at the title of the table and the different categories, as well as the numbers. Think about what the main points of each table are. What are some of the similarities and differences among the different groups of people who vary by one or many factors such as gender, race/ethnicity, and age?

In summary, all of these statistics show the following:

- Men's participation in higher education has leveled off in recent years while women's participation has increased, allowing them to catch up with and even surpass men in the numbers of degrees earned.
- Some important gaps, however, remain. Women are making inroads in every field, but gender inequality still exists in some ways in the kinds of disciplines in which men and women are earning their degrees.
- It is critical that we pay attention to the ways in which gender intersects with race ethnicity, social class, and age because the experiences of all men or all women are not the same. Wealthier white men are much more likely to be increasing their representation in degree programs compared to other men.
- The question of why women are increasingly gaining admission to higher education and completing degrees while men's participation seems to be stagnant is one of much debate. Several suggestions have been made by scholars ranging from individualistic explanations about men's commitment to higher education to social structural arguments about the ways education is organized.

What About the Boys?

The discussion of higher education in the United States shows that women have caught up with and surpassed men in many ways in higher education. This has caused some people to question whether we have gone too far. They are concerned that focusing on the problems in education for girls detracts from our commitment to educate boys. They ask, "What about the boys?" and fear that as women and girls gain access to education, boys will be left out. Are schools designed to support girls and women more than boys and men? Has the pendulum swung in the United States from schools that ignored and discriminated against girls and women to ones that are now privileging them and mistreating boys and men?

As we have noted, some universities and colleges have created affirmative action programs for men and are now even accepting men into their programs with weaker records than the women they are turning away to try to "balance" out the proportion of women and men in the institution.

Recently, critics within the educational system and those in the popular press have sounded an alarm asking whether strides made by girls and women in schools are accompanied by a drag or even a decline in boys' and men's educational attainment. Observations of the suppression of the "warrior narratives" of boys in the schools have caused some to claim that elementary schools are bad for boys. They argue that normal boyish behaviors have been pathologized. The demands that children sit still, raise their hands, and take naps are argued to be ways to discourage boys from liking school and from doing well there. Similarly, the statistics that show women moving ahead of men in finishing high school, enrolling in universities, and completing degrees have been met with assertions that ever since feminists called attention to inequity for girls and women in schools, boys and men have been ignored and have slipped further and further behind.

Michael Kimmel (2000) argues that this social movement is a counterfeminist one. The covert, and sometimes overt, argument is that feminists are to blame for the success of girls as well as for the problems boys face. But are boys' problems caused by feminism or girls? Kimmel says that neither feminism nor girls are the problem; the real underlying issues are racial ethnic inequality and poverty. If the statistics on high school and college graduation are examined carefully, they show that not all men are falling behind. Lower-income men, especially African American and Hispanic men, are rapidly dropping out of education. Racial ethnic inequality and social-class differences play a major role. Look back at Table 5-8 to see that among the wealthiest households, men are more likely to attend college than are women. Focusing on gender in isolation obscures our ability to see racism and class inequities in schools.

Kimmel says that framing the debate as "feminists versus boys and men" is deceptive. First it creates a false opposition between the needs of boys and men and those of girls and women. Kimmel maintains that improvements in education that help girls also help boys. When schools are made **girl friendly**, they become **boy friendly** as well because what they really become is child friendly. Schools that are girl friendly, for example, provide flexible scheduling to allow children to attend to work and family commitments as well as education. They also are closer to children's homes and provide children with toilets and running water. Schools that are made safer to protect girls from bullying and sexual harassment and assault are safer for boys who are also victims of school bullying (UNICEF 2004). Second, blaming feminists causes us to ignore major issues related to education such as cuts in spending on education that hurt both genders. Children, regardless of gender, do not have sufficient materials or services for special needs. Scholarships, work-study opportunities, fellowships, and assistantships for men and women college students have been drastically cut or almost eliminated in recent years, even as the costs of college education rises.

GLOBAL ISSUES IN EDUCATION

Although problems remain, girls in the United States and other wealthy nations have made significant gains in school in regard to equality in attendance and graduation. In many ways today, girls are doing better than boys. The picture at the global level, however, is quite different. In some countries, boys are less likely to attend school. Colombia, Haiti, Lesotho, Madagascar, Malawi, Surinam, and Tanzania are all countries where boys are less likely to go to school than girls are. Taken as a whole, however, girls around the world are less likely to be in school (UNICEF 2004). The gender gap has narrowed significantly in most nations in the past two decades, but 55 percent of children not attending school in the world are girls, and of the 781 million illiterate adults in the world, 500 million are women (World Bank 2009; National Institute for Literacy 2006). The most serious gaps remain particularly in South Asia and Sub-Saharan Africa (World Bank 2010). The nations with the largest gender gaps include Chad, Yemen, Guinea-Bissau, Benin, Niger, Ethiopia, Guinea, Mali and Pakistan, where the enrollment of girls in school is less than 75 percent of that of boys (World Bank 2010). Frequently this gap in education is not by choice but because of discrimination against girls by governments, families, and schools that exclude girls from educational institutions (Pigozzi 1999; Otis 2003). In addition, children are often needed to work to supplement low family incomes, and families fear for the safety of children, especially girls, at school (Henderson and Jeydal 2010). Malala Yousafzai, the Pakistani schoolgirl who survived an assassination attempt by the Taliban in 2012, was targeted for speaking out for the education of girls. Malala miraculously survived a bullet in the head and has continued to speak and write about the importance of schooling for girls in Pakistan and globally, and she has inspired schoolgirls around the world to demand the right to education.

Illiteracy, one of the results of inadequate education among women, is intertwined with other factors, resulting in serious consequences. Low education levels among women are associated with higher rates of pregnancy, lower-paid jobs, decreased income, greater poverty, and higher mortality rates. Sometimes the connections among all these factors are not necessarily obvious. One study in sub-Saharan Africa, for example, found that 30 percent of children whose mothers had no formal schooling were immunized, compared to 70 percent of children whose mothers had a secondary education. Other research has shown that educating women increased the crop production of women farmers and reduced malnutrition of their families (*Economist* 2001).

Educating girls (and boys) is a critical problem around the world, but a number of poor countries have made significant progress by implementing policies that make primary education both free and compulsory, by abolishing secondary-school fees, by prohibiting certain forms of child work, and by compensating poor families for girls' labor. Some of the barriers to girls' education, however, are not so obvious (Global Campaign for Education 2005). Water, for example, may play a critical role in determining whether girls go to school or not.

Unexpected Connections Between Water and Education

We do not usually think of literacy being connected to water and sewage systems, but in fact one of the major barriers to education for girls in poor countries is the lack of access to water and sanitation. In the global South, 1.1 billion people lack access to clean water. Because carrying water is considered women's work in many of these countries, women and girls bear the brunt of that burden. Walking to water sources, waiting in line, and carrying water back home can take up to four hours a day in many places.

This job cuts into the time available for girls to attend school, so access to water is directly related to education. In Senegal, Mozambique, Uganda, and Tanzania, research has shown that school attendance is 12 percent higher for girls who live within fifteen minutes of a water source than for girls who live farther away.

One ten-year-old Bolivian girl explained as she waited to fill her container with water from the community well, "Of course I wish I were in school. I want to learn to read and write—and I want to be there with my friends. But how can I? My mother needs me to get water and the pipe is only open from 10 to 12. You have to get in line early because so many people come here" (United Nations 2006a, 18).

Access to sanitation is also important. If schools do not have toilets, boys are sent into the fields to relieve themselves, but girls must wait all day until they can return to their home or community to find a toilet. Half of the dropouts of girls from school are because of lack of access to water or sanitation. In the global South, 60 percent of the population does not have access to safe sewage systems (United Nations 2006b).

GENDER AND TEACHERS

Gender bias in academic settings is called "**the chilly climate**." Not just students, but teachers, and even the organization of schools, are affected by the chilly climate (Blakemore, Switzer, DiLorio, and Fairchild 1997). Jobs in education are gendered with men at the top. Table 5-10 shows the proportion of women at different levels within the school system from preschool to higher education. In public schools, about 7 percent of superintendents are women, 24 percent of assistant superintendents are women, and 34 percent of principals are women. Even those women who do become principals tend to be relegated to less prestigious positions, as women are 37 percent of grade school principals, 23 percent of middle school principals, and only 8 percent of high school principals (Spade 2001).

In higher education, researchers (Spade 2001) have found a range of economic equity issues. Women make up 38 percent of full time faculty positions but many are clustered in the lowest ranks of the faculty. Seventeen percent of full professors are women and 30 percent of associate professors are women, but 50 percent of the lowest ranks of instructors and lecturers with the lowest pay, fewest benefits, and least voice on the faculty are women (National Coalition for Women and Girls in Education 2008). Within each of these ranks, women receive lower salaries on average. Women are also more likely to be in part-time or temporary positions and to advance in rank or become tenured more slowly.

TABLE 5-10 Proportion of Women in Faculty in Higher Education by Discipline

Discipline	% Women
Law faculty	36%
Business faculty	31%
Computer science faculty	20%
Political science faculty	17%
Physical sciences faculty	12%

Source: General Accounting Office (2001).

Women also express concern about social factors on the job. Women professors feel less supported by their colleagues in their social interactions on campus because of sexist jokes, sexual harassment, and exclusion from social networks. In addition, women faculty find that their students are more demanding and give them lower evaluations, especially if they violate gender norms.

Evaluating Professors

If you have been around a university for even a short time, you have heard teachers talking about annual reviews and evaluations for tenure and promotion. One important piece of evidence used to justify raises, promotions, and granting or denying tenure is student evaluations of teaching. Comparisons of the scores students give professors for their teaching do not find much difference between those given to men and those given to women (Basow 1998; Kardia and Wright 2004). Diana Kardia and Mary Wright (2004), however, argue that the similar numbers hide a dissimilar experience in teaching and in teaching evaluations. They assert that students hold women teachers to different standards and evaluate them more harshly. The similar scores, therefore, indicate that women professors try harder and perform better in the classroom—they are better teachers than men.

Rather than ask students what score they give to teachers when they evaluate them, Kardia and Wright (2004) asked students how they arrived at the scores. Students readily admitted that they had higher expectations of women faculty. One man student explained,

> I think that stereotypes play a big role. I mean if you're looking at a male teacher and he's overbearing, you might just excuse it and say "Yeah, well, you know, he's a professor. He's just doing his job." But if you look at it as a woman professor you'd be like, "Women are supposed to be a lot nicer, and, you know, a lot more friendlier and she's acting like such a bitch." (Kardia and Wright 2004, 8)

Another student said that he would not only judge the woman professor more harshly, but he would respond differently in the classroom. He described his response to a bad teacher:

> I don't think highly of this guy to begin with and I think if he was a woman I would think less of him. . . . I hate to admit it but . . . he's very disorganized and he doesn't articulate his thoughts well. . . . If he was a woman, I would just probably have no tolerance for that. . . . You sit there and you really try to figure out what he's trying to say. You're very attentive, trying to get into it. But if he was a woman, I think I would just sit back and be like, "This is ridiculous." (Kardia and Wright 2004, 8)

Professors are not only evaluated by students; their work is evaluated by other scholars for publication and promotion. Christine Wenneras and Agnes Wold (1997) studied decisions about scholars in Sweden. When they did their study, Sweden had recently been named the leading country in the world in regard to equal opportunities for women and men. Wenneras and Wold (1997) studied how the Swedish Medical Research Council rated women and men on scientific competence, quality of proposed methodology, and relevance of research proposal. They found that the council rated all the women below the least competent men. On other measures of productivity such as publishing, being cited, and quality of publications, however, the women rated equal to the men. In other words, the peer-review system of the

Swedish Medical Research Council rated women scholars much more critically than it did men. When other kinds of measures were used to determine the caliber of the women's scholarship, their peer reviews did not correspond to the real quality and impact of the women's research. The reviewers consistently gave women applicants lower scores than equally productive men. For example, in some cases, Wenneras and Wold (1997) found that women applicants for funding from the Swedish Medical Research Council needed to publish three extra papers in prestigious journals or twenty extra papers in less prestigious journals to be ranked the same as men applicants (Halpern et al. 2007).

THE CORRESPONDENCE PRINCIPLE

Why are schools organized as they are? Samuel Bowles and Herbert Gintis (1978) have tried to explain this through an idea known as the correspondence principle. They argue that much of what we learn at school is preparation for our future roles as workers in a capitalist society. Capitalists need a docile, obedient, motivated workforce, and schools prepare us for this. What happens at school *corresponds* to what happens at work.

Schools teach us these lessons, however, in a "hidden agenda." The teachers do not explicitly tell us how to be good cogs in the wheels of the economic system, but rather the unwritten lessons are built into the organization of the school and the behaviors that are rewarded or discouraged (Illich 1983).

The first lesson is to follow the rules of the social institution, first at school and then in the workplace. Business owners need a subservient workforce with employees who come to work prepared to do what the managers tell them to do in order to make the business run efficiently, productively, and competitively. Schools teach children that they will be successful in the classroom if they are compliant and dependable and that they will not succeed if they are aggressive and independent.

The second lesson is to accept the hierarchy of authority. We learn that some people are in charge and that those whom they supervise need to accept that authority. At school, the teacher controls what the students do and how they will do it. Teachers are also part of a hierarchy, and they will be seen with principals or classroom evaluators, listening to what they must do and how they must do it. At work, the boss is much like a teacher, and the whole system of managers and managed is parallel to the organization of the school and the school system.

The third lesson is that the most important goals of a student are external rewards. Students learn that mastering information and sharing ideas are secondary to the more important issues of exam scores, course grades, and credentials such as passing into the next grade or receiving a diploma or degree. These are all external rewards. An internal reward might be the delight of learning something new, exchanging ideas about issues of importance with others, or successfully completing a project. At work, we will find that our work often is largely focused on the external reward of a paycheck rather than the intrinsic value of the activities we engage in on the job.

Bowles and Gintis's theory does not really speak to the issue of gender in schools, but we can see from the information in this chapter that part of the "hidden agenda" is the lesson of gender. Gender differentiation is built into schools, where boys and girls are frequently separated and treated differently. Many of the differences are not conscious. Teachers usually do not plan to treat their students differently. As we have seen, however, the research suggests that teachers interact quite differently with boys and girls. Schools become a kind of gender factory.

The school hierarchy's levels of authority are also gendered. Teachers are often women, especially in lower grades, whereas those in charge, such as principals, are more often men. These kinds of differentiation in experience and authority are parallel to what we find in the workforce. Gender in the schools corresponds with gender in the workplace.

A second gender issue that we can link to Bowles and Gintis's theory is the way that masculinity seems to conflict to a greater extent than does femininity with the hidden agenda—the rules of schools. In the discussion of the kindergarten warrior, we witnessed the introduction of boys to the contradictory lessons of being a masculine boy and being a successful student. This conflict corresponds to a conflict in the workplace. Aggression in the workplace is strongly associated with lower wages. Every 1 percent increase in aggression is associated with an 8 percent decrease in wages (Andrisanni 1978; Duncan and Dunifon 1998). Women and men in high-status occupations, however, have a somewhat different experience. Women in high-status jobs face significantly larger wage penalties for being aggressive, whereas men in these kinds of jobs are penalized for being withdrawn. The workplace has a hierarchy that places some men in charge of everyone else. Businesses need some men who learn a different set of rules. Although most workers, both women and men, should ideally learn to submit to authority, some workers, mostly men, must learn to be the authorities.

The third issue that correspondence theory cites that can be related to gender is the issue of extrinsic rewards. Here the experience in schools may be more consistent with expectations for men at work than it is for women, or at least the connection is more complex for women. Both boys and girls learn as students to value the extrinsic reward. When they enter the workplace, they are supposed to focus on the paycheck as the key element in their employment. Of course, both women and men work because they earn a paycheck. For women, however, gender "interferes" with their valuing only the extrinsic reward. As we will see in chapter 6, women do a lot of unpaid work. In addition, many of the paid jobs women have do not receive as much pay but may provide greater intrinsic rewards. Working as a teacher or a nurse does not usually result in a big paycheck, but it may feel good to be contributing to the community and the well-being of others.

A fourth issue that links Bowles and Gintis's (1978) theory to gender has to do with a critique of their ideas. Bowles and Gintis's discussion did not leave much room for change or even for resistance to the structure of the social institutions of schools and businesses by students or employees. Scholars who have criticized Bowles and Gintis have noted that no social institution is without critics and that social institutions change as a result of the resistance of those whose lives are constrained by them. The change over time in the treatment of girls and women in primary, secondary, and higher education shows remarkable improvement in the success of girl and women students in the past few decades in the United States and other nations around the world. In many areas, women's and girls' opportunities and successes have met and even surpassed those of boys and men. This progress illustrates the vulnerability of social institutions to conscious change. The women's movement undoubtedly has played an important role in exposing gender inequities and developing policies, such as Title IX in the United States and the Beijing recommendations for nations all over the globe, to create a more equal system. Correspondence theory, however, is still valid because, at the same time as women have entered the labor market in greater numbers, employers need women who have been properly trained in job skills as well as in the lessons of the hidden agenda.

GENDER MATTERS

This chapter has reviewed the organization of education and the experience of participating in schools by tracing through the research on kindergartners to college students and professors. At each stage, we can see how gender is a central feature. Boys and girls face different problems in their earliest years of school, and they continue to face different challenges and participate differently through every level of education.

Schools are both a reflection of the gendered character of their broader context as well as a kind of gender factory that reproduces the inequities between girls and boys and women and men. Access to water and the organization of work are important parts of the social context that shapes education. Gender, however, is not the only dividing line. Race ethnicity, social class, and nation also indicate huge distinctions beyond gender inequity.

In the United States, education is one place where gender equality has been achieved in many respects. But that equality is tempered by inequities by social class and race ethnicity that persist. Other nations have also made great strides in educational equality, but millions of people around the world, men and even more so women, still face serious barriers to even the most fundamental access to education.

The challenges we face in education are at three levels. They include the need to address problems at the interpersonal level of interactions between teachers and students and among students, for example around the question of bullying. We also need to address the issues related to the organization of education, which continues to channel girls and women into gendered fields of study. And finally we need to look at the issues of social context and the interaction of the social institution of education with other social institutions such as government, which often do not provide for free compulsory education or adequate access to water, as well as the organization of the economic institution of the workplace and the job market as they interface with education.

KEY TERMS

ADHD

borderwork

the chilly climate

effeminacy

fag discourse

gender gap in math

gender troublemakers

girl-friendly and boy-friendly schools

historically black colleges

neutralization

No Child Left Behind Act

sexual harassment

symbolic annihilation

warrior narratives

CRITICAL THINKING QUESTIONS

1. Because of the women's relative invisibility in school texts, you may know little about women's contributions to culture and history. More than two hundred women have been inducted into the National Women's Hall of Fame. Choose one woman from the list http://www.greatwomen.org/women-of-the-hall/view-all-women and prepare a brief account of her life and her contributions to share with the class. Alternatively, prepare a report on notable women from other countries or Nobel Prize winners Aung San Suu Kyi, Rigoberta Menchu Tum, Jody Williams, Shirin Ebadi, and Wangari Maathai or on women radicals and revolutionaries such as Rosa Luxembourg, Grace Lee Boggs, or Emma Goldman.

2. The text mentions Bernice Sandler's report on the "chilly climate" that made women feel unwelcome on college campuses. The chilly climate was created by overt and covert behaviors of faculty, administrators, and students, including sexist humor, faculty calling on men more than women in class, and stereotypical comments about women's intellectual abilities. How far has your campus come from those days? Interview two men and two women students about their perceptions of the campus climate, using the following questions:

   • Questions for women
     • What are your impressions of the campus climate for women students?
     • What expectations do you think this college has for women?
     • What views of women are communicated by the student culture, and what roles do women play in that culture?
     • How are women students treated by faculty, administrators, and male students?
   • Additional question for men:
     • What assumptions and expectations does the college communicate to you about how women are to be viewed and treated?
     • What are your assessments of the campus climate?

3. Use the tables from this chapter to write a detailed account of gender, race, and class differences in education that goes beyond the numbers. For example, use what you recall from your own high school experience to discuss gendered high school activities (Table 5-2); recall your thoughts and memories of science and math classes in high school (Table 5-3); describe the ages, race ethnicity, and class of students in your high school and on your campus (Table 5-8).

REFERENCES

American Association of University Women (AAUW). 1999. *Gender Gap: Where Schools Still Fail Our Children*. New York: Marlowe.

———. 2001. *Beyond the "Gender Wars": A Conversation About Girls, Boys, and Education*. Washington, DC: American Association of University Women.

Andrisanni, Paul, ed. 1978. *Work Attitudes and Labor Market Experience*. New York: Praeger.

Arlow, Peter, and Matt Froschel. 1976. "Women in the High School Curriculum." In *High School Feminist Studies*, edited by Carol Ahlum, Jacqueline Fralley, and Florence Howe, xi–xxviii. Old Westbury, NY: Feminist Press.

Aud, Susan, Sidney Wilkinson-Flicker, Paul Kristapovich, Amy Rathbun, Xiaolei Wang, Jijun Zhang, and Liz Notter. 2013. "The Condition of Education 2013." National Center for Education Statistics, May.

Basow, Susan. 1998. "Student Evaluations." In *Career Strategies for Women in Academe*, edited by Lynn H. Collins, Joan C. Chrisler, and Kathryn Quina, 135–56. Thousand Oaks, CA: Sage.

Bazler, Judith A., and Doris A. Simonis. 1991. "Are High School Chemistry Books Gender Free?" *Journal of Research in Science Teaching* 28:353–62.

Bell, John F. 1989. "A Comparison of Science Performance and Uptake by Fifteen-Year-Old Boys and Girls in Coeducational and Single-Sex Schools." *Educational Studies* 15 (2): 193–203.

Bettie, Julie. 2000. "Women without Class: Chicas, Cholas, Trash, and the Presence/Absence of Class Identity." *Signs* 26(1): 1–35.

———. 2003. *Women without Class: Girls, Race, and Identity*. Berkeley: University of California Press.

Biederman, Joseph, Eric Mick, Stephen V. Faraone, Ellen Braaten, Alysa Doyle, Thomas Spencer, Timothy E. Wilens, Elizabeth Frazier, and Mary Ann Johnson. 2002. "Influence of Gender on Attention Deficit Hyperactivity Disorder in Children Referred to a Psychiatric Clinic." *American Journal of Psychiatry* 159 (January): 36–42.

Blair, Cornelia, and Helene Northway. 2001. *Women: New Roles in Society*. New York: Gale Group.

Blakemore, Judith, Jo Young Switzer, Judith DiLorio, and David Fairchild. 1997. "Exploring the Campus Climate for Women Faculty." In *Subtle Sexism*, edited by Niki Benokraitis, 54–71. Thousand Oaks, CA: Sage.

Bowles, Samuel, and Herbert Gintis. 1978. *Schooling in Capitalist America*. New York: Basic Books.

Canada, Katherine, and Richard Pringle. 1995. "The Role of Gender in College Classroom Interactions: A Social Context Approach." *Sociology of Education* 68 (3): 161–86.

Carpenter, Peter, and Martin Hayden. 1987. "Girls' Academic Achievements: Single-Sex Versus Coeducational Schools in Australia." *Sociology of Education* 60 (3): 156–67.

College Board. 2013. *SAT Data Tables*. The College Board. http://research.collegeboard.org/content/sat-data-tables Accessed March 5, 2014. Correll, Shelley. 2001. "Gender and the Career Choice Process." *American Journal of Sociology* 106 (6): 1691–730.

Cox, Emily R., Brenda R. Motheral, Rochelle R. Henderson, and Doug Mager. 2003. "Geographic Variation in the Prevalence of Stimulant Medication Use Among Children 5 to 14 Years Old: Results from a Commercially Insured US Sample." *Pediatrics* 111 (2): 237–43.

Deveny, Kathleen. 1994. "Chart of Kindergarten Awards." *Wall Street Journal*, December 4.

Dewey, John. 1911. "Is Co-education Injurious to Girls?" *Ladies Home Journal*, June 11.

Diller, Lawrence. 1996. "The Run on Ritalin." *Hastings Center Report* 26 (2): 12.

Duncan, Rachel, and Greg Dunifon. 1998. "Long-Run Effects of Motivation on Labor Market Success." *Social Psychology Quarterly* 61: 33–48.

Dwyer, Carol. 1996. "Fighting the Gender Gap: Standardized Tests Are Poor Indicators of Ability in Physics." *APS News-Online* 5 (7). http://www.aps.org/publications/apsnews/199607/gender.cfm. Accessed March 19, 2011.

The Economist. 2001. "The Female Poverty Trap." March 8.

Entwisle, Doris. R., Karl Alexander, and Linda Olson. 1994. "The Gender Gap in Math." *American Sociological Review* 59: 822–38.

McCabe, J., E. Fairchild, L. Grauerholz, B. A. Pescosolido, D. Tope. 2011. Gender in Twentieth-Century Children's Books: Patterns of Disparity in Titles and Central Characters. *Gender & Society*, 2011; 25 (2): 197–226.

FairTest. 2002. "Gender Bias in College Admissions Tests." http://fairtest.org/gender-bias-college-admissions-tests. Accessed March 19, 2011.

Ferguson, Ann. 2001. *Bad Boys: Public Schools in the Making of Black Masculinity*. Ann Arbor: University of Michigan Press.

——. 2011. "Naughty by Nature." In *Gender Through the Prism of Difference*, edited by Maxine Baca Zinn, Pierrette Hondagneu-Sotelo, and Michael A. Messner, 435–442. New York: Oxford University Press.

Ferree, Myra Marx, and Elaine Hall. 1990. "Visual Images of American Society: Gender and Race in Introductory Sociology Textbooks." *American Sociological Review* 61: 929–50.

Fletcher, Michael. 2002. "Degrees of Separation: Gender Gap Among College Graduates Has Educators Wondering Where the Men Are." *Washington Post*, June 25.

Fournier, Janice, and Samuel S. Wineburg. 1997. "Picturing the Past: Gender Differences in the Depiction of Historical Figures." *American Journal of Education* 105 (2): 160–85.

Freeman, Catherine. 2004. "Trends in Educational Equity of Girls and Women." Washington, DC: IES National Center for Educational Statistics. http://nces.ed.gov/pubsearch/pubsinfo.asp?pubid=2005016. Accessed March 19, 2011.

General Accounting Office (GAO). 2001. *Gender Equity: Men's and women's Participation in Higher Education*. Report to the ranking minority member subcommittee on criminal justice, drug policy and human resources, committee on government reform, House of Representatives. http://www.ncaa.org/about/resources/inclusion/gender-equity-legislation-and-case-law Accessed March 5, 2014.Ginty, Molly. 2004. "Mars Mission a Landmark for Female Astronomers." *WeNews*, February 1. http://www.womensenews.org/story/women-in-science/040201/mars-mission-landmark-female-astronomers. Accessed March 19, 2011.

Global Campaign for Education. 2005. "Girls Can't Wait: Why Girls' Education Matters and How to Make It Happen Now." Briefing paper for the UN Beijing +10 Review and Appraisal Global Campaign for Education. *Reproductive Health Matters* 13 (25): 19–22.

Goldman, Larry S., Myron Genel, Rebecca J. Bezman, and Priscilla J. Slanetz for the Council on Scientific Affairs, American Medical Association. 1998. "Diagnosis and Treatment of Attention-Deficit/Hyperactivity Disorder in Children and Adolescents." *Journal of the American Medical Association* 279: 1100–07.

Halpern, Diane, Camilla Benbow, David Geary, Ruben Gur, Janet Hyde, and Morton Gernsbacher. 2007. "Sex, Math and Scientific Achievement." *Scientific American*, November 28.

Hart, Nicky, Noah Grant, and Kevin Riley. 2006. "Making the Grade." In *Medicalized Masculinities*, edited by Dana Rosenfeld and Christopher Faircloth, 132–37. Philadelphia: Temple University Press.

Henderson, Sarah, and Alana Jeydal. 2010. *Women and Politics in a Global World*. 2nd edition. New York: Oxford University Press.

Hinshaw, Stephen P. 2002. "Preadolescent Girls with Attention-Deficit/Hyperactivity Disorder: I. Background Characteristics, Comorbidity, Cognitive and Social Functioning, and Parenting Practices." *Journal of Consulting and Clinical Psychology* 70: 1086–98.

Howell, Joseph. 1972. *Hard Living on Clay Street: Portraits of Blue Collar Families*. Long Grove, IL: Waveland, 1972.

Illich, Ivan. 1983. *Deschooling Society*. New York: Harper and Row.

Illinois Mathematics and Science Academy (IMSA). 1995. *Statement: 1993–1994 Calculus-Based Physics And Mechanics Study*. Aurora: Illinois Mathematics Academy.

Jordan, Ellen, and Angela Cowan. 2004. "Warrior Narratives in the Kindergarten Classroom: Renegotiating the Social Contract?" In *Men's Lives*, 6th edition, edited by Michael S. Kimmel and Michael A. Messner, 103–15. Boston: Allyn and Bacon.

Kardia, Diana, and Mary Wright. 2004. "Instructor Identity: The Impact of Gender and Race on Faculty Experiences with Teaching." *CRLT Occasional Papers*, No. 19. Ann Arbor, MI: Center for Research on Learning and Teaching.

Kimmel, Michael. 2000. "Saving the Males." *Gender and Society* 14 (4): 494–516.

King, Jacqueline. 2006. *Gender Equity in Higher Education*. Washington, DC: American Council on Education.

Kowalski, Kurt, and K. Kanitkar. 2003. "Ethnicity and Gender in the Kindergarten Classroom: A Naturalistic Study." Poster presented at the biennial meeting of the Society for Research in Child Development, Tampa, FL, April.

Lamb, Lindsay M., Rebecca S. Bigler, Lynn S. Liben, and Vanessa Green. 2009. "Teaching Children to Confront Peers' Sexist Remarks: Implications for Theories of Gender Development and Educational Practice." *Sex Roles: A Journal of Research* 61 (5–6): 361–82.

Lee, Valerie, Helen Marks, and Tina Byrd. 1994. "Sexism in Single-Sex and Coeducational Independent Secondary School Classrooms." *Sociology of Education* 67: 92–120.

Leo, Jonathan. 2002. "American Preschoolers on Ritalin." *Society* 39 (2): 52–60.

Liew, Peck-Chong. 2008. "An Analysis of Gender and Ethnic Representations in Chinese and Malay Primary School Reading Textbooks: Grades 2–6." *Dissertation Abstracts International, A: The Humanities and Social Sciences*, 68 (11): 4594.

McCabe, Janice, Emily Fairchild, Liz Grauerholz, Bernice Pescosolido, and Daniel Tope. 2011. "Gender in Twentieth Century Children's Books: Patterns of Disparity in Titles and Central Characters." *Gender and Society* 25, 197–226.

MacLeod, Jay. 2009 *Ain't No Makin' It: Aspirations and Attainment in a Low-Income Neighborhood*. Philadelphia: Westview.

Milner, J. 1977. *Sex Stereotypes in Mathematics and Science Textbooks*. New York: National Organization for Women.

National Center for Education Statistics. 2001. *Digest of Education Statistics 2000*. Washington, DC: U.S. Government Printing Office.

National Center for Education Statistics. 2009. "Percentage of High School Dropouts Among Persons 16 through 24 Years Old, by Sex and Race/Ethnicity: Selected Years, 1060 through 2008." *Digest of Education Statistics*. http://nces.ed.gov/programs/digest/d09/tables/dt09_108.asp. Accessed March 20, 2011.

National Coalition for Women and Girls in Education. 2008. *Title IX at 35: Report Card on Gender Equity*. Washington, DC: National Coalition for Women and Girls in Education. http://www.ncwge.org/pubs-reports.html. Accessed March 20, 2011.

National Education Association (NEA). 2008. Mathematics and Science for Every Girl and Boy: An NEA Policy Brief. http://www.nea.org/assets/docs/HE/mf_PB16_Math.pdf. Accessed March 4, 2014.

National Institute for Literacy. https://www.federalregister.gov/agencies/national-institute-for-literacy. Accessed 3/3/2014.

Nicholson, Christie. 2010. "No Gender Gap in Math." *Scientific American*, January 6. http://www.scientificamerican.com/podcast/episode.cfm?id=no-gender-gap-in-math-10-01-06. Accessed March 20, 2011.

O'Connor, Carla, R. L'Heureux Lewis, and Jennifer Mueller. 2011. "The Culture of Black Femininity and School Success." In *Gender through the Prism of Difference*, 4th edition, edited by Maxine Baca Zinn, Pierrette Hondagneu-Sotelo, and Michael A. Messner, 443–54. New York: Oxford University Press.

Orenstein, Peggy. 2002. "Shortchanging Girls." In *Workplace/Women's Place*, edited by Paula J. Dubeck and Dana Dunn, 38–46. Los Angeles: Roxbury.

Orenstein, Peggy, in association with the American Association of University Women. 1994. *School Girls: Young Women, Self-Esteem and the Confidence Gap*. New York: Doubleday.

Otis, Ginger. 2003. "UN: Women Gain in Political Clout, Lag in Schooling." *WeNews*, May 30. http://www.womensenews.org/story/international-policyunited-nations/030530/un-women-gain-political-clout-lag-schooling. Accessed March 20, 2011.

Pascoe, C. J. 2007. *Dude, You're a Fag: Masculinity and Sexuality in High School.* Berkeley: University of California Press.

Pesticide Action Network. 2010. "Dietary Pesticide Exposure Linked to ADHD in Kids," May 21. http://www.panna.org/resources/panups/panup_20100521. Accessed March 20, 2011.

Pigozzi, Mary Joy. 1999. "Educating the Girl Child: Best Foot Forward?" *UN Chronicle* 36 (2): 39–41.

Rafalovich, Adam. 2005. "Exploring Clinician Uncertainty in the Diagnosis and Treatment of Attention Deficit–Hyperactivity Disorder." *Sociology of Health and Illness* 27 (3): 305–23.

Ridgway, Carolyn, and Christopher Healy. 1997. "Evaluation of Empowerment in a High School Geometry Class." *Mathematics Teacher* 90 (9): 738–41.

Rosser, Phyllis. 1989. *The SAT Gender Gap: Identifying the Causes.* Washington, DC: Center for Women Policy Studies.

Rothchild, Jennifer. 2006. "Gender Trouble Makers: Education and Empowerment in Nepal." New York: Routledge.

Sadker, David, and Karen Zittleman. 2004. "Single-Sex Schools: A Good Idea Gone Wrong?" *Christian Science Monitor*, April 8.

Sadker, Myra, and David Sadker. 1994. "The Miseducation of Boys: Changing the Script." In *Failing at Fairness: How America's Schools Cheat Girls*, edited by Myra Sadker and David Sadker, 42–76. New York: Scribner.

Sapiro, Virginia. 2003. *Women in American Society.* 5th edition. New York: McGraw-Hill.

Shaw, Gina. 2002. "The Ritalin Controversy." *Washington Diplomat*, March. http://www.washdiplomat .com/02–03/a6_02_03.html. Accessed March 20, 2011.

Slackman, Michael. 2007. "A Quiet Revolution in Algeria." *New York Times*, May 26. http://www .nytimes.com/2007/05/26/world/africa/26algeria.html. Accessed March 20, 2011.

Smith, Philip M. 1985. *Language, the Sexes and Society.* Oxford, UK: Basil Blackwell.

Spade, Joan. 2001. "Gender and Education in the United States." In *Gender Mosaics: Social Perspectives*, edited by D. Vannoy, 85–93. Los Angeles: Roxbury.

Staudt, Kathleen. 1998. *Free Trade? Informal Economies at the U.S.–Mexico Border.* Philadelphia: Temple University Press.

Stewart, Lea, Pamela Cooper, Alan Stewart, and Sheryl Friedley. 2003. *Communication and Gender.* 4th edition. Boston: Allyn and Bacon.

Streitmatter, Janice. 1999. *For Girls Only: Making a Case for Single-Sex Schooling.* Albany: State University of New York Press.

Stock, P. 1978. *Better Than Rubies: A History of Women's Education.* New York: Putnam.

Thorne, Barrie. 1993. *Gender Play: Girls and Boys in School.* New Brunswick, NJ: Rutgers University Press.

Timimi, Sami. 2002. *Pathological Child Psychiatry and the Medicalization of Childhood.* Hove, UK: Brunner-Routledge.

Toppo, Greg. 2006. "U.S. Eases Limits on Single-Sex Schools." *USA Today*, October 25. http:// usatoday30.usatoday.com/news/education/2006-10-24-single-sex-education_x.htmAccessed March 5, 2014.

Tsolidis, Georgina, and Ian R. Dobson. 2006. "Single-Sex Schooling: Is It Simply a 'Class Act'?" *Gender and Education* 18 (2): 213–28.

———. 2006a. *Human Development Report 2006: Water Rights and Wrongs.* New York: United Nations. http://hdr.undp.org/external/hdr2006/water/index.htm. Accessed March 20, 2011.

———. 2006b. *Human Development Report 2006: Beyond Scarcity—Power, Poverty and the Global Water Crises.* New York: United Nations. http://hdr.undp.org/en/reports/global/hdr2006/. Accessed March 20, 2011.

——. 2006c. *Report of the Independent Expert for the United Nations Study On Violence against Children.* http://www.unicef.org/violencestudy/reports/SG_violencestudy_en.pdf. Accessed March 20, 2011.

United Nations Department of Social and Economic Affairs. 2013. Water and Gender. http://www.un.org/waterforlifedecade/index.shtml. Accessed March 5, 2014.

U.S. Department of Education, National Center for Education Statistics. 2012. *The Condition of Education 2012* (NCES 2012-045), Indicator 47 http://nces.ed.gov/fastfacts/display.asp?id=72 Accessed March 5, 2014.

——. 2004. *National Postsecondary Student Aid Studies, 2003–2004.* Washington, DC: U.S. Government Printing Office.

Van de Gaer, Eva, Heidi Pustjens, Jan Van Damme, and Agnes De Munter. 2004. "Effects of Single-Sex Versus Co-Educational Classes and Schools on Gender Differences in Progress in Language and Mathematics Achievement." *British Journal of Sociology of Education* 25 (3): 307–22.

Wainer, Howard, and Linda Steinberg. 1992. "Sex Differences in Performance on the Mathematics Section of the Scholastic Aptitude Test: A Bidirectional Validity Study." *Harvard Educational Review* 62 (3): 323–36.

Washington Post. 2002. "Sex Bias Cited in Vocational Ed: Girls Clustered in Training for Lower-Paying Jobs, Study Says." June 6.

Weitzman, Lenore, and Diane Rizzo. 1975. "Sex Bias in Textbooks." *Today's Education* 64 (1): 49–52.

Wenneras, Christine, and Agnes Wold. 1997. "Nepotism and Sexism in Peer Review." *Nature* 307 (6631): 341–43.

Willis, Paul. 1981. *Learning to Labor: How Working Class Kids Get Working Class Jobs.* New York: Columbia University Press.

World Bank. 2009. "Girl's Education: How Are Girls Doing?" January 6. http://go.worldbank.org/1L4BH3TG20. Accessed March 20, 2011.

——. 2010. "Education Is Key to Achieving Millennium Development Goals." August 23. http://data.worldbank.org/news/education-key-to-achieving-MDGs. Accessed March 20, 2011.

6

GENDER AND THE GLOBAL ECONOMY

Walmart employees work for the largest corporation in history owned by the wealthiest people in the world. Their wages are so low many are forced to supplement their income with welfare grants and food stamps in order to survive. Women employees at Walmart are paid even less than men.

Source: AFP/Getty Images.

If you look at a list of the wealthiest people in the world, you will see that four of the top twenty come from one family, the Waltons. They are the four children who inherited Sam Walton's hugely profitable Walmart company. Together they are worth $107 billion, much more than the wealthiest man in the world, Carlos Slim Helu, who is worth $73 billion (*Forbes* 2013). Measured by revenue, Walmart is the largest private employer in the world and the largest corporation in history (Featherstone 2005).

Nearly everyone in the United States and increasingly people all over the world have a Walmart in their neighborhood, a big-box discount department store (sometimes including a grocery store) stacked high from floor to ceiling with just about anything you can think of, open long hours and bustling with customers and workers. If you glance around, you will notice that most of the hourly employees are women (65 percent). Most of the supervisors are men (67 percent). If you were to meet the top managers of each store, you would find that 90 percent of them are men. If you happened to get a look at the paychecks of Walmart employees, you would find that the company has two pay scales, one for women and one for men. Women at Walmart on average earn $5,000 less than men, even though women tend to have higher performance ratings and more seniority. On average, women in hourly positions earn thirty-seven cents less an hour than do men. The pay gap widens as you move up the ladder. Men management trainees make an average of $23,175 a year, compared with $22,371 for women trainees. The four women at the very top earn an average of $279,772, compared to the hundreds of men in senior vice-president positions who average $419,435 a year (Featherstone 2005).

In 2001, women who were current or former employees at Walmart filed a massive nationwide sex-discrimination lawsuit in U.S. District Court against Walmart Stores, Inc. (Case No. C 01–2252 MJJ). In 2003 the suit became the largest class-action lawsuit ever— with 1.5 million participants and 120 affidavits relating to 235 stores (National Organization for Women 2013). The suit charged that Walmart discriminates against its women employees in promotions, compensation, and job assignments and that women who work at Walmart are assigned to the lowest-paying positions and are systematically denied advancement opportunities(Greenhouse 2010). The women lost their case in 2011 when the Supreme Court ruled that "[e]ven if every single one of these charges were true, that would not demonstrate that the entire company operate[s] under a general policy of discrimination" and that if a general policy of discrimination wasn't proven, the women had no legal justification for their case (Reed 2013).

The ruling against the employees has had serious ripple effects on legal cases against discrimination in the workplace. The *Wal-Mart v. Dukes* **decision** has already been cited more than 1,200 times in rulings by federal and state courts resulting in the overturn of jury verdicts, settlements being thrown out, and class actions rejected or decertified, undoing years of litigation. The new rulings based on the *Wal-Mart v. Dukes* case have come in every part of the country, in lawsuits involving a range of workplaces from retailers (Family Dollar Stores) and government contractors (Lockheed Martin Corp.), to business-services providers (Cintas Corp.) and magazines (Hearst Corp.) (N. Martin 2013). The Supreme Court not only ruled against the women of Walmart, it ruled against women across America seeking equity in the workplace.

Despite the legal rulings, most people would view the Walmart case as showing an especially striking system of gender inequality in jobs, pay, and promotion. The grievances of the women at Walmart, however, are not unique. Women today have joined men in the paid labor force, but men are often paid better, promoted faster, and employed in different work altogether.

This chapter looks at gender in the workplace. The chapter is divided into two main sections: paid work and unpaid work, or housework. We begin with a comparison of women and men in the paid labor force and then explore some of the explanations for those differences and the kinds of changes that have been recommended for addressing the inequities. In the second section, we examine unpaid domestic work as it shapes and reflects gender. Finally, our focus shifts to the global economy as the economic context of work and to the ways globalization influences our work lives.

PAID WORK

Who Is In the Paid Workplace?

The entry of women into the paid labor force is one of the key events of the twentieth century. With every decade, more women began to go to work for wages. In 1900 about 20 percent of women in the United States were in the labor force. In the early decades of the twentieth century, African American women were much more likely to be in the paid labor force, and single women and women without children were more likely to be employed. As the years passed, women of all racial ethnic groups, married women, and mothers increasingly began to work for pay. By the end of the century, most women were in paid employment, and 90 percent of them would be in the paid workforce sometime during their lifetime (Bianchi and Dye 2001).

Around the world, these numbers vary from one nation to another. Countries in northern Africa (35 women are in paid labor force for every 100 men in the paid labor force) and the Middle East (39 women are in the paid labor force for every 100 men in the paid labor force) have the lowest proportion of women in the labor force. In nations outside these regions, however, at least half of women are working for wages, and these numbers are rising. While only 14 percent of women are employed in Syria, for example, 67 percent of women in the world are employed, and 82 percent of women in wealthy nations of Europe and North America are employed. When it comes to working for wages, women's lives are more and more similar to men's.

Table 6-1 provides more specific data on the labor force participation rates of men and women in a number of individual countries. The table is divided into three sections. The first section shows a list of nations where men are much more likely to be in the labor force than are women. The second section shows those nations where women and men are most equal in regard to labor force participation. The third section provides data on the most populous nations in the world (China, India, United States, Indonesia and Brazil) and therefore, the places where the greatest number of people are affected by the gap in labor force participation. The first column after each nation shows the proportion of women over the age of 16 who are in the paid labor force and the second column shows the proportion of men who are in the paid labor force. The third column indicates the ratio between the labor force participation of women and men. Notice that the ratio varies from a low of .18 in Syria to a high of 1.06 in Malawi where women are actually slightly more likely to be in the paid labor force than are men.

Table 6-2 displays labor-force participation rates for women and men in the United States. The table shows that women have almost caught up with men in regard to working for wages, although there are important differences among different racial ethnic groups. Hispanic men are most likely to be in the paid labor force, and Hispanic women are least likely. In terms of the proportion of women and men who are engaged in paid work, equality is nearly here. Women now make up almost half (47 percent) of paid laborers in the United States (U.S. Bureau of Labor Statistics 2013a).

Emotional Labor

One way that women's and men's work differs is in the amount and kind of emotional labor involved in their jobs (Hochschild 1983, Lopez 2010). **Emotional labor**, a special kind of work that is invisible, is associated with an increasing proportion of occupations. This kind of work involves face-to-face or voice-to-voice contact between workers and customers. The employee is supposed to display certain feelings like attentiveness and caring and suppress others such as boredom or irritation. Eighty-three percent of workers in the United States are now employed in service sector jobs such as flight attendant, waitstaff, secretary, teacher, salesclerk, and health care worker (Lee and Mather 2008). These all require "emotion work" such as smiling, nodding, greeting, paying attention, and thanking (Bellas 2001).

TABLE 6-1 Gender and Labor Market Participation in Selected Countries, 2013

Lowest Ratio of Women to Men	women	men	women/men
Syria	14	75	.18
Algeria	16	75	.21
Iran	17	75	.23
Jordan	16	69	.24
Saudi Arabia	18	76	.24
Pakistan	23	86	.37
Egypt	25	78	.32
Lebanon	25	75	.33
Morocco	26	78	.34
Yemen	26	74	.35
Highest Ratio of Women to Men			
Malawi	85	80	1.06
Mozambique	87	83	1.05
Burundi	85	83	1.03
Tanzania	90	91	.99
Lao PDR	80	82	.99
Uganda	77	80	.96
Madagascar	85	90	.95
Lithuania	69	73	.95
Ghana	68	72	.95
Finland	73	77	.95
Largest Population in World			
China	75	85	.88
India	30	83	.36
United States	53	64	.83
Indonesia	53	86	.62
Brazil	65	85	.76

Source: World Economic Forum (2013). The Global Gender Gap Report, http://www3.weforum.org/docs/WEF_GenderGap_Report_2013.pdf. Accessed March 3, 2014.

TABLE 6-2 U.S. Labor Force Participation Rates for All Adults over Age Sixteen by Race Ethnicity and Gender, 2012

	All	Whites	Blacks	Hispanics	Asians
Men	64%	66%	54%	69%	68%
Women	53%	53%	52%	50%	53%

Source: U.S. Bureau of Labor Statistics (2013a, 2013b).

A handbook for supermarket checkout clerks provides a prescription for proper emotion work by telling the employees:

> YOU are the company's most effective representative. Your customers judge the entire company by your actions. A cheerful "Good Morning" and "Good Evening" followed by courteous attentive treatment and a sincere "Thank you, please come again" will send them away with a friendly feeling and a desire to return. A friendly smile is a must. (Bellas 2001, 271)

While an increasing number of all employees must do emotion work, women are even more likely than men to be required to do emotion work in their jobs (Bellas 2001). Men's emotion work also often contrasts with women's by the type of emotions that are supposed to be expressed. For example, both nursing and police work demand much emotional labor, and some of the work is similar. Both nurses and police officers are supposed to listen empathetically, express understanding, and motivate others to comply. However, nurses are supposed to show the emotions of caring and nurturance, whereas police officers are supposed to exhibit strength and toughness. Both of these professions are supposed to be emotionally expressive—and sometimes they are supposed to express emotions that are generally similar—but often they must be framed in gendered forms (Steinberg and Figart 1999).

Men and women in the same job may have different expectations about the emotion work they should do. Customers, employers, and co-workers may expect women to be nicer and friendlier and especially to smile more. Women college professors, for example, are evaluated more highly if they are friendly, although men professors are not judged by this criterion (Kierstead, D'Agostino, and Dill 1988; Statham, Richardson, and Cook 1991; Bellas 1999). In a job interview or in salary decisions, women and men may be judged differently depending on whether they express the proper emotion.

In one study, participants viewed a video of someone in a job interview. The person in the interview was asked about his or her experience when a co-worker arrived late and subsequently lost an important account. In one version of the video, the job seeker expressed sadness, and in the other he or she expressed anger. After seeing the video, the participants were asked to assign the person a salary. Angry men were offered the highest salary ($38,000), followed by sad women and sad men. Angry women were offered the lowest salary ($23,000) (Belkin 2007).

Emotion labor adds to the other tasks of a job. It makes work harder. Requiring employees to do emotion work can also cause them to have psychological problems. Performing in ways that are not consistent with their true feelings and constantly having to suppress their own emotions can cause burnout. Some workers, however, resist by refusing to do the emotion work or at least reducing it (Bellas 2001). For example, in this exchange a flight attendant confronts a customer on her flight by refusing to do the continuous emotion work expected of her:

> A young businessman said to a flight attendant, "Why aren't you smiling?" She put her tray back on the food cart, looked him in the eye, and said, "I'll tell you what. You smile first, then I'll smile." The businessman smiled at her. "Good," she replied. "Now freeze, and hold that for fifteen hours." (Hochschild 1983, 127)

Working as a trial lawyer is an occupation that is mostly held by men (88 percent are men) and requires much emotion work. It requires emotional expression and emotional manipulation, two behaviors that are identified with hypermasculinity, or the "Rambo" litigator

(Pierce 2001). Courtroom attorneys must manipulate defendants, witnesses, juries, judges, and opposing counsel through intimidation, persuasion, and aggression. Lawyers also use "strategic friendliness" (Pierce 2001).

A law school text (Berg 1987) advises lawyers to "stride to the podium . . . exude confidence . . . take command of the courtroom" (Pierce 2001, 227). Trial attorneys are also taught to intimidate witnesses in cross-examination, "to control the witness by never asking a question [to] which he does not already know the answer and to regard the impeachment of the witness as a highly confrontational act" (Menkel-Meadow 1985, 54). While they are role-playing in courses on courtroom behavior, law school students are criticized for not being forceful enough or for being too nice (Pierce 2001). They are applauded for looking angry, aggressive, and dominating.

Lawyers and flight attendants both do emotion work, but they use different kinds of emotions to deal with their clients or customers. The job of flight attendant, a "feminine" occupation, requires "feminine" emotion work, including expressing friendliness and deference, all with a constant smile. In contrast, the job of trial lawyer, a "masculine" occupation, calls for a "masculine" range of emotions effective to win over, dominate, and control. Like the inequities of salary and opportunity in work, the differences in emotional labor required in work also fall along lines of gender and also take their toll.

Equal Pay?

The image of men at work and women in the home is no longer consistent with the experience of almost all people in the United States and large numbers all over the world. We have nearly achieved equality in the proportion of women and men in the paid labor force. But has equality been achieved in the workplace in terms of how much pay women and men are receiving for their work? The women at Walmart entered the twenty-first century working for a company that still had two pay scales based on gender. Walmart may lag behind most other companies in moving toward gender equality in pay, but the gap remains throughout the labor market all over the world. Saudi Arabia has the biggest gap, where women earn 16 percent of men's income. Table 6-3 shows the ratio of women's salaries to men's in countries where the gap is much smaller. In these nations, the pay gap ranges from Poland, Spain, and Hungary, where women earn about 94 percent of what men do, to Korea, where women earn about 61 percent of men's pay, on average. In the United States, women now earn about 81 percent of men's wages. The gap has become smaller in the last few decades, but wage inequality remains. After significant improvement in the 1970s and 1980s, progress seems to have stalled since the 1990s.

Every year in April in the United States, a date is declared **Equal Pay Day**. Although this special date is not well known, it is important. What is Equal Pay Day? The average woman in a full-time job would have to work until Equal Pay Day of the next year to catch up with the wages of the average man from the year before. In 2014 it was April 7. Every year, of course, the average individual woman falls further and further behind as this loss is compounded when the three months of pay for January, February, and March pile up year after year (Steinberg 2001).

Look at Table 6-4 to see the pay differences for men and women of different racial/ethnic groups and different levels of education in the United States. White men stand out as

TABLE 6-3 Ratio of Women's Median Earnings to Men's
Median Earnings in OECD Countries, 2012

Hungary	94
Poland	94
Spain	94
New Zealand	93
Norway	92
Belgium	91
Italy	89
Ireland	89
Iceland	88
Greece	88
Denmark	87
Portugal	87
Sweden	86
Australia	86
France	86
Slovak Republic	85
Austria	81
Canada	81
Finland	81
Switzerland	81
United Kingdom	81
United States	81
Czech Republic	82
Netherlands	83
Germany	79
Israel	79
Japan	71
Korea	61

Source: Organisation for Economic Co-operation and Development (2012).

significantly better paid than men in all the other racial ethnic categories and than all women.
Men in each racial/ethnic group make more than women in that category. Education improves everyone's paycheck, but increased levels of education are not enough to allow women
to catch up with men or African Americans and Latinos and Latinas to catch up with whites.

Besides race ethnicity and gender, age also plays a role in the income gap between
women and men. Women and men are very close in median earnings from age sixteen until
about age thirty. They both see their wages rise at about the same rate until they are thirty,
when women's wages seem to stagnate. Men's wages continue to rise until they are in their
early fifties, and then they level off and fall (Regensburger 2001).

Notice the amounts of the differences in Table 6-4. If we compare the annual salaries of
all men and women with bachelor's degrees, men make $16,000 more than women. This is

TABLE 6-4 Median Earnings for Full-Time, Year-Round Workers Over 25 by Sex and Race Ethnicity in the United States, 2007

	High School Grad	BA	MA	PhD
White men	$40,000	$65,000	$75,500	$100,000
White women	29,000	46,000	55,000	70,000
Black men	32,000	50,000	60,000	95,000
Black women	25,000	42,000	55,000	65,400
Asian men	32,000	60,000	75,000	95,000
Asian women	26,000	50,000	67,000	65,000
Latino men	30,000	50,000	68,000	85,000
Latina women	25,000	40,000	52,500	NA
All men	37,200	61,000	75,000	100,000
All women	27,000	45,000	55,000	70,000

Source: National Center for Education Statistics (2008).

enough to pay for a year in college or to buy a car. What about over a decade or over a lifetime of work? The numbers are huge and could make a significant difference in a person's life. For example, over a forty-year career, the gap would amount to about $306,440 in a comparison of all men and all women.

Although the wage gap is still large and cuts across education and race/ethnicity, it has shrunk in the last decades of the twentieth century. For example, in the United States in the 1970s, women earned only fifty-nine cents on the dollar compared to men. Today they earn about eighty one cents for every dollar a man earns. Part of this improvement, however, is unfortunately a result of men's falling wages rather than women's gains (Amott 1999). Furthermore, the closing of the gap has now stalled. (Glynn and Powers 2012).

We can expect this stagnation to continue or for women's wages to decline since most of the jobs for women now being added to the economy are in low-paying and part-time industries like food service and in-home healthcare, jobs that often lack health insurance and pay very little. Nearly 60 percent of the growth was in jobs that pay less than $10 an hour. At the same time, women have taken a substantial hit from shrinkage in public sector jobs that pay more and have benefits. Women have lost close to 500,000 public-sector jobs since the summer of 2009. Men, comparatively, lost 290,000 (McDonough 2013). Now look at the kind of data that are in the tables. These are wages for year-round, full-time workers over the age of twenty-five. These are people who have the most secure, and generally, best-paid jobs. Women (27 percent) tend to be more likely than men (13 percent) to have part-time jobs, but men and women in these less well-paid positions are not included in the table (U.S. Department of Labor 2011). That means that Table 6-4 is showing data that provide the best-case scenario for a small gap. Furthermore, median rather than mean wages are reported in the table. The median is the halfway point between the highest and lowest salaries, in contrast to the mean, which is the average of all the salaries. The median diminishes the effect of people at the very lowest and the very highest ends of the scale, which shrinks the gap as well.

Additional research has shown that the 19 percent gap between women and men is an underestimate of the real picture (Rose and Hartmann 2004). Because women are more likely to work part-time, less likely to work year-round, and more likely to have entire years out of the labor force—often to care for children or other family members—the gap is actually twice as big. If women's part-time, intermittent lifetime employment is taken into consideration, women make only about 38 percent, not 81 percent, of what men earn. Across the fifteen years of a study of women's and men's pay and work histories, the average prime-age working woman earned only $273,592, whereas the average working man earned $722,693 (in 1999 dollars). This amounts to a difference of almost half a million dollars just in the fifteen-year period (Rose and Hartmann 2004).

Unequal Opportunity: The Glass Ceiling, the Glass Escalator, and the Sticky Floor

Besides having different pay, women and men have different ranks in workplaces. Most companies are like Walmart: the higher you go, the fewer women and minorities you will see. Research on a number of corporate headquarters in the United States finds that of all the high-level employees, 37.2 percent are women and 15.5 percent are minorities. Only 16.9 percent of

There is more than one glass ceiling. Women in mid-level positions are prevented from rising to top-level jobs such as CEO or supervisor in skilled trades. Women in the lowest paid, or unpaid positions in factories, offices, and homes are prevented from rising even to those mid-level positions.

Source: Cartoon by Nicholson from *The Australian*; www.nicholsoncartoons.com.au.

the management are women and 6 percent are minorities. At the highest level of management, the numbers fall even more: 6.6 percent of managers at the vice-president level or higher are women and 2.6 percent are minorities. Of Fortune 500 CEOs (chief executive officers), only 4.2 percent are women (Catalyst 2013). Government jobs are a little better, but women and minorities are still underrepresented at the top. Women hold 44 percent of federal jobs, but only 30 percent of higher-level positions. African American women make up 10 percent of federal workers but only 3.5 percent of the top managers and Latinas make of 3 percent of federal workers and 1 percent of top managers (Equal Employment Opportunity Commission 2010).

Although women are strikingly underrepresented in corporate leadership, the United States has a higher proportion of women (15 percent) in the top ranks than all but two other nations (Norway, with 44 percent, and Sweden, with 17 percent). Only 11 percent of the top executives in France are women, and 12 percent of FTSE (Financial Times/[London] Stock Exchange) directors in Britain are women. Norway accomplished equality by introducing legislation in 2003 to boost the number of women on company boards. Norwegian laws now stipulate that businesses must increase the number of women on their boards to 40 percent or face the threat of closure (Davies 2009). Recent French law requires a balanced representation of women and men on boards of directors and supervisory boards in large companies. The government projects that this will result in a 20 to 40 percent rise in the number of women in high level management positions in the next few years (Embassy of France 2013).

Although women do seem to be increasing their numbers on the higher rungs of the corporate ladder all over the world, at the current rate of progress it would take women 475 years to reach equal representation as senior managers (Peterson and Runyan 1999; International Labour Office 2007).

This inability of women to catch up at the highest levels of management is called the "**glass ceiling**": women and minorities seem to be able to only go so far in their jobs because some invisible force is holding them back. Later in this chapter, we explore what these invisible forces might be. The U.S. Department of Labor defines the glass ceiling as "artificial barriers based on attitudinal or organizational bias that prevent qualified individuals from advancing upward in their organization into management-level positions" (L. Martin 1991, 1).

What happens when men enter women-dominated professions? Does a glass ceiling prevent them from rising to positions of leadership? Christine Williams (2000) has looked at these questions in four occupations: nurses, elementary school teachers, social workers, and librarians. Before the Civil War, these jobs were more likely to be held by men than women, but today they are dominated by women.

It seems reasonable that men in women-dominated professions would face similar barriers to those that women face in men-dominated occupations. Williams (2000), however, discovered that instead of confronting barriers, men find themselves welcome and even given preferential treatment when they are tokens. When asked whether he encountered any problems when he applied for positions as a pediatric nurse, for example, one man explained, "No, no, none. . . . I've heard this from managers and supervisory-type people with men in pediatrics: 'It's nice to have a man because it's such a female-dominated position' " (12).

Some men, however, said they had been tracked away from the most woman-dominated specialties, such as obstetrics and gynecology, when they were quickly promoted out of them. The specialties that are considered most appropriate for men in the field are the most prestigious and best paid. Instead of being held back, men face invisible pressures to move up in their professions. Williams (2000) calls this the "glass escalator." Whether they want to ride or not, men are expected to move up and out of the most "feminine" low-prestige and low-paying jobs.

Men's experience in women-dominated jobs also differs from women in men-dominated work settings because both are likely to have men supervisors. The men to whom Williams spoke said that they became very friendly with their supervisor, which provided them with a mentor. One man who was a special-education teacher explained, "Occasionally I've had a principal who would regard me as 'the other man on the campus' and 'it's us against them,' you know? I mean nothing really that extreme except that some male principals feel like there's nobody there to talk to except the other man. So I've been in that position" (Williams 2000, 301).

Openly gay men did not necessarily meet with this kind of support. One nurse said that one of the physicians he worked with preferred to staff the operating room with exclusively men nurses, as long as they were not gay. Although this example is of a prejudiced colleague, heterosexism was especially likely to come from the clients being served. Men who were in the "women's profession" of elementary school teachers, for example, were sometimes accused of being pedophiles. A kindergarten teacher described his problems with stereotypes from parents who had met with his principal:

[The principal] indicated to me that parents had come to him and indicated to him that they had a problem with the fact that I was a male. . . . I recall almost exactly what he said. There were three specific concerns that the parents had: One parent said, "how can he love my child; he's a man." The second that I recall, he said the parent said, "He has a beard." And the third thing was "Aren't you concerned about homosexuality?" (Williams 2000, 301)

Black men may also be unable to get on the escalator. Research on black men who work as nurses finds that they face awkward, unfriendly, and sometimes offensive interactions with colleagues, management, and patients. Black men nurses report that they often do not encounter the deference or even the civility accorded to white men nurses. One man describes his experience as the only black person on the nursing staff: "[The staff] had nothing to do with me, and they didn't even want me to sit at the same area where they were charting in to take a break. They wanted me to sit somewhere else. . . . They wouldn't even sit at a table with me! When I came and sat down, everybody got up and left" (Wingfield 2009, 379).

Patients also treated the black men nurses with hostility. One nurse told of his encounters with patients: "I come [to work] in my white uniform, that's what I wear—being a Black man, I know they won't look at me the same, so I dress the part—I said good evening, my name's Chris, and I'm going to be your nurse. She says to me, 'Are you from housekeeping?' . . . I've had other cases, I've walked in and had a lady look at me and ask if I'm the janitor" (Wingfield 2009, 381).

Discussions of the glass ceiling and the glass escalator focus on jobs at the top. Most women (and men) in the world, however, work in the lowest paid, lowest skills jobs in manufacturing and service. Here the image of a "**sticky floor**" is most appropriate. The garment and electronic industries exploit all their workers, but women tend to have the worst working conditions and the worst pay in these industrial sectors. The sticky floor refers to the fact that women are stuck working long hours for small paychecks in these jobs, with few other options.

In Mexico, these jobs sites are called maquiladoras. **Maquiladoras** are assembly plants that import machinery and materials to Mexico and produce finished export products, which are then sold around the world. The businesses are large multinationals based in the global North, especially in the United States, which include all of the biggest and most familiar corporations such as Ford, Chrysler, Honda, Samsonite, Fisher Price, and General Motors. Workers in the plants, who are mostly women, earn about $6 a day (Center for Reflection, Education, and Action 2000).

Why Is There a Wage Gap Between Women and Men?

Three explanations have been offered for the gap that exists between women and men in pay: (1) discrimination, (2) human capital, and (3) organization of jobs.

DISCRIMINATION. Those scholars who argue that the pay gap is a result of discrimination are called *bias* theorists. They argue that decisions about who will be hired, promoted, or fired and what an employee will be paid are made in ways that discriminate against women. Sometimes discrimination occurs in obvious ways (see Box 6-1). Women are treated differently on the job and sometimes explicitly barred from jobs or promotions. The FBI, for example,

GENDER IN EVERYDAY LIFE   BOX 6-1
MARKING GENDER IN THE WORKPLACE

Darlene Jesperson worked for Harrah's Resort as a bartender for twenty years when her employers decided to fire her because she refused to abide by the new dress code. The dress codes require women employees to style their hair and wear full makeup, including foundation, blush, mascara, lipstick, and nail polish. Men must cut their hair above their collar and to have a clean face and clean fingernails.

Jesperson took her case to court to get her job back but lost the case when the judges decided that Harrah's had the right to require their employees to follow the rules. The decision was made by a panel of judges, however, and not all of them agreed with the ruling. One judge who dissented said that the decision "implies that women's faces compare unfavorably to men's [and that] women's faces are incomplete, unattractive or unprofessional without full make-up" (*Hospitality Industry Quarterly* 2005).

This case shows a surprising level of differential treatment of men and women workers in the twenty-first century. It also, as the judge says, implies not only that women should be treated differently in the workplace but that there is something wrong with women's appearance that needs to be remedied with cosmetics if they are to be acceptable coworkers and employees.

openly refused to hire women until J. Edgar Hoover died in 1972. Women musicians increased their representation in American orchestras from 10 percent in 1970 to 35 percent in the 1990s, as blind auditions became more common. Screens were erected between the musician auditioning for a position and the person making the selections, and rugs were placed on the floor to make high-heel shoes undetectable (Goldin and Rouse 2000). This kind of discrimination was prevalent before the 1970s but has become much less common over the past few decades. In 1963 the Equal Pay Act was passed in the United States, making it illegal to pay workers differently solely on the basis of gender. The Equal Employment Opportunity Commission (EEOC) filed just 393 lawsuits on sex-discrimination grounds in 2003, and this number has been fairly stable in the last decade (see Box 6-2). In a country of 146 million workers, this number is quite small (Ackman 2004). The Walmart case, however, reminds us

GENDER IN EVERDAY LIFE   BOX 6-2
BRINGING A DISCRIMINATION CASE AGAINST AN EMPLOYER

In bringing a case of discrimination against an employer, three types of proof can be used. The first is intent to discriminate. A company document that shows discrimination or an employer's stating in front of witnesses that he or she will treat women (or other groups) differently in hiring, promotion, or pay are examples of this type of proof (Conway, Ahern, and Steuernagel 1999). This kind of evidence is probably rare today, but companies used to have openly separate pay scales for women and men workers and until the 1970s, newspapers listed job opportunities under separate headings for "men wanted" and "women wanted."

A second type is proof of disparate treatment. In these cases, a person in a protected category (by race, color, religion, sex, or national origin) of Title VII of the Civil Rights Act of 1964, which protects people from discrimination at work, is denied a job even though he or she is qualified. Someone from another category is given the job, and the employer claims that the decision was made for some legitimate nondiscriminatory reason. The person denied the job must prove that the reason given is not valid. The prospective employee must show that she or he is as well qualified as the person that was hired or that the criteria used for making the choice were discriminatory. For example, employers in a security-guard business might argue that they must hire only men because customers feel better protected with men guards. Customer preference, however, is not a valid reason for discrimination.

A third type of proof is disparate effects. An employer argues that she or he used neutral criteria to choose which applicant to hire. The person who wasn't hired has to show that the criteria may appear neutral but operate in a discriminatory manner. For example, fire departments formerly had height requirements that discriminated against women and members of racial/ethnic groups who tend to be shorter on average than white men. The height requirements were not necessary to the job, and although they appeared to be neutral, they ended up discriminating (Conway et al. 1999).

that overt explicit discrimination is not entirely a thing of the past. Walmart has been accused of having two pay scales and two tracks for promotion based on gender. Discrimination also occurs more subtly, however.

Nijole Benokraitis and Joe Feagin (1986) suggest that men can use a number of tactics to subtly undercut women with whom they work (Lorber 2000; see Box 6-3). Many of these have positive features and appear to be attempts to help women in some way, but they ultimately work to prevent women from contending and winning in workplace competition. Their subtlety makes these tactics difficult to address or even acknowledge.

Backhanded tactics include the following (Benokraitis 1997):

- *Condescending chivalry*: A supervisor's withholding useful criticism of a woman employee to "protect" her.

GENDER IN EVERYDAY LIFE   BOX 6-3
SEXUAL HARASSMENT AS DISCRIMINATION

Fifty percent of women can expect to experience behaviors at the workplace that legally constitute sexual harassment. Between 30 percent and 66 percent of women students will experience sexual harassment at school. Even though most of this goes unreported, the cost to businesses remains high in the form of sick leave, job turnover, and lost productivity. Private industries have estimated the cost as $6,719,593 annually for each Fortune 500 company (Rundblad 2001). The cost to individual women is significant as well. Sexual harassment can result in feelings of helplessness, confusion, depression, and lower self-esteem and even physical problems like headaches, sleep disturbances, tiredness, and nausea (Paludi 1997).

Harassment can be seen as a continuum from "gender harassment which is inappropriately calling attention to women's or men's bodies, sexuality or marital status, to sexual harassment which is turning a professional, work or student-teacher relationship into a sexual relationship that is not wanted by one of the people involved and that is coercive because the initiator has some power over the other person" (Lorber 2000, 291). The three key words for sexual harassment are *inappropriate*, *unwanted*, and *power*.

Behavior is inappropriate if it is not gender neutral in a situation that should be gender neutral. Gender neutral does not mean cold or hostile. It means cordial and friendly but not in a sexual manner (Lorber 2000).

"Unwanted" means that one person does not want to engage in the interaction. This means that the "test" of sexual harassment is at least partly subjective; it can only be determined by the person who does not want the attention. Sometimes this causes problems because men and women may have different reactions to similar behavior. One researcher (Gutek 1985) found that 67.2 percent of men said they would be flattered if a woman coworker asked them to have sex. Of women, however, 62.8 percent said they would be insulted by a sexual invitation from a man with whom they worked (Lorber 2000).

Power is the final important factor. One effective reaction to harassment is to leave the situation, but power means that a person who feels sexually harassed may not be able to immediately leave. The person who is being harassed may be in a situation in which he or she will have to pay a price for leaving—loss of a good job or of a useful educational opportunity.

Catharine MacKinnon (1979) was the first to define sexual harassment in the 1970s. Her definition became part of EEOC (Equal Employment Opportunity Commission) guidelines in 1980 and was upheld in the courts in the late 1980s in the United States (Lorber 2000). Following the American lead, sexual-harassment policies have spread throughout the world. These policies vary from one region to another because they are tailored to local contexts. In Germany, for example, sexual harassment has been subsumed within non-gender-specific policies that seek to protect all workers from "mobbing," which is defined as systematic and recurrent harassment and insult (Zippel 2006, 123).

- *Supportive discouragement*: Discouraging a woman from competing for a challenging opportunity because she might not make it.
- *Friendly harassment*: Kidding a woman in public for being pregnant or some other aspect of her appearance.
- *Subjective objectification*: Believing that all women fit some particular stereotype.
- *Radiant devaluation*: Offering exaggerated praise for accomplishments that should be expected as routine.
- *Liberated sexism*: Inviting a woman for a drink after work as "one of the boys" but refusing to let her pay for a round of drinks.
- *Benevolent exploitation*: Giving a woman a chance to work on a project to learn the job, but taking full credit for the final product.
- *Considerate domination*: Making decisions for women about what they can handle, for example, as new mothers, rather than allowing them to decide how best to divide their time.
- *Collegial exclusion*: Scheduling networking meetings at times when parents (often mothers) have family responsibilities that may conflict.

Why are men colleagues and managers so hesitant to allow women in? Competition is one explanation, but other men are competitors, too. Why are women so likely to be excluded? Perhaps men fear that if a profession becomes too feminized, it will be devalued. Men may be afraid that if too many women enter their ranks, their profession will become "women's work" and that those in the occupation, including men, will lose prestige, income, and control over resources (Lorber 2000).

HUMAN CAPITAL. A second explanation for the gap in pay between women and men is put forth by **human capital theorists**, who argue that people invest in their own human abilities, including the skills that allow them to move up the ladder at work and receive raises. **Human capital** refers to the talents that we have to do our jobs. They include our attitudes, education, and experience (Wharton 2005). Human capital theorists believe that (1) women do not have as much commitment to paid work; (2) men invest more in themselves than women do; and (3) men obtain more education or job training.

Research has shown that women have similar commitment to their careers as men do. The first human capital claim, therefore, is not correct (Wharton 2005). The other two claims are partially correct, but women may lag behind men in their education and experience not because they choose to invest less in their human capital but for other reasons. Women may be prevented from investing in themselves because of gender barriers in schools and workplaces. Girls and women have made great strides in education and are now surpassing men in many professions. But women still remain somewhat behind in some professions. Furthermore, even when women have similar or even better educations than their male counterparts, their paychecks do not reflect their educational achievement.

Women also are less likely to receive on-the-job training, but the explanation for this is usually that women have fewer opportunities for developing their skills, not that they are making the wrong choices about training. For example, an increasingly global economy is making international experience a prerequisite for executive positions, but men are much more likely to receive international assignments than are women (Antal and Izraeli 1993). As recently as 1988, 36 percent of U.S. companies that posted employees in other nations did not send any women to these assignments (Moran, Stahl, and Boyer, Inc. 1988).

Human capital theory is probably the most prevalent social theory among the general population in the United States, because it rests on an important tenet of the American belief system, **individualism**. Individualism goes like this: "There are abundant economic opportunities. Individuals must be industrious and competitive. Rewards in the form of education, jobs, income and status are, and should be, the result of individual talent and efforts. Therefore, the distribution of rewards is generally fair and equitable" (Rothman 2002, 55).

This ideology is strongly held by the majority of Americans. A recent poll asked people whether they thought success was mostly a result of hard work, mostly a result of luck, or mostly the result of the help of others. Among respondents, 66 percent said that it was the result of hard work, and 12 percent said it was the result of luck or the help of others. Another 22 percent said it was a combination of these factors (UC Berkeley 2010).

ORGANIZATION OF JOBS. The third and most powerful explanation for the gender gap in pay is a social structural one. Social structural explanations point to the ways the workplace and the labor market are organized.

Gender Segregation of the Labor Market. Perhaps the most significant social structural factor is the way occupations are segregated into "men's work" and "women's work." Most sociologists believe that gender segregation of jobs is the most important reason wages are so different for men and women. Men and women are in different jobs, and men's jobs tend to pay better than women's jobs.

Consider two scenarios: As you drive down the interstate and glance in the window of the tractor trailer traveling beside you, you see a woman at the wheel. Although you probably don't make any judgment about the fact that the driver is a woman, you notice it. You go to a party, where your friend introduces her husband and mentions that he is a secretary. You hear someone respond, "That's an unusual job for a man." The distribution of people into jobs by gender is part of our everyday life that often goes unnoticed unless we see someone who is an exception. This categorization of jobs as women's work or men's work is a part of our social scene that has remained remarkably stable despite the growing numbers of women entering nearly every occupation in the paid labor force.

An occupation is defined as **gender segregated** if 75 percent or more of the people who work in that field are of one gender. Because the paid labor force is almost 50 percent men and 50 percent women, a job would not be considered gender stratified if the people who held that job were also evenly divided. When a job reaches 75 percent, it is considered to have tipped into dominance by women or men. Most people work in these kinds of gender-dominated occupations. Nine of the ten most common jobs for women are in women-dominated positions (Bose and Whaley 2001).

Table 6-5 shows the top ten occupations for women in the United States. Secretarial work is the most common occupation for women, and 96 percent of secretaries are women. Register nurse is the second most common job, and 91 percent are women. All the jobs women are most likely to have are overwhelmingly dominated by women.

Men, too, are likely to work in gender-segregated jobs. Table 6-6 shows the top ten occupations for men, and it also shows that men are concentrated in "men's jobs." For example, 97 percent of truck drivers are men, and 98 percent of construction workers are men. All the top ten jobs for men are also occupations in which most of the workers are men.

The gender gap has declined somewhat in recent years, but it remains high and the pace of change is slow. The **occupational sex-segregation index** provides a measure of the gap and ranges from 0 to 100. The number refers to the proportion of women who would need to change occupations to create gender "desegregation" in the labor market. From 1900 to 1960, the occupational sex-segregation index remained fairly constant at about sixty-five in the United States. This means that for the first sixty years of the twentieth century, about two-thirds of women would have had to change their jobs to reach this balance. In the 1970s, the index dropped eight points. It has continued to drop since the 1980s but much more slowly (Bose and Whaley 2001).

TABLE 6-5 Top Ten Jobs for Women, 2010 (Full-Time Workers)

Occupation	% of Workers in Job Who Are Women	Median Weekly Earnings for Women
Secretary	96%	$657
Registered nurse	91%	$1,039
Elementary and middle school teacher	81%	$931
Nurse's aide, home health aide	87%	$427
Customer service representative	66%	$586
Retail sales manager	46%	$578
Cashiers	72%	$366
Office manager	67%	$726
Receptionist	93%	$529
Accountant or auditor	59%	$953

Source: Institute for Women's Policy Research (2011).

TABLE 6-6 Top Ten Jobs for Men, 2010 (Full-Time Workers)

Occupation	% of Workers in Job Who Are Men	Median Weekly Earnings for Men
Truck drivers	97%	$691
Managers (not retail sales)	60%	$1,395
Managers (retail sales)	55%	$782
Janitor	70%	$494
Retail sales	58%	$651
Freight, stock, and material handlers	84%	$508
Construction laborers	98%	$569
Sales rep wholesale and manufacturing	76%	$983
Computer software engineer	79%	$1,590
Chief executive	73%	$2,217

Source: Institute for Women's Policy Research (2011).

Climbing the Ladder of Success. A second social structural feature of the labor market is that not only is it gender segregated, but women's jobs are structured differently than are men's jobs. Many businesses and agencies have systems for promoting employees within the organization. Sometimes these **job ladders** have many people at the bottom and very few at the top, so that the odds of moving up are low. For example, if you visit a hospital, you see many nurses on every floor doing many different kinds of jobs. Only a few nurses become heads of their division, and only a handful become hospital administrators. On the other hand, some jobs have many rungs and only a few people on each step. The sales division of a company that provides auto parts for large manufacturers might have several jobs with only a few people feeding into the next level: a stock clerk, a sales trainee, a sales representative, an assistant sales manager, and a manager. The odds at each level are good that the person will move up into better-paid, more-prestigious positions (Reskin and Padavic 2001).

Women's jobs are more likely to be in positions that have short or no ladders. For example, teaching is a profession that is "feminine" and has no ladder. Teachers might sometimes move into administrative positions, but running a school is quite different from being a classroom teacher, and the odds of becoming a principal are small because there are so many teachers per principal. There are no promotions from one teaching position to another. All the teachers in a school are relatively equal in their responsibilities and rewards (Tomaskovic-Devey 1993).

Women are also segregated into jobs within businesses that are more low profile than men's work. They are less visible to those who are choosing people to promote within the company (Reskin and Padavic 2001). For example, women lawyers are more likely to be assigned jobs in research, and men are more likely to receive assignments in litigation. Both tasks are essential to the work, but courtroom appearances place litigators in the limelight, whereas research is done behind the scenes (Epstein 1993).

Bringing Politics into the Picture. Barbara Reskin and Irene Padavic (2001), however, contend that gender segregation of the labor market is not a sufficient explanation of why women's wages remain lower than men's. They suggest a third explanation, arguing that while the social structural factor of gender segregation of jobs is a key element, politics is even more important. They argue that underlying structural factors such as gender segregation of the labor market and career ladders are issues of power. They assert, furthermore, that focusing on gender segregation will lead us to develop ineffective solutions because we are not tackling the deeper problems that underlie this inequity. Reskin and Padavic believe that the political character of gender is the underlying and more important cause of the wage gap. They explain that "the basic cause of the income gap is not sex segregation but men's desire to preserve their advantaged position and their ability to do so by establishing rules to distribute valued resources in their favor" (Reskin and Padavic 2001, 258). (Some) men have power to make the rules, and they wish to maintain both their power to write the rules and their ability to benefit from them. According to Reskin and Padavic, the cause of low wages for women's work is power differences, and the result is less access to resources for women.

Reskin and Padavic argue that a gender-segregated labor market is a useful tool for maintaining a wage gap. Furthermore, they contend that even if the labor market became less segregated, men would be able to rewrite the rules in a way that would place them and their jobs in a more highly valued and more highly rewarded category.

By looking at causes of the gender gap in wages historically, Reskin and Padavic explain how changing the rules can re-create inequality in a new form. In the nineteenth and early twentieth centuries, men were paid higher wages, and this inequity was defended by the argument that men's work should be more highly paid because men were heads of households and responsible for families and were therefore entitled to a **family wage**. Women, in contrast, were seen as secondary earners working for "**pin money**," while their husbands' wages were the real source of their livelihood. During the twentieth century, women overcame this characterization of their work. Women now are recognized as contributing a large proportion of household income in dual-earner families, and women are more likely than men to be single heads of households. In the United States, 41 percent of women in the labor force are the main **breadwinners** for their households, earning all or nearly all of the money coming in. Twenty-three percent are **co-breadwinners** earning at least a quarter of the household income (Strasser 2013). Today women are indisputably primary breadwinners. The rules, however, have been changed.

The idea of a family wage could benefit women now because women are often heads of households and are nearly always significant contributors to their families' economic status. However, these factors are no longer emphasized. Occupation has become a "better" method of valuing work; and as we have seen, women and men do not have the same occupations.

Just making a distinction between two types of work, however, does not necessarily mean that one will be better paid than the other. Some value has to be placed on the work, making one job more important and, therefore, justifiably better paid. Women have different jobs than do men, *and* women's work is less valued than men's. Engineering work is more highly valued and highly paid than nursing. Truck driving is more valued than working in customer services. Teaching is low paid, and child-care workers are among the very lowest valued and lowest paid occupations. Are these women's jobs really less skilled or less important to society? If they are not, what political struggles will we encounter in trying to rewrite the rules in a way that recognizes the value of women's work?

How Can the Gender Gap in Promotion Be Closed?

Workplaces are resistant to change (Reskin and Padavic 2001). Nevertheless, there are some actions that can be taken to address the problem.

- *Building bridges from one job ladder to another.* In positions where there are few opportunities for advancement, workers could be offered chances to move into another field within a company without losing seniority. For example, clerical workers in dead-end jobs could move to sales divisions, where the likelihood of promotion is greater.
- *Creating formal processes.* Instead of relying on informal personnel decisions that could be biased by individual managers, formal rules and procedures could be established. Rather than guessing which employees might be interested in promotions, management could display written announcements that any worker could respond to.
- *Promoting employee organization into unions.* Unions allow employees to articulate demands that will improve their situation, and they provide vehicles for informing decision makers such as policy makers and management about what their needs are. In addition, unions provide ways to exercise power over political leaders and employers through electoral politics, collective bargaining, and strikes. "On average, unionization raises women's wages by 11.2 percent—about $2.00 per hour—compared to non-union women with similar characteristics. Among women workers, those in unions are about 19 percentage points more likely to have employer-provided health insurance and about 25 percentage points more likely to have an employer-provided pension" (Schmitt 2008).

COMPARABLE WORTH POLICIES. Beyond these specific policies, a broader set of changes may be required to address the wage gap because so many women and men are in gender-segregated occupations. One way of eliminating the pay gap between women and men is to distribute men and women in occupations more evenly and make sure that they receive the same pay for the same work. Given the segregation in the labor market, however, what can be done to provide women and men equitable pay even if they are in different occupations? Comparable worth policy is one answer that has been given to this question.

Comparable worth policy designs systematic ways to evaluate jobs in order to create pay scales that do not discriminate against occupations that are dominated by women. Four factors are typically used: skill, effort, responsibility, and working conditions. Jobs can be evaluated according to these factors, and pay can be assigned based on the scores for each. Those that are most skilled, require the most effort, demand the most responsibility, and take place in the most difficult working conditions would be rated highest and therefore be allotted the highest pay.

These four factors create a good start, but they need to be revised to make sure that they are not used in a way that continues to discriminate against workers in occupations dominated by women. For example, when employers look at the factor of skill, they often do not look at skills associated with clerical work such as knowledge of grammar, ability to write correspondence, and knowledge about organizational shortcuts. Clerical jobs are usually evaluated as "needing no specialized knowledge." Clerical jobs are also usually held by women. In contrast, manufacturing jobs, which are usually held by men, are rated as requiring "limited specialized knowledge."

Responsibility is another issue that will need to be rethought. Sometimes women and men are doing the same tasks in different settings, but the tasks are defined differently and more favorably for the men's jobs than for the women's. For example, managers, who are more often men, and secretaries, who are mostly women, often do the same work running an office. The manager is perceived as exercising authority and responsibility; the secretary is doing similar tasks with a similar result, but her work is not seen as managerial (Steinberg 2001).

The issue of working conditions also needs to be revisited. When they look at working conditions, employers have paid attention to noisy machinery but not to the difficulty of working with incontinent or dying patients or exposure to disease. Men are more likely to work around machinery, and women are more likely to be in caring professions.

SUCCESS STORIES. Although the focus of the discussion has been on the difficulties women have in moving into well-paid prestigious jobs, many women, of course, have succeeded. In many instances, families have played an important role in facilitating that success. Elizabeth Higgenbotham and Lynn Weber (2000) looked at the experience of upward social mobility for white and black women. Besides looking at differences in race ethnicity, they also looked at the social class of the women's families. Some women were raised in working-class families by parents with blue-collar jobs, and some were raised in middle-class families by parents with professional, managerial, or administrative jobs. The women, themselves, however, had all obtained a college education and taken a professional position. White women from working-class families had received the least support for their aspirations from their families. In contrast, middle-class white families expected their daughters to attend college and were better able to provide the financial and emotional help they might need to achieve that goal.

White working-class women were also less likely to have parents who stressed the necessity of having an occupation in order to succeed in life. Nearly all the black families (94 percent), both middle and working class, stressed the importance of getting a good job. By comparison, 70 percent of the white middle-class families stressed this with their daughters, but only 56 percent of the white working-class families stressed it. White women were more likely to feel that their parents emphasized the importance of marriage. One white woman from a working-class family explained her parents' ambivalence about her decision to become an attorney:

> My parents assumed that I would go to college and meet some nice man and finish, but not necessarily work after. I would be a good mother for my children. I don't think that they ever thought I would go to law school. Their attitude about my interests in law school was, "you can do it if you want to, but we don't think it is a particularly practical thing for a woman to do." (Higgenbotham and Weber 2000, 349)

Black women and white women also felt differently about the debt they owed to their family and community for the achievements they had accomplished in establishing their careers. Black women felt that they were obligated to their family for their support. They were especially likely to acknowledge the support their parents had provided in helping them raise their children. White women, in contrast, believed that their accomplishments were a result of their own work. When asked whether she felt she owed a lot to her family and relatives for their help, for example, one white woman who was a judge said, "No, I feel I've gotten most places on my own" (Higgenbotham and Weber 2000, 351).

Success Stories in Engineering. Engineering is one of the most tenacious occupations in regard to gender segregation. Technology in the twenty-first century is central to the global economy. Engineering is the gateway into advanced technology, but women still account for only 13 percent of employed engineers (National Science Foundation 2011). The future for women in engineering, in addition, does not look good, because only 5 percent of people with engineering PhDs are women. Their low numbers in the profession as practicing engineers and as teachers mean that women will have little effect on shaping the technology of the future or on shaping those who will be designing it (Fox 2001).

Engineering has long been associated with men and masculinity because of its ties to the military (Fox 2001). The term *engineering* was first used when military men developed devices for warfare in the fifteenth century. In the United States, the first engineering education was established at West Point Military Academy in 1802. Engineering continues to be associated with the supposedly masculine characteristics of mathematical ability, rationality, and self-discipline (Cardwell 1957).

Moving women into a profession so long identified with men and masculinity is a difficult challenge. Mary Frank Fox (2000), however, has examined the characteristics of universities that have successfully increased the proportion of women in their engineering programs. She has found that institutions like universities can be structured for inequality but that they can also be restructured in ways that promote equality by paying attention to their organization and creating ways that make better use of the talents of underrepresented groups, including women. Universities that have been successful at reducing inequality have the following traits (Fox 1991, 1995, 1996):

- A history of leadership on issues related to increasing participation of women
- Chairs and faculty members who had taken time to consider what constitutes a "good environment" for study
- Clear and standardized criteria for job evaluations
- Written guidelines for evaluating faculty performance and progress
- Open processes in hiring, promoting, and allocating rewards
- Increased opportunities for collaboration between junior and senior faculty, including placement of new people into ongoing projects

Retirement

Retirement marks the end of paid employment, but our work histories have an important effect on our experience of retirement. Because our work lives are so marked by gender, it is not surprising that retirement is also a gendered episode. In a survey of working women in the United States about what worried them most, retirement was reported as one of the top worries (AFL-CIO 2006).

A **pension** is a payment that is made to people who are no longer working. Sometimes it comes from a fund set up by an employer, or it could be a fund an individual sets up for himself or herself, like a savings plan that will not be used until after retirement. Social Security is the public pension program maintained by the government in the United States. When working people decide to retire, many of them rely on Social Security for at least part of their support. Working people and their employers pay into the Social Security fund, and when Americans reach the age of sixty-five they can draw a monthly check from the fund.

Social Security is supposed to treat people equally. Its design, however, is based on the work and social roles of white men. When white women and women and men of minority racial ethnic groups use the Social Security program, they find that it does not treat them as well as it does most white men. Table 6-6 shows the benefits paid to different people by race ethnicity and gender. Table 6-6 shows that men in all categories are paid higher monthly averages for Social Security, but race ethnicity also makes a significant difference. How exactly does Social Security discriminate?

Social Security benefits are tied to income. Because men on average earn more than women, they are more likely to be eligible for maximum benefits ($2,533 a month for full retirement age in 2013). Men are also more likely to be in the paid labor force more years because women often leave the labor market for family obligations. In thirty-five years of employment, men average one year out, whereas women average twelve years out (Harrington-Meyer, Wolf, and Himes 2000). Social Security assumes that recipients have had a long-term stable career in which they have experienced a constant increase in pay over the years (Calasanti and Slevin 2001).

According to the Elder Economic Security Standard Index (Elder Index), a single retired person who rents would need to have an annual income of $20,248 in order to make ends meet. Table 6-7 shows that no category meets this standard. White men come closest with an annual average income from Social Security of $16,176. Women receive only half of this bare-bones income from their Social Security checks.

Social Security was originally deliberately planned to treat women and men differently. The program assumed that women and men were married and that they lived in households where the man was the only breadwinner. Women were thought of as appendages to those men. When wives and widows were added to the program as beneficiaries in 1939, their benefits were not based on their contributions as paid employees but by their relationship—wife—to

TABLE 6-7 Average Monthly Social Security Benefit by Race/Ethnicity and Sex, 2009

Group	Benefit
White men	$1,348
White women	1,025
Black men	1,306
Black women	961
Latino men	1,077*
Latina women	869*
Other men	973
Other women	837

Source: Social Security Administration (2010). * Social Security Administration (2013).

men in paid work. In 1935, when Social Security was introduced, 40 percent of black women were in the labor force, but their activity was ignored (Harrington-Meyer 1996).

The position of appendage to men was accompanied by a lower rate of benefits. Women who obtained "wife and widow" benefits received only half the amount their husbands did. Women who had divorced their husbands were not eligible for any amount. The laws have now changed so that women who were married more than ten years before their divorce are eligible as beneficiaries (Calasanti and Slevin 2001).

Compared to men's benefits, benefits for women are still much more tightly tied to their marital status. Discontinuous marriage because of divorce or widowhood has important effects on retirement income for women more often than for men. In 1995, women who had been continuously married to their husbands averaged only about $85 less than men. However, women who had interrupted marital histories received $356 less than men (DeViney and Solomon 1995). This is a particularly serious disadvantage for black women, who are more likely to marry late or not at all. By age forty-two, 63 percent of white and Hispanic women have been married ten years, whereas only 44 percent of black women have been married that long (Harrington-Meyer et al. 2000).

About 56 percent of full-time workers are eligible for private pensions through their jobs. On retirement, they receive not only Social Security benefits but pensions as well. Employees with jobs that are covered by pensions are disproportionately white, well educated, and work for large companies (Johnson, Sambamoorthi, and Crystal 1999). They are also likely to be men (Stoller and Gibson 2000). The effect of these differences in Social Security and pension plans is greater economic insecurity for women, especially black, Hispanic, and First Nations women (Calasanti and Slevin 2001).

Despite the inadequacy of the Social Security system and its discriminatory character, Social Security is a lifeline for a large portion of the American population. For the average beneficiary, Social Security benefits make up two-thirds of their income. Among those aged 80 or older, Social Security provides the majority of household income for almost two-thirds of beneficiaries and nearly all of the income for one-third of beneficiaries. Without their income from Social Security, the poverty rate among elderly citizens would be 45 percent, but with those benefits it's 10 percent (Bernstein 2012).

When Work Disappears: Masculinity and Homeless Men

The history of Social Security reflects the ideology that unpaid work is part of the social construction of femininity—that to be a woman is to be skilled at domestic tasks like cooking and taking care of children and that women should carry out that work without being paid. Paid work is part of the social construction of masculinity. Jesse Bernard (1981) coined the term "the good-provider role" for the ideas that men are supposed to be good at establishing a career and making money and that a man who cannot hold a job is neither fully adult nor fully masculine (Fuller 2001; Connell 2002).

Robert Connell (2005) describes four **substructures of masculinity**: division of labor, power relations, emotional relations, and symbolization. This chapter focuses on the first of these. Connell notes that paid work is closely associated with manliness in many cultures. And in most countries, men are in fact more likely to be in the paid labor force. Ideologies define working (for wages) as men's realm and consider a man "unmanly" unless he has a regular (paid) job. In a survey in Costa Rica, men were asked what most made them feel like real men. They answered getting a job, having sex, and drinking alcohol.

European scholars assert that the main basis of gender in Europe is the distinction between the household, which is based on gift exchange and is women's world, and the commodity economy, which is based on the buying and selling of labor, which is men's work. This way of thinking about and experiencing gender has been exported from Europe to colonial and neocolonial societies around the world (Holter 2003). In the next section, we examine the household and the exchange of the "gifts" of cleaning, cooking, and child care.

Before moving to that issue, however, let's look at what happens when men do not succeed in their world of buying and selling of labor.

The discussion of poverty shows that many people in the world, men and women alike, are unable to find work that brings them a living wage. Because paid work is so closely tied to masculinity, what happens when men are unable to find a job and earn a living? Homeless men provide an answer to this question. They are stripped of their connection to the symbols of masculinity—a job, money, a car, a house. Some are able to find a way out of their poverty. Others give up and escape only through addiction and death. However, some men survive on the streets by reconstructing their ideas about what it is to be a man (Nonn 2001).

Timothy Nonn (2001) interviewed homeless men in the Tenderloin district in San Francisco. He found that men invented three types of countermasculinities: the "urban hermit," the "cool pose," and the "perfect copy." All three of these allowed the men to cope with the difficulties of living on the street by providing them with feelings of self-worth and allowing them to remain men, despite their break with the symbols and activities associated with dominant views of masculinity.

Urban hermits are mostly white heterosexuals. These men identify themselves as self-sufficient, and many retreat into isolation, spending their time alone in hotel rooms. Despite their failure to succeed in the dominant society, they persist in their belief in individual responsibility for everything that happens to them. They cannot remain men by having a good job and achieving material success, but they can remain men by taking responsibility for their own situation. One disabled man expressed this point of view: "It's a difficult struggle. But you can't blame anybody but yourself. Because it is you yourself. Like with me. It's me myself that has the illness. Not the people of the government. Not the people of the different businesses. And things like that. It's me" (Nonn 2001, 244).

Heterosexual black and Latino homeless men often take on a cool pose (Majors and Billson 1992). Respect is the central feature of this kind of countermasculinity. One man explained, "One of the techniques you use—and this is a prison technique—is getting big. You work out hard. You carry yourself in an intimidating manner. Your body language says, 'I'll kill you if you even think about approaching my space' " (Almaguer 1991, 80).

Homosexual homeless men frequently develop a countermasculinity called perfect copy. This consists of either hypermasculine or hyperfeminine roles. One man described his experience performing the perfect-copy (hypermasculine) role and the response of heterosexual men: "They feel like their manhood or sexuality has been threatened because I'm more butch than they are. I am more of a man than a straight man can be around here. They're threatened. Not only to me but to themselves" (Nonn 2001, 246). Another described how others respond to his perfect-copy (hyperfeminine) role: "I think [they] are very jealous of gay men because we're so open and free with our feelings. We speak what we have to say. We don't hide our feelings. We cry at sad movies. Heterosexual men think that men don't cry" (Nonn 2001, 246). In both cases, the exaggeration of the roles juxtaposed with homosexuality destabilizes stereotypes of manliness.

The Feminization of Poverty

Poverty, of course, is not just a problem for men. In the United States, women are even more likely to be poor. The greater tendency for women to be poor is called the "**feminization**" **of poverty**. Gender, however, does not stand alone, and race ethnicity in particular also plays an important role in determining one's chances of being poor. Table 6-8 shows how gender and race ethnicity intersect. For every racial ethnic group in the United States, poverty rates are higher for women than they are for men. Furthermore, Table 6-8 also shows a large gap in poverty rates by race ethnicity; white women have lower rates than both men and women who are black or Hispanic. Gender is not the only problem, and the feminization of poverty is more descriptive of the situation for whites than for other racial ethnic groups.

Unemployment is an important cause of poverty. Working increases income; however, it does not guarantee that employees will rise above poverty. For example, a full-time, year-round federal minimum-wage job ($7.25 an hour) would gross $14,500 annually, which is below the poverty level for a family of two ($14,710).

Poverty is a critical international problem. The United Nations estimates that nearly half the world (44 percent)—about 3 billion people—live on less than $2 a day. And because of poverty, millions lack access to even basic human needs like water, food, sanitation, and

TABLE 6-8 Poverty Rates in the United States by Race Ethnicity and Gender, 2009 (Percentage Poor in Category)

All people	14.3%
Men	13.0%
Women	15.6%
Black	25.8%
Men	23.9%
Women	27.5%
Hispanic	25.4%
Men	23.4%
Women	27.4%
Asian	12.5%
Men	12.3%
Women	12.6%
White	12.3%
Men	11.2%
Women	13.5%

Source: U.S. Bureau of the Census (2012).

literacy (New Economic Foundation 2006). Table 6-9 shows the proportion of the population living on less than $2 a day in different regions.

The $2 figure does not refer just to the amount of money received by each individual. It is the value of all the goods, money, and services received. A British organization explains that if a woman in the United Kingdom were earning minimum wage (about $7.50 an hour in Britain), paid $2,400 in taxes and was unable to borrow, had no savings to draw on, and received no benefits or free goods from any source, she would have to be supporting eighteen dependents to experience life like those living at the below $2 line (New Economic Foundation 2006).

At the same time that so many people in the world are poor, great wealth has accumulated among others. The assets of the two hundred richest people in the world are greater than the combined incomes of the poorest 40 percent of the people in the world. That gap continues to grow as the wealthiest 5 percent of people in the world receive 82 percent of the income (Munck 2005; Randerson 2006).

To some extent, global poverty is gender blind. Men and women and boys and girls live in dire situations, and the gap is most dramatic between those people who live in the poorest nations and those who live in the wealthiest. Within each nation, however, gender does show up. The poorest of the poor are women and children, who make up 70 percent of the poor people in the world (UN Women 2008; see Box 6-4).

TABLE 6-9 People Living Below $2-a-Day Poverty Line in the World by Region, 2005

Region	Population of Poor People in Millions	Proportion Living Below Poverty Line
East Asia and Pacific	748.3	39.7%
Eastern Europe and Central Asia	50.1	10.6%
Latin America and Caribbean	98.7	17.9%
Middle East and North Africa	58.0	19.0%
South Asia	1091.9	74.0%
Sub-Saharan Africa	551.0	72.2%

Source: Chen and Ravallion (2008).

GENDER IN EVERYDAY LIFE   BOX 6-4
WOMEN AGRICULTURAL WORKERS, HUNGER, AND GENDER

Hunger is a devastating problem for millions of people in the world. In 2013, 8.3 percent of Latin Americans, 13.9 percent of South Asians, and 22.9 percent of Africans were undernourished. Women and girls are even more likely than men and boys to be undernourished in these areas (Ramachandran 2006). In poor households, in particular, the incidence of severe malnutrition is greater among girls. In fact, gender is the most statistically significant determinant of malnutrition among young children, and the most common cause of death among girls below the age of five.

A study in India found that although boys and girls had roughly similar calorie intake, girls were given more cereal, whereas boys were given more milk and fats with their cereal (Bose 2003). Discrepancies exist among adults as well. For example, studies in India have shown a sharp difference in calorie intake among adult men and women, with women consuming approximately one thousand fewer calories a day than men (Development Gateway 2004). Women in Bangladesh eat after the men and children, making do with what is left. A similar pattern prevails in most south Asian countries.

A common coping strategy adopted by households faced with seasonal food shortages involves reduced food consumption by women as a first step, followed by skipping meals, to ensure that the men of the family and the children have the largest portions of food from the meager store (Ramachandran 2006). Even pregnant women are caught up in the cycle of self-denial and food deprivation.

Nutritional deprivation has two major consequences for women: they never reach their full growth potential, and they suffer from anemia. Both are risk factors in pregnancy. High levels of anemia complicate childbearing and result in maternal and infant deaths and low-birth-weight infants (Coonrod 1998).

Ironically, women are the most likely to suffer from food shortage; at the same time, they are also highly likely to be engaged in food production. A large portion of the world's food output originates in the hands of women farmers. In most developing countries, women provide over half the agricultural workforce. However, they have little control over the land they work because laws favor inheritance by sons rather than by daughters or widows.

Bhutan is the only south Asian nation that does not allow discrimination against women socially, economically, politically, or legally. Women are accorded a dominant role in the legal system, especially in family and inheritance law. The law of inheritance reserves equal rights for all children, and in many parts of Bhutan, society is matrilineal.

Households where women have access to their own incomes and exercise decision-making powers tend to have an expenditure pattern different from those dominated by men. Research in Asia, Africa, and Latin America has found that improvements in household food security and nutrition are associated with women's greater access to income and greater power over household decisions on expenditure. Women in poor households spend most of the earnings under their control on basic household needs such as food, clothes, children's education, and health, whereas men tend to spend a significant part of theirs on personal goods such as alcohol and tobacco (Agarwal 2002; Kelkar, Nathan, and Jahan 2003; Ramachandran 2006).

For women farmers to use land more efficiently and thereby make a greater contribution to food security, they need access to land, management control of land-based resources, and the economic incentives that the security of tenure provides (Food and Agriculture Organization 1996).

UNPAID WORK THROUGH THE LIFE CYCLE

Paid work is only a part of the work that takes place in our society. Although a lot of work has moved from families into factories and offices, much still remains as unpaid housework.

Since the 1960s, researchers in the United States have been studying how people spend their time. Thousands of people have filled out twenty-four-hour time diaries describing everything they did in the previous day. Here is what the research found:

1. Women do more housework than men do. Table 6-10 shows the differences in the number of hours women and men spend doing housework every week in twenty-four European nations and the United States. In all the nations listed in the table, women do more housework than men. The gap ranges from a low of 6.5 hours difference in Sweden to a high of 25.2 in Ireland.

TABLE 6-10 Differences in Hours of Housework per week for Men and Women in Europe and the United States

	Mean
Austria	14.4
Belgium	15.5
Czech Republic	12.2
Denmark	7.4
Estonia	10.4
Finland	8.3
France	11.8
Germany	14.7
Greece	24.4
Hungary	15.9
Iceland	15.8
Ireland	25.2
Luxembourg	18.2
Netherlands	13.7
Norway	9
Poland	16
Portugal	21.5
Slovakia	12.5
Slovenia	16.8
Spain	20.4
Sweden	6.5
Switzerland	16.9
Ukraine	11.2
United Kingdom	12.5
United States	10.2

Sources: Voicu, Voicu, and Strapcova (2009); U.S. Bureau of Labor Statistics (2007).

The gender gap in unpaid housework exists all over the world. On average women do about 2 hours and 24 minutes a day more than men in their countries. But the gap varies. Turkish, Mexican and Indian women, for example, spend 4.3–5 more hours per day on unpaid work than men in those countries, while the difference is only about an hour per day in the Nordic countries. In addition, the gap between nations varies. In China, for example, both women (2 hours) and men (1.5 hours) do little unpaid work, and in Australia both women (5 hours) and men (3 hours) spend a lot of time doing unpaid work every day (Miranda 2011).

2. Women who are not in the paid labor force do more housework than women who are in the paid labor force, and men who are not in the paid labor force do more housework than men who are in the paid labor force.

3. Employed women do more housework than nonemployed men.

Besides these differences in the amount of time women and men spend on housework, men and women do different kinds of tasks. Women in the United States are more likely to do cooking, washing dishes, indoor cleanup, laundry, shopping, and child care. Men are more likely to do repairs and maintenance, gardening, and pet care. Table 6-11 shows the proportions of women and men that perform different household tasks in the United States (Newport 2008).

The kinds of tasks people do in their households also differs by gender across nations. The most typical men's jobs around the world are construction and repair work which are activities in which women are rarely involved. Men also slightly more time as women on gardening and pet care. "Women's work" continues to be primarily cooking and cleaning. For example, in international research, 82 percent of women prepare meals on an average day, while only 44 percent of men do. Furthermore, the average time spent by women on cooking is four times the time spent by men (Miranda 2011).

The value of the unpaid work done by women in the United States is estimated to be about $138,095 for stay-at-home mothers for the hours put in as housekeeper, day-care provider,

TABLE 6-11 Proportion of Women and Men in the United States That Perform Household Tasks

Task	Men	Women
Keep the car in good condition	69%	13%
Do yard work	57%	12%
Make decisions about savings or investments	35%	18%
Pay bills	34%	48%
Wash dishes	16%	48%
Do grocery shopping	16%	53%
Do laundry	10%	68%
Care for children on a daily basis	9%	54%
Clean the house	6%	61%
Make decisions about furniture and decorations	6%	60%

Source: Newport (2008).

teacher, cook, computer operator, laundry machine operator, janitor, facilities manager, van driver, chief executive, and psychologist. For women who are also in the paid labor force, the value of unpaid domestic work is $85,876 annually (Wulfhorst 2006; DeFao 2007).

Why Is Women's Work Invisible?

International research on how people spend their time show that unpaid work accounts for one-third of all valuable economic activity (Miranda 2011). Despite the obvious importance of this unpaid housework and the huge amount of human energy and talent it represents, it is often largely invisible. Box 6-5 describing Mr. Moyo's conversation with his doctor illustrates both the heavy load unpaid women bear as workers and the invisibility of their efforts. In the discussion of paid employment, we noted another aspect of work that is often associated with women's jobs and is also invisible—emotion work. One other kind of invisible work largely done by women is called "**sociability work**," which is the work done by volunteers in the community to help support important activities and institutions (Daniels 1985). This might include raising funds for a museum or organizing a marathon to raise money and awareness for breast cancer.

Even though these events take a lot of energy and skill, they appear to be effortless, and the work behind them is usually unseen. The work behind them is also largely done by women (Blackstone 2004). In Amy Blackstone's research on sociability work of women organizing a run for breast cancer to raise money for more and better diagnostic equipment, research, and health education, she found that sociability workers put in up to twenty hours a day motivating volunteers, convincing donors to help pay for tents, and encouraging the community to participate. The work these women do is essential to the community, and the efforts they made are significant; and yet, their work is trivialized. The marathon and its mission are recognized, but the work that enabled the event to occur is not.

Why is this kind of work, along with housework and emotion work, invisible? Arlene Kaplan Daniels (1985) writes that it is invisible because it is "women's work" and is seen as a "natural" part of women's nurturing and caretaking, something to be expected but not recognized. Daniels argues that we cannot seriously understand work if we turn a blind eye to so much work that is going on unnoticed.

Children and Housework

Gender differences also appear in the distribution of housework between boys and girls in families. Boys and girls do different kinds of housework and they spend different amounts of time doing it. Both boys and girls are likely to clean their room and clean their house and neither spend much time taking care of elderly relatives. Girls are much more likely to do the dishes and the laundry, and boys are much more likely to do yard work and take out the trash. The biggest difference seems to be in the amount of time spent caring for younger children. About 38 percent of the girls and 23 percent of the boys say they spend some time during the week taking care of younger children. However, girls spend fourteen hours per week doing child care, compared to only six hours spent by boys.

The burden of housework that teenage daughters carry, especially in low-income families, is significant. Girls are responsible not only for household chores and child care, but also

GENDER IN EVERYDAY LIFE   BOX 6-5

MR. MOYO GOES TO THE DOCTOR

"What is your job?" asked the doctor.

"I am a farmer" replied Mr. Moyo.

"Have you any children?" the doctor asked.

"God has not been good to me. Of fifteen born, only nine alive," Mr. Moyo answered.

"Does your wife work?"

"No, she stays home."

"I see. How does she spend her day?"

"Well, she gets up at four in the morning. Fetches water and wood, makes the fire, cooks breakfast and cleans the homestead. Then she goes to the river and washes clothes. Once a week she walks to the grinding mill. After that she goes to the township with the two smallest children where she sells tomatoes by the roadside while she knits. She buys what she wants from the shops. Then she cooks the midday meal."

"You come home at midday?"

"No, no she brings the meal to me about three kilometres away."

"And after that?"

"She stays in the field to do the weeding, and then goes to the vegetable garden to water."

"What do you do?"

"I must go and discuss business and drink with the men in the village."

"And after that?"

"I go home for supper which my wife has prepared."

"Does she go to bed after supper?"

"No, I do. She has things to do around the house until nine or ten."

"But I thought you said you wife doesn't work."

"Of course she doesn't work. I told you she stays at home."

SOURCE: *Oxfam Gender Training Manual* by Oxfam, Women and Development sub-committee, Suzanne Williams, Janet Seed, Adelina Mwau 1994 is reproduced with permission of Oxfam GB, Oxfam House, John Smith Drive, Cowley, Oxford OX4 2JY, UK www.oxfam.org.uk. Oxfam GB does not necessarily endorse any text or activities that accompany the materials.

do a lot of emotion work in helping their parents handle the troubles and instability they may face in trying to keep the household afloat (Dodson 1999).

Housework remains an important site of gender inequality, and scholars have puzzled about how these differences can persist—especially in light of the changes in the division of paid work. We saw that when it comes to working for wages, women and men are becoming increasingly similar, at least in terms of whether they are in the paid labor force or not. Women and men and boys and girls are also becoming more similar in the division of housework. But why is change so slow?

What's Behind the Way People Divide Up Housework?

Doing housework is part of almost everyone's life, and the gender differences we find in this activity have led to much speculation on the part of scholars about why the work is divided the way that it is. Three theories have been suggested to answer this question: socialization theory, rational choice theory, and feminist theory.

SOCIALIZATION THEORY. Socialization theorists emphasize the early experience of children, especially in their families. **Socialization theory** is a large school of thought with many different ideas about how and where socialization occurs and why it is important. Socialization theorists, however, would agree that we teach our boys and girls skills in certain kinds of housework and that we train them to feel responsible and comfortable with some activities and not others. These scholars would point to the research on children and chores and argue that they provide support for the argument that dividing housework between women and men is a product of the lessons learned by boys and girls about what men and women and boys and girls should feel and do when faced with a dirty kitchen. From a socialization theorist's point of view, the solution to inequity in the division of housework is to teach boys and girls all the skills they will need to take care of themselves and others in households and to teach boys and girls to feel responsible for and comfortable doing all kinds of tasks.

RATIONAL CHOICE THEORY. A second framework is **rational choice theory**. These scholars would argue that as boys and girls we may learn to identify some housework tasks with girls and women and others with boys and men; these childhood experiences are important. The real question in understanding the way in which men and women divide housework, however, comes from their interactions with one another as adults in households. Rational choice theorists argue that women and men enter into negotiations about housework and make rational choices based on questions such as which partner knows how to do the work and which partner has other responsibilities in the paid labor force or brings home a larger paycheck that allows him or her to bargain out of doing housework. Rational choice theorists would solve the problem of injustice by suggesting that couples learn to communicate and negotiate in a fair manner and create ways of dividing housework that rationally take into consideration each individual's skills and other responsibilities and activities.

FEMINIST THEORY. A third framework is **feminist theory**. Feminists argue that the way in which housework is divided cannot represent two equals negotiating an equitable and rational decision because gender inequality interferes with those rational choices. They would point out that who does the housework is both a reflection of gender inequality in families and other social institutions as well as a way in which gender inequality is generated. Housework is both a cause and an effect of the political inequality between women and men. Women do more housework because they do not have as much power as men do.

Furthermore, when women do more housework and when women and men do different kinds of housework, gender is being reproduced.

Feminists maintain that housework is a "**gender factory.**" Men can reaffirm their masculinity by not doing the dishes, whereas women reaffirm their femininity by doing them. The division also reaffirms the relationship between genders—women work for men, men dominate, and women are subordinate (Berk 1985).

To solve this dilemma, feminists argue that people must consciously overcome gender by doing "inappropriate" jobs. Behaving in new ways will create new ways of thinking and feeling that will further break down gender stereotypes. In addition, feminists believe that we need to pay attention to the connection between paid work and unpaid work. As long as women are paid less than men, their ability to negotiate changes in the division of unpaid work will be hampered.

GLOBALIZATION AND GENDER

Both paid employment and the unpaid work in households are embedded in a global system. **Globalization** refers to the integration of the world's economies, political systems, informational networks, and ecology into one large global system (Lenz 2004). This integration touches everyone's life in ways we might not often think about. Think about what you ate for breakfast today. You may have started with a glass of orange juice from Mexico. Then you may have had bread from wheat grown in Canada, prepared in a toaster made in China from steel produced in Russia in an oven fueled by energy from Venezuela. The integration of the production and distribution of goods from many different places in the world is a sure sign of globalization. Economic globalization affects all the issues we have considered so far in this chapter.

Globalization has some benefits, because it means consumers have access to goods from every corner of the world. Globalization also often produces goods more cheaply and potentially allows more people access to those goods. Globalization has huge downsides as well, however, especially for those who live in nations that are referred to as "**developing**" **nations** (Berberoglu 2003).

The United Nations identifies 128 nations in Africa, Latin America, and Asia as "developing." The "least developed" of these include countries such as Afghanistan, Cambodia, Niger, Rwanda, Haiti, and Yemen, which face extreme poverty and most of whose citizens lead difficult lives. Because most of these nations are in the Southern Hemisphere and the richest nations are largely in the North, the terms "global South" and "global North" have come to indicate the gap between countries.

Women in the global South, like women in the global North, are often lower in status and power than are men. For example, women provide 80 percent of the agricultural labor in Uganda and in most of the rest of Africa, but they are much less likely to own land. Only 3 percent of the women in Uganda own land, and this is not unusual in the global South. If women do not own land or other property like cattle, they cannot participate in development programs or receive loans and credit. Only about 1 percent of loans to develop the land are made to women in Uganda, for example (Wamboka 2002).

Women work hard, but they are even more likely than men in poor countries to live in absolute poverty. In Africa, since the 1980s, the proportion of men living in absolute poverty has increased by 30 percent, and the proportion of women in absolute poverty has risen 50 percent (Emasu 2002).

These problems have been exacerbated by international economic pressures. One of the most important of these in the global South is debt. Between 1970 and 2002, African nations received $540 billion in loans from wealthier nations and the World Bank. The **debtor nations** have paid back $550 billion of their debt, but they still owe $295 billion. Yes, these numbers are correct. The difference, of course, is a result of compound interest. When borrowers take a loan, they agree to pay back the amount they borrowed plus the interest accrued—the "price" they pay for getting the loan. The relationship between debtor nations and wealthy nations or the institutions they control, such as the World Bank, creates a situation in which more money is transferred from poor countries to rich countries than vice versa (MacDonald and Gibson 2007; Makwana 2006; Parks 2006).

To continue to pay back the interest as well as the original loans, nations are forced to create **SAPs** (**Structural Adjustment Programs**) and **PRSPs** (**Poverty Reduction Strategy Papers**). SAPs and PRSPs are policies that reduce government spending in poor nations, cutting programs in education, health care, transportation, and other government-funded projects to accumulate money to pay back the interest on loans. SAPs and PRSPs harm the debtor nations and their citizens, regardless of gender, but women are hardest hit because they are already the very poorest members of those countries. In addition, women's responsibilities for children mean that they rely on government programs for food, schools, and medical aid for their children; and when those programs are cut, they have no place to turn (World Resources Institute 1994–1995; Blumberg 1995; Connelly et al. 2000).

Globalization also has important effects on work in wealthy nations like the United States. When work is globalized, jobs are transferred to those places where labor is cheapest. Because American workers are then competing for jobs with very low wage workers around the globe, the pay scales for the jobs that remain in the United States are kept down. Saving labor costs is beneficial to stockholders and investors, but it does not benefit employees in either poor or wealthy nations. In the United States, we have seen the reflection of these changes in an increasingly productive and profitable economy at the same time that the typical worker's real wages have declined since 2001 and problems like homelessness have continued to grow (Tonelson 2000; Berberoglu 2003; Mishel and Eisenbrey 2005; Bernstein 2006). For example, since the **North American Free Trade Agreement** (**NAFTA**) was signed in 1993. NAFTA was an agreement to open up trade between the United States, Canada, and Mexico, making it more profitable and efficient. Since the NAFTA agreement, 794,174 jobs were created in the United States, but another 1,673,453 were lost. The jobs that were lost paid on average 21 percent more than the ones that were gained. We noted earlier in this chapter, for example, that 60 percent of the new jobs being added to the economy were in food service and retail and paid less than $10 an hour with no benefits. During this same period, wages fell between 15 percent and 20 percent in Mexico (Scott 2003; Spieldoch 2005).

These kinds of trends may create more gender equity in pay because men's wages are pushed down to the levels of women's wages. Researchers who have looked at the closing gap in women's and men's pay in the United States in recent years have noted that it may be largely due to sinking or at least stagnating wages among men rather than to rising wages among women. In other words, women are not catching up to men; men are "catching up" to women. Workers in wealthy nations are "catching up" to those in the poorer ones.

What needs to be done to make globalization work as a vehicle to improve people's lives? How can we close the gender gap as well as the eliminate all the other inequities around the world? These questions are ones that scholars have been addressing for some time. A first step to eliminating inequality and injustice is to try to understand what the roots of the problems are. Feminist theory has developed through three phases, as scholars, activists, and policy makers have grappled with these issues. The theories they developed during these three phases are called WID, WAD, and GAD.

WID, WAD, and GAD

Feminist scholars have offered three models for understanding the global economy and creating policies to alleviate the economic difficulties of the world and eliminate the gender gap (Moser 1993; Smyth, March, and Mukhopadhyay 1998). The first of these is called *women in development* (**WID**). This approach maintains that poor nations should model themselves after wealthier ones and that women in all countries, but especially those in the global South, should become more like men by moving into the paid labor force to work alongside men. This approach assumes that the global political economy is sound and that Southern nations need to model themselves after the North and also make sure that women are assimilated into the system at all levels. International economic policies should facilitate these transitions by allowing multinationals to build factories and invest in agribusiness all over the world. Those corporations should be sure to include women in their workforce. One of the most important examples of the kind of discrimination that has existed is in aid programs for agricultural workers. Although our view of "women's work" in the global North is women working in pink-collar jobs such as secretaries and retail clerks, more than 40 percent of working women around the world are employed in agriculture. This proportion is even greater in poorer nations, where 60 to 80 percent of employed women are agricultural workers (Henderson and Jeydal 2010). Aid programs, however, frequently channel funds and farm equipment only to men.

The second approach, *women and development* (**WAD**), is critical of WID, asserting that women already are active workers, even though they may not be receiving wages for much of their work. They point out that like the wife in the story in Box 6-5, women work many hours a day hauling water and wood, raising children, selling goods in the market, and working in the fields, offices, and factories. When unpaid and paid work are both considered, 66 percent of the world's work hours are by women (50% of the population) (UNICEF 2007).

WAD advocates also question whether the model of the Western developed nation is the only or even best way to build effective economies. They believe that international economic policies should recognize the invisible work of women and design ways to support and compensate it. In addition, they argue that a range of possible paths to economic development should be created to avoid some of the pitfalls of Western capitalism, such as environmental degradation and huge gaps between the rich and poor, as well as the inequities between women and men.

The third approach is *gender and development* (**GAD**) (Moser and Moser 2005). These scholars criticize both WID and WAD first of all for treating women as a homogenous group. They shift the focus from gender alone to systems of inequality that include gender but are equally and sometimes more profoundly shaped by other kinds of inequality. They point to the enormous differences in women's experience by race ethnicity, social class, and nation and call for conceptual models and policies that recognize the diversity among women. GAD advocates, for example, would point to the numbers of people living on less than $2 a day, the trafficking in women described in chapter 4, and the problems faced by refugees, who are mostly women and children. These are issues that touch the majority of the world but are not part of the everyday experience of most women or men living in the global North.

GAD also argues that we cannot talk about women in isolation but rather must think of the relationships between women and men—gender relations. In addition, we need to think of gender as not just a force that shapes women's lives but one that creates masculinities as well. For example, we cannot address the problem of violence against women without considering the ways in which violence is part of the social construction of masculinity. GAD activists support policies that look at gender rather than at women in isolation. They also see gender equity as part of a larger exercise of human rights and a as a mission of transforming the global economy into one that is based on human needs and cooperation rather than on profitability and competition.

These three conceptualizations of gender in the global political economy developed chronologically in response to older theories, such as development theory, that ignored women and gender altogether. All three are currently in practice among policy makers, activists, and scholars. There are development programs that are based on the WID view that seek to include women while ignoring other problems of inequality and ignoring the contribution women's work already makes to the world economy. There are development programs that are based on WAD that acknowledge women's contribution and attempt to address the problems associated with women's unpaid labor or informal labor. They also attempt to identify other models for development that are rooted in the cultures and social and physical context of the developing economies rather than assert that the only road to economic development is the one followed by the nations of the global North. The development programs presently underway that are most forward looking and sophisticated fit within the GAD framework.GAD solutions seek to address all forms of injustice and inequality, including the social construction of both masculinities and femininities as well as poverty and other forms of oppression.

Very recently, a fourth stage in the advance of ideas about women and development has emerged. This fourth stage is **WCD**, *women, culture, and development*. WCD scholars criticize WID, WAD, and GAD for not taking culture into account. WCD advocates recommend that we bring culture into our assessment (Bhavnani, Foran, and Kurian 2003). WCD moves away from focusing only on economic issues and attending to the ways that economic issues are tied to broad cultural factors. Furthermore, WCD theorists emphasize the need to look not only at oppression but at the ways in which people seek to resist and alter the conditions in which they find themselves. In addition, if we are to see (and nourish) that resistance, we must look beyond the strictly economic factors to also include the cultural expressions, the threads of everyday life that make up our lives. It is not only economic forces that determine the inequities we see in paid and unpaid work. Our ideas about what women and men are like or should be like play a critical role as well. And, changes in our ideas may play an essential role in motivating people to challenge the status quo.

GENDER MATTERS

" **Dialectical materialism** " is the philosophical term used to describe **Marxist theory**. The word "materialism " in this context means that people from this perspective pay attention to the ways that people use the materials around them to create those things they need to survive. They assume that the core of any human society is the way in which people create and distribute food, clothes, shelter, and all the other material resources they need to stay alive. Since these activities are so essential, they are an aspect of everyone's life and they touch every other activity and relationship in which we engage. Economics is not the only factor in our lives. Sometimes it is not even the most important, but it is always part of the picture.

This chapter has taken a materialist view, reviewing some of the ways gender connects with our attempts to create and distribute those things we need to survive. We have learned that women and men are increasingly similar in some ways that the economy touches their lives: their participation in the paid labor force, their contribution to unpaid labor, the fragile connection they have to access to jobs and income and the things that money can buy. In other ways, huge gaps exist between women and men in all of these areas. But other gaps exist as well.

This review of work, broadly considered, shows us that if we are to create gender equity, we will need to make individual changes in our thinking and behavior. We will also need to change social institutions such as the organization of work and the ways in which our work is valued. In addition, since the problems exist within a global system, we will need to challenge the very largest social institutions that create the context and structure of our work lives.

KEY TERMS

backhanded tactics
bias theorists
breadwinner and co-breadwinners
comparable worth policy
debtor nations
developing nations
dialectical materialism
Dukes decision
emotional labor
equal pay day
family wage
feminist theory
feminization of poverty
gender factory
gender segregated
glass ceiling
globalization
human capital
human capital theorists
individualism

job ladders
Marxist theory
maquiladoras
North American Free Trade Agreement
    (NAFTA)
occupational sex-segregation index
pension
pin money
poverty reduction strategy papers (PRSPs)
rational choice theory
sociability work
social security benefits
socialization theory
sticky floor
structural adjustment programs (SAPs)
substructures of masculinity
women in development (WID); women and
    development (WAD); gender and
    development (GAD); and women,
    culture, and development (WCD)

CRITICAL THINKING QUESTIONS

1. What is the relationship between paid and unpaid work. How does unpaid work support inequality in the work force? How does paid work support inequality in the household? What are some of the ways that households and families are gender factories? How are workplaces also gender factories?
2. The chapter discusses an often invisible dimension of work—"emotion work." Think about the jobs you have held . What kinds of emotion work were you required to do as part of your job? How was the emotion work gendered? Can you think of ways emotion work has racial or class dimensions?
3. In your own words, how would you describe the differences among WID,WAD, GAD, and WCD. Why are these distinctions important?
4. Look at the numbers in one of the tables in this chapter and in your own words summarize what specific information the numbers provide us with. Then think about what the numbers mean. What do they reveal about real people's lives?

REFERENCES

Ackman, Daniel. 2004. "Wal-Mart and Sex Discrimination by the Numbers." *Forbes*, June 23. http://www.forbes.com/2004/06/23/cx_da_0623topnews.html. Accessed March 21, 2011.

AFL-CIO. 2006. *Ask a Working Woman Survey Report*. Washington, DC: AFL-CIO. http://www.aflcio.org/issues/politics/labor2006/wwsurvey2006.cfm. Accessed March 21, 2011.

Agarwal, Bina. 2002. "Are We Not Peasants Too? Land Rights and Women's Claims in India." *Seeds* 21: 29.

Almaguer, Tomas. 1991. "Chicano Men: A Cartography of Homosexual Identity and Behavior." *Differences* 3 (2): 75–100.

Amott, Teresa. 1999. *Caught in the Crisis: Women and the U.S. Economy Today*. New York: New York University Press.

Antal, Ariane, and Dafna Izraeli. 1993. "A Global Comparison of Women in Management: Women Managers in Their Homelands and as Expatriates." In *Women in Management: Trends, Issues, and Challenges in Managerial Diversity*, edited by E. Ganeson, 52–96. Newbury Park, CA: Sage.

Belkin, Lisa. 2007. "The Feminine Critique." *New York Times*, November 1. http://www.nytimes.com/2007/11/01/fashion/01WORK.html. Accessed March 21, 2011.

Bellas, Marcia. 1999. "Emotional Labor in Academia: The Case of Professors." *Annals of the American Academy of Political and Social Science* 561 (1): 96–110. doi: 10.1177/000271629956100107.

———. 2001. "The Gendered Nature of Emotional Labor in the Workplace." In *Gender Mosaics: Social Perspectives*, edited by Dana Vannoy, 269–78. Los Angeles: Roxbury.

Benokraitis, Nijole. 1997. "Sex Discrimination in the Twenty-First Century." In *Subtle Sexism: Current Practice and Prospects for Change*, edited by N. Benokraitis, 5–33. Thousand Oaks, CA: Sage.

Benokraitis, Nijole, and Joe Feagin. 1986. *Modern Sexism: Blatant, Subtle, and Covert Discrimination*. Englewood Cliffs, NJ: Prentice Hall.

Berberoglu, Berch. 2003. *Globalization of Capital and the Nation State*. New York: Rowman and Littlefield.

Berg, David. 1987. "Cross examination" *Litigation: Journal of the Section of Litigation*, ABA 14(1):25–30.

Berk, Sarah Fenstermaker. 1985. *Gender Factory*. New York: Plenum.

Bernard, Jesse. 1981. "The Good-Provider Role: Its Rise and Fall." *American Psychologist* 36 (1): 1–12.

Bernstein, Jared. 2006. "You Know How To Add, Don't You?" *Los Angeles Times*, May 7.

——. 2012. "Straight Talk on Social Security." *Rolling Stone*, April 27. http://www.rollingstone.com/politics/blogs/national-affairs/straight-talk-on-social-security-20120427.

Bhavnani, Kum-Kum, John Foran, and Priya Kurian, eds. 2003. *Re-Imagining Women, Culture, and Development*. London: Zed Books.

Bianchi, Suzanne, and Jane Dye. 2001. "The Participation of Women and Men in the U.S. Labor Force: Trends and Future Prospects." In *Gender Mosaics: Social Perspectives*, edited by Dana Vannoy, 460–72. Los Angeles: Roxbury.

Blackstone, Amy. 2004. "Sociability Work and Gender." *Equal Opportunities International* 23 (3–5): 29–44.

Blumberg, Rhoda. 1995. "Gender, Microenterprise, Performance, and Power." In *Women in the Latin American Development Process*, edited by Christine Bose and Edna Acosta-Belen, 194–226. Philadelphia: Temple University Press.

Bose, A. B. 2003. *The State of Children in India: Promises to Keep*. New Delhi: Manohar.

Bose, Christine, and Rachel Bridges Whaley. 2001. "Sex Segregation in the U.S. Labor Force." In *Gender Mosaics: Social Perspectives*, edited by Dana Vannoy, 228–39. Los Angeles: Roxbury.

Calasanti, Toni, and Kathleen Slevin. 2001. *Gender, Social Inequalities, and Aging*. Walnut Creek, CA: Altamira.

Cardwell, Donald. 1957. *The Organization of Science in England*. London: Heinemann.

Catalyst. 2013. "Women CEOs in the Fortune 1000." Catalyst.org. http://www.catalyst.org/knowledge/women-ceos-fortune-1000.

Center for Reflection, Education, and Action (CREA). 2000. "Making the Invisible Visible: A Study of the Purchasing Power of Maquila Workers in Mexico." Hartford, CT: Author.

Chen, Shaohua, and Martin Ravallion. 2008. *The Developing World Is Poorer Than We Thought, but No Less Successful in the Fight Against Poverty*. New York: World Bank. http://siteresources.worldbank.org/DEC/Resources/Poverty-Brief-in-English.pdf. Accessed March 21, 2011.

Connell, Robert. 2002. *Gender*. Cambridge, UK: Polity Press.

——. 2005. "Globalization, Imperialism, and Masculinity." In *Handbook of Studies on Men and Masculinities*, edited by Michael S. Kimmel, Jeff Hearn, and Robert W. Connell, 71–89. Thousand Oaks, CA: Sage.

Connelly, M. Patricia, Tania Murray Li, Martha MacDonald, and Jane Parpart. 2000. "Feminism and Development: Theoretical Perspectives." In *Theoretical Perspectives on Gender and Development*, edited by Jane L. Parpart, Patricia Connelly, and V. Eudine Barriteau, 51–160. Ottawa: International Research Center.

Conway, Margaret, David Ahern, and Gertrude Steuernagel. 1999. *Women and Public Policy: A Revolution in Progress*. 2nd edition. Washington, DC: Congressional Quarterly Press.

Coonrod, Carol S. 1998. *Chronic Hunger and the Status of Women in India*. New York: The Hunger Project. http://www.thp.org/where_we_work/south_asia/india/research_reports/chronic_hunger_and_status_of_women. Accessed March 21, 2011.

Daniels, Arlene Kaplan. 1985. "Good Times and Good Works." *Social Problems* 32 (4): 363–74.

Davies, Lizzy. 2009. "French Plan to Force Gender Equality in Boardrooms." *Guardian*, December 2. http://www.guardian.co.uk/world/2009/dec/02/french-government-gender-equality-plan. Accessed March 21, 2011.

DeFao, Janine. 2007. "Mother's Work, in Dollars." *San Francisco Chronicle*, May 4. http://www.sfgate.com/cgi-bin/article.cgi?f=/c/a/2007/05/04/BAG79PL5C21.DTL. Accessed March 21, 2011.

Development Gateway. 2004. *News on Food Security, Intra Household Gender Disparities and Access to Food*. Washington, DC: Development Gateway.

DeViney, Stanley, and Jennifer Solomon. 1995. "Gender Differences in Retirement Income: A Comparison of Theoretical Explanations." *Journal of Women and Aging* 7 (4): 83–100.

Dodson, Lisa. 1999. *Don't Call Us Out of Name*. Boston: Beacon.

Equal Employment Opportunity Commission. 2010. Annual Report on the Federal Work Force Part II Work Force Statistics Fiscal Year 2010. http://www.eeoc.gov/federal/reports/fsp2010_2/index.cfm#ID

Emasu, Alice. 2002. "Get the Land, the Rest Will Follow." *AfricaWoman*, Special edition, August/September, 10. www.dailysummit.net/documents/africawoman.pdf. Accessed March 21, 2011.

Embassy of France in London. 2013. Government present gender equality bill. July 9. http://www.ambafrance-uk.org/Government-presents-gender. Accessed February 21, 2014.

Epstein, Cynthia Fuchs. 1993. *Women in Law*. 2nd edition. Chicago: University of Illinois Press.

Featherstone, Liza. 2005. "Down and Out in Discount America." *Nation*, January 3. http://www.thenation.com/article/down-and-out-discount-america. Accessed March 21, 2011.

Food and Agriculture Organization (FAO). 1996. *FAO Focus: Women and Food Security: Women Hold the Key to Food Security*.United Nations. http://www.fao.org/sd/fsdirect/fbdirect/fsp001.htm accessed February 21, 2014.

Forbes. 2013. "The world's billionaires." *Forbes.com*, March 29. http://www.forbes.com/billionaires/list/. Accessed August 25, 2013.

Fox, Mary Frank. 1991. "Gender Environmental Milieu and Productivity in Science." In *The Outer Circle*, edited by Harriet Zuckerman, Jonathan R. Cole, and John Bruer, 108–204. New York: Norton.

——. 1995. "Women and Scientific Careers." *Handbook of Science and Technology Studies*, edited by Sheila Jasanoff, Gerald E. Markle, James Petersen, and Trevor Pinch, 205–23. Thousand Oaks, CA: Sage.

——. 1996. "Women, Academia, and Careers in Science and Engineering." In *The Equity Equation: Fostering the Advancement of Women in the Sciences, Mathematics and Engineering*, edited by Cinda-Sue. Davis, Angela B. Ginorio, Carol S. Hollenshead, Barbara B. Lazarus, and Paula M. Rayman, 265–89. San Francisco: Jossey Bass.

——. 2000. "Organizational Environments and Doctoral Degrees Awarded to Women in Science and Engineering Departments." *Women's Studies Quarterly* 28: 47–61.

——. 2001. "Women, Men, and Engineering." In *Gender Mosaics: Social Perspectives*, edited by Dana Vannoy, 249–57. Los Angeles: Roxbury.

Fuller, N. 2001. "Social Construction of Gender Identity among Peruvian Men." *Men and Masculinities* 3 (3): 316–31.

Glynn, Sarah Jane, and Audrey Powers. 2012. "The Top 10 Facts about the Wage Gap:Women Are Still Earning Less Than Men Across The Board." Center for American Progress, April 16. http://www.americanprogress.org/issues/2012/04/wage_gap_facts.html. Accessed February 21, 2014.

Goldin, Claudia, and Cecilia Rouse. 2000. "Orchestrating Impartiality: The Impact of 'Blind Auditions' on Female Musicians." *American Economic Review* 90 (4) 715–41.

Greenhouse, Steven. 2010. "Wal-Mart Gender Case Divides Court." *New York Times*, April 26. http://www.nytimes.com/2010/04/27/business/27suit.html. Accessed March 21, 2011.

Gutek, Barbara. 1985. *Sex and the Workplace: The Impact of Sexual Behavior and Harassment in Women, Men, and Organizations*. San Francisco: Jossey-Bass.

Harrington-Meyer, Madonna. 1996. "Family Status and Poverty among Older Women: The Gendered Distribution of Retirement Income in the United States." In *Aging for the Twenty First Century*, edited by J. Quadagno and D. Street, 464–79. New York: St. Martin's Press.

Harrington-Meyer, Madonna, Douglas Wolf, and Christine Himes. 2000. "Linking Benefits to Marital Status." *Feminist Economics* 11 (2): 145–62.

Henderson, Sarah, and Alana Jeydal. 2010. *Women and Politics in a Global World*. 2nd edition. New York: Oxford University Press.

Higgenbotham, Elizabeth, and Lynn Weber. 2000. "Moving Up with Kin and Community: Upward Social Mobility for Black and White Women." In *Gender through the Prism of Difference*,

2nd edition, edited by Maxine Baca Zinn, Pierrette Hondagneu-Sotelo, and Michael Messner, 346–56. Boston: Allyn and Bacon.

Hochschild, Arlie. 1983. *The Managed Heart: Commercialization of Human Feeling*. Berkeley: University of California Press.

Holter, O. 2003. "A Theory of Gender, Patriarchy, and Capitalism." In *Among Men*, edited by Soren Ervo and Thomas Johansson, 29–43. Aldershot, UK: Ashgate.

Hospitality Industry Quarterly. 2005. "Ninth Circuit Says Firing Female Employee for Not Wearing Makeup Is Not Discrimination." *Hospitality Industry Quarterly* 16 (1): 3.

Institute for Women's Policy Research. 2011. "The Gender Wage Gap by Occupation." Institute for Women's Policy Research Factsheet. http://www.iwpr.org/publications/pubs/the-gender-wage-gap-by-occupation-updated-april-2011Accessed February 21, 2014.

International Labour Office. 2007. *Equality at Work: Tackling the Challenges*. Geneva: International Labour Office. http://www.ilo.org/global/publications/ilo-bookstore/order-online/books/WCMS_082607/lang--en/index.htm Accessed February 21, 2014.

Johnson, Richard, Usha Sambamoorthi, and Stephen Crystal. 1999. "Gender Differences in Pension Wealth: Estimates Using Provider Data." *Gerontologist* 39 (3): 320–33.

Kelkar, Govind., Dev Nathan, and Rownok Jahan. 2003. *We Were in Fire, Now We Are in Water: Micro-Credit and Gender Relations in Rural Bangladesh*. Working Paper Series, No. 19. New Delhi: Institute for Human Development.

Kierstead, D., P. D'Agostino, and H. Dill. 1988. "Sex Role Stereotyping of College Professors: Bias in Students' Ratings of Instructors." *Journal of Educational Psychology* 80 (3): 342–44.

Lee, Marlene A., and Mark Mather. 2008. "US Labor Force Trends." *Population Bulletin* 63(2). http://www.prb.org/pdf08/63.2uslabor.pdf. Accessed February 21, 2014.

Lenz, Ilse. 2004. "Globalization, Gender, and Work." In *Equity in the Workplace*, edited by Heidi Gottfried and Laura Reese, 29–52. New York: Lexington.

Steven Lopez. 2010. "Workers, Managers,and Customers:Triangles of Power in Work Communities." *Work and Occupations* 37 (3): 251–71.

Lorber, Judith. 2000. "Guarding the Gates: The Micropolitics of Gender." In *The Gendered Society Reader*, edited by Michael Kimmel, 270–94. New York: Oxford University Press.

MacDonald, Theodore H. 2007. *The Global Human Right to Health*. Abingdon, UK: Radcliffe.

MacKinnon, Catharine. 1979. *Sexual Harassment of Working Women*. New Haven, CT: Yale University Press.

Majors, Richard, and Janet Mancini Billson. 1992. *Cool Pose: The Dilemmas of Black Manhood in America*. New York: Lexington Books.

Makwana, Rajesh. 2006. "Cancelling Third World Debt." http://www.stwr.org/aid-debt-development/cancelling-third-world-debt.html. Accessed March 21, 2011.

Martin, Lynn. 1991. *A Report on the Glass Ceiling Initiative*. Washington, DC: U.S. Department of Labor.

Martin, Nina. 2013. "The impact and echoes of the Wal-Mart discrimination Case." ProPublica, September 27. http://www.propublica.org/article/the-impact-and-echoes-of-the-wal-mart-discrimination-case. Accessed February 21, 2014.

McDonough, Katie. 2013. "Women Waiting Tables, Working Retail Account for Most Female Labor Gains." Salon.com, September 19 http://www.salon.com/2013/09/19/women_waiting_tables_working_retail_account_for_most_female_labor_gains/

Menkel-Meadow, C. 1985. "Portia in a Different Voice: Speculations on a Women's Lawyering Process." *Berkeley Women's Law Review* 1 (Fall): 39–63.

Miranda, Veerle. (2011). "Cooking, Caring and Volunteering: Unpaid Work around the World." OECD *Social, Employment and Migration Working Paper* No. 116, http://dx.doi.org/10.1787/5kghrjm8s142-en

Mishel, Lawrence, and Ross Eisenbrey. 2005. "What's Wrong with the Economy?" EPI memorandum. Washington, DC: Economic Policy Institute.

Moran, Stahl, and Boyer, Inc. 1988. *Status of American Female Expatriate Employees: Survey Results.* Boulder, CO: International Division, Moran, Stahl, and Boyer, Inc.

Moser, Caroline. 1993. *Gender Planning and Development Theory: Practice and Training.* London: Routledge.

Moser, Caroline, and Annalise Moser. 2005. "Gender Mainstreaming since Beijing." *Gender and Development* 13 (2): 11–22.

Munck, Ronaldo. 2005. *Globalization and Social Exclusion.* Bloomfield, CT: Kumerian.

National Center for Education Statistics. 2008. "Table 29. Median Annual Earnings of Full-Time, Full-Year Wage and Salary Workers Ages 25 and Older, by Educational Attainment, Sex, and Race/Ethnicity: 2007." http://nces.ed.gov/pubs2010/2010015/tables/table_29.asp. Accessed June 8, 2011.

National Organization for Women (NOW). 2013. "Wal-Mart: Merchant of Shame." http://www.now .org/issues/wfw/wal-mart.html. Accessed February 21, 2014.

National Science Foundation, Division of Science Resources Statistics. 2011. *Women, Minorities, and Persons with Disabilities in Science and Engineering: 2011.* Special Report NSF 11–309. http:// www.nsf.gov/statistics/wmpd/. Accessed June 8, 2011.

New Economic Foundation (NEF). 2006. *Growth Isn't Working.* London: NEF. http://www.neweconomics .org/publications/entry/growth-isnt-working. Accessed March 21, 2011.

Newport, Frank. 2008. "Wives Still do Laundry, Men Do Yard Work." *Gallup,* April 4. http://www .gallup.com/poll/106249/wives-still-laundry-men-yard-work.aspx. Accessed March 21, 2011.

Nonn, Timothy. 2001. "Hitting Bottom: Homelessness, Poverty, and Masculinity." In Michael S. Kimmel and Michael A. Messner, *Men's Lives,* 5th edition, 242–51. Boston: Allyn and Bacon.

Organisation for Economic Co-operation and Development (OECD). 2012. "Table I: Earnings Dispersion, Gender Wage Gap and Incidence of Low Pay." www.oecd.org/els/ETAB_I.xlsx

Paludi, Michele. 1997. "Sexual Harassment in Schools." In *Sexual Harassment: Theory, Research, and Treatment,* edited by W. O'Donahue, 224–49. Boston: Allyn and Bacon.

Parks, J., 2006. "House Passes Jubilee Debt Relief, Battle Shifts to Senate." AFL-CIO, *Ground Report,* April 18. http://www.groundreport.com/US/House-Passes-Jubilee-Debt-Relief-Battle-Shifts-to-/2859495. Accessed March 21, 2011.

Peterson, V. Spike, and Anne Runyan. 1999. *Global Gender Issues.* 2nd edition. Boulder, CO: Westview.

Pierce, Jennifer. 2001. "Rambo Litigators: Emotional Labor in a Male-Dominated Occupation." In Michael S. Kimmel and Michael A. Messner, *Men's Lives,* 5th edition, 225–41. Boston: Allyn and Bacon.

Ramachandran, Nira. 2006. *Women and Food Security in South Asia.* Helsinki: UNU World Institute for Development Economics Research (UNU-WIDER).

Randerson, James. 2006. "World's Richest 1% Own 40% of All Wealth, UN Report Discovers." *Guardian,* December 6. http://www.guardian.co.uk/money/2006/dec/06/business.internationalnews. Accessed March 21, 2011.

Reed, Amanda. 2013. "Walmart and sex discrimination." Say It, Sister! (NOW's Blog for Equality). http://www.now.org/news/blogs/index.php/sayit/2013/06/06/walmart-and-sex-discrimination. Accessed February 21, 2014.

Regensburger, Linda. 2001. *The American Family: Reflecting a Changing Nation.* Detroit: Gale Group.

Reskin, Barbara, and Irene Padavic. 2001. "Sex Differences in Moving Up and Taking Charge." In *Feminist Frontiers,* 5th edition, edited by Laura Richardson, Verta Taylor, and Nancy Whittier, 253–62. New York: McGraw-Hill.

Rundblad, Georganne. 2001. "Gender, Power, and Sexual Harassment." In *Gender Mosaics: Social Perspectives*, edited by Dana Vannoy, 353–62. Los Angeles: Roxbury.

Rose, Stephen, and Heidi Hartmann. 2004. *Still a Man's Labor Market*. Washington, DC: Institute for Women's Policy Research.

Rothman, Robert. 2002. *Inequality and Stratification: Race, Class, and Gender*. 4th edition. Upper Saddle, NJ: Prentice Hall.

Schmitt, John. 2008. "Unions and Upward Mobility for Women Workers." December. Washington, DC: Center for Economic and Policy Research. http://www.cepr.net/index.php/publications/reports/unions-and-upward-mobility-for-women-workers/. Accessed March 21, 2011.

Scott, Robert. 2003. *The High Price of Free Trade*. Washington, DC: Economic Policy Institute.

Smyth, Ines, Candida March, and Maitrayee Mukhopadhyay. 1998. *A Guide to Gender-Analysis Frameworks (Oxfam Skills and Practice)*. London: Oxfam Publications.

Social Security Administration. 2010. "Number and Average Monthly Benefit for Retired Workers, by Sex, Age, and Race, December 2009." *Annual Statistical Supplement, 2010*. http://www.ssa.gov/policy/docs/statcomps/supplement/2010/5a.html#table5.a1.1

——. 2013 "Fact Sheet: Social Security Is Important to Hispanics". February http://www.ssa.gov/pressoffice/factsheets/hispanics.htm

Spieldoch, Alexandra. 2005. "NAFTA through a Gender Lens: What 'Free Trade' Pacts Mean for Women." *Counterpunch*, December 30. http://www.counterpunch.org/spieldoch12302004.html. Accessed March 21, 2011.

Statham, Ann, Laurel Richardson, and Judith Cook. 1991. *Gender and University Teaching: A Negotiated Difference*. New York: SUNY Press.

Steinberg, Ronnie. 2001. "How Sex Gets into Your Paycheck and How to Get It Out." In *Gender Mosaics: Social Perspectives*, edited by Dana Vannoy, 258–68. Los Angeles: Roxbury.

Steinberg, Ronnie, and Deborah Figart. 1999. "Emotional Demands at Work: A Job Content Analysis." *Annals of the American Academy of Political and Social Science* 561 (1): 177–91.

Stoller, Eleanor Palo, and Rose Campbell Gibson. 2000. *Worlds of Difference: Inequality in the Aging Experience*. Thousand Oaks, CA: Pine Forge Press.

Strasser, Annie-Rose. 2013. "Why the Minimum Wage Is a Women's Issue in Three Charts." February 13. Think Progress. http://thinkprogress.org/economy/2013/02/13/1591791/minimum-wage-women-charts/. Accessed February 21, 2014.

Tomaskovic-Devey, Donald. 1993. *Gender and Racial Inequality at Work*. Ithaca, NY: Cornell University Press.

Tonelson, Alan. 2000. *Race to the Bottom*. New York: Union of Radical Political Economists.

UC Berkeley. 2010. "Opinion of How People Get Ahead." General Social Survey. http://sda.berkeley.edu/cgi-bin/hsda3?sdaprog=describe&var=GETAHEAD&sdapath=%2Fvar%2Fwww%2Fsdaprogs%2Fsda&study=%2Fvar%2Fwww%2Fhtml%2FD3%2FGSS10%20%2Fvar%2Fwww%2Fhtml%2FNpubvars%2FGSS10&varcase=upper&subtmpdir=%2Fvar%2Fwww%2Fhtml%2FTMPDIR. Accessed February 21, 2014.

UN Women. 2008. "Women, Poverty and Economics." New York: UN Women. http://www.unifem.org/gender_issues/women_poverty_economics/. Accessed June 8, 2011.

UNICEF. 2007. "Gender Equality—The Big Picture." http://www.unicef.org/education/index_bigpicture.html. Accessed June 8, 2011.

U.S. Bureau of the Census. 2012. "People Below Poverty Level by Selected Characteristics: 2009" (Table 713). *Statistical Abstracts of the United States: 2012*. http://www.census.gov/compendia/statab/2012/tables/12s0713.pdf. Accessed February 21, 2014.

U.S. Bureau of Labor Statistics. 2008. "American Time Use Survey." News release, June 25, 2008. http://www.bls.gov/news.release/archives/atus_06252008.htm. Accessed June 8, 2011.

———. 2013a. "Employment Status of the Civilian Noninstitutional Population by Age, Sex, and Race, 2012" Household Data Annual Averages 2012, Table 3. http://www.bls.gov/cps/cpsaat03.htm. Accessed September 24, 2013

———. 2013b. "Employment Status of the Hispanic or Latino Population by Age and Sex, 2012." Household Data Annual Averages 2012, Table 4. http://www.bls.gov/cps/cpsaat04.pdf. February 21, 2014.

U.S. Department of Labor. 2011. *Women's Employment During the Recovery.* Special report. http://www.dol.gov/_sec/media/reports/FemaleLaborForce/FemaleLaborForce.pdf

Voicu, Mlina, Bogdan Voicu, and Katarina Strapcova. 2009. "Housework and Gender Inequality in European Countries." *European Sociological Review* 25 (3): 365–77.

Wamboka, Nabusayi. 2002. "Closest to Land, Furthest from Cash: Poor Women Less Likely to Own Land or Have Access to Credit." *AfricaWoman.* Special edition, August/September, 2. www.dailysummit.net/documents/africawoman.pdf. Accessed March 21, 2011.

Wharton, Amy. 2005. *The Sociology of Gender.* Malden, MA: Blackwell.

Williams, Christine. 2000. "The Glass Escalator: Hidden Advantages for Men in the 'Female' Professions." In *The Gendered Society Reader,* edited by Michael Kimmel, 294–310. New York: Oxford University Press.

Wingfield, A. (2009). "Racializing the Glass Escalator: Reconsidering Men's Experiences with Women's Work." *Gender and Society* 23 (1): 5–26. doi: 10.1177/0891243208323054.

World Economic Forum. 2013.*The Global Gender Gap Report.* http://www3.weforum.org/docs/WEF_GenderGap_Report_2013.pdf Accessed March 3, 2014.

World Resources Institute. 1994–1995. *World Resources: A Guide to the Global Environment.* Oxford, UK: Oxford University Press.

Wulfhorst, Ellen. 2006. "Study: US Mothers Deserve $134,121 in Salary." *Reuters,* May 3.

Zippel, Kathrin. 2006. *The Politics of Sexual Harassment: A Comparative Study of the United States, the European Union, and Germany.* New York: Cambridge University Press.

7

FAMILIES

Like these men in France, the right to marriage is increasingly being claimed by people all over the world. Many nations now allow gay men and lesbians to marry their partners, thereby gaining the material and social benefits of legal partnership.

Source: Associated Press.

Globalization has created a work world that crosses international boundaries. Companies and jobs move from wealthy nations to poorer ones to reduce the company payroll, factories manufacture products in one country that are sold in another, and service workers provide information and assistance via phones and the Internet. Some jobs, however, cannot be accomplished from far away. **Care work** must take place where the person who needs the care lives. This has created a huge migration of care workers from the global South to the North (UNFPA 2006). Gender has historically shaped migration in ways that made men much more likely than women to migrate. The need for care workers and the association of care work with women has increased the demand for women employees, and for the first time in history half of all migrants today are women. In some places, such as the Philippines, Sri Lanka, and Thailand, women are the majority of those who leave their country. With an average age of twenty-nine, it means that many of them are mothers and, therefore, the care work they do for their own families must go undone or be outsourced to others (Bunting 2005). Rhacel Parreñas (2001) studied these **global chains of care** by interviewing women who came from the Philippines to work as nannies for families in Rome at the same time they were long-distance mothers for their families back home (Hochschild 2000).

Some of the Filipina women had been gone from home for as long as sixteen years and had sent back as much as $400 a month to their families. They were proud of the economic

223

support they provided, talking about how their pay allowed not only their children to attend school but their nieces and nephews. The price they pay, however, is great. One woman explained, "What saddens me most about my situation is that during the formative years of their childhood, I was not there for them. That is the time when children really need their mother and I was not there for them" (Parreñas 2001, 87). Another's loss was felt even more deeply. She said, "The first two years I felt like I was going crazy. I would catch myself gazing at nothing, thinking about my baby. My youngest, you have to understand, I left when he was only two months old" (Parreñas 2001, 89).

One way the women cope with the difficulties of their jobs and the pain of missing their children was to transfer their love to the children they were caring for. One woman described her situation:

> Even though it paid well, you are swimming in the amount of your work. Even while you are ironing the clothes, they can still call you to the kitchen to wash the plates. It was also very depressing. The only thing you can do is give all your love to the child. In my absence from my children, the most I could do with my situation is give all my love to that child. (Parreñas 2001, 86)

When mothers have to leave their children behind, the resulting problems are not just emotional and not confined just to the mothers. On the one hand, the households these women leave benefit from their financial contribution; but children whose mothers migrate from Mexico to the United States to provide care work have significantly higher rates of illness, emotional problems, and behavioral problems (Heymann et al. 2009). Other migrant nannies must leave their own children in grim orphanages while they are away. These women must "choose" either to live in desperate poverty with their children or to make money and live apart (Ehrenreich and Hochschild 2002).

In the United States, some immigrant women have tried to resolve these issues by bringing their children with them. This arrangement allows them to care for their own children, but it may create other difficulties. If the women are undocumented, they constantly face the risk of arrest and imprisonment, which can leave their children stranded without care. Almost 12 million adults live in the United States without proper visas, and about half of them have their children living with them (Passel, Cohn and Gonzalez-Barrera 2013). Some of the children are American citizens (84 percent of children under age six and 63 percent of children ages six to ten) because they were born here, and sometimes they, too, are undocumented. About 5.5 million children living in the United States have at least one undocumented parent (Passel and Cohn 2011). The government has stepped up efforts to catch and either deport or imprison undocumented workers. Homeland Security arrests about 1.6 million people for insufficient documents every year. One study of 900 adults arrested in raids found that most of them were parents with children under age five living with them. When the parents were arrested, informal networks within the community cared for most of their children, who had been left at school or with babysitters when the parents went to work. But some adolescents were left to fend for themselves, and even nursing mothers were not released to care for their infants (Capps, Castañeda, Chaudry, and Santos 2007).

Furthermore, even those who are not subjected to this kind of abuse by the U.S. government work under difficult conditions. Nearly all domestic workers are women, and 98 percent are foreign born. Eighty seven percent earn less than $13.47 an hour despite the fact that most

(60 percent) have worked at their jobs for six years or more. Only 10 percent receive health benefits from their employers. Almost half (43 percent) regularly work fifty hours a week, and 35 percent work sixty hours a week but often never receive extra pay for their overtime. As a result, 37 percent are unable to pay their rent, and 40 percent are unable to buy food or pay for utilities (Domestic Workers United and DataCenter 2010).

Since the 1930s, domestic workers were specifically excluded from labor-law protection in legislation passed in the United States. But in 2010, after a long political battle by Domestic Workers United and its allies, the state of New York signed into the law the Domestic Workers Bill of Rights, which provided domestic workers with rights that most other American workers assume. This law will affect a huge labor force. There are more than two hundred thousand domestic workers in the city of New York alone (Domestic Workers United and Data Center 2010). The new state law "establishes an eight hour legal work day; overtime at time and a half after 40 hours for live-out domestic workers and 44 hours for live-in domestic workers; one day of rest in each calendar week; overtime pay on that day of rest if the worker chooses to work; after one year of employment three paid days off; workplace protection against discrimination, sexual harassment, and other forms of harassment; and workers compensation" if they are injured on the job (Fletcher 2010). Since then, Hawaii and California have followed New York's lead, and Massachusetts will be joining them soon (Flanders 2013). In addition, the federal government has finally agreed to include domestic workers in the Fair Labor Standards Act which guarantees workers a minimum wage, paid breaks, and overtime pay (Dean 2013).

This description of care work reveals tensions between employers and employees, between the government and employees, and between people from one nation (the United States) and another (the citizens of the world who come to the United States to provide care for Americans). It also highlights the issue of gender, because so many of the women who work as caregivers for an employer are also the primary caregivers—as mothers, wives, aunts, daughters, and grandmothers—in their own families. And it shows that when women must leave their homes to engage in care work, the care-giving tasks in their own homes can be passed on to other women, who then are exploited as well because they are prevented from fully participating in their own families.

Family is an institution that currently encompasses a number of tasks and roles that are fraught with dilemma and controversy. Family is also an institution in which gender plays a prominent role. The work we do, the relationships we have with other adults and children in families, and the changes that result from marriage, divorce, and death are experienced differently by women and men. In chapter 6, we examined the division of labor in housework as a gendered experience, and in chapter 8, we will explore violence in families and the ways in which it is shaped by gender. This chapter explores gender in four other important areas in families: marriage, parenting and caregiving, balancing work and family, and divorce.

MARRIAGE

Marriage as a Legal Contract and the Challenge of Gay Rights Activists

Marriage in most countries is a legal contract that is tightly controlled by the government. Only certain people can legally marry, and those who do marry enter into a contract that is largely determined by laws rather than by the parties who are marrying. Although we think of marriage as a personal choice, the marriage contract provides less freedom than other legal contracts. For example, if you wished to sell a car, you could set up nearly any contract to which you and the buyer agreed. The government would interfere with the contract by requiring that certain taxes are paid and that certain assurances of the mileage and ownership of the car were valid, but issues like who can buy and who can sell, when and where the exchange will take place, and the price and payment schedule would be up to you. The details of a marriage contract, in contrast, are specified, and when the contract is ended through divorce, the state makes the final decision over nearly all arrangements.

All the legal restrictions placed on marriage are not bad. Most people agree that only adults should marry one another, and nearly all nations limit marriage to adults. There are about 195 nations in the world today, and 158 have set the legal age of marriage at 18. But many nations still haven't restricted the age of marriage or do not enforce the rules, resulting in a large number of **child brides**. The United Nations reported in 2010 that there were 67 million women age twenty to twenty-four who had become married as children, and these numbers continue to grow as an additional 14 million girls become child brides every year. When men marry girls, gender inequities are created or exacerbated. Child brides are more likely to die from pregnancy and childbirth because they become pregnant before their bodies are fully mature. They are more likely to be raped and physically abused by their husbands and forced to leave school, leaving them more economically dependent and vulnerable than women who do not marry until they are adults (Human Rights Watch 2013).

One important specification of the marriage contract in the contemporary United States that is not supported by human and civil rights activists around the world is the restriction of marriage to only couples that are heterosexual. Although the laws are in flux at this time, gay men and lesbians have the legal right to marry only in a few places, and that right is subject to change as judges overrule previous decisions and people vote to alter the laws from one election to the next. Restricting marriage to heterosexuals only has been criticized because it prevents gay and lesbian couples from making choices about their lives and because it implies that homosexuality and lesbianism are bad or unnatural.

The restriction prohibiting marriage for gay people also creates practical problems. For example, a gay couple may live together for years, pooling their resources, but they will be prohibited from carrying each other on policies for health insurance or life insurance when that benefit is provided by their employer for workers' heterosexual spouses. Other problems arise when a gay or lesbian couple chooses to live together and to take care of each other but do not have the legal right to make decisions about each other's health care as a heterosexual married couple does.

At both the state and the national level, gay rights to marriage have suffered setbacks as well as achieved victories in the past decade. Twenty-nine states still have specific legislation forbidding same-sex marriages (Schoonejongen 2013). In a number of places in the United States, however, concessions have been won. Several employers now provide partner benefits for unmarried partners of their employees, including gay and lesbian partners.

Civil unions have been granted to same sex partners in some states that also allow marriage and some states where same-sex marriage is not legal. Civil unions are certified by a justice of the peace, a judge, or a member of the clergy and grant the couple rights and responsibilities similar to those of marriage for heterosexuals. For example, civil partners can claim each other for tax and insurance benefits, and they have the right to make decisions for each other in a crisis, such as if one is incapacitated and needs decisions made about medical care. In addition, couples who become civil-union partners and decide to separate must go through the family courts and obtain a formal dissolution, similar to a divorce for married couples. Gay marriage advocates, however, believe that these reforms fall short of full legal equality with heterosexual marriage. These advocates for full marriage rights have been successful in an increasing number of states. Marriage is now legal for same-sex partners in Massachusetts, which was the first to legalize same-sex marriage in 2004, Washington, California, Minnesota, New Jersey, Iowa, Vermont, Connecticut, New Hampshire, Maine, New York, Rhode Island, Delaware, Maryland, Hawaii, and the District of Columbia.

At the federal level, progress has also been made. In 1997, the federal **Defense of Marriage Act** (**DOMA**) was signed into law defining marriage as consisting only of heterosexual unions. DOMA allowed states to ignore marriages that have occurred between same-sex partners in other states and denied legally married gay couples federal benefits such as time off under the Family and Medical Leave Act, veterans' benefits, and Social Security. In June 2013, the U.S. Supreme Court struck down DOMA's definition of marriage as a heterosexual union; the majority of the justices said the law violated the constitutional right to liberty. The ruling, which pointed to earlier decisions establishing marriage as primarily a state concern, however, didn't address prohibitions on same-sex weddings by individual states. The ruling has been applauded as an important step forward, but the right to same sex marriage in the United States remains unfinished and will require continued political and legal effort.

The United States is behind many countries in the world on this issue. In 2013, New Zealand joined Argentina, Belgium, Brazil, Canada, Denmark, France, Iceland, Netherlands, Norway, Portugal, Uruguay, South Africa, Spain, and Sweden as the fifteenth nation to allow same-sex marriage. Gay marriage is already legal in England and Wales, and the entire United Kingdom is expected to legalize same-sex marriage by 2014. Like the United States, some states in Mexico, including the largest population center, Mexico city, allow same-sex marriage (Pew Forum 2013). Israel and several nations in Europe extend immigration rights to same-sex partners (Wong 2010). Australia, Venezuela, Ecuador, and a number of European nations recognize civil unions. Many other nations are currently considering extending marriage rights to gay and lesbian couples.

History of Marriage in the United States

Dorothy Stetson (1997) observes that there have been three major periods of marriage and family law in U.S. history. The first was the **doctrine of *coverture***, which defined marriage as a unity in which husband and wife became one, and that "one" was the husband. Stetson quotes an early nineteenth-century document to explain what coverture meant: "By marriage, the husband and wife are one person in law: that is, the very being or existence of the woman is suspended during marriage, or at least is incorporated and consolidated into that of the husband" (Blackstone 1803, 442). Under the doctrine of coverture, married women could not own property. They had to turn over their wages to their husbands. If someone wanted to sue a married woman, she or he had to sue the woman's husband.

The second period was marked by the passage of the **Married Women's Property Laws**, which allowed women the right to own property and to control their own earnings. These laws

GENDER IN EVERYDAY LIFE   BOX 7-1
CYBER/MAIL-ORDER BRIDES

Finding hard data on the number of men who find their wives through catalogs is difficult. Correspondence services like those commonly listed in newspapers advertise "Asian women desire romance" and "Attractive Oriental ladies seeking friendship, correspondence." A Google search for "mail-order" brides turns up more than a million hits, with ads for "Latin women, known for their beauty and loving ways" and "Russian women, petite and pretty." Men who respond to these ads receive pictures and descriptions of women, along with addresses, for a fee (Agbayani-Siewert and Revilla 1995). Research on cyber brides in Eastern Europe have found 219 marriage agencies with a total of 119,649 women on their sites. Nearly half of these are from Russia, and most of the rest were from the Ukraine and Belarus (Hughes 2003).

The Philippines is the major source of mail-order brides from Asia. The Philippines report that nineteen thousand mail-order brides leave that country every year to marry men in other countries (Tolentino 1996). Many of these women come to the United States, although we do not know the exact number (Haley 2009). The system, however, is global, with women coming from all over the world as mail-order brides for husbands throughout the global North. And the practice only appears to be growing, as the Internet makes the arrangements increasingly easier (Lee 2008).

Some of these arrangements result in happy marriages. In addition, the practice in many Asian countries has been argued to be an extension of matchmaking, which has been a part of the culture for centuries and in which women are not passive victims but active participants in selecting and rejecting partners (Lee 2008). But there are some important problems that can occur. The first problem with this practice is the possibility that the women involved are not making their own choices to enter themselves into the service. Researchers have found that mail-order women who seek counseling in Seattle, for example, frequently do not speak English and come from isolated rural areas

were first passed in Mississippi in 1839 and were passed in all the states by the end of the nineteenth century. The case that opened the door for married women to own property in Mississippi was a dramatic example of class and racial ethnic inequality. The "property" which the woman asked the court to allow her to own was a slave. The court ruled in her favor.

Marriage during this period was perceived as a union between two separate and different but equal individuals (Stetson 1997). Women and men had different responsibilities and rights in marriage, but neither was supposed to overshadow the other. The wife was expected to provide services for her husband. One court case, for example, specified that a wife was "to be his helpmate, to love and care for him in such a role, to afford him her society and her person, to protect and care for him in sickness, and to labor faithfully to advance his interests" (Weitzman 1981, 60). Sexual accessibility was also part of these laws, and it was not until

(Mochizuki 1987). One might suspect, therefore, that they did not make a free or informed choice to be listed in the magazines or to marry someone in the United States. Perhaps the choices they had were so limited that they could not really be considered a humane range of options.

Other researchers have found that the level of marital satisfaction among mail-order brides is similar to that of other intermarried Asian women who found their husbands through other means. Mail-order brides, however, report more physical and psychological abuse (Lin 1991).

The ads themselves suggest that the women are chosen, or at least promoted, for their passivity and acquiescence. The advertisements for Filipinas, for example, describe the prospective brides as "pretty, young, faithful, undemanding, family-oriented, feminine in the 'old-fashioned' way and sexually acquiescent to their husbands." The women are also described as good cooks and housekeepers and willing to quickly learn their husband's language (Haley 2009).

The images of the men who are the prospective husbands on the sites portray them as people who will save the women from the difficulties of life in their homelands. "Like the female missionaries of the twentieth century who fulfilled their duty as moral citizens of the world by "uplifting" the natives, men too take on this role of the moral "good guys" who teach Latinas how to assimilate into the dream of liberal capitalism. Chatroom discussions about women marveling over skyscrapers and washing machines in the United States and men's emphasis of women's "traditional" qualities easily slip into colonial ideas of the "natives" as backward, primitive, and uncivilized (Schaeffer-Grabiel 2006, 346).

The idea of a man from a wealthy nation finding a wife from a poor country who is advertised as a commodity illustrates the convergence of gender inequity and national inequality. Although many men and women may find happiness in these arrangements, they illustrate how marriage can represent and validate relationships between two kinds of people with starkly different resources and choices.

1993 that marital rape became a crime in all states in the United States. The husband, in turn, was obligated to provide for the economic needs of his family. The laws that designated men as the "head and master" were overturned in 1979 (Coontz 2006a).

The third doctrine identified marriage as a shared partnership in which spouses would have equal and overlapping responsibilities for economic, household, and child-care tasks. This doctrine has been developing for about forty years in the United States. The greater equality in the legal definition of marriage these changes have brought has been welcomed by many. We have seen, however, that legal equality has not necessarily meant social equality. The division of housework, market work, and child care are still all influenced by gender. Box 7-1 describes another way that equality in the eyes of the law may not create equality in real relationships: the case of "mail-order brides."

In addition, the third doctrine has created problems in some cases when equality between women and men is upheld. For example, changes in laws that make women more equal to men in divorce proceedings are based on assumptions that women are equal to men in their responsibility for children and in their ability to earn an income. The laws assume equality between women and men, which is a valuable reform. Because women and men remain unequal in reality, however, economic problems have developed for divorcing women, as we shall see later in this chapter.

In each of these historical periods, the government has created a legal notion of what a man is and what a woman is and what constitutes a valid or real gender relationship. In the first period, gender was enforced as separate and unequal. The institution of marriage prescribed that women and men are very different from one another and that men were the superior beings. The second period opened up some measure of equality between women and men around economic issues, but it left in place definitions of womanhood and manhood and the different obligations husbands and wives have to each other in marriage.

The third period established the idea of gender equality in the eyes of the law. The current debate around gay marriage marks a fourth period in which another factor, sexuality, is most salient. Those who maintain that marriage should only be allowed between one man and one woman are reminding us again that men and women are not equal. They are different beings who can only unite with someone of the "opposite sex" in marriage. Furthermore, anti-gay marriage laws are telling us that to be properly gendered we need to be heterosexual. For example, the Colorado Family Action organization, a political group lobbying against gay rights and especially the right to marriage, claims that the right of gay men and lesbians to establish domestic partnerships "harms children by sending confusing messages about gender" (Chernus 2006).

Thinking about intersex people or transgender people helps us to see how the narrow definition of marriage as only legal between a woman and a man creates rules about gender. You should recall from chapter 2 that intersex people do not fall into one of the two categories, male or female. Instead they have characteristics—genetic, structural, and/or hormonal—that put them into categories between male and female. Transgender people are those who represent themselves as a gender that is "inconsistent" with their sex. For example, males who might fit clearly into that biological category may represent themselves as women. Whom should intersex and transgender people be allowed to marry? If they represent themselves as women, should they only be allowed to marry someone who represents as a man? What if a partner chooses to become transgender after he or she legally marries? Should the government tell people how we should represent ourselves and whom we should marry?

Marriage Promotion in the United States

So far we have been looking at the ways the government has sought to prevent people from marrying by ruling that marriage is only allowable for one man and one woman. At the same time, ironically, the government has been busy promoting marriage as essential for heterosexuals, especially among women and men who are poor.

Box 7-2 describes the concern that other nations, such as Japan and South Korea, have about the drop in the proportion of people who are marrying. Although the promotion of marriage in those countries has not emphasized any particular social class, it has targeted women

GENDER IN EVERYDAY LIFE   BOX 7-2
PROMOTING MARRIAGE IN JAPAN AND KOREA

Marriage promotion is an issue in many places around the world where governments are concerned about the numbers of people who are choosing to marry much later than previously or not at all (Ganahl 2004). In Japan, a study from Japan Life Insurance shocked the nation when it reported that about half of the country's single women from aged thirty-five to fifty-four have no intention of ever marrying. In addition, nearly three-fourths of women in the same age group said that they never want children. The number of single Japanese women may rise even more dramatically since a new divorce law was adopted that awards up to half of a man's pension to his ex-wife (Hardin 2007). Similarly, in South Korea, around 40 percent of the women are staying single into their thirties as they increasingly prioritize their education and careers. Twenty years ago, only 14 percent of women in South Korea were still single at thirty (Ganahl 2004).

When the Japanese women were asked why they want to remain single, they explained that they wished to maintain a wide spectrum of friends and pursue their careers. The Japanese report also found that employed women were concerned about the work environment, which they perceived as unfriendly to mothers (Retherford and Ogawa 2005).

The response from the government has been highly critical of women. The former prime minister of Japan gave a speech angrily suggesting that women who choose not to become mothers are selfish and should not be entitled to government retirement pensions (Ganahl 2004).

Interestingly, the statistics are even more dramatic for men, although they have not received the same level of criticism. The proportion of men single at age fifty grew from 2 percent to 25 percent between 1970 and 2000. The proportion of women single at age fifty went from 3 percent to 19 percent in those same years. The average age of marriage between 1975 and 2000 increased from 27.6 to 30.8 for men and from 24.5 to 28.8 for women (Retherford and Ogawa 2005).

rather than men. In the United States, both the concern and the governmental policies center around people who are poor. In the past decade, the U.S. government has decided to "promote marriage" as a way to address the problem of poverty. The goal "is to transform single-mother families into families headed by married biological fathers" (Mink 2006, 159).

In 1996, changes in welfare laws created a new program called **Temporary Aid to Needy Families (TANF)**. The laws reward states that increase the marriage rate of the families receiving grants, and states reward couples on welfare who marry. For example, in West Virginia, unmarried families receive $100 less per month than do married families (Solot and Miller 2002). Since 2002, the government has given states $150 million every year for marriage and fatherhood programs. In 2010 the programs were evaluated, and researchers found that the programs apparently had no appreciable effect: marriage rates before and after welfare reforms remained the same (Marsh 2010; Wood, McConnell, Moore, Clarkwest, and Hsueh 2010). But even if they had increased, scholars point out that the assumption that marriage rates are the problem and that increasing marriage among poor people would address poverty is flawed.

There are four errors in the premise of the programs. First, they assume that failure to marry causes poverty. In fact, the reverse is probably true. Poverty seems to inhibit people's ability to marry. Poor people often would like to get married but feel they are not able to take on this responsibility until they are better off financially. Furthermore, to escape poverty, poor single people must marry well. They must find partners who are able to provide for them financially—a tall order in an impoverished neighborhood (Coontz and Folbre 2002).

Second, the program does not acknowledge the issue of quality. Happy, healthy, stable marriages might be a good goal, but not all marriages are healthy and happy. In addition, those marriages that are not healthy and happy are likely to become unstable (Coontz and Folbre 2002). Most people believe that one key ingredient of a healthy, stable marriage is that the partners love one another, which is discussed in the next section.

Third, marriage does not cure the money problem for many poor couples. Almost one-third (27 percent) of low-income children live in families with two parents. In addition, the majority of married low-income parents are employed. Low wages and lack of employee benefits leave married couples and their children with inadequate economic resources.

Fourth, single parenthood does not necessarily lead to poverty. Only a tiny proportion (1.2 percent) of children whose single mothers have college degrees and year-round, full-time jobs are poor (National Center for Children in Poverty 2005). In addition, government programs could eliminate poverty for those single parents who are poor. In many other nations, single parents and their children are provided with safety nets that raise them above poverty (Coontz and Folbre 2002).

Although some politicians argue that the programs have not been given enough time to work, these four weaknesses in the assumption that marriage would cure poverty suggest that the programs are not likely to work regardless of how much time they are given. Politicians who are critical of the marriage promotion programs argue that the federal funds spent on promoting marriage are wasted and that if we want to build stronger families, the money would be better spent on economic supports such as cash assistance, child care, and transitional employment (Marsh 2010).

In addition to those four flaws in Congress's foray into the marriage business, the program also is problematic for another reason: it is an unprecedented intrusion by the government into what most of us believe to be private relationships. We have many reasons for choosing to enter into marriage or not. Making government bonuses and government approval part of those reasons marks a significant and, for many, unwelcome change.

Because women are the majority of adults who receive welfare grants, the marriage program creates an especially questionable situation for women. The organization of the welfare system is shaped by gender, and it influences gendered associations between women and men and can support and perpetuate unequal relationships in which women are subordinated to men. These new rules mean that entitlement to government funds is to be based on the relationships women establish with men. They assume that good, deserving women get married, and bad, undeserving women do not. Those women who tie the knot are entitled to more support. Those women who choose to remain independent of men (at least as wives) are not.

Love and Marriage

Marriage has existed for many centuries, but its meaning has changed significantly over time (Coontz 2006a). In earlier centuries, marriage was primarily an economic arrangement: wealthy people entered into marriage to consolidate wealth, transfer property, and lay claim to political power or to settle wars. Middle-class people married for similar reasons on a smaller scale. And even poor people married to conjoin farms, share tools, and bring more labor into a household. Love was not a reason to get married; nor was the lack of love a reason for divorce, which was usually a result of childlessness or a means to improve one's economic circumstances (Coontz 2004).

In the seventeenth century in Europe and North America, the ideal of a love match and lifelong intimacy as a basis of marriage began to take hold. Since then, love has grown to become the most important reason for marriage. The connection between love and marriage is now a powerful ideology. In a survey of college students in the 1960s, three-fourths of the women said they would marry men they did not love if those men met other criteria such as being a reliable breadwinner, not drinking too much, and not being physically abusive. Only one-fourth of the men said they would marry women they did not love. Today, both women and men say that love is the top priority (Coontz 2004).

Ironically, love is the basis of both the arguments to allow gay men and lesbians to marry and the arguments to allow heterosexuals to remain unmarried. Gay rights advocates who support marriage assert that loving couples should be allowed all of the responsibilities and privileges of legal marriage, regardless of sexuality or gender. Heterosexual couples maintain that it is inhumane and uncivilized for the government to tell parents that to acquire access to support for themselves and their children in programs such as TANF, they must marry even if they do not love each other.

The debates over marriage for gay and lesbian couples and rules requiring marriage for poor people bring into opposition two key issues, gender and love. Those who are against gay marriage and in favor of the government promoting marriage for poor people believe that gender is key. Marriage is for one man and one woman, and every man and woman must be married regardless of love. Those who are in favor of allowing gay marriage and allowing all adults to choose whether they will marry based on their feelings for their partner believe that love is more important than gender. Which do you think is more important? Love or gender?

Widowhood

One final way marriage is different for women is that men are more likely to live out their lives in a marriage, whereas women are more likely to be widowed. Women tend to live longer than men and to marry men who are older than they are. Women are also less likely to remarry after the death of a spouse, and so they are much more likely to be widows than men are to be widowers. Table 7-1 shows the proportion of all women and men over the age of 15 in the United States who were widows or widowers in 2012. The table indicates that race ethnicity creates some differences, but gender differences are striking for all groups.

At every age, men are much more likely to be married and much less likely to be widowed. This gap becomes more pronounced in older age groups. About 40 percent of women over sixty-five are widows while 13 percent of men in this age group are widowed, and on

TABLE 7-1 Proportion of Widows and Widowers Among People over the Age of 15 in the United States, 2012

Race/Ethnicity	Women	Men
White	9.8%	2.8%
Black	8.6%	2.2%
Hispanic	5.2%	1.3%
Asian	6.1%	1.0%

Source: U.S. Bureau of the Census (2012c).

average, widows live about fifteen years after their husband's death (Federal Interagency Forum on Aging-Related Statistics 2004; Administration on Aging 2011). Seventy percent of men over sixty-five live with a wife, whereas only 35 percent of women over sixty-five live with a husband. The living arrangements of widows and widowers is also different. Of women who are widowed or otherwise single, 18 percent live with other relatives, compared to 6 percent of men who live with other relatives. Over a third (37 percent) of women over sixty-five live alone, compared to 19 percent of men over sixty-five (U.S. Bureau of Census 2012a).

In some areas of the world, the problems widows face are even tougher. For example, customary laws in some cultures require that widows marry their dead husband's brother. In other places, widows face extreme poverty and difficult living situations as they are eliminated from households when they lose the link their husbands provided and inherit nothing, leaving them homeless and without any assets to set up a new living arrangement (Peterman 2012). The United Nations estimates that there are 250 million widows globally, 115 million of them live below the poverty line, and 81 million are subject to physical abuse (United Nations 2001).

PARENTING AND CAREGIVING

Both the real experience of being a parent and our ideas about what parents should be like are shaped by gender. Mothers and fathers experience being parents differently, and when we think about what makes a good mother or a good father, we think in gendered terms.

Research shows that, on average, mothers spend more time with their children than do fathers (Aldous, Mulligan, and Biarnason 1998). Race ethnicity, however, makes a big difference. In the United States, African American fathers are more likely to participate in child care than are white fathers (Orbuch and Eyster 1997). Gender, though, remains a strong distinction in parenting. On average in American households with two heterosexual parents, mothers spend about eleven hours per week taking care of their children, while fathers spend just over three hours per week. Mothers are also more likely to be single parents. One in three children in the United States live with a single mother while 1 in 12 live with a single father (U.S. Bureau of the Census 2012c). These numbers reflect strong beliefs about the close link between being a woman and being a mother.

Motherhood Mystique

Gender ideologies, ideas about what it means to be a woman or a man, are closely tied to our ideas about parenting. The idea of being a mother and being a particular kind of mother are strong expectations for women. Beliefs about what makes a good father are quite different, and although they are currently going through some important changes, old ideas persist. For example, a recent poll found that 51 percent of Americans believe that children are better off if their mother stays home, while only 8 percent believe that children are better off if their father stays home (Wang, Parker, and Taylor 2013).

Much of contemporary belief about motherhood idealizes mothering and ignores the problems real mothers face in raising children. The key word here is "belief." Our culture promotes beliefs about mothers that many of us accept. But those beliefs don't necessarily have much to do with either what might be the best relationships between women and children or what real relationships between women and children are like. These beliefs are called the "**motherhood mystique**." The motherhood mystique is based on five principles (Hoffnung 1989; Hays 1999):

1. Women achieve their ultimate fulfillment by becoming mothers. Mothering is supposed to replace all other interests. Fathers, in contrast, are also supposed to be delighted by their children; but men are expected to maintain other interests besides their children.

Mother's Day cards like this help to perpetuate the motherhood mystique which romanticizes mothering and ignores the problems real mothers face in raising children.

Source: Adrian Chinery.

2. Mothers must be involved in every aspect of their children's lives.
3. Mothers are the best providers for all the emotional, social, and intellectual needs of their children. Other people, such as fathers or paid caregivers, can provide for these as backup, but the ideal situation is for children to be primarily or solely in the care of their mothers.
4. Mothers should provide a buffer for their children from the worst of the outside world.
5. Intense exclusive devotion of women to their children is good for children.

Does the motherhood mystique affect all women in the same way? Box 7-3 describes the problems lesbian couples face in dealing with the motherhood mystique. African American women's experience with mothering is also different from the model for middle-class and upper-class white women in the United States. White women have been constrained by the motherhood mystique, but African American women have often been excluded from that role. Historically, slavery and Jim Crow and then poverty forced African American women into the labor market where they often had to care for white children (and their parents) while being prevented from spending time with their own children. Mothering has been central to the role of African American women, but it is more likely to be shared with men and other women, or "othermothers." African American women have organized woman-centered networks of blood mothers and othermothers, aunts, grandmothers, neighbors, and friends to take care of children, sometimes for long periods of time and even as informal adoption (Collins 2000).

WORK AND FAMILY IN LATINO AND AFRICAN AMERICAN FAMILIES. Mothering among African American women has also not been experienced as something that holds women back from other activities, as it is among upper-class and middle-class white women. African American mothers have long been part of the paid labor force. Furthermore, they have used their status, connections, and responsibilities as mothers and othermothers as a motivation and facilitator of their community activism (Collins 2000).

Patricia Zavella (1987) found that Chicanas' experience with motherhood and paid labor were also somewhat different from that of white women. She interviewed Chicanas who worked in canneries in California about the tensions between work and family in their lives and how they made the decision to get a job. The women she interviewed had been encouraged and socialized as girls to become full-time housewives and mothers. A typical pattern was to work outside the home in the early days of their marriage and quit when their first child was born. When it became clear that their husbands' paychecks could not adequately support the household, the women returned to work in the cannery. Choosing to work in the cannery, however, was not perceived as an alternative to their responsibilities as wives and mothers but as an extension of that role (Aulette 2007).

Research on white women in the United States (Gerson 1987) presents two roles for women, that of employee and that of wife and mother, as two opposing possibilities. The women in Zavella's (1987) research saw them as contiguous. The cannery workers fit into another category in which the women seek outside employment not because they wish to move away from their domestic role but because they wish to be better wives and mothers. The Chicanas argue that they choose to go to work because of their obligation to their families.

GENDER IN EVERDAY LIFE   BOX 7-3

LESBIAN MOTHERS

In chapter 2 we described the "standard story": everyone is born a male or female, every male will develop masculine characteristics and behaviors, including being sexually attracted to only females, and every female will develop feminine characteristics and behaviors, including being sexually attracted to only males. We also discussed how every part of this story is flawed and how real people follow many paths among multiple sexes, genders, and sexualities. No matter how invalid the standard story is, however, it retains a powerful influence. Parenting is one those issues that is shaped by the standard story and its influence on our thinking as well as our social institutions.

When lesbian couples become parents they are confronted with the model of parenting that derives from the standard story which assumes/demands that all children are raised in households with one masculine male father and one feminine female mother. Lesbian mothers cannot fit into these models and thus are defined as deviants and incongruent with motherhood ideals. Even finding a language to describe their roles and relationships is a challenge. Should they call themselves both "mom"? Should they take on the heterosexual model designating one person as mom and the other as dad? Should they invent a new language referring to one parent as the mother and the other as the mather?

Margaret and Ruth are lesbian partners. Margaret has a biological son, Cameron, whom she and Ruth are raising as co-parents. Ruth describes how her claim of motherhood has been flatly denied: "Other people are really attached to the idea that there can only be one mom. Every Saturday, Margaret and I take Cameron to Play Center, and there are a lot of other parents there. Even though we know a lot of the parents there because it's a thing for us to go and so we have explained our situation. I feel like most of them don't take me seriously. Just last week, one of them said her kid was having a birthday party and Cameron was invited and said she would see if it was okay with Margaret. I said, "You don't need to ask her. Cameron can go. We don't have any other plans." She told me point-blank that she thought that she should really ask Margaret since she was Cam's mother. I just walked away" (Padavic and Butterfield 2011, 177).

Even more difficult than these social and interpersonal difficulties, however, are the lack of legal rights and legal status connecting them to their children. Karen, another lesbian co-parent, says, "When you can't establish a legal connection, though, it is really hard to feel like a good parent. Right now, I feel like a nanny or mommy's sidekick. . . . And I think that's how my son's teachers view me. I can't sign any of the official paperwork at school. She [my partner] has to do the official important stuff. I get delegated to bring in cupcakes or whatever. Apparently, they will allow us non-moms to do that. . ." (Padavic and Butterfield 2011, 194). Schools, doctors, and the legal system leave a lesbian parent in a constantly precarious position with no legal or social rights regarding the children she feels are her own.

When Zavella asked one woman why she had sought work in the cannery, for example, the woman said, "I did it for my family. We needed the money, why else?" (Zavella 1987, 88). Another woman who was asked this question responded by motioning to her child, who was carrying a large doll, and saying, "That's why I work, for my daughter, so I can give her those things" (Zavella 1987, 134).

Research on employed women often finds that white women choose to work for wages as an alternative to staying home. The Latina women in Zavella's interviews, in contrast, insist that work and family are not two alternatives, but that working for wages is a way of fulfilling their maternal role in their family (Segura 1999).

WORKING MOTHERS AND THE MOMMY WARS. Even though our review of gender in the labor market in chapter 5 showed that a large and increasing proportion of women all over the world are in the paid labor force, the motherhood mystique remains strong. Its assumptions, however, often do not fit well into real women's lives (Hays 1999). In the United States, women from all racial ethnic groups have increasingly entered the paid labor force and now make up nearly half of the employees in the United States. Women with children are also increasingly likely to be employed. In 1993 the labor-force participation of mothers aged twenty-five to fifty-four was 14 percent lower than that of childless women in the same age group. By 2004 it was just 8 percent lower. Mothers' contribution to their family's economic survival is essential. Four in ten mothers are now either the sole breadwinner (a single, working mother) or are bringing home as much or more than their spouse (Boushey and O'Leary 2010). Not surprising, when women do leave work to take care of their children, most of them return to work sooner than did mothers in generations past (Coontz 2006b).

What happens to those women who combine employment and motherhood? Michelle Budig and Paula England (2001) looked at the "**motherhood penalty**" on working women. They found that women's income declined by 7 percent for each child they had. At least four possible explanations exist for the association between lower wages and mothering. First, employers may discriminate against mothers. Laws to protect prospective employees from being asked about marital or family status are vague, nonexistent, and ignored. MomsRising. org has launched a program to expose this situation and to call for laws that can protect mothers from being discriminated against.

Even women who can overcome discrimination are forced to make difficult "choices" because of the organization of work. Mothers may choose to trade higher wages for mother-friendly jobs, or they may interrupt their job history, making them less competitive in the labor market. Finally, mothers may be more distracted and exhausted at work and therefore less productive.

Researchers (Budig and England 2001) have found that that the lower productivity of mothers may be the most significant factor in the wage penalty. They argue that we should not, however, conclude that this is a problem of the mothers themselves, nor is it the responsibility of the businesses that employ them. They assert instead that the rest of us are free riders on the employed mothers who are contributing doubly to the community by raising children and working in the paid labor force, even though they are given little support for their efforts.

Regardless of which route they take, women face problems:

> What this creates is a no-win situation for a woman of childbearing years. If a woman voluntarily remains childless, some will say that she is cold, heartless and unfulfilled

as a woman. If she is a mother who works too hard at her job or career, some will accuse her of neglecting the kids. If she does not work hard enough some will surely place her on the mommy track and her career advancement will be permanently slowed by the claim that her commitment to her children interferes with her workplace efficiency. (Schwartz 1989, 74)

"And if she stays home with her children, some will call her unproductive and useless. A woman, in other words can never fully do it right" (Hays 1999, 434).

Hays (1999) calls the tension between the motherhood mystique and our expectations that adults earn their way through paid labor in our society the "**mommy wars.**" The mommy wars illustrate a dilemma for all women who are required to be good mothers according to the motherhood mystique and to be responsible citizens who work in the paid workforce. Box 7-4 describes how the mommy wars played a role in recent presidential campaigns in the United States, when the images of mothers were represented in the media depictions of First Lady Michelle Obama, Vice-Presidential candidate Sarah Palin, and contender for the Democratic presidential nomination, Hillary Clinton. The mommy wars, however, show up most dramatically in debates about welfare for low-income women.

WELFARE MOTHERS. Welfare in the United States serves about 5 percent of the population at any given time and accounts for 1 percent of the federal budget and 3 percent of state budgets. Despite these small numbers, welfare is a constant issue of political debate. About two-thirds of the people who receive welfare grants are children under the age of eighteen. The majority of adults who receive welfare grants are single mothers. Over the past several decades, government officials have tried to alter welfare policy in ways that bring those mothers into the labor force (Albelda and Tilly 2000). Two important values exist side by side: the work ethic and the family ethic.

The work ethic says that everyone should contribute to society by participating in the paid labor force—by going to work for wages. Doing the job of mothering is not considered work because mothers do not earn wages. The family ethic and the motherhood mystique, however, say that families are the building block of the nation: children should be cared for by their mothers, and children require a lot of attention from their mothers. Poor mothers increasingly are required to enter the paid labor force. They cannot live up to the expectation of being good mothers when they are forced to spend time away from their children. Furthermore, because the motherhood mystique creates an assumption that children are cared for best by their mothers, no alternatives like publicly funded high-quality child care are developed. Children whose mothers are not "good" mothers are left without proper or sufficient adult attention. One welfare mother described her dilemma: "I know I can [go to the job search program and go to school], but who would my kids be eating dinner with? Who would put them to bed if I were to work nights and go to school during the day? Even AFDC [welfare] kids need their moms" (Abramowitz 1996, 41). The motherhood mystique has created an impossible dilemma for her, and it has created a vacuum of care for her children.

The obvious solution to this problem is to acknowledge that the work women do to raise children is worthy of remuneration. The Sloan Foundation notes that Temporary Aid to Needy Families may in fact operate as a form of "paid pregnancy leave" because, as we can see in Table 7–1, the United States is unique in the developed world in its lack of any publicly funded paid leave for new parents (Levin-Epstein 2006). And the "paid pregnancy leave"

GENDER IN EVERYDAY LIFE   BOX 7-4
THE MOTHERHOOD MYSTIQUE IN PRESIDENTIAL CAMPAIGNS

The 2008 presidential elections had more discussion of motherhood in the media than any campaign in almost sixty years (Elder and Greene 2008). A good part of this emphasis on mothers came from the media presentation of three images of mothers through three women who were prominent in the campaign: Sarah Palin, Hillary Clinton, and Michelle Obama. These images were partly a result of what the media chose to focus on and partly a result of what the women chose to promote about themselves in an effort to please the pundits and the voters so that they could succeed in their campaigns.

Sarah Palin, who ran as Vice President in the 2008 campaign, was portrayed as the bad working mother and failed supermom. Palin tried to claim that she was a typical "hockey mom" as well as a world-class political force. The *New York Times* called her an imposter for claiming to be capable of political leadership and taking care of her children, especially her unmarried pregnant daughter and baby with Down syndrome. Overall she was presented as a failure at both paid labor for her professional behavior and at motherhood because of her family's problems and her reliance on a stay-at-home husband to try to keep them from collapsing altogether.

Hillary Clinton, who ran for president in the Democratic primaries, was presented as an unfeeling and absent mother. Clinton tried to distance herself from the mommy wars initially and then was criticized by "onlookers who questioned her gender ("Does she even care about what other women are interested in?"), her age ("Could she still be a mother?"),

program provided by the welfare system is currently eroding, providing less and less support for parents and requiring more and more hours of work outside of families from their participants.

TEMPORARY AID TO NEEDY FAMILIES. In 1996 the U.S. federal government replaced the sixty-year-old Aid to Families with Dependent Children (AFDC) program with a new program called Temporary Aid to Needy Families (TANF) (Burt and Nightingale 2009). TANF included major alterations in existing welfare programs:

1. Welfare is no longer an entitlement. Before TANF, AFDC was guaranteed to eligible Americans. The federal laws required that the state governments provide grants for all needy families that qualified. The new law provides for block grants, which means that the federal government provides a set amount of funds to each state. The states in turn must create their own systems of dispersing the funds. The federal money is now capped at $16.5 billion annually. (This number has remained the same even though the spending power of this amount of dollars has declined by a sixth [Edelman 2009]). When the funds run out, states are not

and the necessity of her mothering ("Does Chelsea even need a mother?") (Dillaway and Pare 2013, 222). In order to address these issues, Clinton eventually had to draw on her motherhood identity by bringing Chelsea into her campaign and talking about so-called family issues. But these efforts were not successful. One MSNBC news analyst went so far as to say that Clinton had "pimped out" her daughter by asking her to accompany her on the campaign trail (Dillaway and Pare 2013).

Media images of Michelle Obama, the first lady during these years, presented her as the intensive stay-at home mother. Originally suspect because ideal images of mothers are white, Obama was able to overcome the suspicions and came closest to fulfilling the mythical image of a good mother (Dillaway and Pare 2013).

Obama referred to herself as Sasha and Malia's mother and mom-in-chief. The media wrote of her commitment to keeping Barack Obama grounded as a good wife should, her skill at being a gracious hostess and loyal spouse, and her efforts to care for her children and make sure that their needs came first. Even when speaking of political causes, Michelle Obama focused on military wives and children's nutrition, both safe topics for a good mother. While Obama was quite successful in the images of good mother, her accomplishments in maintaining this image were at the cost of erasing a good part of her true self as a skilled professional woman—a graduate of Princeton University and Harvard Law School and talented community organizer and political leader.

The experience of these three women in the 2008 presidential campaign shows us the salience of ideologies about gender and parenting and how they interfere with women's ability to take their place in all human activities. The 2008 campaign seems to prove Hays' (1999, 446) comments: "A woman, in other words, can never fully do it right."

legally obligated to provide services, even for families that would otherwise be eligible. Of eligible families, about half do not receive assistance. This proportion is up from 20 percent in 1996 (Fremstad 2004). In 1995, 62 percent of the 14.5 million children then poor were in families that received welfare. By 2012, 27 percent of the more than16 million poor children were living in families receiving assistance from TANF (Kaufmann 2012; Kids Count 2013).

2. Time limits were placed on the number of years people are eligible for grants. TANF, a federal law, states that households are eligible for support for only two years at a time and for five years in the lifetime of any adult in the household, regardless of need. Nine states have opted for shorter limits (for example, Arkansas, two years; Florida, four years; and Utah, three years). The federal law also allows states to exempt 20 percent of their case load from the five-year limit, but many states do not use this exemption (Edelman 2009).

3. Legal immigrants are barred from receiving TANF and food stamps. Undocumented immigrants were already barred from receiving any assistance except for emergency medical care or education for their children.

4. Criteria for receiving disability payments are more stringent.

5. The food stamp program was cut by $27 billion. No legal immigrants are allowed to receive food stamps, and able-bodied adults under the age of fifty are restricted from receiving food stamps for more than three months in a three-year period.

6. States are allowed to place caps on the number of people within a household who are considered eligible for support. Twenty-one states, for example, refuse to pay larger sums to larger households or to parents who have children while they are on welfare. This restriction is based on the assumption that limiting welfare will reduce fertility among recipients. Ironically, lower birth rates are associated with more generous welfare programs in countries in western Europe, Scandinavia, and Canada.

7. Poor families can own larger amounts of assets and still be eligible for assistance. Previously, a family could have only a vehicle worth up to $1,500, a burial plot, and $1,000 in other assets. Now families are allowed to save some money for education or buying a home. Most states allow them to own a car valued at up to $5,000 and an additional $2,000 in assets.

8. States are required to assign all individuals in a welfare household to job-training and job-finding activities. People may be exempt because they are ill, incapacitated, elderly, under sixteen or in school full time, already working at least thirty hours per week, more than six months pregnant, caring for an ill or incapacitated family member in their home, or caring for a young child. States have much flexibility defining these exemptions. For example, Massachusetts allows parents of children under six years old to be exempt to take care of their children (Greenberg 1999). Eleven states require parents of babies over three months old to work, and six states have no exemptions for parents no matter how young their children are (Rowe and Russell 2004).

9. **Medicaid** coverage continues for one year for persons who leave welfare to go to work (N. Walker, Brooks, and Wrightsman 1999).

10. States are not required to provide child care for children of TANF recipients who participate in job-support programs (N. Walker et al. 1999). These changes strengthen the idea that taking care of children is the individual responsibility of parents (who are mostly mothers), and they ignore the work involved in raising children. The policy strongly promotes the work ethic and abandons the family ethic. However, poor women continue to be judged by the ideology of the motherhood mystique (Aulette 2007).

Parenting by Fathers

Changing ideas about gender and, therefore, about what mothering and fathering look like, influence men's and women's behavior and their relationships with children. Structural changes, such as the introduction of women into the paid labor force, have also shifted definitions of gender and the links between being a woman and man and being a parent. Changes in work and family are also altering gender for men. When men do the work of mothers, the feelings and experience of men are altered, and new ways of being men and being fathers begin to emerge. Fathers who play the role of mother begin to behave and think in feminine ways in other areas of their lives.

Barbara Risman discovered in her research on single parents that doing can become being. Risman (1987) surveyed four kinds of parents: single mothers, single fathers, two-parent households where only the father was in the paid labor force, and two-paycheck families. She measured variation in parenting by looking at three factors: time spent in housework, parent–child intimacy, and overt affection. She found that single fathers, single mothers, and housewives spent more time than married fathers or married employed mothers on housework. Single fathers often did not hire others to do the work for them and therefore were forced to take responsibility for these household tasks.

The second factor, parent–child intimacy, was measured by how often children shared their emotions—sadness, loneliness, anger, happiness, pride—with their parents. Here she found that femininity was the most important predictor of parent–child intimacy. Parents who considered themselves more feminine on a range of issues were more likely to report higher rates of parent–child intimacy. This was true regardless of the sex of the parent. Fathers who were more feminine (according to personality scales) were more likely to report parent–child intimacy than mothers or fathers who were less feminine. Single fathers reported levels of femininity similar to those of employed mothers, suggesting that the activity of parenting may create different expressions of personality, which in turn helps fathers build parent–child intimacy.

The third factor was overt affection, which was measured by the amount of physical contact—hugging, cuddling, wrestling—children had with their parents and the kinds of interactions that took place when the parent and child were alone with each other. This factor was affected by the gender of the parent and the parental role. Mothers, regardless of household type, displayed more overt affection. But parents in two-paycheck families were more likely to express overt affection than were single mothers, single fathers, and married fathers in one-paycheck families. In these cases, both single fathers and single mothers reported less overt affection than married mothers in two-paycheck families.

Risman (1987) concludes that the activities of parenting have an important effect on the behavior and personalities of people who do that parenting. Fathers who become the primary parents learn to be capable of caring for their children, and they begin to behave similar to women parents; caring fathers become more feminine. Risman argues that changes in gender, especially in the ways men parent, cannot begin with ideas but with action that engages men in the activities of primary caregivers.

MEN BALANCING WORK AND FAMILY. The "mommy wars" may be slowly eroding the ideas that tie women to motherhood and simultaneously tie men to breadwinning and inhibit men's connections to their children. Ideas about fathers continue to range from seeing fathers as patriarch, moral teacher, and economic provider to gender role model. But our view of fathers increasingly includes the factor of viewing fathers as nurturing parents. Jessie Bernard (1981) was the first to reflect on the rise and fall of the father in the **role of the "good provider"** when she chronicled the association of men with the roles of "head of household" and "provider" and described the psychological consequences for men of such gender-limited roles. She also discussed the transition taking place in our ideas about fathers as centered on activities outside the home to those that include a warm, nurturing component and a shared role for men in family life and work. Today Americans expect fathers to be providers *and* to be involved with their children (LaRossa 2000; Goldberg, Tan, and Thorsen 2009). As the culture of fatherhood (beliefs about what men should be doing with their children) changed significantly in the last few decades, a new style of fatherhood emerged: "A good father is an active participant in the details of day-to-day child care. He involves himself in a more expressive and intimate way with his children, and he plays a larger part in the socialization process that his male forebears had long since abandoned to their wives" (Rotundo 1985, 9). This model is more likely to be talked about than to show up in men's behavior. Today, men express a desire to spend more time with their children, but their behavior often has not kept pace with their aspirations (Townsend 2002). Nevertheless, men from many walks of life are attempting to renegotiate the terrain of work, family, and gender (Aulette 2007).

When Judith Gerson (1993) interviewed men about this new no-man's land, she found that they fell into three categories. One group represented a "**stalled revolution**" seeking to maintain their breadwinning role. The men in this group prioritized their responsibility to provide for their family. They also expected to have their economic contribution translate into authority in their homes. One man explained:

> There has to be a leader. And the responsibility of the leader is to be fair, not just to boss people, but to make decisions, right or wrong. I provide the money, so it's a success. There has to be a system, and that's ours. . . . My wife loves her lifestyle; she's got it made. She drives a new car, has great clothes, her friends, no responsibilities. What the hell does she need a job for? She's got her freedom. What more could you want? (Gerson 1993, 86)

Another group of men, "the **rebels**," chose another path, autonomy over parenthood. They, too, prioritized breadwinning but felt they needed to separate themselves from family rather than to translate their workplace activities into relationships of authority with a wife and children. Some of these men had children but had become estranged. Others had chosen not to have children. One man in this group said, "Nobody has a hold on me. I do as I wish, and if tomorrow I don't want to, I don't have to. It's very important that I never feel trapped, locked in. It leads me away from feeling angry, mad, hostile, all those sorts of things" (Gerson 1993, 109).

The third group tried to integrate paid work and family, especially raising children, and became "**involved fathers**." One man in this group described his experience:

> I thought I was going to be a wild and crazy guy for the rest of my life. I never thought about getting married. But the real me is what's been happening from being married on, not beforehand. Being responsible, getting married, having a child, bringing up a family, becoming responsible for our daughter. This is the real me. (Gerson 1993, 142)

All three of these paths are difficult. Men are faced with the decision of either protecting the privilege of not having to come home to do housework or child care, or accepting arrangements that ease their economic burden or emotional isolation. Men who choose the breadwinner or autonomy route resist family involvement and domestic participation to protect their benefits. However, they also face problems of having to work long hours in the paid labor force to single-handedly support their families, dealing with wives who may not approve of their choices, or being cut off from close relationships altogether (Gerson 1993).

Involved fathers face difficulties, too. First they face the predicament of both spending time making money and spending time with their children. Second, if they want to develop in their careers, they may be asked to travel or to take classes after work, resulting in additional time crunches. Third, even if they are able to balance work and family, they still face the problem of trade-offs of freedom or commitment and their ability to find time for their personal interests in leisure activities, community involvement, or just sleeping late once in a while (Gerson 1993).

Although Gerson found that few men had fully adopted complete equality with their wives, many men were moving in this direction. She cites a *Time* magazine survey that found that more than half (56 percent) of a random sample of men said they would give up one-fourth of their salary for more personal and family time. In the same survey, nearly half (45 percent) said "they would probably refuse a promotion that involved sacrificing hours with their family" (Gerson 1993, 254). More recently, another survey found that these kinds of changes are continuing to develop. Nearly three-fourths (70 percent) of the fathers in their study said they would consider being stay-at-home dads if money was not an issue, and a similar proportion (71 percent) had taken paternity leave when it was offered by their employers (Armour 2007).

THE FATHERHOOD RESPONSIBILITY MOVEMENT. Why is it so difficult to change ideas and practices of fathering? Two competing models for understanding and addressing this issue illustrate Robert Connell's (1995) idea of "**masculinity politics**" (Gavanas 2002). Connell writes that masculinity politics consists of mobilization and struggles where the meaning of masculinity and men's position in gender relations is at issue.

Fatherhood is currently one of the battlegrounds for masculinity politics with two competing wings: the pro-marriage group and the fragile-families group. Both of these positions are part of the **fatherhood responsibility movement**. Both are concerned about what they see as the exclusion of men from the lives of their children. They both cite the growing numbers of children born to single mothers, the high rate of divorce, the large proportion of children awarded to the custody of their mothers, and the lesser role of many men in their children's lives as some of modern life's greatest social evils. Both groups are concerned about children, believe that fathers are essential to children's well-being, and maintain that "the family" is a foundation of society (Gavanas 2002).

The two wings, however, have very different ways of understanding what the roots of the problem are and what should be done to address it. The pro-marriage group is represented by organizations such as the **National Fatherhood Initiative**. This group stresses the importance of gender differences and what they see as the natural difference between fathers and mothers. For them, marriage cements these two human types, men and women, together. They argue, for example, that only men can provide masculine models of risk taking, independence, limit testing, self-regulation, hard but fair discipline, and self-sacrificing protection. Children, therefore, must be raised in heterosexual marriages to satisfy their need for both a mother and a father. They also advocate government intervention to ensure that nuclear families prevail and to promote the proper family values to maintain them (Gavanas 2002). As we saw earlier in this chapter, this group has had some success changing social policy, especially regarding welfare laws, in ways that reflect their promotion of heterosexual families as a key factor in improving fatherhood.

The second faction, the fragile-families group, is represented by organizations such as Partners for Fragile Families. This group emphasizes the similarities between women and men and the need for fathers and mothers to work as a team to raise children. Although this group is not anti-marriage, they also do not believe that marriage is essential to provide strong, effective platforms for raising children. Most important, they do not believe that marriage can guarantee that children will be properly cared for. Their focus is on economic opportunities, especially for fathers (Gavanas 2002).

Fragile-families advocates argue that fathers must have jobs with decent wages and benefits to fulfill their roles as good fathers and good providers. They believe that women and men need to share in this task of breadwinner, but that low-income men, especially low-income men of color, often have not had a chance to play this role because of high unemployment and declining wages. One fragile-families advocate explains, "The stereotypical definition of man in this society is to be able to care for his family, to be a provider. And when a man can't be a provider, he does not engage in that process as a full player" (Gavanas 2002, 225). Fragile-family advocates look to the government to develop job training, job opportunities, and protection of wages and benefits as the solution to the crisis in fatherhood.

Biology and Parenting

"A woman lawyer is exactly the same as a man lawyer. A woman cop is just the same as a man cop. A pregnant woman is just the same as . . . " (Rothman 1989, 248). The discussion so far has emphasized the social character of parenting and the ways the social construction of gender intersects with our ideas, experience, and behavior regarding parenting. Mothers and fathers are the gendered models of parents, and this review of the literature has pointed out how mothering and fathering are different. The underlying argument, however, is that mothers and fathers are not natural categories. Fathers can learn to become better "mothers." Parenting, however, usually also includes a biological component. In nearly every human activity, women and men are the same, or the differences between one woman and another woman are as great as or greater than they are between a woman and a man. Pregnancy and childbirth, however, make some females different from all males. Pregnancy and childbirth also have an especially important connection to parenting.

Both females and males contribute equal amounts of genetic material to a fetus, but it is only the female's body that contributes nine months of gestation and the labor of giving birth. Rothman (1989) argues that this difference is important and should play a role in legal battles, like that in the case of **Baby M**.

Bill Stern wanted a child who came from his sperm, but his wife, Betsy, had multiple sclerosis and had been told that bearing a child might worsen her condition. The Sterns decided to hire Mary Beth Whitehead as a surrogate mother to carry Bill's child. For a fee, Whitehead allowed herself to be inseminated with Stern's sperm and agreed to give the baby to the Sterns. Whitehead, however, changed her mind after the child was born and hid herself and the baby for four months while the courts deliberated the case.

The court said that the contract between the Sterns and Whitehead was not binding. However, because the child was genetically related to Bill Stern, he had the right to sue for custody. According to the court, he and Whitehead were equally parents. The case was then decided on the basis of who would be a better parent: Stern, a wealthy professional, or Whitehead, a working-class wife and mother. In the proceedings, evidence was presented that Whitehead had been a go-go dancer, had dyed her hair, and had trouble with her husband (Rothman 1989, 24). The court decided in Stern's favor.

According to Rothman (1989), the mother's link to the child was incorrectly reduced to that of the father, thereby making them equal parents. Bill Stern and Mary Beth Whitehead had equal genetic links to Baby M. The baby was a product of equal parts of Stern's and Whitehead's genes. Rothman argues that the fact that Whitehead had the additional connection to the child of being a pregnant and birthing mother, however, should not have been dismissed as irrelevant. The court's decision was based on the assumption that men and women are equal. Even though males and females are not equal in their contribution to reproduction, the factors that make them unequal were ignored. The larger contribution (pregnancy and delivery) made by the mother was made invisible. The one way they are equal—their genetic contribution—was the only criterion acknowledged.

Rothman (1989) demands that a new framework be developed that can capture the need for women to be treated as equal to men while not dismissing the unique character of the relationship between biological mothers and their children. She proposes a policy in which the contribution biological mothers make in pregnancy and childbirth and the contribution fathers, mothers, and others make in caring for children after they are born is factored into equations leading to decisions about questions like custody. Specifically, Rothman suggests that policy should be based on the following rules:

1. Infants belong to their mothers at birth because of the unique nurturant relationship that has existed between them up to that moment; genetic ties will not give parental rights.
2. Adoption can only occur after birth, and the birth mother has six weeks to change her mind.
3. All custody cases after six months will be determined by the amount of care provided by the adult with joint custody if this role is fully shared.
4. There is no such thing as surrogacy under this system. Every woman who bears a child is the mother of the child she bears, with full parental rights regardless of the source of the egg or the sperm (Rothman 1989, 254–60).

Another Kind of Family Caregiving: Elder Care

Taking care of children is only one important place where gender shows up in caregiving in families. Care work refers to the unpaid job of taking care of parents, grandchildren, spouses, and other family members, as well as neighbors and other members of the community. Care work includes practical help like mowing the lawn and fixing meals as well as providing emotional support. "Caring" means that the work is both providing for some need of another and feeling affection and responsibility for the person being provided with the care (Calasanti and Slevin 2001). Increasingly, care for older family members, elder care, is a concern in American families.

Most care for older people with disabling and chronic conditions is provided by family members and is called "informal care." About 65 percent of informal care is done exclusively by family and friends. Another 30 percent of care is done by family and friends with some paid help. Only 5 percent of care is provided by paid help alone (Blair and Northway 2001).

Care for a broader group of people than immediate family is more common among African Americans than among whites or Hispanics in the United States (Shirey and Summer 2000). In African American families, grandchildren provide 10 percent of the care for older people (Shirey and Summer 2000). First Nations people are also engaged in broad networks of community members, kin, and extended family in the care of the elderly in First Nations communities (John 1999).

Several changes have occurred in recent decades, which have caused elder care to take a more prominent role in our lives (Singleton 1998):

- Kin networks are becoming more top heavy, with more older family members than younger. For the first time in history, the average married couple has more parents than children.
- Longer life expectancy and lower birth rates are causing shifts to occur in time spent in various family roles. Middle-generation people in the future will spend more years with parents over sixty-five than with children under the age of eighteen.
- Declining birthrates also mean fewer siblings. More people are only children or have only one or two siblings with whom to share the care of their elderly parents.
- Childbearing at later ages means that women are more likely to be simultaneously caring for young children and aging parents.
- High divorce rates eliminate care for many elderly people by their spouses, shifting the responsibility to children of those older people.
- Lack of attention by the government to the growing needs of families and reduced funding for existing social welfare programs is resulting in insufficient support for care activities (A. Walker 1996).

All these changes mean more hours spent in caregiving. Caregivers average twenty hours per week devoted to elder care, and when there is a health or personal crisis they spend even more time. Caregivers often report conflict with their caregiving and their work schedules. Many must take time off work, rearrange their work schedules, and take unpaid leave. Furthermore, at least some working people must keep their caregiving activities a "secret." University faculty, especially women, with family responsibilities, for example, hide their caregiving responsibility to prevent biased, negative career implications. They do not request flex time for fear it will look bad, and they make excuses for absences or missed meetings rather than admitting caregiver responsibilities (Drago and Colbeck 2006).

In addition to the long hours, the tasks themselves are not easy. Care work includes bathing, dressing, feeding, toileting, providing transportation, helping with medication, and doing household tasks. In many sick people's homes, nonprofessional women also use high-tech equipment to deliver treatments for acute and chronic conditions and to treat systemic infection and cancer. They supervise exercise, give mechanical relief to patients with breathing disorders, feed by tubes those unable to take food orally or digest normally, give intramuscular injections and more tricky intravenous injections, and monitor patients after antibiotic and chemotherapy treatments (Glazer 1990). This kind of difficult work may be especially present in care for racial ethnic groups such as Latinos, who have higher health risks for certain diseases such as diabetes that require special kinds of care and cause people to develop disabilities at higher rates earlier in life (Aranda and Knight 1997).

Caregiving, like parenting, is marked by gender differences. Nearly all the work that is done for ill or dependent elderly people in households is done by women. Only among Asian Americans do we find men and women providing care at about the same rate (National Alliance for Caregiving and AARP 1997). According to the U.S. Bureau of the Census, 75 percent of the seven million Americans who provide informal unpaid care are women. Women devote about thirty-five years of their lives to caring for children, grandchildren, and parents (Adams, Nawrocki, and Coleman 1999). People who provide care for these groups simultaneously are called the "**sandwich generation**" because they are sandwiched between caring for older parents and raising their children (Blair and Northway 2001).

Many caregivers, however, are women who are older themselves. The average age of a care worker is forty-six, but 12 percent are over sixty-five, and those in this older category provide the most care for those who are most in need (Calasanti and Slevin 2001). For example, 60 percent of those who care for older people are wives caring for older disabled husbands (Cantor 1994).

A spouse is the most likely person to provide care for a husband or wife. Because men typically marry women who are younger than they are, and because women on average live longer than men do, women are more likely to be giving care than receiving care. When a husband or wife is not available for taking care of a person, however, gender shows up in another form. Adult daughters are next in line, and then daughters-in-law and sisters, followed by sons or brothers (Calasanti and Slevin 2001).

Abel (1986) argues that women take on this responsibility for a number of reasons. First, external sources push them into caring for their relatives. These include a dominant ideology that says that women are natural caregivers, and lower pay for women so that their economic contributions from paid work are more disposable. In addition, women caregivers themselves believe that the sacrifices they make in caring for their parents are necessary and honorable (Aronson 1992).

The organization of society, especially of the government, however, also plays a role in answering the question of why women do so much care work. One woman care worker summed it up: "Who else is going to do it?" (Aronson 1992). The government assumes that individual families, and particularly women in individual families, will take care of the work. Consequently, the government makes little effort to help bring down the costs of providing paid care workers or providing care for those who need it (Calasanti and Slevin 2001). In fact, changes in health care have increased the amount of unpaid care work needed when patients are sent home early from hospitals (Glazer 1990). Today, unpaid care work would cost about $196 billion if caregivers were paid. This is much more than the present bill of $32 billion for home health care and $83 billion for nursing-home care (Shirey and Summer 2000). The work is essential, but it is not publicly valued. Like housework, as described in chapter 8, care work is invisible and highly gendered. It is women's work.

GENDERED STYLES OF CARE WORK. Despite the fact that care work is identified with femininity and done mostly by women, many men participate as well. How do women and men approach the work differently, and what consequences do their activities have for the caregiver's well-being? When women and men care workers are asked about their experience, women are more likely than men to report anxiety, depression, physical strain, health problems, and lower life satisfaction (Shirey and Summer 2000).

Three explanations have been given for this discrepancy in the health effects on women and men caregivers. First, men may have a different style and approach to caregiving. Men's style of caregiving has been called more managerial because they separate caring for and caring about. They are able to separate themselves emotionally from the work, allowing them to provide care but also take time off and maintain outside interests. Women caring for demented partners, in contrast, grieve the lost relationship between themselves and their husbands. They do not seem to be comforted by their caring activities, as men are. The difference is not in the care they provide, but rather in the feelings they have about their caring work (Rose and Bruce 1995).

TABLE 7-2 Percentage of Children in the United States Who Live in a Household with a Grandparent Who Is Head of Household by Race/Ethnicity, 2012

Race/Ethnicity	% Living with Grandparent(s) Who Is Head of Household
White	5%
Black	10%
Asian	4%
Hispanic	7%

Source: U.S. Bureau of the Census (2012b).

Second, men elicit more recognition for the care work they do because it is more "unusual." Family and friends see a man caring for his wife or parents as honorable because he is not only providing care, he is also stepping outside expectations about men and caregiving.

Third, men seem to have larger support networks. For example, sons giving care get more help from their spouses than daughters do. In addition, men, who are often financially better-off, are more able to purchase support (Calasanti and Slevin 2001).

GRANDPARENTS AND CARE WORK. Older people do not just receive care, they often provide care. Of all children in the United States, 5.5 percent (four million households) live in households maintained by a grandparent, and these numbers are rapidly growing (Park 2005; U.S. Bureau of the Census 2012b). Table 7-2 shows the distribution of grandparent-headed households by race/ethnicity.

The numbers show us that the race ethnicity of the different types of households has a lot to do with whether children wind up living with their grandparents. The table doesn't tell us whether the children are living with grandmothers or grandfathers or both, but other research reports that grandparents who are heads of households and raising grandchildren are likely to be women and poor (Bryson and Casper 1999). Grandfathers, however, also play an important role in their grandchildren's lives. Little research has been done on the experience of grandfathers in households raising grandchildren. One qualitative study (Bullock 2005) found that grandfathers faced many difficulties in trying to care for their grandchildren. Although they are not as likely to be as poor as grandmothers are, many did have financial difficulties. Most important, though, the men were not prepared to take care of the children and, therefore, faced other problems. Some of the men spoke of feeling that the task of parenting was one about which they had little choice. One man said, "I don't feel I'm ready to take care of a small child this late in life, but we didn't have any choice. My wife said, we [were] all the child had left. What in the world would have happened to the child if we didn't do it?" (Bullock 2005, 4).

The grandfathers also spoke about feeling that they had not learned the skills of child care and did not feel capable of many of the tasks. One man explained:

I would want to do more as a parent, but I never had to cook, clean, and never had to pick up after the children. So, now I can't just go in the kitchen and make a meal if she is hungry. I don't wash clothes either. Sometimes, I feel like helping more, but I don't really know what to do. Nobody is trying to help me figure how I could do this better. I mean the grandparenting. (Bullock 2005, 5)

The gender histories of the men meant they had divided labor in their families in ways that did not prepare them for caregiving as grandparents.

Care work is highly stratified by gender across age groups. Care work is also stratified by social class and nationality. One option wealthier families from wealthier nations have chosen to help alleviate the care gap is to hire care workers from the global South. However, this choice is not without problems, especially for the women who work as nannies and domestic employees in the United States and Europe, as we saw in the opening scenario.

BALANCING WORK AND FAMILY

What do young men and women want today? Research on young Americans and Europeans finds that they are keenly aware of the obstacles to integrating work and family life in an egalitarian way but that men and women alike wish to forge a lifelong partnership that combines committed work with devoted parenting (Drexler 2010). Amy describes her ideal work–family situation: "I want a 50–50 relationship, where we both have the potential of doing everything—both of us working and dealing with kids. With regard to career, if neither has flexibility, then one of us will have to sacrifice for one period, and the other for another." Michael shares his view, saying:

I don't want the '50s type of marriage, where I come home and she's cooking. She doesn't have to cook; I like to cook. I want her to have a career of her own. I want to be able to set my goals, and she can do what she wants, too, because we both have this economic base and the attitude to do it. That's what marriage is about. (Gerson 2007, 3)

As the men and women in the interviews describe their ideal work–family arrangements, they also are aware that their aspirations might quickly run into rigid, time-demanding jobs and a dearth of child-care or family-leave options. In response, they have developed fallback strategies as insurance in the all-too-likely event that their egalitarian ideals prove out of reach (Gerson 2007).

The second-best strategies are not only different for women and men; they are at odds with each other. Women say that if they cannot find a supportive, egalitarian partnership, they prefer individual autonomy over becoming dependent on a husband in a traditional marriage. Most men, in contrast, say that if they cannot have an equal balance between work and parenting, they will fall back on a neotraditional arrangement that allows them to get married and have children and to put their own work first, relying on their partner to take care of their family life (Gerson 2007).

Rachel illustrates women's backup plan with her fallback strategy: "I'm not afraid of being alone, but I am afraid of being with somebody who's a jerk. I want to be under the right circumstances, with the right person. . . . I can spend the rest of my life on my own, as long as I have my sisters and my friends, I'm OK" (Gerson 2007, 5–6).

Josh, like many of the men, has a different backup plan. He says that if he and his partner are unable to share work and family, he will choose to divide it up along gendered lines, with his wife caring for the children while he provides financially for them. He says:

> All things being equal, it [caretaking] should be shared. It may sound sexist, but if somebody's going to be the breadwinner, it's going to be me. First of all, I make a better salary, and I feel the need to work, and I just think the child really needs the mother more than the father at a young age. (Gerson 2007, 6)

Josh's **plan B** may reveal gender ideas in the United States that are lagging behind other nations. A poll was conducted in several nations in 1983 or 1992 and then again in 2002 asking people if they agreed with the statement "The father of the family must be the master in his own home." In Canada 42 percent agreed with the statement in 1983, but by 2002 only 17 percent did. The numbers also dropped dramatically in Europe. In the United States, however, the numbers rose from 42 percent in 1992 to 48 percent in 2002 (Pearson 2002).

TABLE 7-3 Parental Leave Policies Around the World

Country	Type and Duration of Leave	% Wage Replaced
Afghanistan**	3 months maternity	100%
Australia*	2 years parental	18 weeks paid
Austria*	16 weeks parental +30 months	100% Child care allowance
Belgium*	15 weeks maternity +3 months parental	75%–82% Flat rate
Cameroon**	14 weeks maternity	100%
Canada*	17 weeks maternity 35 weeks paternal +35 weeks for each parent	55% for 17 weeks Wages vary by province 55%
China**	3 months maternity	100%
Chile**	18 weeks maternity	100%
Czech*	28 weeks maternity +3 years parental leave	60% Unpaid
Denmark*	52 weeks maternity +2 weeks paternity +10 weeks parental +52 weeks for child up to 8	100% 100% 60% 60%
Finland*	18 weeks maternity +18 days paternity +26 weeks paternal	70% Flat rate Flat rate
France*	16 weeks maternity	100%

TABLE 7-3 Parental Leave Policies Around the World

Country	Type and Duration of Leave	% Wage Replaced
Germany*	14 weeks maternity +2 years parental +1 year parental	100% Flat rate Unpaid
India**	12 weeks maternity	100
Italy*	5 months maternity +10 months parental	80% 30%
Japan*	14 weeks maternity	67%
Mexico**	12 weeks maternity	100%
Norway*	36 to 46 weeks parental	100% for 36 weeks 80% for 46 weeks
Pakistan**	12 weeks maternity	100%
Poland*	20 weeks maternity	100%
Russia**	28 weeks maternity +1 year	100% Flat rate (minimum wage)
South Africa**	16 weeks maternity	up to 60%
Turkey	16 weeks maternity	66.67%
United Kingdom*	52weeks maternity	90%
United States*	12 weeks parental	Unpaid

Sources: *Huffington Post (2012); **ILO (2010).

International Comparisons of Family Support Programs

Finding solutions to the problem of balancing work and family would help both women and men in families. It would also reduce the gender gap between women and men. Alan Walker (1996) argues that teaching caregivers to better cope with the stresses they face is important but can only partly solve the problems of balancing work and family. More important, he argues, we need to create public solutions by altering social institutions.

This solution sounds monumental and even utopian; but in some nations, just these kinds of structural reforms have been implemented. For example, the work week in the Netherlands was reduced to thirty-eight hours in the 1980s and to thirty-six hours in some industries like health care in the 1990s. All full-time workers in Germany and Sweden (as well as some other nations) receive five to six weeks of paid vacation every year. Paid maternity leaves of at least fourteen weeks are available to all women in the **European Union**. Some countries, like Sweden, provide employed parents an additional paid leave for sixty days to care for a sick child or other close relative (Applebaum, Bailey, Berg, and Kalleberg 2002).

Table 7-3 shows the **parental leave** policies of several nations. (Go to the website listed in the source for a complete list.) Out of 173 countries studied, 168 offer guaranteed leave with income to women in connection with childbirth; ninety-eight of these countries offer four-teen or more weeks of paid leave. The numbers illustrate the kinds of policies that are characteristic of the European Union. For example, Germany and France are the leaders in providing support for family care. The table also shows that some nations that are rela-tively poor, such as Mexico, Cameroon, and Pakistan, provide paid leave for mothers, while wealthy nations such as the United States provide no paid leave. Although in a number of countries many women work in the informal sector where these government guarantees do not always apply, the fact remains that the United States guarantees no paid leave for moth-ers in any segment of the workforce. This leaves the United States, the wealthiest nation in the world, in the company of only four other nations: Lesotho, Liberia, Papua New Guinea, and Swaziland (Heymann, Earle, and Hayes 2007).

Finally Table 7-3 indicates that many nations distinguish among maternity leave, pater-nity leave, and parental leave. Sixty-five countries ensure that fathers have a right to paid parental leave; thirty-one of these countries offer fourteen or more weeks of paid leave. Once again, the United States fails fathers, guaranteeing men neither paid paternity nor paid pa-rental leave (Coltrane 2007). Neglecting fathers has detrimental effects on men who would like to spend more time with their children. It also hurts women by defining them as solely responsible for taking time away from paid work for family care. In addition, it is bad for children because it reduces the time adults are available to care for them.

Family leave policy can be divided into four types (Henderson and Jeydal 2010). The United States is an example of the first type: pro-family and **noninterventionist**. The American government claims to be pro-family, but it also argues that support for families should come from the private sector rather than from government programs. Political leaders encourage private employers to provide their employees with paid family leave or on-site day care, but they do not wish to expand government involvement with policies, funding, and infrastructure for these services.

Germany has represented a second type: the traditional breadwinner model. The German government has promoted two-parent, one-earner families. Programs are gener-ous, but they encourage women to stay home as caregivers while men are employed as wage earners. This model has been changing in the past few years as Germany has sought to enable men to spend more time at home with their children, which allows women more time in the paid workforce.

France is a third type: pro-family and pro-natalist. France is among the most generous nations in the world in its family policies. Women and men have access to paid parental leave. In addition, a number of policies are explicitly designed to promote a higher birth rate, such as long paid maternity leaves, cash benefits for births of children, pension credits for women who have three or more children, and child-care tax benefits (Henderson and Jeydal 2010).

Sweden represents the fourth type, which is an egalitarian model. Sweden has con-sciously tried to encourage families to divide family care in a more gender-equitable manner. The government provides all Swedish families with thirteen months of paid pa-rental leave. Only one parent can take the time off at one time. Two of the months are re-served for fathers only. Other nations, including Norway, Iceland, Denmark, and Germany also reserve a portion of parental care for fathers only (Fox, Pascall, and Warren 2009). Parents in Sweden can take the time off by the hour rather than by the day, and the time may be taken until the child turns eight (Bennhold 2010). For example, a parent can use the time to reduce their work day by working six hours a day and then taking the other two hours as paid leave (Applebaum et al. 2002).

In addition to these alterations of the social institution of government, individual businesses have also changed in Sweden. The pay that parents receive while caring for children amounts to 80 percent of their regular pay, up to a cap of about $54,000 in 2007 (Haas and Hwang 2009). Because men make more money on average in Sweden (as they do all over the world), it is often more advantageous to have the mother rather than the father stay home. However, some companies now add to the government's check to equal 80 percent of all workers' pay, which erases this disadvantage and allows men to take parental leave (Applebaum et al. 2002). In addition, a number of companies in Sweden have implemented policies to assure employees that their jobs and promotions will not be jeopardized if they use the time the government has allotted to them for child care (Haas and Hwang 2009).

DIVORCE

Divorce laws vary from one nation to another and even within nations, such as the United States, where divorce laws are different in every state. Some forms dominate, however. This section reviews a few of the most common kinds of divorce laws: **no-fault** in the United States, no-fault in South Africa, **repudiation** laws in conservative Muslim nations, and reformed repudiation laws in more liberal Muslim nations such as Tanzania. All of these variations both reflect and shape gender arrangements.

Divorce is a common experience in the United States today. From the late 1950s to the early 1980s, the divorce rate rose significantly and then fell a little and leveled off. Although the rate has been flat for more than two decades now, it remains high; and it is estimated that about half of the most recent marriages will end in divorce (Cherlin 1992). Divorce is a key issue in the expression and reproduction of gender in family life. Divorce is experienced differently by women and men, and divorce causes further distinctions between women and men, particularly in terms of finances.

One way men and women experience divorce differently is that women are two to three times more likely to initiate divorce. Between two-thirds and three-quarters of divorces are initiated by wives.

A second way women and men experience divorce differently is in regard to social stigmatization. Although both women and men are still stigmatized for divorcing, the reasons for which they are stigmatized are different. Divorce has become more common, and polls show that people are more tolerant of divorce and divorced people than they were years ago. For example, in the 1960s, the majority of Americans believed that people with children should stay together rather than divorce "for the sake of the children." By the 1990s, only 20 percent still supported this belief (Kosmin and Lachman, 1993), but stigmatizing still exists. The divorced are no longer thought to be sinners or criminals. Divorce, however, continues to set people apart and can represent a mark against them.

Whether those who divorce are stigmatized depends on the way people perceive the specific conditions of the divorce, and these specific conditions vary by gender. Men who have affairs before the divorce are stigmatized as "cavalier homewreckers" (Gerstel 1987, 186).

For women, the key question is whether they have young children. Women with young children are "bad divorcees" when they do not sacrifice their own needs and feelings to try to keep the marriage together.

A third way divorce is experienced differently by men and women is in regard to resulting finances. Women face a 30 percent decline in their incomes after a divorce, whereas men on average see a 15 percent increase (Peterson 1996). Despite the economic difficulties, many women say they still feel more satisfied with their financial situation after the divorce because they feel more in charge, able to make their own decisions, and relieved that they do not have to account to their husbands for their choices (Ahrons 1994). Nevertheless, the decline is significant and it has important consequences for many divorced women. Thirty-nine percent of single women with children live below the poverty level.

The picture for men and divorce is not quite as clear-cut (P. McManus and DiPrete 2001). Some researchers have found that men generally seem to see their economic situation improve after divorce (Smock 1994; Peterson 1996; Bianchi, Subaiya, and Kahn 1999). Some argue that although many men benefit, most men do not. For example, African American men do not benefit as much as white men. Men who lived in households where their wives contributed more to the household income or men who retain custody of their children after the divorce often see declines in their economic situation. Men as a group, however, never see their finances decline as sharply as women do. Divorced women are likely to be poorer than they were when they were married, and they are likely to be poorer than their ex-husbands.

The Gendered Economics of Divorce

What underlies the different economic effect of divorce on women and men? Divorce law in itself in the United States is gender neutral. The laws tell the courts to treat women and men the same. Divorce, however, takes place in a gendered society. Marriage is gendered, divorce court decisions are gendered, and especially the labor market is gendered.

In many households, marriage has a different effect on women's and men's earning capacity. One of the most important investments people make is in their careers and in their ability to earn money. Married couples tend to make these decisions in a way that diminishes wives' earning capacity and enhances husbands' earning capacity (Buehler 1995; Maume 2006).

For example, a couple may decide that one spouse will work while the other obtains an education. Couples may spend money on a special license or membership in a professional organization. They may choose to relocate for one of them to accept a better job or choose to stay in an area so that one person can build seniority, a professional practice, or a pension. If these kinds of decisions are made to improve the earning ability of one partner, they enhance the economic standing of the whole household as long as the wife and husband stay together. After a divorce, however, this investment is usually not considered part of the property to be divided equally, but rather the property of the individual to take with him or her from the marriage. These kinds of decisions are frequently made in ways that favor the husband—partly, at least, because the "payoff" for the investment in a man is greater than it is for a woman. Education, on average, helps everyone raise his or her wages, but men still make more money than women at all education levels. Consequently, the wisest economic decision for a couple is to get the husband educated and into the labor market as quickly as possible and then see to the woman's education.

This strategy, however, does not work well for the woman if the couple parts ways. If wives invest less in their earning capacity, they may leave a marriage with less ability to support themselves. Some wives, of course, do not allow marriage to stand in the way of gaining an education or building a career. But even these wives leave marriage at a disadvantage compared to their husbands, because education and labor-market participation do not necessarily result in equal pay for women.

Table 6-4 in chapter 6 reveals that women with various amounts of education earn less than men at those same levels. In fact, the table shows that women with a college degree earn only a little more than men with a high school diploma. Pay scales vary by race ethnicity and education, but in all comparisons, women earn less than men do. Although divorce laws are gender neutral, gender inequality in the labor market means that women who divorce and stop pooling their income with a husband receive less than half of the household's income.

Alimony is money the court requires one spouse to pay to support another after a divorce. Historically, alimony was a payment a husband was required to make when separating from or divorcing a wife. Theoretically, alimony was a way to overcome the inequity between women and men in the labor market. Divorced women were assumed to be unable to earn as much money as their husbands, and alimony was a method of closing the gap between their incomes. In reality, however, alimony was always rare and the payments were small.

Alimony is now called "spousal support." Many people still believe that most women receive spousal support when they divorce. As in the past, however, only about 14 percent are awarded this kind of support in the United States today (Stetson 1997). Black women are even less likely to receive spousal support than are white women (Shelton and Deen 2001).

Another feature of the gendered context in which divorce occurs is the division of property in the divorce proceedings. The gender neutrality of the divorce laws requires that property be divided equally between the two spouses. What is defined as property, however, may not include some of the most important assets a couple owns. For example, pensions and education are not usually considered assets to be divided, and they go with the individual who has been granted the degree or obtained the pension through his or her work.

Probably the most significant factor in the division of households and property in divorces is the question of child custody. Mothers are much more likely to retain custody of minor children. The property is divided down the middle, but it is awarded to two different-size groups. One half goes to the husband, and the other half goes to the wife and children.

Child support was designed to help even out financial responsibility between the parents, but the awards are not sufficient and support often goes unpaid. Fifty-one percent of divorced custodial parents were awarded child support in 2010. Of that 51 percent, 29 percent had received none of the award, and another 40 percent had received only partial payment (U.S. Bureau of the Census 2012d; Grall 2011,). Noncustodial mothers are equally bad about keeping up with child support when fathers have custody of children. Since most children (82 percent) are placed in the custody of their mothers after divorce, however, nonpayment of child support is primarily a problem for divorced mothers (Grall 2011).

The mean amount received per year is $5,450 for custodial mothers and $3,500 for custodial fathers (U.S. Bureau of the Census 2012d). This amounts to less than half the amount required for child-care costs alone per year. Children, of course, also entail many other expenses besides child care: food, clothing, health care, education, and recreational expenses (Kurz 1995). In addition, child support usually ends at eighteen, although in many families, children are far from financially independent at that age.

Challenges of Divorce for Men

When parents divorce in the United States, nearly all children (82 percent) are placed in the custody of their mothers. We have seen how that creates economic difficulties for many women. However, men who are not custodial parents also face problems when they divorce. Divorce often elicits or exacerbates anger with their ex-wives, but many men want to maintain relationships with their children despite the tensions with their former spouse. Terry Arendell (1995) found that men had three ways of trying to cope with the situation.

One group she called "**traditionalists.**" They had limited contact with their wives and continued to define them as the enemy. These men were especially distressed about their loss of control over their wives and children that resulted from the divorce. Their main way of responding was to disengage, avoiding contact or responsibility for their ex-wives or their children. One traditionalist father explained how he had come to this response:

> I finally decided that I was putting too much into this divorce war with my ex-wife. We've played this game for over four years. So I pulled out. . . . She didn't know when to quit. Someday if my son wants to get to know me he can find me. My daughter, she could care less. She's been totally brainwashed by [the former wife]. (Arendell 1995, 145)

Neotraditionalists, the second type, had some of the same animosity toward their wives but wanted to maintain contact with their children and felt that collaboration with their ex was possible. They wanted to stay close to their children while avoiding their wives. They were especially concerned about being the masculine role model for their children and about sustaining a meaningful relationship with their children, rather than being just a weekend visitor:

> She [the former wife] complains about my teaching them to shoot and hunt; she says it's dangerous and unnecessary. "Too macho," she says. But what's really bugging her is that she can't stand it that I have something to offer them that she can't. They're boys. I understand that. She doesn't. They need this sort of input from me. She can't give them that. (Arendell 1995, 173)

Innovators, the third type, focused on their own parental responsibility for their children rather than their rights as fathers. They did not find it easy to develop cooperation with their wives, but they were willing to be very flexible, rearranging schedules and finding options to create parenting partnerships with their ex-wives. They were more able to set aside their anger at their wives and to dismiss conventional views of masculinity than the other two types of divorced fathers. An "innovative" father said:

> Our relationship is amicable, if that's the proper word. I would describe it that way, an amicable relationship. I don't particularly go out of my way to talk to her. I have my moments and sometimes I really want to talk to her. Other times I don't want to talk to her at all and I just leave. I don't want to be there. We're both concerned about the children. We went together to see the principal. We also went to see the school counselor. Or if my son has a soccer game, we'll be together. (Arendell 1995, 190)

Variation in Divorce Laws in Different Nations

SOUTH AFRICAN DIVORCE LAWS. In 1994 South Africa successfully toppled apartheid government and created a new constitution. A central feature of the constitution, laws, and policies of the new government was the commitment to equality, including gender equity. Changes in the divorce laws reflect this commitment. South African divorce laws are similar to the American version of no-fault. Either party (and since South Africa allows gay marriage, the parties might be a man and a woman, both women, or both men) can file for a divorce. The reasons given for divorce can be traditional ones of fault divorce, such as abuse or abandonment, but they can also include "no-fault" or irreconcilable differences.

South African law, however, differs in some important ways from the American model. Although the South African law, like the U.S. law, is gender blind, it does not treat the two spouses as necessarily equal. Divorce is granted in a gender-blind manner, but property division is done with an eye to acknowledging inequality and coming up with a solution that is fair but not necessarily equal. For example, if one spouse walks away from the divorce with a better job and a better education, that person is granted a lesser share of the property. In addition, South African divorce courts consider child custody along with the divorce. In the United States, these are two separate decisions. The South African court takes into consideration who has physical custody of the children and how that might affect household finances differently for the two divorcing parties.

REPUDIATION IN MUSLIM NATIONS. A third type of divorce law called repudiation exists in some Muslim nations. Repudiation is the unilateral prerogative for a man to terminate a marriage at will without judicial intervention under **Islamic law** (*shari'a*). For example, a Muslim Egyptian man has a unilateral and unconditional right to divorce with few legal requirements (*talaq*). He simply needs to repudiate his wife by saying "you are divorced" three times and register the divorce within thirty days with a religious notary to make it official. A repudiated woman has to observe a waiting period (*'idda*) not exceeding one year, during which she is not allowed to marry another man. An Egyptian woman who is repudiated by her husband is entitled to the deferred dowry, "maintenance" (*nafaqa*) during the waiting period, and compensation (*mut'a*) of at least two years' maintenance (with consideration for the husband's means, the circumstances of the divorce, and the length of marriage) (Otto 2010).

Egyptian law is a reformed version of repudiation. In other nations, under the most conservative repudiation law, a woman's rights to divorce are quite different. If she wishes to divorce, she must go to a religious judge and prove to him that her husband harmed her. The procedure takes years, and judges usually rule against the wife. Even if she successfully divorces her husband, she receives no continued economic support. Under the new procedure in Egypt, the wife must wait six months if she has children or three months if she does not while the judge tries to reconcile the partners. Then the judge must grant the divorce, but the woman has to return all money, property, and gifts that she received during the marriage, and cannot receive alimony (Social Institutions and Gender Index 2012).

In Egypt, recent changes have loosened these restrictions—a wife no longer has to prove she has been harmed—but Egyptian women still face difficulties obtaining a divorce. Egyptian women seeking divorce today often have to make a difficult "choice" of forfeiting their financial rights to avoid burdensome and uncertain court proceedings. If they ask their spouses to divorce them, the process is shortened, but the women lose any right to property accumulated during the marriage or to alimony after (Human Rights Watch 2004).

Repudiation is common in many Arab Muslim nations, although recently laws have changed to eliminate repudiation in several nations. Repudiation laws were changed, for example, in Tunisia and Morocco after they were criticized and contested in court and eventually replaced by no-fault laws. The critics of repudiation laws cited four problems:

1. Repudiation laws do not require court procedure.
2. Only men have the right to divorce.
3. After repudiation, men have no financial responsibility for their wives.
4. The process is too easy for men.

After winning its independence from France in the 1950s, Tunisia implemented a new constitution that guaranteed equality, and the Tunisian Code was established, putting women in an equal position with men in relation to most areas of family life. For example, women have equal duties and responsibilities to men in the running of the family and have equal rights to divorce. Polygamy and the duty of obedience of the wife to the husband—common in some Muslim countries—were abolished (Tamanna 2008). In the 1980s, Tunisia became the first Muslim nation to implement divorce laws that treat women and men equitably.

Morocco also won its independence from France in the 1950s, but despite a constitution that provided for equality under the law, chose to instate a set of family laws that supported gender inequality. Despite the constitutional protection of gender equality, family laws meant that women in Morocco were subjected to discrimination and disadvantage. For example, under the Moroccan Family Law (*Moudawana*), men were free to engage in polygamy and exercise the power of unilateral divorces. Women, on the other hand, had unequal rights to divorce and limited property and inheritance rights. In 2004 Morroco changed its laws to be more consistent with those in Tunisia (Tamanna 2008).

Today divorce laws in both Tunisia and Morocco allow for either the man or the woman to request a divorce, and men can no longer unilaterally declare themselves divorced but must go through legal proceedings in a court. The person who requests the divorce must compensate the nonconsenting person. The law also has special protections for women. A nonconsenting woman must be provided with alimony for life by her divorcing husband. In addition, in Tunisia child custody laws have changed. Children used to be placed in the custody of their mothers until puberty and then transferred to their fathers. Today, child custody is decided on the basis of the best interest of the child. In addition, polygamy is no longer legal. The new laws are better for women than the old ones were, because women can now obtain a divorce on the same grounds and through the same process as men and they can be paid alimony. The progressive divorce laws in Tunisia and Morroco show that Islam is compatible with gender equity in family law (Tamanna 2008). Some disadvantages remain, however, such as the compensation women must pay if they initiate the divorce.

MAKING COMPARISONS. All of these variations in divorce both reflect and reinforce gender. Divorce law is an important vehicle by which the government shapes gender. The laws we have looked at illustrate the distinction between two important ideas: **gender equality** and

gender equity. What exactly are these terms? The World Health Organization (WHO 2001, 9) provides these two definitions:

> Gender equality means equal treatment of women and men in laws and policies, and equal access to resources and services within families, communities and society at large. Gender equity means fairness and justice in the distribution of benefits and responsibilities between women and men. It often requires women-specific pro-grammes and policies to end existing inequalities.

In the review of the no-fault laws in the United States, we see that the laws attempt to ignore gender, but because divorce takes place in a highly gendered social context, the end result of divorce exacerbates differences, especially economic differences between women and men.

Repudiation laws reflect a sharp gender distinction between women and men. The laws are explicitly gendered, and the results exacerbate the inequality between women and men by keeping women in unhappy marriages and impoverishing women whose husbands choose to divorce them. The U.S. laws include more gender equality than do the repudiation laws, but neither provides for gender equity. In both cases, divorce leaves women in difficult economic and social situations after a divorce, no matter how much of an improvement the end of the marriage may bring to their lives in other ways.

Reforms in family law in Muslim nations such as Morocco and Tunisia show how central the question of gender equity is in divorce, and they show that equity is possible in a range of cultures. Much progress has been made in these two nations in regard to gender equality and gender equity, and divorce laws have been an important part of the package.

South Africa appears to attempt to use divorce law as a way to promote both gender equality and gender equity. The laws do not distinguish between women and men; that is, they reflect gender equality. Spouses (regardless of gender) are equal before the law. However, the laws provide for protecting all the parties by (1) incorporating child custody into the divorce proceedings and (2) protecting the more vulnerable people in the divorcing household. These are examples of promoting gender equity.

GENDER MATTERS

Families are one of the first places we think about when we consider the problem of gender inequality. Families are a place where relationships and behaviors are usually highly gendered, and family members negotiate and contest gender as they go about the work that takes place in families. Social institutions beyond families, however, create important contexts that can create, maintain, or break down unequal roles and relationships for women and men, girls and boys. Laws about marriage and divorce as well as government and business policies about family care work are critical factors that can either promote inequality and inequity or serve as vehicles for progressive change. These kinds of changes are being implemented all over the world and are reflected, for example, in the divorce laws in Africa and in family leave policy in Europe. But difficult problems remain.

One of the most important of these is illustrated in the opening scenario. Some gender expectations about women have been altered, and women are increasingly entering the paid labor force. On the other hand, other gender expectations have not changed as rapidly. Women are still expected to take responsibility for the bulk of care work, while in many places, masculinity leaves men without that responsibility or expectation. This has created a care gap that is being filled by women from other nations. But while the migration of global nannies "solves" the care problem for families in the global North and allows greater gender equality between women and men in households in the North, it creates terrible problems for women and their families from the global South. Once again we see that gender is ubiquitous, winding through every aspect of our lives from the most up-close-and-personal to the largest global structures.

KEY TERMS

alimony
Baby M
care work
child brides
civil unions
Defense of Marriage Act (DOMA)
doctrine of *coverture*
European Union
family leave policy
fatherhood responsibility movement
fragile family advocates
gender equality
gender equity
global chains of care
good provider role
involved fathers
Islamic Law *(Shari'a)*
married women's property laws

masculinity politics
Medicaid
mommy wars
motherhood mystique
motherhood penalty
national fatherhood initiative
no-fault
noninterventionist
parental leave
plan B
rebels
repudiation
sandwich generation
stalled revolution
Temporary Aid to Needy Families
   (TANF)
traditionalists, neotraditionalists
   and innovators

CRITICAL THINKING QUESTIONS

1. Look at the table on parental leave policies around the world. How do the policies vary? Who benefits from generous policies that provide financial aid and other kinds of support for parents?

2. The debates over marriage for gay and lesbian couples and rules requiring marriage for poor people bring into opposition two key issues, gender and love. Those who are against gay marriage and in favor of the government promoting marriage for poor people believe that gender is key. Marriage is for one man and one woman, and every man and woman must be married regardless of love.

Those who are in favor of allowing gay marriage and allowing all adults to choose whether they will marry based on their feelings for their partner believe that love is more important than gender. Which do you think is more important, love or gender? Why?

3. What role does gender play in the various forms of divorce outlined in the chapter? How does the experience of men and women differ in each of the variations? Which seems to be consistent with greater gender equity?

REFERENCES

Abel, Emily. 1986. "Adult Daughters and Care for the Elderly." *Feminist Studies* 12 (3): 479–93.

Abramowitz, Mimi. 1996. *Under Attack, Fighting Back: Women and Welfare in the United States.* New York: Monthly Review Press.

Adams, Stephanie, Heather Nawrocki, and Barbara Coleman. 1999. *Women and Long-Term Care.* Fact Sheet No. 77. Washington, DC: AARP Public Policy Institute.

Administration on Aging. 2011. *A Profile of Older Americans.* U.S. Department of Health and Human Services. http://www.aoa.gov/Aging_Statistics/Profile/2011/docs/2011profile.pdf

Agbayani-Siewert, Pauline, and Linda Revilla. 1995. "Filipino Americans." In *Asian Americans: Contemporary Trends and Issues*, edited by Pyong Gap Min, 95–133. Thousand Oaks, CA: Sage.

Ahrons, Constance. 1994. *The Good Divorce.* New York: HarperCollins.

Albelda, Randy, and Chris Tilly. 2000. "It's a Family Affair: Women, Poverty, and Welfare." In *Reconstructing Gender: A Multicultural Anthology*, 2nd edition, edited by Estelle Disch, 363–69. Mountain View, CA: Mayfield.

Aldous, Joan, Gail Mulligan, and Thoroddur Biarnason. 1998. "Fathering Over Time: What Makes the Difference?" *Journal of Marriage and the Family* 60:809–20.

Applebaum, Eileen, Thomas Bailey, Peter Berg, and Arne Kalleberg. 2002. *Shared Work, Valued Care: New Norms for Organizing Market Work and Unpaid Care Work.* Washington, DC: Economic Policy Institute.

Aranda, Marie, and Bob Knight. 1997. "The Influence of Ethnicity and Culture on the Caregiver Stress and Coping Process: A Sociocultural Review and Analysis." *Gerontologist* 37 (3): 342–54.

Arendell, Terry. 1995. *Fathers and Divorce.* Thousand Oaks, CA: Sage.

Armour, Stephanie. 2007. "Workplace Tensions Rise as Dads Seek Family Time." *USA Today*, December 10.

Aronson, Jane. 1992. "Women's Sense of Responsibility for the Care of Old People: 'But Who Else Is Going to Do It?'" *Gender and Society* 6 (1): 8–29.

Aulette, Judy. 2007. *Changing American Families.* 2nd ed. Boston: Allyn and Bacon.

Bennhold, Katrin. 2010. "In Sweden, Men Can Have It All." *New York Times*, June 9. http://www.nytimes.com/2010/06/10/world/europe/10iht-sweden.html?pagewanted=all. Accessed March 21, 2011.

Bernard, Jessie. 1981. "The Good-Provider Role: Its Rise and Fall." *American Psychologist* 36 (1): 1–12.

Bianchi, Suzanne, Lekha Subaiya, and Joan Kahn. 1999. "The Gender Gap in the Economic Well-Being of Nonresident Fathers and Custodial Mothers." *Demography* 36 (3): 173–84.

Blackstone, William. 1803. *Commentaries on the Laws of England.* London: Strahan.

Blair, Cornelia, and Helene Northway. 2001. *Women: New Roles in Society.* Detroit, MI: Gale Group.

Boushey, Heather, and Ann O'Leary. 2010. *How Working Women Are Reshaping America's Families and Economy and What It Means for Policymakers.* Center for American Progress, March 8. http://www.americanprogress.org/issues/2010/03/our_working_nation.html. Accessed March 21, 2011.

Bryson, Ken, and Lynne Casper. 1999. *Co-Resident Grandparents and Grandchildren.* Washington, DC: U.S. Bureau of the Census.

Budig, Michelle, and Paula England. 2001. "The Wage Penalty for Motherhood." *American Sociological Review* 66 (2): 204–25.

Buehler, Cheryl. 1995. "Divorce Law in the United States." *Marriage and Family Review* 21 (3/4): 99–120.

Bullock, Karen. 2005. "Grandfathers and the Impact of Raising Grandchildren." *Journal of Sociology and Social Welfare* 32 (1): 43–59.

Bunting, Madeleine. 2005. "Importing Our Careers Adds Up to Emotional Imperialism." *Guardian*, October 24. http://www.guardian.co.uk/society/2005/oct/24/globalisation.immigrationasylumandrefugees. Accessed March 21, 2011.

Burt, Martha, and Demetra Nightingale. 2009. *Repairing the U.S. Social Safety Net*. Washington, DC: Urban Institute.

Calasanti, Toni, and Kathleen Slevin. 2001. *Gender, Social Inequalities, and Aging*. Walnut Creek, CA: AltaMira.

Cantor, Muriel. 1994. "Family Care Giving: Social Care." In *Family Care Giving: Agenda for the Future*, edited by Marjorie H. Cantor, 1–9. San Francisco: American Society on Aging.

Capps, Randy, Rosa Maria Castañeda, Ajay Chaudry, and Robert Santos. 2007. *Paying the Price: The Impact of Immigration Raids on America's Children*. Washington, DC: Urban Institute. http://www.urban.org/UploadedPDF/411566_immigration_raids.pdf. Accessed March 21, 2011.

Cherlin, Andrew. 1992. *Marriage, Divorce, Remarriage*. 2nd edition. Cambridge, MA: Harvard University Press.

Chernus, Ira. 2006. "Why Are They Afraid to Call It Marriage?" CommonDreams.org . http://www.commondreams.org/views06/1027-22.htm. Accessed March 21, 2011.

Collins, Patricia Hill. 2000. "The Meaning of Motherhood in Black Culture and Black Mother-Daughter Relationships." In *Gender through the Prism of Difference*, 2nd edition, edited by Maxine Baca Zinn, Pierrette Hondagneu-Sotelo, and Michael A. Messner, 268–78. Boston: Allyn and Bacon.

Coltrane, Scott. 2007. "Marriage, Work and Family in Men's Lives." *American Prospect*, March 5.

Connell, Robert. 1995. *Masculinities*. Cambridge, UK: Polity Press.

Coontz, Stephanie. 2004. "The World Historical Transformation of Marriage." *Journal of Marriage and Family* 66 (4): 974–79.

——. 2006a. "Just Which 'Traditional' Marriage Should We Defend?" Press release from Council on Contemporary Families, July 6.

——. 2006b. "Myth of the Opt-Out Mom: The Number of US Mothers Who Also Work Outside the Home Is Actually on the Rise." *Christian Science Monitor*, March 30.

Coontz, Stephanie, and Nancy Folbre. 2002. "Marriage, Poverty, and Public Policy: A Discussion Paper from the Council on Contemporary Families." Presented at the Fifth Annual CCF Conference, New York, April 26–28.

Dean, Amy. 2013. "How domestic workers won their rights: Five big lessons." *Yes!Magazine*, October 9. http://portside.org/2013-10-14/how-domestic-workers-won-their-rights-five-big-lessons. Accessed February 27, 2014.

Dillaway, Heather, and Elizabeth Pare. 2013. "A campaign for good motherhood? Exploring the media discourse on Sarah Palin, Hillary Clinton, and Michelle Obama during the 2008 presidential campaign." *Advances in Gender Research* 17:209–39.

Domestic Workers United and Data Center. 2010. *Home Is Where the Work Is: Inside New York's Domestic Work Industry*. New York: Domestic Workers United. http://www.datacenter.org/wp-content/uploads/homeiswheretheworkis.pdf. Accessed March 22, 2011.

Drago, Robert, and Carol Colbeck. 2006. "Care Givers Hide Actions to Enhance Careers." Paper presented at the annual meeting of the American Association for the Advancement of Science, St. Louis, MO, February 19.

Drexler, Peggy. 2010. "History Is on Women's Side in the Workplace." *WeNews*, March 4. http://womensenews.org/story/commentary/100303/history-womens-side-in-the-workplace. Accessed March 22, 2011.

Ehrenreich, Barbara, and Arlie Hochschild. 2002. *Global Woman: Nannies, Maids and Sex Workers in the New Economy.* New York: Henry Holt.

Edelman, Peter. 2009. "Welfare and the Poorest of the Poor." *Dissent* (Fall). http://dissentmagazine.org/article/welfare-and-the-poorest-of-the-poor. Accessed March 22, 2011.

Elder, Laurel, and Steven Greene. 2008. "Parenthood and the Gender Gap." In *Voting the Gender Gap*, edited by Lois Duke Whitaker, 119–40. Champaign: University of Illinois Press.

Federal Interagency Forum on Aging-Related Statistics. 2004. *Older Americans 2004: Key Indicators of Well-Being.* Washington, DC: U.S. Government Printing Office.

Flanders, Laura. 2013. "California Governor Signs Domestic Worker Bill of Rights." *The Nation*, September 26. http://www.thenation.com/blog/176377/california-governor-signs-domestic-worker-bill-rights. Accessed February 27, 2014.

Fletcher, Bill. 2010. "Victory for an Excluded and Invisible Workforce: Domestic Workers in New York Win Historic Victory!" *Black Commentator*, July 22.

Fox, Elizabeth, Gillian Pascall, and Tracey Warren. 2009. "Work-Family Policies, Participation, and Practices: Fathers and Childcare in Europe." *Community, Work, and Family* 12 (3): 313–26.

Fremstad, Shawn. 2004. *Recent Welfare Reform Research Findings.* Washington, DC: Center on Budget and Policy Priorities. http://www.cbpp.org/cms/index.cfm?fa=view&id=1536. Accessed March 22, 2011.

Ganahl, Jane. 2004. "Women in Asia Are Starting to Say 'I Don't.'" *San Francisco Chronicle*, November 14.

Gavanas, Anna. 2002. "The Fatherhood Responsibility Movement." In *Making Men into Fathers*, edited by Barbara Hobson, 213–44. New York: Cambridge University Press.

Gerson, Judith. 1987. "How Women Choose between Employment and Family: A Developmental Perspective." In *Families and Work*, edited by Naomi Gerstel and Harriet Engel Gross, 270–88. Philadelphia: Temple University Press.

———. 1993. *No Man's Land: Men's Changing Commitment to Family and Work.* New York: Basic Books.

———. 2007. "What Do Women and Men Want? Many of the Same Things." *American Prospect*, March 5.

Gerstel, Naomi. 1987. "Divorce and Stigma." *Social Problems* 34 (2): 172–86.

Glazer, Nona. 1990. "The Home as Workshop: Women as Amateur Nurses and Medical Care Providers." *Gender and Society* 4 (4): 479–99.

Goldberg, Wendy A., Edwin T. Tan, and Kara L. Thorsen. 2009. "Trends in Academic Attention to Fathers, 1930–2006." *Fathering* 7 (2): 159–79.

Grall, Timothy. 2011. "Custodial Mothers and Fathers and Their Child Support: 2009." *Current Population Reports.* http://www.census.gov/prod/2011pubs/p60-240.pdf

Greenberg, Mark. 1999. "Welfare Restructuring and Working Poor Family Policy." In *Hard Labor*, edited by Joel Handler and Lucie White, 24–47. New York: Sharpe.

Haas, L., and C. P. Hwang. 2009. "Is Fatherhood Becoming More Visible at Work? Trends in Corporate Support for Fathers Taking Parental Leave in Sweden." *Fathering* 7 (3): 303–21.

Haley, Pamela Sullivan. 2009. "The Filipina–South Florida International Internet Marriage Practice: Agency, Culture, and Paradox." Florida Atlantic University. *Dissertation Abstracts: Humanities and Social Sciences* 69 (12): 4769.

Hardin, Blaine. 2007. "Learn to Be Nice to Your Wife, or Pay the Price." *Washington Post*, November 26.

Hays, Sharon. 1999. "The Mommy Wars." In *Family in Transition*, 10th edition, edited by Arlene Skolnick and Jerome Skolnick, 432–48. New York: Addison Wesley.

Henderson, Sarah, and Alana Jeydal. 2010. *Women and Politics in a Global World.* 2nd edition. New York: Oxford University Press.

Heymann, Jody, Alison Earle, and Jeffrey Hayes. 2007. *The Work, Family, and Equity Index: How Does the United States Measure Up?* Montreal: Project on Global Working Families.

Heymann, Jody, Francisco Flores-Macias, Jeffrey Hayes, Malinda Kennedy, Claudia Lahaie, and Alison Earle. 2009. "The Impact of Migration on the Well-Being of Transnational Families: New Data from Sending Communities in Mexico." *Community, Work, and Family* 12 (1): 91–103.

Hochschild, Arlie. 2000. Global Care Chains and Emotional Surplus Value. In *On the Edge: Living with Global Capitalism*, edited by Will Hutton and Anthony Giddens. 130–146. London: Johnathan Cape.

Hoffnung, Michelle. 1989. "Motherhood: Contemporary Conflict for Women." In *Women: A Feminist Perspective*, edited by Jo Freeman, 147–75. Mountain View, CA: Mayfield.

Huffington Post 2012 *Maternity Leaves Around the World*. October 24 http://www.huffingtonpost .ca/2012/05/22/maternity-leaves-around-the-world_n_1536120.html. Accessed February 27, 2014.

Hughes, Donna. 2003. *The Impact of the Use of New Communications and Information Technologies on Trafficking in Human Beings for Sexual Exploitation: Role of Marriage Agencies in Trafficking in Women and Trafficking in Images of Sexual Exploitation*. Strasbourg: Council of Europe, Committee for Equality between Women and Men. http://www.uri.edu/artsci/wms/hughes/ pubtrfrep.htm

Human Rights Watch. 2004. "Divorced from Justice." *HRW Publications* 16 (8). New York: Human Rights Watch.

——. 2013. *Q & A: Child Marriage and Violations of Girls' Rights*. Human Rights Watch, June 14. http://www.hrw.org/news/2013/06/14/q-child-marriage-and-violations-girls-rights. Accessed February 27, 2014.

ILO (International Labour Organisation). 2010. *Maternity at Work*. Geneva: ILO. http://www.ilo.org/ global/publications/books/WCMS_124442/lang--en/index.htm. Accessed February 27, 2104.

John, Robert. 1999. "Aging among American Indians: Income Security, Health, and Social Support Networks." In *Full Color Aging: Facts, Goals, and Recommendation for America's Diverse Elders*, edited by Toni P. Miles, 65–91. Washington, DC: Gerontological Society of America.

Kaufmann, Greg. 2012. "This Week in Poverty: Bigfoot, Nessie and Paul Ryan." *The Nation*, October 26. http://www.thenation.com/blog/170849/week-poverty-bigfoot-nessie-and-paul-ryan.

Kids Count. 2013. *Children in Poverty, 2012*. Annie E. Casey Foundation. http://datacenter.kidscount .org/data/tables/43-children-in-poverty#detailed/1/any/false/868,867,133,38,35/any/321,322. Accessed February 27, 2014.

Kosmin, Barry, and Seymour Lachman. 1993. *One Nation Under God: Religion in Contemporary American Society*. New York: Crown.

Kurz, Demie. 1995. *For Richer or Poorer*. New York: Routledge.

LaRossa, Ralph. 2000. "Fatherhood and Social Change." In *Gender through the Prism of Difference*, 2nd edition, edited by Maxine Baca Zinn, Pierrette Hondagneu-Sotelo, and Michael A. Messner, 298–309. Boston: Allyn and Bacon.

Lee, Hye-Kyung. 2008. "International Marriage and the State in South Korea." *Citizenship Studies* 12 (9): 107–23.

Levin-Epstein, Jodie. 2006. *Getting Punched: The Work and Family Clock*. Washington, DC: Center for Law and Social Policy (CLASP).

Lin, J. 1991. "Satisfaction and Conflict in Asian Correspondence Marriages." *Focus* 5:1–2.

Marsh, Julia. 2010. "Marriage Loses Ground as Anti-Poverty Panacea." *WeNews*, July 7. http:// womensenews.org/story/economyeconomic-policy/100706/marriage-loses-ground-anti-poverty- panacea. Accessed March 22, 2011.

Maume, David. 2006. "Gender Differences in Restricting Work Efforts Because of Family Responsi- bilities." *Journal of Marriage and Family* 68 (4): 859–69.

McManus, Patricia, and Thomas DiPrete. 2001. "Losers and Winners: The Financial Consequences of Separation and Divorce for Men." *American Sociological Review* 66: (2): 246–68.

Mink, Gwendolyn. 2006. "Ending Single Motherhood." In *The Promise of Welfare Reform*, edited by Keith Kilty and Elizabeth Segal, 155–215. New York: Haworth Press.

Mochizuki, K. 1987. "I Think Oriental Women Are Just Great." *International Examiner*, May 13.

National Alliance for Caregiving and AARP. 1997. *Caregiving in the U.S.* www.caregiving.org.

National Center for Children in Poverty (NCCP). 2005. "Many Children with Married Parents are Low Income." Fact sheet. http://www.nccp.org/publications/pub_633.html. Accessed March 22, 2011.

Orbuch, Terri L. and Sandra L. Eyster. 1997. "Division of Household Labor Among Black Couples and White Couples." *Social Forces*, 76:301–332.

Otto, Jan (ed). 2010. *A Comparative Overview of the Legal Systems of Twelve Muslim Countries in Past and Present.* Amsterdam: Leiden University Press.

Padavic, Irene, and Jonniann Butterfield. 2011. "Mothers, Fathers and 'Mathers': Negotiating a Lesbian Co-parental Identity." *Gender and Society.* 25(2): 176–96.

Park, Hwa-Ok. 2005. "Grandmothers Raising Grandchildren." *Focus* 24 (1): 19–27.

Parreñas, Rhacel. 2001. *Servants of Globalization: Women, Migration, and Domestic Work.* Chicago: Stanford University Press.

Passel, Jeffrey, and D'Vera Cohn. 2011. *Unauthorized Immigrant Population: National and State Trends, 2010.* http://www.pewhispanic.org/2011/02/01/unauthorized-immigrant-population-brnational-and-state-trends-2010/.

Passel, Jeffrey S., D'Vera Cohn, and Ana Gonzalez-Barrera. 2013. *Population Decline of Undocumented Immigrants Stalls, May Have Reversed.* Pew Research Hispanic Trends Project, September 23 http://www.pewhispanic.org/2013/09/23/population-decline-of-unauthorized-immigrants-stalls-may-have-reversed/. Accessed February 27, 2014.

Pearson, Patricia. 2002. "'Father' Means More than Household Master." *USA Today*, June 13.

Peterman, Amber. 2012. "Widowhood and Asset Inheritance in Sub-Saharan Africa: Empirical Evidence from 15 Countries." *Development Policy Review*, 30 (5): 543–71.

Peterson, Richard. 1996. "A Re-Evaluation of the Economic Consequences of Divorce." *American Sociological Review* 61 (3): 528–36.

Pew Forum. 2013. *Gay Marriage Around the World.* July 16. http://www.pewforum.org/2013/07/16/gay-marriage-around-the-world-2013/

Ray, Rebecca, Janet Gornick, and John Schmitt. 2009. *Parental Leave Policies in 21 Countries: Assessing Generosity and Gender Equality.* Washington, DC: Center for Economic and Policy Research.

Retherford, Robert, and Naohiro Ogawa. 2005. *Japan's Baby Bust: Causes, Implications, and Policy Responses.* Population and Health Series No. 118. Honolulu, HI: East West Working Papers.

Risman, Barbara. 1987. "Intimate Relationships from a Microstructural Perspective: Men Who Mother." *Gender and Society* 1 (1): 6–32. doi: 10.1177/089124387001001002.

Rose, Hillary, and Errollyn Bruce. 1995. "Mutual Care but Differential Esteem: Caring between Older Couples." In *Connecting Gender and Aging: A Sociological Approach*, edited by Sara Arber and Jay Ginn, 114–28. Buckingham, UK: Open University Press.

Rothman, Barbara Katz. 1989. *Recreating Motherhood.* New York: Norton.

Rotundo, E. 1985. "American Fatherhood: A Historical Perspective." *American Behavioral Scientist* 29 (1): 7–25.

Rowe, Gretchen, and Victoria Russell. 2004. *The Welfare Rules Databook.* Washington, DC: Urban Institute.

Schaeffer-Grabiel, Felicity. 2006. "Planet-Love.com: Cyberbrides in the Americas and the Trans-national Routes of U.S. Masculinity." *Signs: Journal of Women in Contemporary Society* 31 (2): 331–56.

Schoonejongen, John. 2013. "Judge Denies N.J.'s stay of Gay Marriage Ruling." *USAToday* October 10. http://www.usatoday.com/story/news/nation/2013/10/10/nj-gay-marriage-stay-denied/2961991/. Accessed February 27, 2014.

Schwartz, Felice. 1989. "Management, Women, and the New Facts of Life." *Harvard Business Review* 67 (1): 65–76.

Segura, Denise. 1999. "Inside the Worlds of Chicana and Mexican Immigrant Women." In *Feminist Philosophies: Problems, Theories, and Applications,* edited by Janet A. Kourany, James P. Sterba, and Rosemarie Tong, 180–88. Upper Saddle River, NJ: Prentice Hall.

Shelton, Beth Anne, and Rebecca Deen. 2001. "Divorce Trends and Effects for Women and Men." In *Gender Mosaics,* edited by Dana Vannoy, 216–26. Los Angeles: Roxbury.

Shirey, Lee, and Laura Summer. 2000. "Caregiving: Helping the Elderly with Activity Limitations." *Challenges for the Twenty-First Century: Chronic and Disabling Conditions,* No. 7. Washington, DC: National Academy on an Aging Society.

Social Institutions and Gender Index (SIGI). 2012. *Egypt, Arab Rep.* OECD Development Centre. http://genderindex.org/country/egypt-arab-rep.

Singleton, Judy. 1998. "The Impact of Family Caregiving to the Elderly on the American Workplace: Who Is Affected and What Is Being Done?" In *Challenges for Work and Family in the Twenty-First Century,* edited by D. Vannoy and P. Dubeck, 201–16. New York: Aldine.

Smock, Pamela. 1994. "Gender and Short-Run Economic Consequences of Marital Disruption." *Social Forces* 73 (1): 243–62.

Solot, Dorian, and Marshall Miller. 2002. *Let Them Eat Wedding Rings.* New York: Alternatives to Marriage Project.

Stetson, Dorothy. 1997. *Women's Rights in the U.S.A.: Policy Debates and Gender Roles.* New York: Garland.

Tamanna, Nowrin. 2008. "Personal Status Laws in Morocco and Tunisia: A Comparative Exploration of the Possibilities for Equality-Enhancing Reform in Bangladesh." *Feminist Legal Studies* 16 (3): 323–43.

Tolentino, Roland. 1996. "Bodies, Letters, Catalogs: Filipinas in Transnational Space." *Social Text* 48: 49–76.

Townsend, Nicholas. 2002. *The Package Deal.* Philadelphia: Temple University Press.

UNFPA. 2006. *State of the World Population, 2006.* New York: United Nations.

United Nations. 2001. *Widowhood: invisible women,secluded or excluded* https://www.un.org/women-watch/daw/public/wom_Dec%2001%20single%20pg.pdf.

———. 2012a. "America's Families and Living Arrangements: 2012." Table A1. https://www.census.gov/hhes/families/data/cps2012.html.

———, 2012b. "America's Families and Living Arrangements: 2012." Table C.4. https://www.census.gov/hhes/families/data/cps2012.html.

———.2012c. "Living Arrangements of the Population 65 and Over, by Sex and Race and Hispanic Origin, 2010." http://www.agingstats.gov/Main_Site/Data/2012_Documents/Population.aspx

———. 2012d. "Monthly Child Support Payments Average $430 per Month in 2010." *Census Bureau Reports,* June 19. http://www.census.gov/newsroom/releases/archives/children/cb12-109.html

Walker, Alan. 1996. "The Relationship between the Family and the State in the Case of Older People." In *Aging for the Twenty-First Century: Readings in Social Gerontology,* edited by Jill Quadagno and Debra Street, 269–85. New York: St. Martin's.

Walker, Nancy, Catherine Brooks, and Lawrence Wrightsman. 1999. *Children's Rights in the United States.* Thousand Oaks, CA: Sage.

Wang, Wendy, Kim Parker, and Paul Taylor. 2013. *Breadwinner Moms.* Pew Research Social and Demographic Trends, May 29. http://www.pewsocialtrends.org/2013/05/29/breadwinner-moms/.

Weitzman, Lenore. 1981. *The Marriage Contract*. New York: Free Press.

Wong, Curtis. 2010. "Same-Sex Marriage around the Globe." *Huffington Post*, July 15. http://www .huffingtonpost.com/2010/07/15/same-sex-marriage-laws-ar_n_647478.html. Accessed March 22, 2011.

Wood, Robert, Sheena McConnell, Quinn Moore, Andrew Clarkwest, and JoAnn Hsueh. 2010. *The Building Strong Families Project*. Princeton, NJ: Mathematica Policy Research. http://www .mathematica-mpr.com/publications/pdfs/family_support/BSF_impact_execsumm.pdf. Accessed March 22, 2011.

World Health Organization. 2001. *Transforming Health Systems: Gender and Rights in Reproductive Health*. New York: World Health Organization.

Zavella, Patricia. 1987. *Women's Work and Chicano Families*. Ithaca, NY: Cornell University Press.

8

VIOLENCE

Violence against women in Guatemala is rampant. Here Guatemalan women demonstrate to end street violence that takes an enormous toll on women.

Source: Associated Press.

Violence against women is the human rights scandal of our times.

Sheila Dauer, "Violence Against Women: An Obstacle to Equality"

Three years ago, here in London, I was a guest at the local Quaker meeting house where a panel of eight women from Israel had been invited to speak. Having spent so much of my life covering "men's" activities in the Middle East—investment and trade, oil and politics as well as outright war—I thought it about time I took a look at what women were doing. The panel included four Palestinians and four Israelis, all from divergent backgrounds: a poet, sociologist, historian, social worker, Christian, Muslim and Jew.

There were some quite direct, pointed questions from the audience about where truth, justice and progress lay. Would Israelis be better off without the occupation of the West Bank and Gaza? Would Palestinians agree to end suicide bombings? The answers varied, both among the Palestinian and Jewish women, and amongst themselves, whatever their nationality.

But when the moderator put the final question, "What, in your opinion, do you think is the worst problem you face?" the answer was surprising. One would have expected the Palestinian women to say, "the occupation of the West Bank and Gaza by Israel since 1967." For the Israeli women, one would have thought the answer would be "security, a right to live in peace with Israel's neighbors and, above all, an end to suicide bombings."

Surprise, surprise. One by one, the eight women stood up, faced the 70 or so in the audience of mostly women and declared: "The militarization of our men." For the Palestinians, seeing their sons subjected to the cannon-fodder rhetoric of ignorant sheikhs, the test of manhood their teen sons were exposed to when it came to throwing stones, or the death and injury of their fathers, sons and brothers were the key points. For the Israeli women, the brutalization of the men they must live with, their sons, brothers and spouses in the Israeli Defense Forces, was the main point. And, unlike the Palestinians, Israelis are required to serve in the Israeli Defense Forces unless they can prove they are conscientious objectors or members of certain Jewish religious denominations.

Pamela Ann Smith, "Mideast Events Vivify Women's 'Worst Problem'"

These two quotes summarize much of our experience and thinking on violence and gender. The first, from Amnesty International (Dauer, 2006), informs us that women experience violence most often as victims. Violence against women is widespread and profound, and a human rights scandal because it is so pervasive, so destructive, and so inhuman.

The second quote tells us about the links between masculinity and violence. The voices are women's, but the focus of their concern is men. The mothers, wives, sisters, witnesses, and victims of violent men tell us that social forces demand that men behave in violent ways to be counted as men. The men and women they hurt are victims of masculinity defined in this way. The men who are the perpetrators are also victims because their humanity is diminished when they behave in "manly" ways required by their leaders, their governments, and their societies.

THE GENDERED CONTINUUM OF VIOLENCE

Perhaps you know of the global epidemic of violence against women that extends from so-called private and personal violence between intimate partners, acquaintances, and strangers to sex trafficking, militarism, and wartime rape, whose main victims now are civilian women and children. The Palestinian and Israeli women quoted by Pamela Ann Smith (2006) in the opening scenario see connections between the violence experienced by women in their private lives and these global horrors. In this chapter, we examine the various points along the gendered continuum of violence and the threads that connect them. We explore how the force and violence required to sustain inequalities link the multiple sites of violence we visit here: street harassment and community-based violence, rape and domestic violence, state-sponsored violence in prisons, militarization and militarism, and sexual violence in conflict zones around the world.

Riane Eisler (1987) argues that gender constitutes all human societies, affecting all our institutions, our values, and now, in the age of nuclear weapons and global warming, our survival. According to her "**cultural transformation theory**," a *dominator model* structures hierarchical societies, which depend on threat and violence to survive. Diverse societies, in Eisler's view, share this underlying commonality. Hitler's Germany, contemporary Iran, the Japan of the Samurai, and the Aztecs of Meso-America are all "rigidly male dominant . . . have a generally hierarchic and authoritarian social structure and a high degree of social violence, particularly warfare" (1987, xix). On the other hand, a different social arrangement—a *partnership model*—organizes societies that are more sexually egalitarian, more peaceful, less hierarchical, and less authoritarian. There have been such societies in human history. Today they include the marginalized preliterate !Kung of Botswana, Angola, and Namibia and contemporary Scandinavian nations.

In this chapter, we survey the gender relations within and between dominator societies. We explore the epidemic of violence against women, connecting it to hierarchies of race, class, sexuality, and nation, as well as gender. We also look at the visitations of violence on and by men to show that men, too, suffer from the systems of violence. For example, bullying and hazing are forms of gendered violence by boys and men against other boys and men, and violent sports are almost exclusively men's domain (see chapter 11). Feminist men's studies scholars argue that bullying and violent sports help to construct and maintain aggressive masculinity. Subordinated men, like women, have been targets of masculine aggression, showing that gender alone cannot explain violence. Gay men are victimized for their sexuality, and men of color for their race ethnicity. Black women and Latinas are more at risk for violence than are white women, and working-class women are less safe than women of the middle and upper classes. The intersecting relations of race ethnicity, class, and sexuality shape gendered power relations and the violence that supports these relations.

The first half of the chapter treats what is often seen as personal or private violence. It reviews studies of street harassment, rape, sexual assault, and domestic violence and introduces some of the work of scholars and activists engaged in challenging these forms of violence. The second half of the chapter explores violence perpetrated or allowed by the state against women and men, including gendered violence in men's prisons and violence against women in conflict zones around the world. A final section introduces readers to the work of international bodies involved in ending violence against women.

SOME STATISTICS ON VIOLENCE

Violence is everywhere, from private homes and city streets to sports arenas, prisons, and workplaces, on national borders, and within states locked in battle with insurgents. **Intimate partner violence**—rape and **domestic violence**—is widespread in the United States and around the world, and women bear the brunt of it. The U.S. Department of Justice estimates that every ninety seconds a person over twelve is sexually assaulted. Almost 90 percent of the victims are girls and women, and 99 percent of the perpetrators are men and boys. Nevertheless, Table 8-1 shows the good news that from 1994 to 2010, the overall rate of intimate partner violence in the United States has declined by more than 63%, although from 2001 to 2010, the rate of decline slowed. Despite this good news, it is still the case that about 4 in 5 victims of intimate partner violence were female. According to Justice Department estimates, there are more than 5 million cases of domestic violence every year, most of them assaults by husbands, sons, boyfriends, acquaintances, and brothers against women. Despite the tenacious "myth of the Black rapist" (which we discussed in chapter 4), domestic violence and rape are primarily intraracial.

Violence between intimates crosses class and income levels, but violence is more likely to occur between poor couples than between more wealthy couples. Indeed, the uptick in domestic violence most recently may be related to rising poverty and unemployment among Americans since the economic crisis of 2008. Persons living in households with lower annual incomes have the highest rates of violence compared with persons in households with other

TABLE 8-1 Intimate Partner Violence, 1993–2010

	Rate per 1,000 persons age 12 or older				Percent change			
	1994	2000	2005	2010	1994–2010	1994–2000	2000–2005	2005–2010
Total Intimate Partner Violence	9.8	5.1	3.8	3.6	−63.6%	−47.9%	−25.2%	−6.5%
Sex								
Female	16.1	8.4	5.8	5.9	−63.2%	−48.2%	−31.2%	3.3%
Male	3.0	1.6	1.7	1.1	−64.5%	−46.4%	9.5%	−39.5%

Note. This table shows that from 1994 to 2010, the overall rate of intimate partner violence in the United States declined by 64 percent, from 9.8 victimizations per 1,000 persons age 12 or older to 3.6 per 1,000. Intimate partner violence declined by more than 60 percent for both men and women during this period. About four in five victims of intimate partner violence were women.

Source: Catalano, 2012, Table 1. Abridged. http://bjs.gov/content/pub/pdf/ipv9310.pdf.

income levels (see Figure 8-1). These statistics may reflect that women with more money and resources are more able to leave violent situations. However, in every income category, women are at greater risk than are men.

In the United States, approximately 1.5 million women are raped or physically assaulted by their boyfriends or husbands each year, and nearly 25 percent of all women have been raped or physically attacked at some point in their lives. Forty percent of women who are assaulted in this way are seriously injured. In contrast, 7.5 percent of surveyed men said they were raped or physically assaulted by a wife or girlfriend at some time in their lives. Lesbian couples report less partner violence (11 percent) than do heterosexual (21 percent) or gay men couples (23 percent). The figures may be inexact, but it is clear that from birth to death, in times of peace as well as war, women face high levels of violence in their everyday lives,

FIGURE 8-1 Average Annual Nonfatal Intimate Partner Victimization Rate, by Income and Gender, 2001–2005.

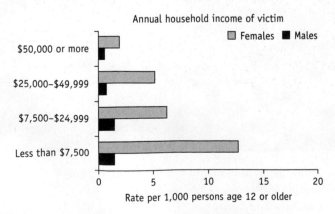

Source: Bureau of Justice Statistics (2010a).

TABLE 8-2 Intimate Homicide Victims by Gender, 1976–2005

Year	Women	Men
1976	1,587	1,304
2005	1,181	329

Source: Truman and Rand (2010).

and men are often engaged in violence against women and other men (Bureau of Justice Statistics 2009, 2010b, 2010c).

Intimate partner violence against women is part of a systematic pattern of gender dominance and control, but the existence of lesbian and gay **battering** demonstrates that violence is related to power over others and is not simply a matter of men's power over women. Still, violence is overwhelmingly men's violence (Table 8-2).

According to the Chicago Foundation for Women (2007), we are in the midst of a global epidemic of violence against women and girls that involves child abuse, street harassment, stalking, bullying, sexual assault, domestic violence, human trafficking, the sex trade, and elder abuse. Violence is one of the leading causes of death worldwide for people aged fifteen to forty. The official statistics may be only the tip of the iceberg, because most violence goes unreported.

"Hegemonic masculinity," power over women and other men, is a familiar form of masculinity that often threatens to erupt in violence.

Source: Sara Naomi Lewkowicz. All rights reserved.

STREET HARASSMENT: A GEOGRAPHY OF FEAR

Safe public space is a precondition for democratic community and a platform for launching popular movements. Black churches in the South functioned as safe spaces that allowed activists to stage the civil rights movement. The student and antiwar movements of the 1960s found safe spaces in universities. Other movements have been connected to the public spaces within which they emerged and grew: Kent State, Tiananmen Square, Stonewall, Selma, and Seattle (Smithsimon 2000). Chapter 10 shows how claiming public space is a central feature of women's peace activism.

Democracy is nurtured not only by political mobilization in public space, but also by the everyday sociability that is the foundation of public interaction and trust. Fear of crime, of strangers, and of dangerous streets destroys trust and, in the view of many, divests citizens of their ability to assemble and to voice their political concerns. In post-9/11 America, fear of others is magnified by militarized policing and increasing surveillance in the public arena (Parenti 1999). Distrust, fear, and surveillance provide the context within which street harassment and street violence are situated.

When some people think about the threat of violence, they bring to mind menacing strangers in public spaces. Although statistics tell a different story—violence is much more likely to occur between people who know each other—we routinely encounter stories of random crime and violence in the news and by word of mouth. Women and girls are warned to take precautions while walking in certain parts of the city or riding on public transportation. Parents and friends, as well as police and city governments, offer safety tips to their constituencies and publics.

If you are a woman reading this book, you are probably familiar with these messages and are vigilant when you are out and about, especially after dark. If you are a man reading this, you may know that women are counseled to be careful in public, but perhaps you have not felt particularly threatened. Nonetheless, women's precautions echo a familiar narrative in contemporary American culture and in sociology: the decline of civic engagement and trust among Americans (Putnam 2000).

The fear of crime and of public violence is gendered. In North America and Europe, street harassment falls near the "merely annoying" pole of the continuum of gendered violence, an irritating but perhaps less threatening fact of public life for women. A study of street harassers in Berlin, Los Angeles, Rome, and Vienna turned up the interesting fact that men in those cities usually only harass women during the day. Why? Wouldn't harassment at night be more intimidating? The authors suggest that this is precisely the reason why men refrain from nighttime catcalls and other annoying encounters with women in public. Such encounters would be "too effective. The woman, not merely annoyed or unnerved but genuinely alarmed, might well be driven to an 'extreme' response (such as calling for help) that the good citizen would not like to have to explain" (Benard and Schlaffer 1993).

What do men say about this behavior? Apparently many harassers do not really think about it. Benard and Schlaffer's interviews with and observations of sixty street harassers revealed that the idea that women disliked this behavior never occurred to most of them. Instead, most saw their harassment as an entertaining sport and believed that women enjoyed the attention. One forty-five-year-old construction worker "portrayed himself as a kind of benefactor to womanhood and claimed to specialize in older and less attractive women to whom, he was sure, his display of sexual interest was certain to be a highlight in an otherwise drab and joyless existence." Twenty percent of the men only harassed women when they were with friends. The authors suggest that this fact shows that harassing women is a means for men to bond with each other, to show solidarity and "joint power" (Benard and Schlaffer 1993, 443).

Although some consider it trivial, street harassment of women is hostile and intimidating and tells women that the streets belong to men. Likewise, our public parks and recreation areas are not always welcoming to unescorted women. Three decades ago, the women's movement took up the ways women were discouraged from engaging in sports and outdoor recreation and lobbied for the passage of Title IX legislation guaranteeing funding for women's athletics. However, women's feelings of vulnerability in the outdoors and their fear of lurking strangers still deny them free use of recreational sites. Wesely and Gaarder (2004) interviewed 128 women, mainly white and college educated, who used South Mountain Park in Phoenix, Arizona, the largest urban park in the United States. They found that women who used the park believed it prudent to develop strategies to keep themselves safe. They told friends where they were going, varied the times they visited the park, exercised in different locations within the park, and only visited the park when accompanied by companions or a dog. These precautions may not be sufficient, as one woman explained:

> Last year, I was hiking on an off-trail . . . with a friend. As we were hiking, we heard male voices and saw a tent and saw some smoke. A little later we stopped to soak our feet in a creek bed and heard a shotgun sound real close. Then we heard hysterical laughter and a lot of obscenities. We quickly got moving and changed directions. We switched trails and went back another way. That's why I don't hike alone anymore. I like to go with someone else. . . . I'd like to get up on Sunday morning and just go out hiking by myself, but I don't. (Wesely and Gaarder 2004, 656)

Women avoided the park at night and carried cell phones for safety. One commented that she feared that if she used the less-traveled trails, she would be "raped, murdered, and left where no one will find me." The women said that catcalls and other forms of harassment ("when guys walk by and turn around and look at you") made them feel less safe.

Street harassment may be a worldwide phenomenon. Women in India face "Eve-teasing" when in public. After ten years abroad, Kavitha Rao (2006) returned to India and to its particular violations against women on the street. She wrote,

> Being back in India brings back memories. I suddenly recall an overnight bus journey when I was 18. I spent the entire night shrinking in my seat to avoid the furtive groping of a man behind me. I remember the elderly man who sat next to me on another bus trip, moving his thigh ever nearer. Like most other victims, I have never complained. I ignore the comments, move out of range or change my seat. Why? Because I was—and am—afraid.

In 2013, stories of gang rapes and violence against women in India were in the news. These events made clear that gender violence in that country is common. Such violence begins before birth, when some parents abort female fetuses (Jha et al. 2011, Gentleman 2006), and continues with high levels of child marriage, teen pregnancy, maternal mortality, domestic violence, and sexual assault, sometimes ending in the death of the victim

(Pazzanese 2013). Some harassers stalk women or throw acid at them (see Box 8-1). Among some men there is tacit approval of this practice. Shiv Sena, the political party that controls large sections of Mumbai, blames women for their troubles because they "wear revealing clothes" or "mingle with men."

GENDER IN EVERYDAY LIFE   BOX 8-1
PATRIARCHY'S BRUTAL BACKLASH: ACID ATTACKS

Kerosene, poison and now, acid—the new weapon against women. Haseena, a 19-year-old girl from a middle-class family, was attacked with acid in 1999 by her boss because she turned down his marriage proposal and refused to continue working in his office. Two liters of pure sulphuric acid were poured on her. In 2000, Noorjahan, a mother of two children who ran a tea cart in front of a factory, was attacked by the factory owner's son. In 2001, Dr. Mahalakshmi, a doctor in Mysore, was attacked with acid by her landlord; later in the same year, Shanthi, a teacher in Mysore, was attacked by her husband. The list goes on.

In the last seven years, sixty-two women in Karnataka have been victims of acid attacks. These are the cases that have been reported or registered according to a recent Campaign and Struggle Against Acid Attacks on Women (CSAAW) report. There could be many more in actuality. The list of sixty-two includes women of all ages, caste, and class backgrounds. All of them were independent women who asserted themselves against coercion, pressure, and violence. All were attacked by someone they knew—acquaintances aspiring to be lovers, husbands, bosses, landlords. It's clear that acid attacks are being used as weapons in the brutal backlash of patriarchy toward women who show any form of agency.

Acid attacks are extremely difficult to treat: the acid seeps into the layers of the skin to cause long-term infection and corrosion. Victims often need multiple complicated and expensive surgeries. Not everyone can afford such treatments. So far, most families have sold their houses and other property to meet the expenses. To make matters worse, only some super specialty hospitals in Bangalore are equipped to treat acid attack victims. Government hospitals (including the burns ward in Victoria Hospital in Bangalore) have no facilities whatsoever to adequately handle such cases. Some doctors are not even aware of basic first aid measures such as flushing acid out of the body immediately after the attack. Many women do not survive because they're unable to access proper medical care after the attack.

And one cannot begin to articulate the emotional trauma of the woman and her family.

There is no law in our country that recognizes acid attack as a crime. Cases are registered under IPC section 326 (causing grievous injury) or IPC section 307 (attempt to murder). There is no law that looks at these attacks as gendered crime. In many cases, the accused person gets out on bail despite these sections being non-bailable and continues to threaten the victim. Police investigations invariably begin with questions on the sexual history and purity of the woman. Most cases that have reached the courts have faced procedural delays. Survivors, who are already coping with so much, have to contend with legal harassment as well. Campaign and Struggle Against Acid Attacks on Women (CSAAW), a coalition of women's rights groups, media activists, and students and concerned citizens, was started in 2003. The group has been working to help victims reclaim their lives as well as demanding that the government respond to their needs. These are some of their broad demands:

- Control over availability of acid, as acid is easily available.
- A specific law that recognizes acid attack as gendered crime against women.
- Proper medical facilities and medical aid for victims. All the government hospitals should be able to provide proper treatment to acid attack victims.
- Necessary rehabilitation for the survivors.

SOURCE: Reprinted with permission from Usha B.N. from Bangalore (2007). Original publication: *UltraViolet*.

Rao suggests that Indian men who harass women are threatened by changes in women's lives. In India, women have been leaving home to take jobs and go to college. Many wear Western clothes. Some Indian men feel threatened by these signs of women's independence. Sexual harassment is the easiest way for men to put a woman in her place and "to assert their traditionally unquestioned male rights."

A growing number of blogs encourage women to "holler back" at harassers and to post their stories of harassment on **HollaBack** websites, along with photos of harassers captured with cell phones and cameras. HollaBack started in New York, but has spread to fourteen cities in the United States and Canada. Stories about the sites have been printed in American, Canadian, Italian, and Swiss newspapers. Hits to HollaBack websites come from as far away as South Africa and South America. In India, Black Noise, a national movement modeled on HollaBack, places photos of harassers on the Internet and organizes "interventions" on the streets.

Literally thousands of stories have been posted on HollaBack websites (you can access these sites at http://www.ihollaback.org/). Some of the stories are of men who do not understand how and why their comments are harassing, similar to the construction worker described earlier, who imagined that he was bringing joy into the drab lives of middle-aged women. Many stories, however, tell of strangers groping women on public transportation, following them home, or threatening them with violence, such as this one, from December 2006:

Tonight around 10 PM, on a train back to her apartment in Williamsburg, a hooded man seated next to my best friend, a 22 year old woman, whispered in her ear "I am going to follow you when you get up." He did follow her, just a step behind, up the subway steps of her stop and out onto the street. With great clarity in a life-threatening moment, she stepped inside a bodega, while he stood outside, waiting for her, and was fortunate to find a couple who were willing to walk her the few steps from the market to her apartment door. When they exited the bodega, the hooded man was still there, waiting for his (potential) victim. Unfortunately, it took the help of two people—a woman to make her feel safe, and a man to protect her—to allow this woman to arrive home unharmed. (Horton 2006)

The HollaBack sites have brought to light an international problem that women confront in their daily lives and have started a public conversation about it. This conversation moves the problem from an individual matter that women face alone to a discussion that gives voice to the victims of harassment and allows them to discuss together the ways to grapple with it (see Box 8-2).

Most stories of harassment that are posted on the HollaBack sites end without physical harm to the mainly white middle-class young women who post them. Violence may be "merely" threatening to many young, white women on the city streets, but street violence is an even more common occurrence in poor and minority neighborhoods, where frequent robberies and shootings keep people on edge. The violence is a result of the lethal combination of gangs, drugs, guns, and police. Mothers in these neighborhoods worry about how aggressive policing, which they see as racist, will harm them and their children (Epstein 2003). Gangs and drug dealers also threaten the street life of these communities. One resident of a poor New York City neighborhood told a reporter, "I had to be worried all the time, you know. Are the children gonna get hit by a car? Is something gonna happen? We've lived in neighborhoods with a lot of drugs, a lot of people getting killed. You'd read about it in the paper the next day and think: Oh, God! That's only two blocks from here" (Epstein 2003, 102).

GENDER IN EVERYDAY LIFE   BOX 8-2
CAREFUL! WOMEN ANSWER BACK

This text is taken from a German feminist poster. It was translated and posted on the blog Feministing, setting off a debate on whether women were justified in preaching violent retaliation for harassment. What do you think? See the comments at http://flickr.com/photos/yog/171269949/.

> If you stupidly stare at a woman, talk rubbish or touch her, you have to be aware that she might insult you loudly, a glass of beer is emptied over you or you might be hit in the face. We strongly advise you to refrain from this kind of harrassments [sic].
>
> Women, migrants, homeless people, transgender people, gays and lesbians are often victims of assaults. Don't look away, interfere!

One outcome of the reign of terror in poor neighborhoods is that residents, especially children, get sick. Poor parents, terrified that their kids will be killed on the street, tend to keep them inside, with the windows shut and the TV on, where they are constantly exposed to contaminants in indoor air and have little opportunity to exercise. The epidemics of childhood asthma, obesity, and diabetes that trouble poor families are outcomes of the wars among gangs, drug dealers, and police. A clinical psychologist quoted by Epstein noted the surprising impact of the reign of terror on neighborhood mothers and their children: "The best parents—the people who are the most upright, the churchgoers, the most protective mothers—keep their kids inside, and they are at the intersection of the asthma and obesity epidemics" (Epstein 2003, 98).

Accounts of life in poor New York neighborhoods reveal several dimensions of gendered violence. There is the violence of gang members and criminals, mainly but not solely men, that threatens neighbors in the community. There is the masculinized and militarized violence of police, chiefly men, whose professional status entitles them to threaten and (literally) push the women and men bystanders around. There is the less visible violence of landlords and public-housing authorities, who fail to provide adequate dwellings for their tenants. This violence gives mothers little peace of mind. They suffer the anxiety that visits those with little control over the dangers they and their children face in the neighborhood. These women suffer the intersecting oppressions of race, poverty, and gender that structure their lives and their prospects.

MEN'S PERSONAL SAFETY AND GENDERED VIOLENCE

Men are supposed to know how to protect themselves from violence, and in fact, most report that they do not feel threatened by public violence or worry about their personal safety. Actually, men's dismissal of public violence does not reflect reality, because men's rates of victimization in public spaces are higher than those of women (Stanko 1990). Perhaps such fearlessness is an example of masculine bravado, a way of being masculine.

Men first learn about gendered dangers as boys, in the context of other boys' violence and threats. Such dangers are masculinized and often sexualized as well. What do boys learn about violence in childhood? Rather than learn to avoid violence, as girls do, many boys must learn to take violence and to dish it out. James Messerschmidt sees violence as a resource for "doing masculinity." Many boys learn as they grow up that aggressiveness and the capacity for violence can affirm their masculinity in the contexts of home, school, and sports (Messerschmidt 2000, 13–14). Using violence against others is learned, among other sites, in school sports (Messner 1992, 64–81) and is supported by peer groups and teachers as they celebrate the dominant gender conventions surrounding boy athletes and girl cheerleaders. Sociologist Don Sabo (1994) recounts how his feelings of inadequacy as a boy shaped his school football career. Feeling "too fat, too short, [and] too weak," Sabo learned to take pain like a man. "Calisthenics until my arms ached. Hitting hard and fast and knocking the other guy down. Getting hit in the groin and not crying. . . . By the time I reported for my first high-school practice . . . I already knew what was expected of me. . . . The way to succeed was to be an animal. . . . Being an animal meant being ruthlessly aggressive and competitive" (Sabo 1994, 12).

Aggression and threat are sexualized as well. High-status boys in grade school and high school maintain their position in the male peer group through heterosexist and misogynist banter or highly competitive "cut talk." Michael Messner describes such a contest he had with a boy named Chris when he was a fifth-grader (Messner 2002, 33):

> I thought I was doing pretty well until Chris hit me with one for which I had no answer: "Messner," he asserted, "blow me!" I didn't know what to say back, and so of course I lost the cut fight. But behind my lack of response was confusion. In my eleven-year-old mind, I knew a few things about sex but was unclear about others. One thing I had recently learned from friends was that there were some men who had sex with other men. They were called homosexuals, and I was told that they were sick and sinful individuals. So . . . if Chris was saying, "blow me" to me, he was in effect asking me to be involved in some homosexual act with him. If homosexuality is such bad and shameful thing, why then did *he* win the cut fight? . . .
>
> Now I can see that insults like "you suck," "blow me," or "fuck you" smuggle into children's and preadolescent groups a powerful pedagogy about sexuality, power, and domination. In short, though children obviously do not intend it, through this sort of banter they teach each other that sex, whether of the homosexual or heterosexual kind, is a relational act of domination and subordination. The "men" are the ones who are on top, in control, doing the penetrating and fucking. Women, or penetrated men, are subordinate, degraded, and dehumanized objects of sexual aggression.

RAPE AND DOMESTIC VIOLENCE

One of the most prevalent myths about rape is that "rapists are hiding in the bushes." In fact, most sexual assaults and rapes of women are committed by their husbands or boyfriends (18% percent), relatives (3% percent), or friends and acquaintances (42% percent) (Rand 2009). It is men who are more likely to be assaulted by strangers. Fifty-four percent of those who violently attacked men in 2005 were strangers, and only 3 percent were intimates (U.S. Department of Justice 2005) (see Figure 8-2). There are indications that efforts to reduce gendered violence are bearing fruit. From 1995 to 2010, the annual rate of female rape or sexual assault victimizations declined 58 percent, from 5.0 victimizations per 1,000 women age 12 or older to 2.1 per 1,000 (Berzofsky, Krebs, Langton, Planty, and Smiley-McDonald 2013).

The most likely victims of rape are young women and girls, and of these, the most vulnerable to rape are young women of color and working-class women. About half of all rape victims are in the lowest third of income distribution (U.S. Department of Justice 2005). Estimates of the rates of sexual violence are difficult to make because more than half of all rapes are unreported, according to the *National Crime Victimization Survey*. Rape crisis counselors believe that underestimates are very significant, because they believe that only one in fifty raped women report the crime to the police.

Men are estimated to be about 19 percent of all victims of rape. Shame, confusion, and fear of being seen as homosexual often make male victims reluctant to call the police. Some believe that most male rape occurs in prison, but research suggests that prison is not the only

FIGURE 8-2 Average Annual Rate of Nonfatal Intimate Partner Victimization, by Type of Crime, 2001–2005.

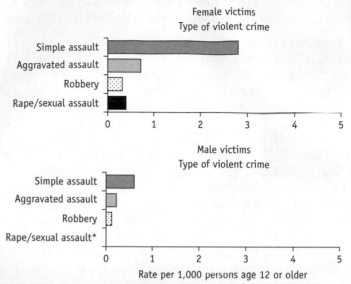

*Information about rape victimization of males is not provided because the small number of cases is insufficient for reliable estimates.

On average between 2001 and 2005, females experienced higher rates of nonfatal intimate partner violence than males in each type of crime.

Source: Bureau of Justice Statistics, 2011.

place men and boys are raped. In Western countries, 5 to 10 percent of men report a history of childhood sexual abuse. A 1991 study of incarcerated and nonincarcerated male rape victims in Tennessee found that men and teenage boys (the more likely victims) are most often raped in remote areas outdoors or while hitchhiking. The assault usually involves penetration of the victim anally, orally, or both. Gang rape is more common in cases involving male victims than those involving female victims. Weapons and serious physical injury are more likely to accompany male-on-male rape (Lipscomb, Muram, Speck, and Mercer 1992; Rand 2009).

Adolescent girls and college women are at risk of becoming victims of "**acquaintance**" or "**date rape**." A 1996 national study found that 25 percent of college women surveyed reported having had unwanted sexual intercourse. Of these women, 84 percent knew their assailant, 57 percent of the episodes occurred on dates, and 41 percent of the women stated that they were virgins at the time of the assault. These data probably underestimate the true incidence of date rape, because students often do not report attempted or completed rapes, nor do they define many such assaults as rapes (Kilpatrick and McCauley 2009). Date rape is more likely to occur in fraternities and is associated with alcohol and gender stereotyping of women (Martin and Hummer 1989, Krebs, Lindquist, Warner, Fisher, and Martin 2007). In the 1996 study, one out of every fifteen male college students admitted that he had raped or tried to rape a female student during the preceding year. A 1998 survey asked young British men whether they would force a woman to have sex. One in eight said they might in a long-term relationship, and one in sixteen would if they had " 'spent a lot of money on her' or if she had 'slept with loads of men' " (Martin and Hummer 1989, 284).

Recent Decline in Rape Statistics

We have seen that there has been a significant decline in rape over the past several decades. Why has this decline occurred? Some argue that the statistics are flawed because so many rapes are unreported so that we do not really know if the numbers have declined, risen, or stayed the same. Some advocates who work with rape victims believe that rape has not declined. Rather, they say, it has moved from the cities, from which the U.S. Justice Department's *National Crime Victimization Survey* draws its statistics, to the suburbs, which are not included in this survey. Other experts, however, believe that the decline is real, and they credit changes that have emerged in laws, policies, and ideas as a result of more than four decades of work by feminists.

Activists have established rape crisis hotlines and services, convinced police and the courts to show greater sensitivity toward rape victims, and convinced news organizations to respect victims' privacy. They have encouraged women to take charge of their own security by sponsoring self-defense classes and "Take Back the Night" demonstrations. College and high school students now learn about the rules of consent and that "no means no." However, as Table 8-2 shows, the greatest decline in gendered violence has not been men's violence against women but homicides of men by wives, girlfriends, and other female intimates. This trend may also reflect the fact that there is more material support for battered and abused women, who need not take the desperate measures they once did to escape a violent home or relationship. These changes and their implications are discussed further later in this chapter.

Accounting for Rape: Evolutionary Theory, Individual Psychology, and Inequality

Although rape may be declining in some places, it remains a major problem throughout the world. Scholars have tried to understand why it persists and why rape is so commonplace. Three kinds of theories have been advanced to explain the prevalence of rape: those that assert that rape is a product of natural selection; those that maintain that rape results from individual psychological deviance and pathology; and those that argue that rape is a political issue and an outcome of power inequalities in society.

EVOLUTIONARY THEORY. In the book *A Natural History of Rape: Biological Bases of Sexual Coercion*, Thornhill and Palmer (2000) maintain that sexual selection propels men to rape. According to their theory, men's proclivities to rape have evolved to enable men to procreate. The theory that men have drives that must be met at all costs is similar to popular notions of men's sexual needs. This theory superficially resembles the views of radical feminists such as Andrea Dworkin and Catherine MacKinnon, who link violence and rape to gendered inequality. However, unlike these feminists, who focus on ways to end male violence, the proponents of natural selection theory contend that men are forever compelled to rape because women, to the disadvantage of the species, tend to resist sex. This logic relieves men of responsibility for their violence ("it's only natural") and makes women complicit in their own victimization. To curb men's natural, hard-wired drives, Thornhill and Palmer (2000) recommend that women should neither flirt nor wear provocative clothing—advice similar to that given by the men of Shiv Sena in India! The natural selection theory of rape assumes that the patterns of sexual violence in the United States are universal; but cross-cultural research shows that the incidence of rape varies greatly from culture to culture. If the biological imperative to rape is as powerful and as universal as Thornhill and Palmer (2000) insist, why does its frequency vary so much across cultures? Why don't all men commit rape?

Are these studies of hunter-gatherer societies relevant to our own postindustrial societies? Although it is bad science to compare large contemporary societies with smaller preliterate ones, there are suggestive parallels. America has one of the most rape-prone of all contemporary cultures. Despite great strides toward women's equality in the United States, men remain dominant economically, politically, and culturally, although in many ways their dominant status is precarious. For many men and their families, resources are diminishing as jobs are outsourced, unemployment grows, and wealth inequality reaches unprecedented levels. As more and more women enter the workforce to share breadwinning tasks with men, many men feel that they have lost their dominant economic position relative to women. They learn from the media and the wider culture that force is the prevalent and legitimate way to pursue national and international goals. No wonder some believe that violence can help them resolve their own problems and worries. This cultural context of violence sets the stage for interpersonal violence.

In this context, what do declining rates of rape mean? We suggested previously that we might credit the decades-long and increasingly international women's movements for publicizing the issues of violence against women and for making important changes in the laws, for educating women and men about gendered violence, and for some women's and men's willingness to work for fundamental changes. The background to these changes includes women's growing labor-force participation, which allows many to leave violent and potentially violent situations, and the growth of organizations devoted to challenging violence against women. Perhaps the current epidemic of gendered violence reflects what Riane Eisler calls a "dying system's violent efforts to maintain its hold" (Eisler 1987, 171) and suggests that we are on the cusp of a new order.

INDIVIDUAL PSYCHOLOGY. Psychological explanations of rape focus on the disturbed and pathological personalities of individuals who have been identified as rapists. Some studies suggest that men who rape children were themselves sexually abused as children. The psychological damage caused by their experience as children results in their aberrant behavior as adults. Other studies focus on rapists' emotional need to dominate and feel power over their victims, their inabilities to relate to women, or their feelings of anger toward and hatred of women.

These explanations may clarify why individuals choose violent strategies to resolve their troubles. However, there are two problems with exclusive reliance on individual psychology to explain violence as a collective phenomenon. First, by ripping individual acts from their social contexts and viewing sexual violence as the conduct of deviant or troubled individuals, we miss seeing the structured dimensions of violence and are blind to the ways social institutions shape our behavior. Second, we are unable to explain why violence is predominantly men's violence. Boys and girls are both sexually abused. Men and women are both likely to feel anger and a desire to control others. Why are men so much more likely to respond by resorting to violence? The contexts within which individual violence erupts—institutions of social control based on violence and a climate condoning violence against women and violence in general—are certainly important parts of the puzzle. Ideas about what boys and men are supposed to be like and the tie between masculinity and violence are critical but often ignored factors by those who explain violence as an individual psychological problem.

Some examples of individualized psychological explanations of violence are the media descriptions of the school shootings that have erupted occasionally in the past decade. These reports ignored the central feature of the shootings: Middle-class white boys were the shooters (see Box 8-3). Michael Kimmel (2000) asks his readers to "try a little thought experiment":

Imagine that the killers in Littleton—and in Pearl, Mississippi, Paducah, Kentucky, Springfield, Oregon, and Jonesboro, Arkansas—were all black girls from poor families who lived in New Haven, Connecticut, Newark, New Jersey, or Providence,

GENDER IN EVERYDAY LIFE   BOX 8-3
COVERAGE OF "SCHOOL SHOOTINGS" AVOIDS THE CENTRAL ISSUE

In the many hours devoted to analyzing the recent school shootings, once again we see that as a society we seem constitutionally unable, or unwilling, to acknowledge a simple but disturbing fact: these shootings are an extreme manifestation of one of contemporary American society's biggest problems—the ongoing crisis of men's violence against women.

October is Domestic Violence Awareness Month, so let's take a good hard look at these latest horrific cases of violence on the domestic front. On September 27, a heavily armed 53-year-old man walked into a Colorado high school classroom, forced male students to leave, and took a group of girls hostage. He then proceeded to terrorize the girls for several hours, killing one and allegedly sexually assaulting some or all of the others before killing himself.

Less than a week later, a heavily armed 32-year-old man walked into an Amish schoolhouse in Pennsylvania and ordered about 15 boys to leave the room, along with a pregnant woman and three women with infants. He forced the remaining girls, aged 6 to 13, to line up against a blackboard, where he tied their feet together. He then methodically executed five of the girls with shots to the head and critically wounded several others before taking his own life.

Just after the Amish schoolhouse massacre, Pennsylvania Police Commissioner Jeffrey B. Miller said in an emotional press conference, "It seems as though (the perpetrator) wanted to attack young, female victims."

How did mainstream media cover these unspeakable acts of gender violence? The *New York Times* ran an editorial that identified the "most important" cause as the easy access to guns in our society. NPR did a show which focused on problems in rural America. Forensic psychologists and criminal profilers filled the airwaves with talk about how difficult it is to predict when a "person" will snap. And countless exasperated commentators—from fundamentalist preachers to secular social critics—abandoned any pretense toward logic and reason in their rush to weigh in with metaphysical musings on the incomprehensibility of "evil."

Incredibly, few if any prominent voices in the broadcast or print media have called the incidents what they are: hate crimes perpetrated by angry white men against defenseless young girls, who—whatever the twisted motives of the shooters—were targeted for sexual assault and murder precisely because they are girls.

What is it going to take for our society to deal honestly with the extent and depth of this problem? How many more young girls have to die before decision-makers in media and other influential institutions stop averting their eyes from the lethal mix of deep misogyny and violent masculinity at work here? In response to the recent spate of shootings, the White House announced plans to bring together experts in education and law enforcement. The goal was to discuss "the nature of the problem" and federal action that can assist communities with violence prevention. This approach is misdirected. Instead of convening a group of experts on "school safety," the president should catalyze a long-overdue national conversation about sexism, masculinity, and men's violence against women.

For us to have any hope of truly preventing not only extreme acts of gender violence, but also the incidents of rape, sexual abuse and domestic violence that are a daily part of millions of women's and girls' lives, we need to have this conversation. And we need many more men to participate. Men from every level of society need to recognize that violence against women is a men's issue.

A similar incident to the Amish schoolhouse massacre took place in Canada in 1989. A heavily armed 25-year-old man walked into a classroom at the University of Montreal. He forced the men out of the classroom at gunpoint, and then opened fire on the women. He killed fourteen women and injured many more, before committing suicide.

In response to this atrocity, in 1991 a number of Canadian men created the White Ribbon Campaign. The idea was for men to wear a white ribbon as a way of making a visible and public pledge "never to commit, condone, nor remain silent about violence against women." The White Ribbon Campaign has since become a part of Canadian culture, and it has been adapted in dozens of countries.

After the horrors in this country over the past two weeks, the challenge for American men is clear: will we respond to these recent tragedies by averting our eyes and pretending that none of this happened? Or will we at long last break our complicit silence and work together with women to turn these tragedies into a transformative cultural moment?

SOURCE: Reprinted with permission from Katz (2006).

Rhode Island. I believe we'd now be having a national debate about inner-city poor black girls. . . . Yet the obvious fact that these school killers were all middle-class white boys seems to have escaped everyone's notice. . . . Yet gender is the single most obvious and intractable difference when it comes to violence in America. Men and boys are responsible for 95% of all violent crimes in this country. (Kimmel 2000, 5)

A second problem with individual explanations is that they draw on biased samples of captured and convicted rapists to develop theories of rape. Such samples overrepresent poor men and men of color, who are most likely to be charged and prosecuted for these crimes and often wrongly convicted and imprisoned. White men, powerful men, and wealthy men who rape may be relatively immune from criminal charges, and therefore are rarely part of such studies (see Weitzman 2000).

POWER INEQUALITY. Kimmel (2004) proposes an alternative to evolutionary and psychological explanations of male violence. He suggests that gender is the *outcome* of inequality, not its cause. In other words, power differences between men and women produce gender domination and subordination, leading to men's sexual entitlement and rape. Gender legitimizes these inequalities by **naturalizing** them. Women seem naturally submissive, and men seem naturally dominant. However, gender is not natural. It is socially constructed along lines of differential power. Kimmel goes further to suggest that the social positions people occupy—for example, their class and racial ethnic locations—account for more differences among them than does gender alone. In this view, Kimmel invokes the theory of "intersectionality." You should recall from chapter 1 that intersectionality helps us see the broad range of social factors that tie us together and the ways that systems of inequality and power based on gender, race ethnicity, and social class intersect to create relationships, sometimes violent, that reflect and maintain those systems of power.

However, the same power relationships that create and nourish inequality and violence also bring forth resistance. Gender inequalities, together with the power and violence that sustain them, shift and change with time. Until the nineteenth century, physical punishment of slaves, children, and wives was legitimate. Indeed, "spare the rod and spoil the child" was a common sentiment that held sway among educators and parents long into the twentieth century. Husbands had the right to punish their wives physically under English common law, but mid-nineteenth-century feminists began to question that right. It was more than a century later, in the 1970s, that the feminist movement against violence had an impact. At that point, feminists successfully labeled several forms of intimate violence including date rape, sexual harassment, and domestic violence. They redefined rape to include forced sex in marriage. They argued that so-called private violence—individual men's use of force against women they knew—was as illegitimate and as criminal as raping or beating strangers. This history shows that what counts as rape or unacceptable violence changes with our changing circumstances and consciousness.

An assumption often underpinning evolutionary and psychological theories of rape is that it is universal because men's bodies have the biological "equipment" to rape and women's bodies the equipment to be raped. These ideas sneak biology back into the discussions of sexual violence. Canadian feminist Susan Griffin (1979, 3) invoked nature when she wrote, "I have never been free of the fear of rape. From a very early age, I, like most women, have thought of rape as part of my natural environment—something to be feared and prayed against like fire and lightning. I never asked why men raped. *I simply thought it one of the mysteries of human nature*" (emphasis added).

Gordon and Riger (1989) called rape "the female fear" and maintained that "every women has it to a degree and all women are affected by it." Helliwell (2000) suggests that these assumptions falsely universalize Western women's experiences. We have seen that not all cultures masculinize men and feminize women as two opposite and unequal genders. Helliwell suggests that Western inequalities of wealth and power between women and men (Kimmel's argument) give meaning and impetus to the practice of rape, but she notes that there are other societies in which rape has no meaning.

A second implicit assumption in some rape studies, and in the popular imagination as well, is that rape is a feature of violent black or third-world cultures. As we saw in the discussion of rape and racism in chapter 4, images and laws regarding rape have a long history of tying together racist ideologies, rape, and relationships among women and men of different racial ethnic groups.

Ending Rape

Cross-cultural data on rape-free societies hold out the possibility of a world without sexual violence. Kimmel's theory that inequality produces gender differences and that gender difference legitimizes and naturalizes inequality suggests that ending inequalities of power, wealth, and status between men and women will help us bring that world into being.

Breaking the silence and turning the experiences of rape into social problems were early steps toward ending sexual violence. As social problems, date rape and marital rape identified actions that were once accepted and were invisible as actionable criminal offenses. Antiviolence advocates encouraged fighting back, overturning the conventional wisdom of an earlier day that women should submit to their attackers to avoid further violence. They renamed raped and battered women "survivors," not victims. They built organizations and services—hotlines, support groups, and rape crisis centers—to tackle these newly identified crimes. They offered training to women in martial arts and ways to reclaim public space. Take Back the Night marches became annual events on many college campuses. Men have been enlisted in the antirape movement, and many have formed their own antiviolence projects (see Box 8-4).

GENDER IN EVERYDAY LIFE   BOX 8-4
MEN CAN STOP RAPE CELEBRATES 10 MILESTONES DURING 10 YEARS OF PREVENTION

Men Can Stop Rape mobilizes male youth to prevent men's violence against women. We build young men's capacity to challenge harmful aspects of traditional masculinity, to value alternative visions of male strength, and to embrace their vital role as allies with women and girls in fostering healthy relationships and gender equity.

1. TRAVELING MEN

Only three days after launching a new website following the incorporation of the Men's Rape Prevention Project on January 13, 1997, the Co-Directors received an email from

North Park College in Chicago, IL, requesting a workshop on its campus, heralding the organization's first out of town trip. During February 1997, Patrick and Jonathan traveled to Chicago where they facilitated an early version of what became one of Men Can Stop Rape's signature exercises, The Continuum of Harm, with 40 North Park College students.

2. FINDING AN OFFICE AWAY FROM HOME

Pat McGann, MCSR's Communication Director, initially started as Volunteer Coordinator in the summer of 1998. Jonathan, Patrick, and Pat worked from their homes and all were unpaid, until the organization hired Jonathan in April 1999 to write grants for four hours a week. By September 1999, enough funding had been secured to allow the three of them to take work out of their homes and move it into Men Can Stop Rape's first office, located in the Josephine Butler Center, a 40-room Renaissance-revival style mansion that formerly served as the Embassy of Hungary and Brazil. The Center was named after one of Washington, DC's most respected activists.

3. BUILDING MEN OF STRENGTH

By 1999, after conducting numerous presentations in DC high schools, the Co-Directors had become frustrated with the limitations of the one-workshop model. That same year, Charles Miles, Director of the Ballou Boys and Girls Club of Greater Washington, contacted the Men's Rape Prevention Project about presenting to the boys in the club. Jonathan and Patrick pitched the idea of five or more workshops. Mr. Miles enthusiastically responded, proposing meeting once-a-week for 10 weeks. After prompting by Mr. Miles to name the group, Jonathan brainstormed the Men of Strength (MOST) Club, and meetings began in January 2000. Under the guidance of Neil Irvin, hired in the spring of 2001 as Community Director, the Club has become the national model for mobilizing young men to prevent violence against women.

4. A CITY OF STRENGTH

In late 1999, John Stoltenberg, Board President of the Men's Rape Prevention Project, was asked by the co-directors to review the organization's information sheet, "What Men Can Do." Trying to come up with more inspirational language, he added to the end of the page, "My Strength Is Not for Hurting." Talk quickly turned to developing a media campaign using the phrase as the theme line. An advisory committee consisting of school administrators, faculty and staff was formed, funding was secured from Barbara Lovenheim and BIL Charitable Trust, and in February 2001, the groundbreaking Strength Media Campaign was launched in all seventeen Washington, DC public high schools. For the first time in the history of the city, bus shelter and bus side ads, REP Magazine, and posters in school hallways and classrooms declared that young men could be strong without using intimidation, force, or violence. And for the first time, all the PSA media materials had the name, Men Can Stop Rape, printed on them.

5. VIRGINIA'S STRENGTH IS NOT FOR HURTING

Immediately after the Strength Media Campaign ended in DC, Men Can Stop Rape began selling the Campaign's posters, which spread across the country like wildfire. Robert Franklin first learned of the posters while at the University of Maine, Orono, but moved to Virginia when he was hired by the slate's Department of Health as Sexual Violence Male Outreach Coordinator. Both he and his supervisor, Rebecca Odor, wanted to use the posters' messages, although in a campaign that would specifically be identified with the Virginia Department of Health (VDH). As a result of this interest, VDH in 2003 was the first in a line of agencies, coalitions, and organizations to license what are now referred to as Strength Mediaworks materials.

6. EARNING SPECIAL DISTINCTION

Every year the Ms. Foundation for Women recognizes those men and women whose work is in line with the Foundation's past, as well as its vision for the future. Men Can Stop Rape was honored to be a part of this tradition as a recipient of the 15th Annual Gloria Awards on May 15, 2003 at the Waldorf-Astoria Hotel in New York City. The entire MCSR staff attended the evening's events, brushing shoulders with Ms. Foundation celebrity guests and supporters like Kathy Najimy, Gloria Steinem, Marlo Thomas, and Phil Donahue. Honored for its pioneering efforts in the men's movement to join with women as allies in ending sexual violence, MCSR earned special distinction as the first organization targeting its services toward men to receive a Gloria Award. Yoko Ono Lennon flew in from L.A. to present the Award to Co-Founders Patrick Lemmon and Jonathan Stillerman, as well as 17-year-old Men of Strength Club member, William Powell.

7. SCHOOLING IN EVALUATION

Lacking expertise in evaluation but recognizing its absolute necessity, Patrick Lemmon submitted a proposal to the Centers for Disease Control and Prevention for a technical assistance grant that would assess best practices for primary prevention programs aimed at preventing young men and boys from committing sexual assault. Neil Irvin, hired specifically to grow the Club as Community Educator, had made substantial inroads so that, in the short span of a year, the number of Clubs had jumped from one to four. This healthy growth and a strong commitment to evaluation prompted the CDC to select the Men of Strength Club as one of four nationwide participants in a two-year evaluation project starting in 2003. Initial results in 2005 led the CDC to declare the MOST Club a promising strategy and to support further evaluation.

8. BE BOLD, BE STRONG, TAKE ACTION

In February 2004, Pat McGann, then Director of Outreach, had a burst of insight: why not have MOST Club members take action in their schools during all of April, Sexual Assault Awareness Month and call it 30 Days of Strength? Neil Irvin, Community Director and now National Director of the Men of Strength Club, embraced the idea and its tagline—Be Bold, Be Strong, Take Action. Committees consisting of two to three Club members at School Without Walls DC Senior Public High School coordinated open meetings for their peers, passed out "Action Sheets" listing weekly awareness and prevention activities, put up 30 Days' messages on the school computers' screen savers, informed the student body about issues of teen dating violence during morning announcements, and hung "My Strength Is Not for Hurting" posters throughout the school.

9. CALIFORNIA DREAMIN'

In late spring of 2005, the California Coalition Against Sexual Assault (CALCASA) initiated an exhaustive search for sexual assault primary prevention campaigns targeting high school age young men so they could decide how best to develop their own campaign. In the end CALCASA chose to license MCSR's Strength Campaign specifically because it offered a positive, integrated, comprehensive approach unlike any other. Starting in September 2005, the bolder, new look of the multimedia component of the My Strength Campaign blanketed the cities and towns of the 66 rape crisis centers across the state. Never before had such a vast array of "My Strength Is Not for Hurting" media materials highlighted positive masculinity. And in conjunction with the media campaign, six MOST Clubs were established in a wide variety of settings throughout California, from urban multicultural to rural white to rural Spanish-speaking. The launch of the Campaign received coverage in a remarkable 150+ news stories, a new precedent for rape prevention initiatives throughout the nation.

10. REACHING ACROSS THE GLOBE

Although Men Can Stop Rape had already licensed media materials outside the United States, Strength Mediaworks traveled farther from home than ever before in November 2005 when MCSR struck up a licensing agreement with EngenderHealth for South African Men as Partners Network and the Western Cape Office on the Status of Women. Twelve posters conveying messages in English, Afrikaans, and isiXhosa, peopled with South African models, and bathed in rich pastels and earth tones, gave Mediaworks a new vibrant look. The posters' positive prevention messages reached South African men across the country during "16 Days of Activism Against Gender Violence"—a worldwide campaign—that ran from International Day for the Elimination of Violence Against Women, November 25, through International Human Rights Day, December 10.

SOURCE: Reprinted with permission from MEN CAN STOP RAPE, INC. www.mencanstoprape.org (2007).

THE DISCOVERY OF DOMESTIC VIOLENCE

Like rape, domestic violence was invisible until it was named by feminists in the 1970s. Of course, many people knew individual women who had been beaten by a husband or boyfriend, or perhaps they themselves had been battered. Each incident seemed no more than an unfortunate event, the outcome of an argument, a sign of individual pathology, the outburst of an out-of-control husband, or a response to a nagging wife. Like the discontent of middle-class housewives identified a decade earlier by Betty Friedan, it was hard to see battering as a large-scale social issue. Domestic violence was another **"problem that had no name,"** raising little public concern until the women's movement discovered it and turned it into a social problem. Feminists rejected the sentimental notion that families were naturally supportive and loving units and the conviction that violence in families was a private matter. They reframed families as sites of political struggle and renamed battering as a criminal act. They drew attention to institutionalized male dominance and looked to police, prosecutors, and judges in the criminal courts to support women's safety by making it easier to bring batterers to justice.

Readers of this book are learning to identify the cultural, political, and social changes in the 1960s and 1970s that helped move domestic violence into the public eye. People were marrying later or not at all and divorcing more often, thereby avoiding or cutting short many potentially abusive situations. A changing division of labor that brought women into the workforce allowed women to attain more education and compressed their childbearing years, so that many women were becoming less dependent on men for support. More directly, the growing movements for women's rights lent weight to the cause of terrorized and beaten women.

Early studies of domestic violence showed that many attacks on women by the men they lived with were prompted by their failures to be "good wives" or to "do family" properly. For example, women were assaulted for not cooking or not cooking well, for failing to do housework, or for failing to be adequately deferential to their men. Interviews with batterers found that men believed it was their right as men to beat wives who disobeyed them. Such violence was most likely to occur in households in which both wife and husband agreed that male dominance and control was legitimate.

Sexual jealousy and possessiveness also precipitated active violence. Batterers often treated other men, but also wives' friends and family, as competitors, and used marital rape as punishment for challenging their claim to women's presence and their bodies (Ptacek 1988).

Laws now criminalize battering in many nations, but even today where the laws are in place, some police and some courts continue to treat violence between spouses as a personal problem that does not belong in the criminal justice system. In the 1970s, when women first attempted to use the criminal justice system to restrain violent men, they discovered that it was at best a crude instrument. Most police were reluctant to arrest men for domestic battery, and many judges shied away from imposing sentences on the men who were brought before them. They were strongly opposed to ousting "good fathers" from their homes and suspected women of making "exaggerated claims" to win benefits from the courts (Radford 1987). Prosecutors and public defenders in Chicago's domestic violence court called some of the women who brought charges against their abusive husbands "abusers" of the criminal justice system, and the court reprimanded them for their false claims and vindictiveness toward men (Wittner 1998).

The laws themselves were difficult to apply to domestic violence cases (Eaton 1986). For example, a woman charged with battery or murder could claim self-defense only if she acted to defend herself from immediate attack. This "reasonable person" standard of the law assumed women should be able to call on their own physical strength to defend themselves in the face of a threat. However, most women's size, strength, socialization, and lack of training in hand-to-hand combat ensured they would be no match for an assailant. If a woman's assault on an abuser took place while he was asleep or was not immediately threatening her, it did not meet the legal standard of self-defense no matter how brutal, unrelenting, and abusive he might have been. The result was that women who retaliated against abusers often faced long prison sentences.

Juries often held stereotyped views of battered women as defendants in criminal cases. Such biases reflected the attitudes of an unsympathetic wider public. A survey conducted in upstate New York in the mid-1980s found that most respondents believed that women were at least partially responsible for the assaults they suffered and thought of them as masochistic or emotionally disturbed if they remained with their husbands (Ewing and Aubrey 1987). An article addressed to attorneys for women who killed abusive mates in self-defense cautioned against constructing a defense around battering as a women's issue, because many jurors could not recognize abuse or would not rule in favor of the women in an effort to preserve families (Thompson 1986). In fact, the assumptions that guided criminal justice professionals and the wider public regarding domestic violence were close to the rationalizations employed by convicted batterers. For example, Ptacek (1988) found that police officers, court clerks, and judges agreed with batterers that wives often provoked the violence husbands visited on them.

In summary, as domestic violence was emerging as a social issue, women who looked for safety and protection from the criminal justice system were learning that institutional practices and practitioners implicated women in their own victimization and excused violent partners. Stereotypes of women informed professionals and the public. There was more interest in preserving families than in women's safety.

Studies of Domestic Violence

During the 1970s and 1980s, the battered-women's movement gained strength and visibility, garnering sympathy for battered women, changing the laws and women's reception in the courts, and influencing national legislation for the protection of victims of domestic violence. Scholars participated in this national awakening to personal violence in families.

Studies conducted by sociologist Murray Straus and his associates stressed that women and men were equally responsible for violence in families. The individual violent acts reported in their national random-sample study of family violence seemed to show that women were as violent as men. These data prompted one of the principal investigators, Suzanne Steinmetz, to coin the phrase, "the battered husband syndrome" and to argue that abuse of husbands was as common as wife battering (Steinmetz 1978; Straus, Gelles, and Steinmetz 1980). Lenore Walker (1979) attributed failure to leave an abusive relationship to "learned helplessness," a psychological explanation that drew on and amplified the stereotype of battered women as passive and helpless.

By the late 1970s, feminist scholars began to question these stereotypes. They argued that Straus's survey data did not take into account the contexts of violence. What if these data were reflecting women's attempts to defend themselves? Was a wife's slap the equivalent of a husband's punch? Was "learned helplessness" an accurate description of women's actions, or was getting away from violent men harder than it seemed? Certainly there was evidence that many abused women looked for help from families, neighbors, doctors, and others (Labell 1979). And why was "family violence" almost invariably men's violence against women and children?

Partially on the basis of such research, activists successfully pressured the courts to provide better legal services to women complainants and to change court procedures. There were dramatic changes in the responses of police and the courts to women's complaints. Increasingly the courts came to accept domestic violence as a crime rather than as a personal trouble. Throughout the 1980s, states passed laws giving police the power to arrest batterers for misdemeanor assaults and required police to provide battered women with information about their legal options and the services available to them. In some cases, police departments adopted a policy of mandatory arrest (Hanmer, Radford, and Stanko 1989, 157).

Kathleen Ferraro (1988) investigated the actual practices of police in domestic violence calls. Police statistics showed that there were 21,000 calls to police coded as family fights in 1984 in Phoenix. Of these, 1,250 resulted in arrests and 2,000 more in detective reports. What happened to the other cases? To answer this question, Ferraro accompanied police on domestic violence calls to observe firsthand the context of police decision making. She found that police attitudes about domestic violence informed their responses. For example, police believed that women could easily choose to leave an abusive household, and if they did not, it proved that their complaints were frivolous. If the violence did not spill out into public space, but remained contained within the home, police saw it as a private fight, in which they had no right to intervene. They were even less likely to consider battering a serious crime when it occurred in minority and low-income households.

Disillusionment with criminal justice solutions to the problem of family violence soon emerged. Even with mandatory arrest policies in place, police often turned a deaf ear to women's complaints and failed to tell complainants about the services and alternatives available to them. Even more chilling, mandatory arrest policies sometimes resulted in women's arrests and, sometimes, in the deportation of abused women who were undocumented. Women still could not count on police protection.

Failures of the police and justice system to protect American women from violence mirrored failures in other parts of the world, although the latter continued to have more consistently gruesome results. For example, men in Bangladesh, Great Britain, Brazil, Ecuador, Egypt, India, Israel, Italy, Jordan, Pakistan, Morocco, Sweden, Turkey, and Uganda have committed honor killings and acid assaults with impunity on women who displeased husbands, fathers, and brothers or violated community standards of female conduct. Police often refused to believe women who asked them for protection and turned a blind eye to these assaults and murders.

From Universality to Intersectionality

By the 1990s, the battered-women's movement had successfully redefined domestic violence as a public problem by arguing that women of every class, racial ethnic group, sexuality, and nationality were subjected to male domination and violence and that the criminal justice system should be the first line of defense for battered women. More than two decades of hard work on behalf of battered women had won the movement notable successes. Police were better informed about domestic violence and were often mandated to arrest abusers. Prosecutors and judges were more aware of the law and more willing to act on behalf of complainants. There was more public awareness of violence against women and more support for holding batterers accountable. Battering was no longer the "problem with no name." Activists had publicized and politicized it, adding terms such as *battering* and *domestic violence* to public discourse. Domestic violence shelters and services were available to many endangered women. The movement's influence on domestic violence policies went all the way to the national level. In 1994 Congress passed the Violence Against Women Act (VAWA), providing $1.6 billion to investigate and prosecute domestic violence crimes and to provide restitution and redress in cases that local prosecutors failed to bring forward. VAWA has been reauthorized several times, most recently in 2013.

Nevertheless, problems accompanied these successes. The "one size fits all" approach to remedies did not take into account the special situations of women of color, poor women, lesbians, and immigrants, who often suffered further abuses at the hands of police or in the legal system. The first generation of antiviolence activists did not dwell on the connections between violence and race or violence and poverty for fear of supporting racist stereotypes and class biases (Sen 1999). In other words, violence against women was treated as the same problem affecting all women. It was not until the 1990s that the problems of violence against women were reframed to recognize how race ethnicity, class, and immigrant status intersected with gender, resulting in different fates for battered women and to call for different solutions.

Activists had assumed that battered women would make use of the services provided them by professionals. They could call the police, go to a safe shelter, or press charges against their abusive mates. For women without additional resources, these routes to safety were difficult, if not impossible solutions. Lacking alternatives, many battered women returned to their abusers. Criminal justice responses to domestic violence could not protect such women if they ignored the underlying structural conditions that made certain women vulnerable. For example, immigrant women needed bilingual and bicultural services to free themselves from their abusers; religious women needed special food and living arrangements; lesbians needed access to services that were not biased against them; and poor women needed affordable housing, accessible shelters, good, inexpensive child care, living-wage jobs, and "humane welfare policy" (Dasgupta 2005; Sokoloff and Dupont 2005).

Researchers began to show how reliance on the criminal justice system for relief from violence had unintended negative consequences for women of color. First, reliance on the police heightened the dangers poor women faced. Women who called the police to intervene when they were threatened were sometimes also arrested. Arrest sometimes set in motion a chain of events that led women to lose their children to foster care. In some cases, after police removed a batterer from the premises, the angry abuser returned to seek retribution. Third, many immigrant women would not call the police, fearing that their immigrant status could be questioned. Fourth, in neighborhoods and communities where police brutality was an issue and where high proportions of the population faced incarceration, a woman calling the police might be labeled a snitch or might fear contributing to stereotyping men of color as violent (Sen 1999).

Beyond Criminal Justice: Marginalized Battered Women at the Center

As it became evident that gendered violence had multiple, interconnected sources and consequences, scholars began to explore the ways that women's specific social locations of race ethnicity, class, and immigrant status shaped their experience of domestic violence and their responses to it (Josephson 2005). The idea that all women were equally at risk from all men missed the convergence of specific inequalities of class, race ethnicity, and nation in the lives of actual women and men. Moreover, listening to the experiences of domestic violence from the most marginalized and least privileged women showed that the criminal justice system also perpetuated violence against them. When white and middle-class women confronted personal violence, it was a terrifying tragedy, but many such women found the resources that allowed them to press for safety and justice. With access to health insurance, they could receive medical attention and psychological counseling. If they were employed in well-paying and secure jobs, they could obtain private legal assistance and find safe places to live. If they called the police, they need not worry that they might lose their children, their citizenship, or their freedom. On the other hand, when marginalized women of color used the criminal justice system, it was very likely to disempower and revictimize them. Aside from the immediate danger to them of calling the authorities, the system also created wider-ranging problems. First, it was disempowering to women if calling the police was the only way they could stop the violence. Second, tax income spent on policing and prisons was money that did not go to shelters, welfare, or affordable housing, leaving women less able to escape violent households. Third, the professional knowledge of workers in the criminal justice system—lawyers, social workers, and police—took precedence over the everyday knowledge of women living with violence.

If criminal justice was not the solution to violence, what was? The specifics of women's situations pointed in new directions: housing for poor battered women, bicultural and bilingual services for immigrants, shelters that accepted lesbians or homeless women, and special food and living arrangements for religious women. Placing women of color at the center of the analysis identified their specific needs. The analysis of the intersecting dimensions of risk among poor women and women of color also helped show the benefits to be gained from uniting personal struggles against gendered violence with community struggles against state violence such as police brutality, prisons, racism, and economic exploitation (Sokoloff and Dupont 2005).

An example is the coalition between the antiviolence organization INCITE! Women of Color against Violence and the human rights organization Critical Resistance, which works to eliminate the prison-industrial complex (see Box 8-5). INCITE! is a national activist organization of radical feminists of color who seek to "end violence against women of color and their communities through direct action, critical dialogue and grassroots organizing." Critical Resistance is an international movement to end the prison-industrial complex by challenging the belief that "caging and controlling people makes us safe." Security and safety will be won, they argue, when all people have their basic needs met for food, shelter, and freedom, exactly what the women's antiviolence movement also promotes (Sudbury 2005).

GENDER IN EVERYDAY LIFE   BOX 8-5

CRITICAL RESISTANCE/INCITE! JOINT STATEMENT: GENDER VIOLENCE AND THE PRISON INDUSTRIAL COMPLEX (2001)

We call [on] social justice movements to develop strategies and analysis that address both state and interpersonal violence, particularly violence against women. Currently, activists/movements that address state violence (such as anti-prison, anti-police brutality groups) often work in isolation from activists/movements that address domestic and sexual violence. The result is that women of color, who suffer disproportionately from both state and interpersonal violence, have become marginalized within these movements. It is critical that we develop responses to gender violence that do not depend on a sexist, racist, classist, and homophobic criminal justice system. It is also important that we develop strategies that challenge the criminal justice system and that also provide safety for survivors of sexual and domestic violence. To live violence-free lives, we must develop holistic strategies for addressing violence that speak to the intersection of all forms of oppression. The anti-violence movement has been critically important in breaking the silence around violence against women and providing much-needed services to survivors. However, the mainstream anti-violence movement has increasingly relied on the criminal justice system as the front-line approach toward ending violence against women of color. It is important to assess the impact of this strategy.

1. Law enforcement approaches to violence against women may deter some acts of violence in the short term. However, as an overall strategy for ending violence, criminalization has not worked. In fact, the overall impact of mandatory arrest laws for domestic violence have led to decreases in the number of battered women who kill their partners in self-defense, but they have not led to a decrease in the number of batterers who kill their partners. Thus, the law protects batterers more than it protects survivors.

2. The criminalization approach has also brought many women into conflict with the law, particularly women of color, poor women, lesbians, sex workers, immigrant women, women with disabilities, and other marginalized women. For instance, under mandatory arrest laws, there have been numerous incidents where police officers called to domestic incidents have arrested the woman who is being battered. Many undocumented women have reported cases of sexual and domestic violence, only to find themselves deported. A tough law-and-order agenda also leads to long punitive sentences for women convicted of killing their batterers. Finally, when public funding is channeled into policing and prisons, budget cuts for social programs, including women's shelters, welfare, and public housing are the inevitable side effect. These cutbacks leave women less able to escape violent relationships.

3. Prisons don't work. Despite an exponential increase in the number of men in prisons, women are not any safer, and the rates of sexual assault and domestic violence have not decreased. In calling for greater police responses to and harsher sentences for perpetrators of gender violence, the anti-violence movement has fueled the proliferation of prisons which now lock up more people per capita in the U.S. than any other countries. During the past fifteen years, the numbers of women, especially women of color, in prison has skyrocketed. Prisons also inflict violence on the growing numbers of women behind bars. Slashing, suicide, the proliferation of HIV, strip searches, medical neglect, and rape of prisoners has largely been ignored by anti-violence activists. The criminal justice system, an institution of violence, domination, and control, has increased the level of violence in society.

4. The reliance on state funding to support anti-violence programs has increased the professionalization of the anti-violence movement and alienated it from its community-organizing, social justice roots. Such reliance has isolated the anti-violence movement from other social justice movements that seek to eradicate state violence, such that it acts in conflict rather than in collaboration with these movements.

5. The reliance on the criminal justice system has taken power away from women's ability to organize collectively to stop violence and has invested this power within the state. The result is that women who seek redress in the criminal justice system feel disempowered and alienated. It has also promoted an individualistic approach toward ending violence such that the only way people think they can intervene in stopping violence is to call the police. This reliance has shifted our focus from developing ways communities can collectively respond to violence. In recent years, the mainstream anti-prison movement has called important attention to the negative impact of criminalization and the build-up of the prison industrial complex. Because activists who seek to reverse the tide of mass incarceration and criminalization of poor communities and communities of color have not always centered gender and sexuality in their analysis or organizing, we have not always responded adequately to the needs of survivors of domestic and sexual violence.

SOURCE: INCITE! Women of Color Against Violence and Critical Resistance (2001).

Andrea Smith, a longtime antiviolence and First Nations activist, a scholar, and a co-founder of INCITE!, explains the importance of this coalition from the vantage point of the women's antiviolence movements:

Any movement seeking to end violence will fail if its strategy supports and helps sustain the prison-industrial complex. Prisons, policing, the death penalty, the war on terror, and the war on drugs all increase rape, beating, isolation, oppression and death. As an anti-rape organization, we cannot support the funneling of resources into the criminal justice system to punish rapists and batterers, as this does not help end violence. It only supports the same system that views incarcerations as a solution to complex social problems like rape and abuse. As survivors of rape and domestic violence, we will not let the antiviolence movement be further co-opted to support the mass criminalization of young people, the disappearance of immigrants and refugees, and the dehumanization of poor people, people of color, and people with disabilities. We support the anti-rape movement that builds sustainable communities on a foundation of safety, support, self-determination, and accountability. (A. Smith 2005, 426–27)

Antiviolence scholar-activists such as Smith believe that organizing against violence should be part of a comprehensive community empowerment agenda involving environmental, peace, human rights, and economic activism for living wages. Within this framework, members of the community would pursue alternatives to the criminalization of violent men while holding batterers accountable and would work to eliminate structural violence such as police brutality, street violence, and mass incarceration (West 2005). These suggestions for change may seem utopian, but they are based on a powerful analysis of gendered violence and its remedies. If nothing else, these visions can set a new direction for activists and scholars.

STATE VIOLENCE AGAINST MEN

As we have seen, private violence is linked in impoitant ways to the criminal justice system. In this section, we look at another link, the gendered aspects of the mass imprisonment of men in the United States (see chapter 10 for a discussion of women's prisons). Since the 1980s, access to welfare, health care, shelter, and higher education—resources that could help poor and working-class women leave violent households and help poor and working-class men realize their potentials and restore their abilities to support and nurture families—has been severely curtailed. The retreat from public protection of vulnerable women and their families is actually a form of state-sponsored violence against women, who may find themselves without safe haven from abusers for lack of affordable alternative shelter or, if forced into homelessness, vulnerable to rape and violent crime on the streets (Fine 1999). The criminalization of poor men of color and their massive incarceration in federal and state prisons is a form of state violence against these men. Together these assaults add up to a major national offensive against poor communities. In many cases, then, the public violence of incarceration compounds and supports the harms of private violence.

The Prison-Industrial Complex

At the end of 2013, 2.2 million people were in prison in the United States—a 500 percent increase over the past thirty years. Serious crime rates in the United States have been declining for the last twenty years, but the number of prisoners serving life sentences has more than quadrupled since 1984 (The Sentencing Project 2013). The United States has the highest proportion of citizens in prison worldwide—716 prisoners for every 100,000 people as of 2013. St. Kitts and Nevis, with 649 per 100,000, and the Seychelles, with 641, rank second and third, respectively. Among **OECD countries**, Israel is second, with 223 per 100,000 (Wing 2013). Contrast these rates with those of Canada (114), Japan (54), Denmark (68), and England and Wales (148). The prevalence of crime in the United States does not explain these figures. Twenty-one percent of the population in seventeen industrialized countries was victimized by crime in 1999, the same proportion as was victimized in the United States. In fact, the increase in prison construction and incarceration has taken place in the face of a 20 percent decrease in the rate of violent crime in the United States since 1991 (Sentencing Project 2013a).

It is likely that one cause of the growing rates of mass incarceration is the for-profit prison industry, which depends on high rates of imprisonment to reap massive profits, as a report on **private prisons** by the American Civil Liberties Union (ACLU) suggests (ACLU 2011).

As incarceration rates skyrocket, the private prison industry expands exponentially, holding ever more people in its prisons and jails. Private prisons for adults were virtually non-existent until the early 1980s, but the number of prisoners in private prisons increased by approximately 1600 percent between 1990 and 2009. Today, for-profit companies are responsible for approximately 6 percent of state prisoners, 16 percent of federal prisoners and, according to one report, nearly half of all immigrants detained by the federal government. In 2010, the two largest private prison companies alone received nearly $3 billion dollars in revenue, and their top executives each received annual compensation packages worth well over $3 million.

Prison construction and mass incarceration began in the era of the Reagan presidency and have become the "social" programs of our time. Public investment in prisons has flourished at the expense of investments in health, education, housing, and other forms of social expenditure. For example, from 1977 to 1995, average funding for prisons nationwide was twice the funding for public colleges (and six to one in Texas). The connection between loss of public funding for social programs and increase of public funding for prisons is often very direct. Between 1988 and 1998, the New York state legislature cut investment in public higher education in the same proportion as it increased funding for prisons. In June 2013, a headline in *Forbes* magazine blared, "Philadelphia Schools Closing While a New $400 Million Prison Is Under Construction" (Stroud, 2013). What happened in New York and Philadelphia is also happening throughout the United States.

What accounts for the prison construction boom? The sharp rise in incarceration has pushed the demand for new prisons, and the building of new private, for-profit prisons increases the demand for prisoners. As prison construction proceeds, new interests are cultivated. Communities, needing jobs and tax dollars, lobby for prisons to be built nearby. Prison guards press for more prisons, looking to enhance their job security, raise their salaries, and increase their benefits. Private firms that contract with the prison authorities for assorted supplies and for cheap labor want to expand their profitability by tapping into the $35 billion a year spent on prisons. Angela Davis compares the institutionalization of private corporate interests in prisons to the "military-industrial complex," the term for the permanent armaments industry allied with the United States military. Davis explains:

> As the U.S. prison system expanded, so did corporate involvement in construction, provision of goods and services, and use of prison labor. Because of the extent to

which prison building and operation began to attract vast amounts of capital—from the construction industry to food and health care provision—in a way that recalled the emergence of the military industrial complex, we began to refer to a "**prison industrial complex**." (Davis 2003, 12)

The vast majority of people caught up in the feverish expansion of prisons are Latino, First Nations, and African American men and, increasingly, women of color.

Sexual Violence in Men's Prisons

It is unusual for men to admit to feeling afraid on the streets and in other public venues. However, men who go to prison do fear sexual assault, and they are right to do so. A 2001 Human Rights Watch report based on a survey of 1,856 adult correctional facilities in the United States, reported 6,241 allegations of sexual violence in prisons and jails in 2006, up from 5,386 in 2004. This report on male rape in U.S. prisons begins as follows:

> A Florida prisoner whom we will identify only as P. R., was beaten, suffered a serious eye injury, and assaulted by an inmate armed with a knife, all due to his refusal to submit to anal sex. After six months of repeated threats and endurance, he tried to commit suicide by slashing his wrists with a razor. In a letter to Human Rights Watch, he chronicled his unsuccessful efforts to induce prison authorities to protect him from abuse. Summing up these experiences, he wrote: "The opposite of compassion is not hatred, it's indifference." (Human Rights Watch 2001, 1)

There are no national data on prison rape, but surveys in men's prisons in several states show that between 20 and 33 percent of male inmates have been forced or pressured into sex or raped in prison. If these figures hold true around the country, at least 140,000 inmates have been raped while under state supervision. Inmates are targeted because of their looks, age, and size; because they are white, gay, or lack "street smarts"; and because they are, in some ways, tagged as "feminine." Prison rapists are usually younger, larger, and stronger than their victims, have been convicted of violent crimes, and are often gang members (Human Rights Watch 2001).

As the preceding quotation from the prison report suggests, prison rape can be brutal and extremely violent. Gang assaults are common, and victims may be viciously beaten and sometimes killed. Human Rights Watch describes the case of one prisoner who entered a Texas maximum-security prison in August 1994 and was attacked within the week by twenty inmates demanding sex and money. When he refused, he was beaten for almost two hours and left to die. Guards said they had not noticed that the beating was happening.

Prison rape is an example of "doing gender" backed up by the threat of overt violence. Victims are forced into sexually subordinate roles, marked as "turn outs" or "punks" who are sexual targets of other prisoners. Once they are labeled, their reputation follows them throughout the prison system. To escape their fate, such prisoners may agree to become the property of another prisoner who will protect them in exchange for sex and domestic labor. The prisoner may be forced to wash his protector's clothes, give massages, cook his food, and clean his cell.

"Owners" of slaves often rent or sell them to other prisoners for sex. Like oppressed housewives, their choices about how to dress and with whom to speak may be controlled by the person who "owns" them. Their name may be replaced by a feminine one. Prison staff regularly ignore these relationships, despite the attempt of victims to report assaults and to gain protection. In men's prisons, violence that creates such differences is as damaging to the victims as is the rape of women. Prisoners suffer nightmares, depression, shame, and self-hatred, just as raped women do. They often become suicidal. Victims are sometimes killed outright by their abusers, or killed indirectly, when rapists infect them with HIV.

Another form of prison violence visited on prisoners is the masculinized sexual violence made familiar to Americans by the scandals of Abu Ghraib in Iraq and the torture of the men incarcerated in Guantanamo as "enemy combatants." There is evidence to suggest that the torture of prisoners is routine in many U.S. prisons. Overuse of solitary confinement, the use of dogs to intimidate prisoners, restraint hoods, belts, and beds, waist and leg chains, Tasers, and other forms of militarized control are ordinary forms of control in prisons (Deen 2006, Magnani and Wray 2006). Such gendered treatment is a stunning violation of prisoners' human rights, and it links domestic terror in prisons to the gendered terror of war in conflict zones.

GENDERED VIOLENCE IN CONFLICT ZONES

Gender and sexual violence are forms of global terrorism that take millions of lives each year. The violence that occurs in families or between intimates is largely invisible. It is also the case that most war victims—civilian women, children, and the elderly—are invisible too (see Box 8-6). The principal victims of violence in wars these days are civilians, often women and children (Marshall 2004b).

There are no longer hard-and-fast boundaries between war zones in which armies clash, and the home front where civilians live in relative safety. Much of this violence grows from the determination of states and corporations to control the abundant natural resources in these regions. For instance, in Congo, at least eighty-five multinational corporations, including some of the largest U.S. companies, covet Congo's minerals, such as coltan (used in cell phones and laptops), cobalt, copper, gold, diamonds, and uranium (Goodwin 2004). Resistance movements and government forces alike sometimes take women and children hostage. In northern Uganda, a years-long conflict was characterized by sexual and gender-based violence against women and girls by the Lord's Resistance Army (LRA) and government forces. UNICEF estimates that more than 32,000 children were abducted by the LRA between 1986 and 2002 and used as child combatants and sex slaves. Ugandan government forces also committed mass rapes. Likewise, in Sierra Leone, one-third of all women and girls were deliberately systematically targeted for rape, sexual slavery, and forced pregnancy during the conflict between 1991 and 2002. To date, there has been little effort to provide justice, care, or reparations for these victims (Amnesty International 2007). In the next section, we look more closely at one country in the throes of militarized violence.

GENDER IN EVERYDAY LIFE   BOX 8-6

THE JUAREZ PROJECT: NAFTA AND THE FEMICIDES

It is important to recognize that the femicide in Ciudad Juarez and Chihuahua does not exist in a vacuum. The problem has its roots in the economic disparity that ravages the U.S.–Mexico border, and we are already seeing this problem spread to other cities facing the same problems.

These murders really accelerated in 1994–1995, which is significant because it was the first few years after the implementation of the North American Free Trade Agreement, or NAFTA. This was a time period when we began to see massive migration of people from the Mexican rural countryside to the cities. Most of these migrants were young men and women, coming alone or with little support structure, trying to earn money to send home to their families. This was because of an economic agricultural crisis created by NAFTA.

NAFTA, a trade agreement designed to eliminate barriers to trade, forced Mexico to reduce price supports for Mexican agricultural producers to "level the playing field" for U.S. producers to sell their goods on the Mexican market. However, the United States, through a major loophole in NAFTA, was allowed to raise already high tax-payer subsidies for our agricultural producers. We did this largely to compete with the European Union and Japan, which also heavily subsidize their agricultural producers. However, these subsidies have allowed producers in powerful industrial countries to drastically undercut producers in the developing world. For example, in Mexico, U.S.-subsidized corn is being sold at about 33 percent below the actual cost of production. This means that Mexican farmers simply can't compete. Not because they don't produce corn efficiently, but because they don't receive the kind of taxpayer subsidies that U.S. producers receive. Now in the United States, a very small percentage of the population still farms the land. Most farming is done by a handful of large-agribusiness companies. In fact, the few small farmers left in this country receive very little support. Seventy percent of subsidies go to only 30 percent of the producers. In Mexico, on the other hand, about a quarter of the population still relies on farming as their primary source of income. This population has been devastated by the flooding of cheap-subsidized agricultural products on the Mexican market. About 1.5 million farmers have had to leave their land and look for work in other sectors. They are moving to the cities, especially along the U.S.–Mexico border, looking for work in the maquiladoras (factories that produce for export), or they are attempting to emigrate to the United States, often as undocumented workers, to look for work they desperately need to feed their families. This migration has created a class of desperately poor and unprotected people, especially women, along the U.S.–Mexico border. In fact, many of the femicide victims were workers in U.S.-owned companies. Most of the victims had not lived in the region for more than a few years. Some of the bodies are unidentified, and it is thought that they may be migrants from southern Mexico or Central America who simply don't have family in the area who know they are missing. Wages in the factories have gone progressively down in the years since NAFTA was implemented as factories replace their workers regularly with new migrants to the area more desperate for work and willing to work for even lower wages. Women, like workers in the region, are treated as disposable commodities. Something to be used up and thrown away.

FEMICIDES OF JUAREZ AND CHIHUAHUA

For more than a decade, the cities of Chihuahua and Juarez, near the U.S.–Mexico border, have been killing fields for young women, the site of over 400 unsolved femicides. Despite the horrific nature of these crimes, authorities at all levels exhibit indifference, and there is strong evidence that some officials may be involved. Impunity and corruption has permitted the criminals, whoever they are, to continue committing these acts, knowing there will be no consequences.

A significant number of victims work in the maquiladora sector—sweatshops that produce for export with 90 percent destined for the United States. The maquiladoras employ mainly young women at poverty level wages. In combination with lax environmental regulations and low tariffs under the North American Free Trade Agreement (NAFTA), the maquiladoras are amassing tremendous wealth. Yet despite the crime wave, they offer almost no protection for their workers. High-profile government campaigns such as Ponte Vista (Be Aware), a self defense program, and supplying women with whistles have been ineffective and are carried out mainly for public relations purposes.

Small advances in the struggle for justice are due to the perseverance of victims' families who cannot be silenced despite the efforts of state and federal authorities to keep them quiet. Campaigns by local, national and international non-governmental organizations are also important. Often grassroots groups work in a climate of threats and defamation by government officials for making one simple demand—STOP THE FEMICIDE!

SOURCE: The Juarez Project (2007).

Guatemala: A Case Study

Rape, torture, and murder is the fate of thousands of women caught in the globalized economic, social, and political transformations located in conflict zones in poor countries such as Mexico, Guatemala, Colombia, and Peru. In Central and South America, thousands of young women, students, housewives, and low-wage workers in maquiladoras (export assembly plants), where they assemble consumer goods such as clothing, shoes, toys, and electronic equipment at a fraction of the cost of production in the United States, have been abducted, tortured, and murdered, their bodies dumped on the outskirts of cities. In 2003 and 2004, 373 women were murdered in Bolivia, 143 in Peru in 2003, and more than 2,200 in Guatemala.

These assaults were first identified and named "**femicide**" (Russell 1992) in the Mexican cities of Ciudad Juarez and Chihuahua, located on the U.S. border, where unknown numbers of women have been found raped, tortured, and murdered since 1993 and where dozens more remain missing (see Box 8-7). The crimes take place in a climate of hypermasculinity and acceptance of violence against women (Amnesty International USA 2005).

GENDER IN EVERYDAY LIFE   BOX 8-7
SPEECH BY MICHELLE BACHELET ON "GENDER-MOTIVATED KILLINGS OF WOMEN, INCLUDING FEMICIDE"

SPEAKER: MICHELLE BACHELET, EXECUTIVE DIRECTOR OF UN WOMEN, MARCH 12, 2013.

As we meet today, we are deep into the 57th session on the Commission on the Status of Women. Dialogue is underway that we hope will strengthen international norms and standards, and result in a plan of action to prevent and end all forms of violence against women and girls.

We are here to discuss the most extreme manifestation of violence against women: gender-motivated killing of women, also called "femicide." We are here to discuss the killing of women, simply because they are women.

This is a harsh reminder that today, in the 21st century, there is still an urgent need to build equality between men and women, equality to live free of violence and discrimination.

Gender-motivated killings of women occur everywhere, in every country and culture of the world. It is an issue of universal human rights and inherent human dignity that concerns us all, involves us all, and requires concerted and urgent action from all of us.

The global extent of femicide is estimated at approximately 66,000 victims per year for the period between 2004 and 2009. This represents about almost one-fifth of all homicide victims for an average year.

We say "estimated" because in the data we have available for most countries many of these killings are not classified as femicide or gender-motivated killings. Thus, it is currently impossible to know its true magnitude, but we can be sure that the problem is much greater than we can determine from the current statistics and evidence.

Special Rapporteur Rashida Manjoo has reported that the lack of investigations, trials and sanctions for acts of violence against women have contributed to an environment of impunity and low confidence in the justice system. This impunity sends a message to society that violence against women by men is not only tolerated, but accepted.

And today, in many countries, we find that impunity is too often the norm, rather than the exception.

It is the obligation of States, as guarantors of the rights of all people, to punish the perpetrators of violence against women and girls and provide services, support and justice to survivors and their families. Today, 160 countries have laws to address violence against women.

Yet all too often the women and girls subjected to violence are violated twice—the first time when they are subjected to violence, and the second time when they seek, and do not find, the services and justice to which they are entitled.

All too often the rate of trials and sanctions for these crimes is very low, and when perpetrators are held to account, they are punished for lesser crimes, given shorter and lighter sentences.

The costs of inaction are evident: the needless, premature and devastating deaths of women and girls, and the suffering and loss experienced by families.

It is time to strengthen justice systems; provide training to the police and judges to eliminate stereotyping and prejudices towards women; improve support services to survivors and families; and dedicate planning and budgeting to preventing violence against women and girls.

Often I am asked what needs to be done, and what UN Women is doing to address this problem. We are working in partnership with other UN agencies, often through the Secretary-General's Campaign UNiTE to end violence against women.

We are encouraged by the work that thousands of women organizations, governments and UN agencies are developing. And the results are promising.

In Latin America, we have developed initiatives to stop impunity, through legal reforms to typify femicide as a specific crime. In Guatemala, for instance, this led to the development of specialized prosecutor units and tribunals. In El Salvador and Nicaragua, there are now policies and procedures to address the crime of femicide, to name just a few examples.

In Mexico, UN Women is providing technical assistance to improve data collection and analysis of femicides. UN Women, the Mexican Parliament and the Colegio de Mexico, an academic institution, developed an innovative methodology for analyzing femicidal violence, its characteristics, trends and new manifestations for a 25-year period. This analysis has been instrumental in defining what femicide is and is currently being replicated in other countries.

One very important initiative that we are supporting is the development of the Protocol for the Investigation of Violent Gender-Based Killings of Women: Femicide for Latin America. This pioneering work is being done with the UN High Commissioner of Human Rights, the Federation of Associations of Human Rights, and the Government of Spain. This protocol will provide guidelines for the effective investigation of violent deaths of women, to ensure that the process takes into account the context, identifies the relation with the perpetrator, and conforms to States' international obligations.

Let me end by sharing some thoughts of what needs to be done to stop impunity and prevent femicide.

First, all countries need comprehensive legal frameworks that create an environment for women and girls to live free of violence and typify femicide as a specific crime. And laws must be implemented, so that cases are diligently investigated, perpetrators brought to trial and the victims or their families offered just reparations.

Second, early intervention by law enforcement and other support agencies is essential for the prevention of femicides. Police forces must develop the capacity to support women´s assessment of the risk they face; provide appropriate and effective protection measures; enforce restraint orders; and refer women to comprehensive social services, including shelters and safe houses.

Third, survivors and families must have access to comprehensive services that ensure access to police and the justice system, shelters, legal aid, healthcare, psychosocial counselling, 24-hour hotlines and long-term support. In all our efforts, we need to engage survivors and place the full human rights of a woman at the centre of any response, so that recovery and justice are supported and the cycle of violence is not perpetuated. And here it is critical to provide services for sexual and reproductive health to protect the reproductive rights of women.

Fourth, it is critical to foster changes in attitudes, beliefs and behaviours that condone or perpetuate violence to prevent violence from happening in the first place. This can be done through awareness-raising, community mobilization, educational programmes, including sexuality education, and support for children and young people who are exposed to violence.

And one thing is certain: Preventing all forms of violence against women requires the engagement of all segments of society, and especially men and boys as partners in gender equality and respectful relationships.

And fifth and finally, Governments need to COMMIT to action. We are very encouraged that so far 50 Governments have answered this call by pledging action to end violence against women and girls through the UN Women COMMIT initiative. I call on all Governments to join. Let us work together to ensure that we keep our promise and women are not at risk of being killed, just because they are women. Let us work for a better and more peaceful world for all.

SOURCE: http://www.unwomen.org/en/news/stories/2013/3/speech-by-michelle-bachelet-on-gender-motivated-killings-of-women-including-femicide#sthash.BWwg5H9t.dpuf.

Some of these attacks on women are directly and indirectly connected to wars that have plagued the region. The Colombian military, as well as right-wing paramilitary forces, have been implicated in rapes and killings of women. Peru's Truth and Reconciliation Commission identified rape as a form of torture during that country's civil wars between 1980 and 2000 (Paterson 2006). The connection of women's murders with militarism is particularly apparent in Guatemala, which suffered a thirty-six-year civil war. Rape and sexual violence were among the tactics used by the armed forces in that country to intimidate and silence opponents.

The overthrow by the U.S. Marines of the democratically elected government of Guatemala in the 1950s inaugurated the decades-long period of state-initiated gendered violence. There were genocidal attacks on the indigenous peasant majority. Between 1960 and 1996, the military threatened, tortured, and killed with impunity. Entire villages were massacred. Women were attacked as "mothers of guerillas," pregnant women had their wombs slit open, and women and girls were gang-raped. Young men from these communities who were suspected of supporting the resistance or avoiding conscription were brutally tortured and murdered. U.S.-backed government troops and their paramilitary allies routinely raped, tortured, and murdered women to destroy targeted villages. Captured women were taken as sex slaves and forced to wash and cook for the troops as well (just as the perpetrators of male prison rape did), strengthening assumptions men may already have about women as providers of sex, food, and clean clothes.

The war has ended, but similar torture and murder of women continues. According to Guatemala's human rights prosecutor's office, rapes and sexual assaults of women increased by 34 percent from 2008 to 2011, while in 9 of every 10 of these cases, those responsible have not been punished (Human Rights Watch 2013). Female murder victims in Guatemala often suffer exceptional brutality before being killed, including rape, mutilation, and dismemberment.

What explains this level of violence against women? What has created killers who show such contempt for and hatred of women? In Guatemala, some men consider women their servants and property. Neither domestic violence nor sexual harassment is a criminal offense in that country. This continuing violence echoes the violence of Guatemala's past. Some suspect that former soldiers, trained in sadistic methods of combat and then demobilized after the war without any plans for readapting them to civilian life or providing them with jobs, are involved in the killing. Some former government soldiers have turned to gangs and organized crime; others work for private security agencies or the police. Militarization of this society damns both women and men. Women live in fear on a daily basis; men shore up their militarized masculinity through violence and intimidation.

A new feature in the struggle against violence in Guatemala, and a global first, is that country's new "femicide courts." In 2012, 708 women died violently there, and an additional 403 women were murdered in the first six months of 2013. In fact, Guatemala is one of the most violent countries in the world, with a murder rate of 48 per 100,000 compared with the global average of 9 per 100,000. The law establishing the specialized courts was approved in 2008 in response to the brutal and sadistic murders of more than 4,000 women over eight years (by 2011, another 1,500 women had been murdered). According to the Guatemala Human Rights Commission (2012) most of the victims were between the ages of 16 and 36. They were students, housewives, professionals, maids, unskilled workers, members or former members of street youth gangs, and sex workers. Many victims were kidnapped, beaten, raped, and tortured, then killed and their bodies left in public areas, among other things, as a warning to other women.

The femicide courts attempt to bring these assailants to justice, but so far there is little evidence of their success. The courts address violence from a gender perspective, analysing each case in the context of inequality, discrimination, and misogyny. The cases before these courts are usually heard by specially trained women judges (Valladares 2013). But convictions are low, and the killings continue to rise. Speake (2012) explains the violence as a continuation of both the 36-year-long brutal civil war and the "deep-rooted patriarchal culture of machismo, where misogyny is widely tolerated."

Thus, the situation in Guatemala, in particular the recent growth of femicide, illustrates the relation between violence against women in "peacetime" and in times of conflict: in Guatemala, the torture and murder of women cannot be attributed solely to the legacy of the civil war; rather, "examining the social support networks of gender-based violence compels us to confront the potential horrors of patriarchy" (Carey and Torres 2010,162). While systematic sexual violence has been a part of conflict, worldwide, throughout history, it is only in recent years that it has gained attention and been internationally recognized as a potential "war crime" by the International Criminal Court, and that international treaties have attempted to legislate against violence against women. However, international human rights legislation enforcement remains weak, and gender-based violence often still struggles to be seen as a human rights abuse (Moser and Clark, 2001). Moreover, international attention to violence against women during conflict, while welcome, does not even begin to address the complex interlinkages between violence against women during conflict and the violence that takes place against them during "peacetime." The targeting of women's bodies in conflict is both an effect and a cause of the acceptability of violence against women. It functions to subordinate women further, and creates a climate where violence becomes more accepted and is committed with impunity. Thus, gender-based violence during conflict cannot be analyzed as fundamentally different from violence in "peacetime": violence against women in the context of armed conflict simply intensifies already existing attitudes and behaviors. As Rehn and Sirleaf state, "violence against women in wartime is a reflection of violence against women in peacetime" (Rehn and Sirleaf 2002, 11).

As the case of Guatemala shows, militarism and conflict intensify the epidemics of violence against women around the world. Rape and sexual assault are part of war. As the "property" of the enemy, women are seen as a way to "get" at men. In addition, military training belittles women. Pornography and prostitution are officially sanctioned as entertainment for soldiers (Enloe 2000). Sexual harassment and rape of women in the military are ongoing problems that are not confined to conflict zones. Domestic abuse on American military bases is widespread, as men (and some women) returning from active duty feel entitled to use violence at home (Marshall 2004a).

WHAT IS TO BE DONE? CEDAW, THE INTERNATIONAL CRIMINAL COURT, AND SECURITY COUNCIL RESOLUTION 1325

Women are not only victims of state terror and war. Women and men have also contributed to the global human rights movement to establish women's most basic right to physical safety. Largely because of grassroots pressure from women's groups around the world, the United Nations has created three promising mechanisms for eradicating gender violence: the **Convention on the Elimination of All Forms of Discrimination Against Women (CEDAW)**, the International Criminal Court, and Resolution 1325 of the UN Security Council.

CEDAW, adopted by the UN General Assembly in 1979, is often called a bill of human rights for women. It calls on governments that sign the treaty to remove all forms of discrimination against women; to ensure women's equal access to political and public life, education, health care, and employment; and to protect their reproductive rights. The United States is one of a handful of nations that has not ratified CEDAW (the others are Sudan, South Sudan,

Somalia, Iran, and two small Pacific Island nations, Palau and Tonga). The existence of this treaty requires countries to examine the conditions of life for women and girls, to report on structures and customs that discriminate against them, and to take action against the barriers to equality. The treaty has been important in stopping violence against women (CEDAW 2014.). In Colombia, the courts ruled in 1992 that the absence of legal recourse then available to a female victim of domestic violence violated her human rights to life and personal security. The state now ensures protection for all such women. Ugandans have created programs and policies to campaign against domestic violence, using state funds for the purpose. In Costa Rica, the courts are authorized to order an abusive spouse to leave home and to continue providing economic support. Training and programs to combat sex crimes are being established, and women officials must handle rape investigations and prosecutions.

In 2001, for the first time, the military was held accountable for sexual violence in a time of conflict. Justice Florence Mumba of Zambia sentenced three Bosnian Serb soldiers standing trial on charges of rape and torture to twenty-eight years, twenty years, and twelve years imprisonment, respectively, the first case of wartime sexual enslavement to come before the International War Crimes Tribunal in The Hague. At the Hague trial, women testified about how paramilitary soldiers entered the "rape camps" and selected women and girls as young as twelve for nightly gang rapes and sexual torture. These sentences were a victory for the international women's movement, which lobbied the United Nations to include wartime rape in the jurisdiction of the International Criminal Court. Rape has also been prosecuted in Rwanda. In 1998 the Rwanda tribunal found former mayor Jean-Paul Akayesu guilty of nine counts of genocide, crimes against humanity, and war crimes. Women are now demanding that they be fully involved in all international efforts to hold armies and security forces accountable for sexual terrorism, as well as in all efforts to maintain and promote peace and security.

Also in 2001, the UN Security Council passed the landmark **Resolution 1325**, giving women the right to participate in conflict-resolution and peace-building efforts. The resolution mandates that participants in peacemaking operations take a gender perspective on conflict and pay special attention to the needs of women and girls in reconstruction efforts. Although Resolution 1325 has not yet been implemented, it frames attempts to bring women's political energies into the work of the UN Security Council, and it has inspired grassroots activists in conflict zones. Women in Melanesia have established women's community media to spread information about the resolution and to inform women about what others are doing to make it a reality at the community level. Women from the Democratic Republic of Congo lobbied for a gender office within the UN peacekeeping mission to that country and have worked closely with that office to spread information about Resolution 1325 and to insert a gender perspective into all levels of government. Women in Kosovo have sponsored television shows explaining the resolution and have built a network of women around the resolution. Iraqi women have used Resolution 1325 to support their call for women's equal rights and responsibilities. Carol Cohn believes that these grassroots efforts "broaden the gaze" beyond the traditional political and military aspects of peace and security. CEDAW, she writes:

> affirms women's rights to protection and participation; and should it be widely implemented, women's experience of conflict and their ability to prevent or end it could be substantially transformed. What could also be transformed by this "broadening of the gaze" is the mainstream belief in the adequacy of restricting one's

vision to the traditional political and military aspects of peace and security. Resolution 1325, as it moves from rhetoric to reality, could potentially transform our ideas about the prevention of war, the bases for sustainable peace, and the pathways to achieve them. (Cohn 2004, 9)

In 2004 the NGO Working Group on Women, Peace and Security was invited to submit a paper, "No Women, No Peace," to the UN High-Level Panel on Threats, Challenges, and Change (NGO Working Group 2004). The paper urges a framework for collective action based on prevention, the participation of women in peace and security, and the protection of civilians. The paper recommends that the United Nations and the international community embrace the full and equal participation of women in peace processes; that they collaborate with women's local peace groups; that they encompass economic development, social justice, and environmental protection in security efforts; that they build a culture of peace growing from equality between women and men; and that they engage men and boys, including young men who have been trained to brutalize and kill, in the struggle for gender equality.

These suggestions are a recipe for fundamentally transforming our gender-divided and violence-generating world by placing women and gender at the center of antiviolence and peace-building activities. They are a formula for promoting the partnership model of society described by Riane Eisler.

The fact that the United States has not signed UN Security Council Resolution 1325 or CEDAW gives U.S. women and men a special responsibility for challenging and changing our country's insularity and its role in perpetuating violent conflict around the world (see Box 8-8).

GENDER IN EVERYDAY LIFE   BOX 8-8
UNSCR 1325 BRINGING WOMEN TO THE TABLE

"Women bring a different perspective to the table," said Dr. Joyce Neu during her first day at the 2013 Bologna Symposium. Dr. Neu, a seasoned mediator who has been engaged in conflict assessment, mediation, facilitation, evaluation, and advising at the official and/ or unofficial level in sub-Saharan Africa, the Baltics, the Balkans, the Caucasus, Cyprus, and Sri Lanka for more than two decades, emphasized the importance of including women in peace talks. "We need to move away from exclusive peace processes, and include women and civil society organizations (CSOs)," she said during our brainstorming exercise on Syria. How do we do this in reality though, when a prerequisite for a seat at the table often is having carried a gun during the conflict? While much still needs to be done, the importance of women's inclusion is being recognized and some mechanisms to push the agenda forward are in place.

WHAT IS UNSCR 1325?

United Nations Security Council Resolution (UNSCR) 1325 was unanimously adopted by the UN Security Council on October 31, 2000. It was the first time that the Security

Council, the most powerful decision making body of the United Nations, responsible for international peace and security, recognized the disproportionate impact of armed conflict on women. For women around the world the adoption of this resolution was hence a long awaited milestone.

UNSCR 1325 recognizes the potential of women's contribution to the prevention of conflict and peacebuilding efforts and demands that member states take effective measures to promote women's rights, including increasing women's representation at all levels of decision-making. Often referred to as the three P's, the emphasis of the resolution is on women's **participation** in conflict prevention, peacebuilding and reconstruction; **protection** of women and girls' human rights during conflict; and the **prevention** of sexual- and gender-based violence (SGBV). Occasionally a fourth P—**promotion** of a gender perspective—is included in the "P's." In moving from seeing women as victims to recognizing them as peacebuilders and decision-makers the resolution also encompasses a transformative element.

UNSCR 1325 further calls on the Secretary-General of the UN to take significant steps to appoint more women to high-level positions within the UN system, such as special representatives and envoys. As Dr. Neu pointed out during one of her sessions, one argument often cited for the low number of women in high-level positions, including as mediators, is that there are no women with the required skills. As Dr. Neu stressed, this argument however, seems somewhat odd, as women have been working as peacebuilders, mediators and negotiators long before the adoption of any Security Council resolution in this regard. Women are often the bridge builders in their communities. They are the ones who hold families and communities together during conflict and the ones who peace them together during the post-conflict period. Indeed, women often have first-hand experience in mediating and building peace.

BUT IS UNSCR 1325 JUST A PIECE OF PAPER OR DOES IT REALLY HAVE AN IMPACT?

Article 25 of the UN charter states that, "the Members of the United Nations agree to accept and carry out the decisions of the Security Council in accordance with the present Charter." Hence, Security Council Resolutions are international law and member states are technically obliged to implement them. However, there is as of yet no accountability mechanism in place and member states implement (or not) at their own discretion. The CEDAW (Convention on the Elimination of All Forms of Discrimination against Women) Committee is currently working on a General Recommendation (GR) on Women in Women in Conflict Prevention, Conflict and Post-conflict Situations. When adopted, this GR would provide authoritative guidance to member states on the measures to be put in place to ensure full compliance with their obligations to fulfill women's human rights during times of armed conflict, and in all peacebuilding processes. The GR would be the first mandatory mechanism for member states that have ratified CEDAW to report on their implementation of UNSCR 1325 (and 1820*).

We still have a long way to go when it comes to the implementation of UNSCR 1325, and women's equal participation in peace processes and decision-making. We here at the Symposium, and the present and future peacebuilders can make a difference because we recognize the importance of including a variety of stakeholders, particularly women, in all our efforts!

With increased attention on sexual violence in conflict UNSCR 1325 was followed by UNSCR 1820 in 2008. 1820 identifies sexual violence as a matter of international peace and security and a tactic of war that calls for a security response. Four more women, peace and security (WPS) resolutions have since been adopted (1888, 1889, 960 and most recently 2106 on June 24, 2013).

SOURCE: Reprinted from Helena Grönberg, "UNSCR 1325 Bringing Women to the Table," Finland, July 1, 2013, International Peace and Security Institute http://ipsinstitute.org/unscr-1325-bringing-women-to-the-table/ Accessed March 6, 2014.

GENDER MATTERS

This chapter has traced the continuum of gendered violence from the most intimate corners of our private lives to spaces as large and diverse as universities and prisons, police forces, armies, and the widest global arenas. Space limitations mean that this chapter only scratches the surface. We could fill many volumes documenting the forms of gendered violence in the world today, and more that trace the violent past. Nor has this chapter begun to explore the work of the peacemakers, those men and women who are laboring to end local and global gendered violence.

What explanations for the epidemic of gendered violence have emerged from this review? First, force is necessary to maintain the inequalities of power and wealth that accrue to the masculinist strata of ruling elites. Naturalizing such inequalities as biologically, evolutionarily, or psychologically necessary has served the status quo, but that unjust order has become harder and harder to maintain. As women and men come to see gender inequalities and gender injustice as part of a world we have made and can alter, they take steps toward ending gender inequality and promoting gender justice.

Second, research by feminists and critical race theorists has broadened and complicated the picture of violence against women. Older ideas that all women were victimized by all men have been jettisoned. We now see that inequalities of race and class place some women in greater jeopardy from sexual and gendered violence than others. We also see that inequalities of race ethnicity, class, gender, and nation shape men's fate as well. We are also learning how these forms of violence are connected, how gendered personal violence can feed off of gendered state violence, as when remedies for personal violence against women shore up a system of criminal justice that visits violence on batterers and battered alike, or when war leaves the mark of sexual terrorism on the postwar society. These new understandings of the ways gendered violence affects individuals, communities, and states suggest pioneering remedies and courses of action.

Does gender matter? In terms of violence and its termination, it is central.

KEY TERMS

acquaintance rape or date rape
battering and domestic violence
CEDAW
cultural transformation theory
femicide
Hollaback
intimate partner violence

naturalizing inequalities
OECD countries
prison industrial complex
private prisons
the problem that had no name
UN Resolution 1325

CRITICAL THINKING QUESTIONS

1. Describe the difference between a dominator society and partnership society.
2. Briefly describe and evaluate the evolutionary theory, individual psychology, and inequality approaches to accounting for rape
3. Agree or disagree. Prisons are a form of institutionalized gender violence that targets men in particular; war is a form of institutionalized gender violence that targets women in particular. Explain.
4. Watch the You tube video "Tough Guise" with some friends (or get a video of Tough Guise 2, the more recent remake of this documentary). Ask them to explain what they learned from the video. What points were made that they thought were most important and consistent with their own observations? What points did they think were not part of their experience?
5. Why has the U.S. refused to sign CEDAW and UN Resolution 1325? Google this question and report on what you find.

REFERENCES

American Civil Liberties Union. 2011. *Banking on Bondage: Private Prisons and Mass Incarceration.* November. https://www.aclu.org/files/assets/bankingonbondage_20111102.pdf. Accessed 2/26/2014.
——. 2006. Women in Prison: An Overview. https://www.aclu.org/womens-rights/words-prison-did-you-know#I. Accessed 2/26/2014.
Amnesty International. 2007. *Sierra Leone: Getting Reparations Right for Survivors of Sexual Violence.* http://www.amnesty.org/en/library/info/AFR51/005/2007. Accessed March 22, 2011.
——. 2013. *Review of the Stop Violence Against Women Campaign* http://www.amnesty.org/en/review-stop-violence-against-women-campaign. Accessed February 26, 2014.
——. 1997. "Women in Prison: A Fact Sheet." http://www.correctionalassociation.org/wp-content/uploads/2012/05/Wome_in_Prison_Fact_Sheet_2009_FINAL.pdf. Accessed February 26, 2014.
——. 2005. "Killings of Women in Guatemala Continue Unchallenged, Says AmnestyInternational." http://www.amnesty.or.jp/en/news/2005/1130_458.html. Accessed February 26, 2014.
Benard, Cheryl, and Edith Schlaffer. 1993. " 'The Man in the Street': Why He Harasses. In *Feminist Frontiers III,* edited by Laurel Richardson and Verta Taylor, 388–91. New York: McGraw-Hill.
B.N., Usha. 2007. "Patriarchy's Brutal Backlash; Acid Attacks." UltraViolet. http://youngfeminists.wordpress.com/2007/09/27/patrarchys-brutal-backlash-acid-attacks. Accessed March 22, 2011.

Berzofsky, Marcus, Christopher Krebs, Lynn Langton, Michael Planty, and Hope Smiley-McDonald. 2013. *Female Victims of Sexual Violence, 1994–2010.* http://www.bjs.gov/index.cfm?ty=pbdetail&iid=4594. Accessed October 30, 2013.

Bureau of Justice Statistics. 2011. *Homicide Trends in the US 1980-2008* http://bjs.ojp.usdoj.gov/content/homicide/tables/intimatestab.cfm. Accessed June 8, 2011.

——. 2010b. *Intimate Partner Violence in the US: Offender Characteristics.* http://bjs.ojp.usdoj.gov/content/intimate/table/vomen.cfm. Accessed June 8, 2011.

——. 2010c *Intimate Partner Violence in the US: Victim Characteristics.* http://bjs.ojp.usdoj.gov/content/intimate/table/vomen.cfm. Accessed June 8, 2011.

——. 2011. Office of Justice Programs. "Nonfatal Intimate Partner Victimization Rate per 1,000 Females, by Type of Crime, 1993–2005." http://bjs.ojp.usdoj.gov/content/intimate/table/tocwom.cfm. Accessed June 8, 2011.

Carey, David, Jr., and M. Gabriela Torres. 2010. "Precursors to Femicide: Guatemalan Women in a Vortex of Violence." *Latin American Research Review,* 45 (3): 142–64.

Catalano, Shannon. 2012. *Special Report: Intimate Partner Violence, 1993–2010.* Washington, DC: U.S. Department of Justice, Office of Justice Programs. http://www.bjs.gov/content/pub/pdf/ipv9310.pdf. Date accessed 2/26/2014.

CEDAW 2014. "Women's Equality, Empowerment, Employment, Education Economic Development." http://www.cedaw2011.org/. Accessed 2/26/2014.

Chicago Foundation for Women. 2007. *What Will It Take?* http://www.cfw.org//Document.Doc?&id=137. Accessed March 22, 2011.

Cohn, Carol. 2004. "Feminist Peacemaking." *Women's Review of Books* 21 (5): 8–9.

Dasgupta, Shamita Das. 2005. "Women's Realities: Defining Violence Against Women by Immigration, Race, and Class." In Sokoloff and Pratt, 56–70.

Dauer, Sheila. 2006. "Violence Against Women: An Obstacle to Equality." *University of Maryland Law Journal of Race, Religion, Gender and Class* 6 (2): 281–289.

Davis, Angela. 2003. *Are Prisons Obsolete?* New York: Seven Stories Press.

Deen, Thalif. 2006. "RIGHTS: Gender Violence a Universal Norm, Says U.N." Interpress News Service, October 9. http://ipsnews.net/news.asp?idnews=35047. Accessed June 8, 2011.

Eaton, Mary. 1986. *Justice for Women? Family, Court, and Social Control.* London: Open University Press.

Eisler, Riane. 1987. *The Chalice and the Blade: Our History, Our Future.* San Francisco: Harper and Row.

Enloe, Cynthia. 2000. *Maneuvers: The International Politics of Militarizing Women's Lives.* Berkeley: University of California Press.

Epstein, Helen. 2003. "Ghetto Miasma: Enough to Make You Sick?" *New York Times Magazine,* October 12.

Ewing, Charles, and Moss Aubrey. 1987. "Battered Women and Public Opinion: Some Realities about the Myths." *Journal of Family Violence* 2 (3): 257–64.

Ferraro, Kathleen. 1988. "An Existential Approach to Battering." In *Family Abuse and Its Consequences,* edited by Gerald Hotaling, David Finkelhor, John Kirkpatrick, and Murray Straus, 126–38. Newbury Park, CA: Sage.

Fine, Michelle. 1999. *The Unknown City: The Lives of Poor and Working-Class Young Adults.* Boston: Beacon Press.

Gentleman, Amelia. 2006. "Millions of Abortions of Female fetuses reported in India" *New York Times,* January 10.

Goodwin, Jan. 2004. "Silence = Rape: While the World Looks the Other Way, Sexual Violence Spreads in the Congo." *Nation,* March 8.

Gordon, Margaret T., and Stephanie Riger. 1989. *The Female Fear.* New York: Free Press.

Griffin, Susan. 1979. *Rape: The Politics of Consciousness*. San Francisco: Harper and Row.

Guatemala Human Rights Commission/USA. 2012. "For Women's Right to Live" http://www.ghrc-usa
.org/Programs/ForWomensRighttoLive/FAQs.htm Accessed 2/25/2014

Hanmer, Jalna, Jill Radford, and Elizabeth A. Stanko. 1989. *Women, Policing, and Male Violence: International Perspectives*. London: Routledge.

Helliwell, Christine. 2000. " 'It's Only a Penis': Rape, Feminism, and Difference." *Signs: Journal of Women in Contemporary Society* 25 (3): 789–816.

Horton, Teresa. 2006. "Billyberg Bastard." http://www.ihollaback.org/blog/2006/12/07/billyberg-bastard/. Accessed March 22, 2011.

Human Rights Watch. 2001. "No Escape: Male Rape in U.S. Prisons." http://www.hrw.org/en/reports/2001/04/01/no-escape-male-rape-us-prisons. Accessed March 22, 2011.

Human Rights Watch. 2013. World Report 2013: Guatemala. http://www.hrw.org/world-report/2013/country-chapters/guatemala?page=2. Accessed 2/26/2014.

INCITE! Women of Color Against Violence. 2011. "Critical Resistance/INCITE! Joint Statement: Gender Violence and the Prison Industrial Complex."http://www.icasa.org/docs/nsac%202012%20workshop%20handouts/d-1%20handouts.pdf. Accessed February 26, 2014.

Josephson, Jyl. 2005. "The Intersectionality of Domestic Violence and Welfare in the Lives of Poor Women." In Sokoloff and Pratt, 83–101.

Katz, Jackson. 2006. "Coverage of 'School Shootings' Avoids the Central Issue." *Dallas Morning News*, October 13. www.jacksonkatz.com/pub_coverage.html. Accessed March 22, 2011.

Kilpatrick, Dean, and Jenna McCauley. 2009. *Factsheets: Understanding National Rape Statistics*. New York City Alliance Against Sexual Assaults. http://www.svfreenyc.org/research_factsheet_149.html. Accessed June 8, 2011.

Kimmel, Michael. 2000. "Manhood and Violence: The Deadliest Equation." *Brother*. Louisville, CO: National Organization for Men Against Sexism.

———. 2004. *The Gendered Society*. 2nd edition. New York: Oxford University Press.

Krebs, Christopher, Christine H. Lindquist, Tara D. Warner, Bonnie S. Fisher, Sandra L. Martin. 2007. *The Campus Sexual Assault (CSA) Study*. National Institute of Justice. http://www.ncjrs.gov/pdffiles1/nij/grants/221153.pdf. Accessed June 8, 2011.

Labell, Linda S. 1979. "Wife Abuse: A Sociological Study of Battered Women and Their Mates." *Victimology* 4 (2): 258–67.

Lipscomb, Gary H., David Muram, Pat M. Speck, and Brian M. Mercer. 1992. "Male Victims of Sexual Assault." *Journal of the American Medical Association* 267 (22): 3064–66.

Magnani, Laura, and Harmon L. Wray. 2006. *Beyond Prisons: A New Interfaith Paradigm for Our Failed Prison System*. Minneapolis: Augsberg Fortress.

Marshall, Lucinda. 2004a. "The Connection between Militarism and Violence against Women." *ZNet*, February 21.

———. 2004b. "Unacceptable: The Impact of War on Women and Children." *CommonDreams.org*, December 18. http://www.commondreams.org/views04/1219-26.htm. Accessed March 22, 2011.

Martin, Patricia Yancey, and Robert A. Hummer. 1989. "Fraternities and Rape on Campus." *Gender and Society* 3 (4): 457–73.

Men Can Stop Rape. 2007. "Men Can Stop Rape Celebrates 10 Milestones During 10 Years of Prevention." http://www.mencanstoprape.org/. Accessed february 26, 2014.

Messerschmidt, James W. 2000. *Nine Lives: Adolescent Masculinities, the Body, and Violence*. Boulder, CO: Westview.

Messner, Michael. 2002. *Taking the Field: Women, Men, and Sports*. Minneapolis: University of Minnesota Press.

———. 1992. *Power at Play: Sports and the Problem of Masculinity*. Boston: Beacon Press.

Moser, Caroline, and Fiona Clark (eds.). 2001. *Victims, Perpetrators or Actors? Gender, Armed Conflict and Political Violence.* London: Zed Books.

National Center for Victims of Crime. 1995. "Sexual Assault Legislation." *Get Help Series.* Washington, DC: National Center for the Victims of Crime

NGO Working Group for Women, Peace, and Security. 2004. "No Women, No Peace: The Importance of Women's Participation to Achieve Peace and Security," Submitted to the UN Secretary-General's High-Level Panel on Threats, Challenges, and Change, April. http://www.peacewomen .org/publications_enews_issue.php?id=94. Accessed March 22, 2011.

Parenti, Christian. 1999. *Lockdown America: Police and Prisons in the Age of Crisis.* London: Verso Books.

Paterson, Kent. 2006. "Femicide on the Rise in Latin America." *International Relations Center Americas Program Report.* http://oreaddaily.blogspot.com/2006/03/femicide-wracks-latin-america.html. Accessed March 22, 2011.

Pazzanese, Christina. 2013. "Understanding India's Rape Crisis." *Harvard Gazette*, September 20. http://news.harvard.edu/gazette/story/2013/09/understanding-indias-rape-crisis/.

Ptacek, James. 1988. "Why Do Men Batter Their Wives?" In *Feminist Perspectives on Wife Abuse*, edited by K. Yliö and M. Bograd, 133–57. Newbury Park, CA: Sage.

Putnam, Robert. 2000. *Bowling Alone: The Collapse and Revival of American Community.* New York: Simon and Schuster.

Radford, Lorraine. 1987. "Legalizing Woman Abuse." In *Women, Violence, and Social Control*, edited by Jalna Hanmer and Mary Maynard, 135–51. Atlantic Highlands, NJ: Humanities Press International.

Rand, Michael R. 2009. "Criminal Victimization, 2008." *National Crime Victimization Survey.* bjs.ojp.usdoj.gov/content/pub/pdf/cv08.pdf. Accessed March 22, 2011.

Rao, Kavitha. 2006. " 'Eve-Teasing' Makes India's Streets Mean for Women." *Women's E-News*, December 11. http://womensenews.org/story/sexual-harassment/061211/eve-teasing-makes-indias-streets-mean-women. Accessed March 22, 2011.

Rehn, Elizabeth, and Sirleaf, Ellen Johnson. 2002. "Women, War, Peace: The Independent Experts' Assessment on the Impact of Armed Conflict on Women and Women's Role in Peace-Building." *Progress of the World's Women Vol. 1.* West Hartford, CT: UNIFEM/Kumarian Press.

Russell, Diana. 1992. *Femicide: The Politics of Woman Killing.* New York: Twayne.

Sabo, Don. 1994. *Sex, Violence, and Power in Sports: Rethinking Masculinity.* Freedom, CA: Crossing.

Sen, Rinku. 1999. "Between a Rock and a Hard Place: Domestic Violence in Communities of Color." *Color Lines* 2 (1): 1–4.

Sentencing Project. 2013. "Incarceration." http://www.sentencingproject.org/template/page.cfm?id=107. Accessed October 30, 2013.

Smith, Andrea. 2005. "Looking to the Future: Domestic Violence, Women of Color, the State, and Social Change." In Sokoloff and Pratt, 416–34.

Smith, Pamela Ann. 2006. "Mideast Events Vivify Women's 'Worst Problem.' " *WeNews*, July 20. http://www.womensenews.org/story/our-daily-lives/060720/mideast-events-vivify-womens-worst-problem. Accessed March 22, 2011.

Smithsimon, Greg. 2000. "People in the Streets: The Promise of Democracy in Everyday Public Space." http://www.livingcity.net.au/resources/publications-others/People-in-The-Streets-The-Promise-of-Democracy-in-Everyday-Public-Space.htm. Accessed March 22, 2011.

Sokoloff, Natalie, and Ida Dupont. 2005. "Domestic Violence: Examining the Intersections of Race, Class, and Gender—An Introduction." In Sokoloff and Pratt, 1–14.

Sokoloff, Natalie, with Christina Pratt, eds. 2005. *Domestic Violence at the Margins: Readings on Race, Class, Gender, and Culture.* New Brunswick, NJ: Rutgers University Press.

Speake, Beth. 2012. "Women's bodies are battlefields: How women's bodies are targeted in times of conflict, and how this relates to violence against women during ' peacetime.' " E-International Relations. http://www.e-ir.info/2012/04/25/womens-bodies-are-battlefields/.

Stanko, Elizabeth. 1990. *Everyday Violence: How Women and Men Experience Sexual and Physical Danger.* London: Pandora.

Steinmetz, Suzanne. 1978. "The Battered Husband Syndrome." *Victimology* 2 (3–4): 499–509.

Straus, Murray, Richard Gelles, and Suzanne Steinmetz. 1980. *Behind Closed Doors: Violence in the American Family.* New York: Doubleday/Anchor.

Stroud, Matt. 2013. "Philadelphia Schools Closing While a New $400 Million Prison Is Under Construction: Could It Be Worse Than It Sounds? *Forbes.* June 17.

Sudbury, Julia. 2005. "Gender Violence and the Prison Industrial Complex: Interpersonal and State Violence Against Women of Color." In Sokoloff and Pratt, 102–14.

Thompson, B. Carter. 1986. "Defending the Battered Wife: A Challenge for Defense Attorneys." *Trial* 2 (2): 74–79.

Thornhill, Randy, and Craig Palmer. 2000. *A Natural History of Rape: Biological Bases of Sexual Coercion.* Cambridge, MA: MIT Press.

U.S. Department of Justice, Office of Justice Programs. 2005. *National Crime Victimization Survey: Rape in America: A Report to the Nation.* http://www.bjs.gov/index.cfm?ty=pbdetail&iid=766. Accessed February 26, 2014.

Valladares, Danilo. 2013. "Guatemala's 'Femicide' Courts Hold Out New Hope for Justice." Truthout. August 12. http://www.truth-out.org/news/item/18136-guatemalas-femicide-courts-hold-out-new-hope-for-justice

Walker, Lenore E. 1979. *The Battered Woman.* New York: Harper & Row.

Weitzman, Susan. 2000. *"Not to People Like Us": Hidden Abuse in Upscale Marriages.* New York: Basic Books.

Wesely, Jennifer, and Emily Gaarder. 2004. "The Gendered 'Nature' of the Urban Outdoors: Women Negotiating Fear of Violence." *Gender and Society* 18 (5): 645–63.

West, Carolyn. 2005. "Domestic Violence in Ethnically and Racially Diverse Families: The 'Political Gag Order' Has Been Lifted." In Sokoloff and Pratt, 157–73.

Wing, Nick. 2013. "Here Are All of the Nations that Incarcerate More of Their Population Than the U.S." August 14. http://www.huffingtonpost.com/2013/08/13/incarceration-rate-per-capita_n_3745291.html. Accessed October 30, 2013.

Wittner, Judith. 1998. "Reconceptualizing Agency in Domestic Violence Court." In *Community Activism and Feminist Politics,* edited by Nancy Naples, 81–106. New York: Routledge.

9

GENDER- AND RACE-BASED ILLNESS: DISEASES OF THE DIVISION OF LABOR

Marching for Reproductive Choice in Minnesota.
Source: Photo by Jennifer Simonson/Minnesota Public Radio News.

We know what makes us ill.

. . .

The pain in our shoulder comes
You say, from the damp; and this is also the reason
For the stain on the wall of our flat.
So tell us:
Where does the damp come from?

Bertolt Brecht, "A Worker's Speech to a Doctor."

Brecht's poems asks us to consider the "causes of the causes" of illness, the social and environmental contexts—homes, schools, neighborhoods, unhealthy food, toxic water and air, violence , injustice (see Farmer 2013). This chapter explores these causes of the causes of health and illness and their intersections with gender and other forms of social inequality. How are illnesses related to gendered divisions of labor? In other words, how do gender and other social inequalities cause particular health problems, and how do they prevent us from achieving health? The chapter begins with a discussion of what health and illness are and how they are related to social structures, social relationships, and social roles. The chapter then looks at some illnesses that have been identified with men or women and traces their history and their connections with other social factors such as race ethnicity, social class, sexuality, and nation. The next section explores the experiences of care workers within the

319

health care system. Then, in the last section, we examine social movements that have emerged in response to gendered health problems and how these movements are tackling problems by calling for restructuring the division of labor.

HEALTH AND ILLNESS AS SOCIAL ISSUES

Health is not simply the absence of disease. The World Health Organization (WHO) considers health a "state of complete physical, mental, and social well-being" (Ruzek, Olesen, and Clarke 1997). A narrow focus on illness itself leaves out the social contexts and forces that shape women's and men's health, such as the fundamental differences of class, race, sexuality, and nation. For sociologists, sickness and health are not simply or even fundamentally biological matters. The causes of disease and injury, the experience of illness, its treatment, and its resolution take shape in a social context.

Undoubtedly, women have made significant progress economically, politically, and socially in the past several decades, but they have not achieved complete equality with men. Economically, women's earnings average less than men's, and women control fewer resources compared with men. Worldwide, women put in more hours of work than men, but women average 30 percent to 40 percent less pay, and often no pay at all for domestic and caring work. Politically, women hold fewer positions of power. In every nation, they are less likely to be decision makers, policy makers, or politicians. Socially, women have lower status than men, as shown in rates of female infanticide and honors awarded. The gender inequalities around sickness and health raise important questions for us to consider:

- How does such pervasive inequality contribute to the diseases that affect women?
- How does men's social, political, and economic dominance contribute to men's diseases?
- What about the health and illness of men who don't dominate, such as men of color, working-class men, and poor men? Does the health status of poor men resemble that of male elites, or does it resemble the health status of the women in their own communities?
- How do race ethnicity, sexuality, and class complicate the health differences between women and men? How does race ethnicity intersect with gender, sexuality, and class (poverty and wealth) to produce different health statuses?
- How shall we envision health? Should our vision include "social health," meaning the health of the community, including health care, housing, decent work, and protection from hunger for individuals (Binford 1996)?
- Is health a human right (Farmer 2003)?
- If health and illness exist within a social context, and not simply in individual men's and women's bodies, how are health and illness embedded in communities, nations, and the globalized world (Ruzek et al. 1997)?

NATION AND LIFE EXPECTANCY

Epidemiology has been called "the basic science of public health." Epidemiologists study life expectancy rates, the distribution and causes of disease, and rates of maternal and infant mortality in different populations (Jackson 2003, 11). These rates suggest that where a person is born has a powerful impact on life and death. For example, look at the differences in life expectancy for a range of selected countries, from the richest to the poorest, shown in Table 9-1.

The rates show that babies born in wealthy nations of the global North can expect, on average, to live many years longer than people born in the poor countries of the global South. A Swedish, Australian, or Canadian baby born in 2013 could live eighty or more years, but a baby from Chad, Somalia, or Afghanistan will be lucky to reach the age of fifty. But there is some good news as well. In 2010, Lesotho had one of the world's highest rates of HIV/AIDS and life expectancy was forty-one years—half as long as in the rich global North. By 2013, the life expectancy in Lesotho had risen to more than fifty-two years, a small improvement probably due to successes in the treatment of AIDS (Nebehay 2013). An interesting exception to the rich country–poor country difference is Cuba, a poor country noted for its first-class public health system. With few resources but a strong commitment to preventive health care for everyone, Cuba is a third-world country whose citizens enjoy first-world health status. In Box 9-1, you can read what a delegation of American medical professionals learned about the Cuban health system after a visit to that country. Their report suggests that a broad system of public health care and preventive medicine can create a successful national health policy. Cuba is an exception among poor and not-so-poor nations in providing its citizens high-quality, accessible health care.

TABLE 9-1 Life Expectancy at Birth in Selected Countries

	Total	Male	Female
Japan	83	79	86
Switzerland	82	80	84
Australia	81	79	84
Sweden	81	79	83
Canada	81	78	83
United Kingdom	80	77	82
United States	78	75	80
Cuba	78	76	80
China	74	72	76
Indonesia	71	69	73
Russia	68	62	74
India	64	63	65
Philippines	72	70	74
Iraq	67	64	72
Sudan	58	57	60
South Africa	55	54	57
Kenya	57	56	57
Rwanda	51	50	53
Nigeria	47	47	48
Swaziland	46	46	45
Angola	45	47	49
Lesotho	41	40	43

Source: Population Reference Bureau (2010, 10–13).

GENDER IN EVERYDAY LIFE   BOX 9-1
A DIFFERENT MODEL—MEDICAL CARE IN CUBA

For a visitor from the United States, Cuba is disorienting. American cars are everywhere, but they all date from the 1950s at the latest. Our bank cards, credit cards, and smartphones don't work. Internet access is virtually nonexistent. And the Cuban health care system also seems unreal. There are too many doctors. Everybody has a family physician. Everything is free, totally free—and not after prior approval or some copay. The whole system seems turned upside down. It is tightly organized, and the first priority is prevention. Although Cuba has limited economic resources, its health care system has solved some problems that ours has not yet managed to address.

Family physicians, along with their nurses and other health workers, are responsible for delivering primary care and preventive services to their panel of patients—about 1,000 patients per physician in urban areas. All care delivery is organized at the local level, and the patients and their caregivers generally live in the same community. The medical records in cardboard folders are simple and handwritten, not unlike those we used in the United States 50 years ago. But the system is surprisingly information-rich and focused on population health.

All patients are categorized according to level of health risk, from I to IV. Smokers, for example, are in risk category II, and patients with stable, chronic lung disease are in category III. The community clinics report regularly to the district on how many patients they have in each risk category and on the number of patients with conditions such as hypertension (well controlled or not), diabetes, and asthma, as well as immunization status, time since last Pap smear, and pregnancies necessitating prenatal care.

Every patient is visited at home once a year, and those with chronic conditions receive visits more frequently. When necessary, patients can be referred to a district polyclinic for specialty evaluation, but they return to the community team for ongoing treatment. For example, the team is responsible for seeing that a patient with tuberculosis follows the assigned antimicrobial regimen and gets sputum checks. House calls and discussions with family members are common tactics for addressing problems with compliance or follow-up and even for failure to protect against unwanted pregnancy. In an effort to control mosquito-borne infections such as dengue, the local health team goes into homes to conduct inspections and teach people about getting rid of standing water, for example. This highly structured, prevention-oriented system has produced positive results.

Vaccination rates in Cuba are among the highest in the world. The life expectancy of 78 years from birth is virtually identical to that in the United States. The infant mortality rate in Cuba has fallen from more than 80 per 1,000 live births in the 1950s to less than 5 per 1,000—lower than the U.S. rate, although the maternal mortality rate remains well above those in developed countries and is in the middle of the range for Caribbean countries. Without doubt, the improved health outcomes are largely the result of improvements in nutrition and education, which address the social determinants of health. Cuba's literacy rate is 99%, and health education is part of the mandatory school curriculum. A recent national program to promote acceptance of men who have sex with men was designed in part to reduce rates of sexually transmitted disease and improve acceptance of and adherence to treatment. Cigarettes can no longer be obtained with monthly ration cards, and smoking rates have decreased, though local health teams say it remains difficult to get smokers to quit. Contraception is free and strongly encouraged. Abortion is legal but is seen as a failure of prevention.

But one should not romanticize Cuban health care. The system is not designed for consumer choice or individual initiatives. There is no alternative, private-payer health system. Physicians get government benefits such as housing and food subsidies, but they are paid only about $20 per month. Their education is free, and they are respected, but they are unlikely to attain personal wealth. Cuba is a country where 80% of the citizens work for the government, and the government manages the budgets. In a community health clinic, signs tell patients how much their free care is actually costing the system but no market forces compel efficiency. Resources are limited, as we learned in meeting with Cuban medical and public health professionals as part of a group of editors from the United States. A nephrologist in Cienfuegos, 160 miles south of Havana, lists 77 patients on dialysis in the province, which on a population basis is about 40% of the current U.S. rate—similar to what the U.S. rate was in 1985. A neurologist reports that his hospital got a CT scanner only 12 years ago. U.S. students who are enrolled in a Cuban medical school say that operating rooms run quickly and efficiently but with very little technology. Access to information through the Internet is minimal. One medical student reports being limited to 30 minutes per week of dial-up access. This limitation, like many of the resource constraints that affect progress, is blamed on the long-standing U.S. economic embargo, but there may be other forces in the central government working against rapid, easy communication among Cubans and with the United States.

As a result of the strict economic embargo, Cuba has developed its own pharmaceutical industry and now not only manufactures most of the medications in its basic pharmacopeia, but also fuels an export industry. Resources have been invested in developing biotechnology expertise to become competitive with advanced countries. There are Cuban academic medical journals in all the major specialties, and the medical leadership is strongly encouraging research, publication, and stronger ties to medicine in other Latin American countries. Cuba's medical faculties, of which there are now 22, remain steadily focused on primary care, with family medicine required as the first residency for all physicians, even though Cuba now has more than twice as many physicians per capita as the United States. Many of those physicians work outside the country, volunteering for two or more years of service, for which they receive special compensation. In 2008, there were 37,000 Cuban health care providers working in 70 countries around the world. Most are in needy areas where their work is part of Cuban foreign aid, but some are in more developed areas where their work brings financial benefit to the Cuban government (e.g., oil subsidies from Venezuela).

Any visitor can see that Cuba remains far from a developed country in basic infrastructure such as roads, housing, plumbing, and sanitation. Nonetheless, Cubans are beginning to face the same health problems the developed world faces, with increasing rates of coronary disease and obesity and an aging population (11.7% of Cubans are now 65 years of age or older). Their unusual health care system addresses those problems in ways that grew out of Cuba's peculiar political and economic history, but the system they have created—with a physician for everyone, an early focus on prevention, and clear attention to community health—may inform progress in other countries as well.

SOURCE: Edward W. Campion, and Stephen Morrissey, 2013, *New England Journal of Medicine* 368 (January 24): 297–99. Copyright © 2013, Massachusetts Medical Society.

GENDER AND LIFE EXPECTANCY

Women's life expectancy is greater than men's in almost every country and region of the world. In the global North, girl babies born in 2010 can expect to live at least five years longer than boy babies born in the same year. In poor countries, where HIV has spread more rapidly among women and where many women have little, if any, access to prenatal care, men may have a slightly higher life expectancy. Less than a century ago in the United States, women's life expectancy was shorter than men's, a difference reflecting frequent childbearing and chronic malnutrition. In developing countries, women's life expectancy is still subject to the risks incurred by frequent childbearing, unattended childbirth, sexually transmitted diseases, malnutrition (family caretakers, wives, and mothers often go without food to feed their families), domestic violence, and HIV. Some differences in life expectancy may be differences of biological sex, not social gender. In the United States today, a woman's life expectancy at birth is seventy-nine, whereas a man's is seventy-two. Human male fetuses die more often than female fetuses, and each year after birth, more males than females die. The long-term result is that by the age of one hundred, there are only eleven men to every hundred women. Biologists believe that among other things, females have a genetic advantage over males in some ways because they have two copies of the X chromosome, which protects them from X-linked diseases such as hemophilia and muscular dystrophy. On the other hand, pregnancy and childbirth create significant health risks for women that until the last century meant that women's life span was significantly shorter than men's all over the globe. Today reproductive health problems continue to be deadly for many women in the global South.

More recently, women have caught up to and surpassed men in regard to life span in many places in the world, causing the longevity gap between women and men to grow, with women enjoying increasingly longer lives than the men in their communities. Very recently, however, the longevity gap between women and men has narrowed as "male" diseases increase among women. Heart disease and stroke are now the leading causes of death for women in the United States (39 percent of all women's deaths) and in most Western countries. Tobacco is another contributor to women's lower life expectancy. Although many more men use tobacco than women (women make up only about 20 percent of the world's smokers), there is evidence that tobacco use among girls is increasing in some countries and regions. In half of the 151 countries recently surveyed for trends in tobacco use among young people, approximately as many girls used tobacco as boys. More girls use tobacco than boys in Bulgaria, Chile, Colombia, Cook Islands, Croatia, Czech Republic, Mexico, New Zealand, Nigeria, and Uruguay. Part of the increase is explained by the fact that women are a major target of the tobacco industry's efforts to recruit new users to replace those who will quit or will die prematurely from tobacco-related diseases. A leading preventable cause of death, tobacco use kills more than 5 million people every year. Most of them are men (3.5 million), but women are rapidly joining their numbers (1.5 million) (World Health Organization 2010b). Currently, more women die each year from lung cancer than breast cancer, uterine cancer, and ovarian cancers combined.

Not all men are equally at risk for poor health. African American men, disabled men, gay men, poor men, and rural men are responsible for men's higher mortality rates. But gender "interferes" with the effect of these social factors. Women with the same kinds of social disadvantages often have lower rates than do men of mortality, disability, chronic illness, and injury.

Most of the closing of the longevity gap appears to be because women are becoming more like men, and as a result, their health has suffered. Perhaps some men's (and women's) recent lifestyle choices—healthier diets, more physical activity, less time spent at work, more involvement with their children—will lengthen their lives. As changes in lifestyle and advances in knowledge about nutrition, exercise, and stress reduction improve, the longevity gap may continue to narrow, at least to some extent, because both women and men are becoming healthier.

In the United States, the impact of racism on life expectancy is startling. Table 9-2 shows that white female babies born in the United States in 2002 can expect to live eleven and a half years longer than African American male babies born in the same year. White male infants can expect to outlive black males by almost six years, and white female infants can expect nearly an additional five years of life when compared with black female infants. The difference in life

TABLE 9-2 Life Expectancy in the United States by Race Ethnicity and Gender, 1930–2006

| | White | | Black | |
	Men	Women	Men	Women
2006	75.7	80.6	69.7	76.5
2002	75.1	80.3	68.8	75.6
1970	68.0	75.6	60.0	68.3
1950	66.5	72.2	59.1	62.9
1930	59.7	63.5	47.3	49.2

Source: Arias (2010, 2).

expectancy between white boy and girl infants narrowed slightly between 1950 and 2002, from 5.5 years to 5.2 years. However, the differences between black and white infants grew, from an advantage to girls of 3.8 years in 1950 to an advantage of 6.8 years in 2002, showing the significance of race ethnicity to the life expectancies of African Americans, male and female.

SEX, GENDER, AND HEALTH: THE GENDERED DIVISION OF LABOR

Toni Schofield and her colleagues (2000) suggest that the key to understanding sex differences in health lies in studying the relations between women and men in the gendered division of labor. Men have often worked long hours in the paid labor force, while women, employed or not, did unpaid household work. Men have also often taken jobs in the most dangerous occupations, in construction, trucking, mines, factories, and the military. In addition, paid work is often done in the context of stressful hierarchies where employees have little control over their work, resulting in high blood pressure, heart disease, and stroke. Higher mortality rates for men may be associated with all these workplace factors. In addition, gender expectations of men require that they refrain from talking about their emotions or disclosing their feelings of depression. Men who are unhappy with their work lives have few outlets for conveying their unhappiness, which then may be expressed in their higher rates of alcoholism and drug use. The great recession of 2010 meant disproportionate job losses for men in men's jobs such as construction and manufacturing compared with women, who did not lose jobs at the same rate as men. But as of 2013, the female unemployment rate has stagnated because of cuts to public sector employment (teaching, government jobs in which women congregate) compared with manufacturing and construction work, jobs which are now hiring men.

What consequences will flow from the fact that women are now about half the paid labor force? Although their stresses are different, with women carrying a greater burden of paid work and men facing unemployment, both women and men will undoubtedly be forced to contend with health problems that accompany these changes.

Women, in this gendered division of labor, furthermore, are responsible for unpaid housework and care work. Housewives and other domestic workers (including men who are farmworkers and landscapers) are exposed to hazards from cleaning products, insecticides, pesticides, pollutants, and a variety of toxic chemicals flooding into households. Wage workers may be alert to the physical and chemical hazards they face on the job, but housewives and domestic workers often use toxic cleaning compounds without adequately understanding the potential of these chemicals to cause cancer and respiratory diseases.

Sometimes housework itself can be equally toxic. Women who are full-time housewives have higher rates of anxiety, depression, and discontent. Women with full-time jobs who share housework and child care with husbands have lower rates of depression and anxiety. However, as we learned in chapter 6, women still do more housework than men. And, in chapter 7, we noted that care work in families is most likely done by women. Especially when women are in the paid labor force and also in charge of caring for children and elders, as well as housekeeping—domestic work that is physically taxing, never done, and often invisible— their physical and mental health may be jeopardized.

The Health Risks and Benefits of Women's Employment in the Global North

Women who are employed are healthier, mentally and physically, compared with those who are not in the paid labor force. Nevertheless, most jobs add significant new health-related stresses to women's days. An indicator of the social origins of many "men's" diseases is the fact that rates of lung cancer, heart disease, and stroke are rising among women along with their rates of labor-force participation. When women go to work for pay, they often also remain responsible for more than an equal share of the necessary child care and domestic work. Many men have not made the reverse trip by substantially increasing their share of this work. Hochschild (1989) called men's failure to take up their fair share of domestic labor as their wives entered the labor force the "stalled revolution." This additional work time for women creates stresses that can translate into high blood pressure, anxiety, lack of sleep, and other sources of ill health.

Some of the workers most pressed for time are women professionals, academics, and managers. These women have transformed the masculine professions of medicine, law, university teaching, and business in profound ways. What they have not changed is the culture of work that demands sixty- and seventy-hour work weeks. The expectation that professionals will give so many hours each week to employers arose in an era when professional men had wives at home who saw to family needs. This work model has remained the same even though households now almost always have all adults in the labor force. As a result, women professionals (and their willing husbands) must figure out how to reconcile long hours at work with time for child care, housework, community activities, and personal renewal.

Poor and working-class women are also pressed for time. Increasingly responsible for sharing the economic support of their families or, as single parents, their families' sole support, they may work at two or more part-time jobs while continuing to be responsible for housework and family needs. The majority of women are employed in service and clerical jobs; the "women's professions" of nursing, teaching, and social work; and in the lower strata of various industries and institutions. Among the health consequences of stereotypically female jobs is burnout resulting from lack of control. Woman-dominated service-oriented jobs and jobs caring for others often evoke feelings of anger and frustration that workers must struggle to handle. Care workers and service workers with the least control over their work and earning the lowest pay are most at risk of experiencing exhaustion, digestive problems, high blood pressure, heart disease, and depression.

Poor women in the United States experience stress with significantly fewer social, financial, and educational resources than professional women. For poor single mothers who are heads of households solely responsible for providing for their families, daily life is a constant struggle. Such mothers may be unemployed or relegated to low-paying jobs, poorly educated, and victims of racism and sexism. They may have to rely on public transportation to shuttle their children back and forth from home to day care. If they work for hourly wages at service jobs, they may not be free to make or receive calls while on the job, to leave the job in an emergency, or to stay away from work on days when their children are out of school or sick. If they have older children, they may worry about their safety if no one is at home when they return from school. This is especially the case when children return to gang-riddled neighborhoods and where there are few adults around who are able or willing to provide protection. As you saw in chapter 7, our welfare system has mandated that everyone must be employed to qualify for assistance. As a result, the grandmothers and aunts who once might have looked out for the children of their extended families must now leave home for work that enriches corporations while they leave behind work that enriches human beings.

Poor Women's Health Risks on the Job in the Global South

Overwhelmingly, it is the poor in developing areas of the world and in the pockets of poverty in industrial nations whose lives are shortened by poverty and disease (Farmer 2003). The poor and powerless live at great risk of life-changing and life-threatening violence, infectious diseases, workplace accidents, lack of medical attention, and the stresses of trying to survive under difficult conditions. As the global economy reorganizes the sites and forms of production, many women and men in poorer countries take jobs in transnational corporations manufacturing products and providing services that were once produced in the global North, while the former jobholders in the North become unemployed or find jobs that pay a lot less. Now it is workers in Southeast Asia and eastern Europe who manufacture textiles or electronics components. Now workers in India and the Philippines take phone calls for American catalog and computer markets. Former farmers and their children grow food for export on large commercial farms in India, China, and Latin America. As in the global North, paid work reduces women's economic and social dependency, relieves them of their isolation at home, and offers them friends and networks of support. On the other hand, long hours of work may keep them from tending family plots that feed their families. For example, Zimbabwean women work on farms growing food for export, even as they and their children experience high rates of malnutrition (Doyal 1995, 159).

In some rural regions of poor countries, housework is especially onerous. In these areas, "housework" involves the arduous labor of carrying water over long distances, tending crops, foraging for wood, and more. It is likely that this heavy labor is a factor in third-world women's poor health and shortened life span. In the global North, the introduction of running water, gas, and electricity in the first third of the twentieth century eased some of the hard physical labor of housework (Luxton 1980), but this transformation has eluded many rural societies in Africa, Asia, and Latin America. One example of activity that may contribute to the discrepancy in infant mortality is the fact that women in these communities cannot afford to rest or to avoid lifting heavy objects during pregnancy, hard labor that often threatens their babies' and their own survival.

In addition, women in poor, rural areas of the world may be exposed to agricultural chemicals, wood smoke from cooking fires, and other domestic fuels. If they do paid piecework at home, they may suffer eyestrain, backache, fire hazards, and exposure to toxic materials (Doyal 1995). Farmworkers around the world, including in the United States, are also exposed to agrochemicals that are wrongly used or badly labeled. The World Health Organization estimates that three million farm workers are hospitalized yearly from pesticide poisoning. Chronic and long-term effects of such exposure include cancers, birth defects, sterility, asthma, eye problems, and damage to lungs, heart, kidney, liver, and the central nervous system. Employers often assign these lowest paid and least valued workers to dangerous and unpopular tasks. For example, on Malaysian plantations, women are 80 percent of the workers spreading herbicides. They work with no protective clothing or equipment for safety. Women who cultivate the cut flowers in the factory greenhouses of Colombia tend the plants during spraying. Fertility problems, stillbirths, and deformed infants are not unusual among such women, along with headaches, impaired vision, nausea, conjunctivitis, rashes, and asthma-like problems. Both men and women suffer from lack of protection in these factory greenhouses, and observers fear that these women's jobs put them at greater risk for damage to their reproductive systems and to the children they may bear. As we discuss later in the chapter, new research on men's health suggests that men's reproductive systems are similarly affected by toxic chemicals and that they also pass on these harms to their children.

The neoliberal free-trade system that eliminates trade barriers and allows corporations to travel the world in search of the cheapest labor with minimal regulation has disrupted local economies, forced massive migrations of people in search of jobs, and accelerated the impoverishment and insecurity of workers around the world. In "The Return of the Sweatshop," sociologists Edna Bonacich and Richard Applebaum (2007) describe the growth of sweatshops—small factories or home operations—that are central to the global garment industry. Typically these businesses violate whatever wage and hour regulations exist in their host countries. Sweatshop workers are not paid overtime, they are not paid minimum wage, and sometimes they are not paid at all. Even if a workplace adheres to the letter of the law, however, the low standards of pay and long hours of work mean that workers still face health problems and poverty. Women working in the textile industry are exposed to cotton dust, which contributes to disabling brown lung disease. Women who sew garments may be sickened by dyes and other chemicals in the cloth they use, they may be injured by sewing-machine accidents resulting from speedups, and they can suffer from fatigue and back strain resulting from long hours of work. Without regulation, these enterprises get away without restricting the onerous conditions of work or providing health care to their employees. The organization United Students Against Sweatshops has worked successfully to force some of these companies to act responsibly. See Box 9-2, "Will Sweatshop Activists' Big Victory Over Nike Trigger Broader Industry Reforms?"

GENDER IN EVERYDAY LIFE   BOX 9-2
WILL SWEATSHOP ACTIVISTS' BIG VICTORY OVER NIKE TRIGGER BROADER INDUSTRY REFORMS?

With the memory of a previous victory over a multinational garment manufacturer still fresh in their minds, student labor activists and Honduran workers are celebrating what they say is another major win—this one against industry giant Nike.

In 2009, Nike shut down two subcontractor plants in Honduras, leaving 1,800 workers without jobs. Under Honduran labor law, the workers were owed severance pay, to the tune of several million dollars. But Nike indicated it had no intention of paying.

Student activists with United Students Against Sweatshops (USAS) were no strangers to labor disputes over Honduran factory closures. Also last year, they picked a fight with Russell Athletic, another major global garment manufacturer, over alleged unionbusting in Honduras after the company shuttered its only unionized plant in the country. After students heaped pressure on a slew of U.S. universities, convincing them to cut their Russell contracts, the company agreed to reopen the plant, scoring a major victory for students and the Honduran unionists.

Building on this experience, students began a campaign to force Nike to pay the 1,800 workers their severance. On Monday, they emerged victorious.

As they had done against Russell, activists crisscrossed the country with workers from the closed plants on a speaking tour at dozens of universities with contracts with the company, meeting with several university administrations. It wasn't long before the prospect of terminating Nike contracts was raised, and the company began to change its position.

It took 89 contract losses before Russell caved. This time, one contract termination at the University of Wisconsin–Madison and the threat of another at Cornell were enough to convince Nike to accede to worker/student demands. The company agreed to pay $1.54 million to their former employees, provide healthcare and vocational training for a limited time, and give priority rehiring to the laid-off workers.

The win against Nike marks the second major victory in one year for USAS and garment workers. The students seem to have developed a winning strategy against massive multinationals they accuse of labor abuse: convincing individual universities to cut contracts with the companies while using traditional and new media to publicly shame the company into straightening up their act.

The method is not a particularly new one. Student labor organizations such as USAS and the Student Farmworker Alliance have utilized it for years, often with success against corporate giants like Yum! Brands and McDonalds. But organizers say they've hit their stride after taking on Nike, one of the garment industry's behemoths, and hope to introduce new standards of responsibility in the global subcontractor supply chain.

"This really is a watershed moment for the student anti-sweatshop movement," said Teresa Cheng, international campaigns coordinator for USAS. "Time and time again, corporations refuse to take responsibility for workers to whom they subcontract production."

Alex Bores, a rising sophomore at Cornell University who participated in the campaign calling for a contract termination—which included a massive student organization outreach effort and a "workout for workers rights," during which students passed out fliers to passing students—said the victory has implications for the entire garment industry.

"Mistreating workers is, sadly, how the apparel industry operates," he said.

"Corporations avoid responsibility [for workers] through the subcontracting system, where they can dictate the actions of factory owners without being held responsible for the devastating effects of their practices."

But, according to Cheng, in the wake of the Nike victory, "students and workers are setting a precedent in which corporations can no longer claim that they don't have responsibility for the workers making their products. "Nike has all the power, and for the first time, it is assuming responsibility for the damage it does in the global supply chain."

With a string of victories under their belt and momentum on their side, USAS isn't planning on slowing down.

"Our goal," Cheng explained, "is that someday, all college apparel will be made in strong union factories where workers can bargain for a living wage and humane working conditions—and that the college apparel sector will serve as a model for the rest of the industry."

SOURCE: Reprinted with permission from Uetricht (2010).

Other global factories rely on the work of women and subject them to health hazards on the job. Women microelectronics workers in east and Southeast Asia (where they comprise more than a quarter of the manufacturing labor force) and in California are increasingly exposed to hazardous chemicals, fumes, toxic substances, and heavy labor. They have three times the rate of headaches, dizziness, nausea, and blurred vision compared with workers in general manufacturing. The strict discipline imposed on this factory labor force, the extremely low pay, and speedups in the work all contribute to high stress levels among workers in this industry. Doyal (1995, 158) suggests that the occasional mass outbreaks of illness in these factories are forms of "covert industrial conflict." In these cases, illness is understood as a form of women's collective resistance to labor discipline, and not a result of germs and viruses (see also Ong 1987).

Sexual and Reproductive Health

Women's sexual and reproductive health depends in large part on the health of their partners and on their ability to control the conditions and frequency of sex. If women do not have control over the terms of their sexual encounters with men, they are at risk. For example, using condoms during intercourse can protect women from STDs, but condoms work to protect health only if women have the ability to negotiate their use with their partner and the right to refuse intercourse altogether. Unfortunately, women do not have this level of social power in many communities. The consequences are evident around the world, as women increasingly fall victim to HIV/AIDS and STDs.

In some communities, women often cede the power to determine sexual behavior to men who are their partners. They may believe that men's "need for sex" takes precedence over their own personal health concerns and agree that men have the right to demand sex from wives and girlfriends, even by force. Often, women's attempts to convince partners to use condoms can provoke rape and battery. Poverty and desperation also coerce sex. Prostitution or taking a sexual partner in exchange for a place to live or food to eat may be the only way some women can support themselves and their children.

When health care is not available, women's risk—and their suffering—increases. Where women have access to public health screening and medical services—Canada, Iceland, Norway, Finland, Sweden, Denmark, and Scotland—deaths from cervical cancer, for example, have declined. Where they do not have access to medical care, their risk of dying from cervical cancer is heightened. Lack of medical care explains the high proportion of reproductive tract infections in many parts of the world. A study of two rural villages in the Indian state of Maharashtra found that 92 percent of women there had gynecological or sexually transmitted diseases (STDs), averaging 3.6 infections each (Doyal 1995, 76). STDs are more socially damaging to women than to men because of the double standard in sexual behavior. In addition, if the disease makes a woman infertile, she may lose her partner and thus her means of support. Additionally, STDs increase the risk of HIV transmission.

In developing countries, women suffer from chronic ailments such as reproductive tract infections, poor nutrition, and communicable diseases. All of these diseases and troubles are connected to poverty. For example, reproductive tract infections in women result from the absence of toilets, the lack of sanitary pads, and the scarcity of privacy. When clean water becomes too expensive, which is the case when international banks force poor countries to privatize water in exchange for loans, poor women must make do with polluted and unsafe water, which affects their reproductive and general health, as well as the health of their children and families members (Box 9-3).

Persistent hunger accounts for the fact that in poor countries of the global South, at least 44 percent of all women are anemic (and 88 percent of Indian women), compared with 12 percent in the global North. The rising number of malnourished women adds to the proportion of high-risk pregnancies women experience and to the continuing high rates of maternal mortality, particularly in sub-Saharan Africa. The underlying causes of these conditions—high fertility, early childbearing, unintended pregnancies, poor nutrition, poverty, and lack of access to adequate obstetric care—are well known and preventable (Mwalali and Ngui 2009). Poor obstetrical care results in the quintessential disease of poverty—tuberculosis—which was reemerging among women and men around the world in the early years of this century (Farmer 2003), but is now slowly declining In fact, TB mortality has fallen over 40% worldwide since 1990 (WHO 2013).

GENDER IN EVERYDAY LIFE   BOX 9-3
WATER PRIVATIZATION

When a water system is privatized, the prices inevitably go up, sometimes as much as 100 percent. One of the arguments for privatization is that private companies will do a better job of maintaining the water system that the national government could. This is untrue—a company that is centered on profits will not do as much to maintain the water infrastructure because that requires pouring money into the system. Jobs are inevitably lost and the quality of the water tends to go down. When water systems are governed for profit, the natural resource is abused.

ACTIONS AGAINST WATER PRIVATIZATION

Perhaps the most well known instance of fighting against water privatization is the water wars between the people of Cochabamba, Bolivia, and private water corporations. The World Bank refused to renew development loans made to Bolivia unless they privatized their water system. Bolivia complied, allowing a consortium of companies, including Bechtel Enterprise Holdings, International Water Limited (owned by Bechtel), and others, to take over the previously state run water systems. The consortium raised the water rates 35% immediately after their takeover of the system to fund improvement projects. However, the consortium never made moves to complete these projects, and the rate hike was widely protested. Eventually, the protestors managed to convince the Bolivian government to return the water systems to the public, after four months of political unrest and military engagement against citizens on behalf of the Bechtel executives.

WHAT ABOUT BOTTLED WATER?

Bottled water is one of the most well-known arms of the privatization machine, but also one of the least recognized as such. When you buy a bottle of water somewhere, two things are happening:

1. That bottle of water has a huge impact on the health of the environment. It takes 17.6 barrels of oil to produce the amount of bottled water consumed in the US alone. Most bottles of water end up in landfills, many of them shipped around the world to developing countries.
2. Huge corporations are making a profit off taking the same groundwater that comes from the tap (draining the ground supply in the process) and selling it back to you [at] 100x the cost of tap water.

Because of this, corporations make millions of dollars off of a resource that used to be free and available to everyone. CEO of Suez Gerard Mestrallet says of water, "[It] is an efficient product. It is a product that would normally be free, and our job is to sell it. But it is a product which is absolutely necessary for life."

Bottled water plays into that way of thinking. It is a resource that is generally free, yet corporations like Nestle, Coca-Cola, and Pepsi Co bottle it and sell it back to the public, often at outrageous prices that are too expensive for many rural poor to afford.

The World Wildlife Fund estimates that the bottled water industry racks up $4 billion in sales each year. Bringing water and sanitation to everyone in the world would cost $10 billion, meaning that if the sales from the bottled water industry alone were redirected to providing clean water systems (not to mention the resources saved without the production of bottled water), that could put a significant dent in the number of people without access to clean water and sanitation.

SOURCE: Americans for Informed Democracy, "Water Privatization," September 25, 2013. http://www .aidemocracy.org/programs/environment/water/water-privatization/.

Racial differences and sexual orientation intersect with the differential risks associated with gender. For example, there are glaring racial disparities in health care among women. In the United States, women have more chronic health problems than men, and women of color are most affected. This is particularly true of poor women, who up until the passage of health care legislation in 2010 have also been likely to be without health insurance (because this legislation did not take effect until 2014, the lack of health care among poor women of color has remained a large problem). African American women face higher rates of violence, childbirth-related illnesses, and death compared with white women. In 1999, 5.9 million mothers caring for young children were without health insurance, and one out of every three of these mothers (4.3 million) was ineligible for Medicaid. In half the states, mothers earning over $9,780 a year (nearly $5,000 below the poverty line of $14,630) were considered too "well paid" to qualify for Medicaid. In Louisiana a mother with two children was ineligible for Medicaid if her earnings exceeded $3,048 a year! Such mothers could not afford preventive care, such as Pap smears and mammograms. As a result, uninsured women were more likely to be diagnosed with cancer at a later stage of the disease, and were therefore at greater risk of dying from it (Guyer, Broaddus, and Dude 2002). Poor African American women had a higher risk of giving birth to babies who died as infants than did women who were either poor or African American, but not both (Kreiger 1990).

The number of women worldwide who die during pregnancy or childbirth has dropped by almost one-half in the past three decades, from 500,000 annual deaths in 1980 to 287,000 as of 2013 (Melgar and Melgar 2010; WHO 2013). Bangladesh, where under-five mortality has fallen 72 percent since 1990, has met and exceeded the goal of cutting under-five mortality rates by two-thirds, as has Liberia. Even though there is great success in reducing the maternal mortality rate in childbirth worldwide, which has declined from 400 maternal deaths per 100,000 live births in 1990 to 210 maternal deaths per 100,000 births in 2010, this rate remains short of the UN target goal of 100 deaths per 100,000 live births by 2015. The problems are lack of prenatal care; assistance of a midwife, nurse, or doctor during childbirth; and contraceptive use to prevent unwanted pregnancies (*New York Times* Editorial Board 2013).

An astonishing statistic is the maternal mortality rate in the United States, which *increased* from 12 to 17 between 1980 and 2008 (Melgar 2010), (making it fortieth out of 181 countries and behind all other industrialized nations [Amnesty International 2010]). Particularly affected are black women, First Nations women, women living in poverty, immigrants, and those who speak little or no English. Black women's mortality rate is nearly four times greater than that of white women. According to Amnesty International's analysis, although recent health care reforms have addressed some problems in the United States, 20 million people are still left without access to affordable care (Amnesty International 2010; Smith 2010). By the time you read this chapter, the Affordable Care Act should have made serious inroads into these maternal mortality rates. Students should search for the latest reports to learn its impact.

Toxins and Reproductive Risk

The comparative data on life expectancy that introduced this chapter makes clear that women and men often face different challenges to their health. Although some of these challenges may be the result of inborn bodily or genetic differences, many, if not most, are social and cultural products of the sexual division of labor. For example, hegemonic masculinity, which promotes risk taking, affects men's health at work and at play, while messages about obesity are generally directed toward women. Recent studies suggest that men are increasingly concerned with body size and that women are becoming less risk averse. Does this suggest that men's and women's health problems are converging? Possibly, but there is also evidence to show that similar health issues have different causes and consequences for men and for women. For example, while alcohol addiction is a problem for some women as well as some men, alcoholic women are more likely than men to be survivors of physical and sexual abuse and are more likely to hide their alcoholism (Disch 2008, 577).

In the interest of maintaining their reproductive health, women have been warned away from cigarette smoking, alcohol, and drug use. The image of "pregnant addicts" giving birth to underweight "crack babies" with a host of health problems fueled the targeting of poor, pregnant black women for prosecution for drug use. Women have often been (and still are) barred from working in the presence of toxins lest they expose their present and future fetuses to harm, whereas men's reproductive systems weren't considered at risk. Daniels (2006) notes that public health warnings to women caution them against the harm they will do to others, whereas warnings to men (about cigarettes, alcohol, or steroid use) warn them about harms they may do to themselves (Daniels 2006, 587).

However, evidence is accumulating to suggest that men's exposures to toxins produce fetal harms to their offspring as well. Toxic chemicals can cause sterility in men and miscarriages in their partners. Soldiers exposed to dioxin (Agent Orange) in Vietnam later had elevated numbers of babies with spina bifida, childhood leukemia, cleft palate, and tumors. Inconclusive though mounting evidence links birth defects of babies to fathers who served in the Gulf War, where depleted uranium from U.S. weapons was widespread (Daniels 2006).

Evidence that men are not immune to reproductive risk overturns basic assumptions on which a century's worth of protective legislation—protecting women, but not men—was based. The message was that women's "bad behavior"—smoking, taking drugs—could and would cause miscarriage and birth defects. For the same reasons, women were barred from industrial workplaces deemed "too dangerous" for them. Likewise, fertile or pregnant women were banned from military service when wartime exposures seemed too risky for them. What, then, does this new health data about men's reproductive susceptibility to toxins imply? Estelle Disch (2008) asks important and thought-provoking questions:

> At what cost would we mandate a workplace safe for the reproductive health of both men and women? If workplace toxins posed a reproductive threat to men, would we be prepared to allow only sterile men to work or shut down industry to make the workplace safe for men? Evidence that work harmed not only men but also men's ability to father healthy children might undermine the very incentives that drove men into toxic workplaces in the first place—the support of their wives and children. . . . If wartime toxins proved a threat to the health of the future children of soldiers, would we ban such weapons of war or refuse to send men to the front lines? Evidence of male-mediated reproductive harm at war threatened the prescription that men rule and protect the nation. . . . Evidence of male-mediated fetal harm

from men's private behaviors threatened to throw into question men's reproductive self-sovereignty—their right to do whatever they pleased with their own bodies.

Indeed. From our point of view, our health demands that we require industries to provide safe, nontoxic workplaces for all workers and insist that states give up war making. What do you think?

Gendered Illness: Believing Is Seeing

Throughout this volume, you have seen how the belief that there are two and only two sex/gender categories sets the stage for the social construction of sex and gender differences. What does it mean to say that "believing is seeing"? "If we believe that men and women fundamentally differ along a number of dimensions, it's easy for us to accumulate evidence that supports our belief and transforms "two fairly similar sexes . . . into two genders with purposefully different characteristics" (Lorber 1993). That is, if we believe that something is true (in this case that women and men are radically different from each other), we will see evidence confirming that belief everywhere, and we will probably ignore or downplay disconfirming evidence. Our beliefs filter out the many ways that in-group differences—differences between women or between men—are at least as significant as the differences separating men and women. In this way, "gendered people do not emerge from physiology or hormones, but from the exigencies of the social order . . . " (Lorber 1993).

Just as sports can be the context for constructing gendered bodies (physically strong men and graceful women), and technologies present the context for constructing gendered skills (mathematical abilities and **nimble fingers**), medicine has constructed gendered maladies. Over the years, all sorts of troubles have been medicalized (defined in medical terms as an illness or disorder) and labeled as characteristic of women or of men (Bell and Figert 2010). "Hysteria" at the turn of the twentieth century, "frigidity" in the 1950s and 1960s, and "anorexia" today are examples of the medicalization of historically specific dilemmas faced by or attributed to women. Such metaphors of illness build on actual physical and mental issues to capture the political conflicts and social anxieties of the historical periods in which they hold sway.

HYSTERIA. Scientific medicine established its authority among middle- and upper-class women at the end of the nineteenth century in the United States. Characterizing sickness as women's normal state, doctors held that childbirth, menstruation, and menopause were pathologies whose presence required that women (at least white middle- and upper-class women) be treated as invalids. And in fact, middle- and upper-class women in that period experienced a wave of invalidism or "hysteria" (from the Greek notion that hysteria was caused by disturbances of the uterus). S. Weir Mitchell, a physician of the day, described the malady:

> The woman grows pale and thin, eats little, or if she eats does not profit by it. Every-thing wearies her,—to sew, to write, to read, to walk,—and by and by the sofa or the bed is her only comfort. Every effort is paid for dearly, and she describes herself as aching and sore, as sleeping ill, and as needing constant stimulus and endless

tonics. . . . If such a person is emotional she does not fail to become more so, and even the firmest women lose self-control at last under incessant feebleness. (quoted in Ehrenreich and English 1972, 103–104)

Feminists such as Charlotte Perkins Gilman (1860–1935) and Olive Schreiner (1855–1920) linked hysteria to the enforced idleness of married women, who were reduced to a state of what Schreiner called "female parasitism" in households that functioned as retreats for successful husbands fresh from battle in the competitive marketplace. Idle women supported by their wealthy tycoon husbands were signs of a man's wealth and business success. The problem was not simply in women's or doctors' minds. The fashions of the day, such as tight-laced corsets and cinched waists, contributed to shortness of breath, constipation, weakness, violent indigestion, and, in the long term, bent or fractured ribs, displacement of the liver, and uterine prolapse, a condition in which the uterus falls into the vaginal canal (Ehrenreich and English 1972).

FRIGIDITY. By the middle of the twentieth century, Victorian conceptions of female passivity and asexuality were transformed by the psychoanalytic doctrine holding that mature and well-adjusted women experienced vaginal orgasms through heterosexual intercourse. That is, women could enjoy sex too, but only the kind of sex controlled and defined by men. Women who did not experience orgasm through intercourse, or who experienced only clitoral orgasms, were called "frigid," a diagnosis that declared that women's inability to enjoy vaginal sex was their own psychological problem. By the 1950s, doctors estimated that an "epidemic" of frigidity had spread to 40 percent of American women (Ehrenreich, Hess, and Jacobs 1986; Ryan 1979).

Throughout the 1960s and into the 1970s, singles lifestyles and singles cultures emerged in large cities, mitigating to some degree the injunction to marry young that had defined young women's choices in the 1950s and limited their sexual experience. In the middle of the 1960s, as you read in chapter 4, Masters and Johnson's sexuality studies challenged the popular and psychoanalytic view with their finding that women had greater orgasmic capacities than men and that all female orgasms were clitoral. Later in the decade, women in consciousness-raising groups began speaking to one another and writing about their sexual experience, producing "an explosion of pamphlets, essays, and discussion exploring women's sexuality without the blinders imposed by conventional assumptions or prudery." The new view stimulated further research, surveys, instruction manuals for masturbation, and a market for sexual toys such as vibrators (Baxandall and Gordon 2000, 158). By the end of the decade, it is fair to say, the doctrine of female frigidity had been put to rest.

EATING DISORDERS. In the latter decades of the twentieth century and into the twenty-first, there has been enormous pressure on women to appear young and be thin. It is widely known that the average weight of successive Miss Americas and of Playboy centerfolds decreased steadily since the 1970s. Even the doll Barbie became thinner over time, helping to impress on little girls that thin is beautiful. If currently marketed Barbie was 5 feet 6 inches tall, her bust, waist, and hip measurements would be 27–20–29. A **"cult of thinness"** seemed to have taken hold, especially among white, upper-middle-class, and educated girls and young women (Hesse-Biber 2007). Institutionally, the decks were stacked for the triumph of this cult. Advertising and popular culture glorified images of youth, whiteness, thinness, and wealth, which intensified women's dissatisfaction with their appearance. At the same time, the weight-loss industry fostered women's fear of weight gain to enhance profits, and job markets discriminated against women who didn't fit the mold. No wonder dieting is ubiquitous in the United States. Where television, films, magazines, and the Internet go, eating disorders follow. On the island of Fiji in 1995, for example, after the introduction of television, reported eating disorders among young women grew from 3 percent to 15 percent. Epidemics of eating disorders have been reported in Argentina, Saudi Arabia, Russia, and China (Edlin and Golanty 2004, 151).

In earlier times, dieting by women was not seen as an illness. Quite the opposite, it was linked to sainthood and was a sign of female holiness and piety (Brumberg 1988). Fasting women today are seen as sick, not holy, and their sickness is named anorexia or bulimia. The medical strategy for treating the problem individualized women's issues with food and failed to address the historical and cultural factors that influenced eating patterns.

The idea that eating disorders are exclusively illnesses of white, middle-class, heterosexual young women is a belief promoted by the failure to consider the intersection of race, sexuality, and class with gender—yet another example of "believing is seeing." Becky Thompson learned from eighteen life-history interviews with women of color and lesbians that their eating problems began as survival strategies that were "logical, creative responses to trauma" brought about by encounters with racism, sexism, poverty, homophobia, and abuse (Thompson 1994, 2). Thompson's multiracial perspective revealed a more complex story of disordered eating as she traced the origins and course of eating problems in the lives of women of color, working-class women, and lesbian women. Bingeing and dieting brought them comfort and relief from their emotional pain. However, Thompson insists that real healing requires that these women develop positive racial and sexual identities, which also necessitates "changing the social conditions that support violence and injustice":

> Making it possible for women to have healthy relationships with their bodies and their food is a comprehensive task: we need to ensure that children grow up free of racism and sexual abuse, that parents have adequate resources to raise their children, and that young lesbians have a chance to see their reflection in their teachers and community leaders. We must confront the myth of a monolingual society and support multilingual education; change a welfare system in which a household that is eligible receives an average of forty cents worth of food stamps per meal; dismantle the alliance of the medical, insurance, reducing, and advertising industries that capitalizes on reducing women's bodies to childlike sizes; refuse to blame women who are anorexic or bulimic; and dispel the notion that large women automatically eat too much. Women must learn to feed themselves along with—not after—others. *Ultimately, the prevention of eating problems depends on economic, cultural, racial, political, and sexual justice.* (1994, 127; emphasis added)

MEN'S BODY CRISES. It is easy to assume that eating disorders are women's problems and women's illnesses, but it is becoming increasingly obvious that there are many men and boys who are dissatisfied, insecure, ashamed, and anxious about their bodies. A national survey of

548 men (Garner 1997) found that men's dissatisfaction with their bodies nearly tripled from 1972 to 1997 (growing from 15 percent to 43 percent of the survey group). This phenomenon, like women's body anxieties, has been medicalized as "muscle dysmorphia," "bigorexia," or "reverse anorexia," a disorder in which a person (usually male) becomes obsessed with the idea that he isn't muscular enough. Whereas people with anorexia see themselves as fat when in fact they're actually very thin, many men feel ashamed of looking too small when in fact they're big. Since the 1980s, there has been a rise in sales of nutritional supplements, cosmetic treatments for men, and men's health and fitness magazines. More and more men develop workout addictions, binge eating, and bulimia.

Some observers believe that the portrayal of hugely muscled characters in cartoons directed to boys fuels this growing syndrome. Indeed, the media broadcast thousands of super-masculine images which have grown leaner and more muscular over time (Pope, Phillips, and Olivardia 2000). GI Joe, Superman, and Batman have been growing larger and more muscular the past two or three decades. If GI Joe were life-size, his chest would be 55 inches and his biceps would be 27 inches, the same size as his waist. Others suggest that, for some men whose masculinity is threatened, muscles may be one of the few ways that they can distinguish themselves from women (Disch 2008).

MASCULINITY AS A HEALTH RISK. Ideologies of masculinity have encouraged men to take up risky pursuits—driving too fast, using drugs and alcohol, engaging in risky sexual behavior, and generally taking chances—or face being thought of as unmasculine or as not "real" men (Waldron 1995). A national sample of boys aged fifteen to nineteen interviewed in 1980 and 1988 purportedly showed the health effects on that generation of pressures to "be a man" (Sabo and Gordon, "Rethinking Men's Health and Illness," 1995). The survey associated traditional attitudes toward masculinity with risky behaviors such as drinking, drug use, and having several heterosexual partners. These behaviors raised the risks of HIV, STDs, accidents, and homicide. For example, young men who drove had substantially higher rates of minor crashes, crashes resulting in injuries, and fatal crashes, compared with young women. Many studies showed that young men were more likely to be aggressive drivers. What was it about being young and male that promoted risky driving? Such aggression has been linked to young men's greater involvement (compared with women and older men) in physical fighting and violent crime and in "sensation seeking," which leads boys to seek out risks, including risks on the road. Moreover, popular culture equates masculinity with reckless driving. The car chase and the game of chicken have long been featured in action movies directed toward teenage boys and young men (Arnett 2002).

More recent studies of driving suggest that many young men continue to be risky drivers (Fergusson, Swain-Campbell, and Horwood 2003) but that they have been joined by young women A 2010 survey by Insurance.com found that auto insurance rates for girls have risen by about $500 for girls over the past few years, while rates for boys have remained flat (Koebler 2012). A 2009 study of teens and distracted driving found that boys and girls were equally likely to report texting behind the wheel; 34 percent of each group say they have used text messaging while driving (Pew Internet 2009). Nevertheless, reports from the United States, Europe, Australia, and a number of other nations show that men continue to be more likely than women to be involved in an accident, and their crashes involve more-serious injuries and property damage.

Men are more likely than women to die of heart disease, although heart disease is now the major cause of death for women in the United States as well. Men also die more readily from homicide, suicide, and drug and alcohol abuse. Research has linked men's mortality from these and other causes of sickness and death with masculine identity, masculine roles, and men's socialization. However, other data suggest that men's mortality may be more directly linked to the vicissitudes of economic change that leave men vulnerable to unemployment and poverty. For example, a study of eastern European men in the 1980s and 1990s found that the greatest increases in male mortality were in regions where the greatest gains and losses occurred in employment. Well-educated men had mortality levels similar to levels in other Western countries, but men with low levels of education, men with low levels of social support, and men with little control over their lives had very high mortality rates. For similar reasons, young men's mortality is rising in several Western countries, especially among disadvantaged minorities in otherwise affluent societies, including African Americans and First Nations people in the United States, and indigenous Australians (McKee and Shkolnikov 2001).

Steroid use among bodybuilders is an example of activity that more clearly originates in an ideology of masculinity. Steroid use is associated with serious illnesses such as liver cysts, elevated blood pressure, and heart disease. The drug can cause wide and erratic mood swings, irrational behavior, increased aggressiveness ("steroid rage"), irritability, and depression. In the United States, the reported rate of **anabolic steroid** use is 6 percent to 11 percent among high-school-age boys, including an unexpected number of nonathletes, and about 2.5 percent among high-school-age girls. In a national survey, the most common reason given for anabolic steroid use was improvement of athletic performance; second was improvement of appearance. A typical user is male (95 percent), an athlete (65 percent), and usually a football player, a heavyweight wrestler, or a weight lifter (Beers, Porter, Jones, Kaplan, and Berkwits 2006).

Anthropologist Alan Klein (1993, 1995) studied the use of steroids among bodybuilders. He found widespread insecurity among these powerful-looking men. Klein's informants explained why they were willing to risk their health by ingesting steroids: "I was small and weak," "My brother got into it . . . cuz his friend used to beat him up all the time," "My parents never gave me credit for anything," or "I was thin." Klein suggests that "the more insignificant" a bodybuilder feels inside, the more he obsesses about "appearing large." Steroids make it possible for bodybuilders to look like powerful men; and that, for men who feel insignificant, is worth the risk. Klein extends this analysis to men who are not bodybuilders. In an article comparing female anorexics to male bodybuilders, Martha McCaughey (1999) disputes Klein's interpretation of bodybuilders' motives, claiming that these men are not trying to become more masculine and that, similarly, the women who starve themselves are not trying to become more feminine. Rather, she argues, both are looking for ways to be less vulnerable in a threatening world. This interpretation seems to support Thompson's view of women's eating problems. However, one could argue that invulnerability is also an aspect of dominant masculinity in Western culture.

According to a 2010 survey by the National Institute on Drug Abuse (NIDA), the use of anabolic steroids (synthetic testosterone) has been declining in recent years, since peak levels were reached by eighth-graders in 2000, by tenth-graders in 2002, and by twelfth-graders in 2004. The rates in 2009 were down by roughly half from those peak years among all eighth-graders but rose, and then fell, among tenth-graders. Among twelfth-graders, use rose significantly in 2001, then declined. In 2010 steroid use rose slightly among tenth-graders and fell slightly among eighth-graders and twelfth-graders. Approximately 4.3 percent of teenage boys and 2.2 percent of teenage girls use steroids (Eaton et al. 2010).

Although most men would probably stop short of steroid use and plastic surgery, watered-down versions of this complex affect significant numbers of men in our society. Consider the lengths to which some men go to appear manly to others: suppressing emotion in public, displaying denial or bravado in the face of physical or mental health problems, reckless driving, binge drinking, exhibiting aggression in their work and private lives, or playing dangerous sports. Steroid use may be understood as a more extreme version of proving one's masculinity, but it is still a part of a cultural legacy that is dangerous to men's well-being as well as to the well-being of those who are the targets of their aggressiveness (Klein 1993, 119). The problem is not confined to the United States. In South Africa, Bollywood drives the use of steroids among boys of Indian descent (see Box 9-4).

GENDER IN EVERYDAY LIFE   BOX 9-4

BOLLYWOOD DRIVES THE USE OF STEROIDS AMONG BOYS OF INDIAN DESCENT IN SOUTH AFRICA

A desire to have six-pack abs like Bollywood actors Shahrukh Khan, Salman Khan and John Abraham is driving Indian teenagers in South Africa to use illegal steroids, a study has claimed.

Jarred Martin at the University of KwaZulu-Natal in Durban investigated the relationship between traditional masculine beliefs, body-image discrepancy and socio-cultural influences on appearance among Indian boys between 13 and 19, the weekly *Sunday Times Extra* reported.

The study followed on an earlier one among all race groups, where boys of Indian-origin showed greater anxiety about their appearance as compared to their white and Black counterparts.

That study also showed that other race groups perceived Indian boys as having a "softer" masculinity, probably because of the close family units that they came from, regarding them to be "mommie's boys."

More than half of the 500 respondents, 57 percent, in the latest study said that they felt pressured to mould their bodies like movie actors.

Although only 5.5 per cent admitted to using illegal steroids, these were mainly from boys who viewed Bollywood films as putting pressure on men to look muscular.

"You see the guys like Salman Khan (who has a screen image of stripping off his shirt regularly). This guy is so popular with the girls. I wouldn't mind looking like Khan," said one of the respondents who spoke to the weekly on conditions of anonymity.

"The only way you can get like that is to use steroids," said another.

"The way in which these cinematic heroes are portrayed is that they always get the girl. They get respect, adoration and envy from other men," Martin said.

"It may be that Bollywood cinema, in its portrayal of its action heroes and leading men as muscular Adonises, simply capitalises on the anxieties of young boys about their masculinity and body image."

But Ekbal Omarjee, owner of the largest distribution company of legal Bollywood product in South Africa, said that this was not entirely the case.

"Yes, we do find boys coming to look for DVD's of Shahrukh Khan in *Om Shanti Om* where he flaunted his six-pack, but the buyers of most of the movies featuring Salman Khan, Hritihik Roshan and the like are young women," Omarjee said.

"It could be that the boys are simply too shy to ask for these DVD's directly."

But whatever the reasons, the use of steroids, both legal and illegal, has been decried by health professionals, particularly because of the high level of cholesterol problems that are a trait of the Indian community.

"The Indian community generally has lower high cholesterol density levels, and a further decrease in it with the use of steroids creates greater risk of heart disease as they grow older," Professor Yoga Coopoo of the Centre for Exercise Science at the University of the Witwatersrand told the weekly.

SOURCE: Reprinted with permission from ExpressIndia.com (2010).

In chapter 11, you will learn more about the ways that violence, pain, and risk of injury are an accepted, perhaps even desired, price of participation in men's sports. Some observers suggest that the sports world gives preference to "hypermasculine competitive sport" in which physical force and violence are valued over skill and gamesmanship (White, Young, and McTeer 1995; Messner and Connell 2007). In the sports world, pain is normal, even welcomed, but succumbing to injury is a sign of weakness. White et al. (1995) note the paradox: that "the systematic destruction of the male body in sport is framed as empowering for masculinity" (177). They conclude that "for male athletes, body mass, physical endurance, risk taking, and forms of body discipline, including pain denial, are integral features of culturally prescribed versions of masculinity" (179–80). Current concerns about the effects of concussions sustained in football and other contact sports suggest that cultural ideals of masculinity may be starting to change.

MASCULINITY AND HEART DISEASE. Some observers suggest that men's greater risk for heart disease is connected to cultural notions of masculinity. Helgeson (1995) reports that studies measuring masculinity-related traits such as competitiveness, self-control, inexpressiveness, impatience, and achievement orientation found three ways that "extreme" masculinity is linked to heart disease: type A behavior, impoverished social networks, and poor health care.

One dimension of social risk is **type A behavior**. This is behavior that is ambitious, competitive, impatient, hurried, angry, and hostile, traits related to masculinity as defined by personality theorists and social psychologists. A type A individual is a "person who is aggressively involved in a chronic, incessant struggle to achieve more and more in less and less time, and if required to do so, against the opposing efforts of other things or other persons" (Sharma 2003). This person is a man (or woman) who hides weaknesses, inhibits emotions other than anger, has little empathy with others, fears homosexuality, and lacks self-knowledge (Helgeson 1995, 76). Research with men has shown a relation between the type A pattern and coronary heart disease.

Lack of a social support network is a second dimension of risk for men. The existence of social support is correlated with qualities associated with femininity but not with masculinity, such as caring, comfort, empathy, and emotional expressiveness. The masculine ideal encourages men to experience and display less emotion than women. Toughness, detachment, and control—"sucking it up"—are standards of manly behavior. Men—and boys—don't cry. Those classic figures of popular culture—the loner, the remote and distant man, the cowboy—need no network of support. Nevertheless, studies show that the extreme individualism that sets the "manly" man apart from others increases his vulnerability to illness and early death when the props of his masculine identity—job, status, sexual potency—disappear (Helgeson 1995, 80).

The third dimension of social risk is men's *unwillingness or inability to seek help for health problems and symptoms*. Manly men solve their own problems, do not admit that they are vulnerable, and endure pain rather than show weakness.

These factors make a strong case for naming stereotypic or "hegemonic" masculinity as hazardous to men's health. Nevertheless, we need to note the class- and race-bound character of this analysis. The competitiveness attributed to all men is really an occupational hazard of men (and women) in specific occupations, in which one's own advancement and tenure depends on winning scarce positions. However, those elites who have "arrived" do not face the dangerous and punishing physical labor allotted to many young men and men of color, or the health-damaging consequences of poverty and homelessness. It makes no sense to place homeless men, working-class men, underclass men, gay men, men with HIV, prison inmates, and men of color in the same health pool as middle- and upper-class white men.

Stratification and Inequality in the Health Care System

The statistics showing the racial ethnic inequalities in life expectancy that began this chapter are indicators of the severe stratification of access to healthcare on a world scale. For example, until recent inroads by women and people of color into the medical profession, doctors were likely to be white men. They still are, although less so. There has been a slow increase in the proportion of women physicians and physicians of color. In 1980, women were 11.6 percent of all U.S. doctors; by 2012, 34.3% of all physicians and surgeons were women. In 2000, women were 40 percent of the medical students in the United States; by 2012, almost half of all U.S. medical students were women (48.3 percent) (Catalyst 2012).

Racial ethnic minorities are also increasing their proportions as medical professionals. In 1980–1981, 85 percent of the medical school students in the United States were white. African Americans were an additional 5.7 percent of all students, Hispanics 4.2 percent, Asians 3 percent, and First Nations peoples 0.9 percent. By 2002–2003, the proportion of white students dropped to 64 percent, and the proportions of students of color rose. Black students were 7.4 percent of all medical students, Hispanics 6.4 percent, and Asians 20.5 percent, but Native Americans remained at 0.9 percent. In 2007–2008, the dominance of whites dropped a little further, to 62.4 percent of all medical students, and the percentage of African Americans remained essentially unchanged. The proportion of Asians grew to 21 percent, though, and the proportion of Hispanic students increased to 7.8 percent. Such slow change has not yet disturbed the basic racialized, gendered, and classed structure of the health care system.

Below physicians and administrators in the health care hierarchy are nurses, who were once predominantly white women (Reverby 1987). Reporting to nurses are nurses' aides, who are mostly immigrant women of color. Aides do the daily work of cleaning, toileting, and feeding patients in nursing homes and hospitals. Black and Latino men make up the janitorial labor force in these settings. Private patients are usually white. We should not forget the many unpaid care workers assisting disabled and elderly family members and friends in their homes, who provide services vital to the system and to those in need.

In the United States, health care has been a for-profit undertaking, provided to those who can afford it, rather than a human right of everyone who needs it. This was not always the case. In fact, for most of the twentieth century, the medical system was comprised of nonprofit organizations and charities. Until the 1980s, profiting from medical care was considered "against sound public policy" (Wang 2010). But a major transformation of American medicine occurred when the Reagan administration deregulated several health-related industries. As Wang (2010) explains:

> For-profit corporations became newly encouraged to take leadership of health care. Deregulating health care into the **free market** was intended to drive down costs and to improve care. After all, medical care in 1980 consumed a whopping 9.1 percent of the nation's GDP. Never mind that after 30 years in the free market, health care costs have doubled to consume 18 percent of the GDP (with a third of these precious dollars wasted on bureaucracy).

A 2003 study concluded that almost one hundred thousand people in the United States die each year because of lack of needed care—three times the number of people who died of HIV at its height (Navarro 2003). Uninsured adults had a 25 percent greater mortality risk than did insured adults and often suffered a lifetime of ill health. Without routine health care, uninsured children may develop chronic diseases and impairments. The problem was not a lack of resources. The United States has for decades ranked highest in health care spending compared with other industrial countries as a percentage of its gross domestic product (GDP). Yet Americans' health status ranks lower than all but one developed nation.

The United States is twelfth of thirteen industrialized nations and twenty-fifth of twenty-nine developed countries in male life expectancy, nineteenth in female life expectancy, and has the highest infant mortality rates.

This health care system has been in profound crisis. Health care had become too expensive for millions of Americans, so that in 2010, almost 50 million Americans had no health insurance. Millions more Americans, at least 10 million of whom were children, were underinsured and thus went without necessary health services and medications. When the new health reform bill passed in March 2010, the United States was the only developed nation in the world without a national health program that guaranteed affordable access to health care for all people.

On March 23, 2010, President Barack Obama signed the 2,409-page health care reform act into law. Its final impact on health care is not yet clear. Some provisions went into effect immediately, and others only took effect in 2014. Cecile Richards, the President of Planned Parenthood, calls the Affordable Care Act "the biggest advance for women's health in 45 years." She continues:

> Here is what progress for women looks like. Starting today, thanks to the Affordable Care Act, American women can get coverage for lifesaving preventive services—including mammograms, immunization, and wellness visits—for free. These preventive services have been a major cause of higher deductibles and co-pays for women. Today, that part of the inequity is history! In addition, today, important new protections go into effect to protect not only women, but their families as well. Insurance companies can no longer drop coverage when someone gets sick, young adults can remain on their parents plans until they are 26, and children can no longer be denied coverage due to a pre-existing condition. Women are often denied coverage for so-called "pre-existing" conditions such as breast cancer or even pregnancy. . . . Women, above all, have much to celebrate. The fact is we have consistently gotten the short end of the stick in our broken health care system. Women are routinely charged higher premiums than men. But, when fully implemented, the Affordable Care Act will end those discriminatory practices. (Richards 2010)

The bill could be better. As written, private insurance companies remain central to health care provision, a fact that proponents of reform believe will limit its effectiveness and affordability. The law maintains the for-profit model of health care, with insurance companies still at the foundation of the system, despite public sentiment in favor of a "single-payer" or social insurance model of health care, such as Medicare for all. On January 11, 2011, the new Republican majority in the House of Representatives voted, unsuccessfully, to repeal the health care law, because they believed that health care reform should be rooted in a free market (Turner 2013). Despite the fact that ACA is now the law of the land, the Republican House has tried to block it. In September 2013, Republicans engineered a shut-down of the Federal government because they could not pass a bill defunding "Obamacare." The repeal of the ACA, like its forerunner, has no chance of success, though, because it cannot pass in the Senate. Even if it were to pass, it would be vetoed by President Obama, who champions health care reform.

Republicans attack women's health care by attempting to defund Planned Parenthood and drastically cut family planning services. The photo is of a Stand Up for Women's Health rally in April 2011.

Source: Associated Press.

CARE WORK: THE PAID OR UNPAID, BUT OFTEN INVISIBLE, FOUNDATION OF HEALTH CARE

In terms of pay, prestige, power, and social status, physicians—until recently, predominantly well-to-do white men—are at the top of the health care hierarchy. Caregivers, those predominantly poor, racial ethnic, and female workers who daily maintain, comfort, and sometimes even heal the sick and dying, are its invisible foundation. Whether unpaid or simply relegated to the lowest pay and status in the health labor force, care workers are essential to the health care system in the United States (Schiller 1993).

Traditionally, women have done the work of care without pay for family and friends. However, women's entry into the labor force, the rise of single parenting, and the increase in people living alone explain why a growing proportion of children, the elderly, and the disabled are being cared for by paid care workers. Like unpaid care work, paid caring is devalued, and the skills required to do it are unrecognized. Employers—hospitals and home-care agencies—cut costs on the backs of these workers (Cancian and Oliker 2000).

The structure and location of the work of caring has shifted since the 1980s, when health insurance supported hospitalization over home care. Since that time, a cost-cutting agenda has propelled the shift to home-based care, where policymakers assumed that the free labor of women, supplemented by the low-wage female labor force of care workers, would take on the extra work of having sicker family members at home. In fact, unpaid as well as underpaid labor is essential to the U.S. health care system. Invisible, its costs hidden, women's caring labor completes and often even supplants the work of paid providers, nurses, aides, and others that hospital administrators have eliminated to cut costs. The work does not go away. It disappears into private homes and families, where its real costs are borne by caretakers.

When the paid labor of medical workers is redistributed to unpaid women family members, a **"work transfer"** has taken place (Glazer 1993). In this case, the work of caring is privatized, moved from the public sphere of hospitals and clinics to the private sphere of homes and families. Think of the enormous changes that follow this shift. Services once provided for a fee now become additional work for household members. Most studies confirm that in this situation, women, whether paid or not, increase the hours and intensity of the work they do. For family caregivers, this increase in family labor comes at a time when women's labor-force participation is almost equal to men's, and in some cases exceeds that of men. Yet private, household-based care of sick and elderly family members may require as much or more time and attention as the care of young children. Invisible or seen as something women are best fit to undertake, free and low-cost care work makes profits for the health care industry, as costs continue to rise precipitously.

Despite the growing need for home care, fewer women are at home to do that work, opening the door for private agencies to take up the slack. This work is associated with high levels of job stress and low levels of job satisfaction (Denton, Zeytinoglu, Davies, and Lian 2002). This comes as no surprise. Home care workers now do what nurses used to do in hospitals, even as they juggle heavy workloads and unpaid overtime. The companionship, compassion, and attention that care workers give their clients is devalued, hardly noticed, and sometimes actively opposed by employers whose focus is on the efficient completion of instrumental (and measurable) tasks (Diamond 1995). Cost-cutting policies and increased control by management mean that care workers have less time for the caring part of their work. Instead, they face limited control over their tasks and schedules, difficult clients, and low wages, as well as "pressures, tensions, anxiety, demoralization, dissatisfaction, frustration, feelings of guilt, and reduced support and supervision" (Aronson and Neysmith 1996).

Of course, this work is stressful for unpaid caretakers of close relatives and friends as well. At least when the work is done for a wage, patients and workers frame the caring relationship as a case of client–worker relations, a frame that may help to limit the expectations of both parties. When relatives do similar work in the home for free, expectations and emotions differ. We may expect to care for our elderly parents, and we may welcome the opportunity when it arrives. However, a little-discussed emotion surrounding caretaking, especially (but not exclusively) unpaid caring by close relatives—a wife, a daughter or son, a cousin, or a mother—is rage. Isolated in their homes with little support, sometimes forced to leave jobs or careers, caretakers may profoundly resent their lot. The feeling often goes both ways, with the invalid perhaps locked into a dependent and unwanted relationship with her or his caregiver. However, feelings of rage and resentment are difficult to express in the face of romanticized notions of selfless caregiving to relatives. The parties to the relationship may try to keep the rage inside, "silenced and repressed" (Schiller 1993, 503).

Rage is more than an individual feeling. It is one of several emotional costs of care work that are socially produced by a society that treats care work as a private good whose costs are borne individually and in isolation. But not for long. Careworkers are organizing, and one of their first victories was the adoption by the Obama administration in September 2013 of regulations requiring that home care workers be paid minimum wage and overtime under the federal Fair Labor Standards Act. You should recall from chapter 6 some of the difficulties faced by home care workers, many of whom are immigrants and links in global chains of care. Box 9-5 describes in more detail the political movement home care workers are building to address these issues.

GENDER IN EVERYDAY LIFE   BOX 9-5
CARING ACROSS GENERATIONS

Caring Across Generations brings together aging Americans, people with disabilities, workers, and their families to protect all Americans' right to choose the care and support they need to live with dignity.

We are a movement of family members, workers, and fellow Americans supported by a growing coalition of organizations advocating for a system of quality, dignified care. We believe every American should be able to choose the care they want based on their needs—and that every American would benefit from being a part of a more supportive care system. Improving the way we provide care for one another will create an economy and a society that works for all of us.

Every 8 seconds, another person turns 65 in our country. At the same time, we are moving into the third decade of the Americans with Disabilities Act and are progressing in our work to become more accessible and inclusive. Changing the way we care offers an opportunity to reinvigorate our economy, strengthen our communities, and uphold our national ideals. By working together we can increase every family's access to the care and support they need at a price they can afford and create millions of high quality in-home care jobs.

OUR POLICY PILLARS

Support for Consumers and Families

We know what it means to be responsible for our families, including seniors and people with disabilities, and we know that care workers are an important part of that support. Caring Across Generations proposes a set of policy solutions to ensure that seniors and people with disabilities receive care and services that are high quality, dignified, and affordable. This includes additional public funding for long-term services and supports, reforming the private market for long term care insurance, and creating refundable tax credits for working age individuals whose incomes are too high for them to qualify for Medicaid but too low to pay for care. Caring Across Generations is also committed to policy reforms that would eliminate the institutional bias in Medicaid. To support family members who are providing care for their loved ones, we propose the creation of a social insurance program to provide paid family and medical leave, as well as social security caregiver credits for those who leave the workforce to provide care.

Job Creation

Americans need care workers and America needs jobs. Already, around 10 million adults, half of whom are under the age of 65, do not get the home care support they need. And with a member of the baby boomer generation turning 65 every eight seconds, America is projected to need 1.6 million additional direct care workers by 2020. The current home care workforce simply cannot support our nation's needs.

Caring Across Generations' policy agenda helps us come together to meet these fast-growing needs—to create jobs and allow every American to live and age with dignity. We can put our country back to work in high quality jobs and help provide the care that America needs at the same time.

Job Quality

Home care is one of the fastest growing industries in our economy, providing critical daily care, services, and supports to millions of individuals and families across the country. However, the quality of home care jobs is very poor. Home care workers often face low wages, few benefits, high turnover, and a high level of job stress and hazards. As Americans, we believe you should get paid a fair wage for the work you do, that you should not have to work when you are sick, that you should not be abused or exploited by your boss.

At the same time, Caring Across Generations is committed to ensuring that increased costs from raising wages and improving benefits do not lead to reductions in services to consumers. In fact, Caring Across Generations supports requiring each state to create a registry connecting consumers and providers of in-home services to help expand care choices for all Americans.

Training and Career Ladders

Caring Across Generations wants to improve the quality of home care in America. Seniors and people with disabilities deserve care workers with the knowledge, skills, and support to do their jobs well. Current federal training requirements for home health aides have not been changed in more than 20 years, and there are no federal standards for training or certification of personal care attendants. This fragmented structure of training requirements hurts workers, too, by limiting mobility between jobs and prospects for career advancement.

Roadmap to Citizenship

Immigration reform presents a remarkable opportunity to address the critical, rapidly growing need for quality in-home care while allowing millions of immigrant care workers to come out of the shadows, improving care and empowering workers to contribute to economic growth.

Immigration reform must ensure that eligibility for legal status and citizenship at any stage is not linked to proof of work and that there are no onerous fines, application fees, or English language requirements. Such measures would effectively exclude many low-wage domestic and home care workers, as well as low-income seniors and people with disabilities, from the road to citizenship.

Our vision for immigration reform also includes providing a legal means for future care workers to enter the country when there is a shortage in the domestic care labor markets. Fair wages and strong job protections, including the right to change employers, to seek citizenship, and to full protections under the federal and state law to the same extent that other US workers are protected, are also integral to stabilizing America's care system while providing quality care for consumers and fair and just treatment for workers.

SOURCE: Reprinted from http://www.caringacross.org/about-us/. All rights reserved by Caring Across Generations © Copyright 2013.

WOMEN'S HEALTH MOVEMENTS

The union organizing drives of care workers are a recent expression of activism that has been important to the shape of health care since the 1960s.

The women's health movement emerged in the United States in the late 1960s, as women began to take stock of the gendered, class-based, and racialized system of medicine that had controlled their health care. What was the social context of this rising activism by women?

- First, the social movements of the 1960s—civil rights, Black Power, La Raza, the American Indian Movement, and of course, women's liberation—promoted both a critical awareness of the ways that existing institutions disadvantaged women and racial ethnic minorities and a growing conviction that ordinary people could make change.
- Second, legislation stimulated by the civil rights movement—the Equal Pay Act (1963), the Civil Rights Act (1964), and Affirmative Action (1965)—contributed to a growing public discourse about the parallel problem of women's rights.
- Third, the contraceptive pill contributed to an increase in premarital sex among white women, often called a "sexual revolution."
- Fourth, women were flooding into the labor force and, as a consequence, were marrying later, having fewer children, and divorcing more than their mothers and older sisters had before them.

These cultural and political shifts help explain the multiple local beginnings of the women's health movement. Meeting in women's "**rap groups**" and conferences, young movement activists began to discuss their own experiences with the medical system, medical experts, and standard medical procedures and began to ask important questions:

- Was the pill safe?
- What were the reasons for the high rates of cesarean sections in the United States?
- Were the routine radical mastectomies and hysterectomies performed on women actually necessary?

- Why did doctors control access to abortion?
- Did treating women's depression as a medical problem deny the very real causes of female unhappiness with their lives (Plechner 2000; Rosen 2001)?

After gathering steam in the 1960s, the movement took off in 1969 (Morgen 2002). In that year, a workshop on women and their bodies led to the founding of the Boston Women's Health Book Collective and to the publication of *Our Bodies, Ourselves* (OBOS), now in its ninth edition. Participants came to the 1969 workshop because they believed that women needed to take back knowledge about and control over their bodies from medical professionals (Ehrenreich and English 1972). The workshop participants decided to gather information about women's anatomy and physiology, birth control, sexuality, abortion, pregnancy, childbirth, medical institutions, and the organization of health care in the United States and to publish their findings. In 1970 the first edition of *Our Bodies, Ourselves* circulated in a newsprint version as a course on women and their bodies. Since the publication of the first edition of *OBOS*, much about women's health care has changed, but much remains the same, as the introduction to the eighth edition shows (Boston Women's Health Book Collective 2005; Box 9-6).

GENDER IN EVERYDAY LIFE   BOX 9-6

"OUR BODIES, OURSELVES": GOING, GOING, GONE GLOBAL

In Asia, it teaches Buddhist nuns how to ease muscle cramps caused by hours of sitting meditation. In Africa, it cautions women not to overeat; a health risk in a region where being overweight is the standard of feminine beauty.

In Latin America, it urges women to rethink the anti-choice stance of the region's Roman Catholic Church. Across the globe, "Our Bodies, Ourselves," the pioneering text that became an underground sensation in the United States after it was first published here in 1970, is adapting itself to the regional variations of women's global reality.

After coming out in its first foreign-language edition in 1976 in Spanish, the text is now available in 17 languages and Braille. It has been published in 15 nations and will soon be released in India, South Korea and Poland. It has sold millions of US copies and—with global distribution—garnered 20 million readers worldwide. In addition, it recently inspired the creation of a similar African health text, "Notre Corps, Notre Sante," which features original content in French and is being distributed to women in 21 African countries.

AN INNOVATIVE APPROACH TO WOMEN'S HEALTH

Created by a group of Boston health activists 35 years ago, "OBOS," as it is widely known, takes health information that was once exclusively in the hands of medical experts and places it in the hands of ordinary women. In all its translations, the book maintains its trademark approach of presenting medical information in the form of communal femi-nine narrative. Testimonials from ordinary women—about everything from menstrua-tion through menopause and beyond—are interspersed with articles, charts, graphs and diagrams. Speaking to readers like a mother or a friend, "OBOS" covers reproduction, contraception, exercise and nutrition.

As it spreads into other languages and other cultures, the text is sparking a variety of consumer health movements. The Armenia version of OBOS has inspired women's activists there to open a storefront health center where they distribute pamphlets about family planning and sexually-transmitted diseases. In Japan, the book spurred its trans-lators to survey 200 clinics and hospitals about their policies regarding women's health. In Latin America, the text provided material for an anti-smoking campaign specifically geared toward women. "Education is the most powerful tool for lifting the plight of women worldwide," says Sally Deane, chair of the board for the Our Bodies, Ourselves collective, the Boston-based non-profit that oversees "OBOS" publications. "We hope to reach a global audience while maintaining our core of personal stories and accurate information about health topics that all women must know."

The creators of OBOS also hope to eradicate health threats that are of specific concern to women. "We're concerned by the rise of religious fundamentalism, which impinges on women's ability to control their reproductive lives," says Judy Norsigian, the executive director of the Our Bodies, Ourselves collective. "We're alarmed by govern-ment cutbacks in developing countries that are preventing women from getting basic health care. We're also concerned that the pharmaceutical industry is blocking the production of generic drugs so developing countries must pay high prices to import them from abroad."

EACH EDITION IS UNIQUE

Back in 1976, when they realized their message could benefit women of all cultures, the creators of "OBOS" translated their original text into Spanish. That success led to more foreign-language texts and the OBOS Global Translation/Adaptation Program, which helps health advocates across the globe amend the book to suit their needs. With a $75,000 annual budget (garnered mostly from foundations), OBOS administrators trans-fer the publication rights for the token sum of one dollar, then provide technical assis-tance with fundraising, negotiating publishing contracts, promoting books and distributing them. Sometimes, health advocates write their own testimonials and use photographs of women from their own countries. Sometimes, they use ready-made wording and graphics provided by the OBOS head office.

With each new publication of "OBOS," women's health advocates work to tell their own stories in their own voices. In their testimonials, they talk about issues that are universal among women: breastfeeding, having an abortion, living with a sexually transmitted disease and going through menopause. They also talk about topics that are unique to their own cultures, such as struggling to gain access to health care in a developing country and struggling to recover from a rape perpetrated by soldiers as an act of war.

The unique set of health needs of each group of readers has led to some surprising spin-offs. In Bulgaria, the shift from Communism to democracy is taking a somewhat anti-Western form. One aspect of that is a widespread antipathy toward feminism, which is seen as Western, anti-male and anti-family. As a result, the Bulgarian translation emphasizes women's rights as consumers, patients and citizens. It refrains, however, from discussing the idea that women are an oppressed or marginalized group. Much of the Serbian adaptation was produced during the prolonged war in the Balkan region in the 1990s, so the privation of readers there was a major consideration. "The authors dropped the nutrition chapter," says Judy Norsigian. "It just seemed terrible to speak of food when people in the region were starving." In Armenia, where a declining birthrate and economic hardship are causing massive emigration from the country, many people are wary of contraception and are pro-natalist. Out of cultural deference, the version published here emphasizes childbirth and gives somewhat shorter shrift to birth control.

Differences like these are reflected in "Our Bodies, Ourselves Transformed Worldwide," a collection of selected English translations of prefaces from international adaptations, which is available on the collective's Web site.

FUTURE PROJECTS

In addition to publishing texts in foreign languages, the Our Bodies, Ourselves collective also has its hands in health projects worldwide. It has distributed 300,000 free books—most of them in English or Spanish—to international groups. It contributes to small-scale projects such as helping Nigerian activists adapt the OBOS text to radio public service announcements and to large-scale programs run by leading health organizations such as the Contraceptive Research and Development Program, Family Health International, the National Women's Health Network, and the World Health Organization.

By the end of this year, women's health advocates hope to launch three new international editions of OBOS. For the Tibetan version (to be published in India, home to a vast community of Tibetan exiles), they are writing about personal hygiene, which is crucial for women living in monasteries that house more than 500 people. For the Korean version, they are addressing parts of the text to Russian sex workers and other foreign women who are flooding into the country in search of employment. For the Polish version, they are expanding the section on reproductive care since basic sex education is not available in the country's predominantly Catholic schools.

In the United States, the collective is about to publish its eighth revision of the English-language text. In the Middle East, the advocates are working to translate and distribute the chapter on childbearing to women in five Arab countries. In China, Nepal, Vietnam, Turkey, Kenya and Brazil, activists are meeting with private funders to drum up financing for new translations. As OBOS international publishing continues to grow, its supporters hope it will continue to reach thousands of new readers; women who likely have nowhere else to turn for accurate health information. "Most books about women's health are not woman-positive or designed to be used by women," says Mavi Kalem, a health advocate working to publish "OBOS" in Turkey. "Of all the books we have looked at, 'OBOS' is the one volume that provides a model that fills these needs. We want women to say, 'I read this book, and it changed my life!'"

SOURCE: Ginty (2004). Reprinted with permission from Women's eNews.

Local activists around the country began developing their own alternatives to the established medical system. They organized feminist clinics and health centers, supported birthing centers over hospital births, encouraged women to enter medical school, and criticized reproductive technologies, medicated childbirth, and cosmetic surgeries. They encouraged women to learn about their bodies and to become active medical consumers. They introduced and promoted alternatives to scientific medicine, including midwifery, acupuncture, and herbalism.

Abortion in the United States

Abortion was legal in the United States and practiced by midwives until about 1880, when restrictions were imposed in the backlash to that century's woman suffrage and birth control movements and in response to the panic over what was then called "race suicide," the declining birth rate among whites. (Ironically, in the 1970s, Black Power activists also called black women's attempts to control their own fertility "race suicide.") These restrictions prevented midwives from providing abortions, and they gave medical doctors greater control over the decision to abort pregnancies.

Making abortion illegal merely drove abortion underground and increased its dangers to women. Women who could afford to do so traveled to Cuba and England, where they had access to hospital abortions. Poor and middle-class women faced the dangers of back-alley abortions or tried to perform abortions themselves with knitting needles and coat hangers, or by swallowing or douching with dangerous chemicals. Some physicians tried to help women. In the 1960s, the Clergy Consultation Service on Abortion operated as a referral service to help women find safe abortions. In 1969, students and housewives active in the Chicago Women's Liberation Union (CWLU) acted on their belief in reproductive rights for all women by organizing to offer low-cost and no-cost illegal abortions, which they learned to perform themselves (Box 9-7). By 1973, when the U.S. Supreme Court, in **Roe v. Wade** (1973), struck down all criminal abortion laws on the basis of women's "right to privacy," the women of the CWLU's Abortion Counseling Service, or "Jane," had already provided more than ten thousand safe abortions.

Roe v. Wade ended the thousands of deaths and the tens of thousands of health complications that occurred yearly as a result of illegal and self-performed abortions. Immediately

GENDER IN EVERYDAY LIFE   BOX 9-7
STATEMENT OF THE ABORTION COUNSELING SERVICE OF THE
CHICAGO WOMEN'S LIBERATION UNION, 1971

This statement is from the informational brochure passed out by the Abortion Counseling Service of CWLU to the women they served. It remains the basic tenet of pro-choice feminism:

> Women should have the right to control their own bodies and lives. Only a woman who is pregnant can determine whether she has enough resources—economic, physical and emotional—at a given time to bear and rear a child. Yet at present the decision to bear the child or have an abortion is taken out of her hands by governmental bodies which can have only the slightest notion of the problems involved. (Abortion Counseling Service 1971)

anti-abortion activists naming themselves "pro-life" began a campaign to restrict and ultimately end legal abortions. They blockaded abortion clinics, threatening and intimidating abortion providers and the women who used their services. As of May 2009, when Dr. George Tiller was shot as he served as an usher in his Wichita, Kansas, church, eight abortion providers had been murdered on account of their work, including four doctors, two clinic employees, a security guard, and a clinic escort. Clinics have been bombed or set on fire, and clinic personnel have been subjected to anthrax threats and acid attacks. The homes of doctors who provided abortions were picketed, and their names and photos appeared on "wanted" posters circulating on the Internet. These tactics created a climate that has contributed to the decline in abortion services, growing state restrictions on publicly funded abortions, and the continuing threat that *Roe v. Wade* could be overturned by the Supreme Court.

BEYOND *ROE V. WADE*: THE STRUGGLE CONTINUES. In 1973 the U.S. Supreme Court overturned all state laws outlawing or restricting abortion on the grounds that they violated the constitutional right to privacy. The debate over this decision is now in its fourth decade. Although surveys show that fully 70 percent of Americans support abortion rights, pro-life activists have had notable success in restricting access to abortions, despite the fact that these rights are now legal. First passed in 1976 and then routinely attached to congressional appropriations bills, the Hyde Amendment prevented low-income women from getting abortions by prohibiting federal funding of abortion through Medicaid. The Supreme Court upheld the Hyde Amendment in 1980. President Ronald Reagan aided opposition to *Roe* by making it his "litmus test" for federal judicial appointees. In 2005 President George W. Bush appointed two anti-*Roe* justices to the Supreme Court, fueling speculation that the law might soon be overturned.

Leslie J. Reagan (1997) describes the long history of abortion practices in the United States since the eighteenth century and the responses to its criminalization. Until the mid-nineteenth century, abortion was legal until about the fourth month ("quickening" or when a pregnant woman first feels the movement of her baby). Physicians campaigned to criminalize abortion, hoping thereby to take business from midwives and "homeopaths." Anti-abortion sentiments were spurred on by nativist (anti-Catholic, anti-immigrant, and racist) sentiments by white groups fearing "race suicide." Even after abortion was made illegal, it is estimated that doctors continued to provide as many as 2 million abortions annually. Widespread availability despite its illegality defined abortion until the 1950s, when availability narrowed considerably, and although some reforms made it available in instances of rape, incest, fetal defects, or risks to mothers' physical or mental health, most women wanted abortions for personal, economic, or social reasons. *Roe v. Wade* was a response to the building pressure for reform of the abortion laws from doctors who were witness to the toll of illegal abortions (5,000 deaths a year), recognition of the discriminatory effects of the law (the lion's share of those 5,000 deaths were of black and Hispanic women), and women activists such as the women of Jane in Chicago. This victory had enormous importance for women. In the year after decriminalization, the maternal mortality rate in New York, for instance, dropped 45 percent. Today barriers to abortion have increased sharply and they have done so in ways that promote inequality. In her review of Leslie Reagan's book, Katha Pollit summarizes the current state of affairs:

> More than 80 percent of U.S. counties have no abortion providers, and some whole states have only one or two. The Supreme Court has allowed states to erect barriers to abortion—denial of public funds for poor women's abortions, parental consent and notification requirements, mandatory delays, "counseling sessions." Anti-abortion zealots have committed arson, assault, and murder in their campaign against abortion clinics. A new generation of doctors, who have never seen a woman die from a septic abortion or been haunted by the suicide of a patient denied help, are increasingly reluctant to terminate pregnancies. Only 12 percent of medical schools teach first-trimester abortion as a routine aspect of gynecology. (Pollit 1997)

Pollit ends her review of Reagan on an optimistic note. Reagan's book, she writes, shows the widespread moderation of most Americans over abortion policies, who reject the "pro-life" doctrine that a fertilized egg is already a baby.

Women of Color and Sterilization Abuse

Women's autonomy depends on their ability to control their reproductive lives, and that includes access to safe contraception and abortion when necessary. Most of the women who participated in the Abortion Counseling Service and those active in the movement nationally were white, college-educated, and middle class. They believed that abortion rights were the key to women's control over their own bodies.

Progressives and socialist feminists involved in this movement were sensitive to racial ethnic inequalities that were pervasive in American society. Perhaps some were even aware that 80 percent of the deaths due to abortions in New York City prior to *Roe v. Wade* were to black and Puerto Rican women. However, the activists who focused on abortion did not at first also make central the issue of sterilization abuse practiced on women of color, which had gone on for many decades.

THE RACISM AND CLASSISM OF STERILIZATION. The United States has a long history of coercive sterilization practiced on poor women and women of color. In both the South and the North, black and poor women and girls had been sterilized by doctors without their consent. In 1973, what members of communities of color had known for many years became a cause *célèbre* when the mainstream media reported on the sterilization of two black sisters in Montgomery Alabama. The twelve- and fourteen-year-old girls were sterilized without their knowledge or their mother's permission on the orders of the Montgomery Community Action Committee, which was funded by the federal Department of Health, Education, and Welfare (HEW) (Davis 1982).

In 1973 the Southern Poverty Law Center filed a lawsuit to end federal funding of sterilizations after finding that between one hundred thousand and two hundred thousand poor women, nearly half of them black, had been sterilized annually under government programs. Women on welfare had been pressured into consenting to sterilization after giving birth. First Nations women were also targeted. By the 1970s, one-quarter of all First Nations women had been sterilized. In the 1960s and 1970s, Mexican American women in California who gave birth to children in public hospitals were sterilized without their informed consent. Activist Ana Nieto-Gomez recalled that doctors "saw themselves as agents of the public, saving taxpayers money" by preventing women on welfare from having more children (Ruiz 1998, 113). The racist aspect of these policies is clear. Whereas women of color were pressured to consent to be sterilized or, which was true in many cases, sterilized without their knowledge or consent, white, middle-class women had difficulty finding doctors willing to perform the operation on them. For these women, most hospitals used the "120 formula"—a woman's age multiplied by the number of children she had should equal 120—for a woman to qualify for sterilization (see Roberts 1997).

Another infamous case is the experiment performed in the 1950s on Puerto Rican women who were used as subjects in the testing of the birth control pill. Physicians touted the pill as the "solution" to the problem of unemployment on the island. Sterilization had been the medical solution prior to the pill, and it was so far-reaching that by 1958, one-third of all women of childbearing age in Puerto Rico had been sterilized.

By mounting resistance to sterilization abuse as well as to restrictive abortion laws, activists demonstrated that there were many consequential differences among women of different race ethnicities and social classes. Sterilization and birth control represented freedom and autonomy for white, middle-class women, but they were tools used by governments to control the reproductive lives of poor and minority women. Black and Latina feminists influenced the reproductive rights movement by raising awareness of these differences, and in so doing, they transformed the abortion rights movement into a more inclusive movement for reproductive freedom (Nelson 2003). By fighting for the rights of the most vulnerable women to be free of forced sterilization and to bear as many children as they chose, women of color broadened the women's rights agenda by bringing "other than white" and "other than middle-class" views of reproductive harms and rights to the center of the burgeoning women's health movements (Eisenstein 2004). They demonstrated that reproductive rights must include the freedom to choose to bear children, as well as the freedom to choose not to bear children. Beyond promoting reforms to legalize abortion and regulate sterilization, they posed new questions for women and families. Realizing the goal of making a woman free to have exactly as many children as she wants, when she wants, if she wants, requires that she have the economic means to support her children as well as equality in her home and community. Otherwise, in what sense is she free to choose? By bringing the reproductive issues of women of color and poor women to the center of the debate, these activists demonstrated how women's rights to health and care mean nothing in the absence of their rights to adequate housing, income, education, and democratic inclusion in the policymaking processes that affect their lives (Silliman, Fried, Ross, and Gutiérrez 2004).

GLOBALIZING STERILIZATION. Forced sterilization has been a worldwide problem (along with forced pregnancies, lack of reproductive health care, and a host of other medically based violations of women's and men's human rights). For many years, beginning in the nineteenth century and continuing long into the twentieth century, the United States had a eugenics program that sterilized thousands of poor people of color in the name of ending "feeble-mindedness," crime, and mental illness. The poor, the illiterate, minorities, epileptics, manic-depressives, prostitutes, alcoholics, the homeless, and criminals were usually the targets. Since the turn of the twentieth century, sixty thousand Americans—men, women, and children, whose only problem appeared to be their racial identity or their poverty—have been sterilized without their consent.

Americans may know more about forced sterilization in Nazi Germany, where four hundred thousand Jews and others were forcibly sterilized, than about their own country's history of forced sterilizations. In fact, some of Hitler's sterilization program was borrowed from the American eugenics movement of the early twentieth century. More recently, several countries struggling with poverty have used forced sterilization as part of a poverty reduction program. For example, Peru's poverty reduction program offered women food and clothing for their children to bribe them into consenting to be sterilized. Under such conditions, these women can hardly be said to have given their consent freely. In some cases, women who gave birth were sterilized without their knowledge. In Japan, where sterilization was practiced until the 1990s, doctors told women that the procedure could be reversed. Not only do forced sterilizations deny people their right to bear children, they are also medically risky. The procedures are often done in poor sanitary conditions, and there is lack of follow-up treatment or medication. Women may die from complications (Woolf 2000).

The work of women of color activist groups such as the Committee for Abortion Rights and Against Sterilization Abuse (CARASA), the National Black Women's Health Project, the National Latina Health Organization, and the Reproductive Rights National Network helped to raise opposition to coercive sterilization programs and to write restrictions such as informed consent, waiting periods, and other protections into U.S. law. However, sterilization programs returned in less coercive guises, such as those that promoted the drugs Norplant and Depo-Provera to poor women. In August 2013, Wyeth Pharmaceuticals withdrew Norplant from the market after many complaints and concerns about its dangers, but another pharmaceutical company, Bayer, is now offering a similar contraceptive implant, Jadelle. The U.S. Agency for International Development has ordered 27 *million* implants for use around the world (but not in the U.S.) (Mosher and Crnkovich 2012).

Similarly, the United States has helped to introduce sterilization into third-world family planning programs. The U.S. Agency for International Development (USAID) has funded programs to bring foreign medical practitioners to the United States to learn sterilization techniques, so that they can return to their home countries ready to sterilize patients. It also funds the Association for Voluntary Surgical Contraception (AVSC), an organization once linked with the eugenics movement, which works in over sixty countries around the globe.

Sterilization programs are only one prong of U.S. policy regarding programs in developing countries that target women's reproductive status. Since the 1970s, the United States has refused to fund programs that provide assistance to women seeking abortions. This policy, further codified by Ronald Reagan as the Mexico City policy or "gag rule," was reestablished by George W. Bush in 2001, and was rescinded on January 23, 2009, shortly after Democratic President Barack Obama took office.

GENDER AND THE GLOBAL AIDS PANDEMIC

Like the black death that swept over Europe in the fourteenth century, killing one-third of the population, and the flu pandemic of 1918 and 1919, which killed between 20 million and 40 million people (including an estimated 675,000 Americans), HIV/AIDS is another global epidemic that has killed and disabled millions around the world. Between 1981 and 2005, more than 25 million people died from AIDS, and an estimated 40.3 million people worldwide were living with HIV (the virus that eventually causes AIDS) or AIDS itself (Centers for Disease Control and Prevention 2005).

In the mid-90s, rates of death from AIDS in developed countries began to decline, thanks to the discovery of highly active retroviral drugs. An unprecedented global response, resulting in the formation of the Global Fund to Fight AIDS, Tuberculosis, and Malaria in 2003, allocated billions of dollars in aid to countries most affected by the epidemic. This unified response suffered from the shortage of health care workers, scarcity of essential medications, and weaknesses in public health systems. Nevertheless, it focused attention on global health issues, strengthened services for maternal and child health, and remains a model for future responses to global epidemics of chronic diseases (Piot and Quinn 2013). AIDS remains epidemic in sub-Saharan Africa, Eastern Europe, and the Caribbean. HIV infection continues to spread in Eastern Europe and Asia, particularly among men who have sex with men, injection drug users, and female sex workers. While diminished, then, the epidemic continues.

What does AIDS have to do with gender? Everything. At first, HIV/AIDS was seen as a disease principally affecting men who had sex with other men or men who injected drugs. More recently, it has become clear that an increasing number of people are becoming infected through unprotected heterosexual sex. Slightly more than half of all people worldwide now living with HIV are women and girls. However, not all women are equally at risk. It is poor women of color, women with the least control over their lives and health, who are most vulnerable (Farmer 2003). In the United States, AIDS disproportionately affects women of color, particularly African Americans and Latinas. While these two populations accounted for less than one-fourth of all U.S. women in 2012, African American women and Latinas represented 67 percent and 15 percent of new AIDS cases, respectively. In 2001, HIV/AIDS was the leading cause of death for African American women aged 25 to 34 and the fifth leading cause of death for same-aged Latinas (American Psychological Association 2006). In sub-Saharan Africa, there are now more new infections among women than among men (Farmer, Connors, and Simmons 1996).

Behavioral and Educational Approaches

The world community, through the United Nations, is searching for a way to control and contain the virus. Many AIDS programs focus on individual behavior and education. For example, supporters of the popular "ABC" approach to preventing the spread of AIDS claim that the program has cut the rates of HIV/AIDS in several countries. The ABC program advises three behaviors to avoid infection: abstain, be faithful, and use condoms. This advice may work for women who have the power to control the situations they encounter in their daily lives, but it is far from reliable for women who are dependent on or subordinated to others.

- Abstinence assumes that women do not engage in sex except when they choose to, but women frequently do not have the choice to say no to sex. All over the world, including in the United States, poor and powerless women are forced to exchange sex for material support. Sex work may be the only work some women can find to feed and house themselves and their children. The use of rape and sexual violence in times of war puts women at great risk. Women and children are abducted or tricked by sex traffickers who take them to parts of the world where they may not speak the language or know how and where to get help. Some women may be at risk of AIDS from injection drug use and have no help or treatment available. All such women have limited, if any, control over their sex lives and are unable to choose abstinence. Even when sex isn't a matter of economic survival or force and violence, societal pressure makes abstinence unlikely. In many places, for example, women who do not bear children are highly stigmatized. And male cultural domination of sexual encounters creates risky situations for women, who may feel that a male partner's desires are paramount and that they cannot assert their right to safe sex or no sex (Doyal 1995, 78).
- Being faithful can prevent infection, but being faithful to a partner who is engaged in risky sexual behavior or is HIV positive will not protect a woman from exposure to HIV. Indeed, husbands who have risky sex with multiple partners are responsible for the explosion of HIV/AIDS among married women around the globe.
- Using condoms or having nonpenetrative sex requires men's cooperation. Many men refuse to use condoms. In some cases, if a woman demands that a sex partner use condoms, she may put herself at risk of being beaten and raped by him. Beatings and violent rape, by the way, increase the risk of HIV transmission through cuts and abrasions to the skin.

Structural Violence and the Women's Epidemic

The HIV/AIDS epidemic feeds on both poverty and inequality. It travels along lines of gender, race, class, and region, "vectors that converge in the bodies and lives of individuals" (Connors 1996, 93). The ABC approach to dealing with the epidemic around the world—and most agency responses—works on the assumption that HIV/AIDS is caused by individual behaviors and is changed by changing those behaviors. Physician and anthropologist Paul Farmer criticizes this view:

To continue to pretend that a two-hour session with an AIDS educator, for example, can measurably increase "self-esteem" in a person who has lived an entire lifetime in a context of violence, discrimination, and abject poverty, or that the problem of "empowerment" lies solely in convincing the subject that he or she has power, regardless of whether this is the case, is to completely miss the mark about why people engage in risk behaviour. (Farmer 2003, 202)

If Farmer is correct, the ABC prevention approach based on educating individuals and exhorting them to take responsibility for their sexual behavior will not work unless there are major changes in women's access to power and resources. Without property rights, basic education, and access to a decent job, many women and girls do not have the social power they need to enable them to claim sexual and social autonomy. Tell a young girl raped by a member of her family, a family friend, or a stranger, to abstain. Tell a wife whose husband has girlfriends or visits prostitutes to rely on faithfulness. Tell a woman to withhold sex from a violent partner unless he agrees to use a condom. Each of these situations is beyond the control of individual women.

In other words, risk is not determined by lack of education about risks, nor is it reliably diminished by more education. These solutions assume that the epidemic can be brought under control when individuals decide to change their behavior (abstain, be faithful, use condoms). But risk is the result of a basic lack of economic equality and social rights that set the stage for what Farmer calls *structural violence*—forms of extreme suffering such as hunger, rape, torture, and AIDS that are visited on the poor and the powerless of the world (Farmer 2003, xiv).

The concept of structural violence focuses attention on the broader social determinants of risk, such as changing patterns of work, family, and sexual relations. For example, some Southeast Asian countries promote sex tourism to increase foreign exchange by recruiting rural women and girls who migrate to cities to help their impoverished families. Their impoverished families are the victims of state policies supporting export and free trade over subsistence agriculture. Also, war puts women at greater risk to be raped by pillaging soldiers. Indeed, a spike in HIV in Rwanda resulted fromthe mass rapes of Tutsi women during that country's genocide in the 1990s.

Growing landlessness creates economic insecurity that encourages women to engage in "transactional sex" with older men in exchange for goods, services, money, or basic necessities. Even in wealthy nations, inner-city blight, the growth of long-term unemployment, and racism structure risk for poor women and women of color.

Men, too, are vulnerable to HIV because of gender expectations. In many, maybe most places in the world, masculinity demands taking risks and being sexually active. To be men, boys learn that they shouldn't back off from danger and that they must be sexually active with at least one woman—and in many places, the more women, the better. These aspects of the social construction of masculinity mean that men may hesitate to be faithful to one woman or to use condoms, lest they seem unmanly. HIV risk for women seems to depend significantly on the men in their lives when the men in their lives are caught up in ideas and practices of masculinity that increase their likelihood of contracting HIV and spreading it to their partners. Gender may be the most significant problem to be solved as we stop the spread of HIV.

Public health advocates argue that we must add three more letters to our toolbox for addressing HIV: GEM. G refers to gender equity, E to economic justice, and M to migration. As long as women remain oppressed and unable to assert control over their sex lives and as long as women and men are trapped in situations of dire poverty and forced by economics or trafficking to migrate, HIV will remain a critical health issue (Dworkin and Ehrhardt 2007).

REFLECTIONS ON GENDER AND HEALTH: FIGHTING BACK AROUND THE WORLD

Farmer's concept of structural violence suggests that poor women must achieve economic security, political power, and cultural respect to defeat the threats to women's reproductive and general health. If they are successful, then universal, comprehensive health services will take precedence over market forces. And, if they are successful, men and children will benefit as well.

The struggles over women's health in third-world or debtor countries are responses to conditions that made it difficult for women to get access to good health care. For example, in many such nations near the end of the twentieth century, free or subsidized health care was cut back or eliminated as required by international lenders such as the World Bank and the International Monetary Fund. Such **structural adjustment** schemes, which were imposed on the debtor nations by the International Monetary Fund (IMF) and the World Bank, put debt repayment ahead of human health. The restructuring affected the availability of food as well, because lenders demanded that local farmers engage in commercial agriculture for export to help raise funds to repay their country's debts. In these ways, third-world debt led to harsh and deteriorating health conditions affecting ordinary citizens—men, women, and children—in the global South.

The global health movement has responded to deteriorating conditions of women's health by bringing together activists from widely differing circumstances. The Latin American movements for women's health have emerged in the context of democracy movements in that part of the world. The south Asian movements arose in the context of sterilization promotion and rising trafficking of young rural women whose families lost the ability to support themselves through subsistence farming when large corporate interests took over peasant land. In Africa, extreme poverty and the HIV/AIDS pandemic are the context within which women's health movements must struggle. In the face of this diversity, a series of UN conferences made dialogue among women on a global scale possible.

These conferences helped feminist activists build transnational networks and develop their vision of reproductive health beyond control over fertility.

Since the 1980s and 1990s, transnational women's organizations—NGOs and transnational coalitions—led by women from the poor nations of the global South—have reshaped the former international consensus that saw control of women's fertility as a means to population control and economic development. These new women's organizations rejected these attempts to use women's reproductive lives as the means to other ends. Instead they embraced and enlarged the concept of reproductive rights by placing it in a human rights framework.

What does it mean to put reproduction into a human rights framework? If reproductive health and health in general are human rights, then it follows that governments must provide the conditions within which such rights are guaranteed. How can a woman exercise her human right to reproductive choice, asks Rosalind Petchesky, if she lacks the financial resources to pay for reproductive health services or the transport to get to them; if she is illiterate or given no information in a language she understands; if her workplace is contaminated with pollutants that have an adverse effect on pregnancy; or if she is harassed by parents, a husband or in-laws who will abuse or beat her if they find out she uses birth control (Petchesky 2004, 19)?

How can health be assured if a woman and her family have no home, no money for food, and no health care? These, too, are fundamental human rights. If reproductive tract infections in third-world countries are linked to the absence of toilets, sanitary pads, and privacy, then adequate sanitation is a woman's right. If high infant and maternal mortality are brought on by the lack of potable water, then potable water is also a woman's right. In fact, the UN General Assembly declared in July 2010 that safe and clean drinking water is, indeed, a human right.

Women from the global South have pioneered in developing this revolutionary framework linking reproductive and sexual health to a wide range of conditions: housing, education, employment, property rights, legal equality, and freedom from abuse, genital mutilation, and gender violence. Petchesky (2004, 48) calls this new direction "a major historical achievement and a mark of the power of transnational women's NGOs and feminist ideas."

GENDER MATTERS

In this chapter, we have explored the many ways that illness and health are gendered around the globe. We have seen how men's and women's social locations, their paid and unpaid labor, their race and class positions, and the political and economic position of the nations in which they live structure their opportunities to enjoy good health or the likelihood that they will fall victim to disease and other bodily harm. Although some risks are apparent to individuals and even avoidable by them, others are not. The hazards of some jobs, the chemical dangers surrounding household work, the inadequacies of health care, or the lack of access to care cannot be offset by individual precautions or undertakings. Health is a collective good that only action at the level of communities and societies can ensure.

In this chapter, we have also seen how women and men have organized to change health systems and health priorities. The language and politics of reproductive rights originated in the women's movements of the 1970s and 1980s as women sought the right to control their bodies. By the 1980s, groups of women of color, such as the National Black Women's Health Project and the National Latina Health Organization, were linking reproductive rights to issues of racism and poverty. In the 1980s and 1990s, a series of UN conferences internationalized the politics of women's health. Participants in these conferences created transnational organizations "to secure women's reproductive and sexual health and rights within a broad context of social development and gender equality" (Petchesky 2004, 35). Although fundamentalists and anti-choice activists seem to have structured the public discussions of reproductive rights and freedoms in many struggles, and although the Supreme Court periodically appears poised to overturn *Roe v. Wade*, women's transnational movements are making progress in linking reproductive health to a wide range of rights: housing, education, employment, freedom from violence, and health services that take priority over market forces. Petchesky (2004, 48) calls this new direction "a major historical achievement and a mark of the power of transnational women's NGOs and feminist ideas," as the statement from the campaign for Solidarity for African Women's Rights (SOAWR), a coalition of groups across Africa seeking to ratify the Protocol to the African Charter on Human and Peoples' Rights on the Rights of Women in Africa, demonstrates (Box 9-8).

The struggle continues. The tide is turning.

GENDER IN EVERYDAY LIFE   BOX 9-8
SOLIDARITY FOR AFRICAN WOMEN'S REPRODUCTIVE RIGHTS

Nairobi, Kenya—On 26th October, 2005, Solidarity for African Women's Rights (SOAWR), a coalition of groups across Africa campaigning for the popularization, ratification and domestication of the Protocol to the African Charter on Human and Peoples' Rights on the Rights of Women in Africa, welcomed the 15th ratification by Togo of the Protocol. The Protocol then entered into force on 25 November 2005, marking a milestone in the protection and promotion of women's rights in Africa and creating new rights for women in terms of international standards. For the first time in international law, this ground-breaking Protocol explicitly sets forth the reproductive right of women to medical abortion when pregnancy results from rape or incest or when the continuation of pregnancy endangers the health or life of the mother. In another first, the Protocol explicitly calls for the legal prohibition of female genital mutilation, and prohibits the abuse of women in advertising and pornography. The Protocol sets forth a broad range of economic and social welfare rights for women. The rights of particularly vulnerable groups of women, including widows, elderly women, disabled women and "women in distress," which includes poor women, women from marginalized populations groups, and pregnant or nursing women in detention, are specifically recognized.

"The 19 national, regional and international organizations of SOAWR have been working tirelessly since July 2003 when the Protocol was adopted for ratification," said Muthoni Wanyeki of FEMNET, a coalition member, in 2005. "This moment is a testament to their work and the work of other civil society groups working across Africa for ratification." The coalition delivered to heads of state a petition for which signatures were collected from across Africa by pen, email, online and by text messaging (SMS) from people encouraging their governments to ratify the Protocol. "To our knowledge, this is the first time that SMS technologies were used on a mass scale on the African continent in support of human rights," said Firoze Manji of Fahamu, the SOAWR member that developed the technique.

"The protocol should not be viewed in isolation," added Hannah Forster of the African Center for Democracy and Human Rights Studies. "It would be prudent to approach its domestication and implementation in consonance with other relevant international instruments," added Gladys Mutukwa of coalition-member WiLDAF. "The coming into effect of the Protocol is just the first step in securing the protection of the human rights of African women," explained Faiza Jama Mohamed of Equality Now, another coalition member. "However our task remains incomplete until state parties exercise the political will to protect, promote and respect these rights."

Since 2005, the SOAWR coalition has expanded and is now comprised of 37 members based in 21 countries—some of whom are regional membership organizations and, through their membership and partners, are working in many more countries. Currently, 29 out of 53 African Union member states have ratified the Protocol, namely Angola, Benin, Burkina Faso, Cape Verde, Comoros, Djibouti, Democratic Republic of Congo, the Gambia, Ghana, Guinea-Bissau, Kenya, Libya, Lesotho, Liberia, Mali, Malawi, Mozambique, Mauritania, Namibia, Nigeria, Rwanda, South Africa, Senegal, Seychelles, Tanzania, Togo, Uganda, Zambia and Zimbabwe. Within the context of the African Union African Women's Decade (2010–2020), SOAWR is calling on all African governments to ratify the Protocol and to urgently develop multi-sectoral action plans for its full implementation.

SOURCE: Brenda Kombo, bkombo@equalitynow.org, 2011.

KEY TERMS

anabolic steroids

care work

cult of thinness

epidemiology

free market

nimble fingers

rap groups

Roe v. Wade

structural adjustment

structural violence

type A behavior

work transfer

CRITICAL THINKING QUESTIONS

1. Briefly describe the current status of legal abortion in the United States and the political debate surrounding it.
2. How does poverty affect the health of women and men? How does it cause health problems? How does it prevent people from finding solutions to their health problems?
3. One of the key factors in the social construction of masculinity is that the requirement has been that men take risks in order to be real men. What are some examples of this kind of risk taking that might be associated with greater incidence of disease? With greater incidence of injury? With less access to medical care?
4. How and why did women of color transform the abortion rights movement into a movement for reproductive health?
5. Interview a person you know who is providing home care for someone. Ask them about a typical day. What work do they do? How did they learn to do the work? What do they do if they need a day off? How do they feel about their work? What pleasure does it bring them? How is it frustrating?

REFERENCES

Abortion Counseling Service. 1971. *Abortion—A Woman's Decision, a Woman's Right*. CWLU Herstory. http://www.uic.edu/orgs/cwluherstory/CWLUFeature/Janebroch.html. Accessed March 23, 2011.

American Psychological Association. 2006. "HIV/AIDS Among Women of Color." January 19. http://www.apa.org/about/gr/issues/hiv/women.aspx. Accessed June 8, 2011.

Amnesty International. 2010. *Deadly Delivery: The Maternal Health Care Crisis in the U.S.A.* London: Amnesty International Secretariat. http://amnesty.org/en/library/info/AMR51/007/2010/en. Accessed 2/28/2014.

Arias, Elizabeth. 2010. "United States Life Tables, 2006." *National Vital Statistics Reports* 58, No. 21. Hyattsville, MD: National Center for Health Statistics. http://www.cdc.gov/nchs/products/nvsr.htm. Accessed March 23, 2011.

Arnett, Jeffrey J. 2002. "Developmental Sources of Crash Risk in Young Drivers." *Injury Prevention* 8:17–23. doi: 10.1136/ip.8.suppl_2.ii17.

Aronson, Jane, and Sheila M. Neysmith. 1996. " 'You're Not Just in There to Do the Work': Depersonalizing Policies and the Exploitation of Home Care Workers' Labor." *Gender and Society* 10 (1): 59–77.

Baxandall, Rosalyn, and Linda Gordon, eds. 2000. *Dear Sisters: Dispatches from the Women's Liberation Movement*. New York: Basic Books.

Beers, Mark H., Robert S. Porter, Thomas V. Jones, Justin L. Kaplan, and Michael Berkwits. 2006. "Anabolic Steroids." In *The Merck Manual of Diagnosis and Therapy*, 1690–92. Whitehouse Station, NJ: Merck Research Laboratories.

Bell, Susan E., and Ann E. Figert. 2010. "Gender and the Medicalization of Healthcare." In *The Palgrave Handbook of Gender and Healthcare*, edited by Ellen Kuhlmann and Ellen Annandale, 107–22. London: Palgrave.

Binford, L. 1996. *The El Mozote Massacre*. Tucson: University of Arizona Press.

Bonacich, Edna, and Richard Applebaum. 2007. "The Return of the Sweatshop." In *Intersections of Gender, Race, and Class: Readings for a Changing Landscape*, edited by Marcia Texler Segal and Theresa Martinez, 289–99. Los Angeles: Roxbury.

Boston Women's Health Book Collective. 2005. *Our Bodies, Ourselves*. New York: Touchstone.

Brecht, Bertolt. A Worker's Speech to a Doctor. 2012. http://structuralhealth.wordpress.com/2012/03/29/a-workers-speech-to-a-doctor/. Accessed 2/27/2014.

Brumberg, J. J. 1988. *Fasting Girls: The Emergence of Anorexia Nervosa as a Modern Disease*. Cambridge, MA: Harvard University Press.

Cancian, Francesca, and Stacey Oliker. 2000. *Caring and Gender*. Thousand Oaks, CA: Pine Forge Press.

Catalyst Knowledge Center. 2012. "Women in U.S. Medicine." http://www.catalyst.org/knowledge/women-medicine

Not cited in the textConnors, Margaret. 1996. "Sex, Drugs and Structural Violence." In *Women, Poverty, and AIDS: Sex, Drugs, and Structural Violence*, edited by Paul Farmer, Margaret Connors, and Janie Simmons. Monroe, ME: Common Courage Press.

Daniels, Cynthia R. 2006. *Exposing Men: The Science and Politics of Male Reproduction*. New York: Oxford University Press.

Davis, Angela. 1982. *Women, Race and Class*. New York. Vintage.

Denton, Margaret, Isik Urla Zeytinoglu, Sharon Davies, and Jason Lian. 2002. "Job Stress and Job Dissatisfaction of Home Care Workers in the Context of Health Care Restructuring." *International Journal of Health Services* 32 (2): 327–57.

Diamond, Timothy. 1995. *Making Grey Gold: Narratives of Nursing Home Care*. Chicago: University of Chicago Press.

Disch, Estelle. 2008. *Reconstructing Gender: A Multicultural Anthology*. 5th edition. New York: McGraw-Hill.

Doyal, Lesley. 1995. *What Makes Women Sick: Gender and the Political Economy of Health*. New Brunswick, NJ: Rutgers University Press.

Dworkin, Shari, and Anke Ehrhardt. 2007. "Going Beyond 'ABC' to Include 'GEM': Critical Reflections on Progress in the HIV/AIDS Epidemic." *American Journal of Public Health* 97 (1): 13–18.

Eaton, Danice, Laura Kann, Steve Kinchen, Shari Shanklin, James Ross, Joseph Hawkins, William A. Harris, Richard Lowry, Tim McManus, David Chyen, Connie Lim, Lisa Whittle, Nancy D. Brener, and Howell Wechsler. 2010. "Youth Risk Behavior Surveillance—United States, 2009." *Morbidity and Mortality Weekly* 59(SS5) Report. http://www.cdc.gov/mmwr/pdf/ss/ss5905.pdf. Accessed June 8, 2011.

Edlin, Gordon and Eric Golanty. 2004. *Health and Wellness*. 8th edition. Sudbury, MA: Jones and Bartlett.

Ehrenreich, Barbara, and Deirdre English. 1972. *Witches, Midwives, and Healers: A History of Women Healers*. New York: Feminist Press at CUNY.

Ehrenreich, Barbara, Elizabeth Hess, and Gloria Jacobs. 1986. *Remaking Love: The Feminization of Sex*. New York: Anchor.

Eisenstein, Zillah. 2004. *Against Empire: Feminisms, Racism, and the West*. London: Zed Books.

ExpressIndia.com. 2010. *Bollywood Drives Steroid Use in S Africa*, July 5. http://www.expressindia.com/latest-news/Bollywood-drives-steroid-use-in-S-Africa/642401/. Accessed March 9, 2011.

Farmer, Paul. 2003. *Pathologies of Power: Health, Human Rights, and the New War on the Poor*. Berkeley: University of California Press.

Farmer, Paul, Margaret Connors, and Janie Simmons, eds. 1996. *Women, Poverty, and AIDS: Sex, Drugs, and Structural Violence*. Monroe, ME: Common Courage Press.

Fergusson David, Nicola Swain-Campbell, and John Horwood. 2003. "Risky Driving Behaviour in Young People: Prevalence, Personal Characteristics, and Traffic Accidents." *Australia and New Zealand Journal of Public Health* 27 (3): 337–42.

Garner, David. 1997. "Survey Says: Body Image Poll Results." *Psychology Today*, February 1. http://www.psychologytoday.com/articles/199702/survey-says-body-image-poll-results. Accessed 2/28/2014.

Ginty, Molly M. "*Our Bodies, Ourselves*: Going, Going, Gone Global." *WeNews*, September 14. http://www.womensenews.org/story/health/040914/our-bodies-ourselves-going-going-gone-global. Accessed March 9, 2011.

Glazer, Nona. 1993. *Women's Paid and Unpaid Labor: The Work Transfer in Health Care*. Philadelphia: Temple University Press.

Guyer, Jocelyn, Matthew Broaddus, and Annie Dude. 2002. "Millions of Mothers Lack Health Insurance Coverage in the United States: Most Uninsured Mothers Lack Access Both to Employer-Based Coverage and to Publicly Subsidized Health Insurance." *International Journal of Health Sciences* 32 (1): 89–106.

Helgeson, Vicki S. 1995. "Masculinity, Men's Roles, and Coronary Heart Disease." In Sabo and Gordon, 66–104.

The Henry J. Kaiser Family Foundation. 2013. The Global HIV/AIDS Epidemic. August 14. http://kff.org/global-health-policy/fact-sheet/the-global-hivaids-epidemic/.

Hesse-Biber, Sharlene. 2007. *The Cult of Thinness*. New York: Oxford University Press.

Hochschild, Arlie 1989. *The Second Shift*. New York: Viking.

Jackson, Beth E. 2003. "Situating Epidemiology." In *Gender Perspectives on Health and Medicine: Key Themes*, Advances in Gender Research Vol. 7, edited by Marcia Texler Segal, Vasilikie Demos, and Jennie Kronenfeld, 11–58. Greenwich, CT: JAI Press.

Klein, Alan. 1993. *Little Big Men: Bodybuilding Subculture and Gender Construction*. Albany: State University of New York Press.

———. 1995. "Life's Too Short to Die Small: Steroid Use among Male Bodybuilders." In Sabo and Gordon, 105–20.

Koebler, Jason. 2012. "Teenage Girl Drivers: No Longer the Safer Bet?" U.S.News and World Report. April 3. http://www.usnews.com/news/articles/2012/04/03/teenage-girl-drivers-no-longer-the-safer-bet. Accessed 2/28/2014.

Kreiger, N. 1990. "Racial and Gender Discrimination: Risk Factors for High Blood Pressure." *Social Science and Medicine* 30:1273–81.

Lorber, Judith. 1993. "Believing Is Seeing: Biology as Ideology." *Gender and Society* 7 (4): 568–81.

Luxton, Meg. 1980. *More Than a Labour of Love: Three Generations of Women's Work in the Home*. Toronto: Women's Educational Press.

McCaughey, Martha. 1999. *Fleshing Out the Discomforts of Femininity: The Parallel Cases of Female Anorexia and Male Compulsive Body-Building*. New York: Aldine.

McKee, Martin, and Vladimir Shkolnikov. 2001. "Understanding the Toll of Premature Death among Men in Eastern Europe." *British Medical Journal* 2001 (323): 1051. doi: 10.1136/bmj.323.7320.1051.

Melgar, Junice Demeterio, and Alfredo R. Melgar. 2010. "New Modelled Estimates of Maternal Mortality." *Lancet* 375 (9730): 1963–64.

Messner, Michael, and Raewyn Connell. 2007. *Out of Play: Critical Essays on Gender and Sport*. Albany: State University of New York Press.

Morgen, Sandra. 2002. *Into Our Own Hands: The Women's Health Movement in the United States, 1969–1990*. New Brunswick, NJ: Rutgers University Press.

Mosher, Steven W., and Elizabeth Crnkovich. 2012. "Norplant Is Back—Under a Different Name." Population Research Institute, October. http://www.pop.org/content/norplant-back-under-different-name

Mwalali, Philip, and Emmanuel Ngui. 2009. "Reduction in Maternal and Child Mortality in Sub-Saharan Africa: The Yo-Yo Effect in Delivering on the Promises." *Journal of Health Care for the Poor and Underserved* 20 (4 Suppl): 149–69. doi: 10.1353/hpu.0.0224.

National Institute on Drug Abuse. 2010. "NIDA InfoFacts: High School and Youth Trends." http://www.nida.nih.gov/infofacts/hsyouthtrends.html. Accessed March 9, 2011.

Navarro, Vicente. 2003. "The Inhuman State of U.S. Health Care." *Monthly Review* 55 (4): 56–62.

Nebehay, Stephanie. 2013. "Life Expectancy Gap Growing Between Rich/Poor World Women—WHO." Reuters Sep 2, 2013. http://in.reuters.com/article/2013/09/02/health-women-idINDEE98100Y20130902. Accessed 2/27/2014.

Nelson, Jennifer. 2003. *Women of Color and the Reproductive Rights Movement*. New York: New York University Press.

Ong, Aihwa. 1987. *Spirits of Resistance and Capitalist Discipline: Factory Women in Malaysia*. Albany: State University of New York Press.

Petchesky, Rosalind Pollack. 2004. *Global Prescriptions: Gendering Health and Human Rights*. London: Zed Books.

Pew Internet. 2009. *Teens and Distracted Driving*. November 16. http://pewinternet.org/Reports/2009/Teens-and-Distracted-Driving.aspx?r=1\. Accessed March 23, 2011.

Piot, Peter and Thomas C. Quinn. 2013. "Response to the AIDS Pandemic—A Global Health Model." *New England Journal of Medicine* 368. June 6. 2210–2218.

Plechner, Deborah. 2000. "Women, Medicine, and Sociology: Thoughts on the Need for a Critical Feminist Perspective." *Social Factors* 18:69–94.

Pollit, Katha. 1997. "Abortion in American History." *The Atlantic Monthly*. May. http://www.theatlantic.com/past/docs/issues/97may/abortion.htm.Accessed February 28, 2014.

Pope, Harrison, Katharine Phillips, and Roberto Olivardia. 2000. *The Adonis Complex: The Secret Crisis of Male Body Obsession*. New York: Free Press.

Population Reference Bureau. 2010. *World Population Data Sheet*. http://www.prb.org/Publications/Datasheets/2010/2010wpds.aspx. Accessed March 23, 2011.

Reagan, Leslie J. *When Abortion Was a Crime: Women, Medicine, and Law in the United States, 1867–1973*. Berkeley: University of California Press, 1997.

Reverby, Susan. 1987. *Ordered to Care: The Dilemma of American Nursing: 1850–1945*. Cambridge, UK: Cambridge University Press.

Richards, Cecile. 2010. "The Affordable Care Act Benefits Women." *Huffington Post*, September 23. http://www.huffingtonpost.com/cecile-richards/the-affordable-care-act-b_b_736927.html.

Roberts, Dorothy. 1997. *Killing the Black Body: Race, Reproduction, and the Meaning of Liberty*. New York: Vintage Books.

Roe v. Wade. 1973. *Findlaw*, 410 US 113 (1973). http://caselaw.lp.findlaw.com/cgi-bin/getcase.pl?court=us&vol=410&invol=113. Accessed March 23, 2011.

Rosen, Ruth. 2001. *The World Split Open: How the Modern Women's Movement Changed America*. New York: Penguin.

Ruiz, Vicki L. 1998. *From Out of the Shadows: Mexican Women in Twentieth-Century America*. New York: Oxford University Press.

Ruzek, Sheryl, Virginia Olesen, and Adele Clarke, eds. 1997. *Women's Health: Complexities and Differences*. Columbus: Ohio State University Press.

Ryan, Mary. 1979. *Womanhood in America*. 2nd edition. New York: New Viewpoints.

Sabo, Donald, and David Frederick Gordon. 1995. "Rethinking Men's Health and Illness: The Relevance of Gender Studies." In Sabo and Gordon, 1–21.

Sabo, Donald, and David Frederick Gordon. 1995. *Men's Health and Illness: Gender, Power, and the Body*. Thousand Oaks, CA: Sage.

Schiller, Nina Glick. 1993. "The Invisible Women: Caregiving and the Construction of AIDS Health Services." *Culture, Medicine, and Psychiatry* 17:487–512.

Schofield, Toni, R. W. Connell, Linley Walker, Julian Wood, and Dianne Butland. 2000. "Understanding Men's Health and Illness: A Gender-Relations Approach to Policy, Research, and Practice." *Journal of American College Health* 48 (6): 247–56.

Sharma, Vijai P. 2003. "Type 'A' Behaviors." *Mind Publications*, December. http://www.mindpub.com/art502.htm. Accessed March 23, 2011.

Silliman, Jael, Marlene Gerber Fried, Loretta Ross, and Elena Gutiérrez. 2004. *Undivided Rights: Women of Color Organizing for Reproductive Justice*. Cambridge, MA: South End Press.

Smith, Stephanie. 2010. "Doubling of Maternal Deaths in U.S. 'Scandalous,' Rights Group Says." *CNN Health*, March 12. http://www.cnn.com/2010/HEALTH/03/12/maternal.mortality/index.html. Accessed March 23, 2011.

Thompson, Becky. 1994. *A Hunger So Wide and So Deep: American Women Speak Out on Eating Problems*. Minneapolis: University of Minnesota Press.

Turner, Grace-Marie. 2013. "It's Fact, Not Anecdote, That ObamaCare Is Turning Us into a Part-Time Nation." *Forbes*. August 27. http://www.forbes.com/sites/gracemarieturner/2013/08/27/its-fact-not-anecdote-that-obamacare-is-turning-us-into-a-part-time-nation/. Accessed February 28, 2014.

Uetricht, Mica. 2010. "Will Sweatshop Activists' Big Victory Over Nike Trigger Broader Industry Reforms?" *In These Times*, July 28. http://www.inthesetimes.com/working/entry/6268/will_activists_victory_over_nike_trigger_broader_industry_labor_reform/. Accessed March 23, 2011.

Waldron, Ingrid. 1995. "Contributions of Changing Gender Differences in Behavior and Social Roles to Changing Gender Differences in Mortality." In Sabo and Gordon, 22–45.

Wang, Dora Calott. 2010. "Is Wall Street Making Life or Death Decisions?" *Huffington Post*, July 26. http://www.huffingtonpost.com/dora-calott-wang-md/is-wall-street-making-lif_b_659897.html. Accessed March 23, 2011.

White, Philip, Kevin Young, and William McTeer. 1995. "Sport, Masculinity, and the Injured Body." In Sabo and Gordon, 158–82.

Woolf, Linda. 2000. "Forced Sterilization." http://www.webster.edu/~woolflm/forcedsterilization .html. Accessed June 23, 2008.

World Health Organization. 2013. "Tuberculosis" Fact Sheet No. 104. February. Geneva, Switzerland: WHO. http://www.who.int/mediacentre/factsheets/fs104/en/. Accessed February 28, 2014.

——. 2012. "Maternal Mortality" Fact Sheet No. 348. May. Geneva, Switzerland: WHO. http://www .who.int/mediacentre/factsheets/fs348/en/. Accessed February 28, 2014.

——. 2010b. "Protect Women from Tobacco Marketing and Smoke." http://www.who.int/tobacco/ wntd/2010/gender_tobacco/en/index.html. Accessed March 23, 2011.

10

POLITICS, PRISON, AND THE MILITARY

Rural Chinese villages are one example of gender inequity in politics that is not often discussed.
But 20 percent of the people on earth live in China, and 49 percent of those 1.4 billion
Chinese live in rural villages which are run by elected Village Committees and where
only 22 percent of those elected are women.

Source: Zheng zhimin—Imaginechina.

When José Luis Rodriguez Zapatero served as prime minister of Spain from 2004 until 2011, he fulfilled his promise to make the government more responsive to women. During his first week in office, the new Spanish government made history twice. First, at the inauguration ceremony, half of the sixteen ministers sworn in as members of Zapatero's cabinet were women. Then, he appointed Maria Teresa Fernández de la Vega the first-ever woman vice premier. In 2008, after his reelection, he brought even more women into his cabinet, including Spain's first woman defense minister, Carme Chacón. Women have been able to serve in the armed forces only in the last twenty years. Chacon herself made news when, visibly very pregnant, she inspected the troops despite the comments of conservative politicians who disapproved of the political and social changes occuring in Spain. Besides these high-level appointments, Zapatero, a Socialist Workers' Party member who calls himself a radical feminist, also tapped women to head several ministries, including those of culture, education, environment, and agriculture. Voters in Spain have played their part as well in this gender revolution, electing 128 women (37 percent) to the 350 seats in the Spanish congress in the 2008 elections. These milestones show how far Spain has come in the three decades since the end of the archconservative dictatorship of General Francisco Franco, when a man had a legal right to "discipline" his wife by beating her and no woman could open a bank account, apply for a passport, or sign a contract without her husband's permission (McSmith 2008).

The new Spanish government not only brought more women into high offices, it also made the government more supportive of women's rights by changing laws and public policy to streamline divorce proceedings, legalize gay and lesbian marriage, and legalize abortion, which had been illegal in Spain except in cases of rape and severe birth defects. Spain also increased police support for battered women and expanded public education on the problem of violence against women. In addition, the Spanish government passed controversial laws banning overly thin models from high-fashion runways. The political leaders declared that girls and young women were adversely affected by images of emaciated women who were supposed to represent feminine beauty. Spanish legislators even passed legislation that obliges men and women to "share domestic responsibilities and the care and attention" of children and elderly family members. The new marriage law requires that couples live together, remain faithful, help one another, and now share with housework and care for family members as part of their spousal obligations (Tremlett 2005).

The news coming out of Spain shows great advances in gender equality in politics. These changes are based on an affirmative action approach, setting goals for increasing the numbers of women at the top of the government and promoting policies that will improve gender equity. What do you think of this kind of affirmative action approach to increasing the numbers of women in high-level political positions?

The strategy in Spain implies that more women in office will mean greater gender equity by paying more attention to women's issues and taking a more supportive approach to programs and policies that serve women. Does it make any difference if more women are in office? If equal numbers of women are in office, will the approach to social issues change? Will the government become more liberal or more conservative? If more women become government leaders, will gender equity issues gain greater attention?

Political office is only one part of the government. How do women and men compare in other branches of the government such as the criminal justice system and the military?

This chapter is organized around the broad issue of gender and politics. We begin by looking at the general topic of politics and power and the state. We then examine three important political arenas within the state: electoral politics, the criminal justice system, and the military. In the last section, we explore the theoretical question of how we define the term "political" and how our ideas about what is political are influenced by gender.

POLITICS AND THE STATE

Politics is the expression and organization of power. In the 1970s, feminists declared that "the personal is political." By this, they meant that power differences and political relationships exist between individuals, even in the most personal areas of our lives with families, friends, partners, and children.

Politics is more commonly understood, however, as a public issue. When most of us use the word *political*, we think about activities such as voting or waging wars. In this chapter, we look at politics in the public arena by examining electoral politics, the military, and the criminal justice system. In doing this, we examine pieces of a large social institution called the "state."

A **state** is broad political complex that organizes and wields power in a society. In the United States, the word "state" is used to describe the fifty political and geographic units that make up the country. For example, we talk about the states of California, Kansas, and Virginia. When social scientists use the term "state," however, they mean something different. Sociologists refer to the state to indicate a social institution that can operate at several levels within a country. In the United States, the state includes the Supreme Court, the president, the armed forces, the Internal Revenue Service, the Bureau of the Census, and Congress at the federal level, as well as governors, legislatures, and more-local bodies such as city councils, school systems, welfare offices, and local police departments. States can be defined as "organizations that extract resources through taxation and attempt to extend coercive control and political authority over particular territories and the people residing in them" (Skocpol and Amenta 1986, 131).

A state, then, is the social institution that makes laws and that uses force (when necessary) to protect itself and enforce its laws. Elected officials, the criminal justice system, and the military are all part of the state. Men and women have different roles and experiences in each of these arenas. Gender is illustrated by who is elected to office, how people are treated by the criminal justice system, and how individuals participate in military operations. This chapter explores each of these three areas—electoral politics, criminal justice system, and the military—to see how gender and politics interact.

ELECTORAL POLITICS

Elections around the world are deeply gendered in several ways. Most obviously, the electoral playing field is dominated by men. Candidates and most behind-the-scenes campaign strategists and consultants—pollsters, media experts, fund-raising advisors, and those who develop campaign messages—are also men. Furthermore, the network news reporters and anchors charged with telling the story of elections are often men. Gendered language permeates our political landscape as elections are described in analogies and metaphors drawn from the traditionally masculine domains of war and sports. Our expectations about the qualities, appearance, and behavior of candidates also are highly gendered. In the United States, for example, we want our leaders to be tough, dominant, and assertive, which are masculine stereotypes in American culture (Carroll and Fox 2005). This section explores the gendered character of **electoral politics** in the United States and around the world.

Voting Rights

The right to vote in a democratic nation is an essential aspect of political activity. The American Constitution withheld this right for a long time from most Americans. For at least a century after the American Revolution, only property-owning white men were allowed to vote. Gender was one of the key criteria for determining whether a person could exercise the right to suffrage. The long, bitter battle for **women's suffrage** lasted many decades, and although it sounds strange to us today, allowing women to vote was feared by many. One senator spoke against the amendment in the early twentieth century, claiming it would "convert all the new harmonious elements of society into a state of war, and make every home a hell on earth" (Flexner 1975, 151). In 1920, Congress finally passed the **Nineteenth Amendment**, giving (white) women in the United States the right to vote.

In 1893, New Zealand was the first nation to allow women to vote, and Australia (except indigenous women), Canada (except First Nations women), and several European nations passed women's suffrage laws before 1920. Many, however, such as France, Italy, and Japan, did not pass women's suffrage until the 1940s. Until 2011, Saudi Arabia remained the only nation where men could vote but women could not. Then, King Abdulla granted Saudi women the right to vote and run for municipal office. Women now make up 20 percent of the lower house (similar to the U.S. House of Representatives) in Saudi Arabia (MacFarquhar 2011). Saudi men were granted the vote in 2005. Before that, their parliament was appointed by the king (Stack 2011).

By the end of the twentieth century, women in the United States had begun to dominate in regard to numbers at the voting booth. Women now make up the majority (51.8 percent) of Americans eligible to vote. Women (63.5 percent) are also more likely to register to vote than are men (60.6 percent). Since 1980, women (61 percent in 2008) have been more likely than men (56 percent in 2008) to exercise their right by going to the ballot box. In 2008, 9.7 million more women voted than men in national elections in the United States (Center for American Women in Politics [CAWP] 2011).

Table 10-1 shows the voter turnout by gender and race ethnicity in the 2008 American presidential elections. The table indicates that black women were most likely to vote and that Asian American women were least likely. Among black, white, and Hispanic Americans, women were much more likely to vote than were men. Asian American men were slightly more likely to vote than Asian American women (Lopez and Taylor 2009).

Besides voting, how do women and men differ in their political activities? Since 1952, the American National Election Studies (ANES) has kept track of political behavior. They (Nagy and Rich 2001) found the following:

- Women are more likely to show up to vote.
- Women are about as likely as men to work for a candidate or party, attend a political meeting, or wear a button or display a sticker or sign.
- Men are still more likely than women to discuss politics, talk to others to try to convince them to support a candidate, and donate money. The differences are small, however, and the difference in donating money may be a result of who is

TABLE 10-1 Who Voted in the 2008 Presidential Election?

Race Ethnicity and Gender	Percentage of Eligible Voters who Voted in 2008
Black women	69.0
White women	68.0
White men	64.0
Black men	61.0
Hispanic women	52.0
Hispanic men	48.0
Asian American men	47.1
Asian American women	46.9

Source: Center for American Women and Politics (2010).

asked to donate to political campaigns. Men report donating money more often than do women. They also report being asked in person, by phone, and by mail more often to make a donation. Perhaps men are not more likely to contribute money to a candidate; they are just more likely to be given the opportunity to make a donation (Conway, Steuernagel, and Ahern 1997).

The Gender Gap in Voting

Women and men also differ in regard to whom they vote for. The **gender gap** refers to the difference between women and men in their choice of candidates and in their opinions on political issues. This term came into use during the 1980s when observers began to notice that women were more likely to vote for more-liberal candidates and referenda than were men (Bourque 2001).

The gap between women and men grew during the 1990s. Women's voting behavior remained fairly stable through the 1980s and 1990s, but men shifted their loyalties away from the Democrats and toward the Republicans during those decades (Seltzer, Newman, and Leighton 1997). By the 2000 election, the gap in voting between women and men was 11 percent. In the 2000 presidential election, men favored George W. Bush by 53 percent to 42 percent, and women favored Al Gore by 54 percent to 43 percent (Connelly 2000). In 2004 the gap narrowed, but women were still more likely to vote for John Kerry than for Bush. Race ethnicity also made an important difference. Fifty-five percent of white women and 62 percent of white men voted for Bush; but among nonwhite voters, only 24 percent of women and 30 percent of men voted for Bush. In 2008, a 7 percent gap remained between men and women voters, as 49 percent of men favored Barack Obama over John McCain, compared to 56 percent of women who favored Obama (CAWP 2008). And the gap expanded again in 2012 when 56 percent of women voted for Obama and 54 percent of men voted for Mitt Romney (J. Jones 2012).

The gender gap indicates differences in the way the majority of men and the majority of women vote, and sometimes the gap makes a difference in who gets into office. These differences are not just ideological, but relate to the different responsibilities and problems women and men have in their everyday lives. Opinion polls and surveys of voting choices show that, compared to men, women are:

- more likely to favor a more activist role for government;
- more supportive of programs to guarantee health care and basic social services;
- more supportive of restrictions on firearms;
- more supportive of same-sex marriage; and
- more likely to favor legal abortion without restrictions. (CAWP 2012)

The positions favored by women voters are more consistent with goals of the Democratic Party. The Republican Party has become identified with opposing those programs that benefit women more than men and that are favored by women voters, such as Medicaid, Social Security, parental leave, and nutritional programs for women and children. The Democratic Party more frequently endorses policies that women are more likely than men to approve of, such as gun control, environmental protection, and government support of health care, education, and job training (Rothman 2002).

The relationship between political party and gender runs both ways. Women are more likely to favor the Democratic Party, and the Democratic Party is more likely to favor women. In the 1990s, for example, Democrats nominated nearly twice as many women for seats in the House as Republicans did (Fox 2000). Republican voters, on the other hand, seem to be more hesitant to support women candidates. A poll in 2004 conducted by the Republican Party asked voters whether they would support a candidate who was a successful business person who had never run for office and whose top priority was reducing government spending and waste (positions traditionally favored by Republicans). Half were told the candidate was a woman, and half were told he was a man. Among Republican men, 57 percent said they would support the man, but only 43 percent said they would support the woman. Among Republican women, 53 percent of Republican women said they would support the man, and only 42 percent said they would support the woman. Democrats had the reverse reaction. Both women and men Democrats were more likely to say they would vote for a woman, given the same choices (Morin 2004).

Gender, however, does not exist in isolation and seems to interact with other factors such as knowledge, parenthood, and race ethnicity. When men and women have little knowledge of political issues, their opinions are similar. As political knowledge increases, the gap widens. Better-informed men tend to become more conservative, whereas better-informed women tend to become more liberal in their political opinions (Carpini and Keeter 2000). The gender gap is also affected by labor force participation. Employed women, for example, overwhelmingly preferred Gore (58 percent) to Bush (39 percent) in the 2000 elections (CAWP 2000).

Parenting also intersects with gender to create differences in political behavior. Women, as compared to men, are more likely to alter their political ideas as a result of becoming parents, but both mothers and fathers are affected by their parenthood. The effects, however, are the opposite for men and women. Raising children has liberalizing effects on the political opinions of women while men who are parents become more conservative (Elder and Greene 2012). Mothers, for example, are more likely to have a liberal opinion of the role of government in providing health care, jobs, and a good standard of living, and they were significantly less likely to support the Iraq war. Fathers, compared to other groups, are significantly less likely to support gay marriage rights.

Race ethnicity is another factor that alters the gender gap. As a group, Latinas, like other women, are likely to identify with the Democratic Party, but Latinas with different national origins have a wide range of opinions on party affiliation. Puerto Rican American women are strongly Democratic, but Cuban Americans are likely to be Republicans. African American women are overwhelmingly Democratic, but so are African American men (Rothman 2002).

The gender gap is important, but it is not the only divide in voting behavior; and, in fact, it is not always the widest one. In 1994 there was a gap of 12 percent between married and single voters, 19 percent between rich and poor voters, 29 percent between urban and rural voters, and 50 percent between black and white voters (Seltzer et al. 1997). These kinds of differences persist (CAWP 2006).

Women Elected Officials

The largest difference between women and men in electoral politics is the proportion of women who are elected by voters and appointed to office by elected officials. The exercise of political leadership by being elected or appointed to office is also probably the most critical political role (Marger 2002). Voting as an individual citizen may be important, but creating policy and voting within elected bodies such as the Senate are vastly more significant.

The numbers of women in public office have slowly increased in the United States since the first woman, Jeanette Rankin, was elected to Congress from the state of Montana in 1916. By the beginning of the twenty-first century, 11,500 men had been elected to the House, but fewer than two hundred women had taken a seat there (CAWP 1998). Only forty-four women have served in the Senate throughout its long history. In 2013, Congress had the greatest proportion of women in history: twenty women senators (20 percent) and seventy-eight (18 percent) women representatives (CAWP 2014a). A full 215 years after Congress was established, Nancy Pelosi was the first woman elected Speaker of the House, the highest rank of a woman in Congress ever achieved. Because the Speaker of the House is second in line to the presidency behind the vice president, Pelosi has also come closest to the presidency of any woman in American history.

The start of the twenty-first century was also record setting for women at the state level. Women were elected governors in five states in 2012 (CAWP 2014b), and women held 22 percent of the 315 other state executive positions in jobs such as lieutenant governor, attorney general, and secretary of state (CAWP 2014c). State legislatures and local governments made more room for women than Congress. By 2013, 24 percent of state legislators were women, and 17 percent of the mayors of cities larger than 30,000 were women (CAWP 2014d). Table 10-2 shows the ten states with the highest percentages of women in their legislatures. Colorado leads the nation, with women serving in 42 percent of their legislative seats.

At the executive level of the federal government in the United States, women have not fared as well. No woman has served as president or vice president, and only ten presidents

TABLE 10-2 Ten States in the United States with the Highest Percentages of Women State Legislators, 2013

State	% of State Legislators Who Are Women
Colorado	42
Vermont	41
Arizona	36
Minnesota	34
New Hampshire	33
Illinois	32
Hawaii	31
Washington	31
Maryland	30
Connecticut	29
Average for all of the United States	24

Source: Center for American Women and Politics (2013).

have appointed a total of forty-five women to their cabinets since George Washington took office. It was 1997 before the first woman, Madeleine Albright, occupied the position of secretary of state, the top seat in foreign policy (Borelli 2000). The United Nations reports that the United States ranks fifty-fifth in 165 nations in political empowerment of women, placing it among countries such as Pakistan (52) and Algeria (57) (Hausmann, Tyson and Zahidi 2012).

Around the world, progress for women has been uneven, although the 1990s seemed to indicate a breakthrough at least in some places. The Scandinavian nations of Iceland, Finland, Norway, and Sweden lead the world in their political empowerment of women (Hausmann, Tyson, and Zahidi 2012). Table 10-3 shows the proportion of women in some national legislatures or parliaments. The table presents information on the top ten nations in regard to the percentage of seats held by women . In 2013, women accounted for 17 percent of the members of parliaments globally. Moreover, of 185 countries with national parliaments, nearly all have at least one woman in parliament. Four nations still have no women in their national legislatures: Micronesia (Federated States of); Palau; Vanuatu; and Qatar. These achievements are also tempered, to some degree, by the fact that only thirty-five countries have so far managed to reach the 30 percent threshold of women in national parliaments, a figure widely considered to signify the point at which women can make a meaningful impact on the work of the parliament.

Rwanda currently has the largest proportion of women in parliament, with 56 percent of the seats. Part of this is probably because the genocide in Rwanda that killed at least eight

TABLE 10-3 Proportion of Women in National Legislatures, 2013

% of Women in National Legislature in Nations with the Largest Proportion of Women in their National Legislature		% of Women in Parliament or National Legislature in Ten Most Populous Nations	
Country	*% of National Legislators Who Are Women*	*Country (in Order of Population Size)*	*% of National Legislators Who Are Women*
Rwanda	56	China	23
Andorra	50	India	11
Cuba	49	United States	18
Sweden	45	Indonesia	19
Seychelles	44	Brazil	9
Senegal	43	Pakistan	20
Finland	43	Bangladesh	20
South Africa	42	Russia	14
Nicaragua	40	Nigeria	7
Iceland	40	Japan	8

Source: Inter-Parliamentary Union (2013). (To see all the countries, look at: http://www.ipu.org/wmn-e/classif .htm.)

hundred thousand people in 1994 left the sex ratio at seven to three in favor of women. Rwanda, however, has also implemented important affirmative action policies that have resulted in many women entering public life as political leaders at the national and local levels of government. For example,

- Thirty percent of decision-making-related positions were assigned to women.
- Local funds and microcredits were provided for production projects led by women.
- In 2003, Article 187 of the new Rwandan Constitution formalized equity promotion structures such as the National Council of Women.
- A **Gender Issues Monitoring Office** was created to facilitate the participation of women in public life and to ensure that development initiatives are egalitarian in generating benefits for both women and men. (Social Watch 2008)

After Rwanda, Andorra, Cuba, Sweden, Seychelles, and Senegal all have women in more than 43 percent of their parliamentary seats. In some places, however, women have lost ground. In eastern Europe, after the fall of communism, women's participation in parliament dropped from 22 percent in 1987 to 6.5 percent in 1993 (United Nations, Department of Public Information 1995). In the Netherlands in the 1990s, the right-wing Protestant party SGP banned women altogether from membership because they believe that the Bible forbids women to be politically active (Reilly 2003). The Netherlands, nevertheless, has a high proportion (39 percent) of women in its parliament.

As a way of seeing what the gender gap in government looks like for the majority of people in the world, Table 10-3 lists the most populous nations in the world in order of their size and shows the proportion of women in their national legislatures. None of them has reached the magic 30 percent mark, with China (23 percent) and Pakistan and Bangladesh (20 percent) coming closest; and five of the ten countries falling short of the international average of 17 percent. Box 10-1 discusses some of the efforts as well as further challenges that persist for people seeking gender equity in politics in the most populous nation, China.

WHAT DIFFERENCE DOES IT MAKE? Women appear to still be outsiders in electoral politics, at least as elected officials. Would it make any difference if women became a larger proportion of political leaders? Four benefits have been attributed to increasing the numbers of women elected officials:

- Increased democratic justice and equity
- More possibility of addressing the interests of women
- Better use of all available resources (Henig and Henig 2001)
- More money for your district

Most people would agree that seeing women in a proportionate number of positions is necessary to the ideals of a democracy. Even if women in public office do not behave in ways that are different from men, their presence is necessary to maintain legitimacy and public confidence in institutions. A commitment to democracy would seem to demand that since

GENDER IN EVERYDAY LIFE   BOX 10-1
NEARLY A BILLION VILLAGERS

Twenty percent of the people on earth live in China, and 49 percent of those 1.4 billion Chinese live in rural villages (Rong and Lifie 2012). In the 1980s, the Chinese began to implement a system of self-government in the hundreds of thousands of villages in the rural areas, shifting power to elected members of Village Committees. This change has been hailed as an important success that has made governance more democratic, improved economic and social development, and advanced women's political status. By 2000, 16 percent of committee members were women, and that proportion rose to 22 percent by 2008. While these accomplishments are significant, the statistics hide important underlying issues. For example, 19 percent of the Village Committees still have no women, and very few have more than one woman. Furthermore, women who are elected to Village Committees are often relegated to narrow roles by being given responsibility for primarily women's issues, especially family planning.

Zhengxu Wang and Weina Dai (2013) conducted research in rural China to examine the current experience of women and men in local governance. They found that both women (97 percent) and men (99 percent) had very high participation rates in the elections for village committees. Regarding non-electoral issues, however, they found less participation and significant gender gaps: 44 percent of women and 76 percent of men said that they had ever participated in the deliberations in a villagers' assembly; 19 percent of women and 41 percent of men had brought suggestions to the Villagers' Committee; 9 percent of women and 22 percent of men had brought governance-related issues to the attention of relevant government offices; and 12 percent of the women and 78 percent of the men said they knew the chairperson of the Villagers' Committee well (Wang and Dai 2013, p. 100).

Wang and Dai (2013) identify a number of issues they believe are the underlying causes for these gender gaps in participation. First, they note that in rural areas in China the education level of women and men is quite different. Twenty-two percent of men and 4 percent of women have completed high school. Sixty-six percent of men and 31 percent of women have only completed junior high school, and 65 percent of women and 12 percent of men only completed primary school. Almost none of the Villagers had attended college. While the education level is low for everyone, it is especially low for women. Education is a critical factor in people's ability to participate in political activities.

Marriage traditions are also important. Women are expected to move to the village of their husbands rather than husbands settling in their wife's village. This means that women are less familiar with the local affairs of their new residence and are unattached to the social networks that might generate participation in civic affairs.

Gender stereotypes may also play a role as the majority (73 percent) of villagers claim that "participating in politics is men's business" and only 27 percent agree that "male and female villagers should play equal roles in politics" (Wang and Dai 2013, 108). Only about half (52 percent) of the women consider themselves as playing a significant role in village affairs compared to nearly all of the men (94 percent).

women are at least half the population, they should constitute a similar proportion of elected officials (Henig and Henig 2001).

A second reason to bring more women into office comes from those who believe that women will behave differently from men in office. They assert that women have at least some different interests from men and that those interests are not as likely to be addressed if decision-making institutions are dominated by men (Henig and Henig 2001). If women are more concerned about issues such as health care, sexual harassment, and family leave, then as their numbers increase we would expect to see these problems and policies to address them given wider coverage by governmental bodies (Kahn and Gordon 1997).

Research shows that women, compared to men, are more likely to campaign on issues rather than on personal traits such as their own integrity, honesty, and intelligence. Women are also more likely than men to campaign on "feminine" issues such as education, health care, and child care. These gender contrasts are true for both Republican and Democratic candidates in the United States. Women candidates are also more liberal within each of the parties, compared to their men counterparts. These differences suggest that more women in elected positions will change the agendas and the debates (Kahn and Gordon 1997), but it is difficult to say how far those differences would go. Research on decisions by women judges, for example, shows that gender does not seem to make much difference. Women judges do not make more feminist decisions in cases, nor are they more liberal (Mezey 2000).

Using all available talent is the third argument given for promoting policies that increase women's participation in elected positions. Women constitute half the population and therefore half the skills and ideas necessary to address social issues. When women are absent, their talents are wasted (Henig and Henig 2001). As we saw in chapter 5, women are increasingly entering institutions of higher education and are obtaining advanced training and degrees. Their ability to use the skills they develop is hindered by their inability to take a leadership role in the government. Furthermore, the opportunity for the community to benefit from their expertise is lost if they are not in representative positions of power.

Finally, electing women to Congress may increase benefits to the district they represent. Researchers at Stanford followed the careers of Congress members from 1984 to 2004 and found that congresswomen secured roughly 9 percent more spending from federal discretionary programs than did congressmen. This amounts to a premium of about $49 million per year for districts that send a woman to Capitol Hill. In addition, they found that congresswomen also sponsored more bills, cosigned more bills, and had larger numbers of cosigners on their bills. In other words, they worked more effectively and collaboratively with their fellow Congress members (Anzia and Berry 2009).

WHY SO FEW WOMEN? There appear to be many good reasons to build an electoral system that is gender equal. Why do women lag behind men in political representation? Scholars have come up with several answers to this question. In the United States, perhaps the most important reason so few women have been elected to office is because they do not often run. The proportion of women holding office at every level of the government is similar to the percentage that entered the race (Seltzer et al. 1997).

The gender gap in regard to running for office may be particularly difficult to address because it appears to be rooted in ideas and expectations already expressed in early adolescence about what it means to be a citizen of a democracy. Researchers in Europe asked more than 72,000 fourteen-year-olds from twenty-two countries about what kinds of political activities they planned to be engaged in when they became adults. The girls were a little more likely than the boys to say they intended to vote. The boys were much more likely to say they intended to run for office (Hooghe and Dassonneville 2013).

When women do decide to run, incumbency is a barrier for women. Incumbents are the people who currently are in office; they have an advantage in an election because they are a known quantity. They have name recognition, and their time in office gives them media coverage. In addition, incumbents often establish themselves as people who can do the job. Incumbents are reelected 95 percent of the time. The problem of running against incumbents is an issue for both women and men who are not currently in office. Because women as a group, however, have been in the political arena for less time, they must either wait for the person who is in office to retire, resign, or die, or they must run elections challenging incumbents.

A third factor that prevents women from gaining office is **gender ideologies**. Some people still believe that women belong at home, not in the House and Senate. Even when these people do think it is acceptable for women to run for office, they associate the characteristics of good leadership with masculine stereotypes. You should recall from chapters 1 and 2 that a major component of dominant ideas about masculinity identifies men with public activities and conflates masculinity with characteristics such as leadership. Man is the default leader. Polls show, for example, that 90 percent of the American public say they would support a woman for president (Seltzer et al. 1997). When they are asked what a good president is like, however, they answer that a good president is one who has the conventional traits of masculinity: strength, self-confidence, determination, and decisiveness. Stereotyped feminine traits such as warmth, gentleness, and compassion are more likely to be associated with lower-level nonexecutive governmental positions, such as judges (Rothman 2002).

Women who have succeeded in holding a high office are often perceived as exceptional women who "act like men" (Peterson and Runyan 1999; Marger 2002). When women "act like men," however, they often face criticism for being unfeminine and unlikable. Women leaders in business and politics are perceived as competent or likable, but rarely both. Furthermore, being unlikable implies fewer social skills and less ability to influence others (i.e., not a good leader). Kim Campbell, who served as prime minister in Canada, explained her dilemma:

> I don't have a traditional female way of speaking. I don't end my sentences with a question mark. I'm quite assertive. If I didn't speak the way I do, I wouldn't have been seen as a leader. But my way of speaking may have grated on people who were not used to hearing it from a woman. It was the right way for a leader to speak, but it wasn't the right way for a woman to speak. It goes against type. (Eagly and Carli 2007).

This kind of gender bias in assessing the leadership skills of women varies cross-culturally. The characteristics of a good leader are defined differently in different nations, but in all cases women come up short, no matter what the criteria. For example, people in the United States and the United Kingdom say that inspiring others is the most important leadership quality. Nordic nations, in contrast, assert that the ability to delegate authority is most significant. In the United States and the United Kingdom, men are perceived as best able to inspire others, whereas people in Nordic nations believe that the men are best at delegating tasks (Belkin 2007).

A fourth factor holding women back from elected office is the link between having a paid job and participating in electoral politics. Women are still more likely than are men to be outside the paid labor force. Being employed in general seems to affect political participation. Women and men who are not in the paid labor force are less likely to participate in electoral politics. Among people who are employed, 42 percent of women and 55 percent of men said they had participated in a campaign. Among people who are not in the paid labor force, 32 percent of women and 45 percent of men say they have been involved in a campaign (Conway et al. 1997).

Among women and men who are in the paid labor force, only some kinds of jobs "track" them into political office. Most political candidates in the United States are drawn from a narrow group of elite occupations. In 2001, 26 percent of the members of Congress were lawyers, 23 percent were executives from business and banking, 19 percent were drawn from public service occupations, and 13.5 percent were educators (Hirschfield 2001). Women are less likely to be in the first two kinds of positions, and as we saw in the chapters on work and education, women in education or public service have less-prestigious positions within those fields.

Women's success in running for office or obtaining a political appointment in the judicial system shows that certain jobs are more likely to track people into political office. It also shows that getting into the right jobs demands getting onto the right educational path. Women have made significant inroads in winning judgeships. Although only four women have ever served on the Supreme Court, three of them currently do. Fifty-two of the 163 active judges currently sitting on the thirteen federal courts of appeal are women (about 32 percent), and about 30 percent of active United States district (or trial) court judges are women (National Women's Law Center 2013). The most important factor in the increase of women in judgeships is access to legal education. The numbers of women in law school increased by ten times since the 1970s (Conway et al. 1997). By the end of the twentieth century, 43 percent of law school students were women (Conway, Ahern, and Steuernagel 1999). Earning a law degree sets people on the necessary pathway to becoming a judge, and women are increasingly getting on the right track.

A fifth factor that may inhibit women's political activity is family obligations and lack of time. Working on a political campaign, running for office, and even voting take time. Voter turnout among men is not affected by the number of children a man has. For women, those numbers are directly related, as 80 percent of women with no children go to the polls, whereas only 57 percent of those women with four or more children say that they vote (Conway et al. 1997). Perhaps these same kinds of time constraints also affect women's participation in running for office. Furthermore, even if these time constraints are not real barriers to women's being effective political leaders, voters may believe that family obligations will interfere with women's work if they are elected to office.

A final factor that may hold some women back from winning office is treatment by the media. In Senate races, women candidates receive less coverage (Kahn 1993). In addition, when journalists do cover women candidates, they often focus on the gender of women candidates and question the ability of a woman candidate to win (Rothman 2002). Some journalists also treat women candidates differently. One woman described her experience with the press while running for office: "[The media covering the race] concentrate[d] on stupid, little things such as clothes, hair, etc., which never comes up with a man. They also use loaded adjectives to describe us, such as feisty, perky, small and lively" (Poole 1993, quoted in Fox 2000, 244).

The differential treatment by the media may be subtle, but because of the enormous amount of coverage of elections, we are exposed to the discrimination over and over, thousands of times. In the 2008 primaries for example, Hillary Clinton and Barack Obama were frontrunners in the Democratic party. Research on the treatment of Clinton with Obama showed that the media referred to Clinton four times more often by her first name while referring to Obama by his last name or by his title, Senator. Calling Clinton by her first name is a way of infantilizing her and detracting from her power and the validity of her run for leadership (Uscinski and Goren 2011).

GENDER AND CAMPAIGNS. Whether a person runs for office and wins an election is affected by gender. Men are more likely to run for office, and they more often win. Men are also more likely to be running against another man in political campaigns (Fox 1997). Does gender also affect the process of elections? What happens when a woman enters the race against a man? Men change their campaign strategy in two ways. First, they are more hesitant to engage in negative campaigning. Fearing that the public might think them ungentlemanly, men who campaign against women sometimes avoid aggressive confrontations. One man candidate told a researcher:

> I don't think it is proper to attack a woman. I was completely constrained in how I went about campaigning. It was a constant struggle to show the proper politeness toward my opponent. Women cannot handle criticism or high stress so I had to watch what I said closely so that I would not appear to be causing my opponent any grief. (Fox 2000, 248)

The second way in which running against a woman changes men candidates is that they go to greater lengths to show they are in touch with women's issues. The men who were running for office in Richard Fox's (2000) research believed that women candidates have an edge with women voters, and therefore the men believed that they must reach out more to the women voters. A campaign aide for a man running for office explained, "The congressman decided that this year we would have a separate group of women supporters. This way, if his woman opponent ran around claiming she was the candidate for women, we could combat this by demonstrating our support from women" (Fox 2000, 251).

Three Models for Reform

Three models have been proposed for evening up the representation of women and men in elected political bodies: meritocratic, affirmative action, and radical (Norris and Lovenduski 1995). The **meritocratic model** sees women as deficient and seeks to remedy those shortcomings. The **affirmative action model** emphasizes the need for policies that can give women "a leg up" to overcome historical discrimination. The **radical model** asserts that the system may need major overhauling rather than just better integration of women into the existing model of politics.

MERITOCRATIC REMEDIES. The meritocratic model assumes that those who merit a reward will gain it. In the case of election results, someone from this standpoint would argue that women need to be more competitive to successfully run for office. They seek ways to narrow the gap by encouraging and training women to run for and fill more political offices, and especially by providing funds for their campaigns. **EMILY's list** is a good example of this approach. EMILY stands for Early Money Is Like Yeast (www.emilyslist.org). Founded in the United States in 1985 by Ellen Malcolm, EMILY is a fund-raising and political training organization that has helped fund successful campaigns for fifty-three members of Congress, four governors, and eleven senators (Bourque 2001).

The EMILY's list model was replicated in Japan, where a network of housewives' cooperatives initiated a movement to bring more women into political office. Their cause was taken up by **WINWIN**, the Japanese version of EMILY's list, which raised money for women candidates in Japan who supported issues such as child care, health care, and environmental protection. Three-quarters of the candidates they supported won, and Japanese women prevailed in more than a thousand elections in 1999, giving them 10 percent of the total races (Freedman 2002). Since the 1990s, WINWIN and other similar organizations such as Shinano have succeeded in increasing women's elected representation by as much as tenfold in some of the areas (Funabashi 2003).

AFFIRMATIVE ACTION REMEDIES. The second model, affirmative action, advocates setting target numbers and quotas for women in political office. This strategy is widespread, and it has been especially successful in Europe. Half of the nations in Latin America (eleven) also have quotas for women's candidates, and about sixty countries throughout the world have now adopted quota laws (Ross 2007).

The structure of party politics has been identified as the key reason that women do not run for office. To win an election, a candidate needs the support of a political party. If the party does not develop an affirmative action policy, women and other underrepresented people are not likely to win elections. In the 1970s, European women tried to gain power outside of political parties by forming their own organizations or caucuses within political parties. In the 1980s, they began to move inside the parties when they decided that their outsider status was not getting them into positions of power. Their efforts to gain a foothold in the parties, however, were hampered by those who did not want them to take on leadership positions and by the women's lack of experience in the organizations.

Advocates of gender equity developed a **quota system** as the solution. Party activists sought to break into the structures by demanding that women fill a minimum number of places on committees within the party so that the number of women in the party leadership would match the number of women in the party. Norway led the way here when their Socialist Party set a quota declaring that 40 percent of their candidates were to be women. Left parties in Denmark, the Netherlands, Spain, and France have now established woman quotas. The Green Party, active across Europe, has the highest quota (50 percent), and Green Party delegations in Germany, the Netherlands, and Sweden now have a majority of women (Henig and Henig 2001).

Affirmative action programs have not remained only at the party level, however. In France, affirmative action became the law of the land in 2000. Because the government funds elections in France, the National Assembly was able to pass a law called *parité* (parity) reducing funds to parties that fail to field equal numbers of women and men candidates. One year after the law was passed, women won 47.5 percent of municipal elections, twice the number they had won in previous years. In India, the numbers are even more astounding.

Since the passage in 1993 of a constitutional amendment reserving one-third of all village council seats for women and those from the lowest castes, one million women took office on village councils or as village heads. Their efforts have resulted in better water, sewer, and transportation systems and more girls in school (Freedman 2002).

The story about the Zapatero election in Spain at the beginning of the chapter was an example of the affirmative action approach. Zapatero declared during his campaign that he would appoint equal numbers of women and men, and when he was elected he kept his promise, appointing eight women and eight men to his cabinet. His approach is common in Europe, but nations all over the world have also created affirmative action programs. In 2000 at the **Beijing + 5 Summit**, a **50/50 program** was championed, and sixty nations in the world now have some kind of gender equity quota system (Gouws 2004). The Sudan, United Republic of Tanzania, Jordan, Antigua, Argentina, South Africa, and Bangladesh provide examples from across the globe of nations that have created quotas for women in office (Azzi 2007).

Some nations, such as Hungary, however, have taken the opposite tack. After employing affirmative action for forty years, Hungarians abolished the practice in the 1990s as part of their transition from a socialist to a capitalist system. The number of women occupying seats in government plummeted from 30 percent to 7 percent (Inter-Parliamentary Union 1997). Because Hungary so quickly went back to low proportions of women in elected office after affirmative action ended, its experience suggests that affirmative action alone will not solve the problem in the long run. Some scholars have suggested more radical reforms.

RADICAL REMEDIES. The third model for improving the representation of women in government is a radical one (Lister 1997). This model calls for restructuring political institutions in a number of ways (Norris and Lovenduski 1995). Those who advocate radical change point to factors in the social organization of elections and representative government that need change. For example, many people have suggested that American elections with only two parties, an electoral college, **gerrymandered districts**, and a winner-take-all approach to voting may lock many people out of true political representation. These factors may create especially difficult barriers for women and people in racial ethnic groups who have only relatively recently been allowed to participate.

One strategy is to increase the numbers of representatives. When larger numbers of seats are available for candidates, parties may feel that they can "risk" supporting women for those slots. Changing legislative bodies by increasing the number of people in the group can improve the chances for women and other underrepresented people to win a seat.

Another structural change that might open up women's chances is to limit terms, which would give more nonincumbents an opportunity to win elections. Because incumbents are more likely to win and men have dominated legislative bodies, men are more likely to be incumbents. Limiting the number of terms a member of Congress could stay in office would allow more new people, many of whom would be women, to run for and win seats.

Increasing the number of political parties is another way to bring a broader range of voices into government. In the two-party system of the United States, for example, women face a huge challenge in being accepted and supported in their bid for seats. If there were more parties, some of which would be newer and less established, with power less entrenched in the hands of those who have traditionally been in power, perhaps women could rise more quickly. In addition, proportional representation, which means that voters choose among many parties and representatives match the proportion of votes allotted, would also open up the opportunities for more diverse legislative bodies.

The radical model also supports making political institutions more woman friendly by initiating practices such as providing day care and keeping family-friendly hours. For example, as part of their quest for gender equity, when the new South African government took power in 1994, one of its first actions was to create a day care center for the children of parents working in parliament.

Finally, the radical model asserts that the culture of political bodies needs to be changed from confrontational, competitive arenas to ones that are more cooperative and compassionate (K. Jones 1993). Remember that one of the barriers to women becoming president in the United States is the kind of characteristics voters believe are necessary for being a good president. Perhaps they believe that a good president is one who is strong, self-confident, determined, and decisive because the context in which an American president leads demands these traits.

If we organized the elected branches of the government in a way that necessitated cooperation and compassion, feminine skills would be perceived as the essential qualities of a good leader. Rather than demanding leaders to be skilled at seeing other Congress members as adversaries and people to be controlled and sanctioned, we could create structures that require that they be team-builders and communicators encouraging everyone to share power and decision making (Eagly and Carli 2007). For example, the two-party system in the United States creates a structure in which there are automatically two sides (no more, no less) to every question and in which these two sides are polar opposites. A parliamentary system, in contrast, allows for a range of positions and demands that people with different interests negotiate coalitions.

POLITICAL INSTITUTIONS: THE COURTS AND PRISONS

Who are criminals? The second major political institution within the state that we explore here is the **criminal justice system**, especially the courts and prisons. Although men constitute about 50 percent of the population in the United States, they make up 74 percent of those who are arrested. Between 1960 and 2000, the proportion of people arrested for serious crimes who are women rose from 10 percent to 26 percent (Small 2000). Between 2002 and 2011, the crime rate for men dropped by 11 percent while the rate for women rose almost 6 percent (FBI 2011). These changes are significant, but crime (at least reported crime) is still generally a man's activity. Prostitution is the only crime for which significantly more women (70 percent of those arrested) than men are arrested. Arrest rates for embezzlement are slightly higher for women compared to men.

As we read in chapter 8, men are also more likely than women to serve time, at least at the state and federal levels. They make up about 93 percent of the prison population, and the conditions of prison life are more difficult in some ways for men. In the past, women prisoners more often had rooms (that they could decorate) rather than cells, could sometimes wear their own clothes, and were less likely to be surrounded by barbed wire or walls. These "homey" conditions, however, were altered in the past decade as sentencing changes escalated numbers. Women are now packed six to a cell, eat army-ration meals, and rarely see the sun (Young and Riviere 2006).

Women prisoners face other difficulties, as well. Because there are few women's prisons, women may be incarcerated a long way from their homes, making family visits more difficult. Women's prisons also have fewer training or recreational facilities, libraries, or medical facilities (Conway et al. 1999). Women prisoners spend about seventeen hours a day in their cells and are allowed outside for one hour a day, whereas men are allowed outside for an hour and a half.

Women also have special health needs that are not addressed in prison. Congress has banned the use of federal funds for abortions for women in prison. If a woman wishes to have an abortion and she can pay for it, she must convince prison officials to take her to a clinic. If she continues with a pregnancy, she is unlikely to receive prenatal care, her prison diet will not meet minimum standards for pregnant women (only 11 percent of the states require appropriate nutritional standards for pregnant prisoners), and she may be forced to go through labor and delivery while shackled (Young and Riviere 2006).

About one-fourth of women entering prison are pregnant or have recently given birth. If they deliver while in prison, they are likely to be shackled—their hands and ankles bound together with locked chains—while giving birth, a violation of responsible medical practice and a form of torture (Ehrlich and Paltrow 2006). Only seven states ban shackles on women prisoners during childbirth; fourteen other states restrict the use of restraints but do not ban them (BBC News 2010). Psychological pain is also inflicted on these women when their babies are taken from them almost immediately after birth or at the time the mother is discharged from the hospital, a practice in forty states. One woman who endured this practice described how she gave birth while she was an inmate of Cook County Jail in Chicago:

> The doctor came and said that "yes, this baby is coming right now," and started to prepare the bed for delivery. Because I was shackled to the bed, they couldn't remove the lower part of the bed for the delivery, and they couldn't put my feet in the stirrups. My feet were still shackled together, and I couldn't get my legs apart. The doctor called for the officer, but the officer had gone down the hall. No one else could unlock the shackles, and my baby was coming but I couldn't open my legs. . . . Finally the officer came and unlocked the shackles from my ankles. My baby was born then. I stayed in the delivery room with my baby for a little while, but then the officer put the leg shackles and handcuffs back on me and I was taken out of the delivery room. (Rebecca Project for Human Rights 2007)

Even if women do not deliver their babies in prison, they face problems finding care for the children. Somewhere between 65 percent and 80 percent of women behind bars are mothers, and most of these have minor children. Most fathers who are in prison (90 percent) report that their children are being cared for by the child's mother. Women in prison do not seem to have this support. Maternal grandmothers are most likely to care for the children, but many children whose mothers are in prison are cared for by older siblings, other relatives, neighbors, church members, and foster care (Young and Riviere 2006).

Sexual violence is another issue incarcerated women face. Amnesty International reports that sexual violence against women prisoners in the United States is widespread. Men show up much more often in Amnesty's reports of torture and abuse of prisoners in the United States, but women are more likely to be raped and to be victims of other forms of sexual abuse at the hands of the male staff (Crossett 1998; Davis 2003).

Young People in the Criminal Justice System

The rates of arrest among juveniles vary by gender. Like adults, boys (70 percent of arrests of people under 18 in 2009) are arrested much more often than girls. Arrests of girls, however, have increased dramatically in recent years, rising 74 percent for white girls during the 1990s and 106 percent for black girls (Gullo 2001).

The reasons for arrest are also different for boys and girls in regard to status offenses, which are activities such as being out after curfew, running away, or drinking alcohol. These activities are considered crimes only when young people participate in them; they are not considered crimes for adults (Belknap 2001). Of children arrested for running away, 55 percent are girls, while boys are the majority (69 percent) of those arrested for curfew violations (U.S. Bureau of the Census 2012).

Boys and girls who are arrested for running away are an indication of the injustice in the system for abused youngsters. Girls and boys who are sexually abused often run away from home as a survival response. This injustice is especially important for girls because sexual abuse is more common among girls. Ironically, girls who run away are more harshly treated by the criminal justice system than are boys. Girls are more likely to be arrested and to be detained (Belknap 2001).

Like many other examples of crime and punishment, young men join gangs more than young women do. But young women are increasingly showing up around gangs and forming their own gangs. The experience of women compared to men is different in gangs and is affected by gender (Valdez 2007). Jody Miller (2001) talked to gang girls in Columbus, Ohio, and St. Louis, Missouri, and found that gender appeared in gang life in three ways. First, sexual assault and other kinds of abuse of girls, especially by people close to them, was a common experience among girls in gangs. Fifty-two percent of young women in gangs have been sexually assaulted. However, girls in gangs claim that this is less of a problem than assault when they are not in a gang. Even though girls are victims of violence when they participate in gangs, they say the violence within a gang is more tolerable and manageable and therefore worth the risk.

Second, gender allows women to restrict their participation in some highly dangerous gang activity, for example, using guns. This protection, however, also works to relegate the women to inferior status within gangs because taking on the most dangerous activities provides the member with status and power. The hierarchy of high status and low status is also used as a basis for violence against subordinate members. In addition, girls do use weapons, although they tend to avoid guns. One young woman explained why she used her fists and knives but no guns: "We ladies, we not dudes for real. We don't be rowdy, all we do is fight. A dude, he quick to go get a gun or something, a girl she quick to pull out a knife" (J. Miller 2001, 140).

Third, gender makes women play particular roles within gangs. The perception that women are less suspected of criminal activity makes them useful for disguising the criminal activities of the men. One young woman in a gang explained:

> Like when we in a car, if a girl and a dude in a car, the police tend not to trip off of it. When they look to see if a car been stolen, police just don't trip off of it. But if they see three or four n****** in that car, the police stop you automatically, boom. . . . When my brother was gonna be locked up, the police was looking at my

cousin Janeeta, she [was in the car with him]. She got a nice little body and face. He let my brother go. . . . He was trying to make on her, you know what I'm saying. Little ways that we got to get them out of stuff sometimes, we can get them out of stuff that dudes couldn't do, you know what I'm saying. So they need us girls. They need us. (J. Miller 2001, 157–58)

Abelardo Valdez (2007) argues that Mexican American girls in gangs have created a "shift in gender" in the Latino communities where they participate. The girls who are in gangs, as well as those who are loosely affiliated with gangs through family, friends, and boyfriends, reject the traditional image of the Latina woman as homemaker and wife. They no longer expect to be supported by men, and so they establish themselves as more autonomous in their personal relationships. But this exchange, which Valdez (2007) calls "**paradoxical autonomy**," is not without difficulties. These girls and women may escape control by individual men, but they continue to face economic challenges as individuals more free to make their own decisions about men and sex but also more alone in providing for themselves in poor communities with few economic opportunities.

The War on Drugs

Although drug use began to decline in the early 1980s, in the late 1980s the U.S. government expanded its efforts to stop drug abuse by increasing arrests and incarceration of drug offenders. The new law-and-order policies of the "**war on drugs**" included mandatory sentencing, longer sentences, "**three strikes and you're out**" legislation, and "**truth in sentencing**," which requires that offenders serve a substantial portion (usually 85 percent for violent crimes) of their sentence. In 2001 the U.S. Patriot Act further stepped up measures to investigate, detain, and arrest (Young and Riviere 2006).

Much of this "get tough on crime" activity, and especially the war on drugs, was directed toward African Americans, although rates of drug use among whites and African Americans are similar. Research on drug use, not arrests for drug use, shows that rates are similar for different racial ethic groups, although the type of illegal drug used varies. In addition to racial ethnic discrimination by police, several other law enforcement techniques result in higher arrest rates among African Americans: the priority placed on outdoor drug venues, the geographic concentration of police resources in racially heterogeneous areas, and especially law enforcement's focus on crack offenders (Beckett, Nyrop, and Pfingst 2006). African Americans are more likely to use crack cocaine, whereas wealthy whites use powdered cocaine. Until 2007, crack had a mandatory sentence of five years for possession or trafficking. Possession of powdered cocaine carried no mandatory sentence. In addition, triggering the mandatory minimum penalty for trafficking required a hundred times more powdered cocaine than crack cocaine (the so-called **100-to-1 quantity ratio**) (Sabet 2005).

In 2010, the **Fair Sentencing Act** eliminated the five-year mandatory minimum sentence for simple possession of crack cocaine and reduced the disparity between the amount of crack cocaine and powder cocaine needed to trigger certain United States federal criminal penalties from a 100:1 weight ratio to an 18:1 weight ratio (*Washington Post* 2010). The Act is an important step in reducing the numbers of people incarcerated, especially African Americans and women, but the numbers of prisoners in the United States and the disparities in sentencing are still remarkable.

The African American population constitutes about 13 percent of the total population in the United States, but black women make up a little more than half (51 percent) of the women's prison population, and black men make up half of the men's prison population (50 percent) (Bush-Baskette 1998). The racial ethnic gap in drug arrests increased dramatically for black people during the war on drugs. In 1976, 22 percent of those arrested for drugs were black. In 1990, 41 percent of those arrested were black. This increase was even more significant for black women than for black men (Bush-Baskette 1998).

The war on drugs has also been a war on women. Before the Fair Sentencing Act, arrests and imprisonment for drugs increased the prison population for both men and women. The increase has now begun to level off, but fourteen times as many people are in state and federal prison in the United States today (331,600 in 2011) for drug-related offenses, compared to the numbers in 1980 (23,700) (Carson and Sabol 2012). Imprisonment of women skyrocketed over this period even more rapidly than the overall arrest rate, with drug offenses as the main reason for this increase. In the mid-1980s, 26 percent of the women in federal prisons were there for drug offenses. By the 1990s, 72 percent were. In women's state facilities, the increase in drug offenders went from 10 percent in 1979 to 33 percent in 1991 (Greenfeld and Snell 1999). Many of the women were swept into prison through mandatory sentencing laws despite the relatively minor roles the women played in the drug trade. Box 10-2 describes one woman's experience. Her story explains that although women are often only peripherally involved, they have less leverage in prosecution and sentencing than do men who are much more central to the drug-dealing activities (Women in Prison Project 2002).

GENDER IN EVERYDAY LIFE   BOX 10-2
MINOR CRIMES, MAJOR SENTENCES: THE CASE OF SERENA NUNN

When she was 19 years old, Serena Nunn was convicted of conspiracy to possess and distribute cocaine and spent 11 years in prison. Her crime? Driving Ralph Nunn (no relation), her boyfriend, to meetings with other drug dealers and taking his messages. Because of stringent federal mandatory minimum sentencing policies, Ms. Nunn, who had no prior criminal record and a minor role in her boyfriend's drug ring, was sentenced to 15 years and 8 months in prison. In contrast, the drug ring leader, who had prior drug, rape, and manslaughter convictions, was sentenced to only seven years because he assisted the prosecution. Ms. Nunn's story mirrors those of many other women who, because of their minor involvement in drug rings, have little information to trade and are left with little bargaining power with prosecutors. They end up facing excessive time in prison; meanwhile, their male counterparts receive reduce sentences in return for their testimony.

Ms. Nunn was luckier than most. Federal, state, and local officials lobbied for her clemency, and U.S. District Court Judge David S. Doty, who sentenced Ms. Nunn, wrote to President Clinton in her support. He argued: "If mandatory minimum rules did not exist, no judge in America, including me, would have ever sentenced Ms. Nunn to 15 years in prison based on her role in the conspiracy, her age and the fact that she had no prior criminal convictions."

Finally, on July 7, 2000, 11 years into her sentence, Ms. Nunn was released with a commutation from President Clinton. While her experience was in many ways a tragedy, Ms. Nunn was able to rise above the injustice and six years after her commutation she completed her law degree at the University of Michigan and now intends to practice law in the public interest or criminal law.

SOURCE: Sentencing Project (2006).

Besides sending more women to jail for longer periods of time, the war on drugs exacerbated gender inequality because stricter drug enforcement caused ripple effects that resulted in a decline in the economic status of women (Danner 1998). Increased spending on prisons required cuts in other government services of 40 percent over eight years in the 1990s. Because women are more likely to rely on services such as welfare, they suffered the consequences of the cuts disproportionately. In addition, women are more likely to be employed in social services and therefore see their jobs disappear when the government shifts spending from social services to prisons. The war on drugs sends more men than women to prison, but women bear a heavier burden of the unintended consequences (Owen 1999).

Since the turn of the century, important changes have been occurring in incarceration rates. While the overall rates remain high, they have leveled off and even begun to fall in state prisons since 2008. In addition, the racial ethnic gap has closed somewhat. Whites are still much less likely to be in prison, but the rates of incarceration for black men fell 10 percent and the rates for black women fell 31 percent between 2000 and 2009. During this same period, incarceration rates for white men rose 8 percent and 47 percent for white women. For Hispanics the men's rate declined by 2 percent while the women's rate rose by 23 percent (Mauer 2013).

In short, fewer black women are entering prison, and more white and Latina women are being incarcerated. Thus, the nearly thirty-year trend of women's incarceration increases outpacing that of men has not abated. Rather, the racial ethnic dynamics of those changes have shifted. What has caused these changes is not yet clear. One hypothesis is that the increase in the numbers of Latina and especially white women being incarcerated is because of an increase in the use of methamphetamines among these population groups. Decline in the numbers of black women may perhaps have been brought about by the Fair Sentencing Act and by changes in court policies that preceded the Act (Mauer 2013). The war on drugs continues to have gendered consequences, although policies have shifted the disparities somewhat by race ethnicity.

Why Are Men So Much More Likely to Be in Prison?

The differences between women and men in the rates of criminal activities and imprisonment are remarkable. Four kinds of theoretical explanations have been offered to try to explain both the difference and the recent closing of the gap: masculinity theory, opportunity theory, economic marginalization theory, and chivalry theory (Small 2000).

Masculinity theory asserts that criminal activity is associated with characteristics of masculinity, such as being aggressive, pushy, hard-headed, and violent. These behaviors are part of being a man in our society, and as a result they make men more prone to committing crimes. Theorists from this point of view argue that as expectations about women and the behavior of women become more masculinized, we should expect that women will become more similar to men and will commit more crimes and become a larger proportion of the prison population (Adler and Adler 1975).

Opportunity theory asserts that property crimes are a result of being in the right place at the right time and that to commit a crime, a person must have certain skills. This theory asserts that men have had greater opportunities to commit crimes because they have been in workplaces where they could steal from their employers, for example. This theory argues that as women enter the workplace, they gain skills, social connections, and opportunities to commit acts such as theft, embezzlement, and forgery (Simon 1975). On the other hand, opportunity theorists note that as women gain greater economic independence, they also improve their ability to leave abusive relationships before they escalate to committing assault or murder of a husband or boyfriend. Opportunity theorists predict that as women continue to take on paid jobs, we will see women committing more property crimes but fewer violent crimes.

A third theory is **economic marginalization theory** (Chesney-Lind 1997). This theory claims that at least some crime results when people are responsible for supporting themselves and their families but don't have opportunities to obtain jobs that allow them to do so. Men have been more likely to be seen as breadwinners, and if the legal job market has been unable to provide them with paid employment, they have sought remuneration from illegal work. These theorists are not optimistic about seeing women's economic fortunes improve just because they are in the labor force. They argue that women are working outside the home more often but remain poor, and crime is an avenue for supplementing their income. They predict that women's criminal involvement will increase as women are more economically independent but still less able to provide sufficiently for themselves and their families (Small 2000).

The National Resource Center on Domestic Violence (NRCDV) provides evidence to support this point of view by describing another way women are vulnerable to economic marginalization. They note that today, women's incarceration is often directly related to the combined impact of rape, battering, and a variety of state violence that fall heavily on their shoulders. According to the NRCDV, "the overwhelming majority of women defendants in the criminal justice system have extensive histories of childhood and adult abuse that may result in homelessness, substance abuse, and economic marginality that force them into survival by illegal means" (S. Miller 2005). Recent changes in welfare, housing, immigration policies, drug enforcement, mandatory arrest, prosecutions, and sentencing policies further criminalize women's efforts to survive, escape, and cope with abuse. Low-income women of color are most at risk (Gilfus 1992).

The fourth theory that attempts to explain why men are so much more likely to be arrested is **chivalry theory** (Steffensmeier and Allan 1996). According to this point of view, women have been similar to men in their criminal behavior in the past, but that similarity was obscured by leniency in the system, making women appear to be less criminal. Men who committed crimes, on the other hand, have been held accountable for their acts. They predict that as chivalry falls away, women's true criminal activity will become more visible and will appear to be greater than in previous decades. This perspective maintains that women's behavior has not changed as much as the criminal justice system's treatment of women.

POLITICAL INSTITUTIONS: THE MILITARY

The military is a third social institution within government that reveals how important gender is. Women have served in the armed services throughout history, but the military is clearly recognized as a masculine institution. In the world, the proportion of women in the military remains small. Ninety percent of the world's armed forces are men, and women are still barred from serving in many countries. It remains one of a few social institutions left in the United States that legally restricts participation by gender.

Women, however, increasingly are participating in the military. What seems to push women into the military or at least allows them to enter? Three sets of factors are important (Bourg and Segal 2001):

- *Demand for personnel.* When a nation or a social movement needs more members, such as in times of war, women are a large resource that can be tapped.
- *Demographic or economic changes.* If the current generation of young men is relatively small, or if unemployment is low, that alters the supply of potential recruits. When fewer men area available to serve, more women are drawn in.
- *Cultural values.* In societies with more egalitarian ideas about gender, or during historical periods when gender equality is emphasized, women are more likely to increase their numbers in the military.

All three of these appear to be significant features of the current social context in the United States. Not surprisingly, women are increasing their numbers and their activities in the military. Today women comprise about 14 percent of the 1.4 million active military personnel. More than 280,000 women have been sent to Iraq, Afghanistan, or to jobs in neighboring nations in support of the wars. Of the more than 6,600 killed in these wars, 152 have been women (Baldor 2013).

Up until 1967, the U.S. military maintained a 2 percent ceiling on women. The quota was lifted in the late 1960s, and in the 1990s significant additional changes took place in military policy. In 1991, Congress repealed laws prohibiting women from flying on aircraft in combat missions. In 1994, women began to be allowed to serve on Navy combat ships. In 2010, submarines were staffed with women for the first time, but women are still not allowed in the Navy's Sea, Air, and Land Teams, SEALS. Table 10-4 shows the breakdown in the proportion of women in various branches of the military and the proportion of women among officers. The numbers vary, but women are certainly a minority in all categories. We may begin to see women's minority status alter with the most recent announcement from the Pentagon that they are formally beginning to lift their ban on women serving in combat, opening hundreds of thousands of front-line positions and potentially elite commando jobs.

TABLE 10-4 Women in U.S. Armed Services, 2013

	% of Positions Open to Women in 2011	Women as % of Enlisted	Women as % of Officers
Air Force	99	19	20
Navy	94	17	16
Army	70	16	14
Marine Corps	62	7	6

Sources: United States Army (2013); Air Force Personnel Center (2013); Navy Personnel Command (2013); U.S. Military.com (2011).

Women in Combat

Combat remains a restricted activity for women around the world. Only seven countries allow women in all combat roles (Australia, Canada, Belgium, the Netherlands, Denmark, Norway, and Spain). Seven others allow women in many combat roles (France, Finland, Ghana, Israel, Japan, United Kingdom, and the United States) (Peterson and Runyan 1999). These policies, however, describe only the official position of women in combat. The United Nations reports that women are much more likely to be unofficially involved in combat than the laws suggest. Since 1990, for example, girl soldiers have been in fighting forces in sixty-four countries (Keairns 2002).

In the United States, the official rules have been changing in the past few decades, culminating in the Pentagon decision in 2013 to begin allowing or even insisting that women serve in combat. While still somewhat controversial, the vast majority of the American public (74 percent) say that they would vote for allowing women in combat (Brown 2013). In addition, observers have noted that, to a large extent, the American military has been largely ignoring their ban on women in combat for quite some time. The recent wars in Iraq and Afghanistan are marked by unclear boundaries, suicide bombers, attacks on supply convoys, and a shortage of American troops. This means that regardless of official assignments, women are in the line of fire and are using weapons to defend themselves and others in direct confrontation with the enemy, including flying combat missions. And many women have died in battle (Benedict 2009).

The laws appear to be lagging behind the on-the-ground reality of the battlefield. Retired Lt. Gen. Claudia J. Kennedy, the first woman to achieve the rank of three-star general, predicts that as the wars continue, more women soldiers will be called up for active duty. She notes that military recruiting is down by 27 percent and estimates that thirty thousand to fifty thousand more soldiers may be needed. She asserts that women "are vital to this mission and should not be segregated. Women soldiers deserve to be treated just as all soldiers should be treated—properly trained, properly equipped and given the proper respect" (Ginty 2005).

Does this gap between the rules and reality mean that women are less well trained and less well armed because they are not officially in combat roles? Is it endangering them or their comrades? Is it disrespectful of women who have died in battle to ignore their combat heroism and sacrifice? These are the issues with which Pentagon officials will grapple in the next three years as they debate the official role of women in combat in all areas of the U.S. military.

Women and Men in the Military Today

The laws changed in the 1990s in the American armed services to allow women into more positions. In 1996, women won their cases at the Citadel as well as the Virginia Military Institute to enter these formerly all-men schools. Expectations for military women appear to have been changing dramatically in the past few decades. Until 1980, for example, women in the Marines did not learn to fire arms. Most of their training resembled charm school. They were issued elaborate cosmetic kits and taught how to apply lipstick and how to properly stamp out a cigarette. They were required to learn how to iron a crisp shirt and sit on a bar stool. At the end of their training, they were tested in their social graces as they sipped punch, strolled around in high heels, and made small talk with the officers (St. George 2002).

Although policy has changed, some problems remain. Some men in the military resist the idea of women in the military. Table 10-5 shows the opinions of men and women currently in the armed services in different ranks about whether women should continue to increase their numbers. The table indicates large differences of opinion between women and men. Women are, not surprisingly, more supportive of more women in the military. Rank also influences opinions. Men in the highest ranks are most likely to believe that there are too many women in the armed services (L. Miller 2000).

Gender and rank also affect opinions about what women should be doing in the military. Among men, 44 percent of men believe that combat roles should be open to women. Among women, 64 percent of enlisted women and 68 percent of officers believe that women should be allowed into combat roles. Race ethnicity also affects the opinion of women in combat. Among black, Hispanic, and those of racial ethnic groups other than white, 68 percent believe women who want to volunteer for combat services should be allowed to do so. Only 18 percent of white officers and 39 percent of white enlisted members share this opinion (L. Miller 2000).

Gender Harassment in the Military

In chapter 6, on work, we examined the problem of sexual harassment. You should recall that sexual harassment was defined as a range of activities from "**gender harassment** which is inappropriately calling attention to women or men's bodies, sexuality or marital status, to sexual harassment which is turning a professional, work or student–teacher relationship into

TABLE 10-5 Soldiers' Opinions About Numbers of Women in the Military

	Enlisted		Noncommissioned		Officers	
	Men	*Women*	*Men*	*Women*	*Men*	*Women*
Too many women in the military	11%	2%	16%	1%	24%	0%
About the right amount	36%	31%	38%	48%	59%	44%
Too few women in the military	33%	50%	22%	38%	7%	49%
Not sure	20%	17%	24%	13%	10%	7%

Source: L. Miller (2000, 417).

a sexual relationship that is not wanted by one of the people involved and that is coercive because the initiator has some power over the other person" (Lorber 2000, 291).

Laura Miller (2000) investigated gender harassment in the military. She defines gender harassment as behavior that is not sexual and is used to enforce traditional gender roles or in response to violation of those roles. Gender harassment tends to target women who are supposedly not feminine enough but can also be used against men who fail to live up to "masculine ideals." L. Miller (2000) argues that women may see their numbers increase and their opportunities expand in the military, but they might not find themselves working in a more supportive or even tolerant environment. Gender discrimination in policy that restricts women in the military may be eliminated, but it might be replaced by more subtle but equally problematic gender harassment.

Gender harassment can take the following forms:

- *Resistance to authority.* A man soldier refuses to follow directions from a superior who is a woman.
- *Constant scrutiny.* Women in the services report that they feel they must work harder and live up to higher standards because they are under surveillance by men who are waiting for them to make a mistake.
- *Gossip and rumors.* An example is a "popular" untrue rumor that some women soldiers in the Gulf Wars made a fortune by setting up a tent and working as prostitutes for the men there.
- *Sabotage.* Equipment and tools being used by women in nontraditional jobs has been reportedly purposely damaged.
- *Indirect threats.* Comments have been alleged about the inevitability of women being raped if they were present in deployments or in infantry or armor units. These comments are often given as concerned warnings, but the end result is to communicate to women that they will be in danger if they challenge the gender lines in combat.

Beyond gender harassment, sexual assault has increasingly been revealed as a pervasive problem in the military. The *Guardian* reported that women soldiers in Iraq faced a higher likelihood of being sexually assaulted by a colleague than they did of dying by enemy fire. The Pentagon estimates that 26,000 rapes and sexual assaults took place in U.S. military in 2012 alone, although only a small proportion of these were reported. Besides the issue of the rapes themselves, reports suggest that those people who did report having been raped were forced out of the military while the rapists were not charged or punished (Wolf 2013).

Why the Hostility Against Women in the Military?

Why do some men in the military see women in the military as the enemy? L. Miller (2000) interviewed men about their hostility toward women and found that it was based on their belief that men are discriminated against in the armed forces. One reason for this is different and easier physical training standards for women. One noncommissioned officer (NCO) explained, "I can't be adamant enough. There is no place for women in the infantry. Women do not belong in combat units. If you haven't been there, then you wouldn't understand. As far as equal rights, some women say they are as physically strong as a man. Then why are [physical training] standards different?" (L. Miller 2000, 421).

Others asserted that women are unfairly advantaged and take advantage of pregnancy for limiting their physical training or labor. Some of the men also said restrictions on women's roles end up advantaging women because they then have better educational opportunities or better assignments, while men are relegated to the combat jobs. They also believe that women get away with more than men do and that quotas exist that result in undeserved promotions for women. White men were especially distressed because they thought that all of these advantages accrued to racial ethnic minorities relative to white soldiers as well (L. Miller 2000).

Remember that these beliefs are not necessarily true. However, the men who expressed them also felt that there was no opportunity for them to talk about their anger. They had been silenced, but their feelings sometimes were expressed in gender harassment. Allowing women into the services and allowing them to participate more fully can be altered by changing policy, but these changes need to be accompanied by uncovering some of these more hidden ideas and the accompanying behaviors.

Masculinity and Heterosexuality in the Military

As we saw in chapter 4, sexuality is a key component in the social construction of gender. The armed forces are an important source of the rules that define proper behavior for women and men as heterosexual. Heterosexuality is a requirement, from the point of view of the military, for a truly masculine man or feminine woman (Bourg and Segal 2001).

In the 1950s, the U.S. military explicitly barred gay men and lesbians from military service. For more than forty years, rules about sexuality became increasingly restrictive. In the early 1990s, however, polls showed that 65 percent of Americans opposed the exclusionary policy. In addition, the General Accounting Office announced in 1992 that the practice of hunting for gay men and lesbians in the military, prosecuting them, and dismissing them from the service was costing $27 million a year (McFeeley 2000). In 1993 these rules were revised to drop the statement that homosexuality is incompatible with military service. The armed services were no longer allowed to ask potential recruits or members about their sexual orientation. This new policy was commonly known as "**don't ask, don't tell**." Gay men and lesbians could still be dismissed from service for engaging in a homosexual act or openly discussing their sexuality, and they could not live with a life partner or seek to marry (Bourg and Segal 2001). "Don't ask, don't tell" was repealed by Congress in December 2010. In 2012, the Army conducted its first gay military marriage for a same-sex couple.

Why Are Differences in the Treatment of Women in the Military Important?

The military plays a significant role in creating and perpetuating gender inequality in three ways. First, gender inequality in the activities of women and men in the military contributes to the continuation of cultural images of masculinity and femininity among military personnel and in the general population who observe members of the armed forces. The military trains its members to identify with and express gender in a stereotyped manner. Men in the military are under constant pressure to prove their manhood by being tough, adversarial, and aggressive. Words such as *little girl*, *woman*, and *lady* have been used as derogatory terms for men who fail to live up to military standards. To fail is to be female (Stiehm 1981). The practice of referring to trainees as "girls" in the service is now officially prohibited (Bourg and Segal 2001).

Second, barring women from some activities in the military limits their access to power and resources such as jobs, job training, or educational benefits. The military, for example, arms its members. Because women are less likely to be in the military and when women soldiers are barred from particular activities such as combat, they have less legitimate access to weapons, weapons training, and the use of weapons than do men (Bourg and Segal 2001).

Third, the association of military service and citizenship means that discrimination in the military can help perpetuate gender inequality in the legal rights of citizens. For example, as we saw in the discussion of elections, getting into a track that leads to political leadership is a key to electing more women to office. The military is a powerful arm of the state. It commands a large proportion of government spending and employs more people than any other single organization in the United States. Those at the top of the organization, not surprisingly, have much influence over public officials. In addition, those who are in public office use their military service as a way of selling themselves to the public. Men with military experience, such as Dwight Eisenhower, Colin Powell, John McCain, and John Kerry have used that credential as a basis for garnering votes or being appointed to important positions. Although public opinion appears to be changing, 45 percent of the American public still believe that women in public office are not capable of effectively handling issues such as the military, war, homeland security, and foreign policy. If women do not have access to high-level, high-profile military positions, including those in combat, they do not have access to this track to political leadership.

Be Careful What You Wish For

Breaking down barriers to gender inequality is a laudable goal. In the case of electoral politics, making women more equal to men would benefit women, men, and the community. Making women more like men in the military and in the criminal justice system is less justifiable. In the case of the criminal justice system, the forces that seem to be associated with greater criminal activity of women, such as greater public participation by women, especially in economic activities, are good; perhaps criminal activity is just part of the package.

In the case of the military, we can see that bringing women into the armed forces on an equal footing with men has some benefits, because the military is an important source of jobs and because it is a powerful institution from which women do not want to be excluded. However, some have grappled with the problem of promoting the practice of more women in the military, particularly when the country is at war. Should our goal be to encourage women to be warriors as skilled as men? Or should our goal be to make men better at the ideas and behaviors associated with women, such as cooperation, compromise, reconciliation, and pacifism?

Women and Peace

The discussion of the military has emphasized the exclusion of women from military work, especially combat. The focus has been on the problems associated with leaving women out and the changes that have been fought for to bring more women into the military and into war making. Internationally, though, women are recognized as instrumental in preventing and stopping armed conflict and in building peace. Both during and after conflict, women

The political institutions of both the military and prisons are dominated by men. Nearly everyone would agree that gaining "equality" by increasing the numbers of women in prison is not a sensible goal. The debate over gender equity in the military is more contradictory, but it also includes those who would argue that women should not seek to be either prisoners or military jailers in places such as Guantanamo.

Source: Associated Press.

have been integrally involved in peace-building processes, seeking solutions to problems such as resource degradation; demobilization and reintegration of former child soldiers; violence against women and children; effects of militarization; and sustainable economic, environmental, and political development (McKay and de la Rey 2001). Women have also been shown to be more likely to support peacemaking efforts; for example, in opinion polls about the Gulf Wars, American women are less hawkish than men. During the Iraq War, a Gallup Poll reported that 62 percent of American women believed that the troops should come home from Iraq by the end of the year, compared to 53 percent of men who took this position.

Like formal combat, however, women are seldom included in formal peace processes. Women are rarely represented among decision makers and military leaders, the usual participants in these processes. This situation is beginning to change with the United Nations Resolution 1325, which calls for the involvement of women in conflict resolution and the peace process. Passed in 2000, twenty-five nations from Liberia and Norway to Nepal and the Philippines have since developed action plans to implement the resolution (Kuehnast 2012). In addition, women have a long history of peacemaking outside of formal roles. Even in the most difficult areas of conflict women have maintained a high profile in trying to build coalitions across national borders to work for peace (Naraghi 2007). Women in Black, an international women's peace organization, for example, works in a highly contentious and politically difficult area, the Middle East (Powers 2003). Women in Black is composed of Israeli and Palestinian women who have marched through the streets carrying banners reading "We will not be enemies." They have also engaged in a broad range of educational and relief activities (Cockburn 2004a, 2004b).

Women in Black began by claiming a public space for women to be heard, standing at public intersections with their signs day after day. This tactic of claiming a public space had been part of the work of the women's group called the Black Sash, which organized against Apartheid in South Africa, and the Madres de Plaza de Mayo, which sought information and justice about the "disappeared" in the years of political repression in Argentina. These organizations were rooted in the work of earlier groups of women that explicitly refused violence, militarism, and war, such as the Women's International League for Peace and Freedom, the oldest women's peace organization, formed during World War I in 1918, the **Greenham Common Women's Peace Camp** in the United Kingdom, and related groups around the world that opposed the deployment of U.S. missiles in the 1980s. Israeli and Palestinian Women in Black stand in public places with high volumes of traffic to call for peace and justice (Women in Black 2008).

Elise Boulding (2000) writes about this technique of "claiming public space for the practice" of peace culture. She notes that because that public space has not been traditionally available to women, they have had to be inventive about claiming it. She argues that women have been "marginal to public decision making in the existing social order" and "have fewer vested interests to protect" (Powers 2003). From these "weaknesses" in women's role in the public world, however, Boulding maintains that women have created strengths in the peacemaking arena because they are more flexible and freer to reach across boundaries between social groups who are at war (Cockburn 2007).

In research on Women in Black, for example, participants spoke of what they believed was one of the most significant strengths of the organization: any question could be put on the table. Unlike formal peace talks that spend so much time delineating which topics will be discussed, Women in Black discusses all issues, no matter how difficult (Cockburn 1998).

Assumptions about the role of women in society and especially in families have also created opportunities for women and girls in peace processes. For example, women from the Democratic Republic of the Congo, Kenya, Liberia, Rwanda, Somalia, South Africa, Sri Lanka, and the Sudan have drawn on their moral authority as mothers, wives, or daughters to call for an end to armed conflict. Women have organized as mothers, either to learn the fate of their children who have disappeared or to prevent their children from being conscripted or deployed to particular conflicts. Such groups include the Mothers and Grandmothers of the Plaza de Mayo in Argentina, the Mutual Support Group in Guatemala, the Group of Relatives of the Detained and Disappeared in Chile, the Association of Women of Srebrenica, the Committee of Russian Soldiers' Mothers in Chechnya, and Code Pink in the United States. The concerns these groups have about their children give them a social legitimacy and a linkage with women from different sides of the conflict (United Nations 2002). The social role of women as mothers would seem to separate them from war and make them less connected to the politics of peace and less authoritative about the issues of war and peace.

These organizations of women, however, have used this "disadvantage" to reveal their particular concern for peace and to give them greater authority in calling for peace and justice.

Boulding is careful to assert that the active role women have played in the peace movement is not because of any "natural" proclivity for peacemaking. She argues that it is the social position of women, as outsiders, parents, and citizens with weaker ties to political and economic interests that often makes them suited to this work. In addition, the social construction of femininity includes nurturance, cooperation, and aversion to conflict, which may make women more interested in and better at working for peace. All of these, however, are part of the social construction of femininity, not a natural inborn tendency of females. This means, of course, that we could reconstruct masculinity to include these traits as well and thereby build a more peaceful world where gender did not push men (and women) in the direction of war.

WHAT IS POLITICAL?

At the beginning of the chapter, we looked at definitions of politics and the connections between the state and political activities. What exactly is political? Does it just mean running for office, holding elected or appointed positions, governing and advocating issues in the established institutions of government, or wielding the instruments of force in the military and the criminal justice system to enforce the decisions made by political leaders? Or should the concept be broader than this and include all the activities in which people engage to link public and private concerns and develop power to bring about change in people's daily lives (Fowlkes 1997)? The first of these is the definition traditionally used by political scientists. Scholars who have paid attention to gender, however, suggest that the second definition also needs to be considered. They assert that politics is a broader set of relationships and activities that defy, shift, or maintain power relationships in the community. Their questioning has challenged our understanding of what is political (Flammang 1997; McEwan 2005).

Scholars who have paid attention to gender puzzled over the activities of women around issues of power in their community and the invisibility of women in what is more commonly thought of as politics proper. They began to uncover a problem with the definition of "political" itself. "The invisibility of women's political activism is, in part, a reflection of the tendency to define politics within the narrow terms of the masculine sphere of formal politics. Once such a restrictive definition is abandoned, it has become almost an alternative conventional wisdom that informal politics represents a more feminized political sphere" (Lister 1997, 147).

As we have seen, men are much more likely than women to be politically active in formal positions as elected officials. Both women and men are active in more informal NGOs. Especially in those concerned with peace, human rights, economic justice, and environmental protection, women are likely to be very active (Peterson and Runyan 1999; Pardo 2000). Within these groups women are often a driving force (Chanan 1992). When formal leadership and formal management positions develop or a local protest campaign shifts to the national level, men begin to take over (West and Blumberg 1990; Lister 1997). But in the grassroots activities, women and men share participation, or women are even more active than men.

Mary Pardo (2000) has examined the political activities of working-class Mexican American women in Los Angeles. The Mothers of East Los Angeles (MELA) provide an example of activism found in many places around the world. MELA is an organization of low-income Latinas that has focused on environmental issues in their community, such as stopping the construction of a toxic waste incinerator, but they represent a group that is not engaged in formal politics. The women come from social categories that are not perceived as power sources. They are not well-paid lobbyists or elected officials. They use networks and tactics that are not associated with politics, such as the contacts they have made working in the parents' club at their children's schools and in the Catholic Church. They also use their role as mothers, not usually thought of as a political one, as the basis of their work. One woman explained how the role of mother intrinsically calls on women to be politically active:

> You know if one of your children's safety is jeopardized, the mother turns into a lioness. That's why Father John got the mothers. We have to have a well-organized, strong group of mothers to protect the community and oppose things that are detrimental to us. You know the governor is in the wrong and the mothers are in the right. After all, the mothers have to be right. Mothers are for the children's interest, not for self interests; the governor is for his own political interests. (quoted in Pardo 2000, 464)

They identify themselves as not part of the world of elected formal politics but the impact they have on formal political institutions is significant. Their work, therefore, challenges our ideas about what is political and who is political.

If we think only about formal politics and elected officials, women's political activities become invisible. If we begin with gender and ask what women do and what men do and how might it be interpreted as political, we are forced to look at the range of ways that women and men experience and express their politics. We have to look at both formal politics and informal politics, and when we do, both women's actions and the activities of "outsider" politics become visible (Lister 1997).

More-inclusive formal politics is necessary for the three reasons outlined earlier: increased democratic justice and equity, more possibility of addressing the interests of women, and better use of all available resources (Henig and Henig 2001). In addition, however, we need to redefine political action and civic virtue in a way that acknowledges informal political activities and organizations that are often the ways that women express their political citizenship. To do both of these things, we need to create ways to connect these two. We need to create grassroots global democracy (Lister 1997).

GENDER MATTERS

When most people think of the word *political*, electoral politics is the image that comes to mind. Campaigns, pollsters, and political office are all colored by gender. This chapter has explored electoral politics as well as two other sections of the political world: the military and the criminal justice system. In each of these social worlds, gender plays a prominent role. Who runs for office, who votes for officials, and who takes the seat in parliaments, Congresses, and executive positions are all marked by gender. In a few places in the world, women have achieved equality, and in many places their numbers are increasing. Men, however, dominate in most places. In addition, masculinity is more closely associated with the skills many of us associate with being a good political leader: strong, authoritative, decisive, and with a track record in business, law, and the military. Armed services are another area where men are dominant. At the other end of the spectrum of power, prisons are also a place where masculinity presides. People with the least political power, those who are incarcerated, are much more likely to be men. In all of these areas, changes are occurring that are bringing more women into elected office, into prisons, and into all corners of the military including combat. All of these areas, however, remain dominated by men in terms of numbers. They also remain dominated by masculinities. They are designed around historical ideas and expectations about men as leaders, criminals, and soldiers.

In contemplating the "outsider" role of women, we are reminded that we have two choices. We can continue to try to gain access for women to all human endeavors. Or we can challenge the institutions by seeking change that will allow men to pull away from the dangerous and inhumane territories of war and crime.

KEY TERMS

50/50 program
affirmative action model
Beijing 5 Summit
chivalry theory
criminal justice system
don't ask, don't tell
economic marginalization theory
electoral politics
EMILY's list and WINWIN
Fair Sentencing Act
gender gap
gender harassment
gender ideologies
Gender Issues Monitoring Office
gerrymandered districts
Greenham Common Women's Peace Camp

masculinity theory
meritocratic model
Nineteenth Amendment
100-to-1 quantity ratio
opportunity theory
paradoxical autonomy
parité
politics
quota system
radical model
state
three strikes and you're out
truth in sentencing
war on drugs
woman suffrage

CRITICAL THINKING QUESTIONS

1. Which of the three theoretical models, meritocratic, affirmative action, or radical, is most persuasive for you? Why do you find it most compelling? What do you think it would take to implement any one of these sufficiently to bring gender equity to electoral politics?
2. What do you think about the latest news from the Pentagon that women will be incorporated into every part of the military, including the most elite combat units? Why do you think this change is taking place at this time?

3. Ask a few of your friends why they believe men are so much more likely to be in prison. Which theoretical model do they fit best (masculinity theory, opportunity theory, economic marginalization, chivalry theory)? What specific comments did they make that make you think they are using one particular framework or the other? Does anyone have a point of view that is not represented by the four theories presented in the text?

REFERENCES

Adler, Freda, and Herbert M. Adler. 1975. *Sisters in Crime: The Rise of the New Female Criminal.* New York: McGraw-Hill.

Air Force Personnel Center. 2013. "Airforce military characteristics 2013." http://www.afpc.af.mil/library/airforcepersonneldemographics.asp. Accessed February 28, 2014.

Anzia, Sarah F., and Christopher Berry. 2009. *The Jackie (and Jill) Robinson Effect: Why Do Congresswomen Outperform Congressmen?* Harris School Working Papers, August 5. http://gsppi.berkeley.edu/faculty/sanzia/Anzia_Berry_8_5_09.pdf Accessed February 28, 2014.

Azzi, Iman. 2007. "Jordanian MP Celebrates Her Post-Quota Victory." *WeNews*, November 29. http://www.womensenews.org/story/the-world/071129/jordanian-mp-celebrates-her-post-quota-victory. Accessed March 23, 2011.

Baldor, Lolita. 2013. *Women in Combat: Leon Panetta Removes Military Ban, Opening Front-Line Positions.* January 23. http://www.huffingtonpost.com/2013/01/23/women-in-combat_n_2535954.html. Accessed February 28, 2014.

BBC News. 2010. "The US Women Shackled During Childbirth." January 9. http://news.bbc.co.uk/2/hi/programmes/from_our_own_correspondent/8449215.stm. Accessed March 11, 2011.

Beckett, Katherine, Kris Nyrop, and Lori Pfingst. 2006. "Race, Drugs, and Policing: Understanding Disparities in Drug Delivery Arrests." *Criminology* 44 (1): 105 37.

Belkin, Lisa. 2007. "The Feminine Critique." *New York Times*, November 11. http://www.nytimes.com/2007/11/01/fashion/01WORK.html. Accessed March 23, 2011.

Belknap, Joanne. 2001. "The Criminal-Processing System: Girls and Women as Victims and Offenders." In *Gender Mosaics: Social Perspectives*, edited by Dana Vannoy, 374–84. Los Angeles: Roxbury.

Benedict, Helen. 2009. "The Plight of Women Soldiers." *Nation*, May 5. http://www.thenation.com/article/plight-women-soldiers?page=0,1. Accessed March 23, 2011.

Borelli, MaryAnne. 2000. "Gender, Politics, and Change in the United States Cabinet: The Madeleine Korbel Albright and Janet Reno Appointments." In *Gender and American Politics*, edited by Sue Tolleson-Rinehart and Jyl Josephson, 185–204. Armonk, NY: Sharpe.

Boulding, Elise. 2000. *Cultures of Peace: The Hidden Side of History.* Syracuse, NY: Syracuse University Press.

Bourg, Chris, and Mady Wechsler Segal. 2001. "Gender, Sexuality, and the Military." In *Gender Mosaics: Social Perspectives*, edited by Dana Vannoy, 332–42. Los Angeles: Roxbury.

Bourque, Susan. 2001. "Political Leadership for Women: Redefining Power and Reassessing Political." In *Woman on Power: Leadership Redefined*, edited by Sue Freeman, Susan Bourque, and Christine Shelton, 84–113. Boston: Northeastern University Press.

Keairns, Yvonne E. 2002. *Girl Soldiers: Challenging the Assumptions.* New York: Quaker UN Office. http://www.peacewomen.org/portal_resources_resource.php?id=135. Accessed February 28, 2014.

Brown, Alyssa. 2013. "Americans Favor Allowing Women in Combat." Gallup, January 25. http://www.gallup.com/poll/160124/americans-favor-allowing-women-combat.aspx. Accessed February 28, 2014.

Bush-Baskette, Stephanie. 1998. "The War on Drugs as a War Against Black Women." In *Crime Control and Women: Feminist Implications of Criminal Justice Policy*, edited by Susan Miller, 113–29. Thousand Oaks, CA: Sage.

Carpini, Michael, and Scott Keeter. 2000. "Gender and Political Knowledge." In *Gender and American Politics*, edited by Sue Tolleson-Rinehart and Jyl Josephson, 21–52. Armonk, NY: Sharpe.

Carroll, Susan, and Richard Fox. 2005. "Introduction: Gender and Electoral Politics in the Twenty-First Century." In *Gender and Elections: Shaping the Future of American Politics*, edited by Susan Carroll and Richard Fox, 1–9. New York: Cambridge University Press.

Carson, E. Ann, and William Sabol. (2012).; "Prisoners in 2011." In *Sourcebook of Criminal Justice Statistics Online*. Washington, DC: Bureau of Justice Statistics

Center for American Women and Politics (CAWP). 1998. *Women in Elected Office*. New Brunswick, NJ: CAWP.

——. 2000. "Gender Gap in the 2000 Elections." http://www.cawp.rutgers.edu/press_room/news/documents/PressRelease_12-00_GG2000.pdf. Accessed February 28, 2014.

——. 2006. "Women Officeholders Fact Sheets and Summaries." http://cawp.rutgers.edu/fast_facts/levels_of_office/index.php. Accessed February 28, 2014.

——. 2008. "The Gender Gap: Fact sheet." http://www.cawp.rutgers.edu/fast_facts/voters/gender_gap.php. Accessed February 28, 2014.

——. 2010. "Gender Differences in Voter Turnout: Fact sheet." http://www.cawp.rutgers.edu/research/topics/documents/genderdiff.pdf. Accessed February 28, 2014.

——. 2011. "Gender Differences in Voter Turnout." www.cawp.rutgers.edu/fast_facts/voters/documents/genderdiff.pdf. Accessed February 28, 2014.

——. 2012. "The gender gap: Attitudes on public policy issues." www.cawp.rutgers.edu/fast_facts/voters/documents/GG_IssuesAttitudes-2012.pdf. Accessed February 28, 2014.

——. 2014a. Women in U.S. Congress 1917–2014. http://www.cawp.rutgers.edu/fast_facts/levels_of_office/documents/cong.pdf. Accessed February 28, 2014.

——. 2014b. Women in State Legislatures. 2014. http://www.cawp.rutgers.edu/fast_facts/levels_of_office/documents/stleg.pdf. Accessed February 28, 2014.

——. 2014c. Women in Statewide Elective Executive Office 2014. http://www.cawp.rutgers.edu/fast_facts/levels_of_office/Statewide-Current.php.

——. 2014d. Women Mayors in U.S. Cities 2013. http://www.cawp.rutgers.edu/fast_facts/levels_of_office/Local-WomenMayors.php. Accessed February 28, 2014.

Chanan, Gabriel. 1992. *Out of the Shadows: Local Community Action and the European Community*. Luxembourg: Office for Official Publications of the European Communities, European Foundation for the Improvement of Living and Working Conditions.

Chesney-Lind, Meda. 1997. *The Female Offender: Girls, Women, and Crime*. Thousand Oaks, CA: Sage.

Cockburn, Cynthia. 1998. *The Space Between Us: Negotiating Gender and National Identities in Conflict*. London: Zed Books.

——. 2004a. "The Continuum of Violence: A Gender Perspective on War and Peace." In *Sites of Violence*, edited by Wenona Giles and Jennifer Hyndman, 24–44. Berkeley: University of California Press.

——. 2004b. *The Line*. London: Zed Books.

——. 2007. *From Where We Stand*. London: Zed Books.

Connelly, Marjorie. 2000. "Who Voted: A Portrait of American Politics, 1976–2000." *New York Times*, November 12.

Conway, M. Margaret, David Ahern, and Gertrude Steuernagel. 1999. *Women and Public Policy: A Revolution in Progress*. 2nd edition. Washington, DC: Congressional Quarterly Press.

Conway, M. Margaret, Gertrude Steuernagel, and David Ahern. 1997. *Women and Political Partici-pation: Cultural Change in the Political Arena.* Washington, DC: Congressional Quarterly Press.

Crossett, Barbara. 1998. "Amnesty Finds Widespread Patterns of U.S. Rights Violations." *New York Times,* May 10.

Danner, Mona. 1998. "Three Strikes and It's Women Who Are Out." In *Crime Control and Women,* edited by Susan Miller, 1–11. Thousand Oaks, CA: Sage.

Davis, Angela. 2003. *Are Prisons Obsolete?* St. Paul, MN: Seven Stories Press.

Eagly, Alice, and Linda Carli. 2007. *Through the Labyrinth: The Truth about How Women Become Leaders.* Boston, MA: Harvard Business School Press.

Ehrlich, Julie, and Lynn Paltrow. 2006. "Jailing Pregnant Women Raises Health Risks." *WeNews,* September 20.

Elder, Laurel, and Steven Greene. 2012. "The Politics of Parenthood: Parenthood Effects on Issue Attitudes and Candidate Evaluations in 2008." *American Politics Research* 40 (3): 419–49.

Federal Bureau of Investigation. 2011. "Ten Year Arrest Trends by Sex." *Crime in the United States, 2011,* table 33. http://www.fbi.gov/about-us/cjis/ucr/crime-in-the-u.s/2011/crime-in-the-u.s.-2011/tables/table-33. Accessed February 28, 2014.

Flammang, Janet. 1997. *Women's Political Voice: How Women Are Transforming the Practice and Study of Politics.* Philadelphia: Temple University Press.

Flexner, Eleanor. 1975. *Century of Struggle: The Women's Rights Movement in the United States.* Cambridge, MA: Harvard University Press.

Fox, Richard. 1997. *Gender Dynamics in Congressional Elections.* Thousand Oaks, CA: Sage.

———. 2000. "Gender and Congressional Elections." In *Gender and American Politics,* edited by Sue Tolleson-Rinehart and Jyl Josephson, 227–56. Armonk, NY: Sharpe.

Fowlkes, Diana. 1997. "Moving from Feminist Identity Politics to Coalition Politics through a Femi-nist Materialist Standpoint of Intersubjectivity in Gloria Anzaldúa's *Borderlands/La Frontera: The New Mestiza.*" *Hypatia* 12 (2): 105–24.

Freedman, Estelle. 2002. *No Turning Back.* New York: Ballantine.

Funabashi, Kuniko. 2003. "Women's Participation in Politics and the Women's Movement." In *Gender and Development,* edited by Mayumi Murayama, 119–51. New York: Palgrave Macmillan.

Gilfus, Mary. 1992. "From Victims to Survivors to Offenders: Women's Routes of Entry and Immer-sion into Street Crime." *Women and Criminal Justice* 4 (1): 63–90.

Ginty, Molly. 2005. "Record Number of Female Soldiers Fall." *WeNews,* March 22.

Gouws, Amanda. 2004. "The Quota Made the Difference." *Network News,* July 3–4.

Greenfeld, Lawrence, and Tracy Snell. 1999. *Women Offenders.* Washington, DC: U.S. Department of Justice.

Gullo, Karen. 2001. "More Girls Go to Jail." *Associated Press,* April 30.

Hausmann, Ricardo, Laura D. Tyson, and Saadia Zahidi, 2012. "World Gender Gap Report 2012." http://www3.weforum.org/docs/WEF_GenderGap_Report_2012.pdf. February 28, 2014.

Henig, Ruth, and Simon Henig. 2001. *Women and Political Power: Europe Since 1945.* New York: Routledge.

Hirschfield, Julie. 2001. "Congress of Relative Newcomers Poses Challenge to Bush Leadership." *Congressional Quarterly Weekly,* January 20.

Hooghe, Marc, and Ruth Dassonneville. 2013. "Voters and Candidates of the Future: The Intention of Electoral Participation among Adolescents in 22 European Countries." *Young* 21 (1): 1–28

Inter-Parliamentary Union. 1997. *Men and Women in Politics: Democracy Still in the Making—A Comparative Study.* Geneva: Inter-Parliamentary Union.

———. 2013. "Women in National Parliaments: Situation as of July 2013." www.ipu.org/wmn-e/classif.htm. Accessed August 27, 2013.

Jones, Jeffrey. 2012. "Gender Gap in 2012 Vote Is Largest in Gallup's History." Gallup, November 9. http://www.gallup.com/poll/158588/gender-gap-2012-vote-largest-gallup-history.aspx. February 28, 2014.

Jones, Kathleen 1993. *Compassionate Authority: Democracy and the Representation of Women*. New York: Routledge.

Kahn, Kim. 1993. "Gender Differences in Campaign Messages: The Political Advertisements of Men and Women Candidates for U.S. Senate." *Political Research Quarterly* 46 (2): 418–502.

Kahn, Kim, and Ann Gordon. 1997. "How Women Campaign for the U.S. Senate." In *Women, Media and Politics*, edited by Pippa Norris, 59–76. Oxford, UK: Oxford University Press.

Kuehnast, Kathleen. 2012. "Gender and peacebuilding." United States Institute of Peace. http://www.buildingpeace.org/think-global-conflict/issues/gender-and-peacebuilding. Accessed February 28, 2014.

Lister, Ruth. 1997. *Citizenship: Feminist Perspectives*. New York: New York University Press.

Lopez, Mark, and Paul Taylor. 2009. "Dissecting the 2008 Electorate: Most Diverse in U.S. History." Pew Research Center. http://pewresearch.org/assets/pdf/dissecting-2008-electorate.pdf. Accessed March 23, 2011.

Lorber, Judith. 2000. "Guarding the Gates: The Micropolitics of Gender." In *The Gendered Society Reader*, edited by Michael Kimmel, 270–94. New York: Oxford University Press.

MacFarquhar, Neil. 2011. "Saudi Monarch Grants Women Right to Vote." *New York Times*, September 25. http://www.nytimes.com/2011/09/26/world/middleeast/women-to-vote-in-saudi-arabia-king-says.html?pagewanted=all&_r=0. Accessed February 28, 2014.

Marger, Martin. 2002. *Social Inequality*. 2nd edition. Belmont, CA: Wadsworth.

Mauer, Marc. 2013. *The Changing Racial Dynamics of Women's Incarceration* Washington, DC: Sentencing Project. http://sentencingproject.org/doc/publications/rd_Changing%20Racial%20Dynamics%202013.pdf. Accessed February 28, 2014.

McEwan, Cheryl. 2005. "Gender Citizenship in South Africa." In *(Un)thinking Citizenship*, edited by Amanda Gouws, 177–98. London: Ashgate.

McFeeley, Tim. 2000. "Getting It Straight: A Review of the 'Gays in the Military' Debate." In *Creating Change: Sexuality, Public Policy, and Civil Rights*, edited by John D'Emilio, William Turner, and Urvashi Vaid, 236–50. New York: St. Martin's.

McKay, Susan, and Cheryl de la Rey. 2001. "Women's Meanings of Peacebuilding in Post-Apartheid South Africa." *Peace and Conflict: Journal of Peace Psychology* 7 (3): 227–42.

McSmith, Andy. 2008. "Closing the Gender Gap: Why Women Now Reign in Spain." *Independent*, April 16. http://www.independent.co.uk/news/world/europe/closing-the-gender-gap-why-women-now-reign-in-spain-809619.html. Accessed March 23, 2011.

Mezey, Susan. 2000. "Gender and the Federal Judiciary." In *Gender and American Politics*, edited by Sue Tolleson-Rinehart and Jyl Josephson, 205–26. Armonk, NY: Sharpe.

Miller, Jody. 2001. *One of the Guys: Girls, Gangs, and Gender*. Oxford, UK: Oxford University Press.

Miller, Laura. 2000. "Not Just Weapons of the Weak: Gender Harassment as a Form of Protest for Army Men." In *Gender through the Prism of Difference*, 2nd edition, edited by Maxine Baca Zinn, Pierrette Hondagneu-Sotelo, and Michael Messner, 409–30. Boston: Allyn and Bacon.

Miller, Susan. 2005. *Victims as Offenders: The Paradox of Women's Violence in Relationships*. New Brunswick, NJ: Rutgers University Press.

Morin, Richard. 2004. "The GOP Problem with Women." *Washington Post*, January 11.

Nagy, Donna, and Aviva Rich. 2001. "Constitutional Law and Public Policy: Gender Equity." In *Gender Mosaics: Social Perspectives*, edited by Dana Vannoy, 312–31. Los Angeles: Roxbury.

Naraghi, Sanam. 2007. *Women Building Peace*. Boulder, CO: Lynne Rienner.

National Women's Law Center. 2013. "Women in the Federal Judiciary: Still a Long Way to Go." December 12. http://www.nwlc.org/resource/women-federal-judiciary-still-long-way-go-1. Accessed February 28, 2014.

Navy Personnel Command. 2013 "Women in Naval Services." http://www.public.navy.mil/bupers-npc/organization/bupers/WomensPolicy/Pages/NavyWomenFactsStatistics.aspx. February 28, 2014.

Norris, Pippa, and Joni Lovenduski. 1995. *Political Recruitment: Gender, Race, and Class in the British Parliament.* Cambridge, UK: Cambridge University Press.

Owen, Barbara. 1999. "Women and Imprisonment in the United States: The Gendered Consequences of the U.S. Imprisonment Binge." In *Harsh Punishment: International Experiences of Women's Imprisonment,* edited by Sandy Cook and Susanne Davies, 81–98. Boston: Northeastern University Press.

Pardo, Mary. 2000. "Mexican American Women, Grassroots Community Activists: 'Mothers of East Los Angeles.' " In *Gender through the Prism of Difference,* 2nd edition, edited by Maxine Baca Zinn, Pierrette Hondagneu-Sotelo, and Michael Messner, 461–77. Boston: Allyn & Bacon.

Peterson, V. Spike, and Anne Runyan. 1999. *Global Gender Issues.* 2nd edition. Boulder, CO: Westview.

Poole, Barbara. 1993. "Should Women Identify Themselves as Feminists When Running for Political Office?" Paper presented at the annual meeting of the American Political Science Association, Washington, DC.

Powers, Janet M. 2003. "Women and Peace Dialogue in the Middle East." *Peace Review* 15 (1): 25–31.

Rebecca Project for Human Rights. 2007. *Mothers Shackled during Labor and Birth.* http://www.rebeccaproject.org/index.php?option=com_content&task=blogcategory&id=57&Itemid=161. Accessed February 28, 2014.

Reilly, Niamh. 2003. *Civil and Political Rights.* Women's Human Rights Net (WHRnet). Accessed February 28, 2014.

Rong, Feiwen, and Zheng Lifie. 2012. *China's Urban Population Exceeds Rural for First Time.* January 17. http://www.bloomberg.com/news/2012-01-17/china-urban-population-exceeds-rural.html. Accessed February 28, 2014.

Ross, Jen. 2007. "Chile Kick-Starts Debate on Gender Quotas." *WeNews,* February 20.

Rothman, Robert. 2002. *Inequality and Stratification: Race, Class, and Gender.* Upper Saddle River, NJ: Prentice Hall.

Sabet, Kevin. 2005. "Making It Happen: The Case for Compromise in the Federal Cocaine Law Debate." *Social Policy and Administration* 39 (2): 181–91.

St. George, Donna. 2002. "Finally In, Facing New Fight." *Washington Post,* April 28.

Seltzer, Richard, Jody Newman, and Melissa Leighton. 1997. *Sex as a Political Variable.* Boulder, CO: Lynne Rienner.

Sentencing Project. 2006. "Serena Nunn." http://www.sentencingproject.org/detail/feature.cfm?feature_id=3. Accessed March 11, 2011.

Simon, Rita. 1975. *Women and Crime.* Lexington, MA: Lexington Books.

Skocpol, Theda, and Edwin Amenta. 1986. "States and Social Policies." *Annual Review of Sociology* 12: 131–57.

Small, Kevonne. 2000. "Female Crime in the United States, 1963–1998: An Update." *Gender Issues* 18 (3): 75–104.

Social Watch. 2008. *Gender Equity Index.* Montevideo, Uruguay: Social Watch.

Stack, Liam. 2011. "Saudi Men Go to Polls; Women Wait." *New York Times,* September 29. http://www.nytimes.com/2011/09/30/world/middleeast/saudi-men-vote-in-elections-for-local-advisory-councils.html?_r=0. Accessed February 28, 2014.

Steffensmeier, Darrell and Emilie Allan. 1996. "Gender and Crime: Toward a Gendered Theory of Female Offending." *Annual Review of Sociology* 22: 459–487.

Stiehm, Judith. 1981. *Bring Me Men and Women: Mandated Change at the U.S. Air Force Academy.* Berkeley: University of California Press.

Tremlett, Giles. 2005. "Blow to Machismo as Spain Forces Men to Do Housework." *Guardian*, April 7. http://www.guardian.co.uk/spain/article/0,2763,1454802,00.html. Accessed March 23, 2011.

United Nations. 2002. *Women, Peace, and Security*. New York: United Nations. www.un.org/womenwatch/daw/public/eWPS.pdf. Accessed March 23, 2011.

United Nations, Department of Public Information. 1995. *Women and Power: Where Women Stand Today*. The Advancement of Women, Notes for Speakers. New York: United Nations.

United States Army. 2013. "Today's Woman Soldier in the U.S. Army." http://www.army.mil/women/today.html Accessed February 28, 2014.

U.S. Bureau of the Census. 2012. *Statistical Abstract of the United States*. Table 324, "Arrests by Sex and Age, 2009." http://www.census.gov/compendia/statab/cats/law_enforcement_courts_prisons/arrests.html February 28, 2014.

U.S. Military.com. 2011. "Enlisted US Marine Females Set Trends." http://www.usmilitary.com/5504/enlisted-us-marine-females-set-trends/. Accessed March 23, 2011.

Uscinski, Joseph, and Lily Goren. 2011. "What's in a Name? Coverage of Senator Hillary Clinton during the 2008 Democratic Primary." *Political Research Quarterly* 64: 884–96.

Valdez, Abelardo. 2007. *Mexican American Girls and Gang Violence: Beyond Risk*. New York: Palgrave.

Wang, Zhengxu, and Weina Dai. 2013. "Women's Participation in Rural China's Self-Governance: Institutional, Socioeconomic, and Cultural Factors in a Jiangsu County." *Governance: An International Journal of Policy, Administration, and Institutions*, 26 (1): 91–118.

Washington Post. 2010. The Fair Sentencing Act Corrects a Long-time Wrong in Cocaine Cases. *Washington Post*, August 3. http://www.washingtonpost.com/wp-dyn/content/article/2010/08/02/AR2010080204360.html. Accessed February 28, 2014.

West, Guida, and Rhoda Blumberg, eds. 1990. *Women and Social Protest*. New York: Oxford University Press.

Wolf, Naomi. 2013. *The US Military's Rape Culture*. June 30. http://www.project-syndicate.org/commentary/the-us-military-s-rape-culture-by-naomi-wolf. Accessed February 28, 2014.

Women in Black. 2008. "A Short History of Women in Black." http://www.womeninblack.org.uk/History.htm. Accessed March 23, 2011.

Women in Prison Project. 2002. "Fact Sheet." New York: Correctional Association of New York. http://www.prisonpolicy.org/scans/Fact_Sheets_2002.pdf. Accessed March 23, 2011.

Young, Vernetta, and Rebecca Reviere. 2006. *Women Behind Bars: Gender and Race in US Prisons*. Boulder, CO: Lynne Rienner Publishers.

11

POPULAR CULTURE AND MEDIA

Popular media continue to present women in highly restrictive roles. Disney movies are one place where some changes have taken place. Disney princesses are now more likely to be shown in physically active roles, behaving heroically, and saving men and boys.

Source: Frank Trapper/Corbis.

Try this the next time you go to the movies. First, count the number of women/girls and men/boys in the film. If there are more than two named women or girl characters, find the scenes where they talk to each other. Are there any? What are they talking about? If they talk about something other than men/boys, how many seconds does the scene last? Does the scene have anything to do with the main point of the movie? You will probably be amazed at how few women play a part in the films, how little they talk to each other, and how few times they talk to each other about anything other than men.

This test is called the **Bechdel test** and was invented in the 1980s by Alison Bechdel, a comic book artist who wanted to bring attention to the "missing" women in the media. Anita Sarkeesian (2012) used the test to review all the films nominated for best picture by the Academy Awards for 2011. Out of the nine nominees, five (*Extremely Loud and Incredibly Close, The Artist, Moneyball, The Tree of Life,* and *War Horse*) failed the Bechdel test either because there were not at least two named woman characters or there were no scenes where two women talked to each other or there were no scenes where two women talked to each other about anything other than boys or men. (Since *The Artist* was silent, nonverbal interactions on screen and subtitles were examined.) Two passed, but just barely: *Midnight in Paris* had one scene where two women characters spoke to each other for about 9 seconds about chairs, and *Hugo* had one scene where two women characters spoke to each other for about

7 seconds. Two films passed the test: *The Descendants* and *The Help*. *The Help*, of course, has its own set of problems and has been widely criticized because of its depiction of black people, racial ethnic relationships, and racism. Although the film had many women characters talking with each other, most of the talk by black women was either black women speaking to white women or black women talking to black women about white women.

How aware have you been of the invisible woman in media? Had you noticed this before when you watched films? Or do the results of the Bechdel test surprise you?

What about media in general? How do the media construct masculinities? Femininities? What does it mean if women and girls are missing from the picture? Do the images vary cross-culturally or within a society by race ethnicity and social class or other social factors? How does sexuality fit into the images? How are gay men and lesbians presented? Do you think the media provide an omnipresent guidebook in our everyday lives about how we should think, feel, and behave in specific gendered ways?

Do you think advertisements, movies, television programs, and other media images help maintain the status quo, or can they challenge ideologies? Or do the media just reflect reality?

This chapter explores these questions. We examine a range of media from advertising, to movies, television programming, the Internet, and social media. We review gender and its intersection with other forms of inequality in media and explore theoretical concepts that can help us understand these issues such as legitimation, hegemony, and symbolic annihilation.

MASS MEDIA AND GENDER

In order for a society, especially one with high levels of inequality, to maintain its stability and popularity, it needs to develop ways to legitimate itself. **Legitimation** involves creating an ideology, a set of beliefs and ideas that explain and justify the existing social organization. Legitimation also requires creating ways to transmit this ideology to its citizens, and this is where mass media play a critical role. **Mass media** consist of the Internet, television, radio, newspapers, magazines, books, CDs, and films. **Commercial media** use these forms to explicitly sell products. Increasingly, the media also include newer outlets called social media that come through our computers, phones, and other electronic devices. Old and new, these all play an important role in both aspects of legitimation, creating an image of our society as the best of all possible worlds, and communicating that message to the common person (Marger 2002).

It is difficult to estimate how important the mass media are, but consider these facts:

- We spend more time watching television and the Internet than in any other activity, besides sleep and work.
- The average American child grows up in a home with three television sets and assorted CD and DVD players, MP3 players, iPods, and computers (Gutnick et al. 2011). Many children have their own TV in their room. And iPhones, Kindles, Netflix, and On-Demand have made a huge array of popular media available every day, all the time. Children spend about four and a half hours a day in front

of some screen. This is equivalent to spending ten weeks a year, twenty-four hours a day doing nothing but watching media images. On an average school day, if children come home from school around 4:00 and go to bed around 9:00, they have approximately one-half hour of screen-free time per day (Dunnewind 2002).

If we add to this older kinds of media, such as newspapers, radio, books, and magazines, we can see that our lives are drenched in media images and sounds that tell us how to view, experience, and act on the world. Gender is one of the critical messages we receive.

In this book, we explore the many ways that gender inequality permeates our lives. Media often legitimates this inequality by creating images and telling us which are valid and which are not.

Gender on Television

Television is a primary source of images of gender. Gender can be portrayed in a range of ways, but two kinds of images are dominant: hegemonic masculinity and emphasized femininity. You should recall from chapter 1 that hegemonic masculinity includes the subordination of women, authority, aggression, and technical competence. Emphasized femininity includes dependence, sexual receptivity, motherhood, and subordination by men (Connell 1993).

Children spend about four and a half hours a day in front of some screen. This is equivalent to spending ten weeks a year, twenty-four hours a day doing nothing but watching media images. The images they view are loaded with messages about gender.

Source: Courtesy of Judy Root Aulette.

In the 1970s, feminists in the **women's liberation movement** in the United States were concerned about the media as a source of gender stereotypes, and a number of studies were done on the images the media presented of men and especially women. The National Organization for Women (NOW) was one of the first to conduct research in this area (NOW 1972). NOW, along with others, came to two general conclusions: first, men were numerically better represented on TV; second, the roles men played on TV were more diverse by factors such as age, appearance, occupation, and character. The roles played by women were less frequent and more limited and more stereotyped.

But haven't television images of gender changed since the previous generation? Surprisingly, subsequent studies in the 1980s, 1990s, 2000s, and as recently as 2011 do not find much change in these two factors (Browne 1998; Furnham and Mak 1999; Coltrane and Messineo 2000; Larson 2001; Stern and Mastro 2004; Smith, Choueiti, Prescott, and Pieper 2012).

Visibility of women compared to men has consistently remained lower on television over the decades. The most recent research in the United States in 2011 found that only 19 percent of children's shows and 22 percent of prime-time programs feature girls and women in at least half of all speaking parts. Imbalance is far more typical. A large percentage of stories on television are male centric, casting boys/men in 75 percent or *more* of the speaking roles (Smith et al. 2012). In addition, when women appear on television, researchers find they are less likely to be the focus of the program compared to men. In a study of domestic comedies with a wife and husband and their children, for example, six times more jokes were by or about the men than by or about the women.

Some progress has been made. Compared to previous decades, women are now less likely to appear in domestic roles or as dependent on men, but men still dominate in terms of numbers. And some stereotypes are remarkably impervious to change: women are young, and men are knowledgeable authorities.

The **hyper-sexualization** of women and girls is also a persistent stereotype. In the most recent studies, researchers have found that in prime time television as well as children's programming, women and girls are sexualized. Girls and women are far more likely than men and boys to be depicted wearing sexy attire (tight or alluring apparel), showing some exposed skin (between the mid-chest and high upper thigh region), thin, and referenced by another character (verbally or nonverbally) as physically attractive or desirous. When girls and women are on screen, they are still there to provide eye candy to even the youngest viewers.

Gender also shows up in the roles women and men play on television. Women comprise 47 percent of the U.S. labor force but only hold 34 percent of all jobs in prime-time programs, and only 25 percent of jobs on children's shows. In 2005, researchers looked at gender in situation comedies and dramas in prime-time American television and found that gender was a critical factor in the kinds of roles played by television characters. They also found that age combined with gender in problematic ways. The researchers looked at the proportion of television characters of different ages and genders compared to their proportion in the real American population. Men in their teens and twenties were underrepresented, as were men over sixty. Men in their thirties, forties, and fifties were overrepresented. Women in their teens and twenties and those in their forties were slightly overrepresented, women in their thirties were dramatically overrepresented, and women in their fifties and sixties were underrepresented (Lauzen and Dozier 2005).

The researchers also examined the kinds of roles women and men played in the shows. They were especially interested in whether there were differences in depicting women and men as leaders who provided guidance or direction to the other characters in the shows. Women and men in their teens, twenties, and thirties were about equally likely to play a leadership role. Older men, however, were much more likely than any other group to play a leadership role. In regard to authority, aging was a positive factor for men.

Age benefited both women and men positively when it came to their occupational status. As women and men aged on the shows, they each tended to have more prestigious jobs, moving from low-status characters like the unemployed and job applicants when they were young to high-status jobs like CEOs in older roles. However, men moved higher than did women, and in comparisons of men and women over sixty, men characters had higher status jobs than did women.

The researchers also looked at goals—whether the character was working toward something as the story line unfolded. On this issue, there were important age and gender differences. Men characters, regardless of their age, had goals. Women characters, until they reached about the age of forty, also had goals. Women over forty, however, were much less likely to have goals than were any men or younger women.

Prime time also stereotypes women and men in regard to the particular kinds of jobs held by characters. Eighty-six percent of characters playing the part of a chief executive of a corporation are men, and 100 percent of chief justices and district attorneys, 70 percent of physicians, 72 percent of high level politicians, and 62 percent of academic administrators are men. In addition, more than five times as many men are shown in scientific occupations, such as computer science and engineering (Smith et al. 2012).

In some ways, images of women have improved on TV, but in many ways the images have remained remarkably similar, continuing to present old stereotypes over several decades. In addition, recently, images of gender have become worse in one regard: violence against women. Research on prime-time programming (except for sports and news programs) on the major broadcast networks (ABC, Fox, CBS, and NBC) finds: violence against women and teenage girls is increasing on television at rates that far exceed the overall increases in violence in general on television; although female victims appeared to be primarily of adult age, there was a 400 percent increase in the depiction of teen girls as victims; domestic violence is trivialized in comedies (Fox stood out for using violence against women as a punch line in its comedies—in particular *Family Guy* and *American Dad*); and there was an 81 percent increase in the incidence of intimate partner violence on television (PTC 2009). This study emphasizes the importance of the images of women of girls as victims of violence, but equally disturbing are the images of boys and men as perpetrators of violence against women. Watching TV tells us that to be a woman or girl is to be a victim and that her victimization is a legitimate form of entertainment. It also tells us that men who are worthy of our attention are violent against women (Kellner 2008).

Reality TV and Gender

In 1973, public television in the United States aired a new program that chronicled the life of a real family named the Louds. Cameras entered the Loud home and followed their lives as the five children in the household negotiated everyday life and their parents separated and eventually divorced. During the filming, one son, Lance, came out to his family as gay and is credited as being the first openly gay character on American TV. The following year, the BBC presented a similar program about a real family in the United Kingdom, the Readings from Berkshire, England. Twenty years later, MTV picked up the idea and ushered in a new genre of unscripted television called reality TV. By 2003, Fox was devoting 41 percent of its airtime during the sweeps to reality shows. Reality television continues to grow in popularity. High ratings, low production costs, and lucrative product-placement revenues make it popular with TV executives, and audiences seem intrigued as well. Unfortunately, despite its cutting-edge character in regard to format, reality TV is now one of the worst spots on the screen regarding gender equity. Reality TV portrays women as "hot, stupid and desperate" and tells us that all men need is wealth to be Mr. Right (Pozner 2004).

Jennifer Pozner (2011) labels reality TV as "pop cultural backlash against women's rights and social progress" as she describes Christine, a bubbly twenty-four-year-old administrative assistant on ABC's template-setting dating series *The Bachelor*. Christine explains why she should win a marriage proposal from some man she doesn't even know yet, instead of the twenty-four other husband-hunting competitors he'd be making out with:"I will make the best wife for Bob because I will be a servant to him. And if he comes home from a long day at the office, I'll just rub his feet, and have dinner ready for him, and just [giggle] love on him!"

VH1 matchmaker Steve Ward, on *Tough Love*, tells us what happens to women who don't win the real life competition and find a husband as he opens every episode saying, "Nobody knows single women like I do. They're lonely. They're clueless. They're needy" (Pozner 2011). Other programs, such as *Wife Swap* and *Trading Spouses*, shows women and men who have failed to meet the gender stereotypes and therefore, have failed as humans in general. The women are bad wives and mothers if they pursue professional or political interests outside the home, and dads are demonized as wimps or poor role models if they are primary caregivers for their kids (Pozner 2011).

So-called reality TV is not really reality, of course. MTV's *Real Life*, for example, filmed 24 hours a day for four months, creating more than 2,000 hours of footage to make an eight-hour series. Producers assemble the clips into pieces that portray the issues in the most dramatic way within templates of characters and relationships they wish to present. But the resulting product is temptingly believable and powerful because of its supposed real grounding. The images we see seem to be ones that are not only true but apparently normal or even exceptional in an enviable way.

LGBT on TV

One of the central features of the dominant images of femininity and masculinity is that women and men must be absolutely heterosexual. LGBT characters were nearly invisible until the 1970s, when a few openly gay characters began to appear in primetime dramas and sitcoms, and daytime soap operas. Gay men and lesbians, however, were rare, and into the 1990s played limited roles as villains and victims in TV crime programs, and comedic relief in shows such as *Ellen* and *Will and Grace* (Peters 2011).

In 2000, a new program was introduced in U.S. and Canadian TV, *Queer as Folk*, which centered around five (eventually six) gay men, a lesbian couple, and a heterosexual activist with PFLAG (Parents and Friends of Lesbians and Gays). This program appears different in many respects. While it primarily maintains the representation of gay men and lesbians as white and affluent, the Showtime series features many gay and lesbian characters who formed a clique within a larger queer community. "Furthermore, beyond depicting love, intimacy, and sex between same-sex partners, the characters enjoyed public sex, sex with strangers, polyamorous relationships, sex for pay, bondage, discipline, and sado-masochism to name only a few of the non-**normative** sexual practices represented on the series" (Peters 2011. 194), While clearly gay, especially in terms of active sexual behavior, the characters fit into a new model of masculinity that is also gay. The "requirement" that to be masculine one must be heterosexual appears to have been altered. The "new" image of a gay man is young, white, with a well muscled, smooth body, handsome face, good education, professional job, and high income (Fejes 2000). And, this image allows men to move from a stigmatized unmasculine role to an acceptable masculine while gay one.

While growing visibility of LGBT people in popular media and challenges to dominant views of masculinity are worth going after, *Queer as Folk* has not been without its critics. Sarah Schulman (1998, 146) writes that the series is economically exploitative, creating provocative but not quite controversial programming in order to go after "**pink dollars**" by gaining customers for its advertisers. "A fake homosexuality has been constructed to facilitate a double marketing strategy: selling products to gay consumers that address their emotional needs to be accepted while selling a palatable image of homosexuality to heterosexual consumers. . . ." Wendy Peters argues, furthermore, that *Queer as Folk* represents what she calls "**narrowcasting**" that has identified a "valuable demographic"—wealthy white gay men—as a niche market with substantial amounts of disposable income to which advertisers wish to present their consumer goods. She argues that other LGBT people who do not fall in the "valuable demographic"—not men, not white, not wealthy—continue to be ignored or stigmatized.

Despite the controversies, there is no doubt that LGBT television has introduced new and visible images of LGBT people to the media. And because sexuality is so central to stereotypes and expectations about gender, LGBT programming has also influenced our thinking about gender. Gay men, for example, are no longer uniformly assumed to be feminine. Rather, a range of gay masculinities has been added to media representations of gender.

LGBT television has also challenged and reshaped gender stereotypes about heterosexual people, especially heterosexual men. Scholars studying the industrialist tradition in the United States before the end of the twentieth century define hegemonic masculinity as emphasizing physical force, occupational achievement, familial patriarchy, frontiersmanship, and heterosexuality (Buerkle 2011). In 2003, a new television program came on air for four years and had an important impact on this definition. *Queer Eye for the Straight Guy* was a popular television program that featured five gay men who chose a heterosexual man every week to make over. Each of the Fab Five were experts in grooming, food and wine, interior design, fashion, or culture. Their task was to "teach a straight man to style his hair, preserve/improve his skin, prepare a somewhat epicurean meal, live in a stylish home, select a fashionable wardrobe, and demonstrate cultural sophistication" (Buerkle 2011, 7). Wesley Buerkle (2011, 74) argues that they not only gave these individual men a makeover, they also gave hegemonic masculinity a makeover, "transforming brute force into physical perfection, occupational achievement into cultural literacy, and frontiersmanship into urban sophistication."

Missing Women in the Television Industry

Gender inequity is also present in the production of television. During the 2011–2012 prime-time season, women comprised only 26 percent of all individuals working as creators, directors, writers, producers, executive producers, editors, and directors of photography on broadcast television programs. This represents an increase of only 5 percentage points since 1997–98 (Lauzen 2012). In addition, it appears that women who are employed in the industry are not dispersed across the programs but are concentrated in a limited number of programs. For example, 30 percent of writers in the industry are women, but 68 percent of all programs have no women writers.

The missing woman in network news is another area of concern, although there has been some improvement in the past few decades. In 2006, 57 percent of local anchors were women. However, women news anchors are still not equal to men. Women anchors' primary value rests on their appearance, whereas men anchors are valued because of their authority and expertise. Men are allowed to shows signs of maturity such as wrinkles and gray hair. Furthermore, as men have left anchor seats and women have increased their numbers, the pay has declined and the median annual pay is now only about $31,320 (Blanchette 2006). Newspapers have even greater gender gaps. The proportion of women working in newsroom has remained steady at about 38 percent since 1999, and the proportion of supervisors in newspapers who are women has also remained almost unchanged at 35 percent.

Another measure of inequality in the newsroom is the sources reporters use for their stories. Women are much less likely to be part of the news being covered. An international study looking at seventy-six countries found that currently about 24 percent of those interviewed on the news are women. In stories about politics and the government, women are least likely to appear (18 percent of those interviewed). In business and economics stories, they are slightly more likely to be interviewed (21 percent). Health and social issues (37 percent) and sports, arts, and entertainment (26 percent) are at the high ends of visibility for women. Women who do appear in news stories are also of lesser status than the men in the news. Foty-seven percent of the ordinary citizens interviewed by the news media are women, whereas 81 percent of experts are men (Project for Excellence in Journalism 2005, Gallagher 2005).

Sunday TV talk shows are a special kind of news programming that identifies experts to talk about the most important issues of the day. They include programs such as ABC's *This Week*, NBC's *Meet the Press*, CBS's *Face the Nation*, and *Fox News Sunday*. In 2011, 86 percent (228 guests) of the one-on-one interviews were of men.

The gender gap showed up dramatically in the news coverage of the 2012 American presidential elections. When Americans have an election, especially a presidential election, newspeople comment non-stop, 24 hours a day on everything from globally critical issues to the most insignificant minutea as it relates to the candidates. Klos (2013) found that in the election coverage in 2012 a much larger proportion of men's voices were being heard while women covering the elections were often relegated to writing and talking about "pink topics" of food, family, furniture, and fashion.

For example, in the ten months leading up to the elections, 77 percent of the people quoted on television regarding the elections were men. On NPR (National Public Radio), 64 percent of those quoted on air were men. NPR provides an especially interesting example because it is often lauded (or criticized) for its liberal stance, and regarding the balance of men and women reporters at the presidential conventions they had seemed to have a gender equal team, with fifty men and fifty women correspondents on assignment. But the gender gap showed sharply in who actually reported the news: 63 percent of the stories filed were by men.

Symbolic Annihilation

Two key findings in the research on media illustrated in the discussion of television images are the greater number of men compared to women and the different images of women and men that are presented, for example, in the roles played in television shows. Men in all media presentations far outnumber women. This issue is part of all aspects of television programming, as well as advertising and films, as we will see next.

Gaye Tuchman and her colleagues (Tuchman, Kaplan Daniels, and Benet 1978) named this invisibility "symbolic annihilation." They argue that when a group and their experience do not appear in the media, it sends a message that they do not matter and that their views are unimportant. Because the numbers of women and girls in the media are smaller than those of men and boys, Tuchman and her colleagues argue that the women and girls have been symbolically annihilated. The message of the nonexistent images is that women and girls must not be as important. Their experiences and ideas are not as interesting or as significant as those of men and boys.

Gender in Advertising

Like mass media, commercial media give us images of what "real" men and women are supposed to be like. Although the audience does not necessarily "buy" the images with which they are presented, advertisements provide confirmation of existing social arrangements and provide a source of stereotypes that become resources for understanding and interacting in the real world. Furthermore, because advertisements provide these stereotypes with flawless people in "magical encounters—the happy family, fun loving youth, and the ubiquitous romantic encounter," they are indeed powerful (Coltrane and Messineo 2000, 367).

ADVERTISING MASCULINITY. What do advertisements tell us about masculine ideals? A historical review of masculine images in advertisements from 1930 to 1980 shows that two stereotypes were remarkably persistent: the sturdy oak (hard-working, good providers) and the big wheel (socially and economically successful) (Frith and Mueller 2003). Two differences in the two historical periods were an increase in the 1980s in younger men and more sexualized images of men.

In the late 1990s, another emphasis became prominent: independence and isolation (Patterson and Elliott 2004). This image is the essence of the earlier ads for the Marlboro man, a cowboy shown enjoying his cigarette alone with his horse in a vast expanse of range with no sign of other humans. In the 1990s, this image of masculinity became increasingly popular.

An additional aspect of the masculine stereotype in advertising in recent years is a growing focus on physicality and especially body size and muscle development. The growth (literally) of the strong, muscular model in the past four decades is illustrated by GI Joe dolls. If GI Joe were a real human, the circumference of his biceps would have grown from 12.2 inches in 1964 to 15.3 inches in 1974 to 16.4 inches in 1994 to a whopping 26.8 inches in 1998. In comparison, Mark McGwire, an athlete known for his strong, muscular, steroid-produced, home-run-hitting arms, has biceps that are 20 inches (*New York Times* 1999).

Along with physical size and bulky muscles, the images tell men they should work hard, acquire wealth, and use violence. Violence appears as an important element of the stereotypes of men in advertisements. Commercials use heroes from history, such as cowboys, conquerors, military men, and crusaders, who were often violent, to signify masculinity. They also use sports heroes in wrestling and martial arts, whose muscles and techniques are associated with power and violence (Katz 1995).

Men and Beer. Advertisements tell men not only what they are supposed to be like, but also how to become a man. Beer commercials, like all advertisements, are designed to sell a product. Along with the product, however, images of masculinity and femininity are also being sold. Beer commercials outline how men can accomplish masculinity. Drinking beer is the way to manliness, and the commercials provide a blueprint for how to become a man by explaining when, why, and with whom men should drink beer. When should men drink beer? Beer signifies the end of the workday and the end of a job well done. In the world of beer, men work hard and they play hard. They must take on challenges of power boating, sailing, and playing sports. Then they reminisce on their triumphs in these challenges while they drink a beer (Strate 2001). "Miller Time" marks the period after work when it is time to drink beer.

Why should men drink beer? According to the ads, beer helps boys grow up. Beer commercials provide a transition in gender from boys to men. The ads show a young outsider who must prove himself to others; then he is rewarded by drinking beer with the older men (Strate 2001). As we will see in the next chapter on sports, the initiation of younger (or at least less experienced) men by older men is part of many cultures. In American culture (and many others), beer is part of this process, and beer commercials provide the model. Beer commercials also tell men with whom they should drink beer. Part of being a real man is drinking beer with the other guys. Unlike the image of masculinity in the cigarette commercials, there are no loners like the Marlboro man. Beer-drinking men travel in groups (Strate 2001).

Finally, beer commercials tell men how to relate to women. Men constitute the largest proportion of figures in the ads, and they are the central characters in beer commercials, but women do sometimes appear. Beer-drinking men should be attractive but detached, cool, and confident when met with the challenge of a woman (Strate 2001).

ADVERTISING GENDER IN THREE NATIONS. The promotion of gender stereotypes is of concern in many nations in the world. Scholars in the United States (Coltrane and Messineo 2000), Turkey (Uray and Burnaz 2003), and Japan (Arima 2003) recently investigated images of people in commercials to see what progress has been made. Are women still being portrayed in limited and stereotyped ways? How are men represented?

Gender in U.S. Advertising. Researchers in the United States have found that television commercials present "packages" of gender characteristics. Box 11-1 summarizes what they have found most recently. Their findings were similar to those for television programming,

GENDER IN EVERYDAY LIFE   BOX 11-1

SUMMARY OF RECENT RESEARCH ON GENDER IMAGES IN TELEVISION
ADVERTISING IN THE UNITED STATES

In 2004, researchers reviewed all the recent studies of television to see what images of
masculinities and femininities were being presented by advertisers in the United States
today (Stern and Mastro 2004). The studies showed the following:

- Television ads underrepresent women compared to men. Men are twice as likely to
  appear in commercials, and voiceovers are largely by men. Men do the voiceovers in
  64 percent of the advertisements for domestic products and 89 percent of the advertisements for nondomestic products. In advertisements for children, boys outnumber
  girls two to one (Sapiro 2002).
- Among women, age makes a difference. Young adult women (compared to girls,
  middle-age women, and older women) are better represented. Older women and older
  men are equally less visible.
- Roles for men are more diverse. Young women, compared to other age groups of
  women, did seem to be catching up with men by appearing in more diverse roles as
  competent, authoritative, and outside the home. Young men and middle-age men,
  however, still far outnumber young women in these kinds of roles.
- Women are associated with domestic cleaning products and cosmetics, men with nondomestic items such as cars, cameras, and electronics.
- Women are likely to be shown inside in a domestic residence; men are shown outside
  in a broad range of settings.
- Women are more physically attractive. For example, 75 percent of women in ads are
  physically fit compared to 25 percent of men (Signorielli, McLeod, and Healy 1994).
- Women are shown in skimpy or sexy clothing and are three times as likely to be sex
  objects (Coltrane and Adams 1997).
- Men are shown in more prominent and dominant positions in the workforce. For
  example, men are more frequently shown as professionals and in positions of authority giving orders, whereas women are frequently shown doing housework or without a
  paid occupation.
- Men are shown in more active roles.
- Similar differences exist in comparisons of children. Boys are active in the ads, and
  girls are passive support figures. Colors, settings, and behavior further emphasize
  stereotypes. Boys wear dark-colored clothes and are filmed against green, gray, and
  blue. Girls wear light-colored clothes against pastel backgrounds. Boys are shown
  outside, whereas girls are filmed inside in bedrooms and playrooms (Frith and Mueller
  2003).

with women and especially older women underrepresented, conventionally attractive, and often scantily clad, while men appear more often in active or professional roles. Since advertising tends to confirm stereotypes rather than challenge them (for fear of alienating anyone in the advertisers' audience), women are still more likely than men to be shown in domestic roles, cooking, cleaning, and doing laundry.

Much of the exploration of gender in advertising, however, has focused on gender to the exclusion of other significant social variables, and it has revealed contradictions in the images of masculinity and femininity. Coltrane and Messineo (2000) argue that race ethnicity needs to be sorted out from gender as a separate powerful factor. When race ethnicity is examined in addition to gender, it helps to explain some of the contradictions in gender images in advertising.

Coltrane and Messineo found that four images emerge from a content analysis of television advertising in the United States:

- *Powerful white men.* White men are twice as likely to be giving orders or exercising authority; for example, as a tank commander barking orders or an authoritative physician in a white coat offering medical advice.
- *White women sex objects.* Twenty-five percent of white women are depicted as sex objects. This is twice the proportion of black women shown this way and three times the proportion of men, black or white. White women are shown as flirting, being checked out by a man, or trying to look pretty in ads like that for a low-calorie cereal with the woman looking at her slim body in a mirror and running her hands over her tight-fitting dress.
- *Aggressive black men.* Black men are three times as likely as white men to be shown behaving in a physically aggressive manner, for example playing rough on a basketball court. Black men are also less likely than any of the other categories to be shown at home: 40 percent of white women, 30 percent of black women, 26 percent of white men, and only 13 percent of black men are shown at home. Whites are shown as married two to three times more often.
- *Inconsequential black women.* Black women are less authoritative than white men, less aggressive than black men, and less engaged in family roles and sexual encounters than white women. They are more likely than white women to be shown in paid employment; but in general, black women are just less visible or less significant to the interactions in the ads than the other categories. Similarly, men and women who are Latino, Asian Americans, and First Nations people are nearly nonexistent in American ads.

Gender in Turkish Advertising. Since the 1980s, important changes have occurred in Turkey, including a significant increase in the number of well-educated working women, an increasing income level, a shift from traditional large families toward small nuclear-type families, and the penetration of Western consumer values. **Gender ideologies** about women and men in families in particular and in society in general are changing. Turkey has also begun to transform from an agrarian society into a postmodern consumer society. One of the major driving forces behind this transformation has been the rapidly growing media, which promote Western lifestyles, values, and consumption. There are now four state-owned and twenty-two private television channels in Turkey. The number of total radio channels grew from 1 in 1992 to 1,200 today. Advertising is increasingly prevalent, although not nearly as pervasive as in the West. In 1996, for example, advertisers in Turkey spent $14 per person, while advertisers in Europe spent $197. But between 1996 and 1997, expenditures on advertising grew by 49 percent in Turkey and only 4 percent in Europe. Messages about gender are an important part of this expanding aspect of Turkish life (Uray and Burnaz 2003).

What images are Turkish television viewers seeing these days? Like commercials in the West, Turkish ads shows different and stereotyped roles for women and men. Media images of Turkish women are similar to those of Western women in their limited age range. Almost all women are young, whereas men span a broader age range. In addition, women are more frequently shown as married and are less likely than men to be portrayed as employed (Uray and Burnaz 2003).

Unlike the West, women outnumber men in Turkish ads. The gender of the primary character, however, varies with the product advertised and follows gender stereotypes. Men are most likely to be primary characters in automobile and accessories, services (mainly financial), and food and drink advertisements. Women, on the other hand, are tied to families and home. Women are more likely than men to be primary characters in body products and home products advertisements, suggesting that their main tasks are to improve themselves and their homes. The main setting in which women appear is the home, whereas men are portrayed mostly out of the home. The connection to home may be the explanation for why women outnumber men, because body and home products, which are mainly purchased and consumed by Turkish women, are the most popular items advertised on television (Uray and Burnaz 2003).

Women in Turkish advertisements also reflect a stereotyped expectation of women's demeanor. Turkish advertisements portray women as more relaxed than men, a behavior traditionally expected of women in Turkish families (Uray and Burnaz 2003).

Gender in Japanese Advertising. The presentation of gender in advertisements in Japan has also been studied (Arima 2003). Researchers have found that, unlike American advertising but similar to the Turkish ads, Japanese women (56.7 percent) outnumbered men (43.3 percent). However, stereotypes in the products they advertise and the roles they play in the ads are similar. Women appear as housewives and product demonstrators in ads for products associated with housework, cosmetics, and services, whereas men are shown as office workers and are linked to electronic products. Like Turkey and the United States, in Japan men of many ages are shown, but women are nearly always young (Arima 2003).

Arima (2003) explored further the gender "packages" presented in Japanese television commercials. Five types of characters were found:

- *Beautiful and wise housewives* (9.4 percent of the characters). They appeared in an apron or kimono, and they advertised food, beauty products, or services to a woman audience.
- *Young ladies attracting people's attention* (20.7 percent of the characters). Most of these were young Japanese women dressed in swimsuits, underwear, or *yukata* (cotton summer sundresses). They appeared at home, in leisure activities, or outside, advertising beauty products and tools used for housework aimed at women. Their appearance and the angles of the shots were designed to attract the attention of the viewer.

- *Young celebrities* (25.6 percent of the total characters). Most were famous young Japanese celebrities, including athletes. They often wore uniforms and acted as providers of the services being advertised and users of products in the role of office workers or salespersons with men colleagues. Men and women in these ads differed in that women were constantly smiling, whereas men appeared serious.
- *Middle-aged and old people enjoying private time* (20.7 percent of the total number of characters). Most were Japanese entertainers in the thirty to sixty age range, and men outnumbered women. They wore casual clothes and appeared at home or in stores with other adults or with adults and children, usually playing parents' roles. They advertised alcohol and tobacco more often than did people in other categories.
- *Middle-aged worker bee* (23.5 percent of the total). Most were men (118 people) and, compared to the other clusters, there was more variety in ethnic background (twenty-three whites, five blacks, and fifteen east Asians in addition to Japanese). They appeared in offices, outside, or in the studio wearing suits with other men, or as masculine animals or cartoon characters. They announced the names of medicines, electrical appliances, or automobiles, or explained the utility or efficiency of products targeted at an audience of men (Arima 2003).

Although these studies from the United States, Turkey, and Japan are not entirely comparable because they use different methodologies, they do suggest similarities and differences among the three societies. In all three nations, gender is expressed in television advertising. Some stereotypes are also common across the borders, such as the limited age range for women and the association of women with domestic products and family and home settings and activities. However, in each nation, gender intersects with different variables. In the United States, race ethnicity takes center stage along with gender. In Turkey the tension between East and West and the newness of commercial media are significant. In Japan, age stands out as an important issue, and the association of men with a serious business image is notable.

Gender in Film

Hollywood generates gender images for filmgoers all over the world. The opening scenario of this chapter showed us what the gender gap looks like in some of the most recent Academy Award winning films. But these problems have persisted throughout the industry for a long time. Screen time is one of the most important gender differences. A review of American films from 1940 to 1980 found that men and boy characters outnumbered women and girl characters about two to one (Bazzini, McIntosh, Smith, Cook, and Harris 1997). Box 11-2 lists the twenty top-grossing films worldwide as of 2012. The list shows that this proportion still holds true. The films that have been seen most widely at the box office around the world are nearly all ones that have a man or boy as a main character; and some of them, such as Avatar, the *Lord of the Rings* films, and the *Pirates of the Caribbean* and *Star Wars* series have almost no women or girls in them. Those women who do appear are in largely insignificant roles.

Some films, of course, do have women in key roles, but their parts tend to come from a narrow range of characters. In the film *The First Wives Club*, Goldie Hawn's character says,

GENDER IN EVERYDAY LIFE   BOX 11-2

TWENTY TOP-GROSSING FILMS WORLDWIDE BY 2012, IN MILLIONS
OF DOLLARS

1. *Avatar* (2009) $2,778
2. *Titanic* (1997) $2,185
3. *Marvels, the Avengers* (2012) $1,512
4. *Harry Potter and the Deathly Hallows Part 2* (2011) $1,328
5. *Lord of the Rings: The Return of the King* (2003) $1,129
6. *Transformers: Dark of the Moon* (2011) $1,123
7. *Skyfall* (2012) $1,109
8. *The Dark Knight Rises* (2012) $1,081
9. *Pirates of the Caribbean: Dead Man's Chest* (2006) $1,066
10. *Toy Story 3* (2010) $1,063
11. *Pirates of the Caribbean: On Stranger Tides* (2011) $1,040
12. *Star Wars: Episode I: The Phantom Menace* (1999) $1,027
13. *Alice in Wonderland* (2010) $1,024
14. *The Hobbit: The Unexpected Journey* (2012) $1,017
15. *The Dark Knight* (2008) $1,002
16. *Harry Potter and the Sorcerer's Stone* (2001) $969
17. *Pirates of the Caribbean: At World's End* (2007) $961
18. *Harry Potter and the Deathly Hallows Part 1* (2010) $949
19. *The Lion King* (1994) $952
20. *Harry Potter and the Order of the Phoenix* (2007) $938

SOURCE: The Movie Times (2013).

"There are only three ages for women in Hollywood: babe, district attorney, and *Driving Miss Daisy*" (quoted in Lauzen and Dozier 2005). This quote turns out also to be true for popular films today.

Research (Lauzen and Dozier 2005) on the 100 domestic top-grossing films in the United States in 2002 concluded that major masculine characters outnumbered feminine characters 73 percent to 27 percent. The researchers also found that most of the men characters were in their thirties and forties, whereas most of the women were in their twenties and thirties. Men had longer and more vital screen lives. The women in films seemed to "remain forever frozen in their 20s and 30s" (Lauzen and Dozier 2005, 437).

Those women characters that did remain in films beyond their thirties saw their mental, physical, and social capacities decline. The older the women were in the films, the less likely they were to lead purposeful lives and to have goals. Men characters, in contrast, saw their leadership and occupational power increase with age. Moviegoers see men in roles as religious, political, and military leaders, setting goals and attempting to reach them. These images reinforce the idea that men are "natural" leaders and that women are not (Lauzen and Dozier 2005).

Moreover, 60 percent of the men but only 35 percent of the women are shown earning a living. In addition, women, especially married women, are likely to be in women-dominated occupations. Single women are more likely to be depicted in gender-neutral jobs or even "men's jobs" (Sapiro 2002).

Both men and women characters are mostly young, and all older people are dramatically underrepresented compared to their real numbers in American society. But the proportion of moviegoers who are fifty or older is increasing, and this age group currently accounts for one-quarter of all the tickets purchased. This buying power may eventually alter the ages of characters on the screen, although judging from the top box-office films, it has not influenced films so far (Lauzen and Dozier 2005). At the other end of the age spectrum are the youngest viewers. The issues affecting them have been studied in G-rated films directed at children moviegoers.

CHILDREN'S MOVIES. Violence in films has been of special concern for researchers and policymakers, and it is of particular interest to scholars interested in gender because of the links among gender, power, and masculinity that we explored in chapter 8. In the film world, "violence is key to the rule of power. It is the cheapest and quickest dramatic representation of who can and who cannot get away with what and against whom" (Gerbner, Gross, Morgan, and Signorielli 1980, 7–8).

In studies of G-rated movies, researchers have found that men and boy characters are dominant, disconnected, and dangerous. Men and boy characters are more prevalent and more important to the story than are girls and women. In a review of 4,000 characters in G movies, men and boys were the majority in every measurement used: 75 percent of all characters live or animated, 83 percent of the characters in crowds, 83 percent of the narrators, and 72 percent of the speaking characters. In addition, little change occurred in these proportions from 1990 to 2004. Women and girls were strongly outnumbered, and the stories of men and boys prevailed. Race ethnicity also figures into these numbers. Among the U.S. population, 36 percent are people of color, but only 15 percent of the characters in the movies are (Eschholz and Bufkin 2001; Kelly and Smith 2006).

In addition to being more prevalent on the screen, boys and men are depicted differently from girls and women, especially in regard to family relationships. Men are only about half as likely (35 percent) as women (61 percent) to be parents. They are also much less often (32 percent of men) in a committed relationship or marriage compared to women (61 percent) (Kelly and Smith 2006).

The contrasts in family roles also depict racial ethnic differences as well as gender differences. Of nonwhites, 35 percent are parents, whereas 53 percent of whites are portrayed as mothers and fathers. Only 22 percent of nonwhites are in committed relationships, compared to 53 percent of whites (Kelly and Smith 2006).

Danger is the third factor observed by researchers of G-rated movies. Forty-four percent of the men and boy characters, 31 percent of white women and girls, and 38 percent of the nonwhite women and girls are depicted as physically aggressive or violent. The gender gap is relatively small, but coupled with the fact that masculine characters also take three times as much screen time, the image of masculine violence is powerful (Kelly and Smith 2006).

While men and boys in G movies are dominant, disconnected, and dangerous, women and girls are depicted as defined by their appearance and longing for romantic love. To be female in G movies is to be beautiful, and beauty is defined in a limited and distorted manner: unrealistically or exaggeratedly thin and narrow-waisted and clad in sexy, revealing clothes (Smith and Choueiti 2010). One old stereotype of girls and women, however, has been abandoned in more recent films: the **damsel in distress**. Feminine characters are about equally likely to be shown in physically active roles, behaving heroically andsaving men and boys as vice versa. Some of the most notable recent scenes include: "Dorothy saving the scarecrow from burning to death; Ariel rescuing Flounder from being eaten by a shark; Belle sacrificing her freedom for Maurice's release from captivity; Mulan taking her father's place in the draft and becoming a soldier in the Imperial Army; and Crysta destroying Hexxus to save all living creatures in the forest" (Smith and Cook 2008, 24).

Sexualization of Girls and Women in Media

The sexualization of women and girls in media are issues of concern not only in films but across the board in media. In chapter 4, we examined the debate around pornography and the exploitation of women and girls. In this chapter we are looking at more subtle kinds of sexualization in media. The Sexuality Information and Education Council of the United States (SEICUS 2004) distinguishes between **healthy sexuality** and *sexualization*: "Healthy sexuality is an important component of both physical and mental health, fosters intimacy, bonding and shared pleasure, and involves mutual respect between consenting partners."

In contrast, sexualization occurs when:
- A person's value come's only from his or her sexual appeal or behavior to the exclusion of other characteristics.
- A person is held to a standard that equates physical attractiveness (narrowly defined) with being sexy.
- A person is **sexually objectified**—that is, made into a thing for an other's sexual use, rather than seen as a person with the capacity for independent action and decision making.
- Sexuality is inappropriately imposed upon a person. (APA 2007, 2)

The American Psychological Association (APA 2007, 3) offers the following examples to clarify their definition of sexualization:

- Imagine a five-year-old girl walking through a mall wearing a short T-shirt that says "Flirt."
- Consider the instructions given in magazines to preadolescent girls on how to look sexy and get a boyfriend by losing ten pounds and straightening their hair.
- Envision a soccer team of adolescent girls whose sex appeal is emphasized by their coach or a local journalist to attract fans.
- Think of print advertisements that portray women as little girls, with pigtails and ruffles, in adult sexual poses.

Sexualization, especially of women and girls, is prevalent on television. In one study, 84 percent of the episodes analyzed contained at least one incident of sexual harassment, with an average of 3.4 per program. The most frequent acts were sexist comments describing women, for example, as "broad," "bimbo," and "dumbass chick." The next most common occurrence insulted women's bodies, especially breasts, using words such as *jugs, boobs, knockers,* and *hooters* (Grauerholz and King 1997).

Music videos are also a well-known source of sexualization of women and men. Of music videos shown on BET, 84 percent have been found to display sexual imagery, including sexual objectification and women dancing sexually (Ward and Rivadeneyra 2002). Lyrics in popular music often sexualize women and/or refer to them in degrading ways (APA 2007):

> "So blow me bitch I don't rock for cancer/I rock for the cash and the topless dancers." (Kid Rock 1998)
> "Don'tcha wish your girlfriend was hot like me?" (Pussycat Dolls 2005)
> "That's the way you like to fuck, rough sex make it hurt, in the garden all in the dirt." (Ludacris 2000)
> "I tell the hos all the time, Bitch get in my car." (50 Cent 2005)
> "Ho shake your ass." (Ying Yang Twins 2003)
> "Bitch, please—you must have a mental disease. Assume the position and get back down on your knees—c'mon." (Eminem 2001)

Magazines are another source of sexualization, and even in our electronic world are an increasingly popular form of media. The number of magazines targeted at teens rose from five in 1990 to nineteen in 2000. Almost half of eight- to eighteen-year-olds report having read a magazine the previous day (Roberts, Roehr, and Rideout 2005). The magazines typically encourage girls and young women to gain the attention of men by presenting themselves as sexually desirable by dressing, "costuming for seduction," in a particular way and using certain products (Duffy and Gotcher 1996). Even articles on exercise emphasize increasing sexual desirability rather than its health effects.

Advertisements in magazines also sexualize women. One study of magazines such as *Time* and *Vogue* from 1955 to 2002 found that 40 percent of the ads featured women as decorative sexual objects (Lindner 2004). In magazines specifically targeted at men, 53 percent (targeted at white men) to 68 percent (targeted at black men) of the images of women depict them as decorative sexual objects (Baker 2005) (see Box 11-3).

The sexualization of women and girls may have important negative consequences for the women and girls who see the images and messages. Studies show they are linked to eating disorders, depression, dissatisfaction with personal appearance, and a greater likelihood of seeking surgical alterations to make themselves appear more like the sexualized images. Trying to imitate the sexualized images in the media, ironically, may create problems in the workplace, as women who are applying for management positions and appear more sexual are judged to be less intelligent and less competent than those who are more conservative in appearance (Glick, Larsen, Johnson, and Branstiter 2005, APA 2007).

The self-objectification of girls that comes with their sexualization has negative consequences in terms of girls' ability to develop healthy sexuality. **Self-objectification** occurs when women and girls "buy" the images and start to behave in ways consistent with them. Self-objectification is linked directly with diminished sexual health among adolescent girls, as measured by decreased condom use and diminished sexual assertiveness (Impett, Schooler, and Tolman 2006). Self-objectification also detracts from the ability to concentrate and focus

GENDER IN EVERYDAY LIFE   BOX 11-3
GOFFMAN AND THE GAZE

Erving Goffman (1979) was one of the first scholars to look at gender in advertising. He explored the poses of women models and argued that these provided powerful, although somewhat hidden, messages about women, turning them into objects and emphasizing their sexuality and vulnerability. His work in the 1970s identified symbolic themes in images of women in advertising that still can be seen today:

- *Body cant or bashful knee bends*. Model curves her body, cocks her head, points her toes, and bends her knee in awkward contorted pose, making herself into a decorative object.
- *Recumbent figure*. Model reclines or semi-reclines on floor, bed, or sofa expressing passivity combined with sexual availability and vulnerability.
- *Psychological or licensed withdrawal*. Daydream or blank stare implying mental incompetence, air-headedness, and passive relationship with surroundings.
- *Engaging gaze*. Sexually seductive expression aimed at camera suggests sexual availability and role of women as sex objects rather than subjects of their own sexuality.
- *Touching self*. Model touches her face making her look girlish, shy, and submissive (Frith and Mueller 2003).

Goffman maintained that advertisements tell us to consume. And when women are depicted as nonthinking, decorative objects, they become part of the "things" to be devoured. Women's eroticized body parts depersonalize the actual human person whose body is being shown. The whole person disappears, and the body parts do not appear to belong to anyone (human). She is no longer a living person but an object to be used by the viewer, buyer, or consumer (Roy 2005).

one's attention, which leads to impaired performance on mental activities such as mathematical computations and logical reasoning (Fredrickson, Roberts, Noll, Quinn, and Twenge 1998; Gapinski, Brownell, and LaFrance 2003; Hebl, King, and Lin 2004).

Gender and the Internet

The Internet is a relatively recent addition to the media with which we interact. About 35 percent of the world population now have access to the Internet. Sixty-nine percent of American households use the Internet, and many other Americans have access through work, school, and libraries (U.S. Bureau of the Census 2010). Despite the fact that the Internet seems an increasingly pervasive part of our lives, research on images of gender on the Internet is only beginning (Beasley and Standley 2002). The research that has been done indicates that women and girls are largely invisible (only 14 percent of all characters in video games, for example, are girls or women). When women and girl characters do appear, they are sexualized through their clothing, behavior, and body shape.

More investigation has been done on gender and the use of the Internet (Ono and Zavodny 2005). In the 1990s, scholars found a cybergap between women and men in the United States, with men much more likely to be using computers and surfing the Internet. By the turn of the century, however, the gap had disappeared and even reversed. In France and the United States, for example, women are now more likely than men to be on the Internet and to use computers at work, and they have better typing skills, allowing them to get around more efficiently (Ono and Zavodny 2005; Day, Janus, and Davis 2005).

Similar trends are found in children's use of the Internet in the United States. Very young girls and boys use the Internet in equal numbers, but girls lead boys in Internet use by middle school (Lenhart, Rainie, and Lewis 2001; Roberts et al. 2005). Overall among school-age children, girls (66.9 percent) are slightly more likely to use the Internet than are boys (65.8 percent) at school or at home (Day et al. 2005).

Factors other than gender, such as race ethnicity, income, and education, are more important distinctions between groups in the United States who use the Internet and those who do not (Calvert, Rideout, Woolard, Barr, and Strouse 2005). For example, 79 percent of white children, 74 percent of Asian children, and 42 percent of Latino and black children have access to the Internet at home (Day et al. 2005).

This change toward greater gender equality, however, has not occurred in all nations. In poorer nations of the global South, fewer women than men have access to the Internet, and the gender gap soars to nearly 45 percent in sub-Saharan Africa, nearly 35 percent in South Asia and the Middle East, and nearly 30 percent in parts of Europe and across Central Asia (Intel 2012). Even in some wealthy nations such as Japan, for example, women lag behind men in their use of the Internet. Japanese women have less experience with computers, and they have weaker typing skills compared to Japanese men.

This contrast between Japanese women and men appears to be related to job experience and perhaps education. Japanese women are less likely to be in the paid labor force compared to American women, and they are more likely to be in part-time and temporary positions. They are also less likely to be in college than are Japanese men, whereas American women are more likely than American men to go to college.

There are also still some differences for women and men on issues related to the Internet in the United States. Men dominate decisions about purchasing computers (Ono and Zavodny 2005). In addition, men and women differ in their perceptions of their skills in using the Internet (Hargittai and Shafer 2006).

Women and men have similar skills in locating information online. They are equally able to find sites for people, data, and organizations and maneuver through the websites quickly and effectively. Other factors, such as age, education, and experience with computers, are important predictors of skill, but gender is not.

When women and men, however, are asked to rate their Internet skills, women give themselves lower scores. One study asked men and women, who tested equal on Internet skills, to rate themselves on a five-point scale, and men's averages were higher. Not one man gave himself the lowest score—novice—and not one woman rated herself with the highest score—expert. When the participants in the study ran into trouble on the Internet, they also had different responses. Men tended to blame the technology, whereas women blamed themselves (Hargittai and Shafer 2006). This confidence among men apparently translates into choosing Computer Science as a profession. Here the gender gap is growing dramatically. In the 1980s in the United States, women made up about 37 percent of students earning a BS in Computer Science. Today women make up less than 12 percent of grads in this discipline (Liebelson 2013).

One of the newest uses of the Internet is what is called **Social Media** and includes outlets such as Facebook, Twitter, Pinterest, Instagram and Tumblr. Facebook is especially popular with 800 million people using the site regularly and 62 percent of American men and 72 percent of American women reporting that they use Facebook accounts averaging about 55 minutes a day on the site (Duggan and Brenner 2013, Special and Li Barber 2011).

Some studies have found gender differences in the use of social media. For example, women are more likely to use Facebook to promote relationship maintenance by posting photographs and communicating with friends, while men are are more likely to spend their time online finding out about events, looking for dates, and playing games (Muscanell and Quadagno 2012).

Besides showing up in different uses of social media, gender also appears in the ways social media can help to enforce or to challenge gender inequality. In Saudi Arabia, women are not allowed to drive and they are not allowed to travel without the consent of a man guardian, their father, husband, brother, son, or other man who is in custody of them. Recently, the Saudi government began texting guardians if they found women boarding international planes just to ensure that their guardians knew of the women's movements. Many Saudi women and men were offended by this new use of social media and began using their own social media, Twitter, to retaliate. Their tweets mocked the government's texting and began to call people to action around the rights of women in the country (France-Presse 2012).

Media Theory

What is the relationship between media and society? Do media determine how we think about gender? Or do viewers play a role, interacting, responding, resisting, and even reconstructing those images in ways that can help create social change rather than maintain the existing systems of inequality? There are two opposing views on the role played by the media and especially television. *Hegemony* **theorists** (Marger 2002) argue that media play a conservative role in society, manipulating and persuading viewers to believe that the status quo is the best of all possible worlds, or even the only possibility. This position was expressed in the beginning of the chapter when we discussed legitimation.

Some theorists, however, would disagree with the assertion that media always legitimate the status quo by persuading people that we live in the best of all possible worlds. They claim that television can elicit responses from viewers that challenge the status quo. Theorists in this second category assert that television can give voice to an otherwise silent point of view or that programming can generate discussion that promotes resistance to hegemonic ideas, including ideas about gender. Stuart Hall is one of the most well-known theorists who takes this point of view, which is called *reception theory* (Hall 1973). He argues that viewers, listeners, and readers are not just passive receivers but rather engage in thinking about and giving meaning to what they take in. Each person, based on his or her social position and background, reinterprets what the media deliver. Our ideas about issues such as gender are a combination of what the media sends and what we make of it, both accepting and resisting different messages.

RESISTING MEDIA. Resistance can take two forms. First, viewers can criticize the characters, images, and values in the presentation. When viewers watch TV programs and enjoy them, for example, they may not be persuaded that the characters or the stories are valid or honorable. Second, resistance can also occur when viewers transform the images into something that is more consistent with their own values or activities, and especially their own interests.

Research on the television program *Beverly Hills 90210* illustrates the first kind of resistance. Viewers were influenced by stereotyped images of young women in the program, but the viewers also reacted and defied the images by criticizing the characters.

90210 was a television show popular in the 1990s about a group of high school students and their families who all lived in the zip code 90210 in Beverly Hills, California, an affluent suburb of Los Angeles. The program presented an image of women as passive, pretty, and nice and, therefore, attractive to cute boyfriends. The message was that women should be allowed speak up and argue with other women, but when it comes to men, women should not say what they think or do what they want if it contradicts men's view of the world. Women should not want sex, but they should want marriage, because marriage is the only solid proof of a woman's worth. Girlfriends must not fight with their boyfriends, and they must be faithful (McKinley 1997).

Although women viewers of *90210* claimed they were not influenced by the program, they admitted to learning about how to dress and behave from the characters on the show. They described the ways they memorized the treatment of social issues like rape, abortion, and drug use so that they could incorporate the ideas and arguments in discussions and decisions about these topics in their real lives (McKinley 1997).

The program also literally influenced their behavior when they altered their schedules so that they would not miss the show. One woman explains her devotion to *90210*:

> I want to be able to hear every word they say. Sometimes I tape it as I'm watching in case anybody does walk in, um, I can rewind it again later and replay that part. I turn my ringer off. I won't answer the phone, I mean—and people know. Sometimes I'll leave a message, I go "You know what I'm doing. Why are you calling?" (McKinley 1997, 209)

The influence of the program on viewers' behavior suggests that hegemony theory is correct in its assertion that television is a powerful force shaping our ideas about gender. On the other hand, the women in this study also spent a lot of time reacting to the program as they watched it and discussing it later with their friends, who were also fans. They did not accept all of the views presented in the program and were critical of the behavior of many of the characters, which illustrates a more active role for viewers than is asserted by hegemony theorists.

Box 11-4 suggests another example of resistance to media images. In this case, women in the global South sift through the messages sent to them from media sources in the global North. They express consciousness of the problems arising from the dominance of Northern

GENDER IN EVERYDAY LIFE   BOX 11-4
NORTH, SOUTH, HEGEMONY, AND RESISTANCE

Where do images of social roles come from? And where do they fit into the global picture of media? Many observers have noted the cultural flow from the North (wealthy powerful nations, especially the United States) to the South (poorer, less powerful nations in Latin America, Africa, and Asia). If you have traveled or lived in the global South, you have probably noticed familiar icons of American culture such as Nike, McDonald's, and Coke. And you have probably heard Justin Bieber and seen Hollywood movies playing in those countries.

Some scholars and political activists worry that the dominance of Northern cultures will damage the Southern cultures. This is called "global intellectual hegemony" (GIH), and it appears to be a major feature of globalization (Gosovic 2000). GIH can promote negative features of Northern culture such as consumerism, cut-throat individualism, unhealthy products, or just bad music, and therefore is certainly a valid concern. However, media images that come from the global North can also play a role in improving people's lives. In research in India, women described the ways that their exposure to global media allowed them to develop alternative ways of thinking and talking about gender relations in their communities. Those alternatives were important to challenging the dominance of men.

For example, one woman described her view of the importance of women entering the paid labor force and earning a living, an idea she developed at least in part from her exposure to media images of assertive "new women." Others spoke of feeling heartened by seeing strong women characters in advertisements, television, or films or in news stories about leadership by women politicians. Although the women expressed concern about the ways the Northern-produced media promote a consumerist ideology and often portray women in derogatory ways, media images of women driving and shopping unchaperoned by men and working in "unacceptable" professional occupations also provided new alternative ideas about womanhood (Ganguly-Scrase 2003).

media images and from the images themselves, but they also use pieces of the messages to wage their own struggles for greater gender equity (Gosovic 2000).

Music Videos. Research on music videos provides another example of the debate between a hegemonic view of the media and the perspective that acknowledges the possibility of resistance against hegemony. Music video fans can protest and challenge the images in an attempt to remove them from the public eye, or they can reconstruct the images in ways that challenge stereotyped views of women and men.

Much has been written about the importance of music videos in young people's lives, particularly, the impact they have on African Americans trying to make sense of their lives, social relations, and the world around them (Emerson 2004). Hip hop artist Chuck D says that hip hop is the CNN of today's youth (Jackson 2007).

Hip hop is also a controversial medium. The discussion earlier in the chapter about sexualization of women and girls in media used some quotes from lyrics of popular songs. The lyrics stand out because they are so blatantly misogynist and racist. The debate over the music has been especially central in hip hop music.

Hip hop emerged in the Bronx in the late 1970s and has been strongly criticized by mainstream media as well as by hip hop insiders. About ten years ago, artists such as C. Delores Tucker, Dionne Warwick, and the National Political Congress of Black Women spoke out against degrading portrayals of women in hip hop lyrics and music videos (Kitwana 2002). More recently, Beverly Guy-Sheftall , a women's studies professor from Spelman College, told a hip hop convention that the nearly naked women in music videos remind her of America's racist past, when women were paraded naked at slave auctions. These depictions are " 'reminiscent of old and obscene racial stereotypes that deprive (black women) of humanity,' she said, adding that the rising influence of hip hop means these images are circulating around the globe. Guy-Sheftall also noted, however, 'it's not the whip, it's the dollar bill' that keeps women oppressed" (Jackson 2005).

The hip hop movement itself is split over the antiwoman and antiblack messages, with many arguing that racist and sexist lyrics and images contradict the essence of hip hop, which is a movement to confront and expose a racist and sexist society in order to change it. Rapper-turned-activist Chuck D shares Guy-Sheftall's view and is trying to bring hip hop back to its roots as a vehicle for challenging the status quo regarding racial and gender injustice. He challenges black men especially to change the industry by confronting the music industry's sexual exploitation of black women with rap music. In a panel discussion on music videos, Chuck D said, "BET is the cancer of black manhood in the world, because they have one-dimensionalized and commodified us into being a one-trick image. We're [shown] throwing money at the camera and flashing jewelry at the camera that could give a town in Africa water for a year" (Zurawik 2007). He concluded, "The only thing that can turn the tide is black men" (Fulwood 2007).

Both Guy-Sheftall and Chuck D are arguing that the CEOs in the industry have distorted hip hop and that the music needs to be transformed so that it respects and honors women and African Americans and promotes images of masculinity that challenge violent, misogynist ideas about what it is to be a man. So far, this discussion has portrayed the debate as one that has two sides: those who promote racist, sexist images and lyrics and those who oppose them and wish to eliminate them from the music. The resisters approach the issue from a hegemonic point of view, arguing that the medium is harmful and needs to be altered.

Another response to the music was explored by Emerson (2004). She argues that the music does not necessarily need to be changed. It is our response to the music that must change, from one of acceptance to one that accepts some of it and rejects other aspects. Furthermore, Emerson asserts that viewers already "censor" out the images and lyrics with which they disagree and accept the ones that they believe are positive for women today. She reviews a number of videos that show both **hegemonic** (and objectifying and exploitative images of women) as well as **counterhegemonic images** and ideas. Her study explores the ways listeners accept the counterhegemonic images and ideas at the same time that they reject the hegemonic ones.

Emerson's (2004) review of music videos of black women musicians shows three types of stereotypical images. First, they emphasize black women's bodies. Like the images of women in the media in general, body types are pretty much limited to thin, young, and pretty.

Second, they present black women as one-dimensional. Not only is their physical appearance limited, but many kinds of women such as pregnant women, women over thirty, mothers, and lesbians are never shown. The roles of women are further limited to being objects of men's desire, and focused on romance and **conspicuous consumption** (Emerson 2004).

Third, the videos show men as "sponsors," always in the background calling the shots. Women's role is primarily as sex object and someone not to be taken seriously. Men appear as the expert, creative geniuses who are guiding the woman musician (Emerson 2004). At the

According to Emerson, however, that is not the only story being told in the videos. At the same time as these negative stereotypes of women are present, women's resistance to the stereotypes is also part of the songs and images. First, the women in the videos embrace their race ethnicity, and they project a sense of pride about being black. Black is portrayed in a positive manner and the black women artists, actresses, models, and dancers in the videos who have darker complexions are emphasized in particular (Emerson 2004).

A second example of challenging negative stereotypes in the videos is in the behavior of the women. At the same time as they are presented in subordinate roles, they are simultaneously depicted as active, vocal, and independent. They assertively express their discontent and challenge interpersonal relationships they find unsatisfactory. The women are shown defining their own identity and determining their own lives. "Speaking out and speaking one's mind are constant themes" (Emerson 2004, 263).

Sisterhood is the third factor providing evidence that music videos can be a forum for black women's resistance to oppressive stereotypes. Women in the videos look to each other for partnership and support. Collaboration musically and in the stories in the videos is a recurring theme.

A fourth, and perhaps the most important, issue in these videos is sexuality. The sexually explicit and objectifying character of music videos is well known. Emerson (2004) argues that there is also evidence of alternative models of women and sexuality. Women and men are frequently shown as coworkers and collaborators, suggesting that women can have relationships with men that are not sexual and are productive and creative for both women and men.

Women's sexuality is also combined with themes of independence, strength, street smarts, toughness, and the ability to act in one's own defense. The women are sexy, and they are objects to be admired and observed, but they are simultaneously glamorous, savvy, and autonomous on their own terms. In addition, women's sexuality is portrayed as active, with men's bodies the object of women's pleasure; men are something to be pursued as well as something to be looked at. In sum, the videos show contradictory images of women, sometimes subordinate, restricted, and designed for men's consumption. Simultaneously, though, the women are shown resisting those roles and creating a more independent and active image (Emerson 2004). The videos show the ways media can legitimate the status quo but also the ways they can be vehicles for challenge and the ways that consumers can choose which messages to take from them.

GENDER MATTERS

This chapter has examined gender across a broad array of media that present us with images that seek to inform us, entertain us, and induce us to buy. The popular media deliver seductive images of gender. The lessons embedded in the images we see on television and in films are not subtle, but they do contain a kind of hidden agenda. Television sitcoms, for example, don't explicitly outline what real men and real women are like, but the invisibility of women and the roles that women and men portray tell us much about who is valued and who is not and how we all should behave if we wish to be part of the dominant culture. How much choice we have in accepting or rejecting those images and ideas is a controversial question within sociology.

Advertisers use gendered images in commercial media to sell their products. If we are to behave appropriately as properly gendered women and men, we must consume certain clothes, food, entertainment, cars, and virtually every good and service offered by commercial interests. There are, though, variations on the images and messages of gender in advertising around the world. A range of other variables intersect with gender, including race ethnicity, age, and global divisions between North and South. One factor remains salient throughout, however. Gender is always part of the picture. What exactly women and men are supposed to be like varies, but the idea that humanity comes in two forms and the line between two categories—feminine and masculine—are always present.

KEY TERMS

Bechdel test
commercial media
conspicuous consumption
damsel in distress
emphasized femininity
gender ideologies
healthy sexuality
hegemonic and counterhegemonic images
hegemony
hegemony theorists

legitimation
mass media
narrowcasting
normative
pink dollars
reception theory
self-objectification
hyper-sexualization sexually objectified
social media
women's liberation movement

CRITICAL THINKING QUESTIONS

1. Some media theories see mass media as a form of mind control, while other theories view mass media as presenting contradictory images that allow audiences to challenge and subvert established authority. Explain both positions. With which position do you agree? Support your case with examples from the text and from your own experience.

2. Think about what your favorite movies are and use the Bechdel test to see how they treat gender. What did you find? Were you surprised? Why do you think films make women invisible?

3. What about your favorite reality tv shows? Does the Bechdel test work on them? If women aren't invisible, what are the images of them on the show? And what about men? How are they portrayed in reality TV? What television shows seem to have moved beyond the stereotypes? What evidence are you seeing that makes you think they are presenting more equitable images?

REFERENCES

50 Cent. 2005. "Get in My Car." http://www.metrolyrics.com/get-in-my-car-lyrics-50-cent.html. Accessed March 2, 2014.

American Psychological Association, Task Force on the Sexualization of Girls. 2007. *Report of the APA Task Force on the Sexualization of Girls.* Washington, DC: American Psychological Association. http://www.apa.org/pi/women/programs/girls/report.aspx. Accessed March 23, 2011.

Arima, Akie. 2003. "Gender Stereotypes in Japanese Television Advertisements." *Sex Roles: A Journal of Research* 49 (1/2): 81–90.

Baker, Christina. 2005. "Images of Women's Sexuality in Advertisements." *Sex Roles: A Journal of Research* 52:13–27.

Bazzini, Doris G., William D. McIntosh, Stephen M. Smith, Sabrina Cook, and Caleigh Harris. 1997. "The Aging Woman in Popular Film: Underrepresented, Unattractive, Unfriendly, and Unintelligent." *Sex Roles: A Journal of Research* 36:531–43.

Beasley, Berrin, and Tracy Collins Standley. 2002. "Shirts vs. Skins: Clothing as an Indicator of Gender Role Stereotyping in Video Games." *Mass Communication and Society* 5 (3): 279–93.

Blanchette, Aimee. 2006. "Disappearing Male TV Anchors." *St. Paul Minneapolis Star*, September 18.

Browne, Beverly 1998. "Gender Stereotypes in Advertising on Children's Television in the 1990s." *Journal of Advertising* 27 (1): 83–96.

Buerkle, C. Wesley. 2011. "Masters of Their Domain: *Seinfeld* and the Discipline of Mediated Men's Sexual Economy." In *Performing American Masculinities: The 21st Century Man in Popular Culture*, edited by Elwood Watson and Marc Shaw, 9–36. Bloomington: Indiana University Press.

Calvert, Sandra, Victoria Rideout, Jennifer Woolard, Rachel Barr, and Gabrielle Strouse. 2005. "Age, Ethnicity, and Socioeconomic Patterns in Early Computer Use: A National Survey." *American Behavioral Scientist* 48 (5): 590–607.

Coltrane, Scott, and Michele Adams. 1997. "Work Family Imagery and Gender Stereotypes." *Journal of Vocational Behavior* 50:323–47.

Coltrane, Scott, and Melinda Messineo. 2000. "The Perpetuation of Subtle Prejudice: Race and Gender Imagery in 1990s Television Advertising." *Sex Roles: A Journal of Research* 42:363–95.

Connell, Robert. 1993. *Rethinking Sex: Social Theory and Sexuality Research.* Philadelphia: Temple University Press.

Day, Jennifer, Alex Janus, and Jessica Davis. 2005. *Computer and Internet Use in the United States: 2003.* Washington, DC: U.S. Bureau of the Census.

Duffy, Margaret, and J. Michael Gotcher. 1996. "Crucial Advice on How to Get the Guy." *Journal of Communication Inquiry* 20:32–48.

Duggan, Maeve, and Joanna Brenner. 2013. *The Demographics of Social Media Users—2012.* Washington, DC: PEW Research Center. http://pewinternet.org/Reports/2013/Social-media-users.aspx. Accessed March 2, 2014.

Dunnewind, Stephanie. 2002. "TV or Not TV, That's the Question." *Seattle Times*, June 25.

Emerson, Rana. 2004. "Where My Girls At?" In *The Kaleidoscope of Gender*, edited by Joan Spade and Catherine Valentine, 259–69. Belmont, CA: Wadsworth.

Eminem. 2001. "Bitch Please II." Eminem Lyrics http://www.azlyrics.com/lyrics/eminem/bitchpleaseii .html. Accessed March 2, 2014.

Eschholz, Sarah, and Jana Bufkin. 2001. "Violence Depicts Power and Masculinity." *Sociological Forum* 16 (4): 654–71.

Fejes, Fred. 2000. "Making a gay masculinity." *Critical Studies in Media Communication* 17:113–16.

France-Presse, Agence. 2012. "Saudia Arabia Implements Electronic Tracking System for Women." *The Raw Story.* http://www.rawstory.com/rs/2012/11/22/saudi-arabia-implements-electronic-tracking-system-for-women/. March 2, 2014.

Fredrickson, Barbara L., Tomi-Ann Roberts, Stephanie Noll, Diane Quinn, and Jean Twenge. 1998. "That Swimsuit Becomes You: Sex Differences in Self-Objectification, Restrained Eating, and Math Performance." *Journal of Personality and Social Psychology* 75:269–84.

Frith, Katherine, and Barbara Mueller. 2003. *Advertising and Societies.* New York: Peter Lang.

Fulwood, Sam, III. 2007. "Blacks Also Are Longtime Critics of Rap, Hip-Hop, Forum Shows." *Cleveland Plain Dealer,* April 19.

Furnham, Adrian, and Twiggy Mak. 1999. "Sex Role Stereotyping in Television Commercials." *Sex Roles: A Journal of Research* 41 (5–6): 413–37.

Gallagher, Margaret. 2005. *Who Makes the News?: Global Media Monitoring Project 2005.* Toronto: World Association for Christian Communication.

Ganguly-Scrase, Ruchira. 2003. "Paradoxes of Globalization, Liberalization, and Gender Equality." *Gender and Society* 17 (4): 544–66.

Gapinski, Kathrine, Kelly Brownell, and Marianne LaFrance. 2003. "Body Objectification, and 'Fat Talk': Effects on Emotion, Motivation, and Cognitive Performance." *Sex Roles: A Journal of Research* 48:377–88.

Gerbner, George, Larry Gross, Michael Morgan, and Nancy Signorielli. 1980. "The mainstreaming of America." *Journal of Communication,* 30 (3): 12–29.

Glick, Peter, Sadie Larsen, Catherine Johnson, and Heather Branstiter. 2005. "Evaluations of Sexy Women in Low- and High-Status Jobs." *Psychology of Women Quarterly* 29:389–95.

Goffman, Erving. 1979. *Gender Advertisements.* Cambridge, MA: Harvard University Press.

Gosovic, Branislav. 2000. "Global Intellectual Hegemony and the International Development Agenda." *International Social Science Journal* 15 (4): 447–56.

Grauerholz, Elizabeth, and Amy King. 1997. "Primetime Sexual Harassment." *Violence Against Women* 3:129–48.

Gutnick, Aviva L., Michael Robb, Lori Takeuchi, and Jennifer Kotler. 2011. Always Connected: The New Digital Media Habits of Young Children. New York: The Joan Ganz Cooney Center at Sesame Workshop. http://www.joanganzcooneycenter.org/wp-content/uploads/2011/03/jgcc_alwaysconnected.pdf.

Hall, Stuart. 1973. *Encoding and Decoding in the Television Discourse.* Birmingham, AL: University of Birmingham, Centre for Contemporary Cultural Studies.

Hargittai, Eszter, and Steven Shafer. 2006. "Differences in Actual and Perceived Online Skills: The Role of Gender." *Social Science Quarterly* 87 (2): 432–48.

Hebl, Mikki, Eden King, and Jingxin Lin Lin. 2004. "The Swimsuit Becomes Us All: Ethnicity, Gender, and Vulnerability to Self Objectification." *Personality and Social Psychology Bulletin* 30:1322–31.

Impett, Emily, Deborah Schooler, and Deborah Tolman. 2006. "To Be Seen and Not Heard: Femininity Ideology and Adolescent Girls' Sexual Health." *Archives of Sexual Behavior* 35 (2): 131–44.

Intel. 2012. "Women and the Web: Bridging the Internet Gap and Creating New Global Opportunities in Low and Middle-Income Countries." http://www.intel.com/content/dam/www/public/us/en/documents/pdf/women-and-the-web.pdf. Accessed March 2, 2014.

Jackson, Camille. 2005. "Misogyny and Rap: 'Chickenhead' Means You." April 11. Assata Shakur Forum.http://www.assatashakur.org/forum/conscious-edutainment-videos-movies-tv/5304-misogyny-rap-chickenhead-means-you.html. Accessed March 2, 2014.

——. 2007. "The ABCs of Hip Hop." Montgomery, AL: Southern Poverty Law Center.

Katz, Jackson. 1995. "Reconstructing Masculinity in the Locker Room: The Mentors in a Violence Prevention Project." *Harvard Educational Review* 65 (2): 163–74.

Kellner, Douglas. 2008. *Guys and Guns Amok: Domestic Terrorism and School Shootings from the Oklahoma City Bombings to the Virginia Tech Massacre.* Boulder, CO: Paradigm.

Kelly, Joe, and Stacey Smith. 2006. *Where the Girls Aren't.* Research brief commissioned by the See Jane Program at Dads and Daughters. SeeJane.org. Duluth, MN: Dads and Daughters.

Kid Rock. 1998. "Fuck Off." http://www.azlyrics.com/lyrics/kidrock/fuckoff.html. Accessed March 2, 2014.

Kitwana, Bakari. 2002. "It's Time for a Renewed Attack on Hip-Hop's Women-Hating." *Cleveland Plain Dealer,* December 2.

Klos, Diana. 2013. *The Status of Women in the U.S. Media 2013.* Women's Media Center. http://wmc.3cdn.net/51113ed5df3e0d0b79_zzzm6go0b.pdf. Accessed March 2, 2014.

Larson, M. 2001. "Interactions, Activities, and Gender in Children's Television Commercials." *Journal of Broadcasting and Electronic Media* 45:41–65.

Lauzen, Martha. 2012. "Boxed In: Employment of Behind-the-Scenes Women in the 2011-12 Prime-time Television Season." San Diego: Center for the Study of Women in Television and Film. http://www.wif.org/images/repository/pdf/other/2011-12_Boxed_In_Exec_Summ.pdf. Accessed March 2, 2014.

Lauzen, Martha, and David Dozier. 2005. "Recognition and Respect Revisited." *Mass Communication and Society* 8 (3): 241–56.

Lenhart, Amanda, Oliver Rainie, and Lee Lewis. 2001 .Teen age Life Online. Pew Research Internet Project. June 21. http://www.pewinternet.org/2001/06/21/teenage-life-online/. Accessed March 2, 2014.

Liebelson, Dana. 2013. "This 17-Year-Old Coder Is Saving Twitter from TV Spoilers (Spoiler: She's a Girl)." *Mother Jones,* May 8.

Lindner, K. 2004. "Images of Women in General Interest and Fashion Advertisements from 1955 to 2002." *Sex Roles: A Journal of Research* 51 (7/8): 409–21.

Ludacris. 2000. "What's Your Fantasy?" http://rapgenius.com/Ludacris-whats-your-fantasy-lyrics#note-22467. Accessed March 2, 2014.

Marger, Martin. 2002. *Social Inequality.* 2nd edition. Boston: McGraw-Hill.

McKinley, Graham. 1997. *Beverly Hills 90210.* Philadelphia: University of Pennsylvania Press.

The Movie Times. 2013. "Top Movies of All Time Worldwide by Box Office Gross." http://www.the-movie-times.com/thrsdir/alltime.mv?world+ByWG. Accessed April 23, 2013.

Muscanell, Nicole, and Rosanna Quadagno. 2012. "Make New Friends or Keep the Old: Gender and Personality Differences in Social Networking Use." *Computers and Human Behavior* 28 (1):107–12.

National Organization for Women (NOW). 1972. *Women in the Wasteland Fight Back.* Washington, DC: NOW, National Capital Area Chapter.

New York Times. 1999. "As GI Joe Bulks Up, Concern for the 98 Pound Weakling." May 30. http://www.nytimes.com/1999/05/30/weekinreview/as-gi-joe-bulks-up-concern-for-the-98-pound-weakling.html. Accessed March 23, 2011.

Ono, Hiroshi, and Madeline Zavodny. 2005. "Gender Differences in Information Technology Usage: A U.S.-Japan Comparison." *Sociological Perspectives* 48 (1): 105–33.

Patterson, Maurice, and Richard Elliott. 2004. "Negotiating Masculinities." *Consumption, Markets, and Culture* 5 (3): 231–46.

Peters, Wendy. 2011. "Pink Dollars, White Collars: *Queer as Folk*, Valuable Viewers, and the Price of Gay TV." *Critical Studies in Media Communication* 28 (3): 193–212.

Pozner, Jennifer. 2004. "The Unreal World: Why Women on "Reality TV" Have to Be Hot, Desperate and Dumb." *Ms. Magazine*, Fall. http://www.msmagazine.com/fall2004/unrealworld.asp. Accessed March 2, 2014.

———. 2011. "Reality TV (Re)Rewrites Gender Roles." *On The Issues Magazine* http://www.ontheissuesmagazine.com/2011winter/2011_winter_Pozner.php. Accessed March 2, 2014.

Project for Excellence in Journalism. 2005. "The Gender Gap: Women Are Still Missing as Sources for Journalists." *Pew Research Journalism Project*. New York: Columbia University. http://www.journalism.org/node/141. Accessed June 8, 2011.

Parent's Television Council (PTC). 2009. *Women in Peril: A Look at TV's Disturbing New Storyline Trend*. Special Report, October. http://www.parentstv.org/PTC/publications/reports/womeninperil/study.pdf. Accessed March 2, 2014.

Pussy Cat Dolls. 2005. "Don'tcha." http://www.azlyrics.com/lyrics/pussycatdolls/dontcha.html. Accessed March 2, 2014.

Roberts, Donald, Ulla Roehr, and Victoria Rideout. 2005. *Generation M: Media in the Lives of 8–18 Year Olds*. Menlo Park, CA: Kaiser Family Foundation.

Roy, Abhik. 2005. "The Male Gaze in Indian TV Commercials." In *Women in the Media*, edited by Theresa Carilli and Jane Campbell, 3–18. New York: University Press of America.

Sapiro, Virginia. 2002. *Women in American Society: An Introduction to Women's Studies*. New York: McGraw-Hill.

Sarkeesian, Anita. 2012. "The Oscars and the Bechdel test." http://www.youtube.com/watch?v=PH8J uizIXw8&feature=endscreen&NR=1. Accessed January 15, 2012.

Schulman, Sarah. 1998. *Stage Struck: Theatre, AIDS and the Marketing of Gay America*. Durham, NC: Duke University Press.

Sexuality Education and Information Council of the United States (SEICUS). 2004. *Guidelines for Comprehensive Sexuality Education*. 3rd edition. New York: SEICUS. http://www.siecus.org/index.cfm?fuseaction=Page.viewPage&pageId=516&grandparentID=477&parentID=514. Accessed March 23, 2011.

Signorielli, Nancy, Douglas McLeod, and Elaine Healy. 1994. "Gender Stereotypes in MTV Commercials: The Beat Goes On." *Journal of Broadcasting & Electronic Media*, 38(1): 91–102.

Smith, Stacey L., and Marc Choueiti. 2010. *Gender Disparity On Screen and Behind the Camera in Family Films: The Executive Report*. The Geena Davis Institute. http://www.thegeenadavisinstitute.org/downloads/FullStudy_GenderDisparityFamilyFilms.pdf. Accessed March 2, 2014.

Smith, Stacy L., and Crystal Cook. 2008. *Gender Stereotypes: An Analysis of Films and TV*. Los Angeles: The Geena Davis Institute on Gender in Media.

Smith, Stacy L. , Marc Choueiti, Ashley Prescott, and Katherine Pieper. 2012. *Gender Roles & Occupations: A Look at Character Attributes and Job-Related Aspirations in Film and Television*. http://www.seejane.org/downloads/KeyFindings_GenderRoles.pdf. Accessed March 2, 2014.

Special, Whitney, and Kirsten Li Barber. 2011. "Self-disclosure and student satisfaction with Facebook." *Computers in Human Behavior* 28(2): 624–30.

Stern, Susannah, and Dana Mastro. 2004. "Gender Portrayals Across the Life Span: A Content Analytic Look at Broadcast Commercials." *Mass Communication and Society* 7 (2): 215–36.

Strate, Lance. 2001. "Beer Commercials: A Manual on Masculinity." In *Men's Lives*, 5th edition, edited by Michael Kimmel and Michael Messner, 505–14. Boston: Allyn and Bacon.

Tuchman, Gaye, Arlene Kaplan Daniels, and James Benet. 1978. *Hearth and Home: Images of Women in the Mass Media*. New York: Oxford University Press.

Uray, Nimet, and Sebnem Burnaz. 2003. "An Analysis of the Portrayal of Gender Roles in Turkish Television Advertisements." *Sex Roles: A Journal of Research* 48 (1/2): 77–88.

U.S. Bureau of the Census. 2010. "Reported Internet Usage for Households 2009." http://www.census .gov/population/www/socdemo/computer/2009.html. Accessed March 23, 2011.

Ward, L. Monique, and Rocio Rivadeneyra. 2002. "Dancing, Strutting, and Bouncing in Cars: The Women of Music Videos." Paper presented at the annual meeting of the American Psychological Association, Chicago.

Ying Yang Twins. 2003. "Bounce U Booty, Shake Your Ass Ho (Work, work, work that back)." http://rapgenius.com/Bg-get-wild-with-it-lyrics#lyric. Accessed March 2, 2014.

Zurawik, David. 2007. "A Daring Look at Hip Hop." *Baltimore Sun*, February 20. http://articles .baltimoresun.com/2007-02-20/features/0702200042_1_beats-and-rhymes-hop-hip.   Accessed March 23, 2011.

12

SPORTS

The 2012 Olympics in London marked the first time in history that every
country that participated sent at least one women athlete. Qatar was one
of the nations that had never included women on their team before.

Source: Reuters/Mike Blake.

Sports are a major aspect of gender and gender ideologies. Athletic events and activities represent and promote images of masculinity and femininity and have been identified as one of the central sites in the social production of masculinity in particular. For women, athletics have been a place of exclusion, expressing the idea that femininity does not include athletic ability and activity. Men and masculinity are closely tied to sports, and women have been outsiders. A list of fifty athletes from around the world who made the most money in the past twelve months ranks athletes from golfer Tiger Woods at the top, who brought in $78.1 million, to football player Matt Schaub at number fifty, who made $22.3 million. The list includes only one woman: Maria Sharapova at number twenty-two, who made $29 million (Badenhausen 2013).

The social construction of femininities that excludes or discourages girls and women from participating in sports has serious consequences even beyond the opportunity to earn money as professional athletes. The United Nations asserts that sports can enhance individual lives and promote broader social goals such as promoting peace. They argue that:

- Sports generate health benefits
- Equip youth with the information, skills, personal and social resources, and the support needed to make key life transitions

- Promote gender equity and empowers women and girls
- Enhance the inclusion and well-being of persons with disabilities
- Help to build relationships across social, economic and cultural divides and build a sense of shared identity and fellowship among groups that might otherwise view each other with distrust and hostility (SDPIWG 2008).

Athletics as they are currently organized, however, are not without problems. The list of the top paid athletes, for example, includes eleven football players and three boxers, all of whom are men. These sports are notorious for being dangerous, causing concussions, paralysis, long-term neurological damage, and even death. Box 12-1 describes the health problems players in the NFL face as a result of head injuries on the field. While men are allowed and sometimes required to be involved in sports and in doing so they reap many of the benefits, they also may put themselves at great risk.

GENDER IN EVERYDAY LIFE   BOX 12-1
THE NFL AND CTE

Mark Fainaru-Wada and Steve Fainaru (2013) write that not only has major league football damaged the brains of most of its players, it has spent two decades covering up the link between injuries on the field and chronic traumatic encephalopathy (CTE). They argue that the National Football League (NFL) used its power and money to discredit scientists whose work showed connections between concussions and CTE.

Dr. Ann McKee, the leading expert on football and brain damage, believes that most NFL players have neurological damage caused by head injuries. Her study is based on fifty-four brains harvested from deceased NFL players which revealed that all but two had CTE (Van Natta 2013).

Although as early as 2000, top neuroscientists warned the NFL that football led to higher rates of depression, memory loss, dementia, and brain damage; officials asserted that concussions were minor injuries that never led to longer term brain damage even though they spent millions of dollars in disability payments to former players after concluding that the hits they took on the field gave them CTE. In 2005 they went so far as to (unsuccessfully) demand that medical journals retract the published work of several independent concussion researchers who reported links between concussions (even mild concussions) and CTE. They were successful, however, in getting their own biased research that claimed there was no connection published in professional neurological journals (Fainaru-Wada and Fainaru 2013). While conducting these contradictory practices, the NFL maintained an aggressive public relations strategy aimed at keeping the public unaware of what league executives really knew about the dangers of professional football.

Research on popular sports programs reveals ten recurrent themes regarding gender that make up the **television sports manhood formula**:

White men are voices of authority.

Sports are a man's world—women athletes are nearly invisible.

Men are foregrounded in commercials.

Women are sexy props or prizes for men's successful sport performances or consumption choices.

Whites are foregrounded in commercials.

Aggressive players get the prize—nice guys finish last.

Violence is natural and manly—boys will be (violent) boys.

Give up your body for the team.

Sports is war.

Show some guts—reckless bravery in the face of danger is what it takes to be a winner and a man (Messner, Dunbar, and Hunt 2000).

Gender stands in the way of enjoying and benefiting from sports for both women and men. This chapter explores the way masculinities shape our ideas and behaviors in athletics by demanding that men and boys participate as aggressive, competitive risk takers. We also examine the ways in which women and girls have been excluded as well as how recent changes in policy have taken place, slowly opening up opportunities in athletics. Throughout the chapter we review the intersection of sexuality and gender and the ways that homophobia and heterosexism have served as powerful tools to stigmatize gay men athletes and to keep women and girls out of the athletic arenas or at least limit their participation and enjoyment of sports. In the last section we consider the theoretical concepts of **assimilation and reform** as possible ways to rethink athletics.

SPORTS AND MASCULINITY

Becoming a man includes demonstrating physical competence (Whitson 1990). Boys begin to display and practice the connection between masculinity and physical interests and skills early on. In the United States, athleticism, prestige, and power for boys crosses race and class lines among even very young elementary school boys. Although not all boys may like sports, and many are not particularly skilled in athletics, all boys to some extent are judged by their ability (or lack of it) in competitive sports (Messner 2001). Physical aggression is associated with status, and popular boys are likely to be those who most skillfully use physical aggression like pushing, shoving, and hitting. One researcher watching first-graders found that not even a half hour went by without boys wrestling around with each other (Hasbrook and Harris 2000).

Michael Messner (2001) interviewed men about the importance of sports in their childhood. He asked them what they remembered about their experience with athletic activities, especially the ways sports helped them develop masculinity. The men experienced sports as so much a part of their life that they said it seemed like something natural. One man explained, "It was just what you did. It's kind of like, you went to school, you played athletics, and if you didn't there was something wrong with you. It was just like brushing your teeth; it's just what you did. It's part of your existence" (Messner 2001, 89–90).

Even though the activities seemed natural, the men also recalled the importance of older men in their lives, especially fathers, and the key role they played in initiating—exposing them and sometimes pushing them—into the male world of sports. One man described his introduction to sports by his father:

> I still remember like it was yesterday—dad and I driving up in his truck, and I had my glove and my hat all that—and I said, "Dad, I don't want to do it." He says, "What?" I says, "I don't want to do it." I was nervous that I might fail. And he says, "Don't be silly. Lookit: There's Joey and Petey and all your friends out there." And so Dad says, "You're gonna do it, come on." And in my memory he's never said that about anything else; he just knew I needed a little kick in the pants and I'd do it. And once you're out there and you see all the other kids making errors and stuff, and you know you're better than those guys, you know: Maybe I do belong out here. As it turned out, Little League was a good experience. (Quoted in Messner 2001, 91)

Boys learn to be athletes, and through those experiences they learn to be masculine. They also learn a particular way of thinking about themselves and relating to others. Messner (2001) calls this "conditional self-worth." By this he means that boys learn that they must compete and they must win to be worthy of other people's concern. It is not enough to just be out there with others playing a game. They must win to be accepted. One man described the importance of being best: "It was expected of me to do well in all my contests—I mean by my coaches, my peers, and my family. So I in turn expected to do well and if I didn't do well, then I'd be very disappointed" (Messner 2001, 94). Being better than the other guy is the key to acceptance. When men learn this way of viewing themselves and the social world around them, it can cause problems in their ability to make intimate connections and express themselves in emotional ways (Messner 2001).

The attraction of sports for boys in terms of bringing them closer to other men in their lives and in the recognition and success they experience crosses social class and race ethnicity lines. These social differences among men, however, do affect their experience with athletics. First, boys from more privileged backgrounds experienced sports almost exclusively in terms of their immediate families. Black and poorer boys were brought into sports because of pressures, often negative, within the community. For example, one black man from a low-income neighborhood described his participation in sports as a survival strategy: "Sports protected me from having to compete in gang stuff or having to be good with your fists. If you were an athlete and got into the fist world, that was your business, and that was okay—but you didn't have to if you didn't want to. People would generally defer to you, give you your space away from trouble" (quoted in Messner 2001, 95).

Second, black and white middle-class boys practiced sports as one activity among many. They saw that the status of the adults around them was linked to their success in fields other than sports, such as school and jobs. Low-income boys, in contrast, saw much more limited opportunities for themselves and the adults in their lives. Sports offered immediate rewards of fun and attention and the potential, although small, of adult professional success. The opportunities for becoming a professional athlete are twice as good for white men compared to black men, but the numbers are miniscule in all groups. The chances of going professional are 4:100,000 for white men, 2:100,000 for black men, and 3:1 million for Hispanic men (Messner 2001).

The descriptions men give of their experience in youth sports sound as if these are primarily a men's theater with fathers and sons playing the main roles. While this a valid description of the main players, women are also part of the action. Women's activities, like much of women's work, however, is invisible (Messner and Bozada-Deas 2009). From chapter 6, on the global economy, you should recall that women are often involved in volunteer work that is essential to the community but remains invisible, unrecognized, and unappreciated. Youth sports are one place where this volunteer work takes place. Men dominate as volunteer coaches, but women do much of the background support work as "team moms." Even women who have been skilled athletes are channeled away from being coaches or assistant coaches and instead assigned tasks such as organizing snacks, gifts, awards, photos, and year-end parties, and making team banners (Messner and Bozada-Deas 2009).

History of Sports and Manliness

The identification of manliness with sports was already a strong theme in the nineteenth century in the United States and Britain. These ideas spread around the world as the British Empire expanded its influence on every continent, and the United States enlarged across North America. Masculinity was threatened, however, at the close of the nineteenth century by political challenges to British imperialism and economic changes in the United States that pushed men out of the rugged independent model of the small businessman and farmer. White men found competition from African American labor with the end of slavery and the waves of immigrants coming into the United States as well as the developing women's movement. The old Davy Crockett and Daniel Boone models of masculinity were washed away, and a crisis in masculinity developed. In Britain a new kind of man was required to ensure that the sun continued to never set on the British Empire (Beynon 2002). Athletic images of masculinity remained a central feature of these "new men" (Kimmel 1990).

Sports in a variety of forms took the place of the frontier and offered a way to reconstruct American manhood. In the last few decades of the nineteenth century, the first tennis court opened in Boston, the first basketball court was built, the American Bowling Congress was established, and the Amateur Athletic Union was founded (Kimmel 1990). The images of sports and masculinity were tied together, establishing enduring myths of masculinity consisting of unstoppable physical power and authority. These continue to influence our thinking about what real men should be like (Beynon 2002).

The link between masculinity and sports has remained strong, but the images have changed somewhat. One feature of the image of the new athletic man of the nineteenth and early twentieth centuries has fallen away in recent years. In early years, sports and sex were seen as opposite poles in men's lives, and athletic activities were believed to be regenerative for men. Athletic ability and activity meant that men were not depleting their stores of sperm and energy and were properly fit to take on all the pursuits required of men. Boys who did not engage in sports were likely to become womanlike, degenerate, and delicate. Men who did not persist in sports would lose control of their sexual desires and eventually succumb to sexual exhaustion. Today athleticism and sexual prowess are both important features of masculinity. Sexual prowess, however, is strictly limited to heterosexuality (Crosset 1990).

Gay Athletes

Robert Brannon (1976) identified four rules for being a man: no sissy stuff; be a big wheel; be a sturdy oak; and give 'em hell. Athletics is the perfect place to display all these attributes. Sports are often segregated in ways that exclude women and any "sissy stuff" they might bring with them. The competitive core of many sports require that participants aspire to be big wheels—better than or in charge of other men. Sturdy oaks show no fear or weakness, and "give 'em hell" is the essence of the pregame pep talk and halftime instructions. Oh, and there is one more rule for being a man: a man must be heterosexual (Anderson 2005).

This fifth rule is strongly defended within sports culture and becomes a huge problem for the many gay men who are also athletes. The rule of heterosexuality is so powerful that within sports culture, athletic skill is identified as a sign that an athlete is heterosexual, and the label of "fag" is thrown around the fields and locker rooms as the worst insult (meaning that an athlete is not as strong, fast, or competitive).

Gay men athletes describe the fear they face of being discovered. One high school basketball player explains, "I fear all the time that others will find out. That people's opinions of me will change if they find out that I'm gay. Like my teachers, they won't think the same of me; they make gay comments and say them in a derogatory manner. Even my own bro will say stuff about gay people. It makes it hard, I'm always thinking in the back of my mind, would you feel this way about me if you knew I was gay?" (Anderson 2005, 79). A professional player asserts that the situation becomes even more difficult, in fact dangerous, as an athlete goes pro. He explains, "The one thing I would never do is talk about it. Never. No one in the NFL wanted to hear it, and if anyone did hear it, that would be the end for me. I'd wind up cut or injured. I was sure that if a GM (general manager) didn't get rid of me for the sake of team chemistry, another player would intentionally hurt me, to keep up the image" (from Freeman 2003, quoted in Anderson 2005, 146).

Some men were able to overcome these barriers and felt that coming out to their teammates was highly beneficial. One man described his experience: "I came out to my best friend, who happened to be on the team. He thought it was great that I was gay, and he encouraged me to come out to another guy on the team. So, I told him, and like, he hugged me! I was so stoked I just wanted to tell everybody. It felt so good to tell people. It still does" (Anderson 2005, 87).

Others described ways they challenged the homophobia among their teammates. One man said, "One day I sat down and just constructed a plan to fight the homophobia. I decided I was going to say something every time they said something homophobic, no matter who it was. My teammates were irritating me, claiming that they didn't mean things the way I was taking them, but I continued to put them in their place when they used homophobia and eventually it faded" (Anderson 2005, p. 99).

Institutional changes such as the establishment of the **Gay Games**, an Olympics-like sporting event held every four years since 1972, also challenge the homophobia of sports and draw more participants than the regular Olympics. Other gay and lesbian sports organizations have increased in the last three decades, and the Gay and Lesbian Athletic Foundation was formed in 2003.

Initiation Rites and Football

In the United States, American football has been identified as a place where boys become men. In fact, football fits the model of a male initiation rite in male-dominated societies that have been observed in many other cultures. An **initiation rite** marks a transition from one social role to another, especially the move from childhood to adulthood. These rites share a number of characteristics cross-culturally (Sabo and Panepinto 1990):

> *Man–boy relationships.* Two key groups are older men initiators and younger initiates.
> *Conformity and control.* Initiates must learn the rules and abide by them to successfully complete the initiation.
> *Social isolation.* Initiates are socially isolated from others in the community, especially women and girls, who may be characterized as dangerous and polluting to the initiation and its goal of full manhood.
> *Deference to men's authority.* Initiates are shown the ladder of success, the way to climb the ladder, and the necessity of deferring to those above them.
> *Pain.* Initiates must show courage and the ability to endure pain to succeed in their initiation.

Football has each of these elements. First, it takes place in a nearly exclusive male theater, with only boys and men interacting. When men recall their football years, they describe their coaches as everything from "almost a god" to "a mean son of a bitch," but they always agree that their coaches played an important role in their "growing up" (Sabo and Panepinto 1990, 119).

Second, officials and coaches exert much control of the players on and off the field through exercise regimes, dietary and dating restrictions, clothing regulations, and study programs, as well as training in athletic skills of the game.

Third, training, playing, showering, traveling, and even sometimes eating takes place away from non–team members. One former college football player described his in-season life:

> We were figuring it out one night before an away-game at Boston College. During the season, we went to classes 5 days a week. We had 3-hour practices 5 days a week followed by team meals. Friday night was psych-up time and Saturday was game day. Sunday we reviewed game films for 3 hours and had a team meeting, not to mention that we were sore as hell and couldn't move worth a damn. The only time we could chase girls was Saturday night after home games, and, even then, the coaches said they'd prowl the bars to catch somebody drinking or breaking curfew. The only things we had time for was going to class, playing ball and jerking off. (Sabo and Panepinto 1990, 120–21)

Fourth, a variety of ranks exist in football, from owners, coaches, and referees to first-string, second-string, and star players, each deferring to the next higher rank. Fifth, injury and pain are obvious components of every game and practice. In addition to hits on the field, players are sometimes inflicted with emotional pain when coaches yell at them or restrict their time on the field or even physically reprimand them. All the while, players are told to "take their knocks" and "toughen up" (Sabo and Panepinto 1990). Football represents an important model of masculine initiation in contemporary American society. Football also strikingly represents the downside of sports: its danger to boys and men.

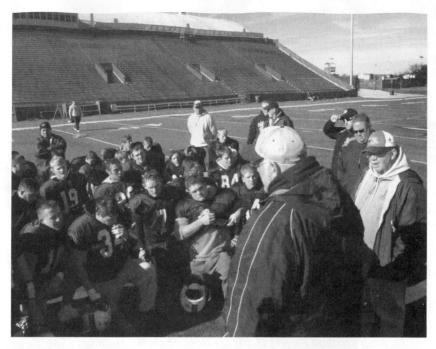

An initiation rite marks a transition from one social role to another, especially the move from childhood to adulthood. In many cultures, these transitions take place as boys learn to become men by emulating and obeying men leaders. Football is one place where this kind of initiation rite takes places in contemporary American society.

Source: Associated Press.

Dangers of Masculinity

Sports are an effective way of creating masculine men, but the kind of masculinity that is promoted in sports is a problem because of the damage it frequently can do to men's bodies (Messner 1992). The physical destructiveness of football epitomizes this problem. Among high school athletes, football is the most common source of serious injury, injury resulting in disability and direct fatality. Professional sports is now the most violent workplace besides the military. A National Football League player is three times more likely to be injured on the job as is a construction worker (Anderson 2005).

Other sports are dangerous as well, particularly those in which men engage. Men and boys are much more likely than women and girls to be hurt and especially to be hurt seriously while participating in sports. Of those injured in sports accidents resulting in long-term disability or death, 85 percent are men (K. Young and White 2000). In research on sports injury and fatality in Canada, water sports (boating, diving, fishing, water skiing, etc.) were the most dangerous, and 87 percent of those injured were men and boys. Motor sports (ATV riding, snowmobiling, etc.) were the second most dangerous, and 90 percent of those injured were men and boys.

Time for a Change?

The connection between masculinity and violence in sports has detrimental physical effects on men, causing them injury and even death. In addition, the link between athletics and endless competition, a winner-take-all mentality, and disrespect for human bodies results in damage to men psychologically. If men achieve success in these goals, they may hurt themselves on the field and they may restrict alternative values and beliefs. If they do not achieve success, they may feel that they are failures, or others may judge them as inadequate.

Boy who engage in high school athletics are more likely to have "stunted identity development." Researchers conclude that the "high status afforded to male athletes was detrimental to their overall psychological development" (Stone and McKee 2002, 98). The celebrity status of boys who were high school athletes apparently prevented them from developing other aspects of themselves and from experiencing high school as a period of "growing up."

In addition to damaging individual men, sports can also damage society. Athletics and athletes are an important source of values, especially for young people who look up to athletes. If sports and individual athletes serve as models for promoting values like excessive competition and disregard of human bodies on the fields that then permeate the rest of society, they do a disservice to society (Burstyn 1999).

Mexican Baseball Players Challenge Hegemonic Masculinity in Sports

Research on historical changes in masculinity from the nineteenth century and cross-cultural contrasts among baseball players show that masculinity is dynamic. Although the dominant form is often accepted, it also sometimes challenged. Kimmel (1992, 166) writes:

> Definitions of masculinity are constantly changing. Masculinity does not bubble up into behavioral codes from our genetic makeup, nor does it float in a current of the collective consciousness, waiting to be actualized by any particular man and simultaneously all men. Masculinity is socially constructed, changing 1) from one culture to another, 2) within any culture over time, 3) over the course of any individual man's life and 4) between and among different groups of men depending on class, race ethnicity and sexuality.

Research on Mexican baseball players illustrates Kimmel's assertion. The term macho is a Spanish word. A macho man is one who displays hypermasculine bravado and posturing, is likely to respond physically to any slight, attempts to dominate women and other men verbally and physically, drinks too much, has many women lovers, and fathers many children. Latino men and men from Spanish-speaking nations have been stereotyped as macho. Researchers, however, have found that these stereotypes are not valid in the family life of the Latino community (Baca Zinn 1992; Hondagneu-Sotelo 1992). Recent research on Mexican baseball players also refutes the macho image of Latinos.

A two-year study of the Mexican baseball team the Tecos found that Mexican ballplayers were less macho than Anglos on the team and displayed clear contrasts to conventional ideas about machismo in three areas: attitudes about children, ability to express vulnerability, and touching between men (Klein 2000).

Mexican baseball players are sensitive and caring of children (Gutmann 1996). In his field notes on the Mexican team, Klein (2000) describes the following scene to illustrate the relationship between the ballplayers and their kids:

> On the field following batting practice and 30 minutes to game time, Romero with his three-day growth of beard looks like central casting's choice for a Mexican bandito. He laughs like a three-pack-a-day convict, but when he holds his little baby girl and zooms her around like a little pink dirigible (she's wearing a pink headband), he's the warmest, most comforting man imaginable. (78)

The Mexican ballplayers also displayed vulnerability, discussing their challenges and failures at home and on the field, sometimes weeping without embarrassment and seeking emotional support from others. Their physical interactions included not only masculine mock boxing but also touching, leaning against, and hugging their teammates. In all of these areas, the Mexican men challenge dominant ideas about masculinity and provide contrasts with the Anglo men on the team (Klein 2000).

SPORTSWOMEN

With all the problems associated with sports and masculinity, we might expect that women would want to avoid athletics. Why are women around the world concerned about bringing more women into athletics? Michael Messner writes, "Increasing women's athleticism represents a genuine quest by women for equality, control of their own bodies and self-definition, and as such represents a challenge to the ideological basis of male domination" (Messner 1992, 197). When women athletes use their bodies to challenge the notions that women are clumsy and weak, they are creating new images and new ways of being for women. They are also creating a new kind of woman who is equal to men on the playing field and off it. In studies of the benefits of sports for girls, researchers (Stone and McKee 2002) have found that girls who are involved in athletics have more positive attitudes about school, higher academic achievement (especially in the sciences), and are less likely to drop out of school. Girl athletes also have stronger self-esteem, lower rates of depression, and greater leadership capacity. Their physical health is also enhanced and they are less likely to smoke or to become pregnant in high school. Box 12-2 summarizes some of the benefits of participating in sports as both spectators and athletes, especially for women.

Women all over the globe are working to bring women into athletics because women in the world of sports have historically been outsiders. In the nineteenth century, women were not even allowed to be spectators at football games (Watterson 2000). Women athletes are still largely invisible in media surrounding athletics, and when they are given attention, they are seen differently. Research on television and leading newspapers shows that 92 percent of sports coverage is about men (Messner, Duncan, and Jensen 1993). Reviews of television sports news programs show that women's athletics are mentioned 1.6 percent of the airtime. Furthermore, after increasing slightly since 1989 (5.3 percent of airtime), coverage of women's sports declined from 8.7 percent of airtime in 1999 to 1.6 percent in 2010 (Messner and Cooky 2010). In addition, in one recent study, all sports news led with men's sports, and 94 percent of the anchors were men (Duncan and Messner 2005).

GENDER IN EVERYDAY LIFE   BOX 12-2
BENEFITS OF SPORTS FOR WOMEN

Why should we love women's sporting events? Sarah Sentilles (2013) has some ideas about this. She says: We can hear the roar of the crowd for women—all kinds of women. "Strong women. Bad-ass athletic women. Teammates. . . . To root for strong women in a patriarchal culture, to root for people who endure pain and frustration and support each other's diverse talents, to root for women who come in different shapes and sizes and sexualities and ethnicities is to root for something more than sport. We're rooting for women who experience sexism at work. For queer women. For women writers and priests and politicians and professors and CEOs. For mothers and daughters and sisters. For survivors."

We see that women's bodies aren't for diets, cosmetic surgeries and being seen posing in a photo shoot—women's bodies are for playing. We don't watch the athletes to see how they look. "We watch them to see what they can *do*: run, shoot, dribble, juggle, slide, push, win" (Sentilles 2013).

We feel a part of women working together to get things done. Team play by the athletes shows us how but even if we aren't playing, as a spectator we feel a part of our community, and especially a part of our community supporting women. Besides, it's healthy, it's fun, and for once we see the good news of women winning (Sentilles 2013).

When women and men athletes are shown, the depictions are gendered. Judith Lorber (2001) notes that in the media, the term *sportswoman* appears to be an oxymoron. Media images of men athletes emphasize strength, power, and violence. Media images of women athletes are more ironic. Images of sportswomen emphasize feminine beauty and grace like those of figure skaters (so that they are not really athletes) or their thin, small, androgynous bodies, like those of gymnasts (so they are not really women but still prepubescent girls) (Lorber 2001).

Other scholars have noted the increasingly sexualized images of women athletes appearing in photos that show little of their athleticism and much of their bodies, clothing, and poses in a sexualized manner (Kane 1996). In the 1990s, women began to make major gains in sports, and men's sports culture responded (Holste 2000). Pat Griffin (1998) explains:

> The hypersexualized images of women athletes function to normalize women athletes for men in the sports culture . . . When it once was enough to feminize women athletes, now it is necessary to sexualize them for men, putting them in their place and making them non-threatening . . . Instead of hearing, "I am woman, hear me roar," we are hearing, "I am hetero-sexy, watch me strip." (Griffin, quoted in Holste 2000)

Although women are still perceived as outsiders in sports, the participation of women in sports skyrocketed in the last quarter of the twentieth century. Donna de Varona won two gold medals in swimming at the 1964 Olympics but could not get an athletic scholarship to college because there were none available for women swimmers. In the United States in 1971, only one of every twenty-seven girls was in high school sports; by 1994, that number was one in three. At the college level in 1972, 31,000 women participated in sports. At the end of the century, 120,000 women did (Oglesby 2001).

One of the most interesting results of the increasing participation of women in sports is the way in which the social and political changes are bringing about physiological changes in women and, therefore, challenging our ideas about "natural" biological differences between males and females. Box 12-3 describes some of the ways athletics has literally reshaped female bodies and what that says about supposedly natural femininity.

GENDER IN EVERYDAY LIFE   BOX 12-3
THROWING LIKE A GIRL

Anyone who has played a game of catch has heard the saying "You throw like a girl." Throwing like a girl means you aren't any good at throwing a ball. You look awkward, and the ball moves slowly and falls short. The thrower uses only a restricted part of the body. Rather than winding up, kicking the leg, and extending arms and legs to put the full force of the entire body behind the pitch, the thrower uses only one arm while moving the rest of the body as little as possible. "Throwing like a girl" is throwing while limiting the use of the body. Bodily restriction takes precedence over fully using bodily ability (I. Young 1980). Throwing like a girl encapsulates the essence of physical femininity. "To be ladylike is to be pretty, graceful, reserved—to be looked at, not to be useful and forceful" (Crawley, Foley, and Shehan 2008, 60).

Crawley, Foley, and Shehan (2008) argue that our ideas and expectations about gender cause women and girls to use their bodies in particular ways, which in turn shape women's bodies in restricted ways. Prescriptions for acting like a lady cause women and girls to restrict their physical bodies and to hold back the true potential of their muscles. Their ability to use their bodies in coordinated, powerful, effective ways becomes atrophied or at least distorted in order to conform to the social demands of gender ideologies. In this way, nurture is determining nature. "Masculine sports are designed to build and highlight large bodies with upper-body strength, whereas feminine sports build smaller, toned, lithe bodies, concentrating on cardio training and size reduction rather than muscle building" (Crawley et al. 2008, 139).

But can nurture be used to allow women and girls to acknowledge and develop their physical potential? If gendered sports performances build gendered bodies, can we reconstruct sports in a way that allows people to build ungendered bodies? Can athletics help each individual to develop our physical potential without the constraints of gender? That is exactly what many women athletes have been doing in the last few decades. They face many barriers as athletic institutions continue to construct women as less competent than men. In the 2010 Winter Olympics, the person who held the international record in the ski jump, a woman, was not allowed to compete in the men's-only sport (Suddath 2010). The reason given for banning her from competing, ironically, was that she might be at an unfair *disadvantage* due to her gender. These kinds of restrictions are prevalent throughout the Olympics. Cross-country skiers in the women's event ski 10 kilometers, while men ski 15 kilometers. Women swimmers in the freestyle event swim 800 meters, while the men swim 1,500 meters. In Judo, women have 4-minute matches, while men's are 5 minutes (Crawley et al. 2008).

Despite these continuing restrictions in many areas, improvements in athletic opportunities have altered women's lives and their bodies. The changes are reflected in the times and distances women athletes are clocking. When given a chance to fully develop their physical ability, women's bodies have shown themselves to be far more competent than previous generations allowed them to be. Cashmore's (2005) research on marathons, for example, shows that "women are now 92.25% as fast as men over the distance today, compared to 1925 when they were only 67.6% as fast as men" (153). Furthermore, women today surpass the speeds that men ran in the marathons in 1925. Men's speeds increased during that time period, but women's increased even more rapidly.

Women athletes provide a persuasive example of how our physical selves, what we sometimes think of as a given, are profoundly influenced by our social experience. Our social context is the "given." But it is a given that can be altered by changing our ideas and the social institutions that embody those ideas.

Title IX

Bringing women into sports has become a part of the feminist agenda around the world. At the UN decade convenings of women around the world, sports are cited in the documents as one of the key issues to be addressed. In the United States, sports for women were given a significant push by passage of Title IX. In chapter 5, we explored Title IX and its importance in developing equity for girls and women in academic institutions. Title IX became law in 1971, prohibiting discrimination in education, and it included discrimination in athletic programs like scholarships and access to sports resources (see Box 12-4). Title IX has had an enormous impact on bringing women into sports in the United States, but problems remain. Spending is still much greater on men compared to women in athletic programs, as 32 percent of recruitment dollars, 36 percent of operating budget, and 43 percent of total athletic scholarship dollars go to women students. Men receive about $133 million more in athletic scholarships than do women (Shakib, Scalir, and Shakib 2003).

In addition, the law remains controversial because some people argue that the demand to level the playing field may have forced some universities to eliminate men's programs when they

GENDER IN EVERYDAY LIFE   BOX 12-4

WHAT DOES YOUR SCHOOL NEED TO DO TO PROVIDE EQUITY
ACCORDING TO THE TITLE IX GUIDELINES?

Here are some of the areas that need to be evaluated to make sure that gender equity is
being achieved:

1. Select sports and levels of competition that effectively accommodate the interest
   and abilities of both genders.
2. Provide equipment and supplies.
3. Schedule games and practice times.
4. Provide travel and per diem allowances.
5. Provide opportunities to receive coaching and academic tutoring.
6. Assign and compensate coaches and tutors.
7. Provide locker rooms and practice and competitive facilities.
8. Provide medical and training facilities and services.
9. Provide housing and dining facilities and services.
10. Publicize sports events.

SOURCE: Shulman and Bowen (2001, 315).

could not fund women's at an equal level. Since its passage, more than 170 wrestling programs,
eighty men's tennis teams, seventy men's gymnastics teams, and forty-five men's track teams
have been eliminated. Some maintain that these cuts are the fault of trying to create gender
equality in sports on campus.

Others, however, assert that the problem is inequality among different sports rather than
attempts to create gender equity. They argue that football and basketball take so much of the
sports budget that other men's sports (as well as women's sports) cannot be supported. Many
people incorrectly believe that college football and basketball teams are revenue-generating
and self-supporting programs, but two thirds of college basketball and football programs, in
fact, cost more than they generate, with an average annual deficit for each school of $9.9 million
(Knight Commission 2009). If colleges did not spend so much money on these two sports
(which are also men's sports), they would have enough money to create gender equity, and they
could also support a broader range of sports for men as well as women.

Title IX advocates further note that 80 percent of colleges are out of compliance. In addition, in 2005, policies were put into place to weaken the law. The 2005 policies allowed colleges and universities to demonstrate whether they had met the interests of the underrepresented
minority, women, by conducting an e-mail survey. If women did not respond or if they had
already chosen to go to another school because the school did not offer an athletic program in
which they were interested, the college could claim that it had met its obligation. This made

Title IX a unique civil rights law, because it demanded that the underserved minority prove their interest in attaining gender equity. The law did not defend the principle of equality. Rather than require the government to protect the principle of equality, the law required the underserved minority to protect its own interest; if it did not, for whatever reason, equality was set aside. Fortunately, this policy was rescinded in 2010.

Despite these difficulties with legislation, women have flooded into sports in the past few decades, and most people credit Title IX with playing a positive role in these changes. Since 1970, the number of women in intercollegiate sports went from 30,000 to 157,000. The numbers of men have remained almost static from 197,446 in 1984 to 206,573 today (Pennington 2002).

Colleges now offer, on average, 8.34 women's sports. At the professional level, women's leagues in basketball, volleyball, and soccer have sprung up. As women have entered sports previously thought of as for men only, the images of women athletes as "skirted skaters" and "tiny tumblers" has been expanded to include "rough muscular women in their 20s and 30s who grunt, grimace and heave each other aside with their hips" (Eitzen and Baca Zinn 2004, 338).

Title IX has had one ironic effect on gender equity. As women's sports have gained support and participants, coaching and administration positions, which were previously nearly exclusively women's positions, are now being taken by men. As a result, women who aspire to coaching and administration have fewer job opportunities (Acosta and Carpenter 2004). In addition, young women have fewer role models in these positions, and gender hierarchies are created with men in dominant positions and women subordinate to them (Eitzen and Baca Zinn 2004).

International Efforts to Bring Women into Sports

At the international level, women in sports have gained attention from people concerned about equality on all fronts. In its recommendations to the nations of the world at the **UN Fourth World Conference on Women in Beijing**, delegates supported three actions that related to sports (Shelton 2001):

- Pay attention to the importance of physical activity and sports in the lives of girls and women.
- Increase opportunities for participation for girls and women in sports.
- Ensure that there are more women in leadership positions in sports.

In 1995, the **International Olympic Committee** pledged to implement these kinds of goals in its documents and activities. Table 12-1 shows that the Olympics increasingly appears to be meeting its goals of greater equity and participation by women athletes, as we see more women athletes competing from more nations. Table 12-1 shows a rise in women's participation in the Olympics from less than 2 percent of the athletes in the 1900 Olympics to 45 percent in 2012, when women competed in twenty-six of the twenty-six sports.

Gender segregation, however, remains in the Olympics. Men still are not allowed to compete in synchronized swimming and rhythmic gymnastics, and women and men do not compete with each other as individuals except in the equestrian events and on mixed teams in tennis and badminton (International Olympic Committee 2012).

TABLE 12-1 Women in the Olympics, 1900–2012

	Number of Women Participants	Women as % of All Athletes	Number of Nations with No Women Athletes
1900	19	1.6	
1920	77	2.9	
1936	328	8.1	
1960	610	11.4	
1980	1,125	21.5	
2000	3,947	38.0	12
2004	4,884	44.0	5
2012	10,800	45.0	0

Sources: Oglesby (2001, 297); Feminist Majority (2004); Whitley (2012).

Barriers to Bringing Women into Sports

Four problems remain in ensuring that women succeed in sports (Shelton 2001). The first problem is sexual harassment. Most girls and women find athletics a source of personal fulfillment, fitness, and fun. However, some are subjected to sexual harassment and even sexual abuse by coaches and managers. This kind of abuse hurts not only the girls and women who are directly victimized. Sexual abuse and harassment also affect other women and girls who hesitate to participate or whose parents will not allow them to participate for fear of abuse (Shelton 2001).

The second problem is related to the pressure to maintain a low body weight. This sometimes leads to what is called the "woman athlete triad": disordered eating, amenorrhea, and osteoporosis (Shelton 2001). Eating disorders are an important health issue for women.

The third problem is the continued barring of women from sports because of cultural and religious constraints. Millions of women in the world live in nations where they are not allowed to participate in public sporting events. In 2008, at least one woman was included on every nation's team that sent athletes to the Olympics. In some of those nations, however, instead of being lauded for their skill and courage, women athletes were stigmatized, harassed, and even threatened for participating. Sarah Attar and Wojdan Shaherkani were the first women representing their country, Saudi Arabia, but their performances were ignored by the Saudi press and marked by slurs calling them prostitutes in Twitter messages originating in their home country (Rogers 2012).

The fourth problem women athletes face is homophobia and heterosexism.

Women Athletes, Homophobia, and Heterosexism

Athletic skills are supposedly part of being masculine. Women athletes, therefore, challenge ideas about femininity. Women who participate in sports, especially sports that are considered the most masculine, are confronted with assumptions about their sexuality and their gender. Are they women or are they men? Are they heterosexuals or are they lesbians? Women athletes must prove themselves heterosexual and feminine in response to the challenges caused by their competence in a "masculine" realm. Instead of being congratulated on their skills, they are discredited for being "unnatural" women.

You should recall from chapter 4 that *homophobia* is the word commonly used to describe negative and prejudiced ideas about homosexuality and about gay men, bisexuals, and lesbians. Heterosexism is another related term that refers to the institutionalization of hatred and discrimination against gay men and lesbians. Homophobia and heterosexism are powerful controlling mechanisms, and people who are labeled gay or lesbian are devalued, stigmatized, discriminated against, and even assaulted or murdered (Pharr 1988; Lenskyj 1991). Both homophobia and heterosexism are found in women's experience in athletics.

Women athletes are often assumed to be lesbians and therefore unacceptable as real women. Research reveals two themes in women athletes' response to this labeling: a silence surrounding the issue of lesbianism and an internalization of the stereotypes concerning lesbianism and women's sport. Both of these disempower women athletes by reducing their ability to form bonds that would enhance their social well-being as well as enhance the strength of their teams' performance. The internalization of the stereotypes—making the ideas their own—diminishes their feelings about themselves, and it makes them critical of their teammates for either being lesbians or for not doing enough to prove that they are "properly feminine and heterosexual" women (Schur 1984).

Women athletes speak of distancing themselves from teammates who are lesbians or who they perceive as not feminine enough. They also often seem to buy into the negative stereotypes that lesbians and women athletes are frequently not heterosexual and not feminine (Blinde and Taub 1992). To counteract the stereotypes, some athletic women have taken to wearing frilly underwear and makeup (Theberge 2000).

One way to cope with being a member of a subordinate group within a system of oppression and privilege is to support stigmatizing labels by asserting that the label is true for other members of the social category, but not for me. This tactic is called **defensive othering** and is illustrated by the women who distance themselves from teammates they perceive to be not feminine enough or not heterosexual enough (Ezzell 2009).

The policing of women athlete's gender and sexuality is not only done among themselves, however. Coaches, fund-raisers, and others associated with promoting the teams and the sports also contribute. For example, professional women hockey players on a championship team in Ontario were told by the coach that he would be unable to raise funds for the team if they wore jeans and work boots (Theberge 2000). Women who are involved in coaching children's teams or teaching sports education are especially likely to be policed.

Homophobia and heterosexism make all women athletes constantly prove themselves "real women," which undoubtedly causes them anxiety. Lesbian athletes face even greater pressures because proving themselves real (heterosexual) women means they must deny a part of their humanity. Homophobia and heterosexism may also interfere with the ability of teammates to form strong bonds that would enhance their sense of camaraderie and their teams' athletic strength. Finally, if women athletes do not "toe the line," they face social exclusion by teammates and coaches, as well as loss of economic and career rewards of positions as players, coaches, and teachers (Lenskyj 1991).

VENUS AND MARS PLAY SPORTS

This review of gender and athletics has exposed many problems with the connection between masculinity and athletics. The conflation of athletics and masculinity causes problems for men, who are forced into participating as proof that they are real men. This can have especially negative effects because of the character of sports as violent, aggressive, and competitive. In addition, the tie between masculinity and sports has excluded women. Both of these issues need to be addressed. Both women and men should be allowed to participate in athletics, but sports also need to be transformed into more humane activities. Alternative versions of sports already exist, and interestingly, they are more characteristics of women's sports. Perhaps rather than trying to include women into men's sports, our focus should be on integrating men into "feminine" athletics.

Sports can be divided into two types: (1) **power and performance sports**, which are highly organized and competitive, and (2) **participation sports**, which are composed of more loosely defined and more informally organized activities. Research on magazine images and articles shows that men's magazines emphasize performance sports, whereas women's magazines stress participation sports (Curry, Arriagada, and Cornwell 2002).

Power and performance sports

1. use physical strength, power, speed, and stamina to dominate opponents and win;
2. include ideas that dedication, hard work, risk, and pain are necessary for excellence;
3. emphasize breaking records;
4. treat the body as a machine that needs to be monitored and controlled through technology;
5. define opponents as enemies that must be defeated;
6. select participants through competition;
7. organize hierarchies of authorities from owners to coaches to athletes.

Participation sports, on the other hand,

1. emphasize connections between people, between mind and body, and between physical activity and the environment;
2. include an ethic of enjoyment, growth, well-being, and expression;
3. express concern for teammates and opponents;
4. experience the body as a source of pleasure and well-being;
5. include participants of many levels of skills, rather than excluding by competition;
6. facilitate cooperation between athletes and coaches;
7. accept competition with, rather than against, others (Coakley 2001; Curry et al. 2002).

ASSIMILATION OR REFORM?

Eric Anderson (2005) summarizes his research on gay athletes by looking at the relationship between gay athletes and their activities and the dominant social structure. He asserts that there are two models for these interactions. Assimilationists desire inclusion in the existing structures. They work for their individual civil rights to be able to be visible gay participants. Assimilationists are sometimes referred to as gay liberation. Reformists, on the other hand, take a more radical position. They want to transform the existing structures to make them more inclusive and less centered on competition and violence. Anderson's view of choosing assimilation or reform can also be applied to thinking about women and men or even more broadly to performance and participation sports.

Assimilation suggests that we maintain the heteronormative, masculine performance model of athletics but that we work harder to allow LGBT and women athletes into the games as long as they will play by the established rules. Reforming athletics presents an even bigger challenge, as it demands that we not only make room for all players but that we change the games themselves.

GENDER MATTERS

Many of us participate in sports primarily as spectators. We consume sports as a form of entertainment within popular culture and as a product of huge sporting interests such as the NFL or the Olympics. Athletics, however, is also often an area of direct experience, and that experience is perhaps one of the most intensely gendered arenas of contemporary life around the world. Athletics is perceived as a requirement for the fully masculine man, while women athletes must prove their femininity if they persist in sports participation. These restrictions create dangers for men because of the way sports are constructed as competitive, aggressive, and sometimes even dangerously violent activities. The restrictions create problems for women who cannot participate or who must fight to remain in the games. They also create problems for women who are allowed to participate only in restricted ways because of gendered constraints and hence fail to develop to their full ability, as we saw in the examination of "throwing like a girl." Both women and men athletes must contend with homophobia and heterosexism as part of the way in which gender shapes and limits participation. These problems have not gone unnoticed, and many activists have been challenging the demand that men participate in sports, especially dangerous ones, and the exclusion of women. Gay men and lesbians in particular have been seeking ways to reconstruct athletics in ways that make them less heterosexist, more inclusive, and better for all our bodies.

KEY TERMS

assimilation and reform
assimilationists
defensive othering
gay games
heterosexism
International Olympic Committee
initiation rite

macho
power and performance sports
    and participation sports
reformists
television sports manhood formula
UN Fourth World Conference on Women
    in Beijing

CRITICAL THINKING QUESTIONS

1. Reforming athletics presents a huge challenge, as it demands that we not only make room for all players, but that we change the games themselves. Think about your favorite sports. What exactly would need to change in order to make them accessible to all players?
2. What do you see as the differences between competitive sports and participation sports? How are these differences tied to gender? What do you think are the gains and losses associated with each type of athletic participation? Have you been involved in either one? What was your experience?
3. Ask someone you know who was an adult before the 1970s (before the passage of Title IX) about their observations about changes in athletics for boys and girls since that time. What do they believe is beneficial about the changes? Do they think there are any negatives associated with the changes?

REFERENCES

Acosta, Linda Jean, and Vivian Carpenter. 2004. *Title IX*. Champaign, IL: Human Kinetics.

Anderson, Eric. 2005. *In the Game: Gay Athletes and the Cult of Masculinity*. Albany: State University of New York Press.

Baca Zinn, Maxine. 1992. "Chicano Men and Masculinity." *Journal of Ethnic Studies* 10 (2): 29–44.

Badenhausen, Kurt. 2013. "The World's Highest Paid Athletes: Behind the Numbers." *Forbes*. http://www.forbes.com/sites/kurtbadenhausen/2013/06/05/the-worlds-highest-paid-athletes-2013-behind-the-numbers/. Accessed March 2, 2014.

Beynon, John. 2002. *Masculinities and Culture*. Philadelphia: Open University.

Blinde, Elaine, and Diane Taub. 1992. "Homophobia and Women Sports." *Sociological Focus* 25 (2): 151–66.

Brannon, Robert. 1976. "The Male Sex Role—And What It's Done for Us Lately." In *The Forty-Nine Percent Majority*, edited by Robert Brannon and Deborah David, 1–40. Reading, MA: Addison-Wesley.

Burstyn, Varda. 1999. *The Rites of Men: Manhood, Politics, and the Culture of Sport*. Toronto: University of Toronto Press.

Cashmore, E. 2005. *Making Sense of Sports*. 4th edition. Abingdon, UK: Routledge.

Coakley, Jay. 2001. *Sport in Society*. 7th edition. New York: McGraw-Hill.

Crawley, Sara, Lara Foley, and Constance Shehan. 2008. *Gendering Bodies*. New York: Rowman and Littlefield.

Crosset, Todd. 1990. "Masculinity, Sexuality and the Development of Early Modern Sport." In *Sport, Men, and the Gender Order: Critical Feminist Perspectives*, edited by Michael Messner and Don Sabo 45–54. Champaign, IL: Human Kinetics.

Curry, Timothy, Paula Arriagada, and Benjamin Cornwell. 2002. "Images of Sport in Popular Nonsport Magazines." *Sociological Perspectives* 45 (4): 397–413.

Duncan, Margaret, and Michael Messner. 2005. *Gender in Televised Sport 1989–2004*. Los Angeles, CA: Amateur Athletic Foundation of Los Angeles.

Eitzen, D. Stanley, and Maxine Baca Zinn. 2004. *In Conflict and Order: Understanding Society*. 10th edition. Boston: Allyn and Bacon.

Ezzell, Matthew. 2009. "'Barbie Dolls' on the Pitch: Identity Work, Defensive Othering and Inequity in Women's Rugby." *Social Problems* 56 (1): 111–31.

Fainaru-Wada, Mark, and Steve Fainaru. 2013. *League of Denial: The NFL, Concussions and the Battle for Truth.* New York: Crown Archetype.

Feminist Majority Foundation. 2004. "Gender Equity in Athletics and Sport." http://www.feminist .org/sports/. Accessed March 23, 2011.

Griffin, Pat. 1998. *Strong Women, Deep Closets: Lesbians and Homophobia in Sport.* Champaign, IL: Human Kinetics.

Gutmann, Matthew. 1996. *The Meanings of Macho.* Berkeley: University of California Press.

Hasbrook, Cynthia, and Othello Harris. 2000. "Wrestling with Gender: Physicality and Masculinities among Inner-City First and Second Graders." In Jim McKay, Michael Messner, and Don Sabo, *Masculinities, Gender Relations, and Sport*, 13–30. Thousand Oaks, CA: Sage.

Holste, Glenda. 2000. "Women Athletes Often Debased by Media Images." *WeNews*, October 17. http://www.womensenews.org/story/athleticssports/001017/women-athletes-often-debased-media-images. Accessed March 23, 2011.

Hondagneu-Sotelo, Pierrette. 1992. "Overcoming Patriarchal Constraints: The Reconstruction of Gender Relations among Mexican Immigrant Women and Men." *Gender and Society* 6 (3): 393–415.

International Olympic Committee. 2012. "Factsheet: The Programme of the Games of the Olympiad Update—July 2012." http://www.olympic.org/Documents/Reference_documents_Factsheets/ Olympic_Summer_Programme.pdf. Accessed March 2, 2014. Kane, Mary Jo. 1996. "Media Coverage of the Post Title-IX Female Athlete: A Feminist Analysis of Sport, Gender, and Power." *Duke Journal of Gender Law and Public Policy* 3:95–127.

Kimmel, Michael. 1990. "Baseball and the Reconstitution of American Masculinity, 1880–1920." In *Sport, Men, and the Gender Order: Critical Feminist Perspectives*, edited by Michael Messner and Don Sabo, 55–66. Champaign, IL: Human Kinetics.

——. 1992. "Reading Men: Men, Masculinity and Publishing." *Contemporary Sociology* 21:162–71.

Klein, Alan. 2000. "Dueling Machos: Masculinity and Sport in Mexican Baseball." In Jim McKay, Michael Messner, and Don Sabo, *Masculinities, Gender Relations, and Sport*, 67–86. Thousand Oaks, CA: Sage.

Knight Commission on Intercollegiate Athletics. 2009. *Quantitative and Qualitative Research with Football Bowl Subdivision University Presidents on the Costs and Financing of Intercollegiate Athletics: Report of Findings and Implications.* Baltimore, MD: Art and Science Group. http://www .knightcommissionmedia.org/images/President_Survey_FINAL.pdf. Accessed March 23, 2011.

Lenskyj, Helen. 1991. "Combating Homophobia in Sport and Physical Education." *Sport Journal* 8 (1): 61–69.

Lorber, Judith. 2001. "The Social Construction of Gender." In *Race, Class, and Gender in the United States*, edited by Paula Rothenberg, 47–57. New York: Worth.

Messner, Michael. 1992. *Power at Play: Sports and the Problem of Masculinity.* Boston: Beacon Press.

——. 2001. "Boyhood, Organized Sports, and the Construction of Masculinities." In *Men's Lives*, 5th edition, edited by Michael Kimmel and Michael Messner, 88–99. Boston: Allyn and Bacon.

Messner, Michael, and Suzel Bozada-Deas. 2009. "Separating the Men from the Moms: The Making of Adult Gender Segregation in Youth Sports." *Gender & Society* 23(1): 49–71.

Messner, Michael, and Cheryl Cooky. 2010. *Gender in Televised Sports: News and Highlights Shows, 1989–2009.* Los Angeles: Center for Feminist Research. http://dornsifecms.usc.edu/assets/sites/80/ docs/tvsports.pdf Accessed March 2, 2014. Messner, Michael, Margaret Duncan, and Kerry Jensen. 1993. "Separating the Men from the Girls: The Gendered Language of Televised Sport." *Gender and Society* 7:121–37.

Messner, Michael, Michele Dunbar, and Darnell Hunt. 2000. "The Televised Sports Manhood Formula." *Journal of Sport and Social Issues* 24 (4): 380–94.

Oglesby, Cynthia. 2001. "Intersections: Women's Sport Leadership and Feminist Praxis." In *Women on Power: Leadership Redefined,* edited by Sue Freeman, Susan Bourque, and Christine Shelton, 290–312. Boston: Northeastern University Press.

Pennington, Bill. 2002. "Men's Teams Benched as Colleges Level the Field." *New York Times,* May 9.

Pharr, Suzanne. 1988. *Homophobia.* Inverness, CA: Chardon Press.

Rogers, Martin. 2012. "Saudi Arabia Ignores Historic Olympic Games." Yahoo news, August 10. http://sports.yahoo.com/news/olympics--saudi-arabia-media-ignore-historic-olympic-games-of-women-athletes-sarah-attar-and-wojdan-shaherkani.html. Accessed March 2, 2014. Sabo, Donald, and Joe Panepinto. 1990. "Football Ritual and the Social Reproduction of Masculinity." In *Sport, Men, and the Gender Order: Critical Feminist Perspectives,* edited by Michael Messner and Don Sabo, 115–26. Champaign, IL: Human Kinetics.

Schur, Edwin. 1984. *Labeling Women Deviant.* New York: McGraw-Hill.

SDPIWG. 2008. *Harnessing the Power of Sport for Development and Peace: Recommendations to Governments.* http://www.righttoplay.com/news-and-media/Documents/SDPIWG_Summary_Report.pdf. Accessed March 2, 2014.

Sentilles, Sarah. 2013. Feeling Thorny: Or 10 Reasons Why I Love Women's Pro Soccer and You Should Too. MS blog, September 4. http://msmagazine.com/blog/2013/09/04/feeling-thorny-or-10-reasons-why-i-love-womens-pro-soccer-and-you-should-too/. Accessed March 2, 2014.

Shakib, Sohaila, Kevin Scalir, and Kuros A. Shakib. 2003. "Title IX: Facts, Figures, Myths, and Reality." *Network News Sociologists for Women in Society* 20 (1): 18–22.

Shelton, Christine. 2001. "From Beijing to Atlanta and Beyond: The International Challenges for Women in Sport." In *Women on Power: Leadership Redefined,* edited by Sue Freeman, Susan Bourque, and Christine Shelton, 171–98. Boston: Northeastern University Press.

Shulman, James, and William Bowen. 2001. *The Game of Life.* Princeton, NJ: Princeton University Press.

Stone, Linda, and Nancy McKee. 2002. *Gender and Culture in America.* Upper Saddle River, NJ: Prentice Hall.

Suddath, Claire. 2010. "Why Can't Women Ski Jump?" *Time,* February 11. http://www.time.com/time/nation/article/0,8599,1963447,00.html. Accessed March 23, 2011.

Theberge, Nancy. 2000. *Higher Goals: Women's Ice Hockey and the Politics of Gender.* Albany: State University New York Press.

Van Natta, Don. 2013. "Book: NFL Crusaded Against Science." *ESPN,* October 2. http://portside.org/2013-10-02/book-nfl-crusaded-against-science. Accessed March 2, 2014.

Watterson, John. 2000. *College Football History, Spectacle, and Controversy.* Baltimore: Johns Hopkins University Press.

Whitley, David. 2012. "Olympics 2012: Women Rule London—No Cynicism Necessary." *The Sporting News,* August 12. http://www.sportingnews.com/olympics/story/2012-08-12/olympics-2012-gabby-douglas-missy-franklin-abby-wambach-female-olympians. Accessed March 2, 2014. Whitson, David. 1990. "Sport in the Social Construction of Masculinity." In *Sport, Men, and the Gender Order: Critical Feminist Perspectives,* edited by Michael Messner and Don Sabo, 19–30. Champaign, IL: Human Kinetics.

Young, Iris. 1980. "Throwing Like a Girl: A Phenomenology of Feminine Body Comportment, Motility, and Spatiality." *Human Studies* 3:137–56.

Young, Kevin, and Philip White. 2000. "Researching Sports Injury: Reconstructing Dangerous Masculinities." In Jim McKay, Michael Messner, and Don Sabo, *Masculinities, Gender Relations, and Sport,* 108–26. Thousand Oaks, CA: Sage.

13

RELIGION

Christianity, like all religions, promotes ideas about gender. Recently, fundamentalist Christians have been presenting images of a "muscular Christianity" for Christian men who are called on to step up as leaders and warriors in the battle against sin and sinners.

Source: Getty Images.

In 2008, Sarah Palin was nominated as the vice presidential candidate for the Republican party. Governor Palin was an outspoken supporter of the most conservative political views of the party, and she was the mother of five children, including an infant. Her views on abortion, gay marriage, the economy, and international affairs made her exceptionally attractive to conservative voters, many of whom are members of conservative religious sects. Her gender, especially coupled with her family obligations, however, caused great anguish as spokespersons for those conservative religious organizations wrestled with the question of whether her candidacy was something they could endorse. **Southern Baptist Convention** churches have strong views on gender and the proper role of women based on their interpretation of Christian scripture. They believe that: "The office of pastor is limited to men," and a wife should "submit herself graciously" to her husband (Baker 2008).

The support of conservative church members is a significant matter for the Republican party, because the Southern Baptist Convention represents 42,000 churches and 16 million members who overwhelmingly identify as Republicans.

Fortunately for the party, Southern Baptist religious leaders were able to reconcile their ideas about women with their support of the McCain-Palin ticket by noting that, according to their reading of the Bible, women cannot be the leaders of men in only two social institutions, church and family. Richard Land, president of the Southern Baptist Ethics and Religious Liberty Commission at the time of the election, explained, "We don't go beyond where the New Testament goes. Public office is neither a church nor a marriage." As long as Todd Palin, Sarah Palin's husband agrees, she is free to take on the role of Vice President and even commander in chief, if the President were to die (Baker 2008).

What do you think about the message about gender given by the Southern Baptist Convention? Are Southern Baptists fundamentalists? What exactly is fundamentalism? Can only Christians be fundamentalists? What religions are most prevalent in the world today, and what do they have to say about what it is to be a man or woman of god? How do women and men participate in religion?

This chapter addresses these questions by reviewing the dominant religions and the images, rituals, and activities of men and women that are part of their beliefs. The chapter begins by discussing what religion is and how important it is in people's lives. Included in this is a discussion of the fundamentalist branches of some religions. We then move to talking about less-dominant spiritual communities and their view of gender and religion. The chapter concludes with a review of classical sociological theorists' ideas about the connection between religion and society.

RELIGION AS AN INSTITUTION

Religion is an important social institution that fulfills many roles. Religions provide humans with answers to the questions we find most serious: Why are we on earth? Is there life after death? What do we need to do to live a good life? Religions also offer practical support, such as providing rituals to mark crucial events like birth, death, and marriage. They bring us emotional comfort or solace when we face difficulties in our lives. In addition, religions can enhance social solidarity and make us feel part of our community (Reineke 1995). In all these aspects of religion, gender is reflected. Men and women are often required to behave differently to be considered godly. Men and women participate in religious institutions in different ways as leaders and as followers. Men and women play different roles in religious rituals and texts.

Religious institutions, like other social institutions, play a dual contradictory role in society as vehicles of both social control and social change. Some religions seek to control behavior and to maintain inequality between women and men. Religions, however, have also served as key resources in justifying, inspiring, and offering material comfort and support, places to meet, and forums from which to challenge inequality.

Religion is somewhat different from other social institutions because of its connection to something greater than human beings or even the earth. Participating in religious institutions and, especially, challenging religious institutions takes on great significance because, for many people, going against the institution not only unbalances human relationships, it rocks the cosmos (Reineke 1995; Gerami 1996).

Importance of Religion Across the Globe

Religion is of great consequence in many societies, but it is especially significant in contemporary American society (Saad 1996). Among Americans, 82 percent say religion is very important or fairly important to them; 88 percent say they believe in God; 63 percent believe the Bible is the word of God; 81 percent believe in heaven; 70 percent believe in the devil; 59 percent say they believe that the apocalyptic prophecies in the Book of Revelation will come true; and more than half (57 percent) of Americans say that it is necessary to believe in God in order to be a good person (Pew Forum 2009; Newport 2007; Gibbs 2002).

Not many societies are as religious as people are in the United States. In a global survey, the United States ranked as the fifth most religious nation in the world behind Nigeria, Poland, India, and Turkey and ahead of thirty-seven other nations from Ireland to Brazil and Japan. The United States is also relatively narrow in its range of religious beliefs. Among Americans, 92 percent claim a specific religion, and 70 percent say they belong to a particular church or other religious organization. Table 13-1 shows the distribution among religions for people in the United States, who are overwhelmingly Christians (75 percent). The fact that such a large proportion of Americans identify themselves as Christians means that the United States is more Christian than Israel is Jewish, Egypt is Muslim, or India is Hindu.

By the Numbers

Americans mostly belong to the world's largest religious group, Christianity (33 percent of the world's population). Christianity along with three other religions—Islam (23 percent), Hinduism (14 percent), and Buddhism (7 percent)—make up the majority of the world's adherents. About 12 percent of the world are non-religious or atheist, and 11 percent are members of other smaller religions, including many different traditional religions in China and Africa (CIA 2010).

One of these smaller religions, Judaism (.22 percent) is often considered a major religion because it is the historical root of the two largest religions today: Islam and Christianity. These three religions are part of the Abrahamic tradition. Jews and Christians share the same sacred text in the **Torah**, which overlaps with sections of the Old Testament of the Christian Bible. Jews and Muslims view Jesus as an important prophet, but they do not believe he was the son of God as Christians do. The gods and prophets of these three religions are all men or at least masculine beings.

Founded approximately six thousand years ago, Hinduism is the oldest religion among the largest four. It is also **polytheist**, which means that Hindus worship many deities, some

TABLE 13-1 What Religion Are Americans?

Religion	% of Americans Who Identify with Each Religion
Christian	78.4
Jewish	1.7
Muslim	0.6
Other	2.4
Atheist, agnostic, and unaffiliated	16.1
No preference or no answer	0.8

Source: Pew Forum on Religion and Public Life (2009).

masculine, some feminine, and some transgendered. A handful of Hindu deities are especially important, but no one god or goddess is most important. Buddhists do not believe in a supreme deity. Instead, they believe that godliness is possible for all humans, regardless of gender, who work to achieve that status. Gender, however, is part of the ideas, rituals, and organization of Buddhism as well.

RELIGION AND GENDER: CONTESTED TERRAIN

Abrahamic Religions

Gender is expressed in religious ideas in two ways. First, religions can teach that women and men are separate kinds of people. They may proclaim and explain that women and men have different missions and standards of behavior. Second, religions can maintain that women and men are not only different, but that women are lesser than men. Although women and men may be equal in relation to the deity, women are subordinate to men (Sapiro 2003). What a religion teaches about gender, however, varies within every religion.

One example of a separate and unequal perception of women and men shows up in religious explanations about the emergence of human life. Eighty percent of societies that have developed supernatural theories about the emergence of humans assert that their god, gods, or other spiritual force ordains that men should rule over women and that a male divine force is the origin of life. The creation story in the sacred texts of the **Abrahamic religions** of Jews, Christians, and Muslims outlines how humanity came into being. One version of the Genesis story tells us that God created Adam to rule over the earth and the animal kingdom. Eve, a physical outgrowth of Adam, was created to serve Adam. The story tells us that men and women have different roles and that women are subordinate to men (Daly 1968; Sanday 1981; Freedman 2002).

Abrahamic religions, however, are not in agreement about gender inequality. Many churches, synagogues, and mosques struggle to assert the equality of all human beings regardless of gender, and their sacred texts illustrate the diversity of opinions about gender. In a second version of the Genesis story, God creates both Adam and Eve simultaneously and as equals. This version leaves more room for finding gender equality among these first humans. Some followers of these religions focus on the version that emphasizes equality, while others prefer the version that emphasizes the subordination of women.

The tension between these two points of view leaves room for debate. For those who see women and men as equals and would like their religion to reflect that belief, there is much discussion about how to interpret religious traditions and religious texts in ways that promote gender equality. In the stories of Genesis, the texts themselves allow for an alternative view. But there are other aspects of Judaism, Christianity, and Islam that are more difficult to interpret. All three of these dominant religions in the United States, for example, worship a masculine god, recognize only men as prophets, and tell many stories that place men in more prominent positions of authority. Box 13-1 describes some of the gendered lessons common to many Sunday Schools, for example, from two sides of the debate within Christianity.

GENDER IN EVERYDAY LIFE   BOX 13-1
CHRISTIAN SUNDAY SCHOOL CURRICULA

Jason Dunnington (2009) studied the curricula that are used to provide religious instruction for young children in Sunday school classes. He found that the curricula are provided by publishing companies that create sets of lessons. These lessons include stories, songs, and crafts as well as narratives that teachers can use to give children information about their religion's beliefs and practices. He looked at two versions of Christian Sunday school curricula, one from a conservative Southern Baptist church and one from a liberal United Methodist church.

He found that the curricula in both churches presented explicit lessons about traditional constructions of gender. The classes all centered on stories from the Bible. Masculine characters were overwhelmingly more prevalent in the stories about God (who is always referred to as a male), Jesus, Old Testament people such as Adam, Noah, and Abraham, and New Testament people such as Paul, Peter, and John. Women such as Mary, Ruth, and Miriam only constituted a small proportion (7.5 percent in the Southern Baptist curriculum and 16 percent in the United Methodist curriculum) of the characters in the stories. Although there are stories in the Bible of women in positive and central roles, such as the stories of Elizabeth (John the Baptist's mother), Mary Magdalene, Martha, Naomi, and Esther, they are not introduced in the Sunday School curriculum. In addition, both women and men characters were shown participating in stereotyped activities. For example, in one story, Christians are bringing support to another Christian community. The women carry babies and food, while the men bring livestock and money.

Dunnington (2009) also found that the stories themselves tended to present men as the more important and more powerful characters. For example, one lesson describes God making people. The teacher's manual for the Southern Baptist class describes Adam and then Eve, his special helpmate:

> God wanted to make something more important than anything He had made. He wanted people to live in the world He had made. First, God made a man. God named the man Adam. Adam lived in a beautiful garden, and he took care of it. Then God made a woman to be a special helper for Adam. Adam named her Eve. Adam and Eve were the first family. God loved Adam and Eve. (quoted in Dunnington 2009, 59)

Dunnington (2009) concludes that there are many factors that go into teaching Sunday school classes. Teachers can teach the information in ways that present more gender-neutral lessons, but that requires going beyond the information in the packaged curriculum.

Catholicism

Catholicism provides another example of the way in which not only religious beliefs but the organization of religious institutions reflect gender inequality. The Catholic Church does not allow women to become deacons or priests. Furthermore, because women cannot be priests, they cannot become bishops, archbishops, cardinals, or popes.

Catholic leaders like John Paul II, who was pope from 1978 to 2005, argued that the ban on women priests is "founded on the word of God and that it is to be held always, everywhere and by all" (Steinfels 1995, 1). The Pope maintained that when the priest serves communion, he is *in persona Christi*. That is, the priest is thought to function "in the person of Christ" and it is essential, therefore, for him to share the same sex as Jesus. There are disagreements, however, about the validity of these ideas among Catholics. Sixty percent of American Catholics, for example, disagree and think that the ordination of women would be a good thing (Steinfels 1995).

Islam

All the major religions today have treated women in unjust ways. Islam is sometimes held up as especially antiwoman. But are these monolithic images of Islam reasonable, or is Islam also a religion that is marked by debate over the question of gender (Armstrong 2002)? When Islam was first founded by Mohammed, Muslims granted women a number of rights that were not available to women in pre-Islamic societies. Islam actually acted as an impetus for greater equality for women in an area of the world and a moment in history when women, globally, were highly restricted. Islam emerged around the year 600, giving women legal rights of inheritance and divorce that Western women would not receive until the nineteenth century.

Muslims use two major sources of religious information. The first is the **Qur'an**, which most Muslims believe is the word of God as it was recorded by Mohammed during the early seventh century. The second source for moral and spiritual guidance are the **hadiths**, which are secondhand reports of Mohammed's personal traditions and lifestyles, which were collected soon after his death to help Muslims apply the dictates of the Qur'an. Together, the Qur'an and the hadiths constitute the source of Muslim law (Read and Bartkowski 2000). In some areas, these documents definitely impose inferior status on women:

- A woman's testimony is only worth half that of a man's in a Muslim court.
- A daughter can only inherit half the share of a son.
- A Muslim man may marry a non-Muslim woman, but a Muslim woman may only marry a Muslim man.
- A man may marry up to four wives.
- Only men have been Muslim clergy, although very recently a few women have become imams in South Africa, China, and other places.

These religious beliefs affect governmental policy in countries where Islam is the dominant religion. Egypt, for example, ratified the United Nations Convention on the Elimination of All Forms of Discrimination Against Women statement (CEDAW). (Of the 194 countries in the world, 187 have ratified CEDAW. The countries that haven't ratified are the United States, Iran, Palau, Sudan, South Sudan, Somalia, and Tonga. When the Egyptians signed the document, they added an exception "out of respect for the sanctity deriving from firm religious beliefs which govern marital relations in Egypt and which may not be called into question." The exception makes a husband responsible to provide financial support for his wife in a divorce. Wives do not have this obligation, and as a result, "the **sharia** [sacred law of Islam] therefore restricts the wife's rights to divorce by making it contingent on the judge's ruling, where as no such restriction is laid down in the case of the husband." As we noted in chapter 7, in many Muslim societies, husbands can seek a divorce without a judge's approval, although women can only seek a divorce if a judge declares it valid. Women, however, can receive financial support from their ex-husbands after a divorce, but men cannot seek such support from their former wives (Deif 2004).

Some of the restrictions on women that are identified as part of Islam, however, are not part of sacred Islamic texts. There is nothing in the Qur'an that says anything about seclusion, education, or paid work for women. Islam does not demand that women be secluded. Seeking knowledge is mandatory for all Muslims, education is no less important for women than for men, and Islam does not oppose women's entry into paid employment (Sanad and Tessler 1990).

THE PRACTICE OF HIJAB. Non-Muslim people often mention veils as evidence of the oppression of women in Islam. Muslims use the term *hijab* for the many variations of this practice today. Some women wear a hijab scarf to cover their heads as part of a contemporary stylish dress. Some wear a veil called a "**niqab**" across the lower part of their face, and others dress in a long, thick, black robe called a "**burqa**," which covers their entire body, with only a small slit through which to see. How do these practices fit with the religion of Islam? Where did they come from?

The Qur'an asserts that both women and men should dress modestly. Neither should wear tight, body-hugging clothing, and men are supposed to be covered at least from waist to knee. Men are also not supposed to wear gold or silk. These restrictions are not as noticeable to non-Muslims as are the clothing practices that have come to be associated with women. The Qur'an also tells women to cover themselves modestly with loose clothing, and many Muslim women also wear head coverings or robes and scarves that cover other parts of their bodies. The Qur'an, however, does not make wearing a hijab obligatory, and many Muslim women do not wear any special head covering. Not until about three centuries after Mohammad died did wearing a hijab or secluding Muslim women in harems emerge. It began at this time because Islam was developing among the Greeks of Christian Byzantium, where women had long been secluded and wore head and body coverings. Muslim women began to copy the veiling of the upper-class Christian women in their community (Armstrong 2002).

In the nineteenth century, colonial armies, accompanied by government personnel and Christian missionaries, came from Europe to places like Egypt as conquerors and occupiers. They claimed that the clothing that covered the head and body of Muslim women was barbarous. In this same period, Christian missionaries were trying to convince people in Africa and Polynesia that they should cover themselves with Western clothes because their method of dress was sinful. Remember that this was the same time period when women in the West wore long, cumbersome, multilayered gowns with unhealthy cinches to show off their waists. Nevertheless, Western military, political, and religious leaders argued that unless the Muslim clothing styles were abandoned and Middle Eastern women became more like the women of the West, the countries would never advance in the modern world (Armstrong 2002).

Lord Cromer, the British consul general in Egypt, was especially outspoken about the need to "liberate" Middle Eastern women by having them shed their head coverings. Cromer, ironically, was also an outspoken critic of the suffrage movements in the Western world, where women were being beaten and force-fed in prisons because they wanted to vote. Cromer was a founding member of the London Men's League for Opposing Women's Suffrage at the same time as he was an outspoken critic of the hijab for women in Egypt. Although he professed to be acting in defense of women's rights in Egypt, his commitment to equality is questionable. Middle Eastern women wearing the hijab were not convinced that shedding it would open the door to freedom. In addition, the long association of colonial occupiers with the call to remove the head coverings resulted in the hijab's becoming an important symbol of Islam and a sign of cultural integrity among the people of the occupied nations. Wearing a hijab was one way that women could stand up for their culture and resist the efforts of oppressive outside forces (Armstrong 2002).

The belief that a hijab does not represent oppression and in fact may mean quite the opposite to those who wear it is still an important aspect of the hijab for many Muslims today. In the 1950s in South Africa, for example, Muslim women wore short skirts and did not cover their heads. When the Iranian people challenged the rule of the Shah of Iran who was put in place by Western forces, especially the United States, the Muslim women of South Africa began wearing long shirts and scarves on their heads as a sign of solidarity with the Iranian people against oppression and neocolonial rule. For these women, wearing certain types of clothing and covering their hair did not represent oppression. Rather, it signified the women's assertion of their political beliefs. The hijab, however, is not a settled issue in Muslim communities, and much debate continues to center on the importance of clothing.

Women and the Hijab in the United States. How do Muslim women in the United States today feel about the hijab? In a study of Muslim women in Texas, the women gave two reasons for wearing a hijab (Read and Bartkowski 2000; see Box 13-2). First, they maintained that wearing one was a way of criticizing Western colonialism in the Middle East. Second, they argued that it was an important aspect of their religious beliefs regarding gender differences and of the need for women to protect their own modesty as well as control the behavior of men. However, covering their hair was not associated with believing that women were inferior to men or should be subordinated to them. Both Muslim women who wore a hijab and those who did not in Texas had similar strong opinions in favor of marital equality and especially women's rights in public life.

Religious advocates of the hijab assert that veils and modest clothing are useful because men often have difficulty controlling their sexual activity when they are around women. They argue, furthermore, that women are not as driven by their sexual urges and are responsible for controlling men's sexuality and protecting themselves. The hijab provides an effective means of protection. One Muslim woman in Texas who advocates wearing a hijab said, "If the veil did not exist, many evil things would happen. Boys would mix with girls, which will result in evil things" (Read and Bartkowski 2000, 404).

Her argument has been criticized by those who claim that it makes women responsible for men's sexual issues and hides women from the outside world in a way that prevents them

GENDER IN EVERYDAY LIFE   BOX 13-2
MUSLIM WOMEN VOICE THEIR OPINIONS OF GENDER AND ISLAM

When American women were asked in a 2005 Gallup poll, "What do you admire least about the Muslim or Islamic world?" the top response was "gender inequality." Face-to-face surveys of a thousand women were conducted in each of eight predominantly Muslim countries—Egypt, Iran, Jordan, Lebanon, Morocco, Pakistan, Saudi Arabia, and Turkey. When asked about their own societies, the majority of women in several of the countries disagreed. Muslim women do not think they are conditioned to accept second-class status, nor do they view themselves as oppressed (Andrews 2006).

They believe they should have the right to vote without influence, work outside the home, and serve in the highest levels of government. They did not see gender issues as a priority in their community, because they believe that other issues are more pressing.

When asked what they resented most about their own societies, they answered that a lack of unity among Muslim nations, violent extremism, and political and economic corruption were their main concerns. Veils, which some Westerners claim are tools of oppression, were never mentioned in the women's answers. Only a handful (Saudi Arabia had the most, at 5 percent) mentioned gender issues at all.

Concerning women's rights in general, most Muslim women polled admired the political equality they associated with the West. Seventy-eight percent of Moroccan women, 71 percent of Lebanese women, and 48 percent of Saudi women polled linked legal gender equality with the West. A majority of the respondents, however, were concerned about the problems of promiscuity, pornography, and public indecency, which they also associate with the West.

One of the most pronounced themes to emerge from the study was the great importance Muslims attach to their faith. An overwhelming majority of the Muslim women polled in each country cited "attachment to moral and spiritual values" as the best aspect of their own societies. In Pakistan, 53 percent of the women polled said attachment to their religious beliefs was their country's most admirable trait. Similarly, in Egypt, 59 percent of the women surveyed cited love of their religion as the best aspect.

They also agree that Islamic principles should guide public policy. Majorities of women in all countries (Morocco, 98 percent; Jordan, 92 percent; Egypt, 90 percent; Iran, 82 percent; Lebanon, 69 percent; Pakistan, 68 percent) surveyed except Turkey (30 percent), which has a secular government, said, "Sharia should be one source or the only source of legislation" (Mogahed 2006).

from fully participating. Covering their hair and heads demonstrates women's obedience to the tenets of Islam and is a sign of how Muslim women disdain profane, immodest, and consumerist cultural customs of the West. However, it also marks a clear distinction between women and men and symbolizes the place of women in the home rather than in more public spaces (Read and Bartkowski 2000).

Covering one's hair and head, however, has an additional twist in contemporary society. Some women argue that veiling is a vehicle for greater participation of women in society and more equal treatment by men. Muslim women in the Texas study assert that wearing a hijab allows them greater access to public life rather than preventing them from participating fully. One woman said, "Women who wear the hijab are not excluded from society. They are freer to move around in society because of it" (Read and Bartkowski 2000, 405). Another stated, "If you're in hijab then someone sees you and treats you accordingly. I feel more free. Especially men, they don't look at your appearance—they appreciate your intellectual abilities. They respect you" (405).

Muslim women who oppose covering their hair and head argue that the hijab represents oppressive social hierarchies and male domination. They also argue that covering their hair and head is a cultural practice, not a religious necessity. They emphasize the fact that the hijab originated outside of Muslim circles because it was practiced in non-Muslim communities in the Middle East long before the arrival of Islam. It is not a Muslim invention, and therefore, they believe it should not be used today as a standard of Muslim religiosity. Muslim women in Texas who did not wear a hijab maintained that other religious practices are more important. One said, "Being a good Muslim means believing in one God, no idolatry, following the five pillars of Islam and believing in Mohammed." Another explained, "Muslim society doesn't exist on the veil. Without the veil you would still be Muslim" (Read and Bartkowski 2000, 409). In addition, critics of the hijab point out that it originated and persists because of men's difficulties in managing their sexuality. One Texas woman argued, "Women are made to believe that the veil is religious. In reality, it's all political" (Read and Bartkowski 2000, 408). They also question the scriptural arguments made by some pro-hijab Muslims. The unveiled Muslim women believe that the Qur'an calls on both men and women to guard their modesty.

The women in this study who did not wear a hijab, however, were careful not to criticize women who did. The unveiled Muslim women said they "construe hijab as a product of patriarchal oppression and assorted masculine hang-ups (e.g., struggles with sexuality, a preoccupation with domination and control) and veiled women cannot legitimately be impugned for wearing hijab" (Read and Bartkowski 2000, 410). Read and Bartkowski's (2000) study shows differences among Muslim women about a specific practice within the religion. Other scholars (Ramji 2007) have found differences among Muslim men and between Muslim women and men around questions of gender within the community.

PERSPECTIVES ON ISLAM IN THE UNITED KINGDOM. Hasmita Ramji (2007) interviewed young Muslim women and men in Britain about their perceptions of what their religion advocated regarding gender. Both women and men asserted that men currently enjoyed greater status within the British Asian Muslim community. They also recognized ways in which the religion and culture of the community not only had gender expectations for women but also promoted ideas about proper masculine behavior. The women believed that gender inequality, especially the restrictions on women, were rooted in a misinterpretation of Islam within patriarchal structures. The men disagreed about what the basis of the inequality was. Some men, especially those who were members of the working class, believed that the inequality was essential to Islam. Other men believed that there was room for interpretation and that the inequality might be eliminated while still maintaining their religious beliefs.

The men in the interviews believed that within Islam it was their responsibility as Muslim men to "bring in the money," "provide a roof over their family's heads," and "look after their wives." Irfan, a 24-year-old bank employee, explained, "It's part of a Muslim man's duty to make sure he has the skills to provide for his family." Similarly, Faizal, a 26-year-old insurance administrator, said, "Islam makes it very clear that it is the man's responsibility to work. If he fails in this, he is failing a religious duty."

Some of the men went further to assert that this responsibility meant that women should not be expected/allowed to participate in earning money or to seek an education to prepare them for employment. Azam, a 21-year-old factory worker, said, "What do women need a degree for anyway? They're not allowed out to work. They can only work inside the home. I certainly won't let my wife work. . . . She'll have to observe *purdah* [segregation of women and men]."

On the other hand, other men, such as Tariq, a 28-year-old pharmacist, refuted this idea, saying,

> There is nothing in Islam that means that women can't work. As long as they observe modesty laws they can do whatever they like. . . . There's a difference in the type of work of course . . . it's not right for a Muslim women to be a fashion model for example . . . where she earns money by showing off her body. Indeed, a suitably employed wife could enhance a Muslim man's cultural capital and community status: I would be proud of my wife if she had a good job, it would reflect well on me. (Ramji 2007)

The young Asian Muslim women in the study had a more-uniform view of these issues. They were strongly in favor of seeking an education and entering the paid labor force. Hafiza, a 22-year-old student, explained, "Our religion says knowledge is the biggest thing that you could ever have, so the more education you have the better." Tahira, a 28-year-old teacher, agreed: "I've stayed true to my religion and found a good job. I've shown my parents that there is no incompatibility with being a Muslim woman and getting an education, a good job . . . and some independence." Shanaz added that not only is working outside for wages compatible with Islam, it allows women to be better Muslims. She said, "I don't think you should have to rely on a man, whether that is your husband, brother or father to provide for you. You should be able to look after yourself. Because when you are independent and not reliant on others you are true to yourself and have a freedom to practise Islam as you want." Hamida, a 29-year-old doctor, agreed, asserting that it is inequality between women and men that is un-Islamic. She noted, "The inequality between [Muslim] men and women that people just accept has no foundation in the Qur'an. It is actually a very un-Islamic practice. Islam is about all believers being equal."

Shamim, a 24-year-old insurance administrator, explained her belief that Islam does not demand that women remain outside the paid labor force and, furthermore, that Muslim men who assert this are just using incorrect religious ideas as an excuse for controlling women.

She said, "There's nothing un-Islamic about going out to work and getting a degree. That's just what Muslim men have been saying to keep women in their place. I have made the effort of doing my Islamic duty and fulfilling my potential. Most of the Muslim men I know my age have done nothing with their lives." For her, making the most of the available education and employment opportunities was a way of both being a better Muslim and creating a more inclusive British Muslim community.

The women also commented on the clothing restrictions that some people in the community advocated for Muslim women. They understood modesty as a requirement of both men and women that was more than merely a matter of clothing. Fatima, a 21-year-old student, explained, "I know what my religion says about women, and it's that we are equal. Observing Islamic teachings on modesty is not about covering yourself head to toe, but about being humble. Are you telling me that these men, who think they are so much better than women, know about being humble? I don't think so!"

The researchers concluded that for the majority of these women, modesty is not about what you wear or who you associate with but rather has to do with the meaning behind your actions. Modesty means "not having a big head," understanding that everything you have is "but for the grace of Allah." In their view, men who suffer from a superiority complex regarding women are not adhering to religious teachings about modesty.

Buddhism

Buddhism, another of the dominant religions internationally, also includes debates around the question of gender. Buddhism was not originally associated with the subordination of women. However, Buddhism today has come to incorporate some gender inequality (Cadge 2004). Buddhists do not worship a masculine deity, and they believe that women and men are equally able to achieve the highest spiritual level of Buddhism. Buddhism began as a gender-neutral story of enlightenment and retains that philosophical belief. As it has developed, however, the religion has come to emphasize masculine qualities of the Buddha and now usually mandates that women must obey men (Freedman 2002). Buddha himself asserted that men and women had equal potential for enlightenment, but some Buddhist writings argue that women are impure and should submit to their husbands, honoring the husband's demands. In addition, the organization of the religion gives men monks higher status than women monks and requires women monks to adhere to eight regulations spelling out their lower status. The regulations require that the women treat all men monks as their superiors and seek out men monks for instruction. Women, in contrast, cannot instruct or admonish men monks (Burn 2000).

The vast majority of Buddhists all over the world—including many Buddhists in the United States—adhere to these practices that subordinate women. Buddhists first came to the United States during the immigration of Japanese and Chinese people in the nineteenth century. Their numbers began to grow in the 1960s, as immigrants from especially Southeast Asia came to the West Coast to settle. Temples were established by the new immigrants as well as by European Americans who converted to the religion. The ideology of the immigrant temples tends to be more conservative and supports the idea that although men and women are equals as adherents of the religion, only men should be monks, who are the teachers and leaders. In addition, there are special prescriptions in the behavior of monks that further separates them from women. For example, monks should not be alone in the presence of a woman, and they should not touch a woman. If an object such as a book is passed from a woman to a monk, the object should be placed on a neutral surface before it is picked up by the monk (Cadge 2004).

The ideology of the convert temples, in contrast, is more likely to advocate gender equality by maintaining that women and men are equally capable of being teachers and leaders. Practices in the temples maintained by European Americans may sometimes correspond to these beliefs, although they do not always. Men continue to serve in the more powerful roles much more often than do women in both kinds of temples (Cadge 2004).

All of the world's religions include restrictions regarding gender. Most often these have placed men in a superior position, but debate continues. Those who wish to acknowledge or shape their religious beliefs, practices, and institutions as places where equality is central are busy challenging aspects of their religions that do not include women on an equal footing. There are others, however, who seek to promote inequality between women and men, and they are called fundamentalists.

RELIGION AND GENDER: FUNDAMENTALISM

The most conservative views of gender come from religions that are fundamentalist. The term *fundamentalism* was first used to describe Christians in the early twentieth century who professed a belief in the literal word of the Bible as a document without error (Ingersoll 2003). We now also use the term to identify many religions that emphasize a conservative view of religion and of gender. For example, we speak of Christian fundamentalists, Jewish fundamentalists, Muslim fundamentalists, and Hindu fundamentalists. Fundamentalist movements are far from monolithic. They tend to converge, however, in their opposition to women's autonomy (Helie-Lucas 1994; Basu 2004).

Shahin Gerami (1996) studied three forms of fundamentalism—Christians in the United States, Muslims in Egypt, and Hindus in India—and found that they are similar in a number of ways. They all maintain that the ideal woman is submissive, asexual, and selfless. Furthermore, motherhood must be the core of women's identity, and family the center of women's lives. For fundamentalists, families are a key feature of controlling and protecting female sexuality, which they believe is dangerous and destructive. Families must, therefore, conform to certain standards, and women need to conform to those families.

Gerami (1996) argues that fundamentalism has been a conservative and discriminatory force in many people's lives, but that, ironically, it has also sometimes been a force for progressive change in reducing gender inequity. Fundamentalism has inadvertently created potential for feminist change because it has made women the center of attention in political debates, especially in the Middle East. What women wear, whether they appear in public alone, and whether they should be employed or vote have all been given center stage in political controversies regarding the relationship between religion and government.

This debate has furthermore encouraged women to examine their religion's sacred texts in an effort to be good women. As they have done so, some are beginning to interpret the texts from a more feminine or feminist point of view. Those women who have interpreted the texts in conservative ways have become an important political force in the struggle to make governments less secular. Those women who have interpreted them in more progressive ways are helping to shape their governments in ways that use what they believe are religious tenets as the basis of creating greater gender equality. They believe that gender equality is not a challenge to their religion; Rather, it is a natural outgrowth of religious teachings (Zoepf 2006).

Muslim Fundamentalism

Although fundamentalism originated among Christians and is currently a strong factor in Christianity, today we hear much about fundamentalist Muslims. The **Muslim Brotherhood** (Sanad and Tessler 1990), a Muslim fundamentalist group, sounds much like fundamentalist Christians in its beliefs that women—especially married women—should be confined to roles of wife and mother and not be permitted to work outside the home. One leader in this group states, "A woman's mission is to be a good wife and a compassionate mother. . . . An ignorant rural woman is better for the nation than one thousand female lawyers" (quoted in Haddad 1980, 80).

What do women living in countries with fundamentalist-controlled governments think about fundamentalist ideas and practices? A survey (Sanad and Tessler 1990) of Muslim women in Kuwait about their opinion of fundamentalism found that they support many of the religious beliefs of the Muslim fundamentalists who run the country:

- They approve of raising Kuwait children according to the teachings of Islam (93 percent).
- They pray regularly (84 percent).
- They approve of the Muslim resurgence taking place in contemporary society (68 percent).
- They prefer religious teachings when making important decisions concerning their lives (51 percent).

Many of the women, however, also had liberal views on women's rights in the workforce and in family law:

- Women should be equal to men in jobs, wages, and promotions (63 percent).
- Laws should be passed that punish men who take more than one wife or that give women the right of separation in such cases (59 percent).
- They approve of women and men working together in the same job setting (57 percent).
- Women should have the right to vote in national elections (48 percent).
- They approve of coeducation in high school and university (47 percent).
- Women should not be required to cease working after marriage to devote full time to their family (47 percent).
- Work in commercial, industrial, and specialized technical positions should be available to women (46 percent).
- Women should have the same rights as men with respect to being able to obtain a divorce (39 percent).
- The hijab is not mandatory (26 percent).

The responses to this questionnaire show that Muslim women in Kuwait are highly religious, but that a large proportion of them also support equality in many aspects of social life. The fundamentalism among these women is strong in regard to religion, and it is fairly strong in regard to social issues; but a large proportion of women, and in some cases a majority, support gender equality that runs counter to the ideologies and practices of their fundamentalist political system. A significant section of the Kuwaiti women in this study sound much like the evangelical feminists in the American Christian fundamentalist community, as we discuss later in this chapter.

Christian Fundamentalism

In the first decades of the practice of Christianity among European immigrants in the United States, both Puritans of the northern colonies and Anglicans of the South based their ideas about gender on their reading of the Old Testament. They asserted that women are supposed to be helpmates for their husbands, be fruitful and multiply, and submit to their husbands. Men were supposed to be the religious authority and the leader of their families (Sapiro 2003).

Among many Christians, these ideas persist. In 2000 the Southern Baptist Convention declared:

> The husband and wife are of equal worth before God, since both are created in God's image. The marriage relationship models the way God relates to his people. A husband is to love his wife as Christ loved the church. He has the God-given responsibility to provide for, to protect and to lead his family. A wife is to submit herself graciously to the servant leadership of her husband even as the church willingly submits to the headship of Christ. She, being in the image of God as is her husband and thus equal to him, has the God-given responsibility to respect her husband and to serve as helper in managing the household and nurturing the next generation. (Southern Baptist Convention 2000)

In the 1960s, religious experience and identity began to change in the United States. Mainstream churches began to lose membership, but participation in smaller fundamentalist Christian churches began to rise. Christian fundamentalists are the most conservative wing of evangelicals. Evangelicals claim that the Bible is literally true and that it can and should serve as a practical guide to everyday living (Stacey 1998). Christian fundamentalism is marked by three tenets (Ammerman 1995):

1. A deep personal relationship with Jesus
2. An emphasis on evangelism, a commitment to spreading the word by sharing their faith with others
3. Belief that every word in the Bible is literally true

This last tenet is especially important in regard to fundamentalist beliefs about gender. Their position on the proper behavior of men and women and appropriate relationships between women and men is drawn from their view of the literal words of the Bible.

They believe that the Bible has given people a plan that must be followed if we are to avoid the collapse of civilization:

> At creation, God designed the family as the foundation of civilization. And for those who followed His directions, He provided a guarantee against structural damage and collapse. God's guidelines are that: Each family member must worship God only, trusting in Him for guidance and protection; A husband and wife must be monogamous, loving each other unconditionally; Children must be treasured, protected, and taught to live by God's laws. (Bush 1996, 4–5)

This description does not mention gender, but fundamentalists believe that the Bible tells them that in godly families, women and men have distinct roles. Fundamentalists are careful to simultaneously assert that women and men are equal and that men's leadership should be administered compassionately. Women, however, must submit to their husbands as leaders of their families, and husbands must accept their authority as head of the home (Diamond 1998).

Christian fundamentalists pride themselves on offering such a clear, unchanging blueprint for gender distinctions:

- Wives should submit to their husbands.
- Husbands should lovingly lead their families.
- Pastoral authority and church leadership roles are for men only.
- As much as possible, women should find their calling at home caring for their families.

As we saw in the discussion of Sarah Palin's candidacy for Vice President at the beginning of this chapter, this blueprint focuses on roles and relationships of women and men in families or in the church. Some fundamentalists, however, did not agree with the conclusion of the Southern Baptist Convention and instead extend these familial and church roles to the rest of society, arguing that women should never take leadership roles in any setting.

One fundamentalist Christian pastor, for example, explained that he would never hire a woman to be principal of his school:

> . . . because there would be male teachers who would then be required to submit to female leadership which we believe would be outside the standard of God. . . . In the microcosm of the family you have two options. If you are a single woman, then you need always to be in the context of submitting yourself to men in general. If you're a married woman, then you need to submit yourself to the authority of your husband. (Ingersoll 2003, 18)

Table 13-2 shows the connection between Christian religious beliefs and opinions about gender. Table 13-2 distinguishes among three categories: those who do not think religion is very important, those who think religion is important but do not consider themselves fundamentalists, and those who think religion is very important and identify themselves as fundamentalists. Among these three groups, fundamentalists are most likely to believe that men should have more power and influence in government and politics (41 percent), in business and industry (34 percent), and in the family (28 percent). Those who do not think religion is

TABLE 13-2 Importance of Religion

	1. Religion Has Little or No Importance	2. Religion Has Great Importance	
		Not Fundamentalist	*Fundamentalist*
In government and politics	8%	21%	41%
In business and industry	11%	25%	34%
In the family	3%	11%	28%

Source: Sapiro (2003).

very important are least likely to believe that men should have more power and authority in these arenas. Religion in general, and especially fundamentalist religion, seems to be associated with more-conservative ideas about what women and men should do outside families as well as inside them.

FUNDAMENTALIST VIEWS OF MASCULINITY. Most of the attention to the connections between fundamentalism and gender issues has focused on women, but fundamentalists also have strong opinions about men. Their view of masculinity has been referred to as "**religious machismo**" (Hawley 1994). Fundamentalists from across a range of religions call on men to reassert themselves in families but also to take on family and community challenges as soldiers in a war against the decline in godliness in the world. This sort of macho, militaristic view of men is an aspect of part of Jewish fundamentalism. For example, the men in Gush Emunim, a highly conservative Jewish sect, wear commando boots and flight jackets with their skullcaps and speak of the perfect match of the Torah with an AK-47 (Hawley 1994). Among fundamentalist Christians, the image of "Onward Christian Soldiers" is promoted as the hard line men should take against communism and other enemies they perceive are against the United States.

The **Promise Keepers** are an example of a Christian fundamentalist organization that has focused its attention on men. Established in 1990 by Bill McCartney, a former football coach for the University of Colorado, the Promise Keepers are dedicated to introducing a new man to America and reestablishing men as the leaders of their families. Men must stand up and be responsible, strong leaders whom their wives and children can look up to.

A book outlining their objectives, *Seven Promises of the Promise Keeper*, tells men:

I can hear you saying "I want to be a spiritually pure man. Where do I start?" The first thing you do is sit down with your wife and say something like this: "Honey, I've made a terrible mistake. I've given you my role. I gave up leading this family and forced you to take my place. Now I must reclaim that role." Don't misunderstand what I'm saying here. I'm not suggesting that you ask for your role back. I'm urging you to take it back. . . . There can be no compromise here. If you're going to lead, you must lead. Be sensitive. Listen. Treat the lady gently and lovingly. But lead! (Phillips 1994, 79–80)

The Promise Keepers believe that women currently dominate American society and that this "unnatural" situation is destroying our nation. Tony Evans, a spokesperson for the group, says, "The demise of our community and culture is the fault of sissified men who have been overly influenced by women. PK [Promise Keepers] is a version of a new kind of 'Muscular Christianity.'" Bill McCartney explains, "You do know, don't you, that we are raising our children at a time when it's an effeminate society. It's not the proper climate. We need young boys that are launched to be men, and that has to be imitated for them by Godly men" (Abraham 1994).

The Promise Keepers' website shows images of men suited up for conflict in military outfits from the Middle Ages with swords drawn. The text calls on men to awaken the warriors and march into battle. McCartney, the CEO of the Promise Keepers, speaking at a 2010 summer conference, addressed the crowd: "How many of you know that a man's man is a godly man?" McCartney's speech lamented the directions the Promise Keepers see the country going in and the problems they find most salient—pornography, homosexuality, dropouts, incarceration rates, and suicide—saying: "It's not the economy guys! It's a famine of hearing and obeying the word of God!" (Promise Keepers 2010).

Besides the call for men to take over leadership, control of sexuality is key aspect of fundamentalist views of gender. Men are to control their naturally strong sex drive, and women are to help men keep themselves in check. Fundamentalist magazines like *New Man*, for example, warn men against reading or viewing pornography, indulging in fantasies about women other than their wives, and masturbating (Diamond 1998). Although men are presented as leaders of their communities, their church, and their family, women are supposed to control men in one area of family life: sex. Like Muslim fundamentalists, Christian fundamentalists assume that women are less easily or quickly aroused sexually and, therefore, must take responsibility for stopping inappropriate sexual encounters between, for example, unmarried people. They assume that strong sexuality is a natural part of being a man but that it must be restrained to live a godly life. Women are assumed to be naturally less interested in sex; if women are sexual, they are regarded as unnatural and dangerous. One evangelist writes, "Sex before marriage . . . develops sensual drives that can never be satisfied and may cause a man to behave like an animal. . . . Some girls become that way, too . . . but most of them don't. When they do, it's the most awful thing that can happen to humanity" (quoted in Rose 2003, 289).

FUNDAMENTALIST FATHERS. What effect have fundamentalist ideas had on family life in households where fathers are attempting to live up to their ideals? Researchers (Bartkowski and Xu 2000) interviewed fundamentalist fathers about their relationships with their children. They measured one factor, paternal supervision, by asking about control over TV viewing. Men who identified themselves as conservative Protestants who frequently attended church turned out to be considerably more likely than other groups—Catholics, modern and liberal Protestants, and those with no religion—to supervise their children's television viewing. However, age and race ethnicity were also significant, because younger and African American fathers were also more likely to supervise TV, regardless of their religious affiliation.

The study measured another factor, affectionate fathering, by asking about hugs and praise. Conservative Protestants and frequent church attendees were considerably more likely than the other categories of fathers to hug their children and praise them when they were good.

The third indicator of fathering the study examined was father–child interaction, which was measured by having meals together, spending leisure time together, helping children with homework, and having private talks. On this measurement, there were no differences among the different groups. Fundamentalist fathers were not more likely to spend time in these interactions than other fathers.

On two of the three dimensions, fundamentalist fathers scored higher than other religious groups. One possible result of this greater participation of men in parenting is that it will create greater equality between mothers and fathers. The researchers caution, however, that stronger relationships between fathers and children could also result in greater gender inequality if men gain greater power and authority within their families and women are left on the sidelines in the supervision of their children (Bartkowski and Xu 2000).

EVANGELICAL FEMINISTS. Christian fundamentalists assert that God does not think that women are lesser than men, but rather that women and men are called to different tasks. The task of leader should fall to men, and the task of helper should be taken by women:

> Seven Affirmations of a Perfect Helper:
> I am the perfect helper for my husband, for God chose me out of all the women in the world especially for him.
> I am the perfect helper for my husband, for I share his hopes and dreams and bear his hurts and frustrations along with him.
> I am the perfect helper for my husband, for I bring him before God's throne in prayer every day.
> I am the perfect helper for my husband, for I encourage and comfort him in strategic moments.
> I am the perfect helper for my husband, for I put his sexual and emotional needs ahead of my own.
> I am the perfect helper for my husband, for I love him unconditionally.
> I am the perfect helper for my husband, for I enable him to become all God wants him to be and I assist him in accomplishing God's purposes. (Wilkinson 1998, 139)

These rules would be difficult for any woman to follow, but they present a special challenge for conservative Christian women. The division of labor between leaders and helpers assumes that both husband and wife share a common view of religion, but in fact, women are more religious than men, as shown in Table 13-3. Women pray more, they depend on religious texts to guide them, and they attend more religious services. In addition, more women than men are fundamentalists, and women are often the most enthusiastic or first in their household to convert. This creates a perplexing situation in which the woman is in fact the spiritual leader in her family—the first or only person to agree with the ideas—but the correct role for women is not leader but helper (Ammerman 1995).

A second problem has to do with different interpretations of the Bible regarding the proper relationship between men and women. Those who believe in the literal truth of the Bible can identify different texts to serve as guides. Those different texts can have very different messages. Some fundamentalists agree with the kinds of passages cited in the discussion of groups like the Promise Keepers, but another voice in the evangelical community is that of

TABLE 13-3 Women Are More Religious Than Men in the United States

	% of Men	% of Women
I attend religious services weekly or almost weekly.	34	44
Religion is an important part of my life.	49	63
I have an absolute belief in a personal god.	45	58
I believe religion can answer today's important questions.	59	73
Religion provides a great deal of guidance in my day-to-day life.	40	56
I pray at least once a day.	49	66
I read the Bible at least weekly.	29	43

Sources: Winseman (2002); Pew Forum on Religion and Public Life (2007).

evangelical feminists, who also call themselves Biblical feminists or Christian feminists. They share many beliefs with fundamentalists about the importance of living directly by the word of the Bible, cultivating a close personal relationship with Jesus Christ, and bringing the "good news" to others. Evangelical feminists, however, have some important differences as well.

First, they claim the right of women to be leaders within the Christian community. They also assert that the Bible uses inclusive language, for example, by speaking of God as a being without sex rather than as a male. Third, they challenge the scriptural basis for the subordination of women, noting that passages cited for this purpose are taken out of context or misrepresented. When it comes to relationships between women and men, evangelical feminists argue that the Bible teaches that husbands and wives must be mutually submissive to each other and that an unequal marriage is an un-Christian one (Stacey 1998).

Hindu Fundamentalism

The third largest religion in the world is Hinduism, which originated in the ancient land that is now India. Hindus believe in a cosmic spirit that is everywhere, they worship many gods and goddesses, and they do not believe that women have a lesser standing in relationship to these deities. For the most conservative Hindus, however, a woman's role in life is to be a good wife, bear sons, treat her husband as a god, and facilitate her husband's spiritual journey. Children take their caste, or social position, from their mother, so a woman who has sexual relations with a lower-caste man pollutes herself, endangers her future children, and subjects the whole community to danger. The chastity of unmarried women, therefore, is of great concern (Reineke 1995). Hindu fundamentalism, like Christian and Muslim fundamentalism, appears to be a growing force (Rastogi 2007). Conservative Hindu fundamentalists like the **Ram Janambhumi** in India advocate highly restrictive codes of conduct for women (Ramsukhdas 1992):

- Women should not choose their own husbands.
- Women should not demand an inheritance from their fathers.
- Women should accept harsh treatment by mothers-in-law.
- Women should "pay attention to the comfort of her husband even at the cost of her comfort," treating their husband as a god and rising early to clean the house.

- If her husband beats her, a woman should accept it as punishment for sins she committed in a previous life.
- If a man's wife has an abortion, he should abandon her; and the only acceptable form of birth control is celibacy.

One of the most egregious practices of some fundamentalist Hindus is **suttee**, which is portrayed by them as a high form of religious commitment. Suttee is a tradition in which a wife throws herself on the burning pyre of her dead husband. The practice has been illegal for a century, but it occurred as recently as 1987, when Roop Kanwar jumped on her husband's pyre and became an honored person among some fundamentalist Hindus. A religious cult has since formed around her, which reveres her as a devout Hindu (Shaw and Lee 2004).

Hindu men also have specific obligations. They must marry a good woman to sire sons and grandsons and advance toward *moksha*, liberation or salvation from *samsara*. Samsara is what many Americans call reincarnation and refers to a long cycle of moving to different levels of spirituality to the bliss of moksha (Reineke 1995).

WOMEN IN THE PULPIT

So far, we have been observing the gender inequality that still exists within religions. Women have been struggling successfully in many religions, however, to take their place alongside men in leadership. In some Christian churches, women are fully participant and important leaders at the highest level, serving the Eucharist, leading the congregation, hearing confessions, baptizing, entering the holy of holies, and preaching to or teaching men (Shaw and Lee 2004).

The first woman ordained as a minister in the United States was Antoinette Brown (Blackwell) of the Congregational Church in 1853. By the end of the nineteenth century, 3,400 women had been ordained in a dozen Christian denominations including the Churches of Christ, American Baptists, and the Disciples of Christ. A backlash in the early twentieth century, however, caused the numbers to plummet. By 1950, only 2.1 percent of ordained religious leaders were women (Nesbitt 1997). In the 1960s and 1970s, in the wake of the women's liberation movement, women clergy's numbers again began to grow as women became ministers in nearly all Protestant denominations and rabbis in all the branches of Judaism. In 1980, Marjorie Matthews became the first woman to be elected bishop of an American church, the United Methodists.

By the end of the twentieth century, 62 percent of religious workers, both clergy and lower-level staff, were women. In the United States, women now make up more than half of the students preparing for the ministry and about one-fourth of students studying for advanced theological degrees. In addition, 21 percent of teachers of theology are women (Bonavoglia 2006). In the United Kingdom, for the first time, more women than men were ordained by the Church of England in 2006 (Seltzer and Soguel 2008).

Public opinion has also changed. Seventy-one percent of Americans polled say they favor opening up the clergy to women. These beliefs have not been fully put into action, however. Only 14 percent of official church and synagogue leaders are women (Nesbitt, Baust, and Bailey 2000). Half of the Christian denominations in the United States still do not ordain women.

The three biggest denominations that oppose the ordination of women are the Roman Catholic Church (the largest religious body in the United States), the Southern Baptists (the largest Protestant denomination in the country), and the Lutheran Church, Missouri Synod (Christiano, Swatos, and Kivisto 2002). The Vatican has taken this issue so seriously it has identified the "attempted ordination" of women as one of the gravest crimes under church law, placing it in the same category as clerical sex abuse of minors, heresy, and schism. Catholic women who agree to a ceremony of ordination and the bishop who conducts it are excommunicated (Hooper 2010).

Holiness and Pentecostal denominations have taken the opposite side on leadership for women in their congregations. Despite their conservative positions on many social issues related to gender, they have the largest proportion of women in the clergy. This may be at least partly because not many men are available to take the positions because their congregations are 90 percent women (Gilkes 2000). In addition, the Pentecostal Church has a long tradition of challenging barriers to racial ethnic and gender parity (Sanders 1996).

Very recently, reversals in the admission of women to church leadership have occurred in the Southern Baptist Convention. Hundreds of women had been ordained since 1964, when the church opened up leadership to women, but in 2000, the Southern Baptist Convention declared, "While both men and women are gifted for service in the church, the office of pastor is limited to men as qualified by Scripture" (Sapiro 2003, 237).

This absolute barring of women from the priesthood is also the position of the Roman Catholic Church. Pope John Paul II felt so strongly about the ban that he forbade a Benedictine sister to even discuss the issue when she attended the first Women's Ordination Worldwide Conference in Dublin in 2000. In 2009, an American archbishop was appointed to investigate the largest organization of Catholic nuns in the United States, after the Vatican accused the group of promoting "certain radical feminist themes incompatible with the Catholic faith." The report they issued in 2012 harshly criticized the nuns and called for reform. The Archbishop was especially critical of the nuns' liberal position on homosexuality and their support of Obamacare. In response to the report, Sister Beth Rindler of Detroit, who is part of the National Coalition of American Nuns as well as a member of the LCWR, said she was shocked by the report and believes it is a gender issue between the Vatican men and the American nuns. "The church in Rome believes in the patrimony of God. But we believe that God created men and women equally. That's where we clash" (Common Dreams 2012).

Despite their conservative opinions regarding gender, the Vatican may have to alter its view to preserve the church. The sharp drop in the numbers of men entering the Catholic priesthood has opened a window for women to take over many of the tasks of parish priests.

The number of priests in the United States has plummeted to about half the levels of the 1960s, when each priest ministered to about 700 parishioners. By the end of the twentieth century, each priest was responsible to more than 1,400 members. In addition, there are now more Catholic priests over the age of ninety than under the age of thirty (Christiano et al. 2002; Bonavoglia 2006). The situation is even worse in other nations, where, for example, the ratio of priest to parishioners is 1:7,000 in South America and 1:4,700 in Africa. In the United States, 16 percent of parishes are without a resident priest; and worldwide, more than one-fourth of Catholic parishes do not have a priest in residence.

The response has been for laypeople to take over many of the paid positions in parish ministry. Today, approximately thirty thousand lay ministers are filling empty positions where priests are not available in the Catholic Church, and 82 percent of these lay ministers are women (Bonavoglia 2006). The women who hold these positions, however, are restricted from performing many important rituals. For example, they cannot administer last rites. Even though they may be the religious representative closest to a family who has a member nearing death, an unknown priest must be called to say the prayers of last rites.

Many religions, of course, do allow women to complete training as priests and ministers, to take on leadership positions, and to perform all the most important rites. The women, however, may face additional barriers as they attempt to take leadership of congregations. These barriers have been called the "stained glass ceiling." Like women in many occupations, women in the ministry tend to have difficulty getting hired and often remain in lower-level and midlevel jobs despite interests and qualifications similar to men who rise more quickly through the ranks.

Women clergy with the same training as men are still less likely to be senior pastors, and they earn about $5,000 less than men in annual salary and benefits (Gushee 1997; Nesbitt et al. 2000; Christiano et al. 2002). In the mainline Protestant denominations, women make up 20 percent of lead or solo pastors, but women account for only 3 percent of the pastors at the top of the pay scale, largely those who lead big congregations (Carroll 2006).

Men and women clergy also have different career trajectories. Men move from smaller to larger and wealthier congregations, and from supervised to solo roles. Women get tracked into positions like assistant minister for children's education. The women remain in smaller, less wealthy churches and they are kept in assistant-level positions (Christiano et al. 2002). In their second decade in ordained ministry, 70 percent of men moved on to medium-size and large congregations, whereas only 37 percent of women led medium and larger congregations (Carroll 2006).

Although women have been held back from official participation in the highest ranks of their religions, they continue to be the backbone of the church. Regardless of whether the church allows women to be priests, women dominate the congregation in their numbers and participation. Sundays may be run by men clergy, but the rest of the week, a local church is the domain of the women (Christiano et al. 2002). Women have long been responsible for many tasks, such as caring for the altar, teaching Sunday School, serving food, fund-raising, providing outreach to the poor and ill, and directing the choir.

THE DA VINCI CODE AND ANCIENT RELIGIOUS VIEWS OF WOMEN

A recent popular film and book, *The Da Vinci Code* by Dan Brown (2003), illustrates another way women have been excluded from official positions within the Christian church. In this case, women who were key figures in the early Christian church are invisible in the current sacred texts. Brown's book speculates that Jesus was married to Mary Magdalene and had children who have continued the line to the present. The novel and film are fiction, but the issues have been debated for a long time among religious scholars (Brock 2003).

Some scholars point out, for example, that during the Easter season, one important story is often excluded from the services and programs. According to the Christian Bible, Mary

Magdalene was the primary witness to the most important moment in Christian mythology, the resurrection of Christ. She was the only one to see him after he had died and ascended to heaven. The Easter Sunday gospel, however, focuses on the men in the story, who never even see Jesus after his death (Bonavoglia 2006).

The role of Mary Magdalene in the early Christian church is only part of the debate around **goddess worship**, however. Most anthropologists believe that artifacts suggest that ancient pre-Christian Europeans worshipped goddesses because of women's ability to reproduce human life. The connection of males to reproduction may not have been known thousands of years ago, and females were, therefore, seen as the only source of human life. Figurines as old as twenty-five thousand years have been found that appear to exaggerate the bellies and breasts of pregnant women (Miles 2001). Most ancient art shows images of female bodies and mothers holding babies. The very earliest creation stories known describe a goddess mother as the source of all being (Eisler 1988).

In more-recent ancient societies, such as the Greek and Roman, religions were polytheist, and female gods were prevalent. Some of them were major deities, such as **Isis**, an Egyptian goddess whose temples appear in places such as Pompeii, Italy. Isis was believed to have introduced agriculture to her people. The goddess **Ninlil**, in the religion of the people in Mesopotamia, was said to have taught the people in her region to farm. The idea of a single masculine god is fairly recent in human history, first appearing about six thousand years ago with the emergence of Judaism.

Riane Eisler (1988) writes that this evidence suggests that two major forms of spirituality and social organization have marked human history. Today our religions and our societies are centered on men. Women are subordinated in both the spiritual and material worlds. She refers to this as the "**dominator model**" (see chapter 8). Looking back at the archaeological evidence, however, Eisler observes that another form predated the dominator model and lasted for a longer time, since most of the time humans have been on earth was before the emergence of men's dominance. Eisler calls this other model the "**partnership model**." It was not matriarchal, nor was it patriarchal. Rather, these ancient societies were ones of equality between women and men and a reverence for the special life-giving abilities of women's bodies through reproduction, birth, and breastfeeding. Eisler argues that we must reach back to these partnership roots if we are to transform our world into a more humane and sustainable one.

Today some people are reaching back to these ancient polytheist roots to find a religion that is more gender equitable and more consistent with their beliefs in the sanctity of the natural world. **Wicca** is one example that arose in Britain the middle of the twentieth century. Wiccans focus on the connection among humans, spirits, and the natural world, and many base their rites and rituals on what they believe was characteristic of ancient Celtic religions that created stone circles all over the British Isles. A mother goddess is a key character in the Wiccan religion.

Ecofeminism is another recent spirituality movement that appeared in the twentieth century that celebrates female biology and claims that humans must use the skills of women to pull back from the environmentally destructive features of contemporary societies. Many ecofeminists believe that women are closer to the earth and closer to life because of their reproductive and nurturing roles and are therefore better suited to provide spiritual and practical guidance. Other ecofeminists maintain that these skills are part of women's makeup but are not natural. Rather, the capacity for caring is part of women's social experience because of our ideas about femininity and the kinds of activities women are encouraged or required to engage in. In any event, ecofeminism represents an alternative to mainstream religious ideas and leadership.

RELIGION AS A FREE SPACE IN OPPRESSIVE CULTURES

Is religion always oppressive for women? Although this chapter has shown how religion often shapes gender in ways that devalue women and restrict them, this is not always the case. Many women are involved in their religious communities and find them places of support and expression (Neitz 1998). Women in Pakistan, for example, live in a society that restricts women, but religion sometimes provides a place for them to express themselves and seek respite from the oppression of their everyday lives.

In demonstrations for equality, Pakistani women chant "Had I been a boy, I could have, I would have, I may have," expressing deep feelings about the repression of their gender (Shaheed 1998). Controlled by a conservative religion, women's families and their government bar them from moving around freely, fully participating in paid work, and interacting with others, especially men who are not close relatives. Women are identified by their relationships with the men in their families rather than as individuals in their own right. Women have few choices about whom they will marry or whether they will stay married, even to an unsatisfactory husband. One woman in Pakistan summed it up: "A woman is considered inferior to men and she has to do everything with their permission" (Shaheed 1998, 151).

Pakistan is a highly religious society that is dominated by Muslim fundamentalists. The women in Shaheed's (1998) study, however, did not see religion as the root of their oppression. Quite the opposite, they viewed religion as an arena in which they could find freedom in an otherwise restricted world. Prayer time provided a respite from daily work. Women could take a break from their chores and create a physical and spiritual space for themselves to worship.

The women also welcomed religious events like *dars* (lectures) and *Khatms* (collective reading of the Qur'an or Sharif or celebrations marking an individual's first complete recitation) as opportunities for social interactions that are otherwise unattainable for most women. Women, unlike men, are not often allowed into the streets, markets, tea shops, and workplaces to socialize. Religious events provide them with a chance to socialize and support one another and to feel a sense of public participation and belonging (Shaheed 1998).

RELIGION AS A BASE OF RESISTANCE

Women Activists in Sri Lanka

The Hindu community in Sri Lanka is another place where women's lives are highly restricted. The women in the community, however, have used religious rituals that are exclusively for women as a form of resistance. In the late 1980s and early 1990s, sixty thousand young people who had protested the government's violations of human rights disappeared in

Sri Lanka. "Bodies rotting on beaches, smoldering in grotesque heaps by the roadsides, and floating down rivers were a daily sight during the height of state repression" (Alwis 1998, 185). An organization of women, calling themselves the **Mother's Front**, emerged to challenge the murders and the conditions that led to the protests.

The women used religious activities to make their case. They grieved the deaths of their children and husbands at temples, breaking coconuts and beseeching the deities to return their family members, and cursing those who were responsible. Weeping and wailing, they chanted, "Premadas [the president], see this coconut all smashed into bits. May your head too be splintered into a hundred bits, so heinous are the crimes you have perpetrated on my child" (Alwis 1998, 191). In any other context, these actions would not have been tolerated, but the government found it difficult to restrain the religious grieving of the Mother's Front. It could not deny them the right to weep and curse because that is what is expected of women in the religious ritual of funerals. The actions of the women received widespread media coverage and alerted the public to the crimes of the state.

Religion in the American Civil Rights Movement

One of the most important social movements of the twentieth century was the civil rights movement directed at abolishing the apartheid of Jim Crow in the United States and establishing social and legal rights for African Americans. This movement was tightly embedded within the Christian church and provides another example of the progressive role religion can play in political struggles, and in particular, the ways religion can be used to challenge gender inequality by facilitating women's effective political participation. The civil rights leaders whose names are most familiar to us, such as the Reverend Martin Luther King, Jr., were religious leaders. The songs we think of when we picture the civil rights movement came from the gospels sung by the church choir. The church served as a critical forum for resistance and provided material and spiritual support for those who fought against racism.

Research on the role of women in the black church and in the civil rights movement and on the role of religion in those women's lives shows that gender, social action, and religion are tightly tied together. Women did not hold visibly dominant or formal positions of power in the church or the civil rights movement. Black women, however, were the backbone of both of these (Gilkes 2000).

As far back as the era of slavery, researchers have documented powerful black women prophets who served as spiritual leaders and teachers in the slave community (Collier-Thomas 1998). Men slaves described their early socialization in both religion and politics as beginning with hearing their mothers and aunts, biological and fictive kin, praying for freedom. Famous black women abolitionists such as Sojourner Truth and Harriet Tubman were active religious leaders (Painter 1996; Clinton 2004). Truth served as a minister in the Adventist church, and Tubman used the scriptures and music from the AME Zion church in her work as a "conductor" on the Underground Railroad (Gilkes 2000).

More recently, in the middle of the twentieth century, the church was an important resource for the black women who participated in the civil rights movement. The church operated as a training ground for learning the essential skills of leadership, "running meetings, managing treasuries, keeping minutes, electing officers" (Gilkes 2000, 187). Churches also created a ready-made set of social connections among individuals and between communities.

Religion also provided a powerful spiritual set of tools, giving women strength and courage to confront bosses, police, public officials, and racist organizations. One woman explained that Jesus was her role model. Because he was "able to keep his commitments and make sacrifices, she was able to keep hers" (Gilkes 2000, 188).

The black church was gendered in a manner that disempowered women, excluding them from formal leadership positions. Nevertheless, the church provided women with resources that they then used to push forward the civil rights movement, where although they were not identified as formal leaders, they in fact played an effective and essential role.

Women in religious organizations that address issues of inequality continue today to press for change in organizations such as NTOSAKE, the Women's Leadership Training Program, the Georgia Citizens' Coalition on Hunger, and Interfaith Worker Justice (Gamaliel Foundation 2010; Idealist 2007; Interfaith Worker Justice 2007). In all of these organizations, religion serves to facilitate and support the work and to empower the women who work within them (Caiazza 2006).

CHALLENGING RELIGIONS FROM WITHIN

These examples among Muslims, Hindus, and Christians illustrate ways in which the existing church and its gender hierarchies have been used by women to support their political

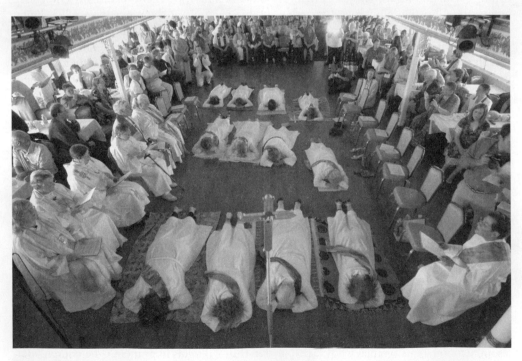

After the eight women in this photo were ordained as priests, the Catholic Church excommunicated them. The Vatican continues to assert that only males may become priests even though many lay women are practicing priests' rituals in their parishes because of a shortage of priests all over the world.

Source: Copyright © Pittsburgh Post-Gazette, 2013, All Rights Reserved. Reprinted with permission.

work. Wiccans and ecofeminists represent a challenge to religions from the outside. They have set up an alternative set of rituals and beliefs that oppose those of mainstream religions, especially the centrality of men in those religions. However, many people have also challenged the religious institutions themselves, demanding that they alter gender hierarchies and allow women greater equity.

Catholic nuns are an example of challenges to the church coming from within. In the early 1960s, Pope John XXIII revolutionized the church by authorizing a number of changes. Many nuns interpreted his writings by replacing their habits with more conventional street wear, leaving convents to live independently, and pursuing careers in academia and social work to the exclusion of their traditional work within the church's hospitals and schools. Since then, other changes have evolved. Some nuns have replaced the traditional daily prayers with one that mentions more women. Some have opposed the church hierarchy's teachings on controversial issues such as abortion, same-sex marriage, and women's ordination.

Catholics for Choice have organized to try to change the church's position on abortion, and despite the ban on ordaining women priests, at least eight women have been ordained as Catholic priests since 2002 (Bonavoglia 2006). Corpus is an organization of Catholics who support married priests, and Dignity is an organization championing the rights of gay and lesbian church members. Led by lay members (nuns are considered laity, not clergy, according to the church), these and other feminist Catholic groups have been created to challenge the church from within. Because they have invested their lives living by the gospel as they understand it, Catholic members of these organizations do not want to leave the church, although they disagree with many of rules established by the Vatican (Farrell 1996). As we saw earlier in this chapter, these challenges have been met with heavy criticism from the Vatican.

Conservative Muslim women in Syria have formed groups called *Qubaisiate*, which educate girls and women about religious texts. Girls memorize the Qur'an and are taught the principles of Qur'anic reasoning. In the past, the older girls were told, "This is Islam, and so you should do this." The women were made to feel that they could not really ask questions. In these new schools, however, the women say that when the occasion arises, they are able to reason from the Qur'an on an equal footing with men. One woman observed, "People mistake tradition for religion . . . . Men are always saying, 'Women can't do that because of religion,' when in fact it is only tradition. It's important for us to study so that we will know the difference" (Zoepf 2006). Recent findings by a scholar at the Oxford Center for Islamic Studies in Britain suggest that these "new" schools, however, may be part of an ancient history. Mohammad Akram Nadwi, a Sunni *alim* or religious scholar, has rediscovered a long-lost tradition of Muslim women teaching the Qur'an, transmitting hadith, and even making Muslim law as jurists. In 1998 Akram began to search for women who were hadith scholars, expecting to find a few dozen examples. His research has already uncovered eight thousand women over the past 1,400 years (Power 2007).

The recent history of Judaism presents another example of a successful challenge within a mainstream religion (Pinsky 2005). The twentieth century was a period of remarkable change in Judaism. Before the 1900s, it had been a long-standing practice that only men could become rabbis. In 1972, Reform Judaism, and in 1983 Conservative Judaism, began to allow women to be rabbis. The Shalom Hartman Institute in Jerusalem ordained women as orthodox rabbis for the first time in 2008 (Wagner 2008).

In 1922 the first public celebration of a **Bat Mitzvah** occurred, which allowed a girl to participate in the ceremony of coming of age and joining the community as a responsible adult. Before that, only boys could celebrate **Bar Mitzvah**. Reform and Conservative Jewish women can now participate in important rites, such as publicly reading the Torah, serving as a cantor, and being counted as part of the *minyan* (a quorum required for public worship). Women still, however, cannot carry a Torah scroll while praying in Jerusalem, because it is against civil laws. A supreme court ruling prohibits women from reading the Torah at the holy site. If they attempt to, they are arrested by the police, fined, and barred from returning to the Western Wall for thirty days (Ben Gedalyahu 2010).

Conservative Judaism still retains some distinctions between women and men, but reform Judaism has accepted women and men as equals. Whereas other Jews believe that children can only claim Jewish descent through their mother's line, reform Judaism now maintains that if one parent is Jewish, father or mother, then the child is automatically Jewish as long as the child is raised as a Jew. Feminist rituals and feminist interpretations of theology are being practiced in the Reform synagogue.

What Difference Would More Gender-Equal Religions Make?

Making women and men more equal in the ideologies and practices of religions is an important goal of many feminists, but what difference would these changes make? One area that scholars have considered in relation to this question is the gendered use of language by religions.

The words that dominant religions use to describe God are gendered. Christians, for example, usually speak of God as the Father, the Lord, and the Son. Some churches now use gender-neutral language, and some people argue that in any event this is just a matter of words and that they have a gender-neutral meaning. It would be difficult, however, to substitute the feminine versions of these words, like *goddess* for *god*, *lady* for *lord*, *queen* for *king*, or even *mother* for *father* (Sapiro 2003). If women remain in marginalized support roles in religious institutions, they have less influence on decisions and practices regarding doctrine, programming, curriculum, and language (Nesbitt et al. 2000). Could increasing the numbers of women clergy alter our view of what is god like? If more women were in the leadership of religions, representing god, would the congregation begin to think about god and religion differently?

Table 13-4 shows the results of a survey by the National Opinion Research Center (NORC) that asked people what words they identify with the images of God. NORC is a large research organization that conducts random polls of Americans. Table 13-4 shows the ranking of the different words mentioned. Most of the words are masculine and a few are gender neutral, but the feminine words rank last in the poll with only 3.2 percent of the respondents mentioning "mother." You might have noticed that the question itself uses a masculine word for deity, *God*.

However, other feminine words could be associated with god such as healer, friend, lover, and spouse. If we shifted to a more "feminine" view of god, might our view of religion and religious behavior change? Thinking about god as like a man, father, or lord makes us think of women as not godlike and feminine attributes as not godly (Shaw and Lee 2004).

TABLE 13-4 Is God in the Image of Man?

What Images Do You Associate with God?	% of Respondents
Masculine	
Master	48.3
Father	46.8
Judge	36.5
King	20.6
Gender neutral	
Redeemer	36.2
Creator	29.5
Friend	26.6
Healer	8.3
Lover	7.3
Liberator	5.5
Spouse	2.6
Feminine	
Mother	3.2

Note: Participants could choose more than one image.

Source: National Opinion Research Center (1989, 156–59).

It also means that our image of god does not include some of the most highly valued components of maternal care, love, and friendship.

Language is not the only area scholars have thought about in their consideration of the effect of bringing women into more leadership roles in the church. Besides changing our ideas about god and godliness, the increased numbers of women in church leadership can also change the churches themselves. One study of women who took over clergy activities in Catholic parishes that lacked a priest showed that women's less-authoritarian style in addition to their lay status caused the churches to become more democratically administered in contrast to the traditional model (Christiano et al. 2002).

FEMINIST THEORETICAL MODELS

This chapter has reviewed several religions, each with many connections to gender. Feminists who explore religious beliefs and practices take a broad range of positions about how to assess them and also how to change them to make religion more a part of the movement for gender equity. Johanna Stuckey (1998) has revised a framework originally proposed by Carol Christ (1983) to try to categorize the different feminist approaches. Stuckey argues that feminists fall into one of four categories.

The first is called ***Revisionist***. Revisionist feminists take the least extreme position. They argue that contemporary religions are not inherently discriminating and may in fact be an important tool in creating progressive social change. The task of feminists is to identify the "liberating message at the core of a tradition" (Stuckey 1998, 17). They would look to the example of the way Christianity was used by the civil rights movement or how Hindu funeral rituals were used by the Mother's Front in Sri Lanka as illustrations of how an established religion could be a strong force to challenge the status quo even if some aspects of its beliefs and organization are conservative.

The second framework is called ***Renovationist***. Feminists with this point of view argue that religions must be changed if they are to serve as progressive tools. Current religious beliefs, images, and rituals themselves must be altered. They might point to the creation of the Bat Mitzvah by Jewish feminists as an example where one of the most significant rituals of the faith was altered to allow girls along with boys to come of age and enter the community as adults through a religious ceremony (Stuckey 1998).

The third framework is called ***Revolutionary***. Revolutionary feminists take one step further by not only changing various ideas and rituals associated with a particular established religion but by bringing in the images and traditions of other religions. Revolutionary feminists suggest that we need to restructure established religions by blending their beliefs and practices with those of other non-masculinist religions, in particular those from goddess spirituality of ancient societies but also from First Nations, Celtic, and African traditions. The discussions over the role of Mary Magdalene in the Christian church popularized in ***The Da Vinci Code*** provide an example of a potentially revolutionary framing of Christianity. Those feminists who write about the important role Mary Magdalene may have played in early Christian history and argue for bringing her into contemporary Christian theology are reaching back to pre-Christian ideas about women in religious belief and adding those ideas to conventional contemporary views of Christianity (Stuckey 1998).

The fourth framework is called ***Rejectionist***. Feminists who hold this point of view have left the traditional religions to construct spiritual traditions of their own. Wicca is an example of this last framework. Rejectionists believe that the religions that dominate in contemporary society are so masculine-centered that they must be abandoned and new religions established that are based on equality of humans (Stuckey 1998; Daly 1968).

CLASSICAL SOCIOLOGICAL THEORY ON RELIGION

An important question that emerges in our review of the connections between gender inequity and religion is why religions are organized as they are. How do religious institutions and practices connect with other social institutions and the broad organization of societies in general? Sociologists have been interested in these questions about religion since the emergence of the discipline. Two classical theorists associated with sociology, Emile Durkheim and Karl Marx, wrote extensively about religion, and their perspectives still represent key debates in the field around the question of the role of religion in society.

Durkheim argued that religion was a core social institution existing in all societies. He believed that its role was to serve as a glue holding people together. Religion provided a set of ideas that members of a society shared, which made them feel committed to the group and their participation in it. According to Durkheim, religion provided an answer to the questions of what is right and wrong and therefore helped each generation be socialized into the society, helping to strengthen the group and ensuring its survival.

Karl Marx agreed with Durkheim that religion provided a uniform set of ideas that helped maintain the status quo. He believed, however, that this worked against the interest of most people who were being exploited by dominant individuals and groups who used religion as a way to keep people from seeking social change. Marx was concerned with the fact that so many people were ruled by so few and that the political and economic structures of contemporary societies use the majority of people to provide an abundant life for a few who are at the top. He argued that religion is one important way that this unfair situation was maintained. Religious rituals and ideas lead people to believe that the current system is the only possible moral way to organize society and that challenging it not only goes against the ruling class, it also confronts the sacred powers that created our society. According to Marx, religion is a result of the political and economic organization of a society, and it is used as a tool to preserve the status quo. According to Marx, religion offers oppressed people a heart in a heartless world, but at the same time, religious leaders and religious texts also often discourage them from taking action to change the world into a more humane and joyful place.

How would these two theorists see the connections between religion and gender today? Durkheim would argue that the rituals and organization of religions do indeed provide a blueprint for gender. They give us rules about what it is to be a good man or a good woman and how women and men should relate to one another. Durkheim would assert that these rules are good because they provide stability and comfort. The rituals, holidays, and texts help us know our place and know what to expect of others.

Marx would assert that knowing our place and what to expect of others hinders any progress toward greater gender equity. Religion in a gender-biased society (as all societies are) only helps to support inequality and reproduce it with every new generation. Marx would point to the rise of fundamentalisms around the world as an indication of the powerful force of religion in maintaining political relationships within and between nations. He would suggest that although religion may bring us comfort in a difficult world, those who are interested in progressive social change will need to confront religious ideologies and institutions that operate as roadblocks to justice and equity.

GENDER MATTERS

In this chapter, we have seen that gender permeates religion. Although there are debates within religions and criticisms from without, religious institutions are fairly transparent in their expression of gender. They establish clear rules about gender, and those rules are expressed in rituals, texts, ideologies, and leadership hierarchies. However, classical theorists remind us that the interplay between gender and religions does not take place in a vacuum. Powerful political forces may use religion to maintain stability or inequality, or they may use it to facilitate change.

The literature on gender and religion reveals the prevalence of gender in every aspect of our lives. It shows up in the most mundane areas such as Sunday School craft projects as well as the most profound beliefs about which humans are more godlike or in rules about who may communicate with and about our gods. The chapter also shows, however, that these are all contested terrains. They have changed throughout history and continue to be challenged and altered by the conscious efforts of religious activists as well as by the changing social contexts of global and local politics.

KEY TERMS

Abrahamic religion

alim

Bar/Bat Mitzvah

Catholics for Choice

dars and *Khatms*

Da Vinci Code

dominator model and
  partnership model

ecofeminism

evangelical feminists

fundamentalism

goddess worship

hijab, niqab, and burqa

Isis and Ninlil

Mother's Front

Muslim Brotherhood

polytheist

Promise Keepers

Qur'an and hadiths

qubaisiate

Ram janambhumi

revisionist, renovationist, revolutionary,
  and rejectionist feminists

religious machismo

samsara and *moksha*

sharia

Southern Baptist Convention

suttee

Torah

Wicca

CRITICAL THINKING QUESTIONS

1. Describe the three feminist approaches to religion cited in the text. Apply each theory to a religious tradition with which you are familiar. For example, if you are Catholic, how would you apply revisionist, renovationist, and rejectionist thinking to Catholicism, and what would be the outcomes?

2. If Karl Marx and Emile Durkheim were alive today, what do you think they would notice about the political activities, especially those that relate to gender issues, of religious leaders, particularly fundamentalist religious leaders? How would these two theorists see the connections between religion and gender today?

3. What difference would it make if women were leaders in religions today? If texts were reinterpreted to emphasize gender equity? And if language of sacred rites and texts were altered so that they were gender free?

REFERENCES

Abraham, Ken. 1994. *Who Are the Promise Keepers?* New York: Doubleday.

Alwis, Malathi. 1998. "Motherhood as Space of Protest: Women's Political Participation in Contemporary Sir Lanka." In *Appropriating Gender*, edited by Patricia Jeffery and Amrita Basu, 185–99. New York: Routledge.

Ammerman, Nancy. 1995. "North American Protestant Fundamentalism." In *Sociology and Religion*, edited by Andrew Greeley, 416–25. New York: HarperCollins.

Andrews, Helena. 2006. "Muslim Women Don't See Themselves as Oppressed, Survey Finds." *New York Times*, June 8.

Armstrong, Karen. 2002. "The Curse of the Infidel." *Guardian*, June 20.

Baker, Mike. 2008. "Southern Baptists Back Palin Despite View on Women's Role." *USA Today*, October 10. http://usatoday30.usatoday.com/news/religion/2008-10-02-palin-baptists_N.htm. Accessed March 2, 2014.

Bartkowski, John, and Xiaohe Xu. 2000. "Distant Patriarchs or Expressive Dads?" *Sociological Quarterly* 41 (3): 465–86.

Basu, Amrita. 2004. "Hindu Women's Activism in India and the Questions It Raises." In *Feminist Frontiers*, 6th edition, edited by Laurel Richardson, Verta Taylor, and Nancy Whittier, 458–67. Boston: McGraw-Hill.

Ben Gedalyahu, Tzvi. 2010. "Woman Uses Torah Scroll to Wail at the Law at Western Wall." *Israel National News*, July 12. http://www.israelnationalnews.com/News/News.aspx/138556. Accessed March 17, 2011.

Bonavoglia, Angela. 2006. *Good Catholic Girls*. New York: HarperCollins.

Brown, Dan. *The Da Vinci Code*. New York: Doubleday.

Burn, Shawn. 2000. *Women Across Cultures*. Mountain View, CA: Mayfield.

Bush, Rosaline. 1996. "The End of Innocence." *Family Voice*, February: 4–5.

Brock, Ann. 2003. *Mary Magdalene, the First Apostle: The Struggle for Authority*. Boston: Harvard Divinity School.

Cadge, Wendy. 2004. "Gendered Religious Organizations: The Case of Theravada Buddhism in America." *Gender and Society* 18 (6): 777–93.

Caiazza, Amy. 2006. *Called to Speak*. Washington, DC: Institute for Women's Policy Research.

Carroll, Jackson. 2006. *God's Potters: Pastoral Leadership and the Shaping of Congregations*. Grand Rapids, MI: Eerdmans.

Christ, Carol. 1983. "Symbols of Gods and Goddesses in Feminist Theology." In *The Book of the Goddess, Past and Present*, edited by Carl Olson, 231–51. New York: Crossroads Press.

Christiano, Kevin, William Swatos, and Peter Kivisto, eds. 2002. *Sociology of Religion: Contemporary Developments*. New York: Rowman and Littlefield.

CIA. 2010. *World Factbook*. https://www.cia.gov/library/publications/the-world-factbook/geos/xx.html. Accessed March 2, 2014.

Clinton, Catherine. 2004. *Harriet Tubman*. New York: Little Brown.

Collier-Thomas, Bettye. 1998. *Daughters of Thunder*. San Francisco: Jossey-Bass.

Common Dreams. 2012. "Vatican Orders Crackdown on 'Radical Feminist' US Nuns." April 20. http://www.commondreams.org/headline/2012/04/20-0. Accessed March 2, 2014.

Daly, Mary. 1968. *The Church and the Second Sex*. Boston: Beacon Press.

Deif, Farida. 2004. *Divorced from Justice: Women's Unequal Access to Divorce in Egypt: Human Rights Watch*. New York: Dickinson University Press.

Diamond, Sara. 1998. *Not by Politics Alone: The Enduring Influence of the Christian Right*. New York: Guilford.

Dunnington, Jason. 2009. *Learning Gender at Church*. Dissertation, University of Oklahoma. *Dissertation Abstracts International, A: The Humanities and Social Sciences* 69 (11): 4512.

Eisler, Riane. 1988. *The Chalice and Blade*. New York: Harper and Row.

Farrell, Susan. 1996. "Women, Church, and Egalitarianism." In *The Power of Gender in Religion*, edited by Susan Farrell and Georgie Ann Weatherby, 39–50. New York: McGraw-Hill.

Freedman, Jo. 2002. *No Turning Back*. New York: Ballantine Books.

Gamaliel Foundation. 2010. "Ntosake." http://www.gamaliel.org/AboutUs/OrganizationalChart/NationalTables/NTOSAKE.aspx. Accessed March 17, 2011.

Gerami, Shahin. 1996. *Women and Fundamentalism*. New York: Garland.

Gibbs, Nancy. 2002. "Apocalypse Now." *Time*, June 23.

Gilkes, Cheryl. 2000. "Exploring the Religious Connection." In *Women and Religion in the African Diaspora*, edited by R. Marie Griffith and Barbara Savage, 179–98. Baltimore: Johns Hopkins University Press.

Gushee, Steve. 1997. "Female Ministers Gradually Finding Acceptance." *Denver Post*, September 27.

Haddad, Yvonne. 1980. "Traditional Affirmations Concerning the Role of Women as Found in Contemporary Arab-Islamic Literature." In *Women in Contemporary Muslim Societies*, edited by Jane Smith, 61–86. Cranbury, NJ: Associated University Presses.

Hawley, John. 1994. *Fundamentalism and Gender*. New York: Oxford University Press.

Helie-Lucas, Marie-Aimee. 1994. "The Preferential Symbol for Islamic Identity." In *Identity Politics and Women*, edited by Valentine Moghadam, 391–407. Boulder, CO: Westview.

Hooper, John. 2010. "Vatican Makes Attempted Ordination of Women a Grave Crime." *The Guardian*, July 15. http://www.guardian.co.uk/world/2010/jul/15/vatican-attempted-ordination-women-grave-crime. Accessed March 16, 2011.

Idealist. 2007. "Georgia Citizens' Coalition on Hunger." http://www.idealist.org/view/asset/NP3F23zZ8zMD/. Accessed March 24, 2011.

Ingersoll, Julie. 2003. *Evangelical Christian Women*. New York: New York University Press.

Interfaith Worker Justice. 2007. (Website.) http://www.iwj.org/. Accessed March 24, 2011.

Miles, Rosalind. 2001. *Who Cooked the Last Supper?* New York: Random House.

Mogahed, Dalia. 2006. "Perspectives of Women in the Muslim World." *Gallup Muslim ThinkForum*, June 6.

National Opinion Research Center. 1989. *General Social Survey*. Chicago: NORC.

Neitz, Mary Jo. 1998. "Feminist Research and Theory." In *Encyclopedia of Religion and Society*, edited by William Swatos, 184–86. Walnut Creek, CA: Altamira.

Nesbitt, Paula. 1997. *Feminization of the Clergy in America: Occupational and Organizational Perspectives*. New York: Oxford University Press.

Nesbitt, Paula, Jeanette Baust, and Emma Bailey. 2000. "Women's Status in the Christian Church." In *Gender Mosaics*, edited by Dana Vannoy, 386–97. New York: Oxford University Press.

Newport, Frank. 2007. "Americans More Likely to Believe in God Than the Devil, Heaven More Than Hell." *Gallup*. http://www.gallup.com/poll/27877/americans-more-likely-believe-god-than-devil-heaven-more-than-hell.aspx. Accessed March 24, 2011.

Painter, Nell. 1996. *Sojourner Truth*. New York: Norton.

Pew Forum on Religion and Public Life. 2007. "The Stronger Sex—Spiritually Speaking." http://pewresearch.org/pubs/1135/religious-fervor-sex-differences. Accessed March 24, 2011.

———. 2009. "US Religious Landscape Survey." http://religions.pewforum.org/comparisons#. Accessed March 24, 2011.

Phillips, Randy. 1994. "Spiritual Purity." In *Seven Promises of a Promise Keeper*, edited by Al Janssen and Larry Weeden, 73–80. Colorado Springs, CO: Focus on the Family.

Pinsky, Dina. 2005. "You (Don't) Gotta Have Faith." In *Still Believing*, edited by Victoria Erickson and Susan Farrell, 102–12. Maryknoll, NY: Orbis.

Power, Carla. 2007. "Reconsideration: A Secret History." *New York Times*, February 25.

Princeton Religion Research Center. 1996. *Emerging Trends*. Princeton, NJ: PRRC.

Promise Keepers. 2010. "Promise Keepers Denver Conference." http://www.promisekeepers.org/. Accessed June 8, 2011.

Ramji, Hasmita. 2007. "Dynamics of Religion and Gender amongst Young British Muslims." *Sociology* 41 (6): 1171–89.

Ramsukhdas, Swami. 1992. *How to Lead a Household Life.* Gorakhpur, India: Gita Press.

Rastogi, Sonya. 2007. *Indian Muslim Women's Education and Employment in the Context of Modernization, Religious Discrimination and Disadvantage, and the Rise of Hindu Fundamentalism and Muslim Identity Politics.* Dissertation, University of Maryland, College Park. *Dissertation Abstracts International, A: The Humanities and Social Sciences* 68 (4): 1666.

Read, Jen'nan Ghazal, and John Bartkowski. 2000. "To Veil or Not to Veil?" *Gender and Society* 14 (3): 395–417.

Reineke, Martha. 1995. "Out of Order: A Critical Perspective on Women in Religion." In *Women: A Feminist Perspective,* edited by Jo Freeman, 430–47. Mountain View, CA: Mayfield.

Rose, Susan. 2003. "Christian Fundamentalism." In *Women: Images and Realities,* edited by Amy Kesselman, Lily McNair, and Nancy Schniedewind, 286–92. New York: McGraw-Hill.

Saad, Lydia. 1996. "American's Religious Commitment Affirmed." *Gallup Poll Monthly,* January.

Sanad, Jamal, and Mark Tessler. 1990. "Women and Religion in a Modern Islamic Society." In *Religious Resurgence and Politics in the Contemporary World,* edited by Emile Sahliyeh, 195–218. Albany: State University of New York Press.

Sanday, Peggy. 1981. *Female Power and Male Dominance: On the Origins of Sexual Inequality.* New York: Cambridge University Press.

Sanders, Cheryl. 1996. "History of Women in the Pentecostal Movement." *Cyberjournal for Pentecostal-Charismatic Research,* October 1. http://www.fullnet.net/np/archives/cyberj/sanders.html. Accessed March 24, 2011.

Sapiro, Virginia. 2003. *Women in American Society: An Introduction to Women's Studies.* 5th edition. New York: McGraw-Hill.

Seltzer, Sarah, and Dominique Soguel. 2008. "More News to Cheer." *WeNews,* November 17.

Shaheed, Farida. 1998. "The Other Side of the Discourse: Women's Experience of Identity, Religion, and Activism in Pakistan." In *Appropriating Gender,* edited by Patricia. Jeffery and Amrita Basu, 143–64. New York: Routledge.

Shaw, Susan, and Janet Lee. 2004. *Women's Voices, Feminist Visions.* New York: McGraw-Hill.

Southern Baptist Convention. 2000. "The Baptist Faith and Message." http://www.sbc.net/bfm/bfm2000.asp. Accessed March 24, 2011.

Stacey, Judith. 1998. *Brave New Families.* Berkeley: University of California Press.

Steinfels, Peter. 1995. "Vatican Says the Ban on Women as Priests Is 'Infallible' Doctrine." *New York Times,* November 19.

Stuckey, Johanna. 1998. *Feminist Spirituality: An Introduction to Feminist Theology in Judaism, Christianity, Islam, and Feminist Goddess Worship.* Toronto: Center for Feminist Research at York University.

Wagner, Matthew. 2008. "Hartman Institute to Ordain Women Rabbis." *Jerusalem Post,* October 1. http://www.jpost.com/JewishWorld/JewishNews/Article.aspx?id=88492. Accessed March 24, 2011.

Wilkinson, Darlene. 1998. "A Wife's Role." In *Issues in Feminism,* 4th edition, edited by Sheila Ruth, 136–48. Mountain View, CA: Mayfield.

Winseman, Albert. 2002. "Religion and Gender." *Gallup,* December 3. http://www.gallup.com/poll/7336/Religion-Gender-Congregation-Divided.aspx. Accessed June 8, 2011.

Zoepf, Katherine. 2006. "Islamic Revival Led by Women Tests Syria's Secularism." *New York Times,* August 29.

14

GLOBALIZING, ORGANIZING, AND MAKING THE WORLD A BETTER PLACE

Worldwide around 115 million acres of farmland are leased to foreign investors, mainly in Africa. Small farmers are forced off their lands in order to make way for export food crops and biofuels.

Source: Aaron Mascho/AFP/Getty Images.

We never fail to be amazed at how the feminist movement has transformed and continues to transform households, lives, and livelihoods around the world to different degrees and in different ways, rendering the life experiences of many women literally unrecognizable in the terms of a generation ago. Here we are thinking of everything from the increased participation of women in public life, to the social recognition of and responsibility for domestic violence, to the proliferation of options of gendered embodiment. This is not to deny that these achievements are partial and embattled, but rather to affirm that they are recognizable and widespread.

J. K. Gibson-Graham 2006

To Gibson-Graham, feminist thinking has not simply transformed the ways we live now, but has created new ways of imagining the ways we might live together. Gibson-Graham focuses on the changes in women's lives, but men's lives too have been altered. Indeed, the rethinking and reconstruction of gender has transformed the entire human landscape. By producing a politics oriented to the "local, the daily, the bodily," feminism has mobilized major changes in how we see and act in the world. Capitalism and globalization may appear impenetrably powerful and permanent, but feminism has led the way toward another vision of possibilities and alternatives. In this chapter we trace the emergence of these possibilities.

What is globalization? Does it refer to the declining importance of local social arrangements? Does it mean that the world is becoming more and more Westernized, Americanized, neoliberal? Does it refer to the expansion and global triumph of capitalism, the growth in power of global corporations? This characterization of globalization certainly describes much of what we see going on around us. But might these events also turn out to be the final gasp of the old order and the precursor to revolutionary transformations that are emerging in local spaces and that can bring the world's people justice and sustainable economies?

The neoliberal view of globalization is that it sweeps away cultural and political differences and allows for economic growth, thereby assuring freedom and democracy. But who will benefit from this economic growth, whose freedoms will be protected, and who will participate in the running of these supposed democracies? The neoliberal view of globalization couples it with free markets, freedom from state regulation, and the dominance of private over public ownership. When neoliberals advocate for free markets, they promote the idea that corporations should be able to move to wherever they find the best opportunities to grow their projects.

The 1980s marked a turning point for neoliberalism that sparked a huge surge in neoliberal ideology and practice. Then-President Ronald Reagan and U.K. Prime Minister Margaret Thatcher took neoliberalism forward in the 1980s by deregulating business and industry and privatizing formerly public domains. Privatization was supposed to produce more efficient and economical goods and services, but it has not done so. It has, however, cut wages of workers, reduced protections to the environments, and increased the profits of corporations. Furthermore, it has enhanced the growth of some of the most inhumane industries in our economy. In 1983, Reagan privatized U.S. prisons. Today, the largest owner and operator of for-profit prisons, the Corrections Corporation of America, earns yearly revenues over 1.7 billion dollars. Private prisons are a big business, and stockholders's profits increase when the numbers of people who are incarcerated increase. Since the opening of private prisons in the 1980s, there has been a tripling of the U.S prison population.

In this era, the International Monetary Fund (IMF) imposes neoliberal conditions on loans to poor countries through its Structural Adjustment Programs (SAPs). You should recall from chapter 6 that these programs require debtor nations to tighten their belts so that they are be able to pay back their debt plus interest to lenders such as the World Bank. SAPs restrict public spending that supports state welfare programs, eliminates worker protections that might restrict business, privatizes public utilities and services (water, health, education), and expands the private market from biotechnology to agriculture and pharmaceuticals by awarding intellectual property rights to corporations that develop transgenic seeds and genes engineered to produce food and drugs (Walby 2009, 1–14). Critics of neoliberalism argue that these examples show that globalization is a process brought about by corporate power that extends itself over the world, increasing inequality between the wealthiest nations and the poorest ones, enlarging the gaps between the rich and poor within nations, and supporting and exacerbating gender inequities.

The story of globalization's triumph begins in the aftermath of World War II, when the rich industrial world led by the United States discovered mass poverty and "underdevelopment" in Asia, Africa, and Latin America (Mintz 1986). The United States had emerged from the Second World War with its factories at full production, while the economies of Europe and Japan were in tatters. American businesses needed the resources of the mines, land, and water in the global South to grow their enterprises. They also needed the labor of the world's workers, and they needed to turn the entire globe into an open market for the goods they began to produce. In this historical moment, the project of "development" became the focal point for restructuring the two-thirds of the world that was not yet industrialized or producing for global markets. As Europe and Japan were restored, they too followed the lead of the United States; and as the decades of the last half of the twentieth century unfolded, the global South was also increasingly incorporated into the world marketplace, but in a more dependent way as suppliers of resources, labor, and trade.

Some have argued that what was happening in the global South in the last half of the twentieth century was a social upheaval similar to the upheaval that shook western Europe prior to the industrial revolution in the 1700s. Then, **peasants** and craftspeople were cut off from free access to their traditional agricultural lands and forests—the "collective economic assets of the poor." No longer were they able to graze their sheep on "common land" or hunt in the forests for food. The **enclosures**, as they were called, pauperized the vast majority of the rural population and drove them to the towns and cities, where they eked out a living by hiring themselves out for wages (Engels 1973). In the New World, Europeans stole land from First Nations people and chased them onto reservations. In both cases, the common lands of the people were seized and privatized, while the expropriators made their fortunes.

In our time, neoliberal policies have privatized more than land and forest. In the name of development, "an enormous number of people who were involved in agriculture with direct access to the production of their existence were expropriated and displaced, and the lands on which they farmed 'mobilized' for large-scale, market-oriented agriculture, creating huge urban masses of superfluous people" (Araghi 2000, 145). What has happened to those "urban masses of superfluous people" numbering in the millions? They are part of the largest migration in world history, as unemployment and poverty have driven them from their home countries. In 2010 there were an estimated 214 million international migrants, an increase of almost 40 million since 2000.

Migrants in the past have tended to be men. Today, however, women are increasingly joining their ranks, and at least half of migrants now are women searching for and finding work in the global job market in order to support their children and families (International Organization for Migration 2010). Migration sometimes creates an economic solution to poverty for those who migrate; but their wages are low, and the sacrifices they and their families make are enormous.

As we have seen throughout the text, gender plays a central role in these historic social movements. We cannot understand the globalization of the world economy or the acceleration of migration as a critical feature of these changes without looking at gender. Walby (2009) calls first- and third-world women's massive entry into paid labor since the 1970s and their heavy representation in the most "modern" and growing of these labor forces—service work, particularly caring work and domestic labor for pay—the "**second great transformation**."

The first "**great transformation**," famously described by Karl Polanyi (1944), brought men into the capitalist economic order as wage workers:

> The hallmark of the first great economic transformation that was the development of capitalism and industrialization was free wage labour. Labour was simultaneously freed and constrained in new ways, which were implicated in the transformation of all other social relations. Free wage labour made possible new forms of political combination and practice, generating both new forms of independence and new forms of collectively experienced subordination. But, with a few contested exceptions, these were the experiences of men only. Most women remained outside these new economic relations, experiencing them only indirectly, and vicariously, through their husbands and fathers. (Walby 2009, 109–110)

The second great transformation, which can be dated from the 1970s, pulled women from the domestic sphere into the world of wage labor. For women of the global South, this great transformation involved leaving home for other countries. Barbara Ehrenreich and Arlie Hochschild (2002) describe this feminization of migration that began in the last third of the twentieth century and is continuing in the twenty-first century. Millions of women— overwhelmingly women of color—have migrated (and are migrating) from poor to rich countries to be nannies, maids, and sex workers. Their choices are to live with their children in desperate poverty or to leave their children and families behind at home and come to the United States, Italy, Hong Kong, Saudi Arabia, and other parts of the wealthy world to care for the children and the households of the elites and the middle class, to serve the sexual desires of men from wealthier parts of the globe, to provide commercial food, cleaning, and other services to the women and men of the corporate stratum in global cities (Sassen 2002), or to provide entertainment and services in the massive tourist industry (Ehrenreich and Hochschild 2002).

This gendered migration reflects a worldwide gender revolution in which men have lost the position of family breadwinners. Today, favored employees are women—cheaper than men, reputedly more docile, and certainly with the undervalued skills of caring for others and **reproductive labor**. Additionally, while women migrants are the major and often the sole support of their families at home, they also contribute significantly to their governments as well. For example, despite the worldwide economic crisis, in the first eight months of 2010, Filipino workers (mainly domestics and nannies) sent back $13.7 billion in remittances to their families. In 2008, remittances of $25.3 billion from these overseas workers equaled roughly three percent of Mexico's gross domestic product (GDP). In countries such as the Philippines, Mexico, Indonesia, Sri Lanka, and Bangladesh, remittances from migrant workers have provided foreign-exchange revenues that are vital to sustaining these national economies.

The caring labor transferred to the rich countries through the low paid work of poor women of color from around the world replaces the valuable (though unpaid) but increasingly scarce caring labor of working women from the global North who can no longer provide it and of the governments of the receiving nations, which have not stepped up to fill the gap. What Hochschild (2002) has named the "**care deficit**" has been growing in the global North as full-time work for mothers and wives becomes standard for working-class and middle-class women. Women's difficulties are increased as employers retain the male model of long hours and demanding jobs for professional and managerial women—and other women—attempting to build careers.

Whether in careers or not, the number of hours of work in the United States has increased significantly more for women than for men, even while global inequalities in men's and women's wages have also increased. Much of the caring labor that has been transferred from the global South to the North, from poor countries to rich, is hidden away in private households, creating the illusion that the narrow stratum of executive and professional women in the North are "doing it all," when" doing it all" is possible mainly because of this largely invisible labor force. Especially in the United States, where there is no public child care, no medical or (paid) family leave, where school and library budgets have been slashed and afterschool programs cut, the need for caring labor is extensive. Just as women of color in early twentieth-century America made it possible for wealthy white women to opt out of the struggle against women's consignment to the domestic sphere rather than insist that men share family work and public work with them (Palmer 1989), women of color from around the globe now step in to overcome the care deficit, allowing the lack of a social safety net for parents to continue without challenge. Gender in the North appears to be disappearing as women enter the paid labor force. If we look behind the scenes, however, we see that gender inequity remains a potent force, as the labor of one set of women (from the South) replaces the labor of another (from the North).

In addition, as Northern children gain new quantities of love in this extraction of love and care from the global South, children left behind at home suffer while their caregivers scramble to provide for them at the same time that their mothers and fathers are working in faraway places. Hochschild draws important lessons from this relationship:

> The notion of extracting resources from the Global South in order to enrich the North is hardly new. It harks back to imperialism in its most literal form: the nineteenth-century extraction of gold, ivory, and rubber from the Colonies. That openly coercive, male-centered imperialism, which persists today, was always paralleled by a quieter imperialism in which women were more central. Today, as love and care become the "new gold," the feminine part of the story has grown in prominence. In both cases, through the death or displacement of their parents, Southern children pay the price.

> Imperialism in its classic form involved the North's plunder of physical resources from the South. The brutality of that era's imperialism is not to be minimized, even as we compare the extraction of material resources from the South of that time to the extraction of emotional resources today. Today's North does not extract love from the South by force: there are no colonial officers in tan helmets, no invading armies, no ships bearing arms sailing off to the colonies. Instead, we see a benign scene of Southern women pushing baby carriages, elder care workers patiently walking, arms linked, with elderly clients on streets or sitting beside them in Northern parks.

> Today, coercion operates differently. Although the sex trade and some domestic service is brutally enforced, in the main the new emotional imperialism does not issue from the barrel of a gun. Women choose to migrate for domestic work. But they choose it because economic pressures all but coerce them to. That yawning gap between rich and poor countries is itself a form of coercion, pushing Southern

mothers to seek work in the North for lack of options closer to home. Given the prevailing free-market ideology, however, migration is viewed as a "personal choice." Its consequences are seen as "personal problems." In this sense, migration creates not a white man's burden but, through a series of invisible links, a dark child's burden. (Hochschild 2002, 26–27)

Paradoxically, as the need for care work grows, its value declines, just as does the value of food crops compared to manufactured goods. "Just as the market price of primary produce keeps the Third World low in the community of nations," writes Hochschild, "so the low market value of care keeps the status of the women who do it—and ultimately all women— low (2002, 27). Every child deserves "loving, paid child care," and every society needs to value care "as our most precious resource" (2002, 28).

THE DEVELOPMENT PARADIGM

The post–Second-World-War U.S.-led development project aimed to bring the "two-thirds world" into world markets and to introduce peasants (subsistence farmers) and industrial workers to global production and consumption, overturn the **sustenance economy** (in which people work to provide for themselves and one another, instead of for the market), and impose a capitalist growth economy on these regions. Small family farms and peasant farming traditions that produced crops for local consumption were undermined, as global financial organizations such as the World Bank and multinational corporations sought to integrate rural society into the international economy by taking peasant land and imposing as "development" the system of commodity food production for export (Box 14-1: The Global Land Grab).

Many of the farmers who resisted these transformations of rural production were women, who were left out of such development plans because the experts who devised them assumed that only men were engaged in productive activities or had the technological potential for industrial farming. According to Carolyn Sachs:

> [d]evelopment planners have tended to assume that men are the most productive workers. There has been worldwide failure to evaluate the contribution of women to productive activity. Approaching agricultural development from a Western perspective, planners define the US agricultural system as the ideal. Women's contribution to agricultural production in the United States has remained invisible. . . . Programs for women have been in health, family planning, nutrition, child care and home economics. . . . For women, the consequences of development include increased work loads, loss of existing employment, changes in the reward structures for their work, and loss of control of land. (Sachs 1985, 127; quoted in Escobar 1995, 172)

The assumption that women were not producers was long supported by the statistics gathered into common economic categories (Waring 1990). Giving birth, home caring, gardening, educating children, keeping to a family budget, volunteer work in communities, work done for friendship or reciprocal or community responsibilities, and all work done at home without pay wasn't counted as productive work. But imagine the world without this work—it would come to a standstill!

GENDER IN EVERYDAY LIFE   BOX 14-1
THE GLOBAL LAND GRAB

The food and financial crises of 2008 ignited a massive round of "land grabbing" in the Global South, with foreign agribusinesses leasing and buying large tracts of land to produce both food and fuel crops for export. Despite the canceling of a few highly controversial leases, these land deals have continued largely unabated, with international institutions increasingly trying to re-frame them as potential development opportunities. The idea that nations simply have a stock of "unused" or "reserve" agriculture land overlooks the massive displacement of peasant farmers and pastoralists already underway.

MAPPING THE LAND GRAB

The land grab is difficult to map, with thousands of deals reported in the popular press from Sub-Saharan Africa to Latin America, and South and Southeast Asia to Central Europe. Catalogs of press reports are available from GRAIN (http://farmlandgrab.org) and the International Land Coalition (http://www.landcoalition.org/cpl-blog).

Because of the secrecy involved, the speculative nature of the process, and the lack of a central registry, precise locations and acreage for all land deals are unknown. Recent estimates include the following:

- "between fifteen and twenty million hectares of farmland in poor countries have been subject to transactions or talks involving foreigners since 2006";
- "upwards of twenty and even thirty million hectares transacted between 2005 and mid-2009";
- "twenty to fifty million hectares in play, out of [a] potential 200–800 million available";
- "over $100 billion for the acquisition of upward of 50 million hectares"

Africa and Southeast Asia were home to some of the first mega-land deals that helped call public attention to the story. In 2007, ZTE (a Chinese telecommunications company) announced a 2.8 million hectare deal to produce agrofuels in the Democratic Republic of Congo. In 2008 and '09, massive public outcry forced the governments of Madagascar, Indonesia, and the Philippines to renege on or postpone the projects. In the case of Madagascar, the government collapsed under pressure from popular movements against a 1.3 million hectare 99 year land lease with the South Korean firm Daewoo Logistics to produce corn for export back to South Korea.

While transnational land grabbing took off in the wake of the 2008 food crisis, growing demand for agrofuels (e.g., in Europe) and industrial crops (e.g., in China) had produced a string of land deals in Africa and Southeast Asia before it started. "The trick here is not just to harvest crops but to harvest money."

WHO IS BEHIND IT?

Governments, private investors, sovereign wealth funds and hedge funds are all involved. Governments throughout the Middle East and East Asia are looking to decrease their reliance on market-mediated food imports by locking up land access in other countries. Large-scale investments, in turn, can be attractive to host governments who see big land deals as a chance to bring jobs and infrastructure by, as national leaders in Laos put it, "turning land into capital."

- *Governments seeking a more secure and stable food supply* are buying and leasing foreign land to circumvent the volatile global market.
  - Governments grabbing land for food security include: "China, India, Japan, Malaysia and South Korea in Asia; Egypt and Libya in Africa; and Bahrain, Jordan, Kuwait, Qatar, Saudi Arabia and the United Arab Emirates in the Middle East."
  - Water is a primary concern for many of the countries involved as well. Saudi Arabia, for example, faces not only dependence on international food markets, but growing water scarcity as aquifers dry up as a result of decades of irrigated wheat farming.
- *Private investors* Farmland started out as a way to diversify and hedge against the global financial bubble. Spurred on by high commodity prices and strong government mandates for agrofuels, it has since taken off as its own hot commodity. According to investor Howard Buffet, fund managers have claimed 15–20% return on investment in African farmland, and advertised land leases at under $3.00/hectare per year with country governments committing 70% of financing.
  - Private investors also include local elites, government officials and other business interests. Peasant farms are being bulldozed in Cambodia for example, under a new 10,000 hectare sugar concession given to a member of the ruling political party.

MECHANISMS FOR LAND GRABBING

Long-term leases, concessions, purchases and now, coercive contract farming arrangements are all mechanisms for grabbing up foreign farmland.

As a result of popular opposition to foreign land giveaways, Laos has been trying to implement a "cooperative investment" model based on the principle of contract farming. These efforts, however, are becoming entangled in latent disputes about the legal relationship between "village" and "state" land, leading to a combination of low and coerced participation.

THE ROLE OF INTERNATIONAL INSTITUTIONS

After decades of calling for increased investment in agriculture, neither the FAO nor the World Bank is condemning the land grab outright. In June 2008 in response to the food crisis, FAO head Jacques Diouf came out in favor of "innovative new solutions" to global hunger, but changed tone three months later, expressing fear that new land deals create "a neocolonial pact for the provision of nonvalue-added raw materials" to investors.

The World Bank was noticeably silent on land grabs when the story broke (Lamb 2009, slide 18) and is now promoting a voluntary code of conduct with seven principles for "responsible and successful" land grabbing. The UN Conference on Trade and Development agreed to collaborate on the principles. Neither institution has the authority to enforce a code of conduct.

The World Bank has also been accused of facilitating the land grab through its advisory and technical assistance programs at the Foreign Investment Advisory Service and the International Finance Corporation.

CIVIL SOCIETY RESPONSE

GRAIN led the way in cataloging and mapping land deals in 2008, and has since been joined by the International Land Coalition. Civil society is increasingly mounting an organized global resistance. In a recent statement the international peasant movement La Via Campesina with GRAIN and the FoodFirst Information and Action Network demanded an immediate end to the land grab, and to the World Bank's tacit support for land takeovers. According to the statement:

> The WB's principles attempt to create the illusion that land grabbing can proceed without disastrous consequences to peoples, communities, eco-systems and the climate. . . . Farmer's and indigenous peoples organisations, social movements and civil society groups largely agree that what we need instead is to:
>
> 1. Keep land in the hands of local communities and implement genuine agrarian reform in order to ensure equitable access to land and natural resources.
> 2. Heavily support agro-ecological peasant, smallholder farming, fishing and pastoralism, including participatory research and training programmes so that small-scale food providers can produce ample, healthy and safe food for everybody.
> 3. Overhaul farm and trade policies to embrace food sovereignty and support local and regional markets that people can participate in and benefit from.
> 4. Promote community-oriented food and farming systems hinged on local people's control over land, water and biodiversity. Enforce strict mandatory regulations that curb the access of corporations and other powerful actors (state and private) to agricultural, coastal and grazing lands, forests, and wetlands.

SOURCE: Reprinted by permission of the Institute for Food and Development Policy (2010). 398 60th Street, Oakland, CA 94618. www.foodfirst.org.

Raj Patel (2009, 67–68) comments on the invisible reproductive labor of women:

To reproduce workers requires more than making babies: It's a long process of child-rearing, feeding, clothing, housing, educating, socializing and disciplining, and the costs of this are the source of perhaps the most fundamental misevaluation, worldwide—the market's treatment of women's work in the home. The daily work of rearing children, maintaining a household and engaging in civic work—the unpaid slabs of work that feminists have called "women's triple burden"—remains unpriced worldwide. Were all unpaid work to be remunerated, the sum was estimated in 1995 to be $16 trillion. . . . Back in 1995 this was more than half of the world's total output. What's worse, this miscalculation isn't innocent. It's *because* this reproductive work has been naturalized as women's work, and because women's work is unpaid, that there can be such a large paid economy. Because their work is uncounted, women appear to have "free" time, time that is used by development agencies to explain why women are able to "burden share," to pick up some of the slack where public services fail. This sexism spread to the wage economy too— according to the International Labour Organization, women in most countries earn between 70 and 90 percent of what men earn for the same work, though in some places, particularly in Asia, that figure is lower.

The primary objective of capitalist production is not to provide for people's needs (what Marx called "**use values**"), but to make profits (Wood 1999). But what if meeting the needs of community members were the objective of our work? This would be work whose aim is life and well-being for all, not the production of profit for some. If we were to value such work, if we were to gather statistics about reproductive work as essential work, we would appreciate the tremendous productivity of the world's women.

Many observers have found the development discourse economistic (the reduction of all social facts to their economic dimension) and **masculinist** (because it focuses on the activities of men, while women's lives and women's work remains invisible—as, for example, in Box 6-5 in chapter 6, "Mr. Moyo Goes to the Doctor"). In addition, it dismisses the majority of humanity by drawing on the idea that the North is the model for all other nations to emulate and only Northern knowledge and Northern experts can overcome the cultural constraints keeping people in the South poor (Carruyo 2007). Even worse, the South is held accountable for the scarcities and poverty that have actually resulted from the imposition of capitalist production relations. In other words, problems that are caused by businesses and governments from the North are blamed on the people of the South. For example, Vandana Shiva (2005, 33–34) claims that capitalist globalized agriculture increases hunger, erodes and depletes the soil, pollutes groundwater, and extinguishes diversity. It spreads health hazards (*E. coli*, salmonella), obesity, and pesticide residues and destroys healthy, local eating habits.

There are many corpses littering the field of industrial agriculture. For example, the United States and other rich nations capture new markets at the expense of Southern countries when they sell their produce on the world market for far less than the cost of its production. Are lower prices on the world market signs of the greater efficiency of U.S. agriculture? Not at all. American corn is subsidized by the U.S. government so that the large corporate farms that grow it on thousands of monocultural acres are able to dump it, for example, in Mexico, where it has contributed to the impoverishment of millions of small corn farmers and the loss of their lands. Similar practices have led to similar results in Africa. Arturo Escobar suggests that the "problems" of development are Northern inventions that are used to justify U.S. interventions in the name of development assistance (Escobar 1995, Carruyo 2007). Behind the global markets and unfair competition between Southern peasants and Northern corporations is the pressure to adopt the intensive agricultural model of technological inputs that use oil, fertilizers, machinery, pesticides, and hybrid and genetically modified seeds in order to grow commodity crops for the world market, crops that fill the coffers of transnational corporations.

BEYOND THE RURAL: EXPORT PROCESSING ZONES

Until the 1970s, development experts ignored women, whom they saw as marginal to production, which was the main focus of their attention. The experts, economists, and development agents involved in programs designed to increase technical expertise for large-scale farming recognized only men as engaged in productive activities. This view became a self-fulfilling prophecy. Male farmers were the beneficiaries of technical improvements, were given land,

Dominican women employed in a factory in a **free trade** or **export processing zone (EPZ)** in 2005. EPZs are industrial areas set up by governments to attract multinational companies, using incentives such as exemption from labor laws, tax breaks, and duty free imports of raw materials. In EPZs, workers work long hours for very low pay. Working conditions are often dangerous (1,129 Bangladeshi working women lost their lives in 2013 when the factory in which they were making clothes for Walmart and other large companies collapsed).

Source: Associated Press.

and were enticed to produce crops for markets and to participate in cash economies. Women were relegated to subsistence activities, and when such activities became mechanized (as when grain mills replaced the mortar and pestle), the control of the activities and the technologies went to men (Escobar 1995, 172).

It was not until the promotion of Southern industrialization through export processing zones (EPZs) that women became visible as producers. Nevertheless, women remained the lowest paid, most exploited, and least skilled workers. EPZs have been a major source of employment for rural migrant women as rural livelihood options have become increasingly limited. EPZs are labor-intensive manufacturing centers located in developing countries that produce clothing, electronic goods, shoes, toys, and other consumer goods. By 1999, there were 3,000 free-trade zones in 116 countries, employing 43 million people, mainly young women (Economy Watch 2010). Since the 1970s, millions of women have gone to work in these zones. Corporations that establish factories in the zones receive tax breaks, gain access to a cheap and reputedly docile labor force, benefit from antiunion labor laws imposed by the host country, and are forced to compete with few, if any, employers.

With few restrictions, most factories in export processing zones inflict environmental damage on their hosts, have poor safety and health standards, commit labor rights abuses, and demand compulsory overtime. Women may be fired at the employers' convenience for involvement in union activity and for pregnancy, and they are subjected to sexual harassment and discrimination in wages and benefits. There is a high turnover rate in the zones and a continuous supply of young women from the countryside to take the place of workers who leave or are fired.

To those who point out the abuses of these workplaces, others counter that the young women who work in the zones are liberated from patriarchal families. However, the factories themselves impose patriarchal restrictions on their young female employees. For example, the *Bangkok Post* reported in 2007 that while women workers were "the backbone in the export manufacturing industries," they were poorly paid, badly protected against occupational health hazards, faced mass layoffs when the export economy faltered, earned lower wages than men, lacked opportunities for training and promotion, and were pressured to resign when they got pregnant or got older. In the American protectorate of Saipan, young Chinese women employed in American textile factories were forced to sign contracts that barred them from having boyfriends and from having children if they became pregnant (Democracy Now 2006).

The development project of the global North is promoted and pursued by means of a **discourse**, a way of seeing and knowing, that casts Southern workers, especially women, as ignorant, indolent, and incapable of civilized life. Are third-world economies failed economies? Is the Northern way of living the only way? This is the view from above, from the wealthy world, from capitalist production, from the men who rule. How is this world seen by peasants, workers in the free-trade zones, people who migrate to find work and leave their children behind, women, the poor?

TWO MORE GLOBAL ECONOMIES

Vandana Shiva (2005, 13), the Indian environmental and anti-globalization activist, writes that the capitalist economy is only one of three major economies in the world today. An economy is a system for producing and distributing the goods and services people need for their survival. The capitalist economy produces goods for the market and distributes them only to those who can pay the prices. Capitalists are not primarily interested in providing for people's needs or for paying attention to the "hidden" costs to the environment. Rather, they are interested in making the greatest profit by reducing wages, expanding markets, and keeping hidden costs to the environment invisible.

Shiva writes that although global capitalism is certainly the dominant economy, two other economies exist: the sustenance economy and nature's economy. As we have noted, market-based development—the capitalist economy—has been a spectacular success for the very wealthy, the banks, and the multinational corporations. For the vast majority of the world, however, capitalism has been an equally spectacular failure. Billions of people in the world capitalist system strive every day to live on a dollar or two a day. The damage wrought by capitalist "development" is everywhere to be seen. The globalized workers who travel the world to find work are better off than the former peasants, who end up in the slums of Mumbai, Rio, Mexico City, or Dakar. The homeless and near-homeless slum dwellers of those global cities are about two-fifths of the economically active population of the developing world, where they work in unskilled, unprotected, and low-wage informal industries according to Mike Davis, who calls these workers the " 'active' unemployed, who have no choice but to subsist by some means or starve" (Davis 2004).

The third economy Shiva describes is nature's economy. Nature's economy, according to Shiva, "consists of the production of goods and services by nature—the water recycled and distributed through the hydrologic cycles, the soil fertility produced by microorganisms, the plants fertilized by pollinators" (2005, 16). Little of this productivity is valuable within market economics. Nature's economy therefore is taken for granted, ignored and abused. For example, scientists believe that "colony collapse disorder," the name of the huge annual die-off of bees in the United States, is the result of the liberal use of insecticides and fungicides on commercial fruit and vegetable crops (Philpott 2013). This example illustrates the way that wealth generated in the market is in conflict with wealth generated by nature. It looks as if we will live to see the consequences of our profligate use of nature's economy as global climate change proceeds.

In a sustenance economy, people work to provide for themselves and one another. A global sustenance economy preceded the development of capitalism, and it persists as an alternative means to survival. Like the natural economy, however, when the sustenance economy comes into conflict with the needs of the capitalist economy to expand or profit sufficiently, the sustenance economy is pushed to the side or destroyed. Because the gender division of labor throughout the world makes women predominantly responsible for the work of "reproduction" (reproducing human life *and* well-being through nurturing, care, and emotional support), the sustenance economy is, for the most part, the women's economy. Market economies depend on the sustenance economy, although it is officially, statistically invisible. When health care is privatized, mothers and other women look after the ill in the family; when livelihoods are destroyed by globalization, women and men work more jobs and more hours to feed their families. Southern poverty has grown from the depletion of Southern resources by the colonial powers over several centuries. More recent attacks on the sustenance economy come through privatizing water, patenting seeds, and corporatizing agriculture.

FEMINIST POLITICAL ECOLOGY: BEYOND PRODUCTION

Feminist political ecologists look closely at the sustenance economy and at the reproductive labor that supports the productive economy. They see the reproductive economy as a women's economy, the outcome of the gender division of labor that consigned women to reproductive work. They expand the notion of productivity ("reproductivity!") from its association with markets and money wealth to a wider conception that includes reproducing human life and well-being through nurturing, care, and emotional support. Bearing children, teaching and nurturing them, caring for the sick, the old, and extended family members, working in volunteer community organizations are all part of the reproductive economy. Its logic is social reciprocity, not profit and acquisition. Although it is invisible and doesn't "count" in the official statistics, this work is the basis and support of the capitalist productive economy. Without these two economies, the capitalist economy would not exist. The capitalist market economy, however, is cannibalizing the sustenance and nature's economies and therefore destroying the pillars on which it relies as well as its own ability to operate. How can we find a way out of these contradictions?

A Provisioning Economy

Feminist political ecologists offer alternatives to capitalist globalization (Salleh 2009). They expand the concept of economy from the narrow focus on markets, money, and property to a wider conception of human activities that meet human needs, a "distinctively feminist economics" that includes care, reciprocity, women's domestic work, and the social reciprocity that sustains people in communities and other nonmarket economies. Mary Mellor calls this economy a "provisioning economy," an economy that will meet human needs and cultivate human potential without destroying the planet (Mellor 2009, 253).

A provisioning economy would start from the embodiment and embeddedness of human lives, from the life of the body and the ecosystem, from women's work and the vitality of the natural world. Prioritizing the life-world of women's work would mean that patterns of work and consumption would be sensitive to the human life cycle. Necessary production and exchange would be fully integrated with the dynamics of the body and the environment. Provisioning of necessary goods and services would be the main focus of the economy, in which all work would be fulfilling and shared. The idea of sufficiency would come before the dynamics of the market or the profit motive. Priorities would be determined by the most vulnerable members of the community, not its "natural" leaders as defined by economic dominance (Mellor 2009, 264).

The capitalist economy has gained its power through the marginalization and exploitation of women, colonized peoples, working people, and the natural world. Feminist political ecologists imagine a future in which **the commons**—our shared wealth—will be restored, and market excess and polluting trade will give way to local production and reciprocal exchange. Is this utopian? Is utopian thinking a waste of time? Is it possible to create a provisioning system that will meet human needs and enhance human potential without destroying the planet?

Local Knowledge

What if we were to take local knowledge seriously? Taking local knowledge seriously entails questioning the received wisdom of the development discourse. Does growth improve or harm the environment? Is "sustainable growth" an oxymoron? Does the Gross Domestic Product measure human well-being? Is the economy simply "the market"? Where shall we look for answers?

Globalization is a big idea, and people who think about globalization often succumb to the idea that big thinking is required of anyone who tries to understand it. However, lately some scholars are "thinking small;" that is, they are turning to the local as a place to begin. Actually, feminist and Marxist thinkers have pioneered beginning from the local or with the view from below. Marx's work was about political economy from the perspective of the working class. Feminist theorist Dorothy Smith adapts Marx's method to begin from the standpoint of women and all people in their daily lives to learn how factors external to

GENDER IN EVERYDAY LIFE   BOX 14-2
AFRICAN FARMERS AND ENVIRONMENTALISTS SPEAK OUT AGAINST A NEW GREEN REVOLUTION IN AFRICA

Oakland, CA: A new report from the Oakland Institute, *Voices from Africa: African Farmers & Environmentalists Speak Out Against a New Green Revolution in Africa*, issues a direct challenge to Western-led plans for a genetically engineered revolution in African agriculture, particularly the recent misguided philanthropic efforts of the Gates Foundation's Alliance for a New Green Revolution in Africa (AGRA), and presents African resistance and solutions rooted in first-hand knowledge of what Africans need.

The report finds a lack of accountability, transparency, and stakeholder involvement in philanthropic efforts such as AGRA. "Despite the Gates Foundation's rhetoric of inclusion and the claim that their investment in agricultural development benefits the growing majority of the world's poor who rely on agriculture, a leaked Gates Foundation confidential report on their Agricultural Development Strategy for 2008–2011 actually emphasizes moving people out of the agricultural sector," said Anuradha Mittal, Executive Director of the Oakland Institute and the editor of the report. "Their intention is to reduce dependency on agriculture, but their strategy report does not specify where or how this new 'land mobile' population is to be reemployed," she continued.

AGRA claims to be an "African-led Green Revolution," and features Kofi Annan at the helm as its chairman; however, African civil society has rejected the idea that one man can speak on behalf of over 50 countries and 680 million people. It is also not apparent from the foundation's Agricultural Development Strategy report whether—or how—the Gates Foundation consulted with African farmers before launching their multi-million the local shape the local. It is equally important to discover how people in their local, every-day, every-night worlds act back on those external forces. The view from above, from the rich world, reduces the economy to the market. It treats the cultures and values of agricultural, industrial, and service workers in the global South as backward and without merit in the globalized world. It devalues peasant practices geared toward the satisfaction of needs and the provision of livelihoods, and substitutes Northern values of acquisition, accumulation, and profit (Escobar 1995, 168) (Box 14-2).

Like Smith, Kum-Kum Bhavnani and her colleagues have introduced ideas that bring our attention back to the view from below in their study of development and globalization. Their "Women, Culture, and Development" paradigm centers on women and sees culture as "lived experience," making visible how subordinates and lower classes work toward social change (Bhavnani, Foran, Kurian, and Munshi 2009, 6). They criticize mainstream development scholarship as elitist, Eurocentric, top-down, and focused on Northern ways of life.

dollar development strategy for the continent. Some of the foundation's external advisors have long partnered with biotech companies: for example, Ruth Oniang'o is featured on Monsanto's website claiming that there is an urgent need for food biotechnology in Africa, and Gates Foundation potential grantee Calestous Juma has urged the G8 to put biotechnology on the agenda for Africa and discard the application of the precautionary principle because it interferes with the development of new technologies.

"Africa does not need dumping of food aid by rich countries that destroys local efforts to produce. Not the imposition of industrial-style agriculture based on chemicals and 'high-yielding' seeds, with the paradoxical outcome of greater production of a few food crops accompanied by even worse hunger and environmental degradation," said Diamantino Nhampossa, a contributor to the report and Executive Coordinator of the União Nacional de Camponeses (National Peasants Union) in Mozambique and member of the Via Campesina's International Coordinating Committee for the Africa Region.

The battle over genetic engineering is being fought across the world, between those who champion farmers' rights to seeds, livelihood, and land, and those who seek to privatize these. While promotional campaigns for technological solutions to hunger regularly feature a handful of African spokespeople who drown out the genuine voices of farmers, researchers, and civil society groups, there is widespread opposition to genetic engineering and plans for a New Green Revolution for Africa. Voices From Africa is based on the essays and statements of leading African farmers, environmentalists, and civil society groups, and brings to light the real African perspectives on technological solutions to hunger and poverty on the continent—and the solutions that the people on the ground believe would bring true development.

SOURCE: Voices from Africa (2009). Reprinted with permission from The Oakland Institute. www.oaklandinstitute.org.

It would be better, they argue, to focus on the realities of subordinate people's lives in the South and to own up to the failures of development policy, including the privatizing of basic needs, water, and health care, perpetual wars in the South, and of course massive poverty (13).

Beginning in the everyday world of poor Southern people shows a reality very different from the imaginings of Northern experts. For example, Hume Johnson shows how generations of Afro-Caribbean women played critical roles in labor and community resistance, turning the street into "theaters for collective actions," despite "extraordinary sexism and racism aimed at silencing and excluding them from public participation." These women, outspoken, feisty, noisy, and aggressive troublemakers, emerged out of the failures of structural adjustment programs that produced debt, massive unemployment, impoverishment, inequality, deterioration in health and education, criminality, and violence. Afro-Caribbean women, Johnson writes, were the major casualties of austerity programs imposed on Jamaica by the World Bank. In response, the poor relied on themselves, turning the street into economic space for sidewalk vendors, higglers, peddlers, and hawkers. Women—domestics, washerwomen, babysitters, drug traffickers, and prostitutes—took over the space with their "creative entrepreneurship." For these poor women, resistance is a must against what they see as the encroachment of the modern capitalist state, big business, and other superordinate groups on their livelihood.

The development orchestrated by the state has failed poor Caribbean women and others like them by not serving their interests and not taking account of their struggles. But rather than succumbing as victims of inequity and marginalization, these **subaltern women** have "refused" development. In so doing, they expose its flaws and calamitous effects on the poor and revise the terms dictated by globalization. They effect development on their own terms and at their own convenience. Indeed, rather than necessarily "buying into" the trappings of modern capitalism by merely selling consumer goods, they see capitalism as an inescapable, requisite aspect of the struggle to survive poverty and improve their lives. By resisting efforts by the Jamaican state to streamline their operations and remove them from the street, these women reimagine development. They demand that it become more equitable and livable (Johnson 2009, 24).

Bhavnani and Bywater (2009) show how "the world's most marginalized people" were affected by the top-down development scheme to privatize the water of the people of Cochabamba, Bolivia. When the government agreed to sell the city's water to Bechtel (Dick Cheney's company, by the way) for forty years, bills increased 300 percent, people were forbidden to collect rainwater, and women were denied access to community wells. Households reduced household water use by limiting baths, washing, and cleaning, but still there was not enough to irrigate crops. In response, rural women joined with lower-, middle-, and some upper-class urban women and men, youth, factory workers, neighborhood associations, and peasant co-ops to form coalitions and organize resistance. Ultimately, they were successful, and the privatization agreement was revoked.

Likewise, in 2002 in Plachimada, Kerala, India, villagers organized resistance when a Coca-Cola bottling plant, built on 35 acres of former farmland, polluted their drinking water with high levels of sodium, chloride, cadmium, and lead. On Earth Day, 1,500 people blocked the factory gates demanding that the plant be shut down and that the company be held responsible for destroying the groundwater and people's livelihoods. Coke's unregulated use of groundwater was a form of privatization. The company, after all, was using a public resource for its own gain. Despite opposition from the company, police, politicians, and the local village council, the struggle continued until international publicity and scientific analysis of the water led to the cancelation of Coke's bottling license.

Such actions, write Bhavnani and Bywater, "demonstrate that globalization from above—capitalist globalization—is not inevitable. People on the edge of society can shape the direction and nature of globalization" (2009, 58). And women are key shapers. Stories like these are everywhere. Women in Senegal have worked to eliminate female genital mutilation in their villages and also take care of the women whose job it is to conduct such cutting. Women rubber tappers in western Brazil have created organizations that increase literacy and challenge the domestic violence in their lives. It is the poor, nonwhite peoples of the third world who are leading the resistance to "the apparent juggernaught of capitalist globalization" (2009, 61).

John Foran interprets these events as part of a new political culture that is nurturing more democratic routes to power, more participatory political systems and popular demands for social justice. These are matters the world is learning from an international movement of resistance to capitalist globalization led by indigenous communities such as the Zapatistas.

The Zapatista movement in southern Mexico originated in the damage done by the International Monetary Fund (IMF), the World Bank loan agreements, and the Mexican state's anti-democratic policies. This movement includes considerable grassroots organizing by women unnoticed by the media, "the pieces of the first global revolution" that seek "to replace the money values of the current system with the life values of a truly democratic system" (Foran 2009, 158, quoting Kevin Danaher and Roger Burbach). Foran claims that this revolution is radically different from those that went before. Quoting Patrick Reinsborough:

> When we say we want a better world, we mean it. We want a world that reflects basic life-centered values. We've got the vision and the other side doesn't. We've got biocentrism, organic food production, direct democracy, renewable energy, diversity, people's globalization, and justice. What have they got? Styrofoam? Neoliberalism? Eating Disorders? Designer jeans, manic depression, and global warming? (Foran 2009, 159)

The work of Bhavnani and her colleagues promoting the "Women, Culture, and Development" paradigm shows the grounded intelligence of local actors, especially women, in confronting the injustices that capitalist development brings their way.

How Will We Change the World?

An assumption of many progressive scholars and activists in the global justice movement is that large-scale mobilized power is the only way to challenge globalization. Small, local, grassroots initiatives would be inadequate to challenge these massive global forces. Global power is obvious; local economic projects have no chance.

J. K. Gibson-Graham suggest otherwise. They write:

> As feminists, we are reminded of the incredible power of discussions around kitchen tables and village wells that formed much of the political practice of a women's

"movement" of global proportions. It is important not to underestimate the magnitude and extent of this movement. It transformed and continues to transform households, lives, and livelihoods around the world to different degrees and in different ways, rendering the life experience of many women literally unrecognizable in the terms of a generation ago. The "upscaling" or globalization of a feminist politics did not necessarily involve formal organization, coordinated actions, and alliances (although some of these followed upon the "second wave"). Indeed the movement has remained largely discursive, often personal, un- or under-resourced. Perhaps it is the continually revitalizing and transformative energy of this relatively unorganized movement that encourages us to pursue a different kind of politics, outside the global/local binary. (2002, 35)

We have all been subjected to the discourse of development and, more recently, to the discourse of globalization. Just as development has been a chimera, justifying the harms done to the third world, so too, perhaps, is globalization. We believe in globally marshaled power, and that belief keeps us from seeing other possibilities that are right before our eyes. For inspiration, information, and the knowledge that can guide us toward the future we imagine, we need to look for stories of noncapitalist economic arrangements that exist here and now (Mondragón, for example, the local farmers' market, feminism as a global force).

We are lucky to live in these revolutionary times. Let us listen and learn from the poor, the weak, the women, the workers, the higglers and street people, the young and the old. They are us.

KEY TERMS

care deficit	masculinist
the commons	peasants
discourse	reproductive labor
enclosures	subaltern women
export processing zones or free trade zones	the sustenance economy
the first and second great transformations	use values

CRITICAL THINKING QUESTIONS

1. What is the Second Great Transformation? How is it related to or similar to the Great Transfomation of the seventeenth century? How is it different?
2. Describe the global land grab.
3. What is the purpose of Export Processing Zones? In what ways are they useful to the women employed in them, and in what ways are they destructive?
4. Describe the three economies, and give examples of each.
5. What is the significance of reproductive labor?
6. What is the importance of "thinking small"?
7. What changes would you like to make in the world?

REFERENCES

Araghi, Farshad. 2000. *The Great Global Enclosure of Our Times: Peasants and the Agrarian Question at the End of the Twentieth Century*. New York: Monthly Review Press.

Bhavnani, Kum-Kum, and Krista Bywater. 2009. "Dancing on the Edge: Women, Culture, and a Passion for Change." In *On the Edges of Development: Cultural Interventions*, edited by Kum-Kum Bhavnani, John Foran, Priya Kurien, and Debashish Munshi, 52–66. New York: Routledge.

Bhavnani, Kum-Kum, John Foran, Priya Kurian, and Debashish Munshi, eds. 2009. *On the Edges of Development: Cultural Interventions*. New York: Routledge.

Carruyo, Light. 2007. *Producing Knowledge, Protecting Forests: Rural Encounters with Gender, Ecotourism, and International Aid in the Dominican Republic*. University Park, PA: Pennsylvania State University Press.

Davis, Mike. 2004. "Planet of Slums." *New Left Review* 26 (March–April). http://www.csub.edu/~mault/davis.htm. Accessed March 17, 2011.

Democracy Now. 2006. "Forced Abortions & Sweatshops: A Look at Jack Abramoff's Ties to the South Pacific Island of Saipan and How Tom DeLay Became an Advocate for Sweatshop Factory Owners." January 4. http://www.democracynow.org/2006/1/4/forced_abortions_sweatshops_a_look_at. Accessed March 20, 2011.

Economy Watch. 2010. "International Free Trade Zone." http://www.economywatch.com/international-trade/free-trade-zone.html. Accessed December 14, 2010.

Ehrenreich, Barbara, and Arlie Russell Hochschild, eds. 2002. *Global Woman: Nannies, Maids, and Sex Workers in the New Economy*. New York: Henry Holt.

Engels, Frederick. 1973. *The Condition of the Working Class in England*. Moscow: Progress Publishers.

Escobar, Arturo. 1995. *Encountering Development: The Making and Unmaking of the Third World*. Princeton, NJ: Princeton University Press.

Foran, John. 2009. *From Old to New Political Cultures of Opposition: Radical Social Change in an Era of Globalization*. In Bhavnani et al., 143–66.

Gibson-Graham, J. K. 2002. "Beyond Global vs. Local: Economic Politics Outside the Binary Frame." In *Geographies of Power: Placing Scale*, edited by Andrew Herod and Melissa Wright, 25–60. Malden, MA: Blackwell.

———. 2006. *A Postcapitalist Politics*. Minneapolis: University of Minnesota Press.

Hochschild, Arlie. 2002. "Love and Gold." In Ehrenreich and Hochschild, 15–30.

Institute for Food and Development Policy. 2010. *Food First Fact Sheet: Harvesting Money—The Global Land Grab*. http://www.foodfirst.org/sites/www.foodfirst.org/files/pdf/Land%20Grabbing%20Fact%20Sheet.pdf. Accessed March 17, 2011.

International Organization for Migration. 2010. *World Migration Report*. http://www.iom.int/jahia/Jahia/policy-research/migration-research/world-migration-report-2010/cache/offonce;jsessionid=EE302968FE5A5ED567019856F34762DE.worker02. Accessed December 17, 2010.

Johnson, Hume. 2009. "Ode to 'Quasheba': Resistance Rituals among Higgler Women in Jamaica." In Bhavnani et al., 22–37.

Lamb, John. 2009. "Achieving a Global Consensus on Good Policy and Practices." PowerPoint presentation for the World Bank's Sustainable Commercial Agriculture, Land and Environmental (SCALE) Management Initiative. World Bank. http://siteresources.worldbank.org/INTEAPREGTOPRURDEV/Resources/JohnLamb2.pdf. Accesses February 11, 2014.

Mellor, Mary. 2009. "Ecofeminist Political Economy and the Politics of Money." In *Eco-Sufficiency and Global Justice: Women Write Political Ecology*, edited by Ariel Salleh. London: Pluto Press.

Mintz, Sidney. 1986. *Sweetness and Power: The Place of Sugar in Modern History*. New York: Penguin.

Palmer, Phyllis. 1989. *Domesticity and Dirt: Housewives and Domestic Servants in the United States, 1920–1945*. Philadelphia: Temple University Press.

Patel, Raj. 2009. *The Value of Nothing: How to Reshape Market Society and Redefine Democracy*. New York: Picador.

Philpott, Tom. 2013. "The Mystery of Bee Colony Collapse." *Mother Jones*, July 31.

Polanyi, Karl. 1944. *The Great Transformation: The Political and Economic Origins of Our Time*. Boston: Beacon Press.

Sachs, Carolyn. 1985. *Women: The Invisible Farmers*. Totowa, NJ: Rowman and Allanheld.

Salleh, Ariel, ed. 2009. *Eco-Sufficiency & Global Justice: Women Write Political Ecology*. London: Pluto Press.

Sassen, Saskia. 2002. "Global Cities and Survival Circuits." In Ehrenreich and Hochschild, 230–53.

Shiva, Vandana. 2005. *Earth Democracy: Justice, Sustainability, and Peace*. Cambridge, MA: South End.

Voices from Africa. 2009. *Voices from Africa: African Farmers and Environmentalists Speak Out Against a New Green Revolution in Africa*. http://www.oaklandinstitute.org/voices-africa-african-farmers-environmentalists-speak-out-against-new-green-revolution-africa. Accessed March 20, 2011.

Walby, Sylvia. 2009. *Globalization and Inequalities: Complexity and Contested Modernities*. London: Sage.

Waring, Marilyn. 1990. *If Women Counted: A New Feminist Economics*. New York: HarperCollins.

Wood, Ellen Meiksins. 1999. "The Politics of Capitalism." *Monthly Review* 51(4). September.

GLOSSARY

50/50 program. International program to increase the numbers of women in elected office by establishing quotas.

100-to-1 quantity ratio. Mandatory minimum penalty requires a hundred times more powdered cocaine than crack cocaine.

Abrahamic religion. Judaism, Christianity, and Islam are all monotheistic religions that trace their origins to Abraham.

Abstinence-only sex education. Focuses on advising people not to have sex if they wish to avoid sexually transmitted diseases such as HIV. Abstinence-only has been strongly criticized because it assumes that people, especially women, always have control over whether they will be engaged in sex. It also assumes that people can and will abstain completely from sex.

Accountability. One of the practices that helps to enforce appropriate gender performance. Audiences hold individuals accountable for the expected performance of gender. A man who wears a skirt, or a woman who rejects her children, does not perform gender according to expectation.

ADHD. Attention-deficit/hyperactivity disorder (ADHD) is a relatively recently diagnosed disorder characterized by impulsivity, inattention, and in some cases, hyperactivity. Increasing diagnoses of ADHD have prompted some to question the veracity of these diagnoses and to worry about the consequences of medicating children and teens on the basis of questionable diagnoses.

Affirmative action model. One of three models for addressing gender inequity in politics, this model emphasizes the need for policies such as quotas that can help women to overcome historical discrimination.

African Union. Established in 2001 and comprised of fifty-four African nations, the union was formed "to rid the continent of the remaining vestiges of colonization and apartheid; to promote unity and solidarity among African States; to coordinate and intensify cooperation for development; to safeguard the sovereignty and territorial integrity of Member States and to promote international cooperation within the framework of the United Nations" (http://www.au.int/en/about/nutshell).

Agency. The ways that people seek to change their social circumstances, to dismantle existing ways of thinking and acting, and to create new ideas and new social institutions. The capacity to act.

Alim. A Muslim scholar.

Alimony. Payment awarded by the court in a divorce settlement originally intended to support women but now called spousal support and may be awarded to men as well. Alimony is increasingly rare and has never been awarded to more than a small proportion of divorced people.

Androcentric policies. Organized around or focused on the experience and needs of men and neglectful of women.

Androcentrism. Male-centeredness. One of three "lenses of gender" (also, gender polarization and biological essentialism) identified by psychologist Sandra Bem.

Assimilation and reform. Two opposing theoretical and political positions regarding eliminating the gender gap in sports. Should we work to assimilate women into existing athletic institutions and practices, or should we seek to radically reconstruct them for both women and men?

Baby M. Legal custody case involving a biological father and a woman who agreed to bear his child and give it up for adoption to the father and his wife. The judge in the case was criticized for deciding the case on the basis of the DNA connection alone and ignoring the contribution women make through pregnancy and childbirth.

Backhanded tactics. Tactics used by men to subtly undercut women with whom they work include the following: condescending chivalry, supportive discouragement, friendly harassment, subjective objectification, radiant devaluation, liberated sexism, benevolent exploitation, considerate domination, and collegial exclusion.

Bar/bat mitzvah. Jewish initiation ceremony of a boy (bar) or girl (bat).

Battering and domestic violence. These are among the most common and least reported crimes in the world. Women of every class, every nationality, every race, and every age may experience this form of violence from husbands, sons, friends, lovers, and others.

Bechdel test. Invented in the 1980s by Alison Bechdel in order to bring attention to the "missing" women in the media.

Beijing+5 Summit. Meeting that took place five years after the 1995 UN Fourth World Conference on Women in Beijing.

Believing is seeing. The idea that beliefs order people's views of the world. The reverse of the familiar saying, "seeing is believing."

Bias theorists. One of three explanations for the pay gap between women and men. Bias theorists argue that decisions about who will be hired, promoted, or fired and what an employee will be paid are made in ways that discriminate against women.

Bigger Thomas, Jezebel, Uncle Tom, Aunt Jemima. Racist stereotypes of African Americans based on characters in the book *Uncle Tom's Cabin* and other popular culture such as ads for pancake mix.

Binaries. Idea that factors such as sex, sexuality, or gender can be categorized into two exclusive opposites. Sociologists argue that in real human bodies and lives all of these factors are not binaries: male or female, masculine or feminine, heterosexual or homosexual. Rather, they are ranges of possibilities that include any number of variations.

Biphobia. The dominant ideology about sexuality places people into one of two categories: homosexual or heterosexual. Biphobia is the fear of the space between categories and the discrimination against people who cannot or choose not to categorize themselves as one or the other.

Black Power Movement. Loosely organized mid-twentieth century group of anti-racist and civil rights organizations such as SNCC and the Black Panthers that argued for more radical changes to end racism in the United States.

Body reflexive practices. A concept developed by R.W. Connell in *Masculinities* to understand practices that incorporate mind, body, and social situation in material (flesh and blood) bodies within a social world. Bodies are "brought into history" by being shaped socially: an athlete's body, masculine and feminine bodies, warrior's bodies.

Borderwork. Interaction between schoolboys and schoolgirls that affirms gender differences. Examples are chasing and pollution rituals. A term used by Barrie Thorne in *Gendered Play*.

Breadwinner and co-breadwinner. A person who earns most of the money to support a household is the breadwinner for their household; co-breadwinners earn at least a quarter of the household income.

Care deficit. In the book *Global Woman*, Arlie Hochschild identifies a "care deficit" that is the result of the migration of millions of third-world women to the first world to do the work that first-world women, who have moved *en masse* into the labor force, can no longer do. While they care for first-world children and families, their own families at home struggle under a lack of care.

Care work. Refers to the paid and unpaid work of taking care of parents, grandchildren, spouses, and other family members, as well as neighbors and other members of the community. "Caring" means that the work is both providing for some need of another and feeling affection and responsibility for the person being provided with the care.

Catholics for Choice. Activist organization of Catholics who support legal abortion rights and the ordination of women priests.

Child brides. Formal marriage of people younger than 18.

CEDAW (Convention on the Elimination of All Forms of Discrimination Against Women). United Nations agreement that defines discrimination against women and outlines national actions to end that discrimination. CEDAW has been ratified by 189 of 196 countries in the world. The countries that have not ratified it are the United States, Iran, Palau, Somalia, Sudan, South Sudan, and Tonga.

Chilly climate. A term first used by Bernice Sandler in a 1982 report on what she called the chilly campus climate. The chilly climate refers to the many small and often hard-to-see ways that women are pushed back, made to feel inferior intellectually, excluded, and otherwise prevented from succeeding in higher education.

Chivalry theory. One of four theories to explain the gender differences in criminal behavior. Chivalry theorists argue that women may commit as many crimes as men but are treated more leniently and therefore not arrested or not punished.

Civil rights. Rights granted by governments and legal systems, in contrast to human rights that are granted to us because we are human and may or may not be recognized as legal rights.

Civil unions. Legal unions certified by a justice of the peace, a judge, or a member of the clergy which grant a couple (heterosexual or LGBT) rights and responsibilities similar to those of marriage for heterosexuals.

Commercial media. Any public communication, such as advertisements, billboards, films, or magazines, that are designed to increase sales or generate profits.

Commission on the Status of Women (CSW). Established in 1946 by the UN Economic and Social Council to promote the rights of women in political, economic, civil, social, and educational fields.

Comparable worth policy. A policy that designs systematic ways to evaluate jobs in order to create pay scales that do not discriminate against occupations that are dominated by women. Four factors are typically used: skill, effort, responsibility, and working conditions.

Compulsory heterosexuality. Refers to our assumption that everyone is heterosexual, unless proven otherwise. Adrienne Rich argued that compulsory heterosexuality is especially problematic for women, because it demands that women be dependent on men, who are generally dominant over women, for their sexual identity.

Conspicuous consumption. Buying and displaying expensive and un-necessary items in order to appear powerful and attractive.

Criminal Justice System. Refers to the entire system of defining crime and punishment, finding people who have committed crimes and administering punishment.

Cult of thinness. Young American women's intense involvement with weight loss and dieting. See Sharlene Hesse-Biber, *The Cult of Thinness* (Oxford 2006).

Culture of poverty thesis. The theory used by Daniel Patrick Moynihan in his report, written for President Lyndon Johnson and published in 1965, "The Negro Family: The Case for National Action." Moynihan blamed the matrifocal (mother-headed) families of inner city African Americans for black poverty, a classic case of "blaming the victim."

Cultural transformation theory. In *The Chalice and the Blade* (HarperCollins), Riane Eisler argues that there are two basic models of society: the dominator model and the partnership model. The dominator model ranks some humans over others and is backed up by force or the threat of force. This model is androcentric (its basis is patriarchy and male domination) and hierarchical (diversity entails either inferiority or superiority). The partnership model (an earlier social arrangement) links members of society together instead of ranking them hierarchically and is based on an equal partnership between men and women in society.

Damsel in distress. Image of women in films that portrays them as incompetent and weak and needing men to save them.

Dars and khatms. Among Muslims, dars are lectures and khatms are collective readings of the Qur'an or Sharif or celebrations marking an individual's first complete recitation.

DaVinci Code. A popular film and book by Dan Brown (2003), which illustrates the way women have been excluded from official positions within the Christian church, for example, the invisibility of women who were key figures in the early Christian church in current sacred texts. The book is fiction but draws on debates among religious scholars about how and why women were excluded.

Debtor nations. Those nations, most of whom are poor, that owe trillions of dollars to international organizations such as the World Bank because of the accumulation of interest on the original loans.

Decriminalize. To remove from the status of both legal and illegal. Some advocates for sex workers advise decriminalizing sex work rather than working to make it legal.

Defense of Marriage Act (DOMA). Defense of Marriage Act (DOMA) was signed into law defining marriage as consisting only of heterosexual unions in 1997. In 2013, DOMA's definition of marriage was struck down by the Supreme Court.

Defensive othering. A way to cope with being a member of a subordinate group within a system of oppression and privilege by supporting stigmatizing labels but asserting that the label is true for other members of the social category, but not for oneself.

Developing nations. Nations with extreme poverty and most of whose citizens lead difficult lives.

Dialectical materialism. Philosophical term used to describe Marxist theory. The word "materialism" in this context means that people from this perspective pay attention to the ways that people use the materials around them to create those things they need to survive. Dialectics refers to the contradictory and dynamic character of social life.

Doctrine of coverture. Legal definition of marriage as a unity in which husband and wife became one, and that "one" was the husband.

Doctrine of separate spheres. The idea that women's place is in the private, domestic sphere; men's place is in the public sphere of business and politics. In the late eighteenth century and well into the nineteenth century, the ideology of separate spheres explained and justified the gendered division of labor among members of the growing urban middle classes.

Doing gender. Rather than being something we "have," gender is something we perform in interaction, in other words, something we *do.*

Dominator model and partnership model. Eisler's (1988) theory that two major forms of spirituality and social organization have marked human history: the dominator model in which religions and society are centered on men and women are subordinated in both the spiritual and material worlds; and the partnership model which predated the dominator model and was based on gender equality and a reverence for the special life-giving abilities of women's bodies through reproduction, birth, and breastfeeding.

Don't Ask, Don't Tell. Armed services policy repealed in the United States in 2010 in which gay men and lesbians could not be asked about their sexuality but could still be dismissed from service for engaging in a homosexual act or openly discussing their sexuality, and they could not live with or marry a life partner.

Double standard. The assumption that it is more natural and moral for men to be sexually active and for decent normal women to be less interested in sex and less sexually active.

Dukes decision. Supreme Court decision in 2011 against the women who contested Walmart's pay scales and promotion practices as sex discrimination. This ruling in favor of the employer is now being used as a precedent in other cases of sex discrimination.

Ecofeminism. Celebrates female biology and claims that humans must use the skills of women to pull back from the environmentally destructive features of contemporary societies.

Economic marginalization theory. One of four theories to explain gender differences in criminal behavior. Economic marginalization theorists claim that at least some crime results when people are responsible for supporting themselves and their families but don't have opportunities to obtain jobs that allow them to do so.

Effeminacy. Characteristics of a boy or man with the qualities or characteristics associated with girls and women.

Electoral politics. Related to running for office and voting.

Emily's List and WINWIN. Two examples, one from the United States and one from Japan of the meritocratic approach to addressing gender in equity in politics by raising funds for women candidate.

Emotional labor. Involves face-to-face or voice-to-voice contact between workers and customers. The employee is supposed to display certain feelings like attentiveness and caring and suppress others such as boredom or irritation.

Emphasized femininities. Dominant images of the supposedly ideal woman; includes dependence, sexual receptivity, motherhood, and subordination by men.

Enclosures. In the seventeenth century, Acts of Parliament enclosed or privatized common land in England. Before the enclosures, this land was often cultivated by peasants. One result of these acts was that peasants without land to support themselves and their families left the countryside for work in factories in the cities.

Epidemiology. The study of health and disease in different populations.

Essentialism. Sandra Bem's third lens of gender, biological essentialism, rationalizes and legitimizes the other two lenses (androcentrism and gender polarization) by treating them as the inevitable consequences of the intrinsic biological natures of women and men.

Equal pay day. The average woman in a full-time job would have to work until Equal Pay Day of the current year to catch up with the wages of the average man from the year before.

European Union (EU). Union of twenty-eight European nations formed after the Second World War to promote political stability and economic cooperation. The EU is comprised of three major social institutions: the European Parliament, which represents the EU's citizens and is directly elected by them; the Council of the European Union, which represents the governments of the individual member countries; and the European Commission, which represents the interests of the Union as a whole.

Evangelical feminists. Religious fundamentalists who believe in living directly by the word of the Bible, cultivating a close personal relationship with Jesus Christ, and proselytizing. They differ from other fundamentalists in their additional belief in the equality of wives in families and the right for women to take leadership roles in religious institutions.

Fair Sentencing Act. Eliminated the five-year mandatory minimum sentence for simple possession of crack cocaine and reduced the disparity between the amount of crack cocaine and powder cocaine needed to trigger certain U.S. federal criminal penalties from a 100:1 weight ratio to an 18:1 weight ratio.

Family leave policy. Provides for people to take time off work to care for newborns or sick family members which can be divided into four types: pro-family and noninterventionist; traditional breadwinner model; pro-family and pro-natalist; and egalitarian.

Family wage. Enough to support a family with only one employed member of the household.

Fag discourse. C.J. Pascoe's study of a California high school, *Dude You're a Fag*, found that labeling other boys as fags is part of a "fag discourse" that helps white boys to bond and to sooth their anxieties about their masculinity. The fag discourse also helps white boys to police hegemonic masculinity among their peers.

Fatherhood responsibility movement. Includes two contrasting wings: a pro-marriage group and a fragile-families group.

Female genital cutting or female genital mutilation (FGM). Refers to the practice in some cultures of cutting, "circumcising," or partially or totally removing external female genitalia for non-medical reasons. It has no health benefits and harms girls and women in many ways.

Feminist theory. One of three theories to explain why women usually do more housework. Feminist theorists argue it is because women do not have as much power as men do. Furthermore, when women do more housework and when women and men do different kinds of housework, gender is being reproduced.

Feminization of poverty. The tendency for women to be poorer than men. This poverty gap varies by race ethnicity, social class, and nation.

Fragile families advocates. Emphasizes the similarities between women and men and the need for fathers and mothers to work as a team to raise children; however, they believe that in order to build families the economy needs to provide jobs with decent wages.

Free market. A market economy that is not regulated by a government.

Fundamentalism. First used to describe Christians in the early twentieth century who professed a belief in the literal word of the Bible as a document without error. We now also use the term to identify many religions that emphasize a conservative view of religion and of gender.

Gay games. An Olympics-like sporting event held every four years since 1972, they describe themselves as the world's largest sports and culture festival open to all under the founding principles of participation, inclusion, and personal best.

Gender equality. Equal treatment of women and men in laws and policies, and equal access to resources and services within families, communities, and society at large.

Gender equity. Fairness and justice in the distribution of benefits and responsibilities between women and men. It often requires women-specific programs and policies to end existing inequalities.

Gender essentialism. The idea that there are innate differences between men and women, that these are universal and do not vary with the context. A common essentialist idea is that women cannot do math. Another is that men cannot care for children.

Gender factory. Housework is considered a gender factory because it is an activity that reflects and reproduces gender inequality. Men can reaffirm their masculinity by not doing the dishes, whereas women reaffirm their femininity by doing them.

Gender gap. The differences in voting patterns between women and men; women tend to vote for more liberal candidates and issues.

Gender harassment. Inappropriately calling attention to women or men's bodies, sexuality, or marital status; gender harassment is often used to enforce traditional gender roles or in response to violation of those roles.

Gender Issues Monitoring Office. Established in Rwanda to ensure gender equity. For the past several years, Rwanda has had the highest proportion of women in political leadership of any nation in the world.

Gender is omnirelevant. Gender is relevant in every interactional situation. Test this theory. Can you think of situations in which your gender did not play a part?

Gender ideologies. Widespread beliefs about what men and women are like and should be like.

Gender polarization. A lens of gender identified by Sandra Bem (along with androcentrism and biological essentialism). Gender polarization identifies the use of gender differences to explain all aspects of human experience.

Gender segregated. An occupation is defined as gender segregated if 75 percent or more of the people who work in that field are of one gender.

Gerrymandering. Creating oddly shaped districts in order to manipulate the representation of elected officials.

Girl-friendly and boy-friendly schools. Schools that take into account the different learning styles and situations of girls and boys in specific cultures.

Glass ceiling. Artificial barriers based on attitudinal or organizational bias that prevents qualified women from advancing upward in their organization into management-level positions.

Global chains of care. Refers to the situation when a woman from a wealthy country enters the paid labor force and is unable to care for her family. She then hires a woman from a poorer country to come and care for her children and household. This leaves the family of the poorer woman without someone to do the care work or reliant on other poor women to care for them.

Global North and South. The division of the world into wealthy nations that are mostly located in the northern half of the globe and poor nations that are primarily in the southern hemisphere.

Globalization. Integration of the world's economies, political systems, informational networks, and ecology into one large global system.

Goddess worship. The practice of ancient pre-Christian Europeans who worshipped goddesses because of women's ability to reproduce human life. The connection of males to reproduction may not have been known thousands of years ago, and females were, therefore, seen as the only source of human life.

Good provider role. Dominant role for men in the United States during the twentieth century which meant that men were expected to be focused on earning money for the families but not providing nurturant care for their children. This role is increasingly being challenged.

Great transformation. Karl Polanyi's term for the changes that ushered in capitalism and market society. While premodern economies were based on reciprocity and redistribution, modern societies after the great transformation were reshaped by the unrestrained free market that, he argued, malformed society and human nature. Some have named the massive movement of women into the labor force in the last third of the Twentieth Century the "second great transformation."

Healthy sexuality. In contrast to sexualization, healthy sexuality is an important component of both physical and mental health, fosters intimacy, bonding, and shared pleasure, and involves mutual respect between consenting partners.

Hegemonic and counterhegemonic images. Hegemonic images are those that represent women and men in stereotyped and exploitative ways. Counterhegemonic images challenge hegemonic ones by offering alternative images that emphasize positive human traits.

Hegemonic masculinity. The culturally exalted form of masculinity that is linked to institutional power, such as that displayed at the top levels of the military, business, and government. Includes factors such as the subordination of women, authority, aggression, and technical competence.

Hegemony. Dominance of one social group over another.

Hegemony theorists. Argue that media play a conservative role in society, manipulating and persuading viewers to believe that the status quo is the best of all possible worlds, or even the only possibility.

Heteronormativity. The assumption that heterosexuality is the only normal and natural form of sexuality and that anyone who is not heterosexual is deviant or bad.

Heterosexism. Refers to the institutionalization of hatred and discrimination against LGBT people.

Heterosexual matrix. A concept used by philosopher Judith Butler that refers to cultural expectations and norms surrounding the performance of sex and gender.

Heterosexual privilege. Personal behaviors and public policies that assume that heterosexuality is the only valid form of sexuality. Some examples include the right to publicly acknowledge one's partner or to legally marry him or her.

Heterosexuality. Being sexually attracted to or engaging in sex with someone of the "opposite" sex. For example, males who have sex with females.

Hijab, niqab, and burqa. Hijab is the practice among many Muslim women of wearing a scarf to cover their head and hair. The niqab is a veil worn across the lower part of the face, and a burqa is a long, loose robe that covers the head and body.

Hijra. In south Asian culture, a hijra is a male, usually a eunuch, who adopts a feminine identity, assumes feminine gender roles, and wears women's clothing. Many hijras live together in all-hijra communities, and many are sex workers.

Historically black colleges. Institutions of higher education in the United States established before 1964 to serve the black community.

HIV. Human immunodeficiency virus, which is spread through contact with semen, blood, and breast milk and interrupts the body's immune system's ability to fight against opportunistic infections.

Hollaback. A movement to end street harassment (sexual harassment in public spaces) that asks victims of harassment to document and share incidents of street harassment on the Web. Street harassment is a way to exercise control over people (women, LGBTQ folks, working class people, differently sized people, and other subordinated groups). On their website they write, "By holla'ing back you are transforming an experience that is lonely and isolating into one that is sharable. You change the power dynamic by flipping the lens off of you and onto the harasser. And you enter a worldwide community of people who've got your back." See http://www.ihollaback.org/about/.

Homophobia. Literally the fear of homosexuals but used more broadly to refer to the discrimination against and hatred of lesbians, gay, bi-sexual, and transgendered (LGBT) people.

Honor crimes. When women and girls are killed because they have allegedly brought shame on the family. The behavior they are most often accused of is having sex outside of marriage.

Hooking up. The practice of finding casual sex partners.

Human capital theorists. One of three explanations for the gap in pay between women and men, these theorists emphasize the ways that people invest in themselves by such activities as getting an education or social networking. Human capital theorists believe that most anyone who wants to succeed can make these investments and they will be rewarded with money and other social benefits.

Hyper-sexualization. An overemphasis on sexuality. For example, many feminists have been concerned with the hyper-sexualization of girls in advertising and popular media that show them in "sexy" adult clothing and stances.

Individualism. Tenet of the American belief system that asserts that there are abundant opportunities for individuals to succeed if they are industrious and competitive. Therefore, the distribution of rewards is generally fair and equitable.

Initiation rite. Marks a transition from one social role to another, especially the move from childhood to adulthood.

International Olympic Committee (IOC). Body of representatives from nations that participate in the Olympics; this committee organizes and oversees the events and seeks to protect, support, and encourage athletes from all nations.

International Women's Year, 1975. The United Nations sponsored the first of a series of international women's conferences in Mexico City which recommended that the UN declare 1976–1985 the Decade for Women, during which the UN would address the needs of women throughout the world.

Intersectional analysis. Sociological theory often identified with Patricia Hill Collins emphasizing the crosscutting inequalities that complicate gendered differences.

Involved fathers. In contrast to the stalled revolution and rebels, involved fathers try to integrate paid work and family, especially raising children.

Isis and Ninlil. Examples of early goddesses. Isis was believed to have introduced agriculture to her people in the Mediterranean region; Ninlil, in the religion of the people in Mesopotamia, was said to have taught her people to farm.

Job. A seemingly neutral category that actually embeds the idea of the split between work and home. The job is a category that assumes that workers in jobs are not at home, are not taking care of children, and have the time and ability to be present and to take direction from employers.

Job ladders. A system for promoting employees that requires many layers of inequity among different jobs through which employees can strive to move up.

Legitimation. Involves creating an ideology, a set of beliefs and ideas that explain and justify the existing social organization.

LGBTQ. Lesbians, gay men, bi-sexuals, transgendered people, and those questioning their sexuality.

Macho. A macho man is one who displays hypermasculine bravado and posturing, is likely to respond physically to any slight, attempts to dominate women and other men verbally and physically, drinks too much, has many women lovers, and fathers many children.

Mail-order/cyber brides. Wives who are found by men who search Internet sites that advertise women, usually from poorer nations in Asia or Russia, who are looking for a husband from a wealthier nation.

Maquiladoras. Assembly plants usually owned by large multi-national corporations that import machinery and materials to Mexico and produce finished export products, which are then sold around the world. Notorious for low wages and dangerous working conditions.

Married women's property laws. Allowed women the right to own property and to control their own earnings.

Marxist theory. Classical theory in sociology developed by Karl Marx and his colleague Frederick Engels. Marxist theory takes dialectical and materialist view of social life and society.

Masculinity politics. Consists of mobilization and struggles where the meaning of masculinity and men's position in gender relations is at issue.

Masculinity theory. One of four theories developed to explain differences in rates of criminal behavior by gender. Masculinity theorists assert that criminal activity is associated with characteristics of masculinity, such as being aggressive, pushy, hard-headed, and violent. These behaviors are part of being a man in our society, and as a result they make men more prone to committing crimes.

Mass media. Vehicles for sending information to large numbers of people, such as the Internet, television, radio, newspapers, magazines, books, CDs, and films.

Medicaid. Health care coverage for poor families as part of the welfare system in the United States.

Meritocratic model. One of four models for addressing gender inequity in politics; this model sees women as deficient and seeks to remedy their shortcomings.

Mestiza. A mestiza is an amalgam of many races—indigenous, European, Asian—and of multiple sexualities, and therefore part of all races and nationalities. In her being, the mestiza has a complexity to understand multiple sides of situation. Sharing many identities, the mestiza can make new worlds.

Microinequities. Gestures, tones of voice, and other subtle differences in treating women or people of color in classrooms; treatments which can undermine classroom performance.

Miscegenation/anti-miscegenation laws. Refers to marrying across racial ethnic lines. Laws in the United States made marriage between white people and people from other racial ethnic groups illegal until the 1960s.

Misogyny. The hatred of women.

Mommy wars. The tension between the motherhood mystique and our expectations that adults earn their way through paid labor in our society.

Monster ethics. A term used by Alice Dreger to describe the treatment of intersex infants in the twentieth century and possibly continuing today. Doctors were counseled to lie to their intersex patients and their families or withhold information from them, and to perform life-changing surgeries on children who didn't fit normative expectations about sexed bodies. After surgery, they failed to review the impact of such treatments on the individuals who were treated. Dreger assumed that these practices were specific to cases of intersex infants. However, in a 2004 essay (http://www.isna.org/articles/how-wrongiwas), Dreger discovered that medically changing otherwise healthy individuals to fit social norms was widespread (circumcision, ADHD, growth hormones). In other words, Dreger claimed that monster ethics remains normal and goes beyond the treatment of intersex individuals.

Mothers Front. An organization of women in the Hindu community in Sri Lanka in the 1980s and 1990s which emerged to protest the government's violations of human rights and murder of thousands of young people.

Motherhood mystique. Ideology about motherhood that idealizes mothering and ignores the problems real mothers face in raising children.

Motherhood penalty. Decline in women's income with every child they have.

MSM (men who have sex with men). Men who do not identify as homosexual or bisexual but who engage in sex with other men. Also popularly referred to as down low (DL)/trade.

Muslim Brotherhood. Islamic political organization focused on creating nation states that base their laws and policies on principles and documents of Islam.

Narrowcasting. Targeting commercial television shows to wealthy white gay men as a niche market with substantial amounts of disposable income.

National fatherhood initiative. Stresses the importance of gender differences and what they see as the natural difference between fathers and mothers.

National Organization for Women (NOW). Was founded by a group of lawyers, academics, writers, business executives, and government employees in 1966 to work for the elimination of legal barriers to women in government, the work force, educational institutions, and labor unions.

Natural attitude. A belief in the reality of the lived, everyday world as it is directly apprehended and experienced.

Naturalizing inequalities. Systems of inequality are constructed by people in society, but these gain power when they appear to be part of the natural order of things.

Neoliberalism. Supports free (unregulated) markets and the privatization of state welfare provisions. Neo-liberals believe that corporations should have total freedom to pursue profits around the globe, that trade unions should be curbed, and that the social safety net should be greatly reduced or eliminated.

Neutralization. Barrie Thorne's term, the opposite of "borderwork," in which children diminish or eliminate gendered markers of differences among themselves.

New Left. Loose coalition of anti-war, women's rights, and civil rights activists in mid-twentieth century America. They differed from the old left, which was more class conscious and focused on labor issues.

Nimble fingers. The proliferation of free trade zones is an aspect of globalization in which factory production is located in areas of the world where labor is cheap. Young women are the cheapest workers in cheap labor countries. Manufacturers often explained that they hired young women to work in these factories because of their "nimble fingers." "Nimble fingers" were treated as a natural ability of unskilled women (who were paid as unskilled workers), but in fact they were the product of training received from mothers and female kin who taught the women to sew at home. Women's "nimble fingers" are in demand as low wage vegetable packers in Mexico, garment workers in China, and cotton harvesters in Egypt.

Nineteenth Amendment. Ratified in 1920, gave (white) women in the United States the right to vote.

No Child Left Behind Act. A 2001 Act of Congress that supports high stakes testing in public schools. Supporters argue that this type of accountability raises school standards nationally. Critics argue that the act focuses on the wrong kind of learning—responses to standardized testing, teaching to the test, and undermining creative teaching and learning.

No-fault. Divorce laws that allow people to divorce because they no longer wish to be married rather than requiring them to develop a case against their spouse justifying the divorce and identifying who is at fault for the breakup of the marriage.

Nongovernmental Organizations (NGOs). Organizations that focus on social issues and provide services and political leadership, often referred to as non-profits in the United States.

Normative. The supposedly correct way of doing something. The problem, of course, is who will define what is correct?

North American Free Trade Agreement (NAFTA). International agreement established in 1994 between three countries in North America: Canada, the United States, and Mexico. NAFTA eliminates many trade barriers that improve the ability to move goods and labor among the three countries and therefore the profitability of multinationals. The effects, however, have created many serious problems for workers, small businesses, especially farmers in Mexico, and the environment.

Occupational sex-segregation index. Provides a measurement of the proportion of women who would need to change occupations to create gender "desegregation" in the labor market.

OECD countries. Thirty-four countries, including most of Europe, Australia, Canad,a and the United States, that have signed the Convention on the Organisation for Economic Co-operation and Development, which is designed to preserve and promote capitalism.

Opportunity structures. The means available to succeed. Women and people of color often don't have equal access to the opportunity structures available to men and/or white people.

Opportunity theory. One of four theories to explain differences in criminal behavior by gender. Opportunity theorists assert that property crimes are a result of being in the right place at the right time and that to commit a crime, a person must have certain skills.

Optimum gender of rearing model. A system developed by medical specialists in the 1950s to treat children with intersex, who believed that intersex children would become "real" girls or boys if they were assigned a gender by the age of 18 months.

Parental leave. Policies that provide for time off work for mothers or fathers to care for newborn or sick children in contrast to maternity leave, which is allotted only to women, and paternal leave, which is allotted only to men.

Paradigm shift. In *The Structure of Scientific Revolutions*, historian of science Thomas Kuhn focused on revolutions in scientific understanding of matters that could not be explained by accepted scientific theories and methods ("normal science") of the time. A well-known paradigm shift was the transition in the early twentieth century from the worldview of Newtonian physics to Einstein's relativistic worldview.

Paradoxal autonomy. Used to describe young women associated with gangs in low income neighborhoods who are freer to make their own decisions about men and sex than other women but who are also more likely to be solely responsible for their survival in communities with few economic opportunities.

Parité. French law that reduces campaign funds for parties that fail to field equal numbers of women and men candidates.

Pension. A payment that is made to people who are no longer working from funds accumulated during their years of employment.

Pin money. Income earned that is perceived as being insignificant to the household.

Pink dollars. Money to be made by advertising to the LGBT community.

Plan B. Fallback strategies young people develop as insurance in the all-too-likely event that their egalitarian ideals for sharing work and family with partners prove out of reach.

Politics. The expression and organization of power in any social relationship or institution.

Polytheist. People who worship many gods and goddesses, such as ancient Greeks and Romans and contemporary Hindus. The idea of one god with a masculine image emerged about 6,000 years ago.

Power and performance sports and participation sports. Power and performance sports are highly organized and competitive, such as professional football, and participation sports are comprised of more loosely defined and more informally organized activities, such as exercising at the gym or jogging with friends.

Prison industrial complex. In May 1973, New York Governor Nelson Rockefeller signed into law strict mandatory prison sentences for the sale or possession of illegal drugs, a law that began the growth and development of the prison industrial complex. The subsequent rapid expansion of the prison population is taking place under the political influence of private prison companies and businesses that profit from supplying goods and services to government prisons. In response, the prison abolition movement includes those who wish to eliminate prisons completely.

Promise Keepers. An example of a Christian fundamentalist organization that has focused its attention on men. Established in 1990 by Bill McCartney, a former football coach for the University of Colorado, the Promise Keepers are dedicated to introducing a new man to America and reestablishing men as the leaders of their families. They believe men must stand up and be responsible, strong leaders whom their wives and children can look up to.

Pro-sex feminists. Are against censorship because they view it as an attack on free speech and civil rights and argue further that pornography can have benefits for women.

Purity balls and promise (abstinence) rings. Prom-like events where girls are escorted by their fathers to whom they pledge their virginity. Their fathers then present them with promise rings to remind them of their pledge.

Qur'an and Hadiths. According to Muslims, the word of God as it was recorded by Mohammed during the early seventh century. The second source for moral and spiritual guidance are the hadiths, which are secondhand reports of Mohammed's personal traditions and lifestyles, which were collected soon after his death to help Muslims apply the dictates of the Qur'an.

Qubaisiate. An Islamic women's society in Syria which educates girls and women about religious texts.

Queer theory. An approach to exploring the connections between genders and sexualities that asserts that the links between biological sex, social gender, and desire are infinitely variable and are socially constructed, acted, and reenacted as we relate with one another.

Quota Systems. Affirmative action programs to bring more women into political leadership by setting quotas of women in party leadership and in candidates for office.

Race ethnicity. Both race and ethnicity are social factors that are intertwined; we have combined the terms to remind us that neither has anything to do with biology but both are socially constructed and enormously socially consequential.

Radical model. One of three models to address the problem of gender inequity in politics. This model suggests that the system may need major overhauling of structures and ideologies rather than just better integration of women into the existing political institutions and practices.

Ram janambhumi. Conservative Hindu fundamentalist organization in India that advocates highly restrictive codes of conduct for women.

Rap groups. During the 1970s, women in the women's liberation movement gathered in "rap groups" where they discussed issues ranging from housework and sexuality to war, employment, and child care.

Rational choice theory. One of three theories about why women usually do most of the housework. Rational choice theorists argue that women and men enter into negotiations about housework and make rational choices based on questions such as which partner knows how to do the work and which partner has other responsibilities in the paid labor force or brings home a larger paycheck that allows him or her to bargain out of doing housework.

Rebels. Men who chose autonomy over parenthood. Like men in the stalled revolution, they prioritize breadwinning but feel they need to separate themselves from family rather than to translate their workplace activities into relationships of authority with a wife and children.

Reception theorists. Theorists who assert that television can give voice to an otherwise silent point of view or that programming can generate discussion that promotes resistance to hegemonic ideas, including ideas about gender.

Relative numbers and tokenism. In Rosabeth Moss Kanter's study of the relations between women and men in a corporation, she argued that the small number of women amidst a large number of male employees explained the fact that women were only symbolically included in the work of the corporation, that men only made symbolic gestures to include women as equals.

Religious machismo. Describes religious political organizations such as the Promise Keepers that call on men to reassert themselves in families and to take on family and community challenges as soldiers in a war against what they believe to be the decline in godliness in the world.

Reproductive labor. Reproductive labor, in some ways another term for care work, ranges from biological reproduction to the socialization of children, the care of bodies, love and tenderness, providing food and clothing within families, and so forth. This labor traditionally taken place in the home for free and was rarely recognized as real work. Now this work has been commodified, as increasingly workers (often immigrant women) are hired to take the place of employed mothers and wives.

Repudiation. The unilateral prerogative for a man to terminate a marriage at will without judicial intervention under Islamic law (shari'a).

Resources for doing gender. When we "do" gender, we use many props. For example, many couples follow the rule for height difference between women and men. Relatively taller men and shorter women are props for doing gender.

Revisionist, rejectionist, renovationist, and revolutionary feminists. Four feminist approaches to inequality in religion that call for varying degrees of change.

Roe v. Wade. In 1973 the U.S. Supreme Court held, in *Roe v. Wade*, that under the due process clause of the Fourteenth Amendment, women have a right to privacy that extends to their decisions to have an abortion in the earlier months of pregnancy without legal restriction, and with restrictions in later months.

Samsara and moksha. Among Hindus, moksha is the liberation or salvation from samsara. Samsara is what many Americans call reincarnation and refers to a long cycle of moving to different levels of spirituality to the bliss of moksha.

Sandwich generation. Refers to middle-aged adults sandwiched between caring for older parents and raising their children.

Second wave feminism. Term used to describe the emergence of feminism in the United States in the middle of the twentieth century. It included two branches: one spearheaded by the National Organization for Women (NOW), focused on reform of the political and economic system. The second arm of second-wave feminism, often called the women's liberation movement, was made up of young women, many of whom identified themselves as socialist feminists and/or lesbian feminists. They were former civil rights activists, Vietnam War protesters, community advocates, and student militants.

Self-objectification. Occurs when women and girls "buy" hypersexualized and sexually objectifying images and start to behave in ways consistent with them.

Sex tourism. Typically involves men from the global North traveling to countries and regions in the global South for the purpose of engaging in sexual acts with local sex workers, many of whom are illegally trafficked or are children.

Sex work. Engaging in sexual activities for pay. Includes prostitution but is a more general and less stigmatizing term.

Sexual harassment. Turning a professional, work, or student–teacher relationship into a sexual relationship that is not wanted by one of the people involved and that is coercive because the initiator has some power over the other person.

Sexual identity/orientation. Refers to how people identify or classify themselves sexually. Sexual identity may differ from one's fantasies or behavior.

Sexual minority. Categories of people whose sexual identity is not of the dominant "exclusively" heterosexual type and is therefore subject to stigma and discrimination.

Sexual scripts. Shared cultural instructions for "normal" sexual behaviors. These behaviors are different for men and women.

Sexually objectified. Made into a thing for an other's sexual use, rather than seen as a person with the capacity for independent action and decision making.

Sharia. Laws based on the teachings of the Qur'an and Hadiths which Muslims believe are derived from the word of God. Some nations base their civil law on Sharia.

Sociability work. Tasks done by volunteers in the community to help support important activities and institutions.

Social media. Websites and applications that can be used on electronic devices that enable large numbers of people to network, sharing information about themselves and ideas and activities in which they would like to engage others. Facebook and Twitter are two currently popular examples.

Social security benefits. The public pension program maintained by the government in the United States and funded by taxes on employees' paychecks during their work years.

Socialization theory. One of three explanations for why women usually do most of the housework. Socialization theorists argue that we teach our boys and girls skills in certain kinds of housework and that we train them to feel responsible and comfortable with some activities and not others.

Southern Baptist Convention. Represents 42,000 churches and 16 million members and develops and promotes ideologies they believe are consistent with the Southern Baptist faith.

Stalled revolution. Contemporary men who continue to seek to maintain their role as breadwinners and dominant in the households and not share in childcare and other unpaid care work.

Standard story. The widespread belief in gender binarism, or the classification of humans into two distinct types of human on the basis of sex and gender.

State/nation state. The social institution that makes laws and uses force (when necessary) to protect itself and enforce its laws.

STD/STI. Sexually transmitted disease and sexually transmitted infections.

Sticky floor. Similar to the glass ceiling, the sticky floor refers to workers stuck in low-paying jobs working long hours, with few other options.

Stigma/othering. A negative label that sets a person apart from others, links the labeled person to supposedly undesirable characteristics, and then discriminates against them.

Structural Adjustment Programs (SAPs) and Poverty Reduction Strategy Programs (PRSPs). Reforms required by the World Bank of debtor nations that demand that poor nations that owe money to the World Bank make cuts in social spending in order to find funds to repay their debt.

Structural violence. Medical anthropologist and physician Paul Farmer writes that the division between the affluent and the poor is an example of structural violence, which makes it impossible for the poor to access medical care. In his writings, Farmer describes how "racism, sexism, political violence, *and* grinding poverty" inflict violence and suffering on the poor. Some examples of structural violence from the United States are Hurricane Katrina and the U.S. prison system.

Structuration. Anthony Giddens' theory about the relationship between social structures and human agency. How are individual actions related to social structure? How does structure inform individual actions?

Student Nonviolent Coordinating Committee (SNCC). The younger wing of the civil rights movement active in the 1960s, noted for its leadership of sit-ins, freedom rides, and the dangerous work of registering black voters in the rural South.

Subordinated masculinities. Include sexually marginalized gay men, "sissies," "mother's boys," and "wimps." The intersections of class and race ethnicity produce other forms of subordinated or marginalized masculinity, men rendered socially invisible or outside the gender order.

Substructures of masculinity. Idea developed by Raewyn Connell that includes division of labor, power relations, emotional relations, and symbolization.

Sustenance economy. In *Earth Democracy* (2005), Vandana Shiva writes about three economies: the market economy, nature's economy, and the sustenance economy. The sustenance economy is the site of societal reproduction, the women's economy, the economy of the vast majority of humanity. According to Shiva, it "includes all spheres in which humans produce in balance with nature and reproduce society through partnerships, mutuality, and reciprocity." As austerity and globalization threaten livelihoods, women work longer, have less time and resources for domestic labor and care work, and the sustenance economy becomes weaker.

Suttee. A tradition among some Hindus in which a wife throws herself on the burning pyre of her dead husband. It has been illegal for more than a century but is still practiced in some areas.

Symbolic annihilation. The invisibility of women in media. In the twentieth century, girls were "symbolically annihilated" in children's literature.

Television sports manhood formula. A review of popular sports programs reveals ten recurrent themes regarding gender that make up the television sports manhood formula. The formula emphasizes violence, gender inequality, and racial ethnic inequality.

Temporary Aid to Needy Families (TANF). The reformed welfare system established in the 1990s in the United States.

Third wave feminism. Brought our attention to the diversity of gender especially within the United States and the persistence in particular of racial ethnic inequality and its ties to gender inequality.

Thomas theorem. W. I. Thomas, an early-twentieth-century sociologist and part of the "Chicago School" of sociology, and his wife Dorothy wrote that "if men [*sic*] define situations as real, they are real in their consequences."

Three strikes and you're out. Baseball-inspired slogan to describe laws implemented in the U.S. War on Drugs that mandated long prison terms for people who were found guilty of crimes three times. This policy sent many people to prison for life for three minor crimes.

Title IX. A law mandating equal funding for girls' and women's sports; it has been responsible for women's gains in educational institutions and in high school and collegiate athletics.

Torah. In Judaism, the law of God according to the first five books of Hebrew scripture.

Traditionalists, neo-traditionalists, and innovators. Three responses to divorce among men with varying degrees of engagement with their ex-wives and children.

Trafficking. Moving people across borders and around the world in order to exploit their labor. Includes modern-day slavery and forced labor, particularly to perform sex work.

Transgender. When a person's gender identity does not match that person's assigned sex category. An umbrella term for different types of gender-variant people.

Transnational feminism. Emphasizes the diversity of women around the world, and in particular critiques the view that a feminist view that may be valid in the global North is equally valid in the South.

Transnational capitalism. The spread of the capitalist system throughout the world as a result of globalization of the economy and the dominance of capitalist nations such as the United States as well as the dominance of corporations whose historical roots were in the United States, Europe, and Japan but now float around the globe without ties to any particular country.

Transwomen (MTFs) and transmen (FTMs). Transwomen are male-to-female (MTF) transgender persons who were assigned the male sex at birth but who identify as female. Transmen are female-to-male (FTM) transgender persons who were assigned the female sex at birth but who identify as male.

Truth in sentencing. Laws implemented in the 1980s and 1990s that require that offenders serve a substantial portion (usually 85 percent for violent crimes) of their sentence.

Two-spirit people. Many Native American or First Nations communities prior to European contact institutionalized roles for multiple gender and sexual variations. Some First Nations men took up the roles, work, and dress of women, and some First Nations women lived, partially or entirely, as men, hunting and pursuing war alongside them. Some of these individuals married people of their own biological sex, while others married members of the other sex. The term "two-spirit," a translation of the Anishinabe/Ojibwa term "niizh maleitoag," was coined by members of the Indian community in 1990 at the third conference of American Indian gays and lesbians in Winnipeg, Canada.

Type A behavior. Type A behavior is said to be the behavior of "short-fused," competitive, irritable, and stressed workaholics who are candidates for heart attacks.

UN Fourth World Conference on Women in Beijing. Held in 1995, this conference represented the culmination of two decades of work since the 1975 declaration of International Women's Year. The highlight of the conference was the establishment of goals for nations to achieve regarding gender equity in a broad range of areas such as women's human rights, poverty, the girl-child, and violence against women. These goals have been reviewed every five years since 1995.

War on Drugs. Slogan created in the 1980s to describe the upsurge in arrests and incarceration of people for drug-related offenses in the United States.

Warrior narratives. Young boys bring their fantasies about displaying masculinity in play to school, where they learn that teachers do not allow these kinds of play. While boys' fantasies of masculinity are repressed in school, the dreams of little girls about motherhood, domestic life, and beauty are encouraged.

Waves of Feminism. Conceptualization of social movements that demarcate dates and activities into sections called waves. American feminists often divide the twentieth century American feminist movement into three waves.

Welfare-state capitalism. Economic and political system which seeks to maintain a free-market economy by providing some relief from the problems associated with it, such as poverty and unemployment, by developing policies that provide programs such as Food Stamps and unemployment benefits.

Wicca. A pagan religion that emerged in the twentieth century in the United Kingdom but was rooted in the practices of pre-Christian religions, especially ancient Celts. A mother goddess is a key character in the Wiccan religion.

Woman-Identified Woman. A term introduced in the 1970s by lesbian feminist activists who maintained that lesbians were at the forefront of the struggle for women's liberation because lesbian lives were centered around women, rather than men.

Woman Suffrage. The right for women to vote and run for office.

Women in development (WID), women and development (WAD), gender and development (GAD), and women, culture, and development (WCD). Four models for understanding the global economy and creating policies to alleviate the economic difficulties of the world and eliminate the gender gap.

Women's liberation movement. Social movement that emerged in the mid-twentieth century promoting gender equality, usually associated with the more radical branches of the movement.

Work transfer. The process of transferring paid service work to the unpaid work of housewives.

INDEX